LEARNING FROM SAVANNAH

LEARNING FROM

SAVANNAH

FROM IDEAL CITY TO ELASTIC URBANISM

DAVID W. GOBEL | ROBIN B. WILLIAMS

THE UNIVERSITY OF GEORGIA PRESS | ATHENS

A Wormsloe
FOUNDATION
PUBLICATION

Athens, Georgia 30602
www.ugapress.org

Designed by April Leidig
Set in Garamond by Copperline Book Services
Printed and bound by Sheridan Books

The paper in this book meets the guidelines for permanence and durability of the Committee on Production Guidelines for Book Longevity of the Council on Library Resources.

Printed in the United States of America

30 29 28 27 26 P 5 4 3 2 1

EU Authorized Representative
Easy Access System Europe—
Mustamäe tee 50, 10621 Tallinn, Estonia
gpsr.requests@easproject.com

Library of Congress Cataloging-in-Publication Data
Names: Gobel, David Walter author | Williams, Robin B., 1964– author
Title: Learning from Savannah : from ideal city to elastic urbanism / David W. Gobel, Robin B. Williams.
Description: Athens : The University of Georgia Press, [2026] | Includes bibliographical references and index.
Identifiers: LCCN 2025039174 | ISBN 9780820374598 hardback | ISBN 9780820374604 paperback | ISBN 9780820374628 ebook | ISBN 9780820374611 pdf
Subjects: LCSH: City planning—Georgia—Savannah | Grid plans (City planning)—Georgia—Savannah | Architecture and society—Georgia—Savannah | Architecture—Georgia—Savannah
Classification: LCC NA9127.S59 G63 2026 | DDC 720.9758/724—dc23/eng/20251120
LC record available at https://lccn.loc.gov/2025039174

To our patient, gently prodding wives,
Fun and Odette

CONTENTS

PREFACE

THIS BOOK HAS ENJOYED a long gestation period. Its genesis can be traced to 1997, when we, the authors, began planning an academic conference on the city square to be held in February 1999 by our newly formed Architectural History department at the Savannah College of Art and Design (SCAD). This symposium enabled us to join with scholars from around the world in exploring how Savannah's most famous urban feature related to other cities. Soon after, SCAD's exhibitions staff invited us to curate an exhibition of photographs about Savannah; originally focusing on the city's squares when displayed at the annual meeting of the National Trust for Historic Preservation hosted by SCAD in Savannah in 1998, *Jewels in the Crown* subsequently traveled to the Octagon Gallery in Washington, D.C., where it opened in November 2000. For the D.C. exhibition we decided to go beyond the squares to illustrate the city's urban plan. Commissioning additional photographs, we attempted to tell the story of Savannah's plan not just through images of buildings but also through the pattern of how those images were hung on the gallery walls to address the plan's logic, what we called "The Architecture of the Savannah Plan," the exhibition's new subtitle. A short essay for an accompanying brochure was the narrative seed of this book.

Our musings about Savannah continued to be enriched by hosting the annual meetings of the Society of Architectural Historians (SAH) and the Vernacular Architecture Forum (VAF) in 2006 and 2007, respectively. The opportunity to author the guidebook *Buildings of Savannah* (University of Virginia Press, 2016), part of the SAH's Buildings of the United States series, allowed us to distill what we already knew about Savannah and discover much that we did not. These experiences, along with other essays we published along the way, helped us realize that the more we analyzed Savannah—its plan, its buildings, its monuments, its landscape features—the more we discovered new layers and complexities. In the words of our colleague at the University of Georgia, Mark Reinberger, "Savannah is the gift that keeps on giving."

Also greatly informing our study has been the day-to-day experience of walking, cycling, and driving on the streets of Savannah and through its squares and other public spaces. We both have given countless walking tours to various groups, including professors and students from other schools' architecture and planning programs, who are always eager to discover the city's secrets. In 2005, the Washington, D.C., chapter of the American Institute of Architects (AIA) held a Regional and Urban Design Knowledge Community roundtable called "Learning from Savannah." Clearly we are not alone in believing the city has much to offer as an urban and architectural model.

ACKNOWLEDGMENTS

WE COULD HARDLY NAME all those who have aided us, inspired us, and provided us with insights over these many years. Our families have been a steady source of support, encouragement, and feedback, helping us stay focused and always challenging us to be clearer and more concise. Our colleagues in the Department of Architectural History at SCAD have also played no small role. The work of E. G. Daves Rossell and our former student Marisa Gomez Nordyke in compiling the 2007 VAF guidebook has been particularly important, as has the work of Daves Rossell, Patrick Haughey, and Karl Schuler as coauthors of our 2016 guidebook, *Buildings of Savannah*. Our students have provided us with countless insights in their theses, research papers, presentations, and observations, and through their penetrating questions during class discussions and on field trips. Among these students, Nathaniel Walker has gone on to publish important and insightful articles on Savannah. Throughout our journey, the Savannah College of Art and Design has supported our efforts in numerous ways, most notably with presidential grants to fund our early research and writing.

Numerous colleagues at other institutions have provided us with helpful feedback as we have shared our research in lectures, tours, and conference presentations. We are deeply indebted to a host of experts who have graciously shared their wisdom and knowledge directly with us, including Leopold Adler II, Stanford Anderson, Malcolm Bell III, Philip Bess, John Deering, John Duncan, Vince Graham, Mark Reinberger, Beth Reiter, John Reps, Christian Sottile, Carroll William Westfall, and Tom Wilson. We also extend much gratitude to the archivists and librarians at the Georgia Historical Society, the Kaye Kole Genealogy and Local History Room at Savannah's Bull Street Library, the Georgia Archives, the Moravian Archives, the Hargrett Rare Book and Manuscript Library at the University of Georgia, the SCAD Jen Library Archives and Special Collections, and, above all, the City of Savannah Municipal Archives and its energetic and congenial director, Luciana Spracher.

The writing of this book has been improved greatly by corrections and suggestions made by many readers and editors. Our anonymous peer reviewers have played an enormous role in this regard, as has the editorial staff at the University of Georgia Press. Others have helped us in developing our illustrations, including Leeza John, Marcel Williams, and Geoffrey Taylor. Colin Williams created the precise digital base map used for many of our diagrams, and Hamilton Brindley applied his skillful hand in drawing illustrations that capture the humanistic spirit of Savannah's architecture.

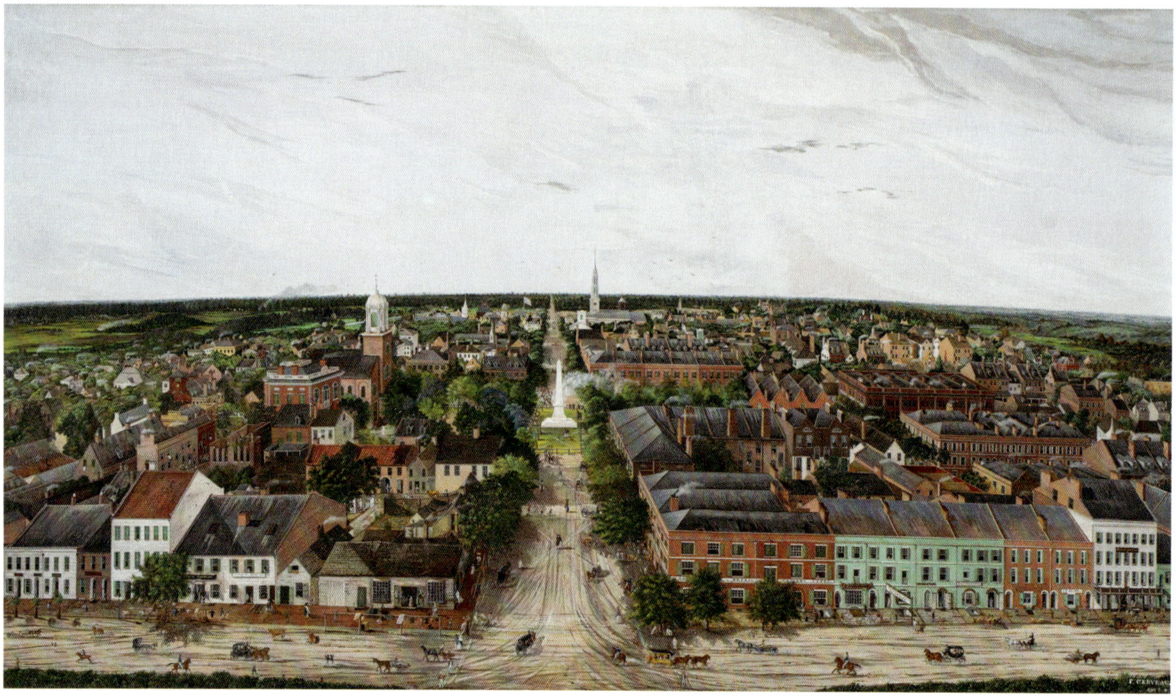

FIGURE 1. *Panorama of Savannah*, Joseph Louis Firmin Cerveau, 1837, watercolor on paper, 27½" × 49½". Courtesy of the Georgia Historical Society, Savannah.

INTRODUCTION

IDEAL AND REAL IN THE SAVANNAH PLAN

. . . you mean the city whose establishment we have described, the city whose home is in the ideal; for I think that it can be found nowhere on earth.
—PLATO, ca. 380 BC

All Houses and Gardens are laid out in *Mathematical Equality*; which will make a fine shew, when they come to Perfection.
—JOHANN BOLTZIUS, 1734, describing Savannah one year after its founding

Savannah, Georgia, more than most cities in the world today, bears the imprint of its utopian founding. Conceiving of a city that satisfies all human needs and desires by composing a masterplan of orderly, geometrically disposed streets, public spaces, and building lots has been a long-standing project in Western history (figure 2). From Plato's *Republic* to Le Corbusier's *Ville Contemporaine*, philosophers, political reformers, and visionary architects have devised such plans. The problem with these imaginary cities is, of course, their unreality. Many, like Thomas More's *Utopia*, belong only to fiction. Others, like the hypothetical plans of Renaissance architect Pietro Cataneo, were drawn on paper but never realized (figure 3). Still others, such as the sixteenth-century star-shaped city of Palmanova that was designed to defend the Venetian Republic (figure 4), or the nineteenth-century Owenite community of New Harmony, Indiana, were built but failed to achieve their intended goals and so remain as curious artifacts, reminders of best-laid plans gone awry. A few cities founded with idealistic motives have grown into thriving metropolises, but their original plans have been so thoroughly compromised that their ideal origins have become unrecognizable to those who walk their streets today. Two famous examples of this last group are the American cities of Philadelphia (Greek for "brotherly love") and New Haven, whose very names divulge their utopian origins but whose plans have lost their ideality.

Savannah stands out in the age-old story of the ideal city. It began as a utopian experiment, resembling a typical Renaissance plan, and like so many others, it quickly failed to fulfill its promised goals. But Savannah's plan transcended its founders' ambitions, such that it is remembered today not as a failure but as one of the nation's most celebrated urban plans. So renowned is this plan that residents and tourists are often told—wrongly—that Savannah is "America's first planned

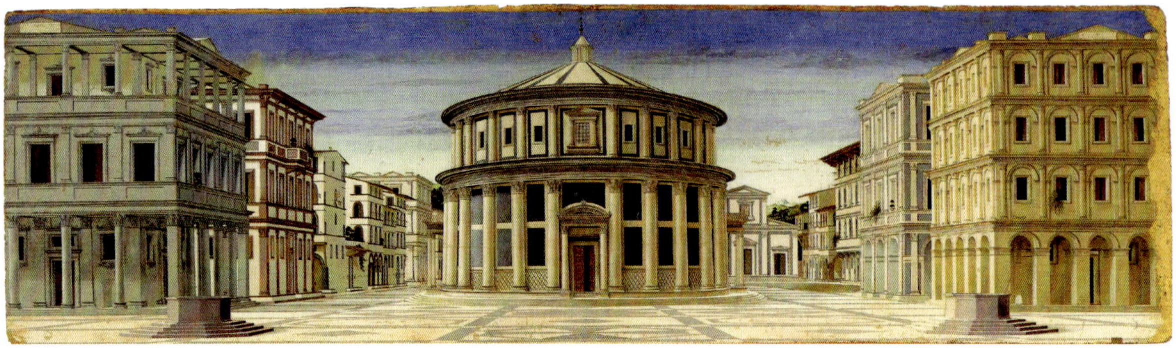

FIGURE 2. *View of an Ideal City*, anonymous, ca. 1470, oil and tempera on wood panel, 26½" × 94½". Galleria Nazionale delle Marche, Urbino, Italy. Public domain via Wikipedia Commons.

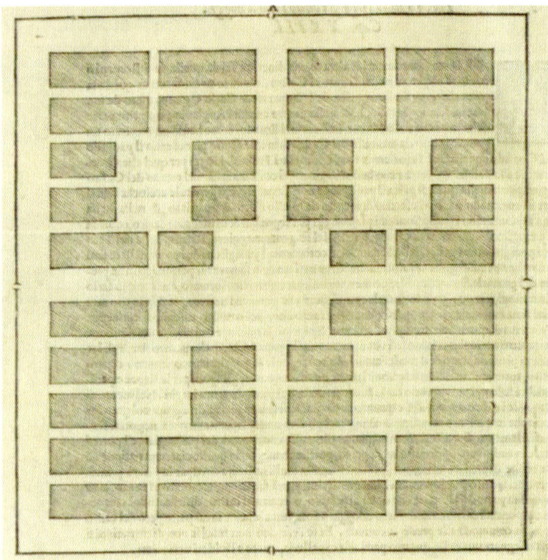

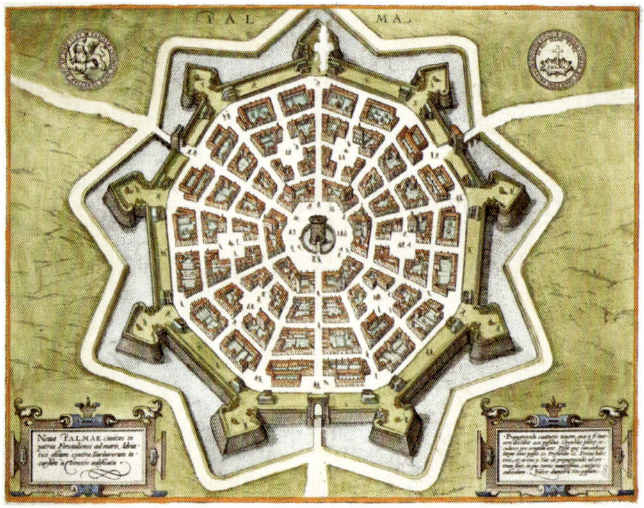

FIGURE 3. (*Left*) Plan for a fortified town, woodcut illustration from Pietro Cataneo, *L'architettura* (Venice, 1567), p. 48. Internet Archive scan of copy at the Getty Research Institute.

FIGURE 4. (*Right*) *Palmanova*, designed by Vincenzo Scamozzi and Giulio Savorgnan, 1593–98. Map drawn in 1593 by Joris Hoefnagel and published in Georg Braun and Frans Hogenberg, *Civitates Orbis Terrarum*, book 5 (Cologne, 1618), p. 68. Courtesy of the Toronto Public Library via Wikimedia Commons.

city."[1] Savannah's achievement, its reputation as a well-planned city, surely warrants further investigation. Indeed, for decades planners, architects, urban designers, and their students have visited the city to glean what lessons Savannah has to teach regarding the design and construction of cities. In this book, we seek to unpack those lessons by investigating and analyzing both the design and implementation of Savannah's original plan, its transformation and expansion into a working plan for a real city, and its impact on the architecture set within it.

The Savannah Plan

The "Savannah Plan" is the name employed throughout this study to refer to the distinctive layout of streets, squares, blocks, and building lots that shapes the historic core of the city—an area a little less than one square mile. The key feature of this plan is the ward, a modular neighborhood unit comprising public and private building lots arranged around a public square and knitted together by a rhythmic pattern of streets (figure 5). The private (residential) building lots are organized into blocks called tythings. The public building lots are autonomous blocks called trust lots. Each Savannah ward is an ideal city plan in miniature, bearing resemblance to countless historic examples of orthogonal, centrally focused town plans. In the Savannah Plan, however, the ward plan is repeated twenty-four times with thirteen subtle variations in a grid of five rows and up to six columns (figure 6). Acting as warp and woof, streets of varying widths run through the city's urban fabric, knitting the blocks and squares of the wards into a composite pattern. This

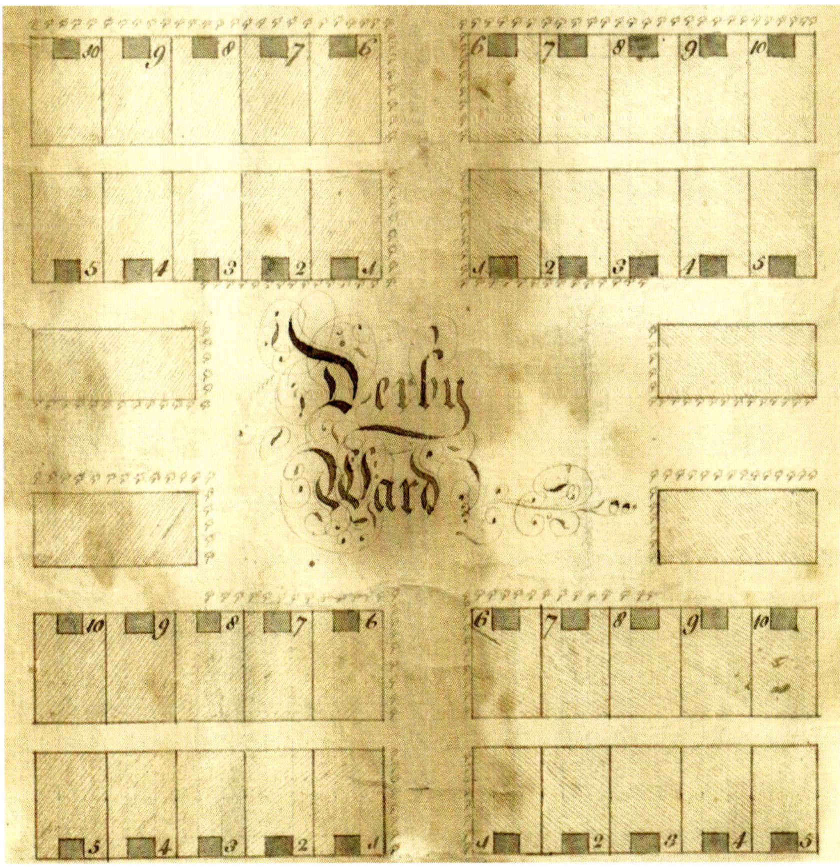

FIGURE 5. Derby Ward as a typical ward; detail taken from the oldest extant plan of Savannah, *A Plan of the Town of Savannah*, ca. 1735–40. By permission of the Archives of the Moravian Church, Bethlehem, Pennsylvania.

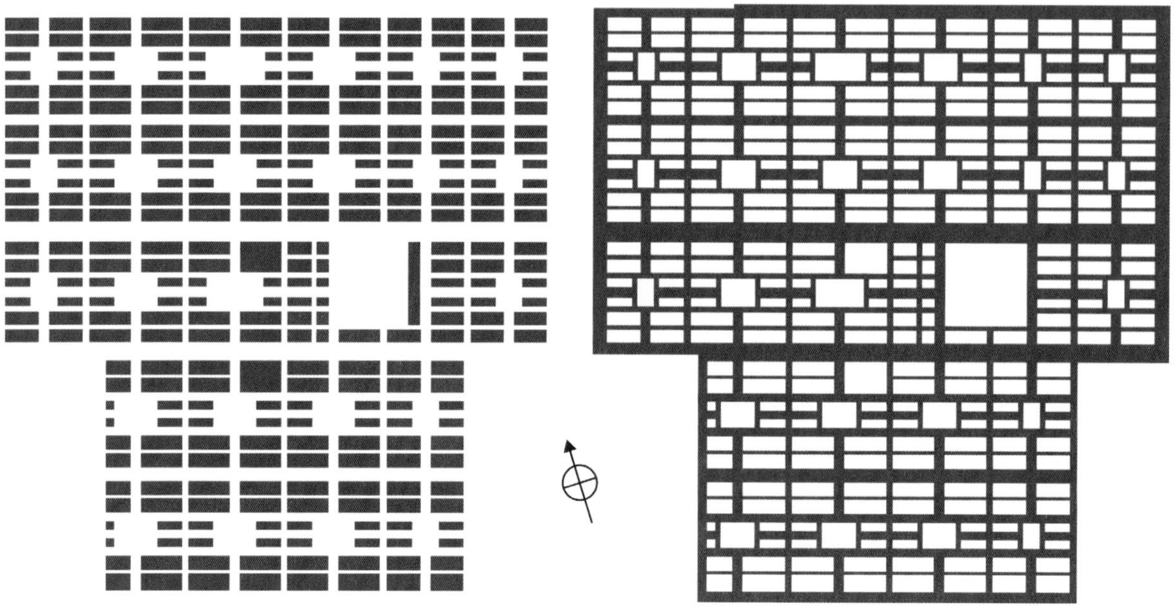

FIGURE 6. Double diagram of the twenty-four-ward Savannah Plan as a network of streets and as a pattern of blocks and squares. Diagram by Robin B. Williams.

essential structure was sewn together by adding wards incrementally, from the first four in 1733 to the final three in 1851. Although certain features have been modified, the integrity of the ward plan has been surprisingly well maintained.

The Savannah Plan is commendable in many ways. Its walkability and human-scaled architecture are among its most profound and immediately felt virtues, but its greatest quality is its elastic ability to hold the real and ideal together in dynamic tension. Savannah is a very real place—it's no utopia—but it bears the unmistakable imprint of the ideal town plan laid out at its founding. Evading the fate that has befallen so many other utopian designs, the Savannah Plan has maintained its essential geometric order while simultaneously adapting to changing needs, circumstances, and social values.

The Savannah Plan cannot be understood, however, merely as an abstract drawing or a set of principles. The geometry of the plan is made real by the physical components that compose the city's urban fabric: its streets, squares, trees, monuments, and buildings. Our book examines the symbiotic relationship between the plan as an idea and its actual implementation over time. We believe that it is in the agile interplay between the layout of Savannah's urban plan and its richly crafted fabric of buildings and landscape features that Savannah's greatest lessons can be learned. It is in the give-and-take of this dialogue that the secret to Savannah's ideality is found.

Savannah's dialogical nature derives from the often-overlooked fact that its plan is the creation of a succession of designers over an extended period, not the work of a single individual or of a moment in history. James Edward Oglethorpe, representing the "Trustees for establishing the colony of Georgia," rightly deserves credit for laying out the initial scheme for Savannah in 1733. His achievement has been celebrated and studied by many, including Thomas Wilson in his book appropriately entitled *The Oglethorpe Plan*.[2] By all accounts, Oglethorpe's visionary layout for Savannah stands as a masterplan in the utopian tradition. What is often forgotten, however, is how dramatically Oglethorpe's plan of Savannah differs from the plan that was implemented over time. Foremost among the differences is how Oglethorpe's plan was limited and fixed in its layout of six wards. Oglethorpe and the Trustees envisioned Savannah as a low-density, agrarian town. As Wilson astutely observes, it was never meant to grow.[3] In 1752, less than two decades after Savannah's founding, the egalitarian and agrarian ideals of the Georgia Trustees were abandoned, and through several incremental steps beginning in 1791, the urban plan was expanded into the town Common to produce the mid-nineteenth-century plan that is praised today. Although the expansion replicated the ward conceived by Oglethorpe, urban growth had not been his intention.

Thus the Savannah Plan is not a masterplan by a master designer but a working plan that was repeatedly modified, expanded, and refined by various surveyors, city engineers, and political leaders to accommodate changing civic ideals and circumstances over the course of a century and a half. Ever since its essential completion in the 1850s, planners, architects, and citizens have continued to modify, amend, and refine the plan. Elements of the Savannah Plan—its block scale, street widths, lanes, landscape elements, and, in some neighborhoods, squares—continued to shape the city's urban form as it grew outward into automobile-oriented suburban districts. Even today, long after the city has run out of municipal land on which to expand the plan, private developers in Savannah continue to employ its elements and emulate the architecture it generated. The Savannah Plan is an ongoing project.

The Allure of the Plan

Savannah may not be among the most famous cities in the world, but it has had no shortage of admirers over the past two centuries. What is celebrated most is nothing spectacular; it is simply a town whose orderly streets, squares, and buildings present a compelling vision of urban life. "Of all the cities in America, none impresses itself more vividly upon the imagination and the memory than this little green bowery city of the South," wrote Scottish poet Charles Mackay in *Life and Liberty in America* in 1859.[4] Some years earlier, the Virginia novelist William Caruthers had one of his protagonists observe that Savannah "is nobly built, and is laid out on a magnificent scale. . . . Talk of Philadelphia, and New-York, and Boston, and Richmond, and New-Haven—Savannah outstrips them all, both in artificial and natural beauty."[5]

In the latter half of the twentieth century, Savannah once again attracted adulation. Writing in 1960, famed Italian journalist and novelist Italo Calvino was effusive in his praise, calling Savannah "THE MOST BEAUTIFUL CITY IN THE UNITED STATES. . . . It is one of the only American cities to have been built with unique urban planning, of extreme rational regularity and variety and harmony."[6] Travel magazines and newspapers have routinely sung the praises of Savannah, but unlike so many other "great cities," Savannah is lauded not so much for its museums, cultural attractions, natural features, food, or even architecture as it is for its urban plan. A 1997 *Washington Post* article by Roger Lewis, for example, claimed Savannah as "one of America's greatest town planning paradigms, a model of rational, geometric composition aesthetically vitalized by an extraordinary array of public squares . . . that have become the city's hallmark."[7] A 1986 travel section article in the *Toronto Star* claimed that "MANY cities around the globe spend great amounts of civic energy trying numerous master plans in search of a sense of character, [or] focus on some other elusive element to give them a unique aura and appeal. This town [Savannah] has been blessed with everything they're seeking since its birthday in 1733."[8]

Urban planners and historians have long felt the same way. In his renowned 1967 book *Design of Cities*, Edmund Bacon called the Savannah Plan "so exalted that it remains as one of the finest diagrams for city organization and growth in existence."[9] A. E. J. Morris noted in his influential 1972 textbook *History of Urban Form* that "whatever its origins and whoever assisted him, Oglethorpe's name coupled with that of Savannah merits a far higher position in urban history than hitherto accorded."[10] Unquestionably, it is the individuality of the plan that has driven scholars such as Turpin Bannister, John Reps, and Stanford Anderson to study the formal sources and historical development of the city.[11] Thomas Wilson's more recent books are further evidence of a growing body of scholarship dedicated to explaining and debating the origins of the plan. Regarding the forms and ideas associated with the founding of a city, we can think of few case studies that have sustained as much scholarly attention as Savannah has.

This book builds on the work of these scholars by exploring how the Savannah Plan evolved into its present form and how it continues to evolve in response to changing social, economic, and technological conditions. Our investigation goes beyond existing literature by integrating a study of the city's architecture with our study of the plan. Savannah's historic architecture has been cataloged and researched by many local and national scholars, most especially those concerned with matters of historic preservation. Rather little of this literature, however, explores the distinctive practices and forms that characterize Savannah's architecture in relation to the broader history of architecture or the interaction between the architecture and the city's urban plan. We intend to synthesize these concerns as we seek to learn from Savannah as a model of urban and architectural form.

The Persistence of the Plan

An important part of being "real" is not being held captive to the past. It is tempting to assume that Savannah has garnered praise and attention because it somehow escaped the forces of modernization, in the manner of such celebrated cities as Venice or Siena. Indeed, today's prospective visitors to Savannah are often promised an immersive antebellum experience. Historic preservationists, architects, and planners likewise approach Savannah as a "historic city" with a "historic district." Nevertheless, as much as we admire and care for its history and historic content, we must emphasize that Savannah is an ongoing venture; it is a modern city with an illustrious history, not a historic relic. Its historical development has not, until recently, been guided by a bracketing of its "historic" content. In a 2024 article on the website of an advocacy group called Strong Towns, the group's chief technical advisor complained about the "regulatory amber" that has left Savannah "frozen under glass, making it nearly impossible to allow the traditional pattern of development."[12] This book seeks not to advocate for any regulatory policies but to learn from the city's urban and architectural lessons with the knowledge that Savannah's history is far from finished.

Savannah has been confronted by the same forces of change and destruction that have so dramatically affected other American cities. Major urban fires devastated the city several times from 1796 to 1889. New transportation and building technologies—the railroad, the streetcar, the automobile, and the skyscraper—have left an imprint on the city's urban fabric. The Central of Georgia Railway, established in 1833, had by the 1850s constructed one of the nation's most advanced railroad complexes on the western edge of the city. The embrace of early skyscraper technology by 1895 and the construction of multiple high-rises during the early 1900s reflected the city's openness to change and new ideas. Like most other cities in the post–World War II era, Savannah saw the departure of residents and businesses to the city's growing suburbs, prompting local leaders to experiment with large-scale urban renewal projects, notably the construction of a new civic center and county courthouse, which obliterated parts of the plan. Nor has the city been immune to racial, social, and economic inequities.

The ability of the Savannah Plan to transcend the forces of change is due in part to the esteem with which Savannahians have long regarded it, an esteem that has engendered what French writer Bernard-Henri Lévy observed to be "a rare but all the more precious case of metrophilia, or city-love, in America."[13] Lévy was impressed by "the way the inhabitants love their town." It may well have been a case of metrophilia that prompted the municipal government in the 1790s to expand the town "agreeably to the old Plan of Savannah"—that is, using the planning formula devised by Oglethorpe—even though its social and economic goals were contrary to those of the city's founders. This decision set up the growth pattern that civic leaders followed for the next sixty-five years in the course of six more expansions. Despite the rather ignominious end of the founding Trustees' control of the Georgia colony, municipal officials in Savannah even retained the nomenclature of the utopian plan (trust lots, the Trustees' Garden).

The establishment of the Georgia Historical Society in 1839 heralded the beginning of a long-standing tradition of preserving the cultural heritage of the city, thus nurturing generations of historians focused on Savannah's built environment. Savannah, having survived the Civil War largely unscathed—thanks to General Sherman's decision to occupy the city rather than torch it—faced new threats in the years that followed. In 1871, city officials fought an unsuccessful legal battle against a street railway company to prevent streetcar tracks from passing through the city's squares. When in the 1920s "automobilists" lobbied to cut roads through the squares, city officials and a majority of citizens fiercely opposed the proposal.[14] Although their efforts failed to prevent U.S. Route 17 from severing three squares in 1935, the decade-long battle galvanized Savannahians to protect and beautify the remaining squares and prepared them for further rounds of preservation battles over the squares in 1945–46, 1953, and 1962, while the fights to save buildings in the 1950s and beyond have been led by the Historic Savannah Foundation, established in 1955.

Not only has the Savannah Plan withstood the relentless forces of time and modernization, it also has adapted and changed in innovative ways. As the plan expanded in the nineteenth century, inventive new features were introduced. When new wards were laid out in 1801, the former southern edge of the town was transformed into a 140-foot-wide boulevard, South Broad Street (now Oglethorpe Avenue), establishing a new feature in the plan—the tree-lined median (possibly its first appearance in American urbanism)—that would be replicated on Liberty Street and several other streets and become a defining characteristic of the city (figure 7).[15] The plan also mutated in response to changing social needs, with the discarding of land use restrictions on the various blocks defined by the founding Trustees and, more radically, the amalgamation of adjacent blocks to create larger building sites. The power of the plan to accommodate innovation is yet further evidence of its elastic nature.

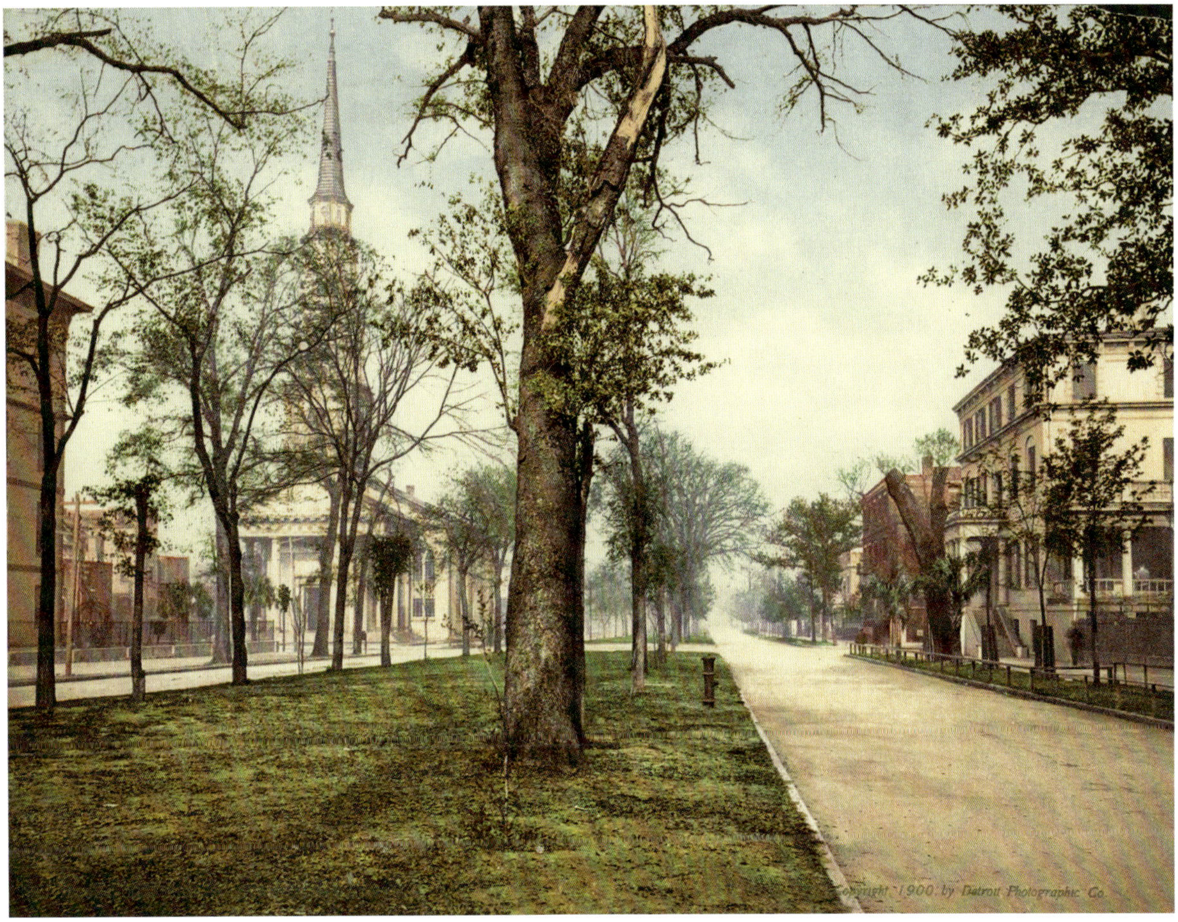

The Power of the Plan

FIGURE 7. *Oglethorpe Avenue* (South Broad Street), looking west across Bull Street, ca. 1900, photochrom print, Detroit Photographic. Library of Congress, Prints and Photographs Division.

The Savannah Plan's power is plainly revealed in the architecture it fosters. Savannah's public and private buildings are governed in their distribution, scale, composition, and ornament by the organizing patterns of the city's wards, building lots, streets, and squares. Public buildings are dispersed across wards in a way that avoids the conventional concentration of political power around a single urban node. Residential and commercial buildings are similarly scattered. Civic and utilitarian streets of varied widths, prominent trust lots, less prominent tything lots, and, of course, public squares at the heart of each ward create hierarchies both within the wards and across the entire Savannah Plan. The resulting tension between the dispersed uniformity and competing hierarchies of the plan elicits architectural responses that are as rich in their complexity and nuance as the plan itself. Buildings on trust lots, for example, almost always face the square they front, while secondary entrances or dependent buildings occupy the rear of the site fronting the utilitarian street at the edge of the ward. Yet trust lot buildings respond to this configuration in numerous creative ways in terms of scale, layout, style, materials, function, and so on. The architecture *of* the plan shapes the architecture *in* the plan.

No single building stands out as being original, and even the components of the plan itself are quite ordinary, yet Savannah's built environment has a character that is authentically its own. The habits of its buildings, building forms, and details are peculiar to the city. The plan, with all its idiosyncrasies, must be recognized for its power to establish the city's distinctive sense of place. Exceptional as it is, Savannah has lessons that apply to all cities, lessons that are not easily discovered nor reduceable to a simple formula. Savannah's lessons are about the difficult task of balancing competing principles such as regularity and flexibility, uniformity and difference, and modernity and tradition. They are also about how architectural and landscape design are shaped by planning decisions and vice versa. Savannah is a vivid case study of how this symbiotic process works, one that can shed light on the architecture and planning of many other cities.

Learning from Savannah

To investigate the architecture of the Savannah Plan is to learn how Savannah has embraced both the ideal and the real. To do this requires a sustained analysis of the ideas and ideals that informed the plan, the events and decisions that gave it life, and the formal qualities of the plan and its architectural and landscape elements. We seek to learn from Savannah by analyzing its urban plan and its architecture from a variety of perspectives: its origins, development, form, meaning, and legacy. Section 1 explores how the plan came into being and how it was transformed from the utopian "Oglethorpe Plan" into the flexible, incremental, and multiauthored "Savannah Plan." Section 2 analyzes the component parts of the plan—its DNA, so to speak—and then identifies lessons that can be learned from the many paradoxical patterns produced by and embedded in the Savannah Plan as a whole. Section 3 explores how the parts and patterns of the urban plan have played a decisive role in shaping Savannah's architecture and landscape design. Here we find the paradox of ordinary architecture that is made extraordinary by the plan. Section 4 moves beyond the Savannah Plan in two different senses: first, by exploring how the city grew beyond the twenty-four wards and squares that make up the Savannah Plan into the surrounding garden and farm lots with suburban reverberations of the plan, and second, by exploring the legacy of the Savannah Plan in places near and far from Savannah both historically and in the present day. The final chapter ponders one of the most perplexing questions posed by the plan: Given that it is so admired, why has it not been replicated?

The Savannah Plan is elegant in its simplicity and logic but wily in its adaptability and nuance. Like any other city plan, it is merely a pattern of lines and rectangles that describe a network of streets, squares, and building lots. How it has organized and shaped the city and its architecture over time, however, is anything but simple. In these pages we describe and attempt to unlock the subtle mechanics of the Savannah Plan as they have functioned from the city's founding to the present. In doing so we hope to shed light on what makes Savannah one of the most admired cities in the United States.

SECTION ONE

BEING AND BECOMING SAVANNAH

AN EVOLVING, MULTIAUTHORED PLAN

A work of art is never finished, merely abandoned.
—PAUL VALÉRY, 1933

The work of a single man remains necessarily meager and dies when scarcely born.
—ANTONI GAUDÍ, 1901

Like a Shakespearean sonnet or a Bach fugue, the Savannah Plan is admirable for its unity of design and its unique identity. Unlike such artistic masterpieces, however, the Savannah Plan does not belong to a single designer or moment in time. Its initial design was undoubtedly the work of James Oglethorpe in 1733, but as it is experienced today, the Savannah Plan can only partially be credited to its founder and his time period. Many of its features deviate significantly from Oglethorpe's initial plan both in form and in function. The Savannah Plan, therefore, should not be confused with what has been called the Oglethorpe Plan. The Savannah Plan is a unified and cohesive design that was produced by many authors working over more than a century, a period interrupted by two wars, several disastrous fires, economic downturns, and two regime changes. In fact, the plan has continued to absorb and reflect social, technological, and political changes while maintaining its distinctive character to the present day. Surely this uncanny ability to change and yet remain essentially intact holds lessons for urban designers today. This is the story of how Savannah itself learned from Savannah.

The lessons of the Savannah Plan are paradoxical. The ability of the plan to change and yet not change—to be one thing and then become another while maintaining its essential unity of design—is among the most intriguing of its paradoxes. It might be explained by employing another simile: The Savannah Plan functions as the city's genetic code, its DNA. As with any individual human, its genetic code is uniquely its own, but this code does not prevent it from growing or changing in shape, size, or personality. What we are calling the Savannah Plan is at once a timeless idea and a spatial-temporal reality; it is a work of art, but one that is caught between being and becoming.

CHAPTER ONE

CONCEIVING AND IMPLEMENTING THE PLAN, 1732–1752

Whoever then is a Lover of Liberty, will be pleas'd with an Attempt to recover his fellow Subjects from a State of Misery and Oppression, and state them in Happiness and Freedom.

Whoever is a Lover of his Country, will approve of a Method for the Employment of her Poor, and the Increase of her People, and her Trade.

Whoever is a Lover of Mankind, will join his Wishes to the Success of a Design, so plainly calculated for their Good: Undertaken, and conducted, with so much Disinterestedness.

—BENJAMIN MARTYN, secretary for the Georgia Trustees, 1733

In the distribution of the Town the Streets should be spacious and laid out by Line and a large Square reserved for a Market place, and for exercising the Inhabitants, on the sides of which may be the Church, Infirmary for the Sick, an House for new Comers, Town House and other publick Buildings.

—JAMES OGLETHORPE, ca. 1732

The Savannah Plan in the Trustee Era

The Savannah Plan began as a diagram for a new society in a new world. Like John Winthrop's "City upon a Hill" or William Penn's "greene Country Towne," James Oglethorpe's Georgia was a bold experiment in human polity, one that was to be carried out in the boundlessly promising but still mysterious wilderness of America. Like its predecessors, the Georgia colony was a radical attempt to recast the relationship between city and country, to create a society harmonious with itself and with nature. Like other political experiments, the enterprise undertaken by the Georgia Trustees was a predictable failure. And yet, like several other American colonial endeavors, the principles for which it stood and the lessons it continues to teach resonate with the ideals of the American founding. The carefully formulated regional plan of Savannah and its hinterland played a key role in the society envisaged by the Georgia Trustees, but it too failed to function as its founders intended. The urban component of that regional plan, the Savannah Plan of today, retains the essential elements of its original design, but with its fourfold expansion to twenty-four wards, its lush

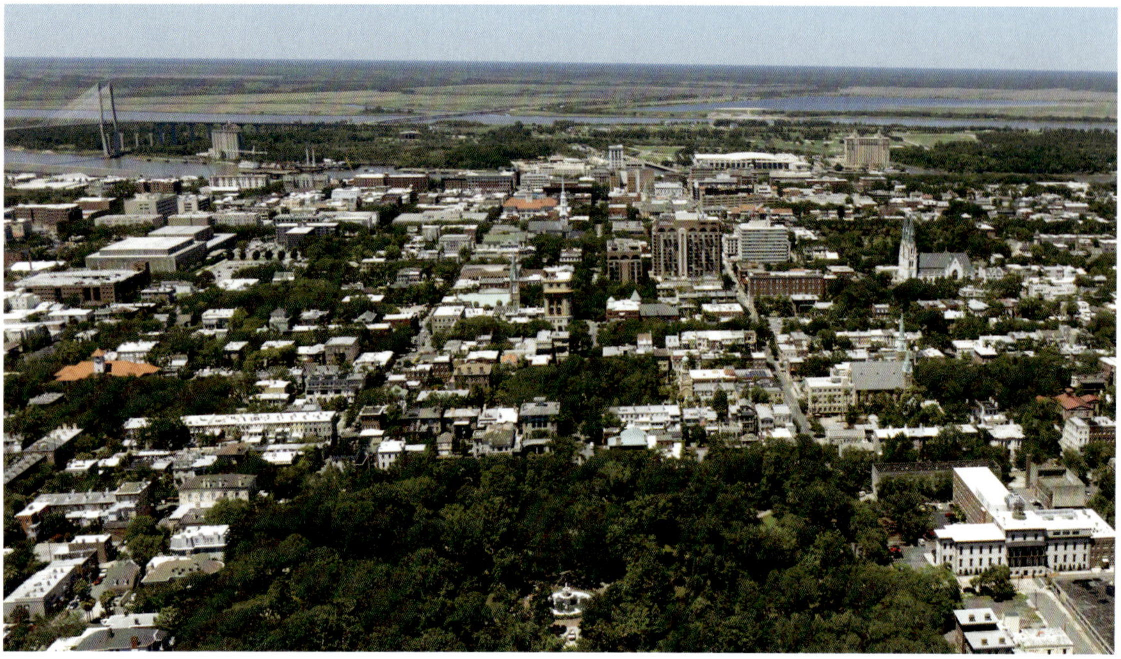

FIGURE 8. Detail of *An Aerial View of Savannah, Georgia*, looking north. Digital photograph by Carol M. Highsmith, 2017. Library of Congress, Prints and Photographs Division.

landscape features, and its rich architectural fabric, it is far from what Oglethorpe or his fellow Trustees in eighteenth-century England ever imagined it would become (figure 8).

The events and circumstances surrounding the establishment of the Georgia colony have been amply documented and ably analyzed.[1] Numerous letters, journals, pamphlets, and documents have been preserved, and many have been transcribed and republished.[2] Many scholars have studied these documents and provided critical accounts of the Georgia founding from a variety of perspectives, offering diverse explanations regarding the motivations of the Trustees. What's indisputable is that King George II signed a charter on June 9, 1732, granting lands south of the Savannah River and north of the Altamaha River to the Trustees for establishing the colony of Georgia.[3] The charter granted the Trustees the authority to raise funds and to establish settlements and plantations and govern them for a period of twenty-one years, after which the colony would revert to the control of the Crown. King George's stated purpose for supporting the colony was to extend compassion to "our Poor Subjects [who] are through misfortunes and want of Employment reduced to great necessities insomuch as by their labour they are not able to provide a maintenance for themselves and Families." This was done by paying their expenses and settling them in Georgia, where "Cultivating the lands at present wast[e] and desolate they might not only gain a Comfortable Subsistence for themselves and families but also Strengthen our Colonies and Encrease the trade Navigation and Wealth of these our Realms."[4]

The charter further explains how settlements in this region would provide security against warlike "Indian Enemies." Unstated in the charter, but widely understood by Parliament and the Crown, was the need to secure Britain's claim to the territory between the Carolinas and Florida, which the Spanish claimed as theirs. The Georgia charter of 1732 thus represents an important chapter in the geopolitical and social history of Great Britain.

Of the twenty-one Trustees listed in the Georgia charter, fourteen were members of Parliament, two were scientists, and five were ministers of the Church of England. A total of seventy-one Trustees served terms of varying length over the twenty-year existence of the organization. They came to the Trust with a variety of interests and abilities and were not always in agreement about goals and methods, but their motto, *Non sibi sed aliis* (Not for self but for others), represented their common desire to serve the needy through selfless charity. Fundraising and promotion occupied much of their energy, but the Trustees were also responsible for the governance of the colony, a task they were not equipped to fulfill.

James Oglethorpe was the group's visionary founder and the only Trustee to visit the Georgia colony. Motivated by his celebrated leadership as chair of a parliamentary committee on prison reform, Oglethorpe conceived the idea of planting a charity colony as a means of resettling debtors from prison, an objective that was only partly realized. He found a key ally in Viscount John Perceval (titled the first Earl of Egmont in 1733), who served on the prison reform committee and as one of four associates of a charitable trust managed by the Reverend Thomas Bray, the Associates of Dr. Bray. This philanthropic group was charged with the administration of a bequest granted by Abel Tassin d'Alonne to support the instruction of "Negroes" serving on British plantations in the Christian religion.[5] Bray was a noted social reformer with a concern for Christian evangelism and education, especially in the American colonies. He was the founder of the Society for Promoting Christian Knowledge (SPCK) and the Society for the Propagation of the Gospel in Foreign Parts (SPG). To the D'Allone trust, Bray added legacies from his own estate intended for the funding of libraries in Britain and the colonies. Upon Bray's death in 1731, Oglethorpe and Perceval were able to expand the membership of the Associates of Dr. Bray, add new sources of funding, and refocus its scope to include the founding of a charitable colony. It was from these alliances that the Georgia Trust was born.

Promotional pamphlets confirm that the Trustees were driven by a desire to alleviate rising urban poverty in England by providing the "worthy poor" with an opportunity to start their lives afresh in the New World. A second pressing concern was the plight of Protestants fleeing religious persecution on the continent.

Large numbers of Huguenots, Palatines, Salzburgers, Moravians, and other groups were struggling as placeless refugees in early eighteenth-century Europe. "The Protestant Interest in Europe hath declin'd very much since the Treaty of Westphalia," wrote Trustee secretary Benjamin Martyn in *Reasons for Establishing the Colony of Georgia*.[6] The promotion of Protestantism in its various forms was a repeated theme in the sermons given during the annual joint meetings of the Trustees and the Bray Associates, as it was also an emphasis in the missionary efforts of the SPCK and SPG.[7]

The Trustees' plan for the Georgia colony was a utopian experiment in social, political, economic, and religious reform. Like the Augustan poets and satirists of their day, the Georgia Trustees believed that British society had been poisoned by self-interest, greed, and moral decay. Growing urban poverty and the failure of the privileged classes to properly provide relief or moral guidance to the poor created a culture of despair and dissipation. "We hear, that Publick Spirit is lost among us, and that no one pursues any Dictates but those of his Interest," wrote Martyn. "It is Time to awaken People," he continued, "to a Love of their Country, to see her Welfare, and to promote it. Virtues may become a Habit in a Nation, as well as in a private Man."[8] The Trustees conceived the Georgia colony as an answer to this call. It would be a republic of virtue, rooted in the principle of "Agrarian Equality." Perhaps the most eloquent expression of this vision is found in an anniversary sermon preached by Philip Bearcroft to the Trustees in London in 1738. Drawing inspiration from both the Roman Republic and the Hebrew prophet Micah, Bearcroft explained his hope for the Georgia colonists:

> That they may apply with Pleasure and Alacrity, to the Cultivation of their Farms . . . which will naturally raise such a general Industry, and virtuous Emulation through the Colony, that with the free-born Romans of Old, they will quit the Plough only to transact the Business of their rising State; and that finished, hasten back to the Labors of the Field, and at the Close of them, sit with their Wives and Children, under their own Vines and Fruit-Trees, and enjoy Themselves, in a virtuous Frugality, under the happy Influence of this Agrarian Law.[9]

The Georgia colony was thus conceived as a free society of landowning citizens equally distributed across the land, cultivating habits of virtue as they cultivated their gardens and farms. Appeal to the "Agrarian Law" appears repeatedly in the literature of the colony.[10] Oglethorpe refers to it in a letter to the Trustees as "Agrarian Equality, one of the first principles on which you set out."[11] Like other political reformers of their day, Georgia proponents appealed to Hebrew, Greek, Roman, and Saxon precedents to justify their plan. Their concept of agrarian law is believed by several scholars to be rooted in neo-Harringtonian thought.[12]

Whatever its ideological sources might have been, the Georgia experiment was a critique of developments in eighteenth-century England—the consolidation of agricultural lands into the hands of the landed elite, the displacement of the rural poor through the Enclosure Acts, and the rapid growth of urban centers. It was also a repudiation of the plantation culture in nearby South Carolina, which similarly saw the rapid rise of a planter elite dependent on slave labor. To ensure the Georgia colony's success as an egalitarian, agrarian republic, the Trustees famously instituted prohibitions against land speculation, the consumption of rum, the practice of Roman Catholicism, and the importation of enslaved Africans.[13] These prohibitions soon became sources of resentment for many colonists. Except for the ban on Catholics, all the restrictions would be rescinded before the end of Trustee rule.

To support their venture, the Trustees waged a multifaceted promotional campaign appealing to a variety of constituencies and interests. In addition to making moral arguments on behalf of the poor and the persecuted, they crafted pragmatic appeals concerning the political and economic interests of Britain. Supporting the Georgia colony was not simply an act of charity, the Trustees argued; it was an investment in national prosperity. A 1732 promotional tract contended, for example, that the indebted poor were a costly drain on the British economy and that sending them abroad would enrich the nation, not only by reducing national expenditures but also by creating new wealth and extending national interests in the colonies.[14] Indigents could be turned into productive citizens by granting them a new start in a distant colony.

Geopolitical concerns more pressing to the Crown and Parliament were also addressed: French, Spanish, and Native American interests converged and often collided at the southern frontier of the British colonies. The Carolina colony was threatened in the early eighteenth century by attacks from the French and Spanish; the Spanish further destabilized British rule by forming alliances with Native tribes and encouraging enslaved Africans to run away from their captors to find freedom in Spanish Florida. From 1715 to 1717, the Yamasee War unnerved many Europeans in the Carolina colony, precipitating significant changes in its governance.[15] Proprietary rule came to an end in 1719, and a policy of systematic settlement was instituted in the newly established Crown Colony of South Carolina by its second royal governor, Robert Johnson. The Township Act of 1730 codified Johnson's plan to establish South Carolina towns of twenty thousand acres, "laid out in square plats," contiguous with a river, and with a town common not greater than three hundred acres; each settler would be granted both a town lot and a farm lot totaling fifty acres, the same total that the Savannah Plan would offer.[16] These towns, to be populated by poor Protestants from the continent, were to be built in part as a counterstrategy to the plantation system that had characterized much of the earlier settlement of the Carolinas.[17] Although some of these towns were built, Parliament was keen to expand British settlements south of the Savannah River in territory whose sovereignty was contested by the Spanish Crown.

Beyond national defense and territorial control, the Trustees promoted the Georgia colony for its potential agricultural production as a way of enticing London merchants to invest in the project. Promotional pamphlets highlighted the colony's warm and salubrious climate, perfectly suited for cultivating crops that could not grow in England. Of particular interest was silk production. Expert consultants advised the Trustees that Georgia was so well-suited to growing mulberry trees and raising silkworms that it would quickly be able to supply all of Europe with silk, which would enrich England and reduce its dependence on imports. Other crops, including vineyards, olives, coffee, and cotton, were thought to have high-yield potential in this tropical paradise as well. The Trustees funded the Trustees' Garden, the first experimental botanical garden on the continent, for the purpose of identifying plants that would flourish in Georgia.[18]

Despite their altruism and tireless efforts, the Trustees failed to achieve their goals. The collapse of their experiment in social, economic, and moral order is well documented and has been carefully analyzed, though opinions have varied regarding the causes of the failure.[19] Criticism of the venture came soon after its implementation. As early as 1735, "clamorous malcontents" among the colonists began to grumble, bringing charges of mismanagement and neglect against Oglethorpe. More troubling were increasing complaints about foundational policies of the colony. Rules established by the Trustees were seen by many as overbearing, intolerant, and unrealistic. Many colonists objected to the tail-male policy of land tenure, under which property that was granted could not be sold but could only be inherited by "the Heirs Male of their Bodies for ever; And in Case of Failure of Issue Male Revert to the Trust, to be Granted again to such Persons as the Common Council of the said Trustees shall think most for the Advantage of the Colony."[20] The ban on slavery was proclaimed intolerable, and the prohibition of rum, which was generally ignored, was viewed as unjustifiable. The Trustees were charged with falsely exaggerating claims about the climate and fertility of the soil. Oglethorpe left the colony and quit the Trust in 1743, dispirited and facing numerous accusations. In June 1752 the Georgia Trustees gave up their charter to Parliament and disbanded, one year before the charter was to expire. Only one of the original Trustees, James Vernon, remained until the end.

Although their social, economic, and political goals were largely unrealized, the Trustees successfully founded a state and city that carry the imprimatur of their urban and regional planning and a legacy that continues to be celebrated by the popular use of place-names such as the "Trustees' Garden" and terms such as "trust lots" and by events like the Trustees Gala, held annually to commemorate Georgia's founders.

Building the Plan

Oglethorpe personally led the first boatload of 114 colonists across the Atlantic as a veritable *oikist*, a city founder in the manner of the ancient Greeks. Though he was given no official governing role, he was the only Trustee to travel to Georgia. Oglethorpe had knowledge about and enthusiasm for architecture and city planning. In his pamphlet *Some Account of the Design of the Trustees* he makes extensive references to Vitruvius's *Ten Books of Architecture* as well as to other architectural treatises.[21] For these reasons, we presume that Oglethorpe was the designer of Savannah's urban plan, but no document explicitly proving this attribution has been found.[22] No signed drawing exists.

On February 12, 1733, the Georgia colonists "arrived at Yamacra[w] Bluff, the place which Mr. Oglethorpe had pitched upon for our intended settlement," wrote Peter Gordon, bailiff of the colony.[23] Foreshadowing the four wards that would soon be laid out, the settlers pitched four large tents that day, perhaps to accommodate the four groups overseen by the four tythingmen appointed by Oglethorpe while still on board the ship.[24] On February 16, Colonel William Bull, "being a gentlem[a]n of great experience in making of settlements" and surveyor general of South Carolina, arrived to assist Oglethorpe in laying out the town.[25] Another observer noted that on February 20, "Mr. Oglethorpe and Colonel Bull marked out the square, the streets, and the lots for the houses."[26] Oglethorpe himself wrote, "I have marked out the Town and Common; half of the former is already cleared, and the first House was begun Yesterday in the Afternoon."[27] A slight discrepancy appears in Gordon's journal, which reports that on March 1, "the first house in the square was framed, and raised, Mr. Oglethorp[e] driving the first pinn."[28] In any case, these earliest accounts tell of a city founded with methodical foresight and a sense of destiny.

The four wards laid out by Bull and Oglethorpe are the modular neighborhood units that constitute the plan. In *A View of Savanah as It Stood the 29th of March, 1734*—an engraved copperplate print published in London by Paul Fourdrinier and commonly referred to as the "Gordon View," because the name of the Trustees' bailiff, Peter Gordon, appears on the print—we see these wards, just one year after Savannah was founded, eerily etched onto a perfectly flat clearing in the wilderness, a colonial *tabula rasa* (figure 9).[29] Two more wards were added under Oglethorpe's direction soon after the first year, yielding a town of six wards. A plan

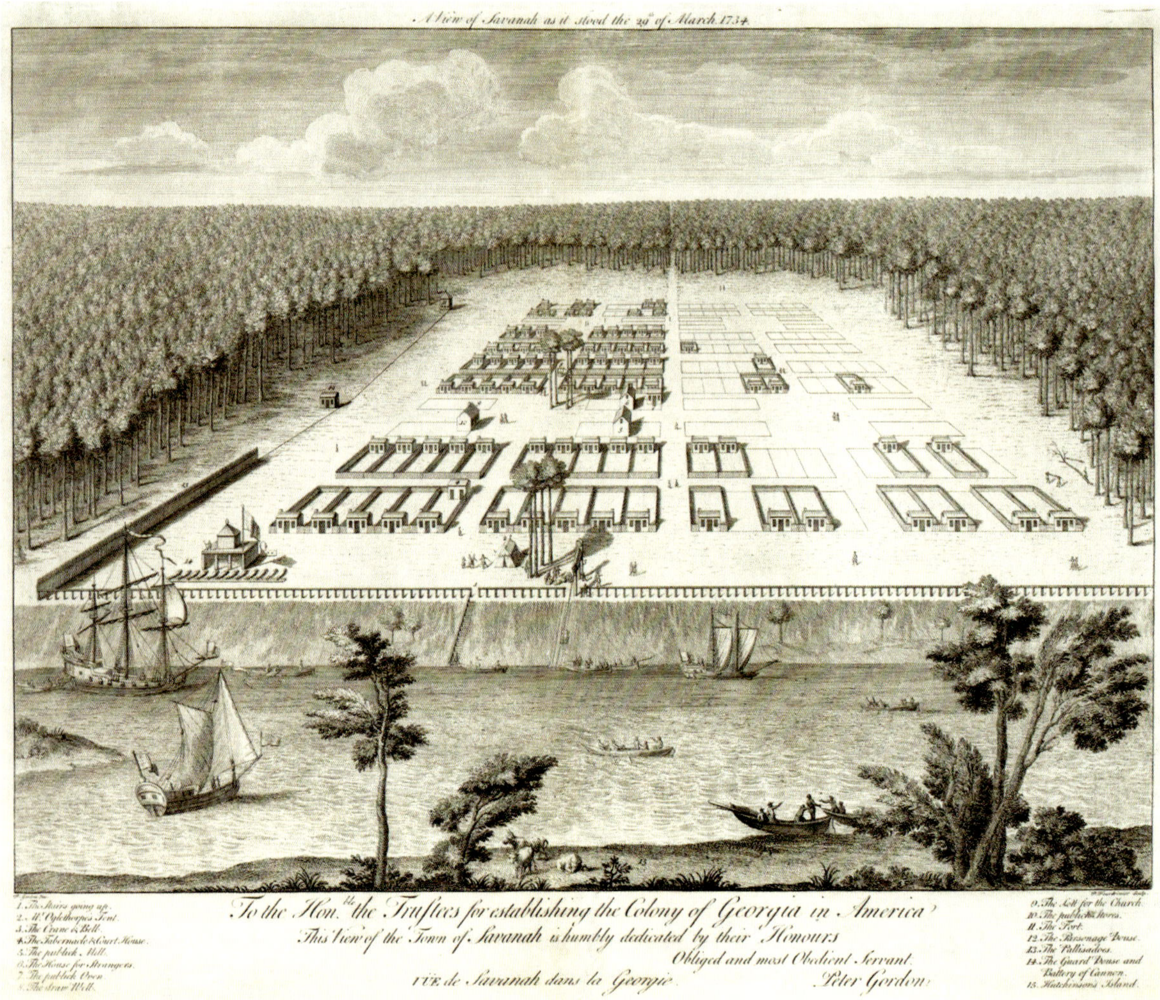

FIGURE 9. *A View of Savanah as It Stood the 29th of March, 1734,* copperplate engraving of a watercolor sketch probably by George Jones, though usually attributed to Peter Gordon; engraved by Paul Fourdrinier (London, 1734). Library of Congress, Prints and Photographs Division.

dating to 1735–40 that is now in the Moravian Archives in Bethlehem, Pennsylvania, shows these six wards neatly drawn to scale (figure 10). A verbal description of the Savannah Plan as it appeared in 1735 was penned by Oglethorpe's secretary, Francis Moore:

> Each Freeholder has a Lott in Town 60 Foot by 90 Foot, besides which he has a Lott beyond the Common, of 5 Acres for a Garden. Every ten Houses make a Tything, and to every Tything there is a Mile Square, which is divided into 12 Lotts, besides Roads: Each Free-holder of the Tything has a Lott or Farm of 45 Acres there, and two Lotts are reserved by the Trustees in order to defray the Charge of the Publick. The Town is laid out for two hundred

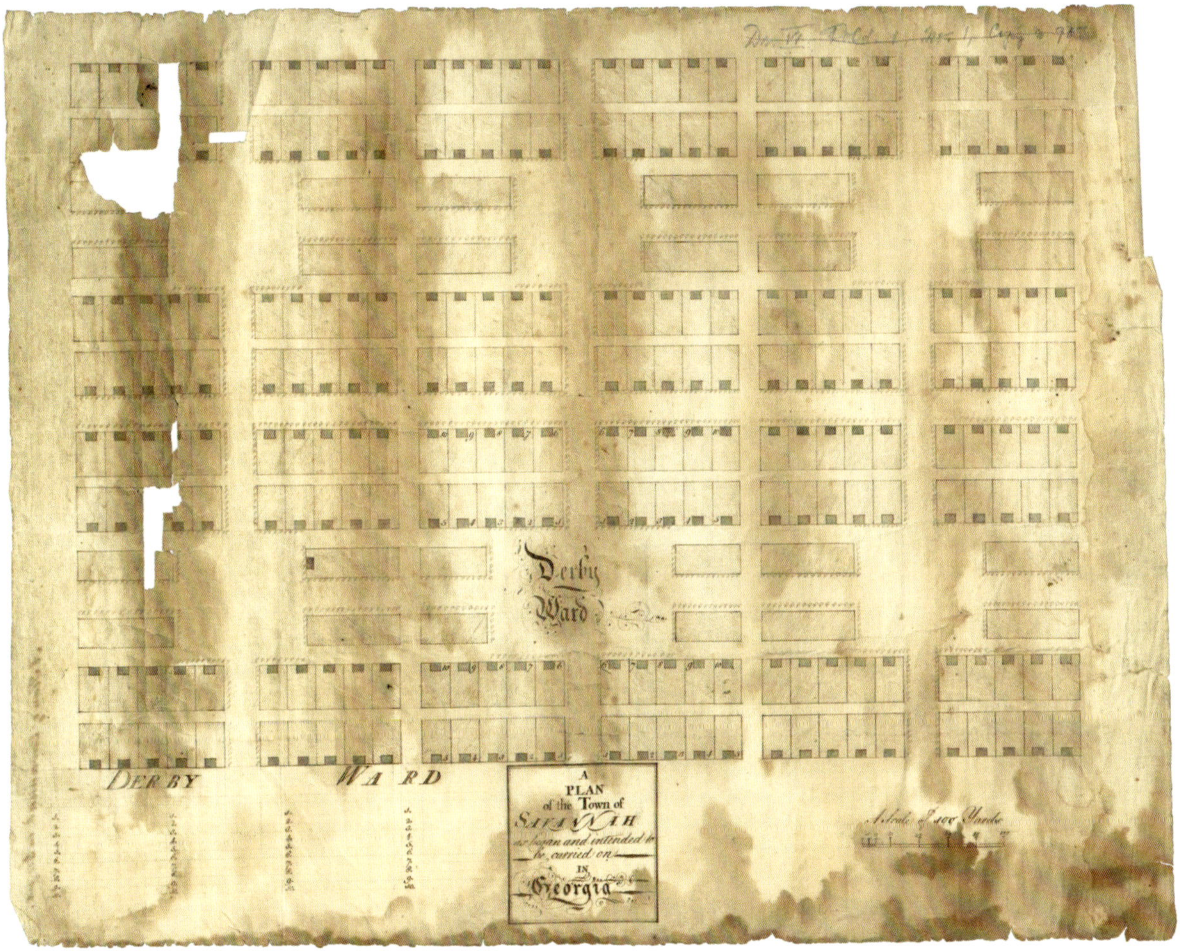

and forty Freeholds; the Quantity of Lands necessary for that Number is 24 Square Miles; every 40 Houses in Town make a Ward, to which 4 Square Miles in the Country belong; each Ward has a Constable, and under him 4 Tything Men. Where the Town-Lands end, the Villages begin; four Villages make a Ward without, which depends upon one of the Wards within the Town. The Use of this is, in case a War should happen, that the Villages without may have Places in the Town, to bring their Cattle and Families into for Refuge, and to that Purpose there is a Square left in every Ward; big enough for the Out-wards to encamp in.[30]

FIGURE 10. *A Plan of the Town of Savannah as Began and Intended to Be Carried On in Georgia*, ca. 1740. Ink on paper, 12½" × 16½". By permission of the Archives of the Moravian Church, Bethlehem, Pennsylvania.

The original plan was a mathematical and geometrical transcription of the Trustees' vision of an ideal, egalitarian, and agrarian community. Each of the six wards "within the town" centers on a public square surrounded by four tythings, groups of ten house lots. The five lots in each half of the tything are separated by a lane (alley) running east–west. Four public lots (later called trust lots) reserved for civic institutions as designated by the Trustees face each square, two on the east side of the square and two on the west side. The plan's orthogonal grid is formed by weaving together four types of east–west streets and two types of north–south streets. The width of these streets varies by type from 22½ feet to 75 feet. Each ward is bisected by a north–south street and an east–west street, each 75 feet wide, in the manner of an ancient Roman castrum or new town plan.

Beyond the town lots, extending into the pine barren to the south, were the town Common, garden lots, and farm lots. The Common was originally a simple rectangular band separating the town plan on three sides (narrower on the western side) from the garden lots. We see it delineated on a regional map dated 1751 that was drawn by surveyor Henry Yonge (figure 11). The garden lots and farm lots are depicted in several different versions of a plan that dates to the 1760s (figure 12).[31] In the latter plan, the Common has been expanded along either side of the central road. The garden lots are shown as squares bisected diagonally to form two 5-acre parcels and clustered into one-mile-square blocks subdivided into seven-by-seven grids (or portions thereof). These blocks align with the continued mile-square grid of the farm lots.[32] Broad roads separate the mile-square groupings of garden lots, the central road being labeled "White Bluff Road." A small brownstone mile marker inscribed "White Bluff ROAD 1" survives from this original phase of the plan (figure 13); it stands just south of present-day Henry Street, exactly one mile from the south edge of South Broad Street (now Oglethorpe Avenue), the early

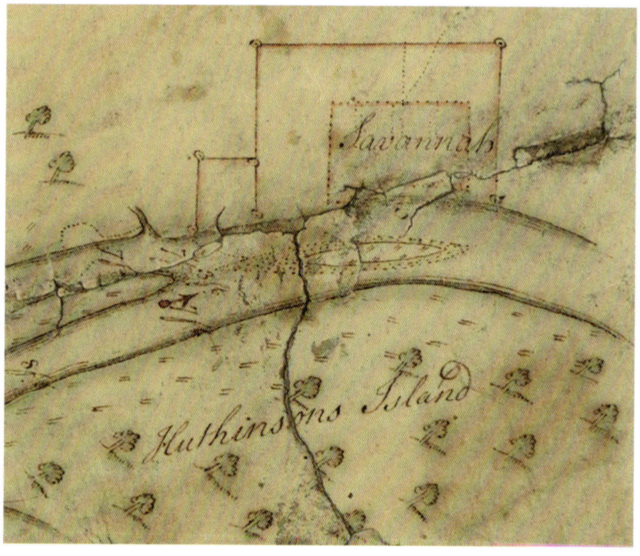

FIGURE 11. Detail (reoriented) showing the outline of the town plan, Common, and Trustees' Garden, from *A Plan of the Inlets & Rivers of Savannah & Warsaw in the Province of Georgia* by Henry Yonge, 1751, pen and ink and watercolor. Library of Congress, Geography and Map Division.

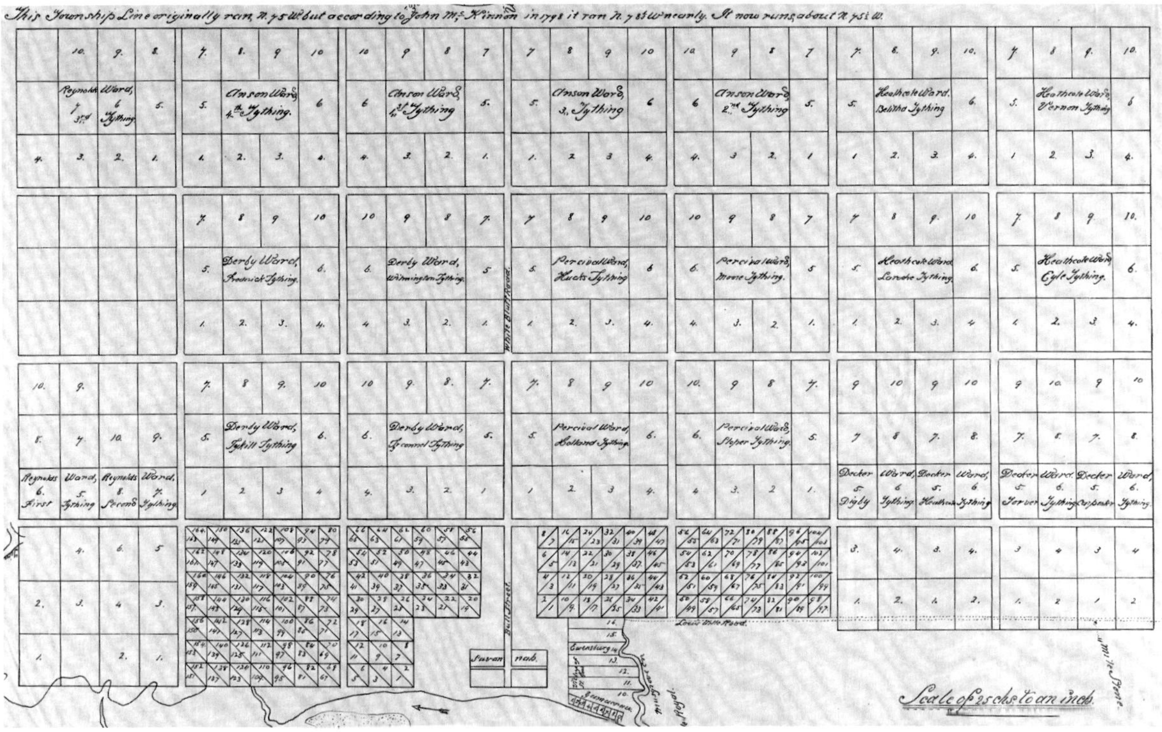

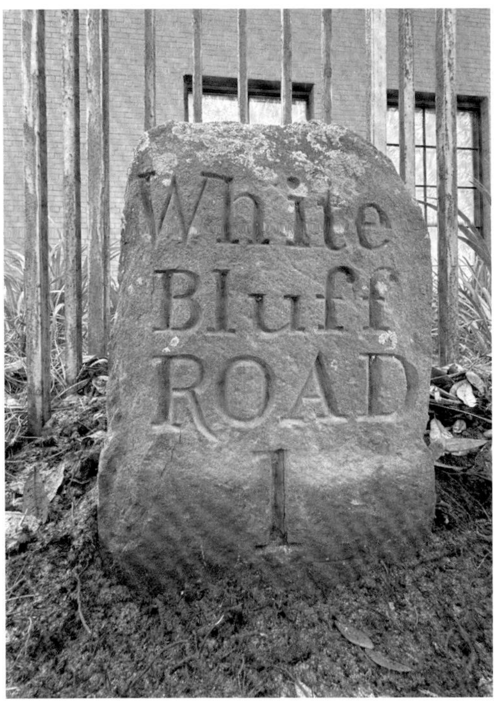

FIGURE 12. (*Above*) Copy of a plan of Savannah and its garden and farm lots dating to ca. 1760–62; the original map has been lost. Courtesy of Hargrett Rare Book and Manuscript Library, University of Georgia Libraries.

FIGURE 13. (*Left*) Eighteenth-century milestone on present-day Bull Street just south of Henry Street, indicating the distance to the southern edge of Savannah, which corresponded exactly to the south edge of Oglethorpe Avenue. Photo by Robin B. Williams, 2024.

southern boundary of the town. Farm lots were organized into groups of ten 45-acre lots and one 90-acre lot (also called a "trust lot") set aside for the Trustees and correlating to their in-town tythings.[33]

The further extent of this regional plan is depicted in an intriguing engraved map of the "County of Savannah," dated 1735, which shows the extension of a mile-square grid into the surrounding forest to the south and west (figure 14). This map shows the "villages" in which settlers were each granted a single fifty-acre lot. Two adjacent villages are shown as developed within this grid: Highgate and Hampstead, both of which are rendered as having radial street plans.[34] Three other villages—Thunderbolt, Joseph's Town, and Abercorn—are depicted beyond the grid. The remaining forty squares are shown as dense forests. How much of this plan was surveyed is uncertain. It is known that in October 1742 the newly appointed public surveyor, Joseph Avery, reported to the Trustees that "the Garden and Farm Lots of the Town of Savannah are not Run out as they ought, but remain in Confusion . . . and some of the people complain that they never had Run out, and so they cannot know where they are."[35] The County of Savannah map is remarkable for how accurately it represents the city of Savannah and its suburbs as they exist today.[36] Many of its boundaries correspond to present-day streets in what is today known as midtown Savannah (figure 163). The gridded area depicted on this map corresponds roughly to the size of the present city (excluding recently annexed outlying lands).

In addition to gridded townships and fifty-acre farm plots, the Trustees granted five-hundred-acre plantations to "private adventurers" willing to pay their own way and bring their own servants.[37] Here again, the Trustees' land policy was a calculated attempt to create a limited-scale agrarian economy. As such, it was a strategic critique of both the large-scale estate farming resulting from the British Enclosure Acts and the slavery-based plantation economy of South Carolina.

The town, garden, and farm lots were assigned to freeholders by lottery. A colonial newspaper recorded that on July 7, 1733, a ceremony was held at which "the people proceeded to the Square. The Wards and Tythings were named, each Tything consisting of ten Houses, and each Ward of four tythings. An House Lott was given to each Freeholder. All the people had a very plentiful Dinner, and in the Afternoon, the Grant of a Court of Record was read, and the Officers for that Court were appointed."[38] Property titles were formalized by the Trustees in January 1734.[39] Evidence of the Trustees' fervor in protecting their land system can be seen in rules they published in 1735:

> All Lots are to be preserved separate and undivided, and cannot be united in order to keep up a Number of Men equal to the Number of Lots for the better Defence and Support of the Colony.
>
> No Person can lease out his House or Lot to another without Licence for

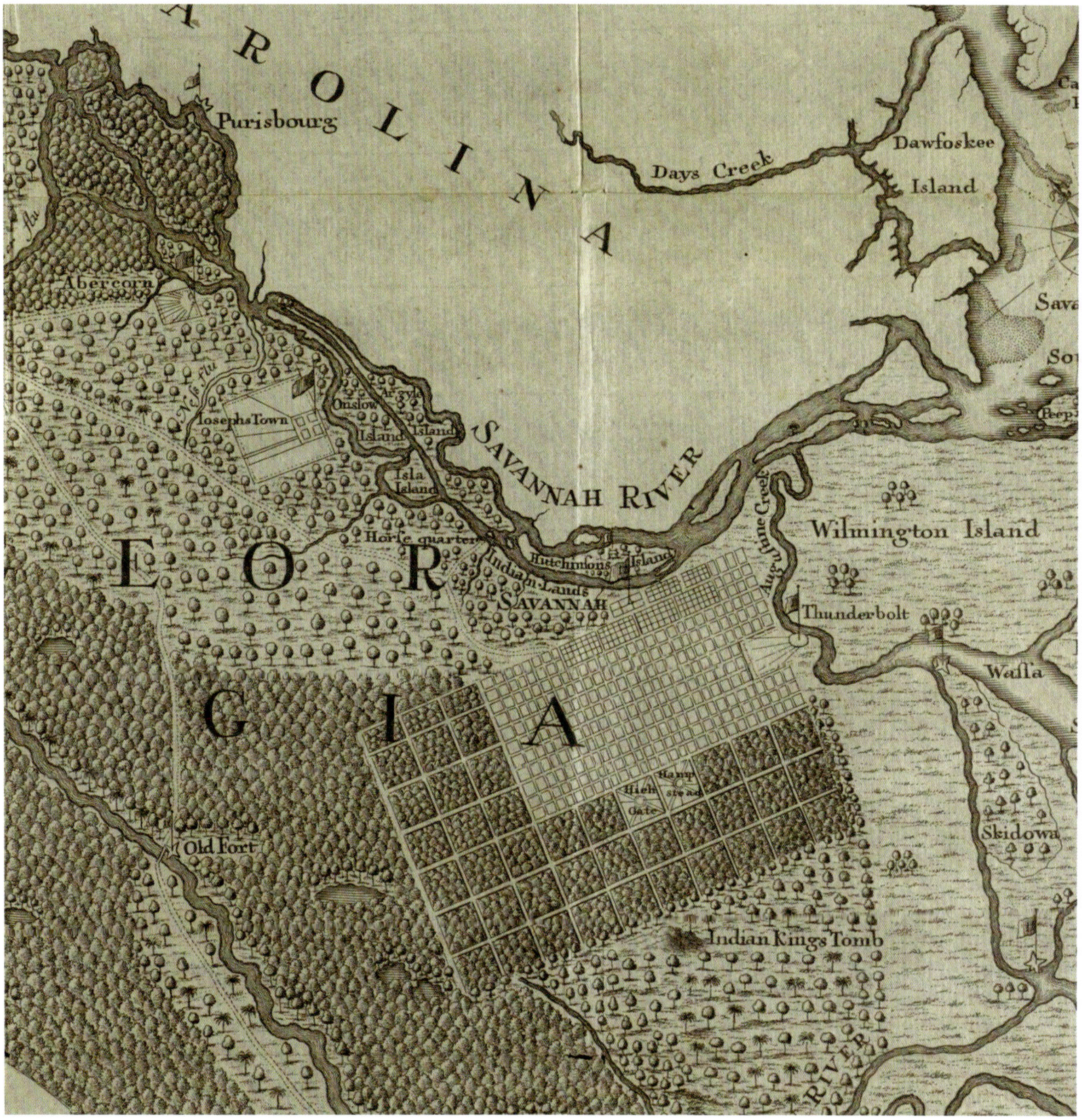

FIGURE 14. Detail of *A Map of the County of Savannah*, map by Tobias Conrad Lotter, dated 1735, printed by Matthäus Seutter and published in Samuel Urlsperger, *Der Ausfürliche Nachrichten von den Salsburgischen emigranten* (Halle, 1747). Courtesy of Hargrett Rare Book and Manuscript Library, University of Georgia Libraries.

> that Purpose that the Colony may not be ruined by Absentees receiving and spending their Rents elsewhere. Therefore each Man must cultivate the same by himself or Servants.
>
> And no Person can alienate his Land, or any Part, or any Term, Estate or Interest therein, to any other Person or Persons, without special Licence for that Purpose, to prevent the uniting or dividing the Lots.[40]

The social, economic, political, and military fabric of their experimental society was carefully woven together by the orderly town plan and its corresponding system of gardens, farms, and villages.

Sources of the Plan

Discovering the sources of Oglethorpe's plan has occupied the attention of numerous scholars for many years. Many have pointed to the precedent of the fashionable seventeenth- and eighteenth-century residential squares in the West End of London, where many of the Trustees lived.[41] Plans for rebuilding London after the fire of 1666 have also been suggested as models for Savannah.[42] A widely published but anonymous Dutch engraved plan labeled "Nieuw Moodel" shows the destroyed portion of London reconfigured according to an orthogonal street grid punctuated with four "market" squares, fourteen church squares, and prominent lots for the exchange and city hall (figure 15).[43] More intriguing for their similarity to Savannah are three rebuilding plans by cartographer Richard Newcourt that now reside in the London Metropolitan Archives. Each of these plans is radical in its proposed reconfiguration of London.[44] The first extends the rebuilding of

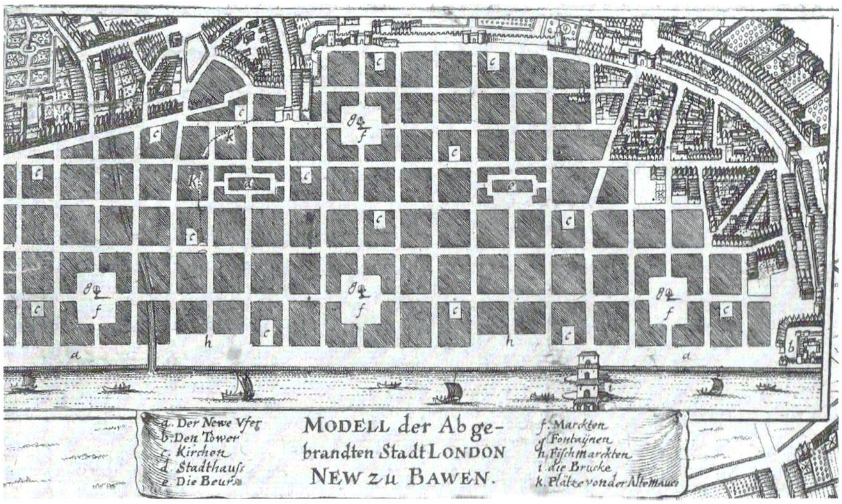

FIGURE 15. Anonymous engraved plan for rebuilding London after the 1666 fire, labeled *Modell der ab gebrandten stadt London new zu bawen*; detail from a broadsheet entitled *Platte grondt der verbrande Stadt London* (Frankfurt, ca. 1666). Beinecke Rare Book and Manuscript Library, Yale University.

London beyond the burnt districts, turning the entire city into a walled rectangle (figure 16). This is divided into fifty-five parishes, comparable to Savannah's wards, with each parish divided into quadrants surrounding a churchyard and church at the center.[45] At the center of the city is a capacious square, four times the size of an individual parish. Four other large squares are shown in each quadrant of the city, an arrangement used in the layout of Philadelphia a few years later. Despite the similarities to the Savannah Plan, however, it seems unlikely that Oglethorpe or any of the Trustees could have known about Newcourt's unpublished plans, which remained in private possession well into the twentieth century.[46]

Alternative theories of origin abound. John Reps once made a strong case for the influence of English new towns in Ireland, particularly the 1622 plans for Londonderry and Coleraine, though he later argued that the Piazza San Carlo, laid out in the expansion plan for Turin in 1682, may have been the model that inspired Oglethorpe.[47] Laura Palmer Bell suggested a more exotic prototype: a 1705 English engraving of the extension plan of imperial Beijing.[48] Mark Reinberger finds

FIGURE 16. *Proposed Plan for Rebuilding London*, pen and ink drawing by Richard Newcourt, 1666. London Metropolitan Archives, City of London CLC/481/MS03441, Newcourt maps of London, p. 8, 1666.

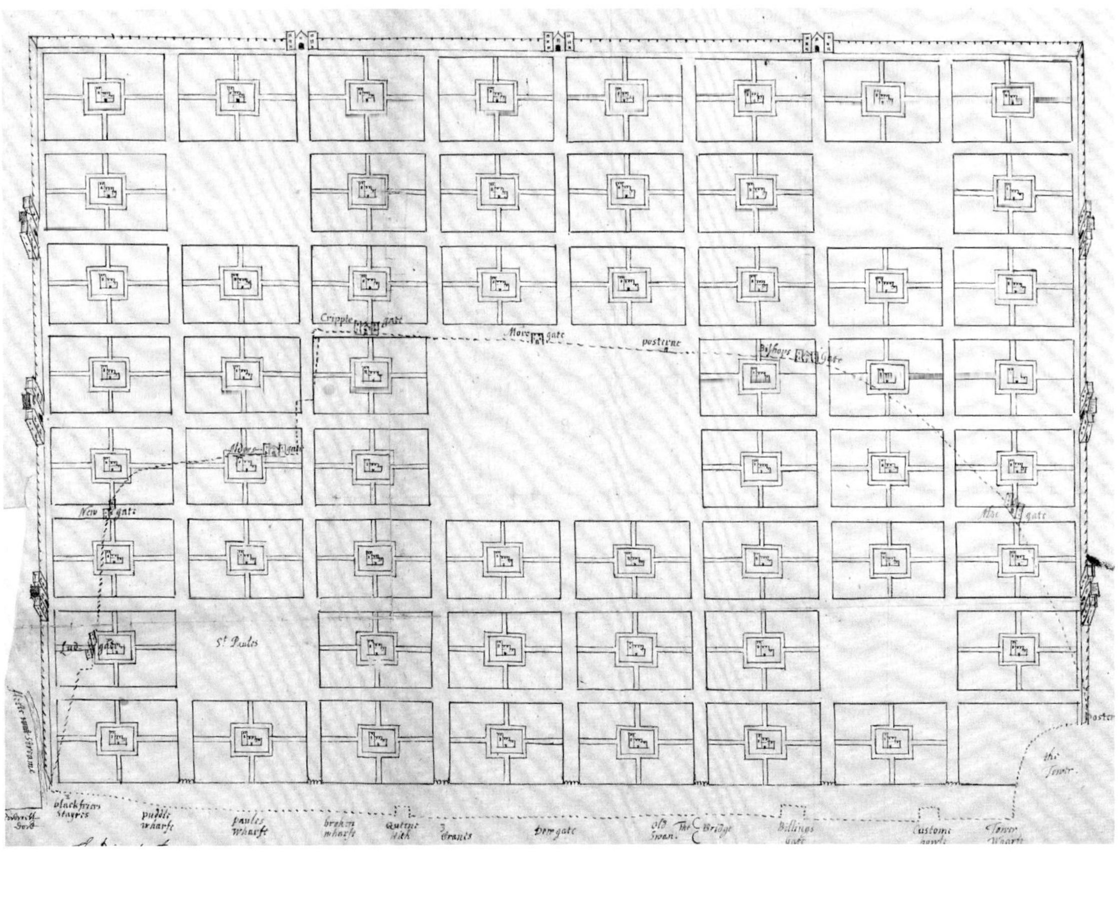

symbolic meaning in the arithmetical relationships of the component parts of the plan, suggesting the influence of Freemasonry in its creation.[49] Stanford Anderson sees some clear connections between the Savannah Plan and eighteenth-century garden design.[50] Intriguing comparisons are also made to the Renaissance tradition of ideal city plans, and especially to centralized military plans. Such sources are favored by Turpin Bannister, who identified a military encampment plan by English writer Robert Barret in 1598 as a direct influence.[51] Following Bannister's theory that military town planning was influential on Oglethorpe, Nathaniel Walker has identified another possible source in a hypothetical town design by Leonhard Christoph Strum published in 1718.[52] City planner Edmund Bacon made a casual but keen observation in linking the Savannah Plan to the hypothetical town plans published by Pietro Cataneo in the 1567 edition of his treatise *L'architettura* (figure 3).[53]

These many attempts to discover the "source" of the Savannah Plan have enriched our understanding of its meaning and significance. Many of the proposed sources are credible, but none are universally accepted as correct. It seems likely to us, as it does to many of the scholars just mentioned, that the inventors of the plan were influenced by multiple sources.

Comparative Colonial Plans

Oglethorpe's plan of Savannah has also been compared with other American colonial town plans. Numerous scholars have noted how its orthogonal grid and agrarian ideals typify Anglo-American urbanism in the eighteenth century.[54] Oglethorpe's fastidious gridding of the Lowcountry landscape can be seen as an expression of Enlightenment rationalism, a Lockean or Cartesian impulse to order nature, but it can also be seen as characteristic of American urbanism. The square grid, exemplified by the six-mile square described by the anonymous Puritan author of the 1635 "Essay on the Ordering of Towns" and by the famed Land Ordinance of 1785 (the Jefferson grid), is seen by authors such as John Stilgoe as a defining feature of the American landscape.[55] For European settlers building cities in the American wilderness, the grid was not only an expedient for efficient land development but also what Michel Foucault would call an *episteme*—an apparatus for both interpreting and implanting meaning into the landscape. The grid aligned the land with political, economic, moral, and aesthetic order.

Agrarian ideology, and with it a suspicion of the city, is likewise both an undercurrent in the Georgia experiment and a pervasive theme in American political thought from the seventeenth century to the present.[56] William Bradford promoted the "plain country life and the innocent trade of husbandry."[57] Thomas Jefferson wrote to James Madison of his belief that "our governments will remain

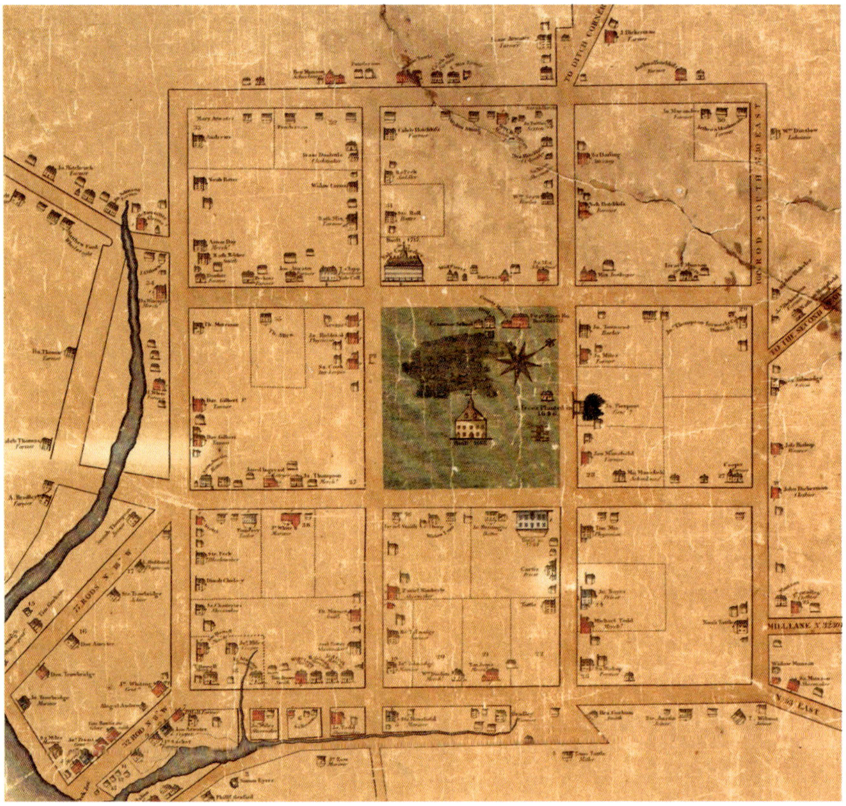

FIGURE 17. Detail of *A Plan of the Town of New Haven with All the Buildings in 1748*. Hand-colored engraving by James Wadsworth, published by Thomas Kensett, 1806. Beinecke Rare Book and Manuscript Library, Yale University.

virtuous for many centuries; as long as they are chiefly agricultural."[58] Agrarian ideology permeates the promotional literature of the Georgia colony and receives frequent mention in the records of the Trustees.

The oldest known town plan in English colonial America is that of New Haven, founded by John Davenport in 1638 and laid out by John Brockett in 1641 (figure 17).[59] The New Haven plan is a nine-square grid with the central square reserved as a town common or green. Each square is 52 rods or 286 yards per side. The central green was not only a common pasture but also the town square, in which were found the primary public institutions, the most notable of which was the meetinghouse. This configuration provided a model for New England towns in the late eighteenth and early nineteenth centuries to preserve centrally located commons as public parks. New Haven's original garden and farm lots were located outside of the nine-square plan. Historians have suggested a variety of precedents for Davenport's ideal plan, including Vitruvius's instructions on laying out cities, but some believe that Davenport found inspiration in the Bible, either in the encampment of the Israelites or in Ezekiel's vision of a square city.[60] Sylvia Fries

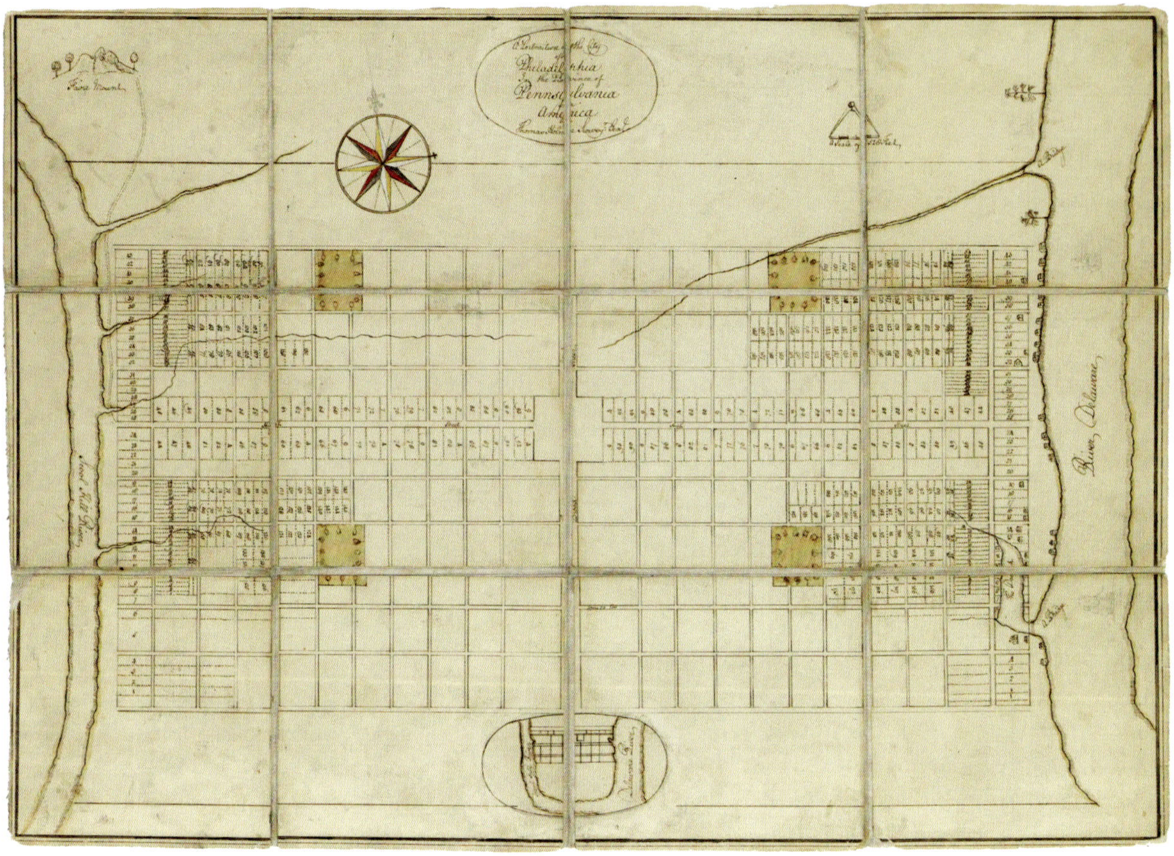

FIGURE 18. *A Portraiture of the City of Philadelphia in the Province of Pennsylvania in America*, hand-colored, engraved map by Thomas Holme, printed in London, 1683; from the collection of the Historical Society of Pennsylvania. Wikimedia Commons.

interprets the New Haven plan as the purest expression of the New England Puritans' planning ideals more generally, which had been described in "Essay on the Ordering of Towns."[61] The block sizes (if that's what they were meant to be) of the New Haven plan are enormous, with each square being more than sixteen acres. All but the central square (the green) were subdivided into quadrants in 1784.[62]

Philadelphia's town plan, as depicted in *A Portraiture of the City of Philadelphia* (1683), a map drawn by Surveyor General Thomas Holme in collaboration with William Penn, was clearly on the minds of the Georgia Trustees (figure 18). Trustee secretary Benjamin Martyn, when comparing the Georgia colony with Pennsylvania, called the Philadelphia plan "as fine a City as most of Europe."[63] Penn's original vision was for "a greene Country Towne, which will never be burnt, and allways be wholsome."[64] Although this original vision for a sprawling collection of ten-acre house lots, each associated with five-hundred-acre farms, was modified in Holme's plan, it retains the spirit of the green country town. Agrarian ideals, religious liberty for dissenting Protestants, the use of promotional literature, proprietary rule, and orthogonal city planning are among many similarities shared by Penn's "Holy Experiment" and Trustee Georgia. Holme's Philadelphia plan is an enormous one-by-two-mile grid extending east to west from the Delaware River to the Schuylkill River.[65] The two principal streets are 100 feet wide, while the secondary streets are 50 feet wide. The blocks are generally large, the smallest being 425 feet by 500 feet. A central square of ten acres appears in Holme's plan, bisected by the principal north–south and east–west streets; this square was to be surrounded by "houses for public affairs, as a meeting-house, assembly or state-house, market-house, school-house, and several other buildings for public concerns."[66] Four lesser squares (one in each quadrant) of eight acres each "for the like Uses, as the Moore-fields" constitute an innovative feature in the plan, made even more striking by Holme's depiction of organized patterns of trees in these squares.[67]

The essential imprint of the plan can still be discerned in the street plan of modern Philadelphia, but it has been modified in a variety of ways. Two observations should be highlighted. First, because few early settlers were interested in purchasing lots on the west side of the city, the actual pattern of growth for the commercial city favored the Delaware River, moving only gradually westward. This pattern of development effectively denied the centrality of the central square, which was only realized in the late nineteenth century. Second, the large blocks drawn in the plan, like those of New Haven, were soon subdivided by the ad hoc insertion of narrow streets, alleys (cartways), pedestrian footways, and courts. Soon after American independence, however, attempts were made to revive and restore the badly neglected squares of the original Penn plan. As Elizabeth Milroy has shown, the *Portraiture* plan had in the days of the early republic acquired symbolic status; it came to be seen as a founding document.[68] A similar veneration of Oglethorpe and the Trustees can be seen among the early members of the city council of Savannah as they began to replicate the original ward plan in 1791.

Geographically closer to Savannah is Charleston, which was laid out following a plan known as the "Grand Model," drawn as early as 1670 and largely implemented in 1694.[69] According to Thomas Wilson, the English philosopher and physician John Locke "was the principal drafter of the detailed instructions on how Charleston was to be laid out (a city plan) and how it was to be linked to the surrounding region (a regional plan)."[70] The original drawing has disappeared, but subsequent maps and descriptions demonstrate that it too was an orthogonal plan featuring a central square, described as a "piazza," which was bisected by wide streets. In 1722, John Herbert and William Bull, who would assist James Oglethorpe in laying out Savannah a decade later, resurveyed the Charleston plan.[71] A hierarchy of street widths (seventy, fifty, and thirty feet) was also specified. Although the province of Carolina was by no means a charity colony, the visionary Lords Proprietors

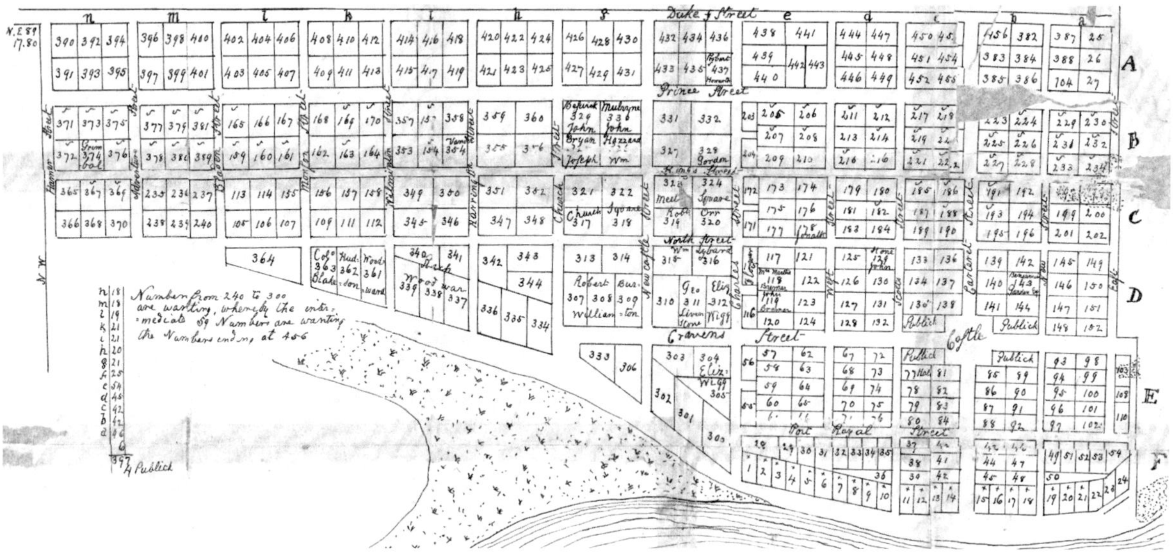

FIGURE 19. Detail of *Plat of Beaufort*, dated 1711; hand-drawn by H. A. M. Smith after a lost map at the South Carolina Department of Archives and History and published in *The South Carolina Historical and Genealogical Magazine* in 1908 (vol. 9, no. 3, p. 140).

of Carolina adopted the experimental Fundamental Constitutions of Carolina in March 1669, and the Grand Model is thought by some to be a product of this vision.[72] The rational ideality of the Grand Model plan is hard to detect in the city today, as the central square was compromised by the encroachment of public buildings by the end of the eighteenth century, and the network of streets is far from a precise orthogonal grid.

The smaller town of Beaufort, South Carolina, established in 1711, was laid out with a similar grid plan featuring a central square. Henry Smith's copy of an early but undated plat map in the South Carolina Archives shows this square, labeled "Castle," bisected by the two widest streets and flanked at its quadrants by lots labeled as "publick" (figure 19).[73] Like Charleston's piazza, however, this square is today an ordinary intersection (Carteret and Craven Streets).

Closer still to Savannah in time, place, and purpose was the now-extinct town of Purrysburg, South Carolina.[74] In 1732 Jean Pierre Purry founded Purrysburg on a bluff on the South Carolina side of the Savannah River, about fourteen miles upriver from the future site of Savannah, in what is today unincorporated Jasper County. Purry, a wine merchant, entrepreneur, and scientific visionary from Neuchâtel, Switzerland, outlined a plan to establish a colony as early as 1724 in a report presented to the Duke of Newcastle.[75] This promotional tract argued the advantages of exploiting the natural "boundless wealth" of South Carolina by enlisting Protestant refugees from the continent to colonize it. Purry even suggested that this newly colonized territory could be called "Georgia."[76] Purry's plan was initially approved by the Carolina Proprietors in 1726, but the attempt failed because the proprietors reneged on their offer to support the colonists. Following the demise of proprietary rule and the subsequent Township Act of 1730, which was meant to secure the Carolina border by establishing towns along it, Governor Robert Johnson approved the establishment of Purrysburg, which was to be settled by about three hundred colonists, mostly from Switzerland. Purry, meanwhile, had solicited the Bray Associates, who looked favorably on the venture and granted him £200. In December 1731, James Oglethorpe purchased a one-quarter interest in the Purrysburg venture.[77] Because the landing at Purrysburg was a major ferry crossing, commerce with Savannah and Georgia was vigorous from 1733 until the mid-nineteenth century. Even so, the Swiss town was already in decline as a viable community by the end of the eighteenth century. General Sherman's army destroyed what remained of the town in the winter of 1865.[78] No buildings or streets remain today. Purrysburg's town plan, recorded in a plat map of 1765, was a simple though partially skewed orthogonal grid of about 625 acres extending 6,996 feet along the Savannah River. The plan shows 455 numbered house lots, each about 210 feet square (approximately one acre). The streets were uniformly 66½ feet wide.[79]

An earlier failed attempt at colonization in this territory should also be mentioned. In June 1717, near the end of the tragic Yamasee War, the Carolina Proprietors granted all the land between the Savannah and Altamaha Rivers to Sir Robert Montgomery to establish a province called the Margravate of Azilia.[80] Montgomery described his plan with scientific precision in a promotional tract entitled *A Discourse Concerning the Design'd Establishment of a New Colony to the South of Carolina, in the Most Delightful Country of the Universe*. The accompanying copperplate engraving represents his visionary *Plan Representing the Form of Setling the Districts* as a walled precinct measuring twenty miles on each side, to be laid out on a "level, dry, and fruitful Tract of Land" (figure 20). The entire settlement is defended by "sufficient Numbers of Men, . . . dwelling in the fortified Angles of the Line." At the center of this symmetrical, gridded plan is the Margrave's house, which "contains all sorts of publick Edifices." Surrounding the Margrave's residence is the "City," a square "full of Streets crossing each other." The city is surrounded by trees and a "large void Space, which will be useful for a thousand Purposes, and, among the rest, as being airy, and affording a fine Prospect of the Town in Drawing near it." Beyond the town are 116 one-mile-square estate lots, each with a house in the middle. In each quadrant of the estate lands is a four-mile square park, or "forest," "in which are propagated Herds of Cattle of all Sorts."[81] Not surprisingly, Montgomery was unable to raise enough interest or capital to see Azilia materialize, and Montgomery's charter expired at the end of three years. His plan seems far-fetched in many ways, particularly its generous scale. Its strong centralized design and fortified boundary appear to have little in common with Oglethorpe's plan, and yet it is comparable in some of its features, including its balanced integration of regional and urban planning, its emphasis

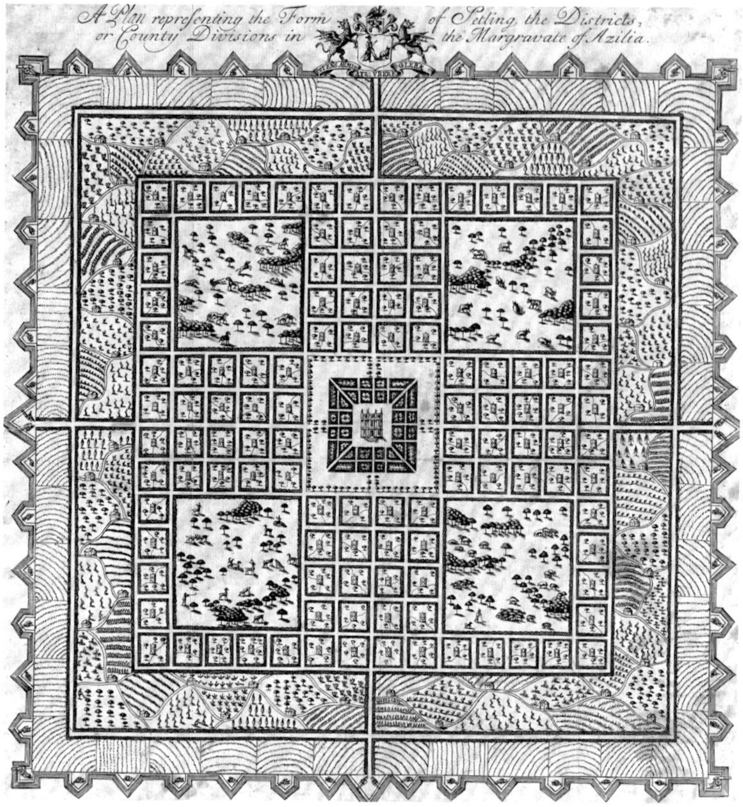

FIGURE 20. *A Plan Representing the Form of Set[t]ling the Districts, or County Divisions in the Margravate of Azilia.* Engraved plan published in Sir Robert Montgomery, *A Discourse Concerning the Design'd Establishment of a New Colony to the South of Carolina, in the Most Delightful Country of the Universe* (London, 1717), 12½" × 12½". Courtesy of the John Carter Brown Library.

on mathematical and geometrical equality, its use of the one-mile grid, and the primacy of landscape features.

The combination of a town plan comprising six squares surrounded by a common, garden lots, and larger farm lots found one last echo at the end of the eighteenth century in Canada, in what was then part of the Province of Quebec (but which became the Province of Upper Canada in 1791). The 1788 *Plan of the Harbour of Toronto with the Proposed Town and Settlement* bears a striking resemblance to the original regional plan laid out by Oglethorpe (figure 21).[82] The basic grid plan of the town involved square blocks bisected by secondary streets (a far simpler configuration than the Savannah Plan), with six of those blocks allocated to squares, each defined on its edges by red rectangles presumably representing public buildings. A common surrounds the town on all sides, as in Savannah, and beyond are "town" lots and even larger farm lots. The plan was never implemented. Five years later, the town of York (later renamed Toronto) was established with a modest arrangement of eight square blocks, a fraction of the size of this regional plan. That the grandiose 1788 plan never materialized underscores the commendable achievement of the Georgia Trustees in implementing their plan.

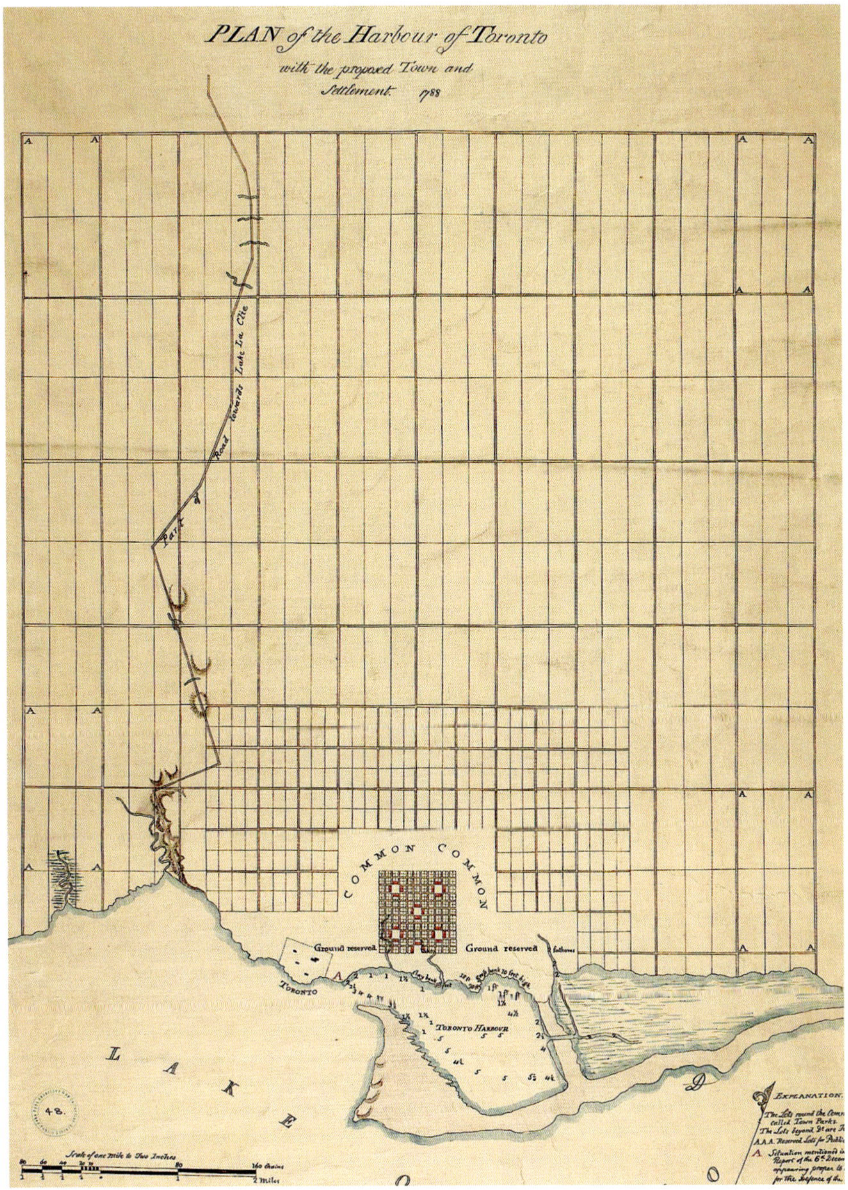

FIGURE 21. *Plan of the Harbour of Toronto with the Proposed Town and Settlement*, plan by John Collins, 1788, $33\frac{1}{16}$" × $24\frac{13}{16}$". Toronto Public Library; licensed under public domain via TPL Digital Archive.

Comparative Town Plans in Oglethorpe's Georgia

Oglethorpe's commitment to the Savannah Plan can be evaluated by comparing Savannah to Georgia towns subsequently planned and built under Oglethorpe's leadership. Four of these merit discussion: two are extant Georgia towns, Augusta and Darien; two others, Frederica and Ebenezer, disappeared as towns soon after their founding.

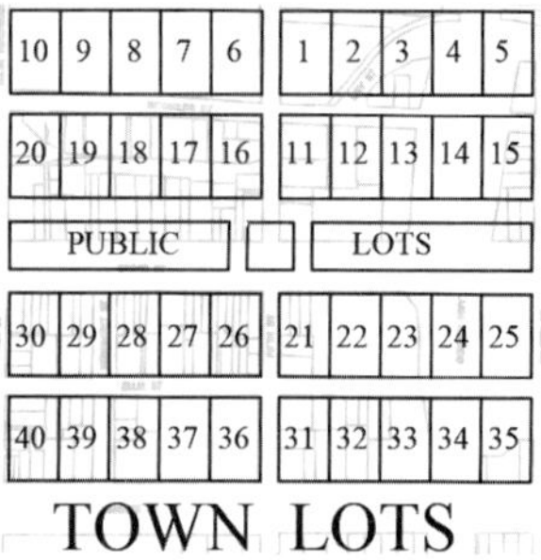

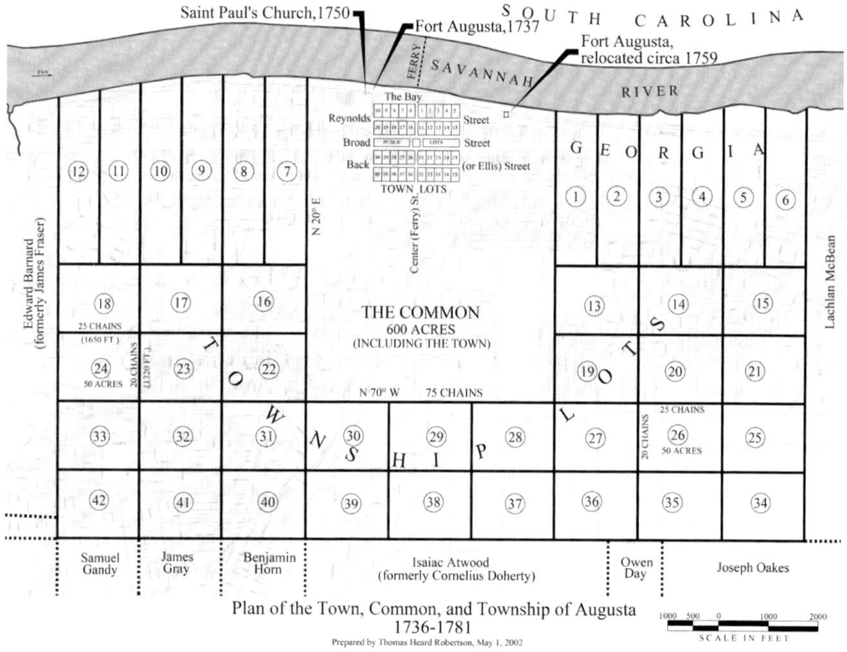

FIGURE 22. Colonial plan of Augusta, reconstructed by Thomas Heard Robertson Jr., in "The Colonial Plan of Augusta," *Georgia Historical Quarterly* 86, no. 4 (Winter 2002): 531. *Above*: Detail of central section. Courtesy of Thomas Heard Robertson Jr.

Augusta was founded just below the fall line of the Savannah River, across the river from a Native American village called "Savannah town" by Europeans and not far from the English Fort Moore. On June 14, 1736, in response to a request made by a group of Indian traders from South Carolina, Oglethorpe instructed surveyor Noble Jones to lay out a town with "40 House Lotts each of an Acre, the largest Streets not narrower than 25 yards; a Square in the Center, & Lotts for Publick Buildings on each Side the Square. All the Publick Lotts together not to consist of less than 4 acres, the Common to consist of 600 acres, and the Lotts next [to] the Town to be 50 acres, but only to each of those who have 500 acres."[83] Essential components of the Augusta plan (figure 22), including farm lots, town lots, public lots, a public square (though only one), and a common, are similar to aspects of the Savannah Plan, but the house and public lots are far larger, and no garden lots are mentioned. Although portions of this plan were executed, significant modifications were made in subsequent years, making the Oglethorpe-era plan unrecognizable. No historic drawing of the colonial plan exists, but Thomas Heard Robertson Jr. reconstructed the intended plan, which shows it to be a supersized version of one Savannah ward surrounded by a common and farm lots beyond.[84]

At the southern border of the colony, Oglethorpe founded two new towns in 1736. Frederica was built as a military garrison on a high open field on St. Simons

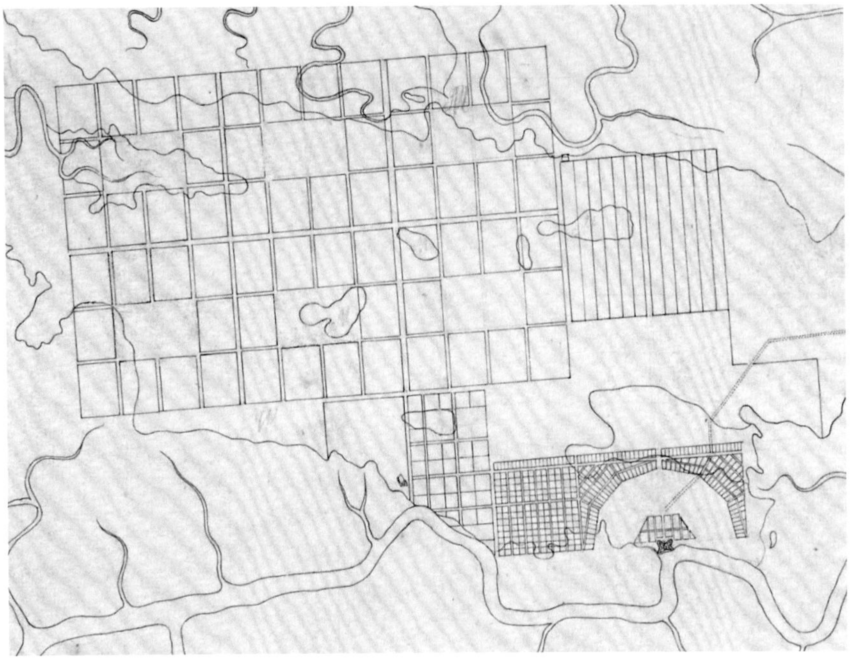

FIGURE 23. Detail of *Map of Saint Simons and Jekyll Islands with Fortifications* by John Thomas the Elder, 1738. British Library. Map reproduction courtesy of the Norman B. Leventhal Map and Education Center at the Boston Public Library.

Island, where the Georgia colony was under imminent threat of a Spanish attack.[85] Extending from a fortified battery facing the Frederica River, a trapezoidal palisade surrounded a town with an orthogonal grid of streets and lanes comprising eighty-four numbered house lots of sixty feet by ninety feet (the same size employed in Savannah). A broad central street (seventy-five feet wide) connected the fort with the northern city gate, which gave access to a roughly semicircular common. The town plan was laid out by Swiss surveyor Samuel Auspourger.[86] It was described by Francis Moore and recorded in a map dated 1796.[87] An earlier, unfinished map of St. Simons dating to 1738 and now in the British Library shows the common to be about one thousand feet deep, polygonal in shape, and surrounded by radiating garden lots (figure 23). The map indicates what appear to be farm lots and villages to the northeast of the town (at upper left). This grand plan together with the substantial tabby foundations remaining on the site suggest that Frederica was intended to become a town rivaling Savannah in its size and significance. However, the town languished after the Spanish threat disappeared in the later eighteenth century and exists today only as an interpretive archaeological site.

About sixteen miles north of Frederica, a group of Scottish Highlanders, recruited by Oglethorpe to settle and defend the southern border of Georgia, founded the town of Darien in January 1736.[88] The site was a high bluff near the mouth of the Altamaha River, about one mile from the abandoned Fort King

George, a pre–Trustee era outpost. The town was surveyed under Oglethorpe's direction in the summer of 1736, with one large square (720 feet) surrounded by four ranges of town lots, a common on the east and north, and acreage lots beyond.[89] It presumably followed the "Rules of the Year 1735," which stipulated that "Towns will have each of them a Lot Sixty Feet in Front and Ninety Feet in Depth whereon they are to build an House and as much Land in the Country as in the whole shall make up Fifty Acres."[90] Darien was largely destroyed by the Spanish in the War of Jenkins' Ear (1739–48). However, on June 2, 1767, the governor and council ordered that

> a Reserve of Land be made for a Town at Darian [*sic*] where the Old Town formerly Stood, And that Lots be of Dimensions laid down in a Plan thereof already prepared. And also that two hundred Acres of Land adjoining the said Town be in like Manner reserved for the Public. And that the Town be Accordingly laid out.[91]

The town survey was carried out by Lachlan McIntosh.[92] A plan now in the Georgia Archives presumably represents this rebuilding (figure 24). It shows a one-ward version of the Savannah Plan, including a central square of 430 feet by 370 feet,

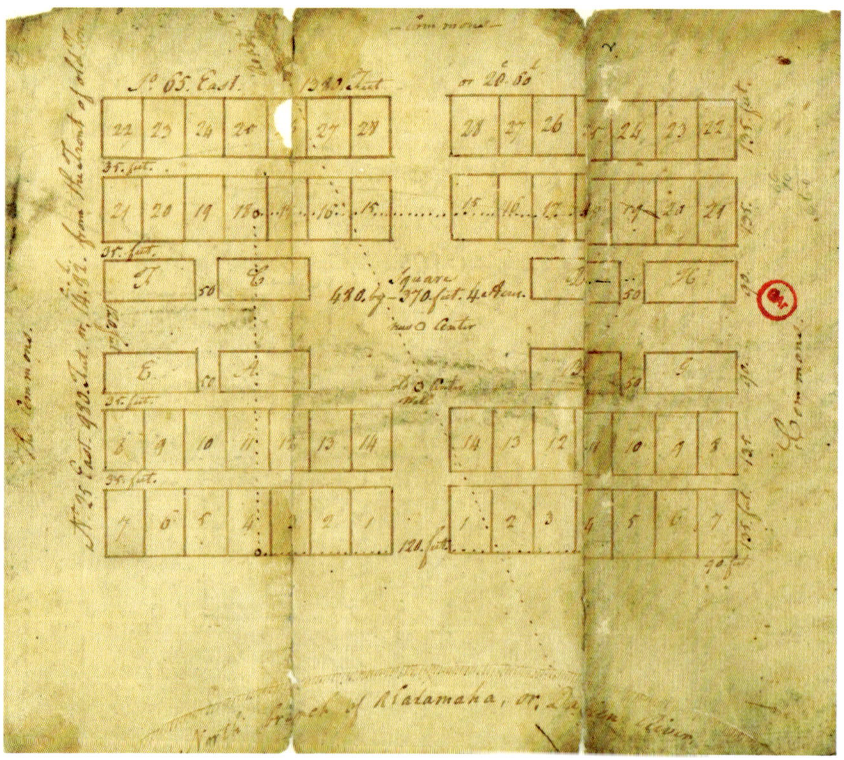

FIGURE 24. Detail of *Plan of the New Town of Darien*. Hand-drawn map signed by Lachlan McIntosh, 1767, pen and brown ink on paper. Courtesy of the Georgia Archives, Historic Map File.

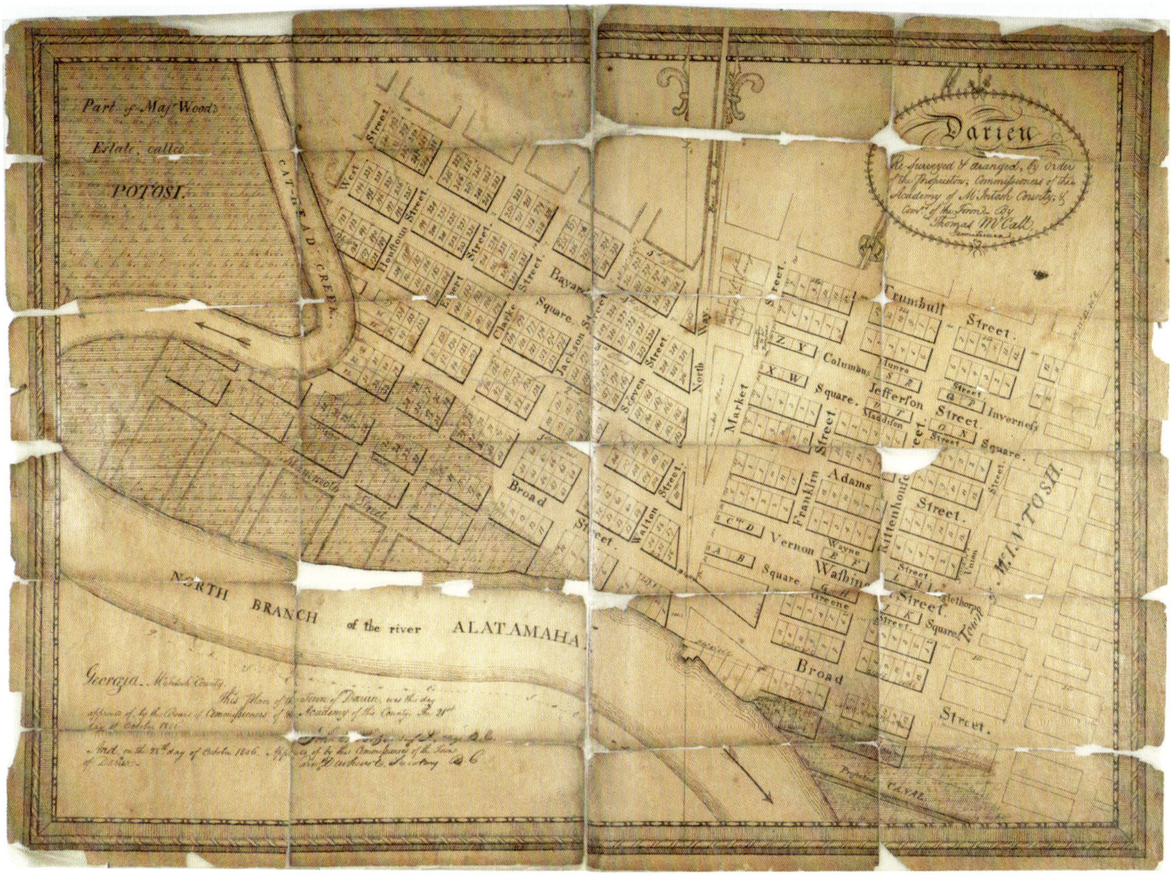

bisected by two broad streets (120 feet wide), with eight trust lots and four tythings each containing fourteen house lots of 90 feet by 135 feet. All the components are larger than the typical Savannah ward, yielding an area of about 25.75 acres, compared to 10.5 acres in Savannah.

After being destroyed again in the Revolutionary War, Darien rebounded as a port in the new republic. A survey map by Thomas McCall from 1806 shows that the single ward had multiplied into four wards, with two more wards suggested but cut off by the edge of the map (figure 25). The basic imprint of this plan persists today but with numerous modifications. Two squares remain, but because of the low density and small scale of the surrounding buildings and changes to the street grid, the squares appear more rural and informal in character than Savannah's urban squares.

The best known of Oglethorpe's other towns is Ebenezer, also founded in 1736. Initially called New Ebenezer, the town was established for Salzburger refugees,

FIGURE 25. *Plan of the Town of Darien: Resurveyed & Ar[r]anged, by Order of the Proprietors; Commissioners of the Academy of McIntosh County; & Comrs. of the Town* by Thomas McCall, 1806. Ink on paper, 29½" × 21". Courtesy of the Georgia Archives, Historic Map File, hmf0045.

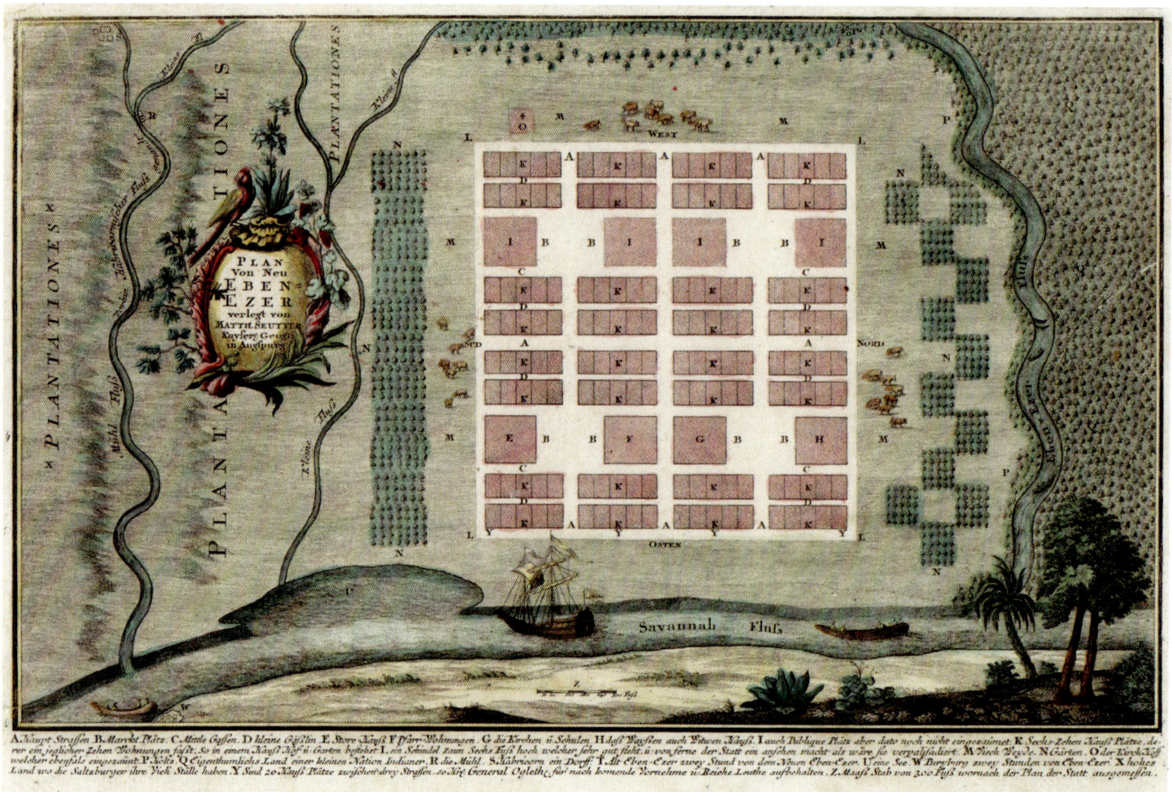

FIGURE 26. *Town Plan and Common of New Ebenezer.* Hand-colored, engraved print by Tobias Conrad Lotter, published by Matthäus Seutter as *Plan von Neu Ebenezer* (Augsburg, 1747). Image from the Barry Lawrence Ruderman Map Collection, courtesy Stanford University Libraries.

who moved to a site on the Savannah River after abandoning their original 1734 settlement (which came to be called "Old Ebenezer") less than six miles away.[93] The plan of Ebenezer is depicted in an exquisite, hand-colored map engraved by Tobias Lotter and published by Matthäus Seutter in Augsburg in 1747 (figure 26). This plan is similar but not identical to the description given by Philip Strobel in 1855:

> The new town was laid off after the plan of the city of Savannah, and covered an area of a quarter of a mile square. This space was divided into small squares, each containing ten building lots, and the latter numbered one hundred and sixty. Three wide streets passed through the town from east to west, which were intersected at right angles by four others running from north to south; beside which were a number of narrow lanes, but these extended in only one direction—north and south. Four squares were appropriated to the sale of produce, and called "market-places," and four were reserved as public parks or promenade grounds. Two-thirds of a square were appropriated to the church,

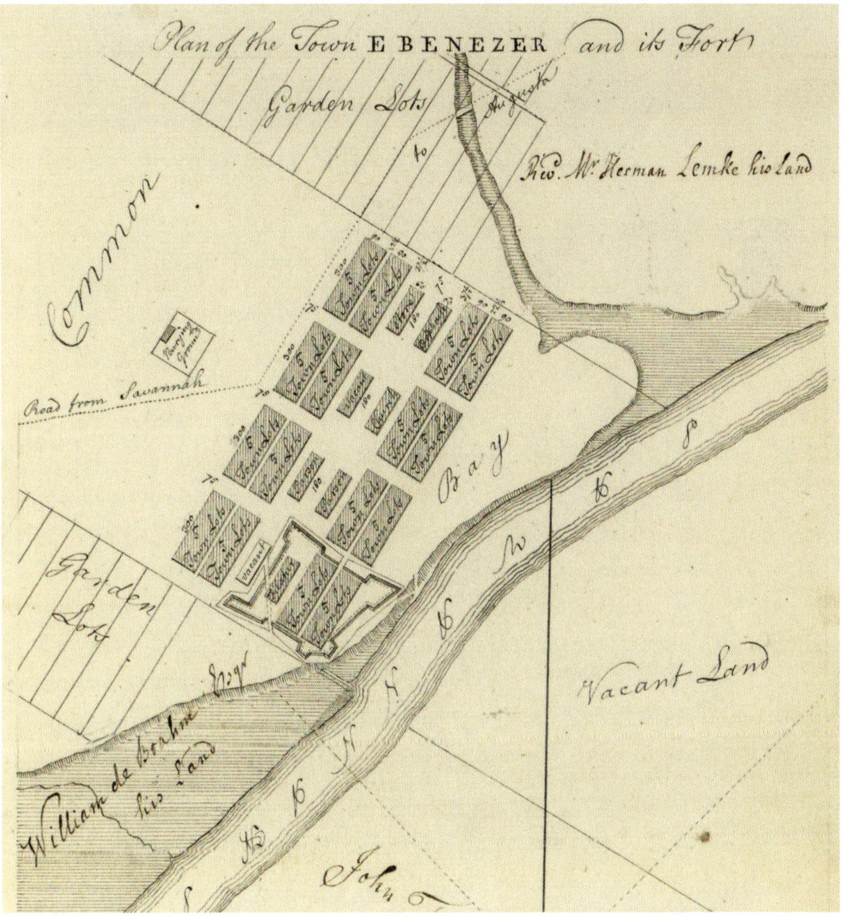

FIGURE 27. Detail of *Plan of the Town of Ebenezer and Its Fort* by William Gerard de Brahm, ca. 1757, in "History of the Three Provinces South Carolina, Georgia, and East Florida." MS Am 824, p. 111. Houghton Library, Harvard University.

parsonage, and academy, and an equal quantity to the orphan asylum and the public storehouse respectively. On the east, a short distance from the town, was the cemetery. On the north and east was a large pasture for cattle, and on the south was one for sheep and goats. On the north and south, garden-lots were laid out, and still farther south, beyond Little Creek and Mill Creek, and upon their waters, the farms were located, each consisting of fifty acres. . . . The whole plan of the town, with its environs, was well conceived, and one can but admire the great judgment displayed in the whole arrangement.[94]

This mile-square, four-ward plan differs, however, from the surveyed map by William Gerard de Brahm in 1757 (figure 27). De Brahm shows only two wards, one of which is compromised by the presence of a fortification. The wards are nearly identical to the original Savannah wards, even in their street dimensions, with two significant differences. First, the trust lots are centered longitudinally with the tythings so that a third square is created between the two wards. This creates an ambiguous relationship of square to ward. Another significant difference is in the garden lots, which are approximately the same size as those in Savannah, but instead of being triangular, they are long, narrow plowing strips, much more like the garden lots one would find in a medieval English village.[95] Ebenezer initially flourished under the exemplary discipline and direction of the Salzburgers, but the town was largely abandoned after the Revolutionary War. Today all that is left is the handsome Jerusalem Church, the oldest extant church in Georgia—built in 1767–69 on land originally laid out as a trust lot, though no street grid is detectable today.[96]

The towns founded soon after Savannah under Oglethorpe's direction attest to the Trustees' allegiance to the basic arrangement of the Savannah Plan. We see an initial commitment to the system of town, garden, and farm lots; the use of public and residential lots; the establishment of a town common and the creation of public squares; and the employment of unusually wide principal streets and secondary streets half their width. But we also see modifications that might be interpreted as critical refinements of the plan. The change in the configuration of garden lots at Ebenezer suggests this. Not seen, however, are any plans that replicate all parts of the Savannah Plan. Though it belongs to a family of Georgia town plans from the Trustee era, the Savannah Plan was distinctive even in its own day and is remarkable for enduring intact.

CHAPTER TWO

EXPANDING AND ADJUSTING THE PLAN, 1752–PRESENT

The Mayor and Aldermen wish to be empowered to lay off all that part of the Common, on the East and West sides of the City . . . to lay out lots on the ground so taken in . . . agreeably to the old Plan of Savannah as nearly as the same can conveniently be done.
—Savannah City Council minutes, May 18, 1790

The city is fast extending its limits. The Common will soon disappear before the *march of houses* (if you please), and "Hodgson's park," which now affords a pleasant walk and resting place, will ere long be at our doors.
—*Savannah Daily Republican*, editorial, February 10, 1851

James Oglethorpe's Savannah Plan was intentionally limited in its size, but it was never static. It grew and changed even in the first years of the colony. Surveying began on February 20, 1733, "on *the square*," suggesting that a single ward, most likely Derby Ward, was laid out first.[1] By July 7, the original four wards and their sixteen tythings had been named after the Trustees, transforming the plan into a memory map of its founders. By the fall of 1735, however, six wards were in place.[2] That the two added wards were called simply the "upper new" and "lower new" wards suggests that they were perceived as additions, but the overscaled size of Johnson Square from the outset suggests it was meant to enjoy a central location among the three wards closer to the river. These six wards would suffice until 1791.

Adapting and Refining the Plan Under Crown Rule

Although many of the Trustees' rules and intentions were overturned, the essential components of Savannah's town plan were preserved during the period of royal governorship. This is not to suggest, however, that Georgia's first royal governor, Captain John Reynolds, was a booster for Savannah. In fact, soon after his arrival on October 29, 1754, Reynolds proposed moving the colony's capital from Savannah to a new town about seventeen miles to the southwest on the Ogeechee River. The town he chose, Georgetown, had been founded in February of that year under the leadership of the provincial president Patrick Graham. Reynolds renamed the

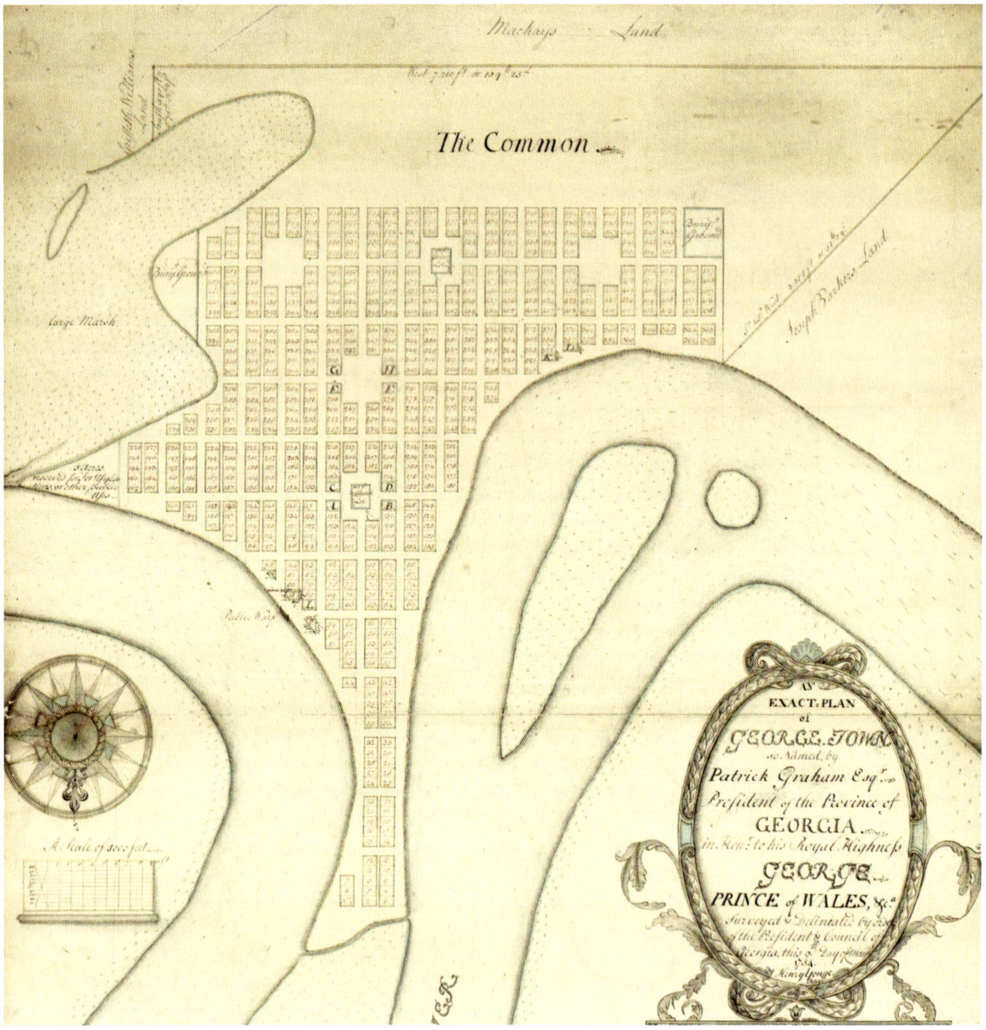

FIGURE 28. Detail of *An Exact-Plan of George-Town [Hardwick] So Named by Patrick Graham, Esqr., President of the Province of Georgia, in Honr. to His Royal Highness George, Prince of Wales, &ca.*, 1754. Pen and ink and watercolor. Library of Congress, Geography and Map Division.

site "Hardwick," after his sponsor Philip Yorke, first Earl of Hardwicke and Lord Chancellor, in the spring of 1755.[3] A description in the colonial council records and a corresponding plan show that the town was designed as a grid of streets (75 feet wide) and lanes (20 feet wide), with house lots of 120 feet by 80 feet and five "publick squares" bisected by north–south and east–west streets (figure 28).[4] Hardwick never functioned as the colonial capital, and although much of the site was inhabited by the early nineteenth century, by the time of the Civil War it had virtually disappeared.

Meanwhile, Savannah was prospering under royal governance. Large-scale rice plantations cultivated by enslaved Africans, who were allowed in Georgia beginning in 1751, were bringing increased wealth and population growth to the colony and to its principal city. The Reynolds administration instituted one significant change to the Savannah Plan in 1755, ordering that half of the "Publick Lots" (trust lots) be granted to private individuals and that they be divided into two sixty-by-ninety-foot lots, back-to-back.[5] Changing the rules about the use of trust lots would increase the number of residential properties, and it would also change how the plan worked politically, socially, and architecturally.

Among those granted public lots in 1755 were two surveyors general for the colony, Henry Yonge and William Gerard de Brahm. They would split the back-to-back halves of Lot X (the northeast trust lot) in Anson Ward, the present-day site of the Owens-Thomas House.[6] Both would play an important role in the development of the Savannah Plan. Yonge's frustration in surveying properties in Savannah led him to give a report to the colonial assembly in December 1756 advocating for an improved planning process.[7] One of the chief problems facing the assembly as the town was growing was the confused state of property surveys and deeds. This confusion was the result of incomplete or contested property surveys and the complicated procedure for acquiring clear title to property under the Trustees.[8] Yonge noted that Savannah had many vacant "Town Lotts, Garden and Farm" with no clear title of ownership, thus preventing "many persons [who were] inclined to build" from moving into the town. More significantly, he noted that the town Common needed to be "ascertained" and, perhaps, enlarged because not enough lots remained available for the growing population. Yonge was directed by the assembly to document these concerns and return with a report.

The threat of war with Spain, France, and Native Americans loomed in Georgia in the latter half of the 1750s, complicating the planning process in Savannah. Soon after the arrival of Governor Henry Ellis in 1757, de Brahm designed a circuit of trenches, wood-reinforced bastions, and wooden towers around the six wards of the town.[9] Although these fortifications remained incomplete as late as November 1760 and may never have been completed, they appear in a carefully drawn map and accompanying silhouetted profile view of Savannah that de Brahm included in an unpublished report completed more than a decade later (figure 29).[10]

On May 1, 1760, the Royal Legislature passed "An Act for the Better Regulating the Town of Savannah, and for Ascertaining the Common Thereunto Belonging," a town planning act aimed at restoring and preserving the integrity of the Savannah Plan, even as work on the fortifications continued. The act addressed issues related to health, safety, and cleanliness and required the dismantling of encroachments on the "Streets, Squares, Lanes or Alleys belonging to or within the Town of Savannah." Yonge's earlier concerns about ascertaining the Common appear to be reflected in this legislation, as it carefully defined the boundaries of the Common and stipulated that

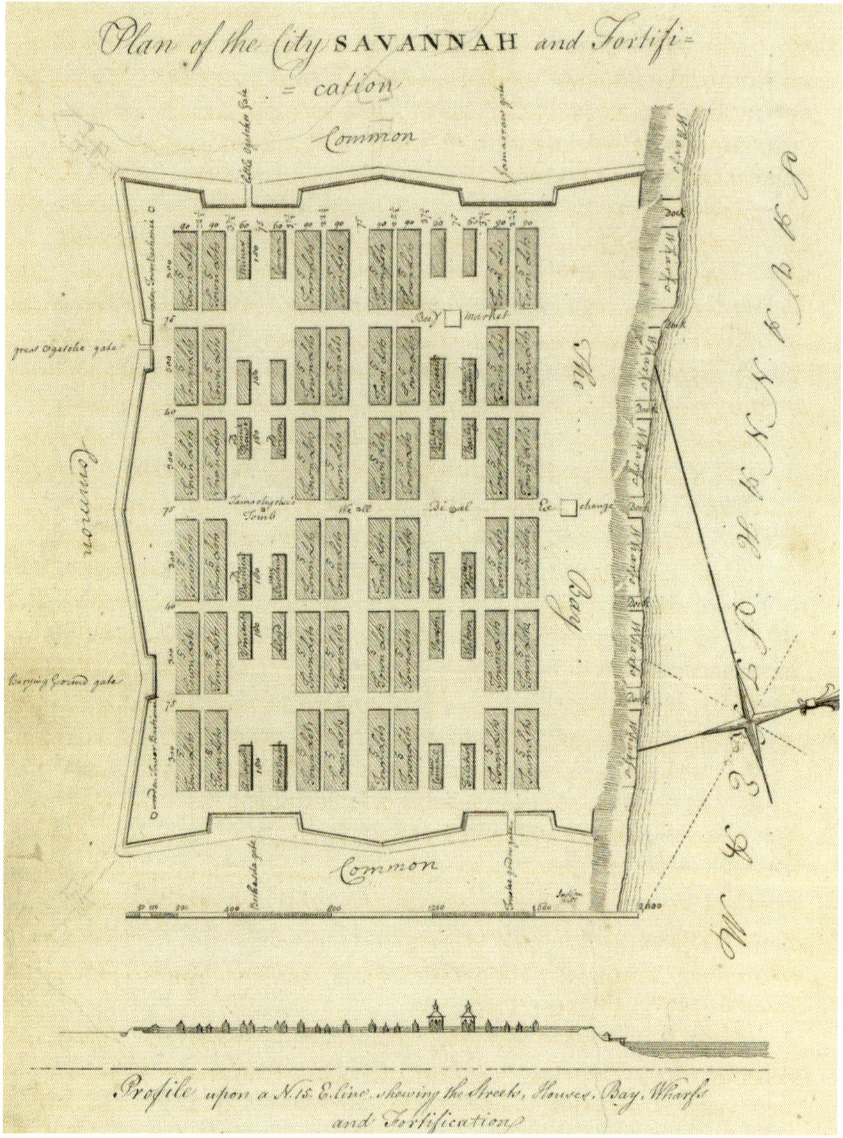

FIGURE 29. *Plan of the City of Savannah and Fortifications* by William Gerard de Brahm. Plan of 1757 in a drawing completed no later than 1771 in "History of the Three Provinces South Carolina, Georgia, and East Florida," MS Am 824, p. 126. Houghton Library, Harvard University, Cambridge, Mass.

all the squares, streets, lanes and passages described in the plan of the said town in the surveyor-general's office, and which have been heretofore accustomed or made use of by the inhabitants of the said town, shall be and continue the common property of the lot holders in the said town, and shall not be alien[at]ed or granted away for any purpose whatsoever than by act of the general assembly.[11]

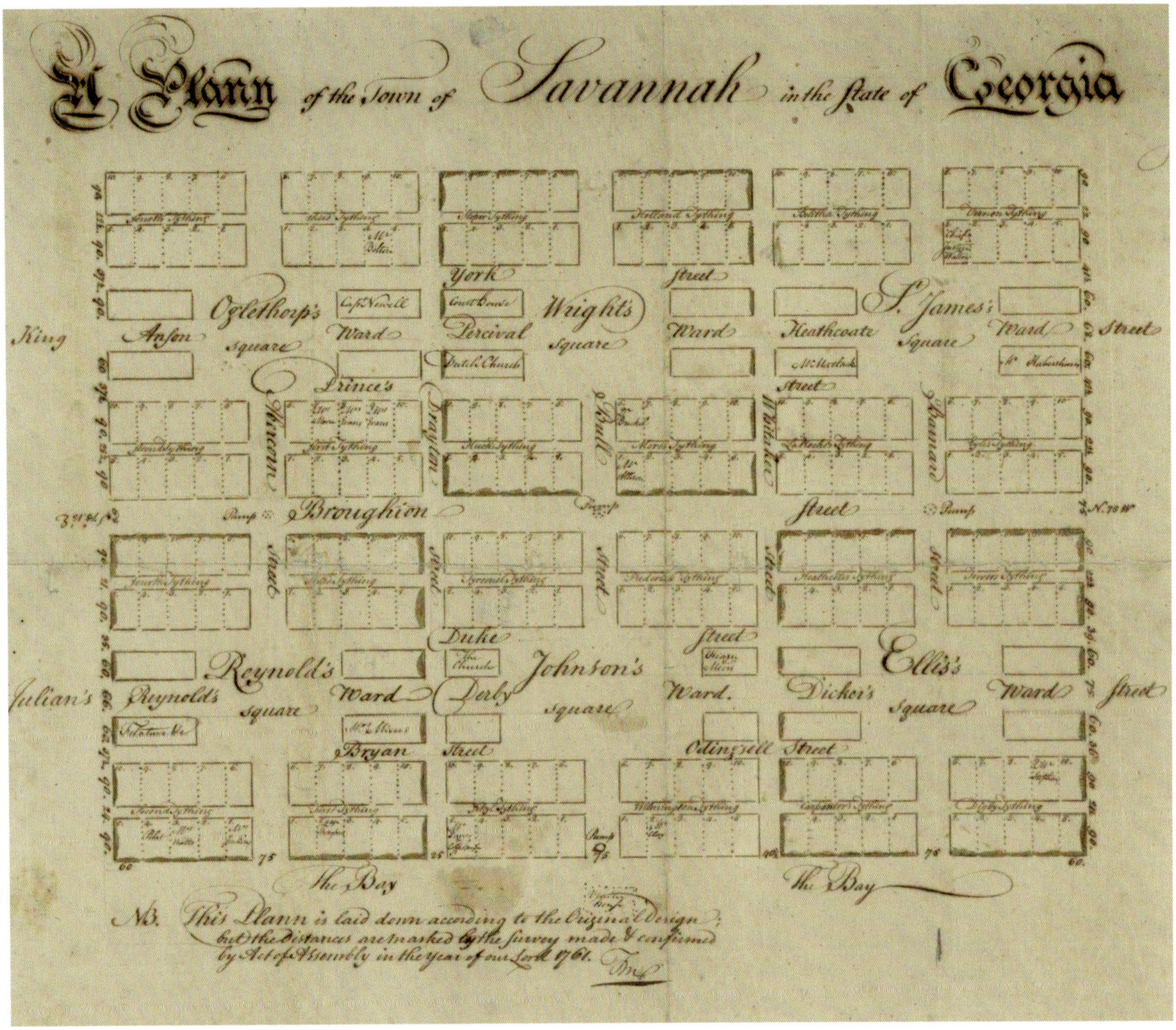

FIGURE 30. *A Plan of the Town of Savannah in the State of Georgia*, copy of a plan ordered by an act of the colonial assembly in 1761. Marian S. Carson Collection, Library of Congress.

The next spring, with the colony now under the rule of its third royal governor, James Wright (who had arrived in 1760), the colonial assembly instructed "the Surveyors General to draw a plan of the Town of Savannah from a Survey agreeable to the Original Plan, describing all the Lotts, Streets, Squares and Lands in the said Town."[12] A copy of that plan, now in the Library of Congress, specifies that it "is laid down according to the original design; but the distances are marked by the survey" (figure 30). The dimensions noted on this plan reveal that the streets and lots as surveyed did not conform exactly to the originally specified dimensions of the town plan. Deputy Surveyor Thomas Shruder's town plan of 1770 showed

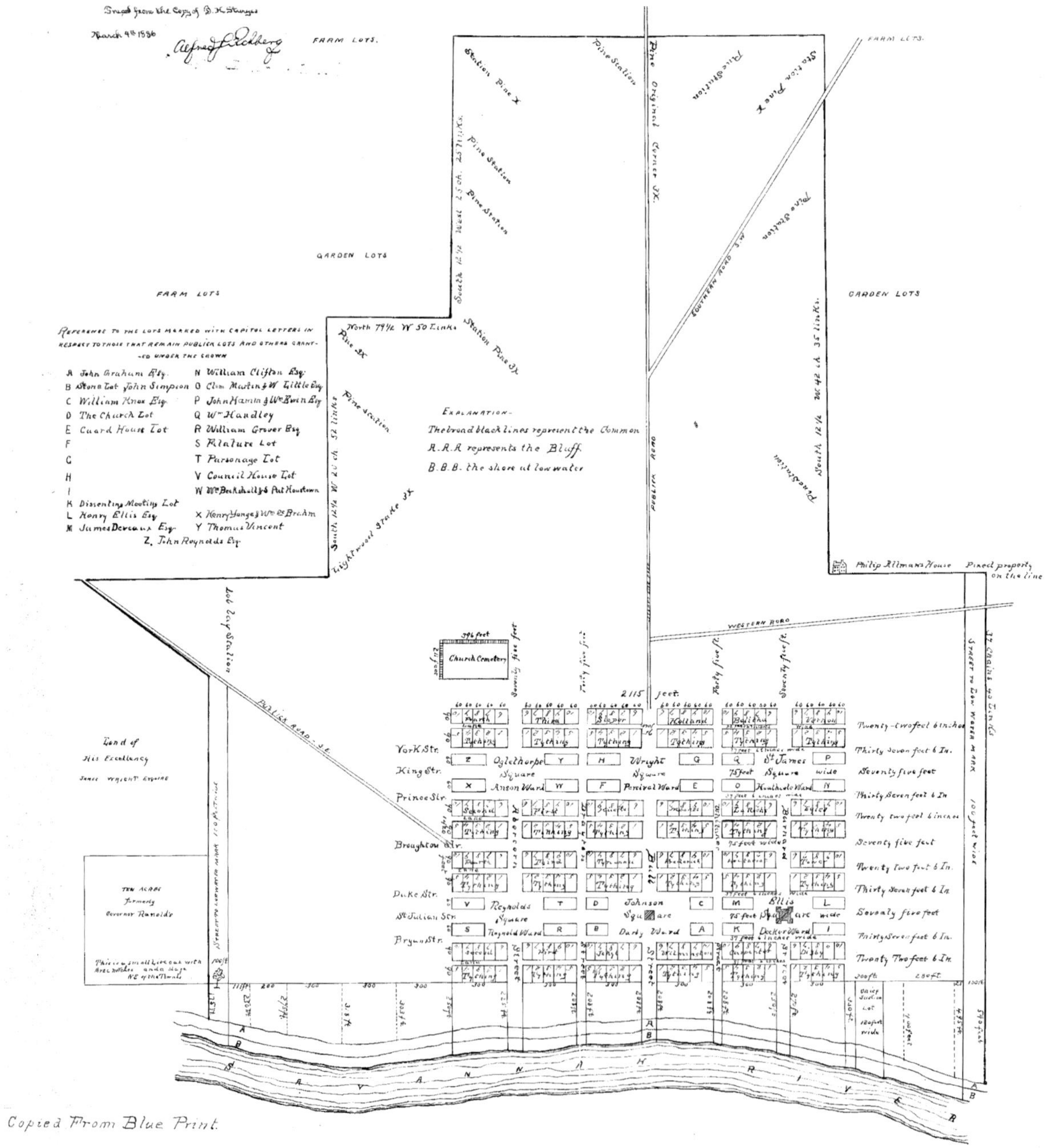

FIGURE 31. Plan of town and Common of Savannah by Thomas Shruder, 1770. This late nineteenth-century tracing is one of several versions of this map. Courtesy of the City of Savannah Municipal Archives, Engineering Department, General Maps, Item #JJ-04VA.

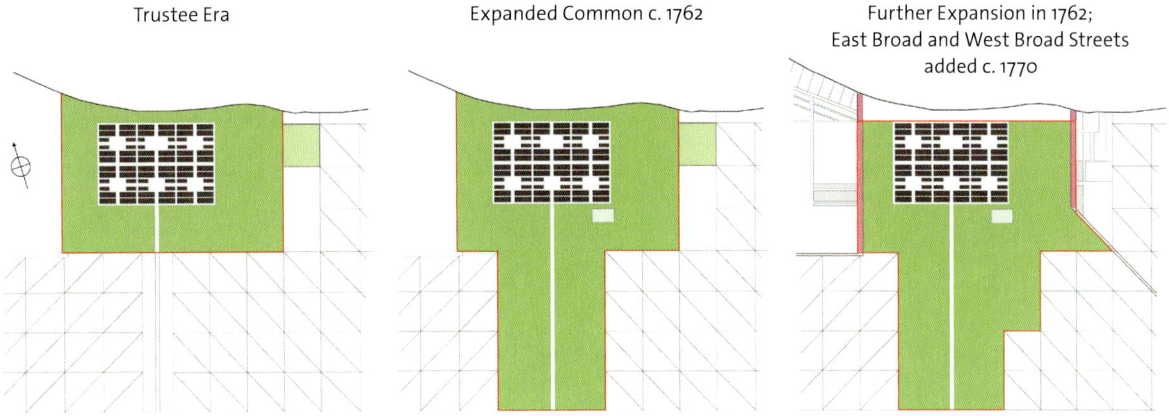

FIGURE 32. Colonial modifications to the Savannah Common. Diagram by Robin B. Williams.

that those dimensions had been rectified (figure 31), suggesting the surveyors' office had readjusted the street and lot boundaries to make them more accurately reflect the original plan—the first in a long history of actions preserving the city's distinctive plan.

As the town plan was being readjusted, the Common was enlarged. By early spring of 1762, the equivalent of sixteen garden lots flanking either side of Bull Street became part of the Common. This change, for which no documentation can be found, is illustrated in the T-shaped Common depicted in figure 12 (Bull Street is labeled "White Bluff Road" as it passes between the farm lots). On March 4, 1762, the assembly passed "An Amendment to the Act for Regulating the Town of Savannah," enlarging the Common further by appropriating four garden lots to the east of the town lots, thus extending the Common to the edge of the Trustees' Garden.[13]

Shruder's measured drawing of the town plan and Common, dated February 5, 1770, shows the changes made in 1762 together with several other modifications.[14] Perhaps the most curious feature in Shruder's drawing is the triangular protrusion extending from the eastern edge of the Common. This appears to be the consequence of a land exchange involving Governor Wright described in the March 4, 1762, act (figure 32). In total, the Common was expanded by adding the land of twenty-one former garden lots, or 105 acres. Why this was done is not clear, but it was remarkably foresighted in facilitating the future expansion of the Savannah Plan. The most significant new feature in the 1770 plan is two 100-foot-wide broad streets—East Broad Street and West Broad Street—bounding the eastern and western edges of the Common. These important additions suggest that expansion of the town plan was anticipated as early as 1770, even if no such expansion of Oglethorpe's ward system would occur until two decades later.

The intended role of the Common and its expansion in the growth of the Savannah Plan remains obscure.[15] Oglethorpe had planned for the Common to function much as it would in other English colonial towns, writing that "without the Town a Mile square which amounts to 640 Acres might be reserved as a Common for the pasturing of the Cattle and all within Musket shot of the Works should be cleared. This open space will contribute greatly to the health and security of the Town as well as to the conveniency of the Inhabitants."[16] Town commons in England and in the colonies were used for communal grazing of livestock, military exercises, burial grounds, ropewalks (a facility for the manufacturing of rope, typical in port towns), and other extra-urban activities. The peripheral location of many colonial commons suggests that they were often seen as land for potential future urban growth.[17]

It seems reasonable, therefore, to believe that the colonial assembly increased the size of the Savannah Common to prepare for an expansion of the town plan. Why the royal council did not take this next step, however, remains a mystery, especially since the town greatly prospered under royal rule between 1760 and the American Revolution.[18] Meanwhile, the Common was put to an increasing number of uses, many of which would create impediments to future expansion of the town. Among these were at least four separate burial grounds, an academy, a jail, a hospital, a ropewalk, and a tobacco inspection station.[19] A map by Mossman Houstoun dating to between 1810 and 1812 illustrates several of these features (figure 35).

The Revolutionary War prompted the erection of a new and more elaborate set of fortifications around the six wards of the town plan. More than half a dozen surviving battle maps show the town plan of British-controlled Savannah surrounded by the attacking American and French allies and depict offensive and defensive earthwork fortifications built for the siege of Savannah in October 1779. Although those fortifications must have obliterated previous structures built in the Common, little trace of the fortifications exists today aside from the Spring Hill Redoubt, whose location is marked by a cairn and stone outline on the south side of Louisville Road in Battlefield Park.[20] A 2005 reconstruction of that redoubt stands nearby.

Expanding and Enhancing the Savannah Plan

The establishment of a new nation, a new state, and a new municipal government inaugurated a period of almost seventy years during which the Savannah Plan grew from six to twenty-four wards, following the original pattern established by Oglethorpe but with subtle yet significant modifications (figure 33). Formal planning resumed in the 1780s as the city began to rebuild following the American victory. The newly formed state legislature passed acts in 1785 and 1787 "for better regulating the Town of Savannah and the Hamlets thereof."[21] These had to do with cleaning streets, building a hospital, and drawing a new plan of the city—the old plan having been lost in the war. In December 1789 Savannah formally incorporated as a city, empowering it to form a municipal government composed of a city council along with a mayor and aldermen, who were elected the following March. Among its early priorities was the expansion of the Savannah Plan. As the city experienced rapid growth in the early days of the republic, the municipality oversaw a series of eight major expansions of the Savannah Plan into the Common from the 1790s through the 1850s, with each expansion using the Oglethorpe-style ward as the basic modular unit of growth. For the elected officials and city surveyors, fitting new wards into the irregular Common required dexterous adjustments to the module and its parts. Throughout each expansion, the elasticity of the Savannah Plan enabled its designers to stretch and compress its constituent parts as needed.

EXPANDING THE PLAN TO THE EAST AND WEST

The first expansion was initiated on May 18, 1790, when the council of the newly incorporated City of Savannah ordered that a plan be drafted to "lay off all that part of the Common on the east and west sides of the City . . . *agreeably to the old Plan of Savannah* as nearly as the same can conveniently be done."[22] In other words, the council planned to develop three new Oglethorpe-style wards and squares on two sides of the Common, a decisive act in the history of the Savannah Plan. The stated purpose of this proposal was to raise revenue for the city by selling the land. Approval for the first expansion was complicated by the question of ownership of the Common. As the town planning act of 1760 stipulated, it was "the Common Property of the Lot holders in the said Town, and shall not be aliened or granted away for any Purpose."[23] After months of debate, a majority of lot holders agreed to grant authority to the council to sell parts of the Common, and a bill to lay out the new wards was passed on September 28, 1790. The resulting nine-ward city plan is illustrated in a map documenting the extent of the large urban fires in 1796 (figure 34).

The three new wards along the Strand—Warren and Washington to the east and Franklin to the west—doubled the number of wards in the first row, extending the limits of the town plan to the East Broad Street and West Broad Street boundaries that had been delineated on Shruder's survey map of 1770, along the edges of the East and West Commons (figure 31). The new wards adopted the plan configuration of the original six, but they were made about 18 percent narrower on their east–west dimension than the earlier wards, as if the full-size wards had been squeezed. To fit the new wards into their allotted spaces in the Common, the surveyors reduced the number of lots in each tything from five across to four,

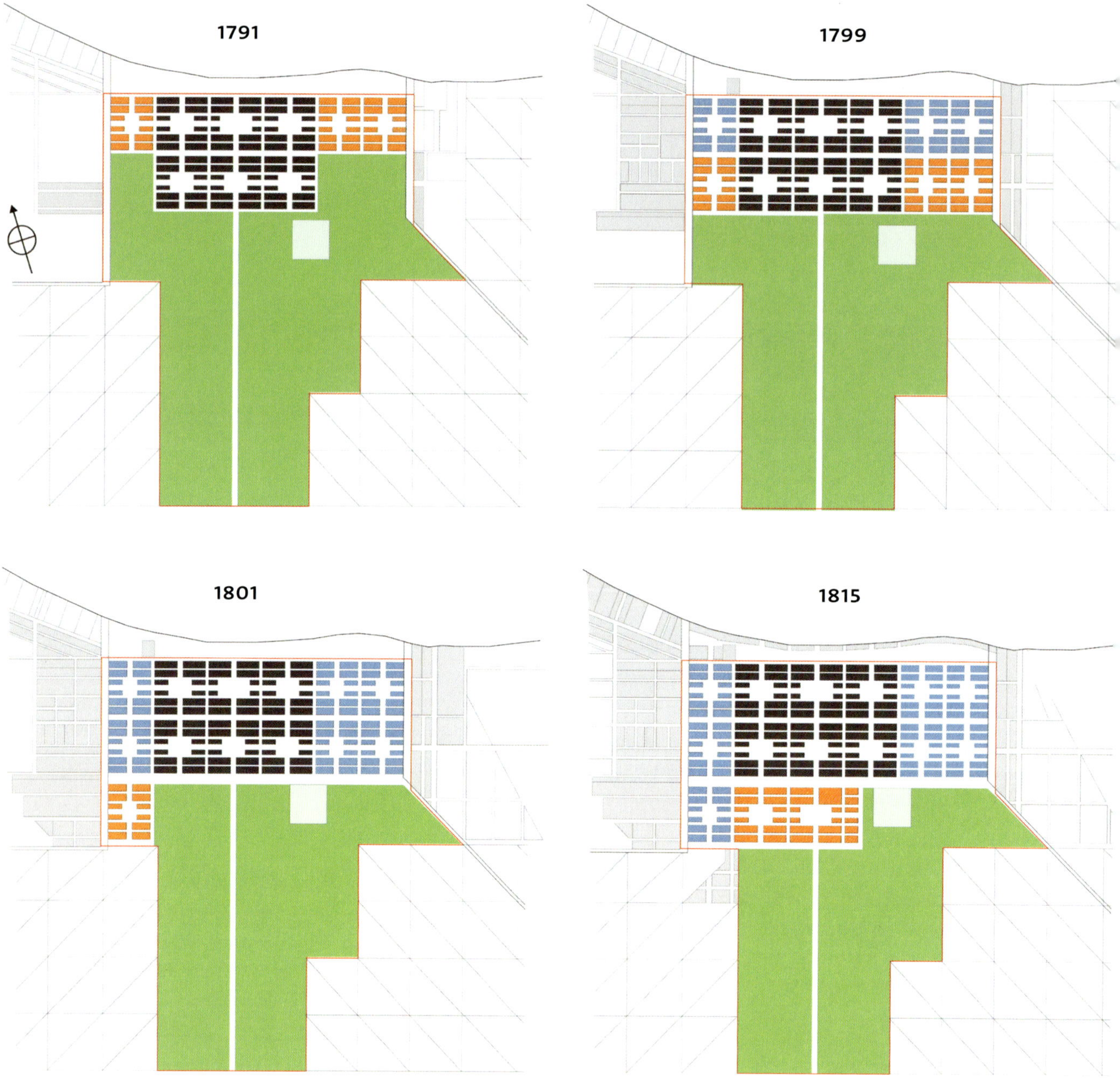
1791
1799
1801
1815

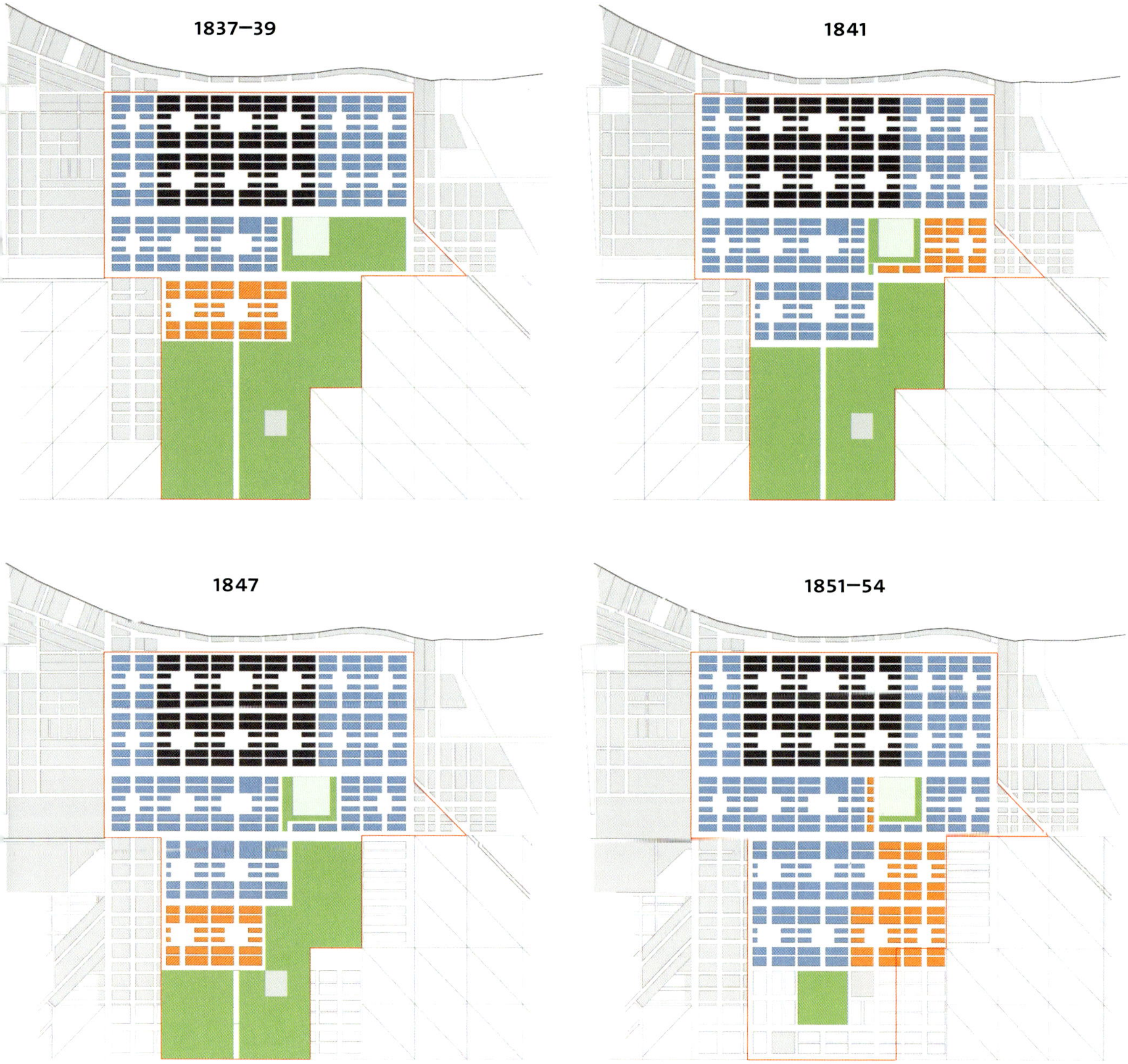

FIGURE 33. Eight major expansions of the Savannah Plan. Diagram by Robin B. Williams.

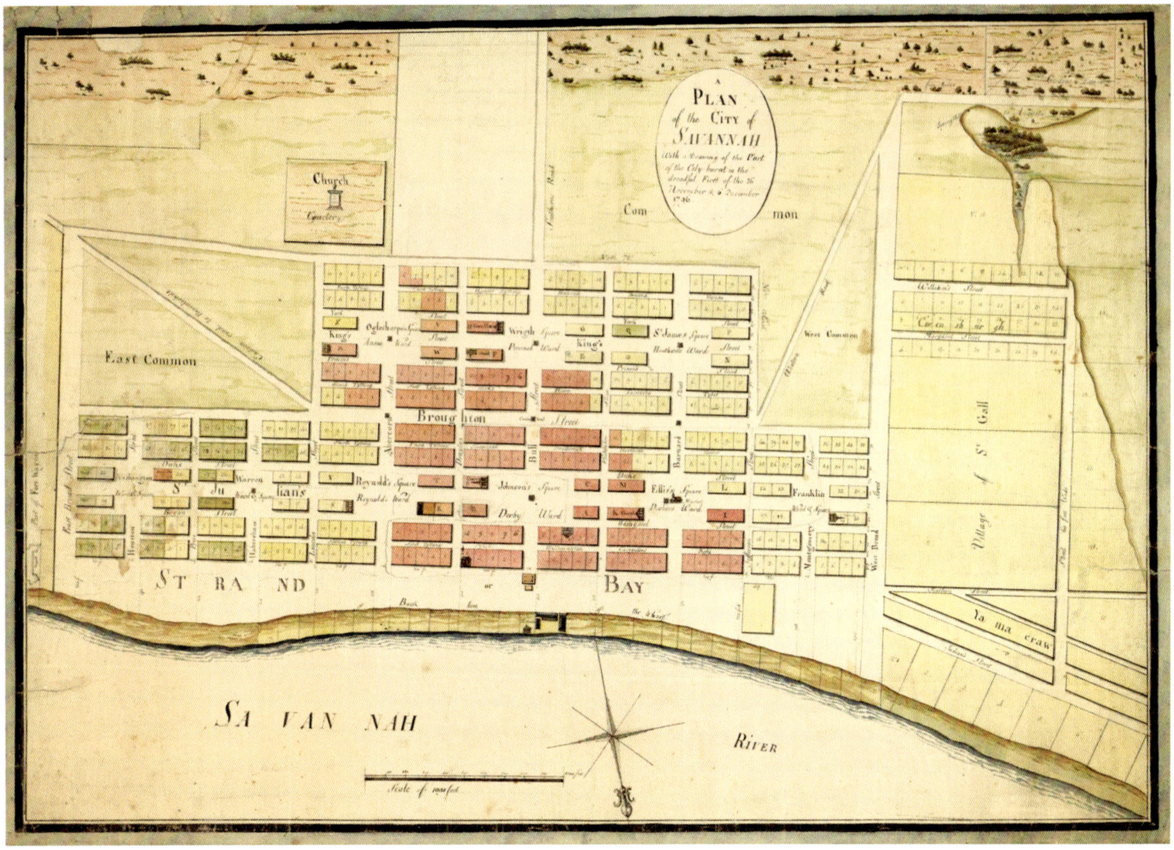

FIGURE 34. *Plan of the City of Savannah*, ca. 1796, showing the first expansion of the original town plan into the East and West Common. The map documents the extent of damage caused by fires on November 26 and December 6, 1796. Pen and ink, pencil and watercolor, 19¼" × 28". Marian S. Carson Collection, Library of Congress.

thereby decreasing the east–west dimension of each ward by 120 feet. This adjustment, along with leaving the trust lots unchanged in size, had the effect of reducing the size of the public squares in these wards by half, giving them a noticeably more intimate scale.[24] A second expansion followed in 1799, when the addition of a corresponding set of three wards—Columbia and Greene to the east and Liberty to the west—located directly south of the three created in 1790 increased the size of the plan to twelve wards in two rows.

SOUTHWARD EXPANSION OF THE PLAN

The platting of Elbert Ward in April 1801 initiated a third row of wards south of the previous two. Jackson Ward and Brown Ward followed in 1815—delayed by the War of 1812—and then Crawford Ward, though not until 1841. Due to preexisting site conditions, the incremental development of these wards gave rise to significant

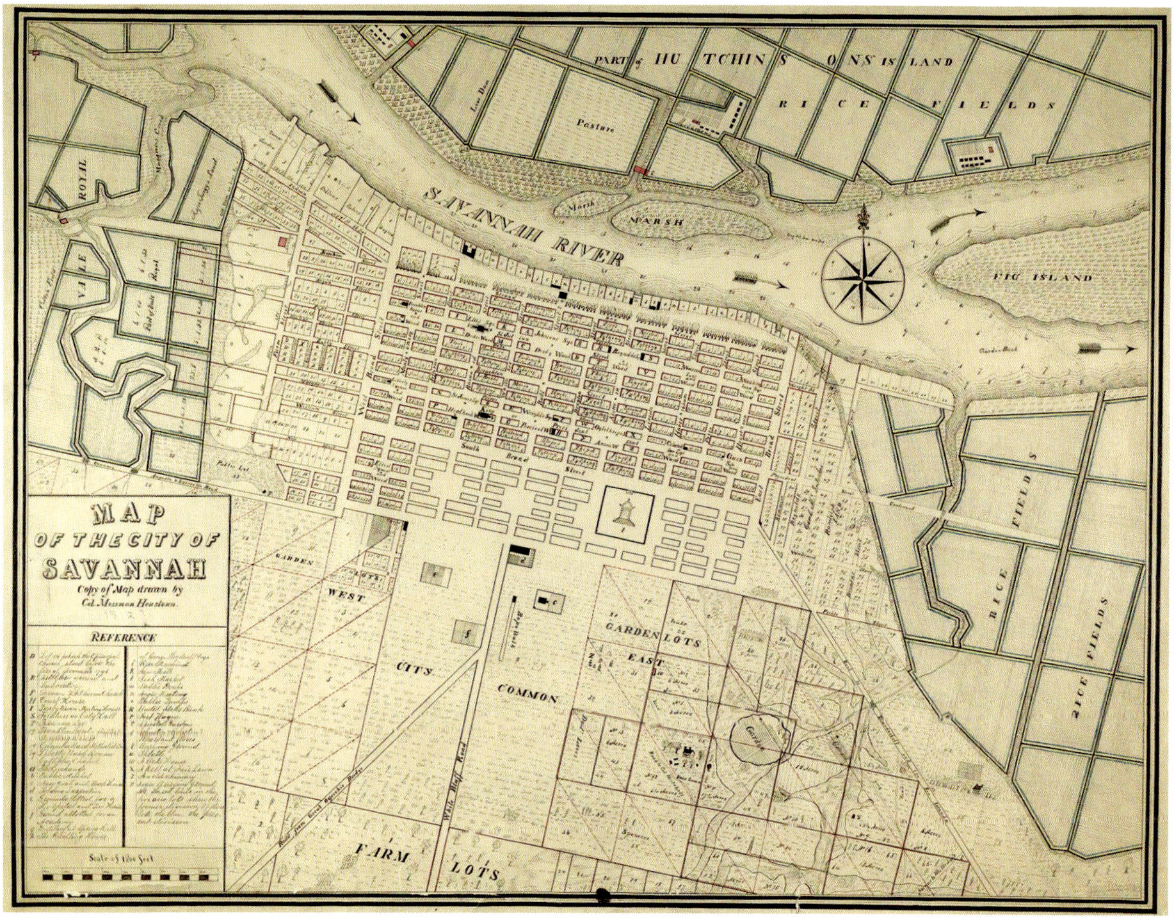

FIGURE 35. *Map of the City of Savannah*, copy of a map drawn by Colonel Mossman Houstoun, 1810–12. Colored ink on paper, 22¼" × 29⅜". Courtesy of Hargett Rare Book and Manuscript Library, University of Georgia Libraries, Rare Map Collection.

irregularities but also to innovative adaptations in the plan. The Mossman Houstoun map shows how the city surveyors attempted to negotiate existing conditions as they expanded the modular ward system during these third and fourth expansion campaigns (figure 35).[25] Similar maps produced in 1813 and 1818 show subtle variations (figures 36 and 37).

In the third-row wards, the width of the lanes was increased from 22½ feet to 32½ feet, and the east–west streets flanking the square were increased from 37½ feet in width to 40 feet. These adjustments added a total of 25 feet to the north–south dimension of the wards. This stretching of the modular ward seems to have allowed the eastern and western wards to extend to the southern edges of the East and West Commons, but it also seems that these increased dimensions were understood as civic improvements, refinements to the plan.

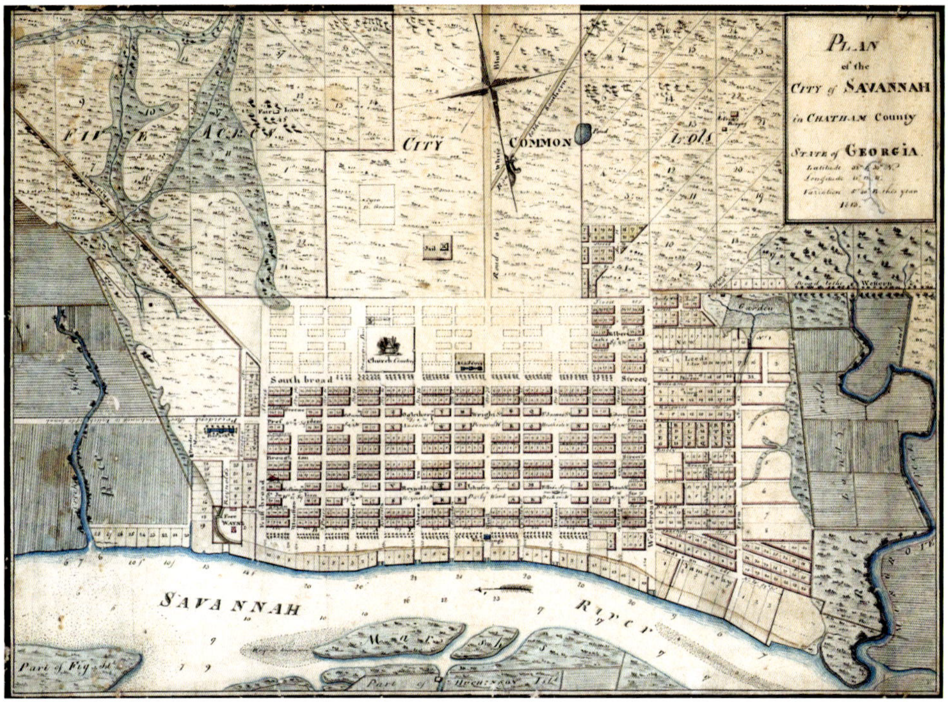

FIGURE 36. *Plan of the City of Savannah in Chatham County, State of Georgia*, 1813. Ink and watercolor on paper, 20" × 27". Courtesy of the Davenport House Museum, Savannah.

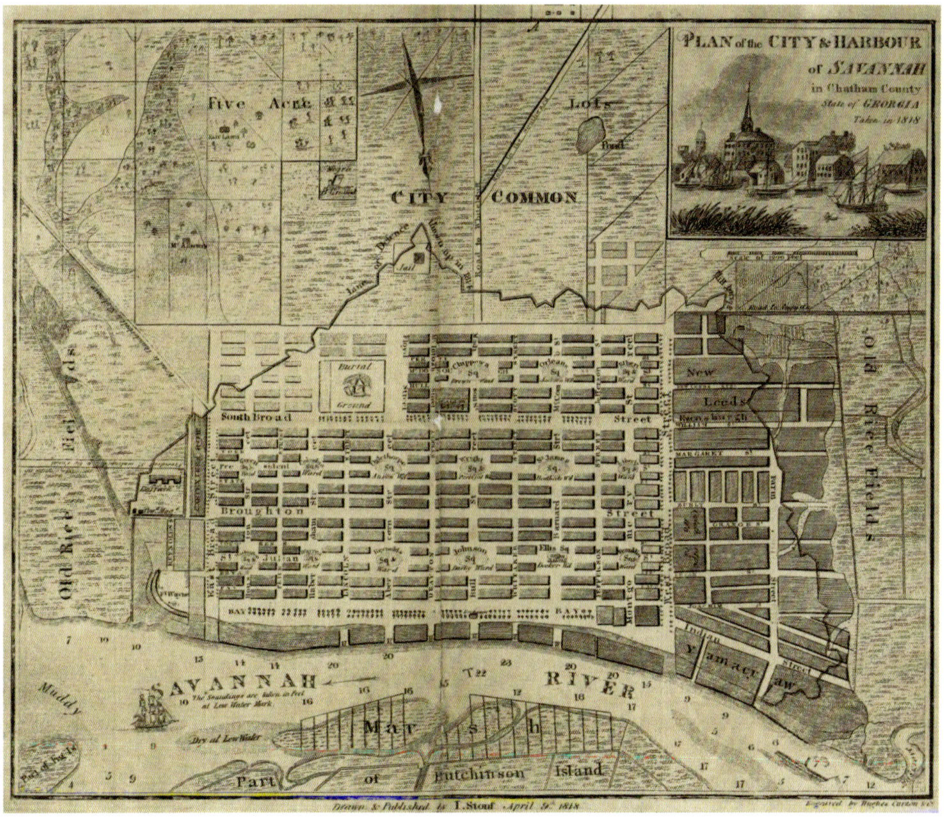

FIGURE 37. *Plan of the City & Harbour of Savannah in Chatham County*, drawn and published by Isidore Stouf, engraved by Hughes Curzon & Co., 1818, 8½" × 10⅜". Courtesy of Hargrett Rare Book and Manuscript Library, University of Georgia Libraries.

THE CREATION OF a grand east-west civic street—South Broad Street (now Oglethorpe Avenue)—dividing the third row from the original wards introduced a new feature to the Savannah Plan. Laid out with a width of 140 feet, nearly double that of 75-foot-wide Broughton Street that divided the first two rows, South Broad Street was comparable to the widest avenues in the newly established national capital plan for Washington, D.C. (1791), and, notably, to Broad and Greene Streets in Augusta, Georgia (1784 and 1791), but few other American cities of that time had streets of such breadth.[26] Between 1809 and 1813, the city planted two rows of pride of India (*Melia azedarach*, also known as chinaberry) trees along the center of the street, forming an allée that echoed the tree rows planted in the Strand in the 1790s (figure 7). South Broad Street's prodigious width can thus be explained by its function as a public promenade—though, as with the widening of other streets in the third row, it might also be the result of filling the extra space between the southern edge of new wards on the southern edge of the East and West Commons.

An intriguing third possible reason for the width of South Broad Street was the presence of a small burial ground interrupting its pathway. In 1733 James Oglethorpe granted a parcel of land of unspecified size in the Common just south of Percival Ward for Jewish burials.[27] Petitions to enlarge and enclose this cemetery were made to the colonial council in 1762 and again in 1770, but these requests went unfulfilled. An April 7, 1770, "Memorial" opposing the petition argued that the expanded burial ground

> would become a Nuisance and in some measure prevent the extending the Town that way, and would also be a means of lessening the Value of many of the Lots, as they apprehend no Person would choose to buy or rent an House whose Windows looked into a Burial Ground of any kind, particularly one belonging to a People who might be presumed, from Prejudice of Education to have imbibed Principles entirely repugnant to those of our most holy Religion.[28]

Jewish burials were thereafter relegated to a pair of private walled cemeteries on a garden lot southwest of the Common, known to this day as the Old Jewish Burial Ground and the Mordecai Sheftall Cemetery.[29] Although no historic maps or views show the original Jewish burial ground, the memory of its presence remained strong enough that Adelaide Wilson, writing in 1889, maintained that the width of South Broad Street was "extended to include within its space the unmarked place of burial" of the mother of Benjamin Sheftall, "in token of appreciation" of his valuable services as a patriot in the Revolutionary War.[30] In 1983, on the 250th anniversary of the founding of Savannah, the trustees of the Mordecai Sheftall Cemetery erected a commemorative monument on the west side of Bull Street in the Oglethorpe Avenue median.

A much larger and less expendable cemetery posed a yet greater obstacle to the replication of Oglethorpe-style wards along the third row. Known since 1896 as Colonial Park Cemetery, Savannah's primary Protestant burial ground remains today the greatest aberration in the Savannah Plan. Although Oglethorpe was instructed by the Common Council of the Trustees in 1732 to create a "burial place at a proper distance from the Town,"[31] it appears that a pair of tything lots in Percival Ward served this purpose until 1750, when the present burial ground was established in the South Common.[32] Although no documentation can be found for its original establishment, public ordinances record three enlargements (1763, 1768, and 1789), bringing it to its final size of five hundred by five hundred feet in 1789.[33]

Wrapping the plan around this burial ground clearly perplexed city surveyors of the 1810s and 1820s, as maps from this period illustrate. One solution, illustrated on the 1813 map, was to place half a ward—two tythings, two trust lots, and half a square—to either side of the cemetery (figure 36). A few years later, on the 1818 map, the proposed half ward to the west had been simplified to a set of six equally long blocks (establishing their present form), with the sets of tything blocks reduced to match the length of the central trust lots, likely to allow room for the rows of trees planted around the cemetery in 1807 (figure 37). In both maps, two pairs of tything blocks flank the southern boundary of the cemetery. The 1820 map of Savannah by city surveyor John McKinnon records an open buffer space (planted with double rows of trees) surrounding the west, south, and east sides of the cemetery, with simplified blocks aligning with the blocks in adjacent wards beyond (figure 38). Progressively during the nineteenth century, the broad spaces on the east and west sides of the cemetery were developed as well, with simple rectangular blocks added to the west in 1853 and a large undivided block attached to the east side for the county jail and police barracks.[34] The open space immediately south of the cemetery, where McKinnon shows rows of trees, remains a public park today.[35]

Liberty Street, another wide east–west street, defines the southern edge of the third row of wards. Named and located in the same 1801 ordinance as South Broad Street, the 1813 map designates the still-undeveloped Liberty Street as being 85 feet wide. This dimension was determined by the southern edges of the East and West Commons, which were bordered by garden lots in which suburban development had already begun. When the city began platting a fourth row of wards (the fifth expansion) in 1837, however, Liberty Street was officially established as 130 feet in width within the narrower part of the Common between Tattnall Street

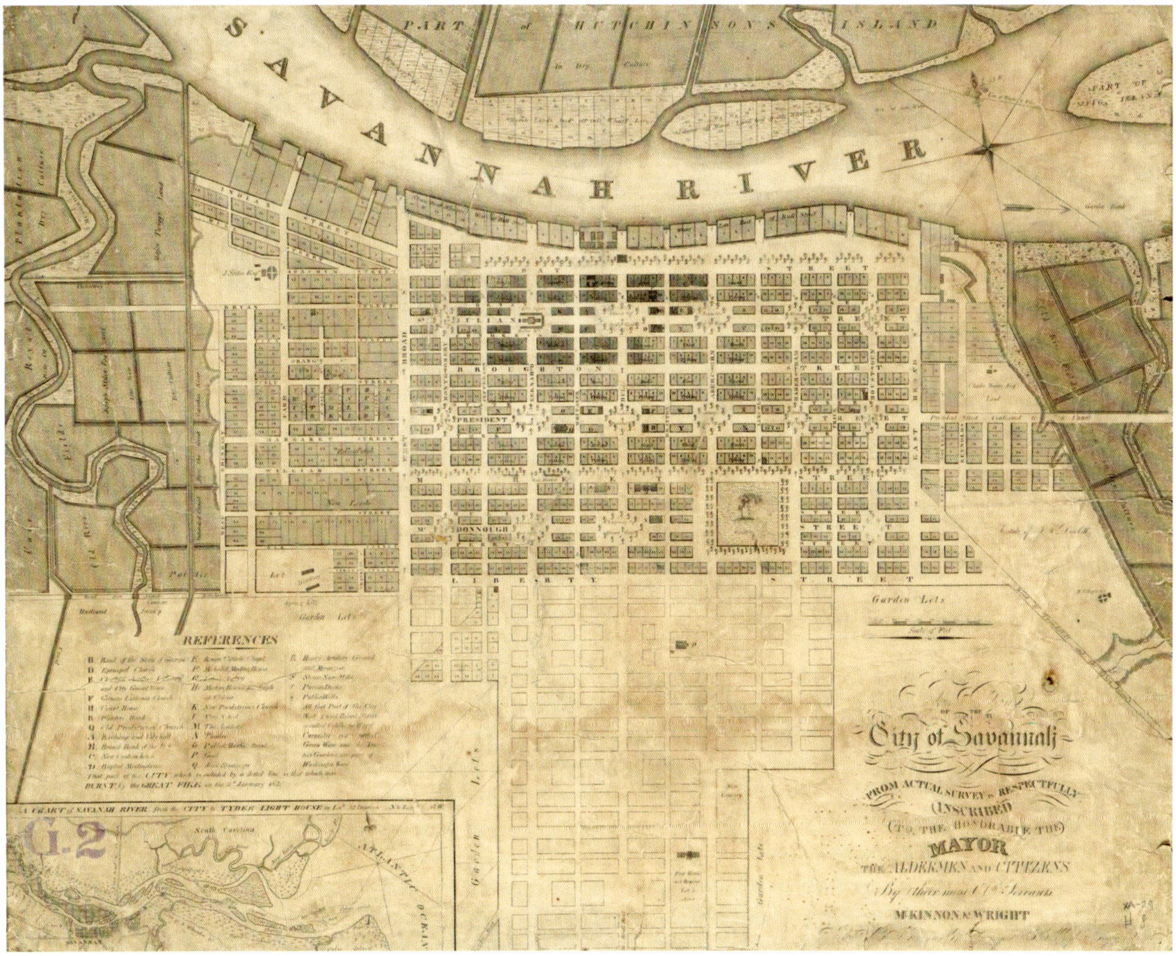

on the west and the west edge of the garden lots on the east, as seen in an 1840 map by city surveyor Charles Stephens (figure 39), and it was extended further eastward beyond East Broad Street, as shown in the Edward Vincent map of 1852 (figure 40).[36] Like South Broad Street (Oglethorpe Avenue), Liberty Street received a green median of paired trees, though the median was only 30 feet wide. Oglethorpe Avenue and Liberty Street introduced generous and verdant public spaces into the Savannah Plan. They became linear versions of the squares at the center of each ward, competing with them in attracting monuments and flanking prominent buildings.

As the fourth row of wards was being established, the western edge of the Common south of Liberty Street posed a new challenge to the city surveyors. Running along the border of garden lots that had already been developed as house lots, this

FIGURE 38. *City of Savannah from Actual Survey*, drawn by John McKinnon, engraved by C. C. Wright, 1820, 24¾" × 30¾". Courtesy of the City of Savannah Municipal Archives, Engineering Department, General Maps, Item #XA-029.

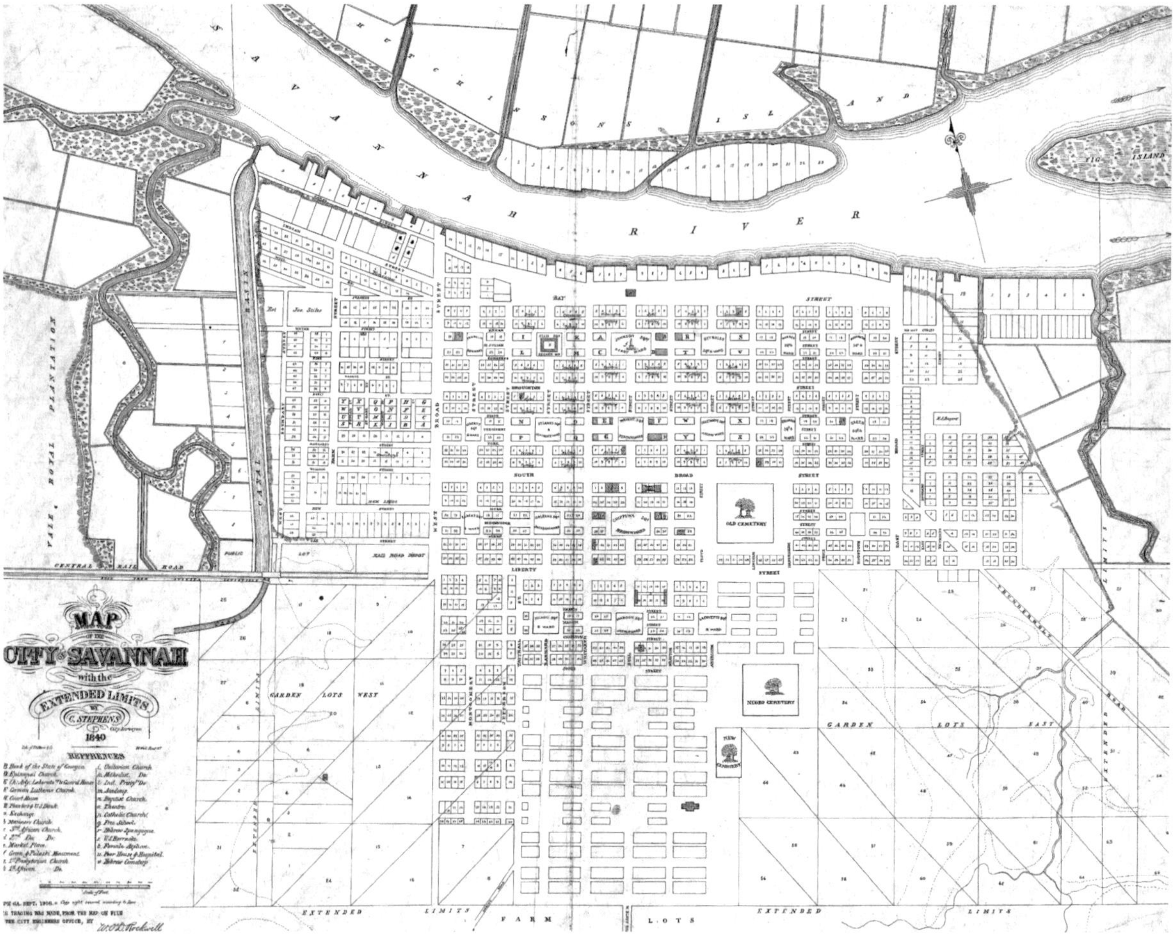

FIGURE 39. *Map of the City of Savannah with Extended Limits*, drawn by Charles Stephens, 1840 (tracing of a published lithograph, dated 1908). University of Georgia Libraries, Map and Government Information Library, Athens, Georgia, as presented in the Digital Library of Georgia.

edge was defined by a street (Tattnall Street) that was not aligned with the street grid of wards to the north. To fill this narrower portion of the Common, in 1820 McKinnon proposed a dramatic adjustment of scale to the Oglethorpe ward formula, with two rows of "super wards" significantly larger than all previous wards to form fourth, fifth, and sixth rows of wards extending to the southern boundary of the Common at today's Gwinnett Street. McKinnon's motive appears to have been to maximize the available land left in the Common, which was too much for three rows of conventional wards but too little for four rows (figure 38).

McKinnon's 1820 "super ward" plan was not adopted. However, with the establishment of Pulaski Ward in 1837, the north–south dimensions of each ward were nonetheless stretched by increasing each tything block from 90 to 100 feet deep,

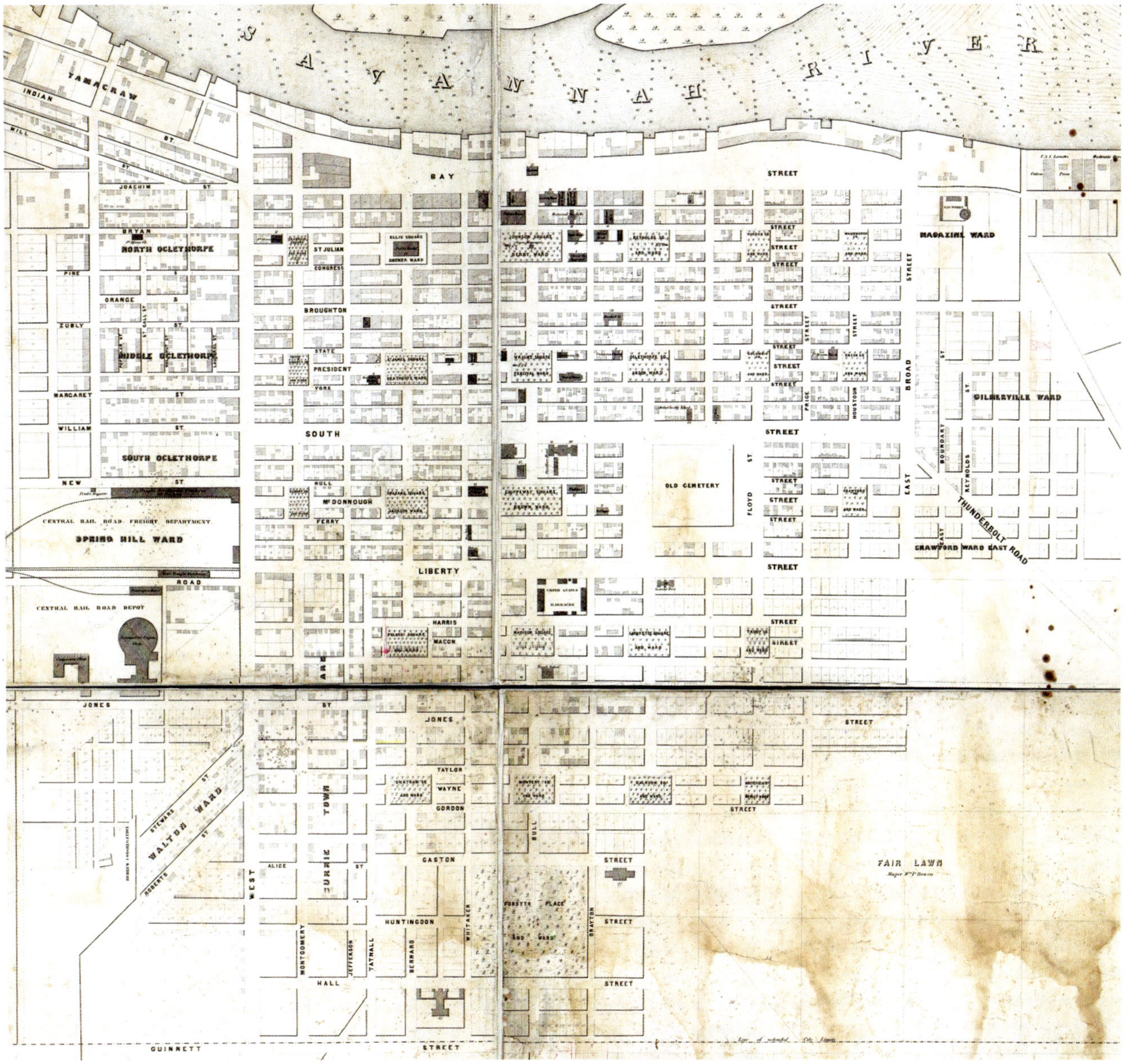

FIGURE 40. Detail of *Vincent's Subdivision Map of the City of Savannah, Chatham County, State of Georgia, Shewing All the Public and Private Buildings, Lots, Wards, etc., Together with All the Latest Improvements, from Surveys and Authentic Records*, hand-drawn original by Edward A. Vincent, 1852 (published as lithographic print by Snyder and Black, 1853). Courtesy of Hargrett Rare Book and Manuscript Library, University of Georgia Libraries, Rare Map Collection.

adding 40 feet to each ward. All wards south of Liberty Street would follow this tything dimension. Additionally, modifying the three central east–west streets in each ward from 40-75-40 feet to 60-60-60 feet added 25 more feet. More dramatically, the city devised a definitive solution for abutting the western section of the Common by using a truncated, asymmetrical ward. Chatham Ward followed this pattern to its south in 1841 (part of the seventh expansion). The east half of each ward is full scale, with tythings comprising the usual five lots abreast. The west half of each, however, comprises only three lots per tything block and diminutive trust lots only 60 feet deep (one-third the normal depth). Significantly, the central square follows the pattern of other wards (unlike the asymmetrical solution proposed by McKinnon). The on-ground experience within the ward, especially from within the square at the center of each ward, gives no sense of this asymmetry that is so obvious in the plan. It is a testament to the cohesive power of the Oglethorpe planning formula that even when the components are of unequal size, the overall harmonious order and balance remain.

On the east side of the South Common, a similar misalignment with the planned city to the north, as well as the presence of two cemeteries, presented still more challenges to the surveyors planning the eighth expansion during the 1850s. The city's "Negro Burial Ground," established in the Common by the colonial assembly in 1763 and expanded in 1789, was moved to a location further south in 1810.[37] A burial ground for "strangers" was established nearby in 1819.[38] Both of these cemeteries are neatly drawn on Stephens's map of 1840 (figure 39), which, like McKinnon's map two decades earlier (figure 38), shows hypothetical layouts for future wards. Stephens left both cemeteries untouched in his plan. In 1844, however, the council made plans to relocate the cemeteries, making this space available for the creation of new wards.[39] The council's decision followed the recommendations of the city's Health and Cemetery Committee to move the cemeteries away from the town lots as a health preventative. Unsettled by a series of yellow fever epidemics and attracted by a national trend to build suburban landscape cemeteries, the city purchased a former plantation to the southwest of the city to create Laurel Grove Cemetery in 1850 (visible in the lower left corner of the 1852 Vincent map, beyond what is shown in figure 40). The city ordered a mass exhumation of bodies from the Negro Burial Ground in 1855.[40]

The Completion of the Savannah Plan

After six decades of adding new wards by squeezing, stretching, and truncating them to make them fit within the irregular constraints of the Common, the Savannah Plan was essentially completed on March 13, 1851, when the city council approved the "laying off" of Calhoun, Troup, and Wesley Wards—the eighth expansion. Numerous problem-solving decisions remained. Several wards remained incomplete, awaiting the full platting of their building lots. This would be accomplished by 1854, once the city had acquired property from adjacent garden lots and resolved the problem of relocating the Negro Burial Ground and the Strangers Burial Ground. One final change was made in July 1851 when the city increased the depth of the tything lots along the southern edge of the fifth row of wards, the blocks facing Gaston Street (only the half of each tything south of Gordon Lane), making them 120 feet deep instead of the conventional 100 feet used for the rest of the tything lots in these wards. This innovation allowed townhouses on the north side of Gaston Street to have small front gardens, an unprecedented feature for townhouses on east–west streets within the area of the Savannah Plan. What made these house lots even more appealing was the view they would have of a newly established public park across Gaston Street.

The Savannah Plan did not fill the Common entirely. Instead of adding another Oglethorpe-style ward south of the fifth row, the city chose, months after the twenty-fourth ward had been established, to fill the central ten acres of the remaining area of the Common (sandwiched between the City Hospital and the county jail) with a single ward-sized public park named Forsyth Place. Set between Whitaker and Drayton Streets and centered on Bull Street, Forsyth Park (as it came to be called) terminated the twenty-four-ward Savannah Plan as if it were a supersized square (figure 40). It would be surrounded by a grid of streets and blocks that no longer followed Oglethorpe's ward system apart from continuing the tything block sizes and generous scale of east–west streets.[41] Why did the city end its program of replicating the modular Oglethorpe system when enough land was available to create at least one more ward? There is evidence that public enthusiasm for the Savannah Plan had waned. Some Savannahians had become advocates for the emerging park movement promoted by American luminaries such as Ralph Waldo Emerson, William Cullen Bryant, and Andrew Jackson Downing in the 1840s.[42] In words that could easily have applied to Savannah, Downing advocated precisely for the need to create a large park, rather than small squares, for New York City.[43] Savannah's Forsyth Park would precede by seven years the establishment of New York's Central Park.

Each of Savannah's eight discrete expansions of the plan involved a dexterous balancing act: maintain the essence of Oglethorpe's planning formula while making the extra wards fit within the irregular confines of the Common. The city's commitment to perpetuating the urban component of the Oglethorpe Plan and the skill of its surveyors in executing this goal must be admired. Their achievement is even more impressive when one considers the sixty-year time frame from the first expansion in 1791 to the last in 1851. No single individual could have been responsible for projecting and implementing all these expansions. As authors of the maps on which so many of the proposed expansions appear, the city surveyors and engineers deserve much of the credit for this remarkable accomplishment. In blending idealism and practicality, they introduced a range of thirteen ward sizes and shapes that helped foster an even greater degree of architectural variety and subtle hierarchies throughout the wider downtown district than Oglethorpe's own plan would have achieved if expanded at constant dimensions.

Growth Outside the Plan: The Four Edges of the Common

The population of Savannah grew steadily under Crown rule, but the Savannah Plan did not. Instead, it became more densely inhabited as house lots and trust lots in the plan were subdivided. Most of the city's population growth in the colonial era, however, occurred through private development of land outside of the original six wards, to the west and east beyond the limits of the Common, in what came to be referred to as Savannah's hamlets and suburbs. Growth also occurred to the north along the riverfront, in the wharf lots that were established descending from the bluff. Development along the edges of the Savannah Plan in the colonial era played an important role in the later development of the plan.

The West Common, as it is referred to in some eighteenth- and nineteenth-century documents, was bounded not by garden lots but by land allotted at the founding of the colony for use by the Yamacraw tribe (figure 33).[44] The town planning act of May 1760 refers to this land as "the Lots lately laid out between Musgrove's Creek and the said Town."[45] Official development of the Yamacraw land began with its cession to the Crown in the Treaty of Savannah of 1757, but sanctioned development began in 1760 after the settling of claims by Mary Musgrove, the daughter of a Muscogee Creek woman and a White trader from South Carolina who served the early Georgia colony as a translator for Oglethorpe.[46] An adjacent parcel of land south of the former Yamacraw land was deeded by Jacob Matthews, Musgrove's second husband, to William Ewen in 1741.[47] This property came to be known as Ewensburg. At least six lots of former Yamacraw land were deeded first to Joseph Gibbons and then, in 1761, to the minister of the Independent Presbyterian meetinghouse, John Joachim Zubly, after which this land was known in some documents as "St. Gall," after Zubly's birthplace in Switzerland. Another amendment made to the 1760 act in 1761 declared that land south of Ewensburg and north of the northern edge of the garden lots, "sixteen acres of land laid out for the use of the public, joining the common of the said town, and known by the name of the Spring, shall be held, deemed, and reputed, as public lots and lands, and reserved for the use of the public only."[48] Several maps from the Revolutionary War era indicate structures in this general vicinity.

The lots developed in the Yamacraw district to the west of the original wards provided much-needed real estate to accommodate the growing population, but they were not initially considered part of the town of Savannah. This changed in 1787, however, when the Georgia state legislature passed "An Act for Better Regulating the Town of Savannah, and the Hamlets Thereof," incorporating "the hamlets of Ewensburgh and Yamacraw" into the city and declaring them to "constitute the seventh, and be known by the name of Oglethorpe's ward."[49] Ironically named after the initial author of the Savannah Plan, Oglethorpe Ward was an anomalous, privately developed district outside of Oglethorpe's carefully structured public plan and bore no resemblance to it (figure 36). In the nineteenth century, the ward continued to grow, attracting immigrants and free African Americans. By the twentieth century, Oglethorpe Ward—known once again as Yamacraw—had become a notorious slum, the most densely populated neighborhood of the city. In 1938 it became the site of Savannah's first major slum-clearance; the old blocks of wooden worker housing (mostly in the form of Savannah cottages, as seen in figure 166) were replaced by housing blocks set in grassy open spaces, with most of the earlier streets removed. A similarly anomalous hamlet developed on the east side of the Common, adjacent to the northwest corner of the garden lot squares, the area originally developed as a ten-acre experimental garden known as the Trustees' Garden. By 1748 it was largely abandoned, and in 1755 it was deeded to Governor Reynolds as private property.[50] Like the westside hamlets, residential lots in the former Trustees' Garden area and the three former garden lots south of it were developed in the years following the Revolutionary War.[51]

During the first decade of the nineteenth century, some private development also occurred to the southwest of the original plan on the five-acre triangular garden lots. Initially these developments, like those in the Yamacraw district, disregarded the Savannah Plan formula. The first such development occurred in the triangular garden lot closest to the town, in the area where the Common shifted eastward along the south side of what is now Liberty Street (figure 35). Unlike the earlier private developments, this informal grid had its north–south streets aligned with Jefferson and Montgomery Streets within the city across the Common to the north (whereas its east–west streets would not align with the later expansions of the Savannah Plan). Subsequent development of garden lots followed suit, creating numerous misalignments of streets and building lots around the perimeter of the Common.

The narrow, irregular strip of land along the thirty-to-forty-foot-tall bluff above the Savannah River played a crucial role in the development of Savannah from the town's beginning, and yet the land has always remained distinctly outside of the Savannah Plan. Considered common land, it is referred to as being "in front of this town" in some colonial documents.[52] It was later referred to as "the Strand." The 1734 Gordon View depicts a fence running along the edge of the bluff, below which are "The Stairs going up" and "The Crane and Bell" (figure 9). Atop the bluff are "Mr. Oglethorpe's Tent" and a building to the east labeled "The Guard House and Battery of Cannon." By the 1740s, mention of a public wharf and warehouse appears in the colonial records, and by 1749 private individuals were making petitions to build wharves and storage buildings "under the bluff."[53] Under Crown rule, wharf lots began to be sold to private individuals. The de Brahm map of 1757 shows these lots inserted between "docks" that align with the north–south streets of the plan (figure 29). An open area labeled "The Bay" appears between the top of the bluff and the northern edge of the town.

The wharves were accessed by extending the north–south streets (as well as an alignment for the future Jefferson Street) from the plan to the river as public rights-of-way, as shown on the Shruder map of 1770 (figure 31). Later maps show the absence of public rights-of-way north of the 1791 expansion wards, which may indicate that the wharf lots extending across these areas had already been sold prior to the establishment of those wards. By 1813, rights-of-way had also been established in alignment with Lincoln and West Broad Streets, while the Jefferson Street alignment had been lost (figure 36). A final additional right-of-way, aligned with East Broad Street, was introduced shortly afterwards, as documented on the 1818 map (figure 37). Extending the plan to the water's edge, these eight rights-of-way defined the lengths of successive warehouse blocks and permitted a visual connection between the area inside the plan and the river.

The wharf lots and their warehouses became the economic engine of the city from the mid-eighteenth century into the twentieth century. After the Revolutionary War, these buildings grew taller, rising above the bluff. By the middle of the nineteenth century, a row of three-to-six-story brick-and-stone warehouse buildings formed an undulating architectural wall between the town and its port—interrupted only by the eight rights-of-way—by following the curvature of the river, whose fast current during outgoing tides prevented the extension of piers from the shore into the river (figure 41). Masonry retaining walls, mentioned as early as 1820, and cobblestone-paved ramps (first installed in 1843), built and paved with ship ballast dumped on the wharves, enabled vehicles to ascend and descend the bluff.[54] The retaining walls also defined stepped lanes running behind the warehouses (Factors Walk), allowing the buildings to be accessed on their south side directly at the second floor and via bridges to the third and fourth floors. River Street gradually took form at the river level, running between the warehouses and the riverfront and providing access to the first floor of the warehouses on their north side; it was initially paved with cobblestones—later replaced by

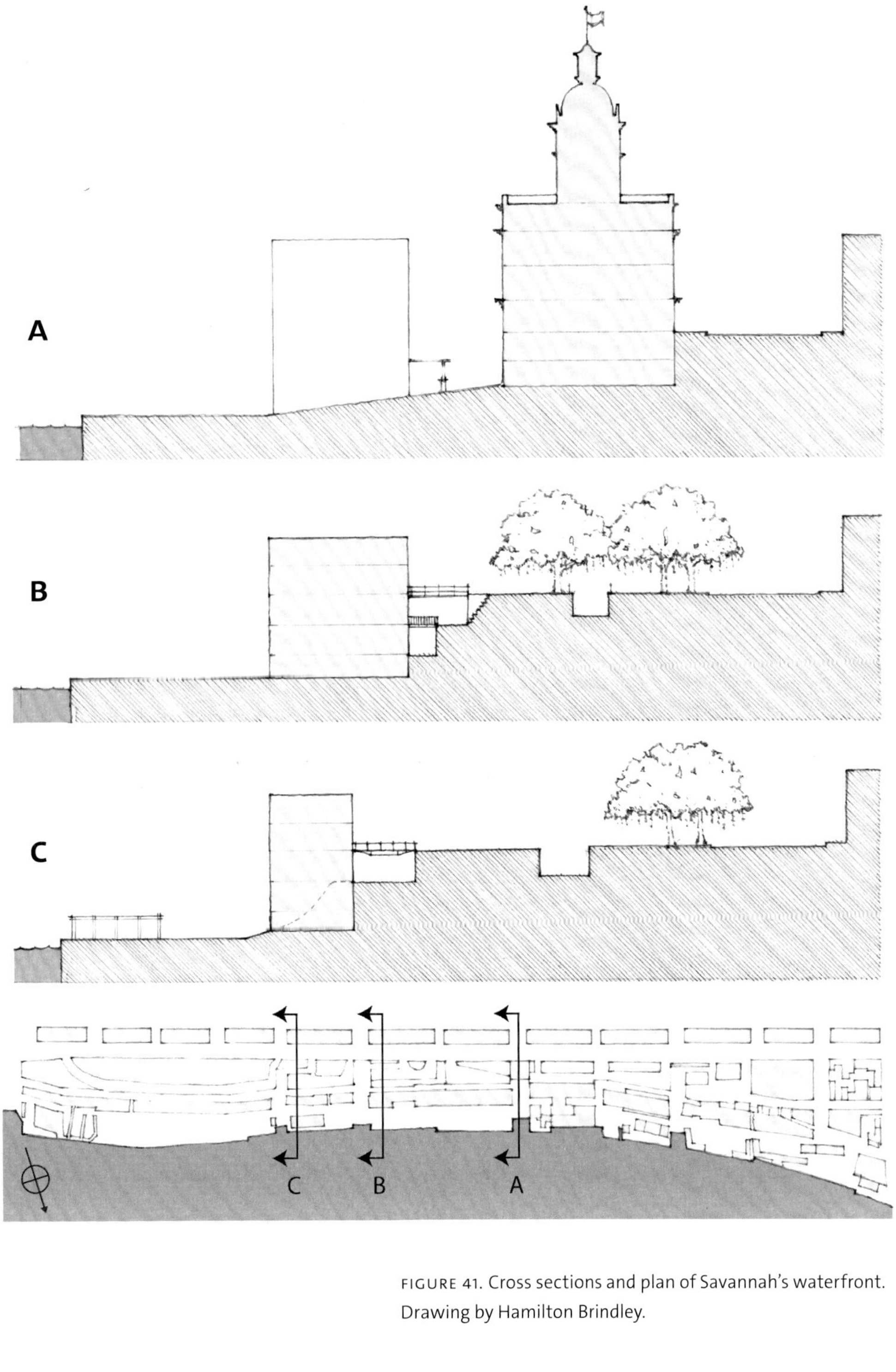

FIGURE 41. Cross sections and plan of Savannah's waterfront. Drawing by Hamilton Brindley.

granite Belgian blocks (typical in industrial areas)—and had two lines of railway tracks installed during the late nineteenth century.

Threatening, Disrupting, and Restoring the Savannah Plan

Following its completion in the mid-nineteenth century, the Savannah Plan faced immediate challenges posed by the city's growth and the introduction of new transportation and building technologies. In 1851, the same year the city established Forsyth Place, the Central of Georgia Railway began constructing its innovative thirty-three-acre multipurpose complex along the west side of West Broad Street, just outside the plan. Its introduction heralded a period of increased industrialization for the city in general and for the western suburbs in particular, helping steer to the south and east most of the suburban residential developments during the second half of the nineteenth century and throughout the twentieth century. The growth of the suburbs and the need to connect them with the downtown area presented the first real challenge to the integrity of the plan. First streetcars and then automobiles would directly impact fifteen of the twenty-four squares. Four of Savannah's squares would be lost, though two of those would later be restored.

In 1871, a streetcar company received permission to run tracks along Abercorn Street through the center of its squares. Although there was a significant public outcry at the violation of an 1806 state law explicitly prohibiting nonpedestrian traffic through the squares, the Georgia Supreme Court ruled in favor of the streetcar company—using as its justification earlier uses of squares, such as for markets and public mills, for which, the justices assumed, wheeled vehicles must have needed access to the squares. Significantly, they also concluded, wrongly, that the original function of the squares "was not as parks, or of pleasure grounds."[55] By the early twentieth century, streetcar tracks ran through twelve of Savannah's twenty-four squares and skirted three others (figure 42).

The forces of modernization and transportation redoubled their assault on the squares in the 1920s when proposals were made to direct automobile traffic through several squares and to use others as parking lots. In 1935, following a decade of heated debates—characterized as a battle of "progress versus beauty"—the city's three westernmost squares (Franklin, Liberty, and Elbert) were sacrificed to accommodate unimpeded traffic flow along U.S. 17 (figure 43).[56] The west side of downtown had long been associated with industry and with minority and lower-income residents. As Nathaniel Walker argues, the decision to run U.S. 17 on Montgomery Street was due to the street's role as a "racial border," dividing the predominantly Black area along West Broad Street from the predominantly White central area of downtown.[57] Running the highway on Montgomery removed most

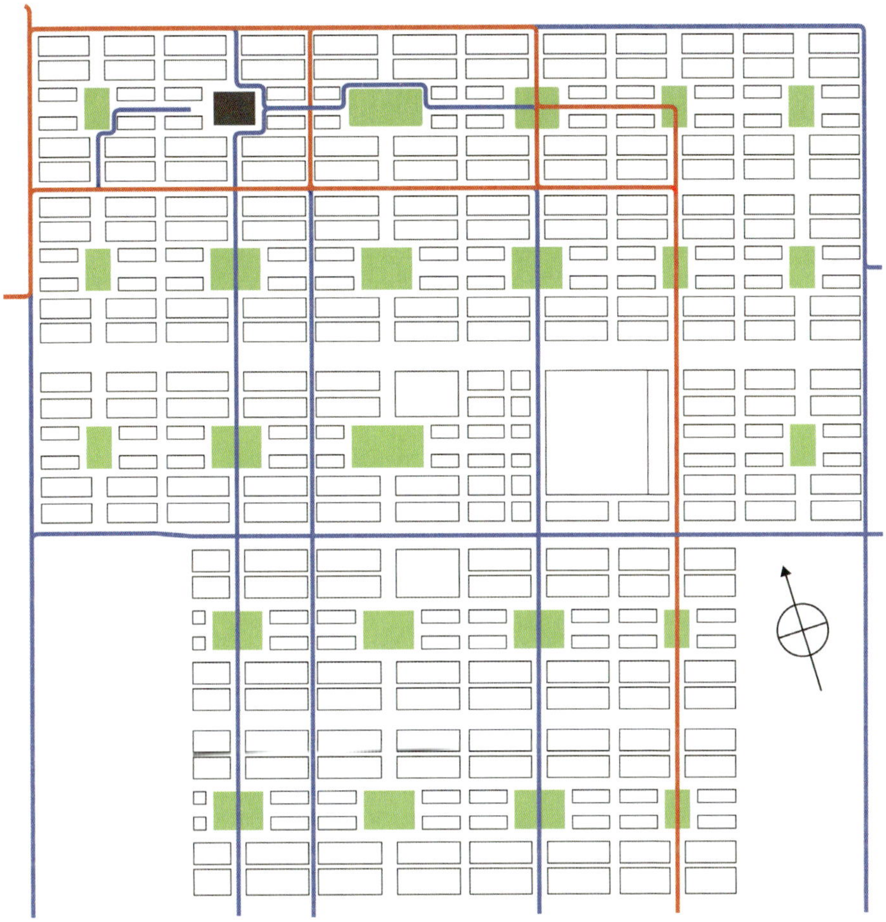

FIGURE 42. Streetcar lines through Savannah's squares. Beginning in 1872, streetcar lines in downtown Savannah expanded to pass through twelve squares and skirt three others, including the City Market building (shown in dark gray). All routes shown existed until at least 1914. By 1939, only the lines marked in red remained, and those were removed in 1946. Diagram by Robin B. Williams.

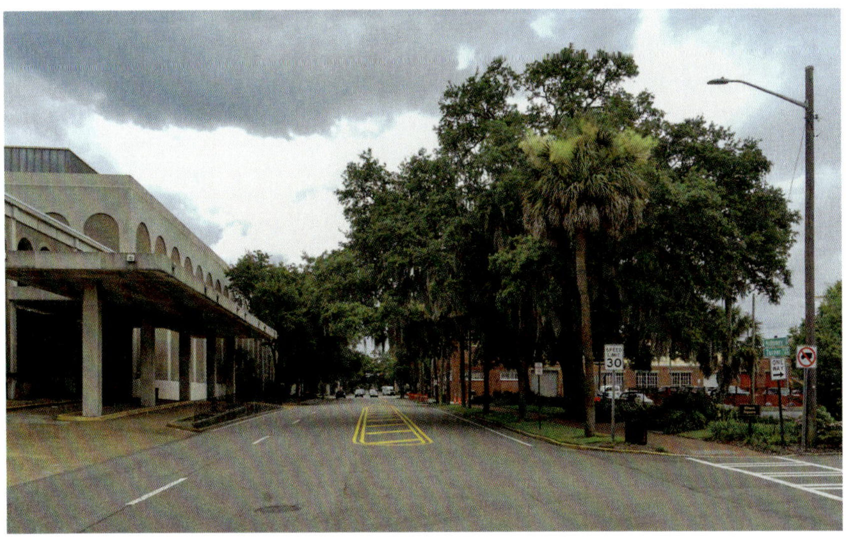

FIGURE 43. Montgomery Street looking southward across the remnant of Elbert Square (on the right). The entrance to the Savannah Civic Center appears on the left. Photo by Robin B. Williams, 2024.

of the street's three squares, which were principally used by Black residents. Proposals to run streets through other squares emerged again after World War II with the removal of streetcar tracks in 1946, but these never materialized.

AUTOMOBILITY AND SUBURBAN FLIGHT

The broader impact of automobiles on the Savannah Plan began in the 1920s with the implementation of one-way streets. Although the plan's wide streets allowed downtown Savannah to accommodate the demands for on-street parking and traffic circulation better than the typically narrower streets of other older cities, automobiles and the forces of suburbanization during the second half of the twentieth century posed the greatest threat to the integrity of the Savannah Plan.

The postwar explosion in private vehicle ownership led to a dramatic increase in facilities catering to automobiles—namely, dealerships, gas stations, repair garages, and, to accommodate the growing number of private vehicles entering downtown, parking lots and parking garages (figure 144). The demolition in 1950 of the Wetter House, one of the city's grandest historic mansions, for a used car parking lot, despite opposition from local preservationists, was a harbinger of the car's destructive influence. Ironically, the humble carriage house belonging to the Wetter House was spared to serve as the office of the used car lot; it is now incorporated as a picturesque roofless ruin behind the Savannah Cultural Arts Center. The Lincoln Parking Garage, erected in 1955, was part of the first wave of large-scale parking structures and surface parking lots in downtown Savannah. With an entrance appropriately oriented to the utilitarian Lincoln Street on its west side, the garage covers the western pair of trust lots in Warren Ward and the central civic trust street in between while turning its back on Warren Square. More consequential was the multilevel parking garage built over the entirety of nearby Ellis Square, the city having granted a private company a fifty-year lease for the site the year before. This garage replaced the 1872 City Market, the third market building on the square since the eighteenth century, after a contentious preservation battle the year before failed to save the venerable structure (figure 44).

The old City Market was a victim of larger postwar trends beyond the need for parking; the rise of suburban neighborhoods farther from downtown, the proliferation of refrigerators (which reduced the need for daily trips to the market), and the change in shopping habits resulting from reliance on cars all conspired against traditional farmers' markets. The loss of the City Market catalyzed the local preservation movement, spurring the creation of the Historic Savannah Foundation in 1955 to fight, successfully, the demolition of the Davenport House for yet another parking lot.

The late 1950s witnessed a diminished respect for the integrity of the Savannah Plan as automobile-oriented businesses began to have a greater presence in

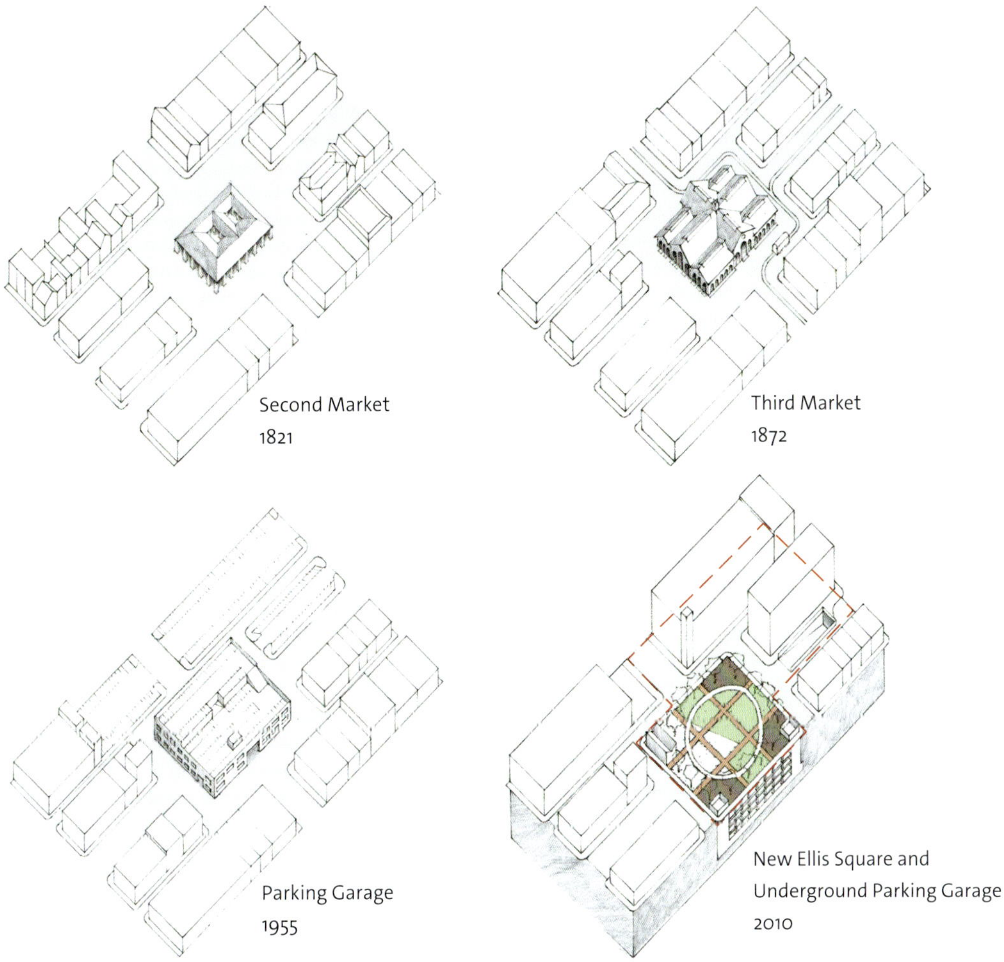

FIGURE 44. Ellis Square—four stages of evolution. Drawings by Hamilton Brindley.

the downtown landscape. In 1959 a suburban-style one-story strip mall complex covered the entirety of the northwest tything in Crawford Ward, with the stores facing the parking lot that fronted Oglethorpe Avenue and utilitarian Price Street. Disregarding the centripetal inward pull toward a square, the mall turned its back on the predominantly African American Crawford Square. Farther west on Oglethorpe Avenue, the Downtowner Motor Inn, erected in 1965 on the northern half of the northwest tything in Jackson Ward, acquired most of the southern half of the tything and its lane three years later, creating a consolidated site on which the motel erected a large addition and a sizable parking lot. The construction of an elevated and curving off-ramp at the eastern terminus of Interstate 16 in 1960–67 severely disrupted the vibrant African American commercial district by spanning West Broad Street (now Martin Luther King Jr. Boulevard) before sloping

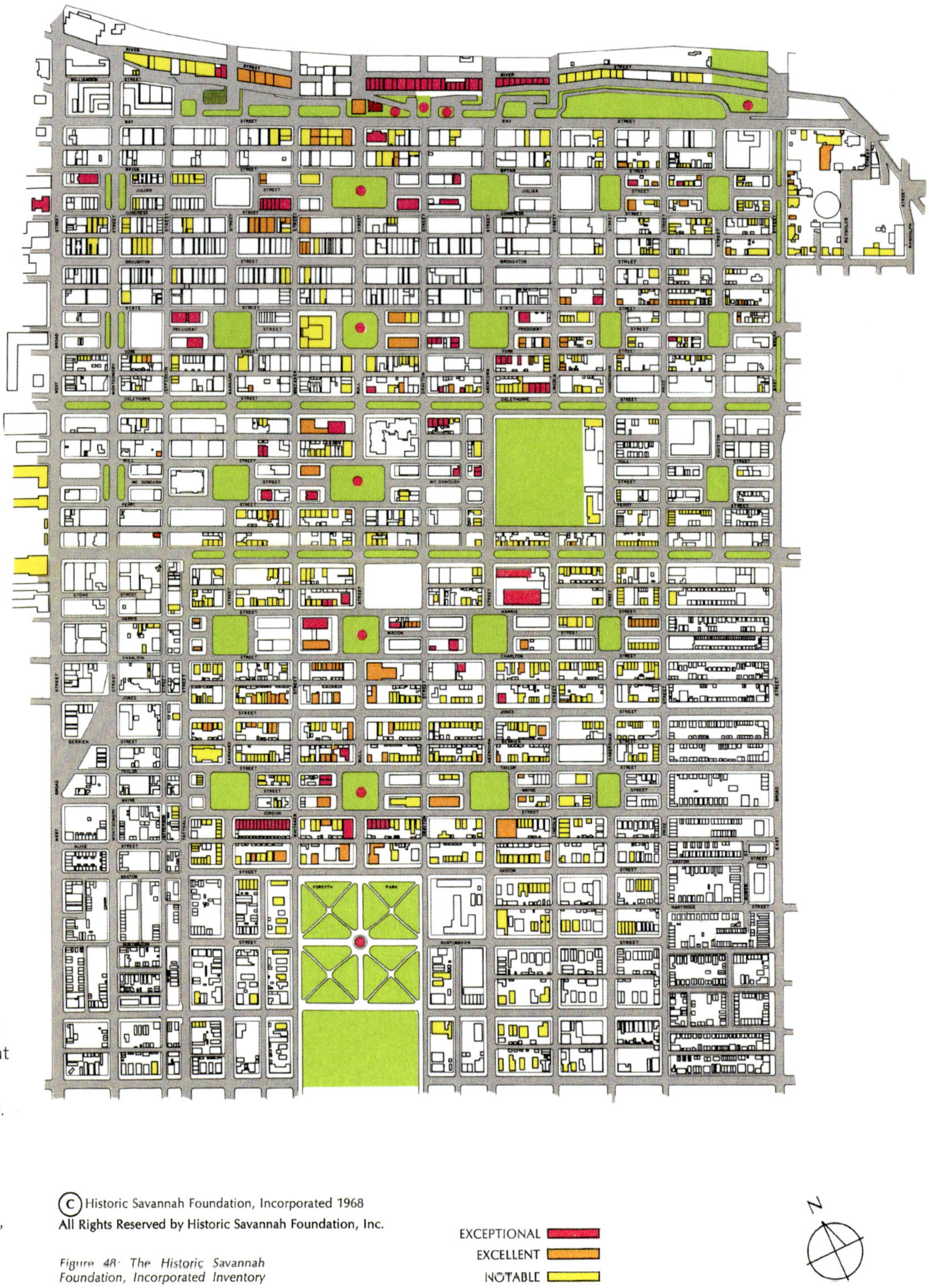

FIGURE 45. Historic Savannah Foundation inventory of significant buildings rated by perceived significance. Historic Savannah Foundation, *Historic Savannah* (Historic Savannah Foundation, 1968), between pp. 57 and 58.

downward to connect with Montgomery Street. Although the overpass did not directly impact the layout of the twenty-four-ward Savannah Plan, it transformed Montgomery Street into a one-way northbound regional traffic corridor and led to the building of two enormous urban renewal projects along its length within the plan, the Savannah Civic Center and the Chatham County Courthouse complex.

HISTORIC PRESERVATION AND URBAN RENEWAL

The growing influence of the historic preservation movement led in 1966 to federal passage of the National Historic Preservation Act, which among its functions recognized the historic significance of individual buildings and districts, encouraging their preservation and protection. Among its earliest accomplishments was the designation of Savannah's downtown as a National Historic Landmark District that same year. It remains among the largest NHLDs in the country. In 1968 the Historic Savannah Foundation, seeking to preserve and protect historic structures, published *Historic Savannah*, a survey and inventory of significant buildings and monuments in that district (figure 45). This work was impressive for its scope—though, as one might expect, it reflected a biased valuation of the downtown's architectural assets, privileging houses, churches, and select public buildings while largely ignoring commercial, industrial, and vernacular buildings, with the notable exception of the waterfront warehouses. The hierarchies of the Savannah Plan also shaped the survey's valuations, with most buildings on trust lots being recognized, while no building fronting a lane (such as any of the historic carriage houses) was identified. More significantly, few buildings from the predominantly African American areas flanking downtown received recognition, reinforcing the perception that these areas were eligible for redevelopment.

The 1960s also witnessed the expansion of large-scale government-sponsored projects aimed at revitalizing downtown areas under the banner of urban renewal. In Savannah, the west side of downtown was ripe for renewal. The conversion of Montgomery Street into U.S. 17 in 1935, severing its three squares, precipitated the replacement of the surrounding urban fabric of houses and stores with auto-related businesses, many of which required large parking lots. The closure of the large Central of Georgia Railway complex fronting West Broad Street in 1963 sapped the area's economic vitality. The arrival of the Interstate 16 off-ramp diminished the area's economic and social integrity. To help renew the west side of downtown, the city government created the Savannah Civic Center (1968–73), a 305,000-square-foot multievent complex comprising an arena, a large theatre, and a public ballroom (figures 46 and 47). Typical of urban renewal projects, it ignored the preexisting urban fabric, with the building covering the east half of Elbert Ward and its parking lot covering a tything, two trust lots, and streets in Jackson Ward. Designed as a single grouped mass, this enormous building stands

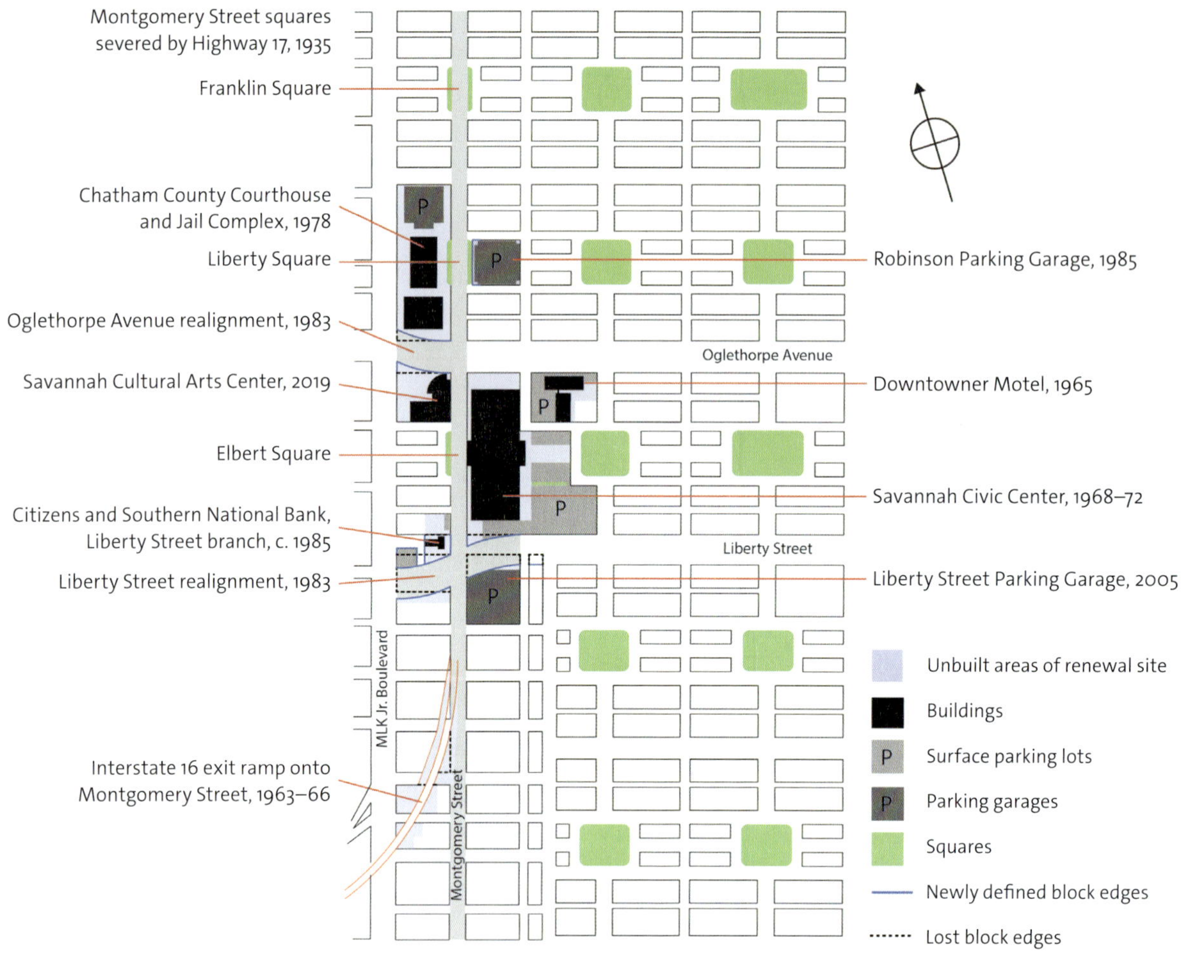

FIGURE 46. Urban renewal projects along Montgomery Street. Diagram by Robin B. Williams.

dramatically at odds with even the largest earlier buildings within the Savannah Plan and has effectively functioned like a wall, orphaning the blocks of the plan to its west from the rest of the downtown area.[58] Typical of its era, the building sits back from the street, leaving unused and unloved open space in front of its north, west, and south sides, further distancing it from its urban setting.

Farther north along the west side of Montgomery Street, and nearly as destructive as the Civic Center, is the Chatham County Courthouse complex (completed in 1978), which occupies the whole western half of Liberty Ward, consolidating its tythings, trust lots, streets, and lanes into a single large site (figure 46). Different from the Civic Center's single mass, the courthouse complex involves three buildings—a central courthouse flanked by a courthouse annex (replacing a county jail building that was demolished in 2018) and a parking garage—

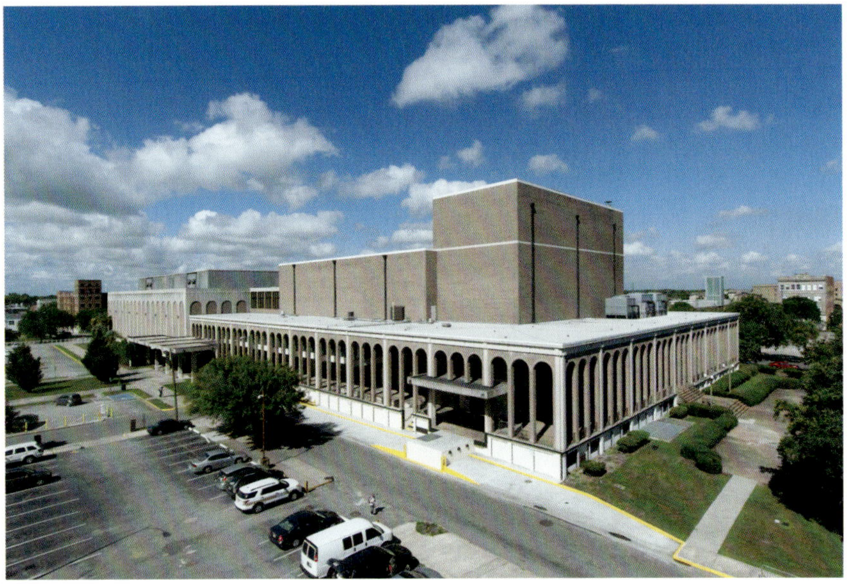

FIGURE 47. Savannah Civic Center, designed by Nowell & Ritzert, 1968–72. Photo by Robin B. Williams, 2014.

separated by pedestrian walkways, which diminish the wall-like effect but do not align with the existing streets of the Savannah Plan. Compounding the complex's destructive impact on the plan, in 1985 the city erected the Robert E. Robinson Parking Garage across Montgomery Street, atop the eastern trust lots and central trust street of Liberty Ward. Easing traffic flow around these large projects also motivated the curving realignments of Liberty Street and Oglethorpe Avenue between Montgomery Street and Martin Luther King Jr. Boulevard in the 1980s so that they directly connect with Louisville Road and West Oglethorpe Avenue, respectively, west of the plan.

RESTORING THE SAVANNAH PLAN

Growing appreciation for the city's architectural history and urban integrity encouraged the 1973 creation of the Historic District Board of Review (HDBR) to "provide for the protection of historic buildings, structures, appurtenances, and places that are of basic and vital importance."[59] Appointed by the mayor and aldermen, this volunteer board of citizens regulates new construction and the alteration or demolition of existing structures within the locally defined downtown historic district (which is larger than the National Historic Landmark District). The strict set of design guidelines, encoded in a "design manual," enforces compatibility with the city's design traditions that historically occurred organically.[60]

The tremendous success of the historic preservation movement in Savannah propelled the restoration of Franklin Square, the northernmost of the three

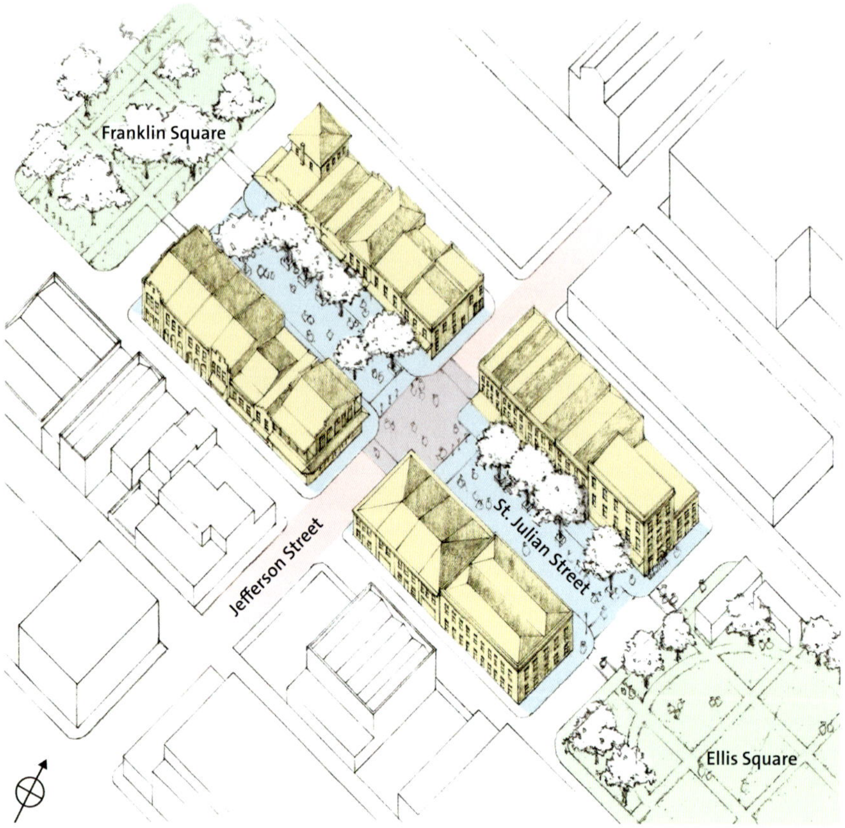

FIGURE 48. St. Julian Street pedestrian mall and City Market, designed by Gunn Meyerhoff and Shay, 1985. The intersection of St. Julian and Jefferson Streets constitutes a *woonerf*. Drawing by Hamilton Brindley.

Montgomery Street squares severed by U.S. 17 in 1935. First proposed in 1973 by the city council,[61] reinstatement of the square was completed in 1985. Remarkably, the long-standing tradition of the square serving as a gathering place for day laborers, curtailed for fifty years, resumed upon the square's restoration and continues to the present. This restoration corresponded with a concurrent project to convert the adjacent two blocks of St. Julian Street, the central seventy-five-foot-wide east–west civic trust street, into a car-free pedestrian mall dubbed "City Market," repurposing the name of the lost market building on Ellis Square at the east end of the mall (figure 48). Such conversions had begun nationally in 1959 with a pedestrian mall designed by Victor Gruen in Kalamazoo, Michigan, in an effort to revitalize a downtown main street by emulating the suburban shopping experience.[62] While many such pedestrian malls had a deleterious effect on the street they were attempting to reinvigorate, the City Market mall on St. Julian Street is a notably successful exception, benefiting from its generous width and location within the Savannah Plan. The mall's intersection with Jefferson Street, unmarked by traffic signage, merges pedestrian and automotive mobilities in a shared space, in the manner of a Dutch *woonerf,* a "living street" or "living yard."

The successful revitalization of downtown Savannah since the 1990s, supported in part by the City Market pedestrian mall, made inevitable the removal of the Ellis Square parking deck at the end of its fifty-year lease in 2004. Through a public-private partnership with the owners of the tything block and trust lot northeast of the square, the City of Savannah spearheaded the restoration of Ellis Square and the surrounding urban fabric, the adjacent lots having been parking lots for decades (figure 44). Underneath the square, the private lots, and the streets between them, the city created a massive underground parking garage, dexterously accessed from Whitaker Street through one of the buildings, but with one of its exits carved ungraciously out of St. Julian Street east of the square. The new multifunctional park, completed in 2010, differs conspicuously from Savannah's older squares by combining the conventional grid of pedestrian paths and live oak trees with playful, active-use design elements and practical features such as aboveground restrooms.[63]

Recent development trends have revealed increased public engagement in protecting and restoring the Savannah Plan. A federal government initiative to build an annex overlooking Telfair Square to complement the U.S. courthouse on the western trust lots overlooking Wright Square resulted in an initial proposal in 2017 that once again spanned two trust lots and the central trust street. The broad, squat, and modestly designed proposal met with spirited local opposition to the destruction of yet another part of the plan, the section of President Street where the only entrance to the proposed annex was located, and to its unsympathetic design. Through multiple meetings with a local committee,[64] the General Services Administration dramatically revised the annex design, resulting in a smaller building whose massing, orientation, and height more sympathetically conform to architectural patterns shaped by the Savannah Plan. Most importantly, the revised project preserved the street grid by retaining President Street as a visually open corridor.

The growing momentum to restore the Savannah Plan wherever possible has fueled the campaign to demolish the Savannah Civic Center and restore Elbert Square, as well as the tythings, trust lots, and streets that were obliterated by the Civic Center project.[65] The completion of a new multipurpose event venue (Enmarket Arena) west of downtown in 2022 has rendered the arena portion of the Civic Center redundant; removal of the arena, along with the parking lots, has been approved by the Savannah City Council. The potential removal of the Johnny Mercer Theatre portion of the center has been more controversial, pitting advocates of the full restoration of the Savannah Plan against those wishing to save and transform the theatre, whose 2,600-seat size is unlikely to be replaced. In

June 2024, the Savannah City Council voted to demolish the arena and renovate the theatre and ballrooms.[66]

The Savannah Plan is enjoying a renaissance at the present time. The squares are more neatly manicured than ever before. The local and regional economy is booming. Tourism has exploded, precipitating a proliferation of new hotels, restaurants, and shopping and entertainment venues. Meanwhile, preservationists and city officials are pursuing policies to protect and restore elements of the plan as never before. Vacant and derelict properties are being filled or revitalized. New construction projects abound. Lost tything blocks, trust lots, and streets are being reconstructed. The Savannah Plan has never been static. It is now entering a new phase in its development, one that will require commitment and skill comparable to that of the Trustees, surveyors, city officials, and citizens of the past three hundred years.

SECTION ONE CONCLUSION

COLLABORATIVE ELASTIC URBAN DESIGN

The First Honours of the ancient World were paid to the Founders of Citys.
—JAMES OGLETHORPE, 1731

This relationship between a collective artifact, which is necessarily an urban artifact, and the individual who proposes and single-handedly realizes it can only be understood through a study of the technics by which the artifact is manifested.
—ALDO ROSSI, 1966

The Savannah Plan has no real origin date. It has no single author. What it has is an illustrious story and a recognizable identity. Its story can be told by recounting the formation of the Georgia Trustees in the 1730s, but other groups and individuals preceded them in their desire to found an egalitarian, agrarian utopia; and so the story must begin earlier, perhaps with the enlightened political ideals of John Locke or James Harrington, or with the inventors of the ideal urban plans of the Renaissance. The Trustees themselves drew connections between their project and the practices and ideals of the ancient Romans. Some of their cheerleaders found their progenitors in the ancient Greek philosophers, others in the Hebrew prophets. The ideological pedigree of the Savannah Plan is deeply rooted in the history of city making. The plan's distinctive form bears the imprint of this rich heritage.

The Savannah Plan was "marked out" on Yamacraw Bluff by James Oglethorpe on February 12, 1733, but its story soon changed. Although the Trustees' social, economic, and political plan failed within two decades, Savannah grew nevertheless. As its circumstances changed, the urban plan steadfastly remained. In 1791, thirty-one years after the Trustees ceded control of the colony, it began to be reimagined and expanded. For the next sixty years, into the 1850s, it was continually amended and reconfigured to become an amplified version of itself. Damaged and threatened with utter destruction in the automobile age, it withstood repeated assaults in the twentieth century. Recent regeneration efforts, modifications, and refinements suggest that the Savannah Plan will continue to evolve throughout the twenty-first century.

The story of the Savannah Plan is a story of continuity and change. Not only has its identity persisted over nearly three centuries of change, but it also has been enriched and refined by those changes. A long-lasting collaborative process has strengthened the plan, but its ability to endure the rigors of this process is found in its inherent flexibility, its ability to be shaped, replicated, reconfigured, and reconstituted without losing its essential identity. We examine this elastic quality of the Savannah Plan further in the following section.

SECTION TWO

PARADOXICAL PATTERNS

ANALYZING THE SAVANNAH PLAN

Of all the cities in America, none impresses itself more vividly upon the imagination and the memory than this little green bowery city of the South. It stands upon a terrace about forty feet higher than the river, and presents the appearance of an agglomeration of rural hamlets and small towns. . . . Twenty-four open spaces, as large as, or larger than, Bedford Square, with a pump in the middle, a church or a bank at one side, and neat wooden and stone houses around, the open spaces being laid out into walks and drives, and thickly planted with trees, among which the flowering China-tree or pride of India, the oleanthus, and the evergreen oak, are the most prominent—such are the component parts and general aspect of Savannah.
—CHARLES MACKAY, 1859

What beguiled the Scottish poet Charles Mackay about Savannah was its paradoxical nature. He saw a city that appeared to be one thing and yet was actually another, a city that was simultaneously one and many, a city of unity and diversity, of uniformity and variety. Indeed, paradox abounds in the Savannah Plan, a plan that both attracts and bewilders because it is simultaneously simple and complex. The component parts that constitute the city's urban form and the tacit rules that govern their arrangement are simple to describe, but the effects produced by their implementation are complex. Like many cities in the world, Savannah was laid out as an orthogonal grid of streets, squares, and blocks. Unlike the uniform grid plans of so many American towns, however, the Savannah Plan is a complex network of modular cells composed of building lots knitted together by a rhythmic pattern of streets and squares of varying sizes, more like a tartan than a gridiron. Its parts are familiar, while their arrangement is uncommon (figure 49). In the next two chapters, we embark on a sustained analysis of the plan. We begin by examining its basic parts and then explore how they work together to form a complete urban fabric.

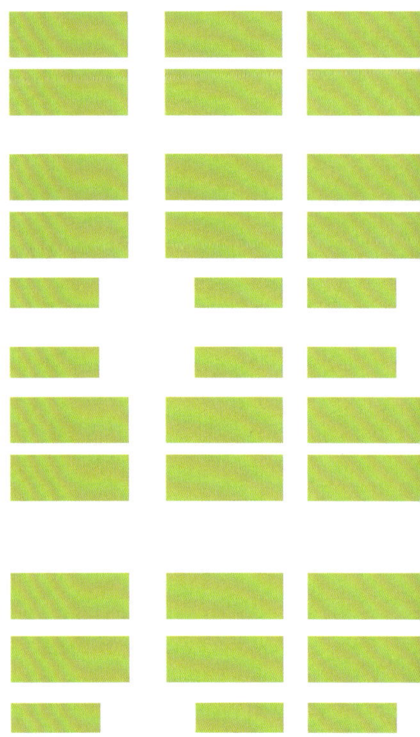

Among the plan's most noteworthy attributes is the relative smallness of its blocks, a quality that seems even more noteworthy when seen in contrast to the relative spatial generosity of the city's streets and squares. While a typical Savannah

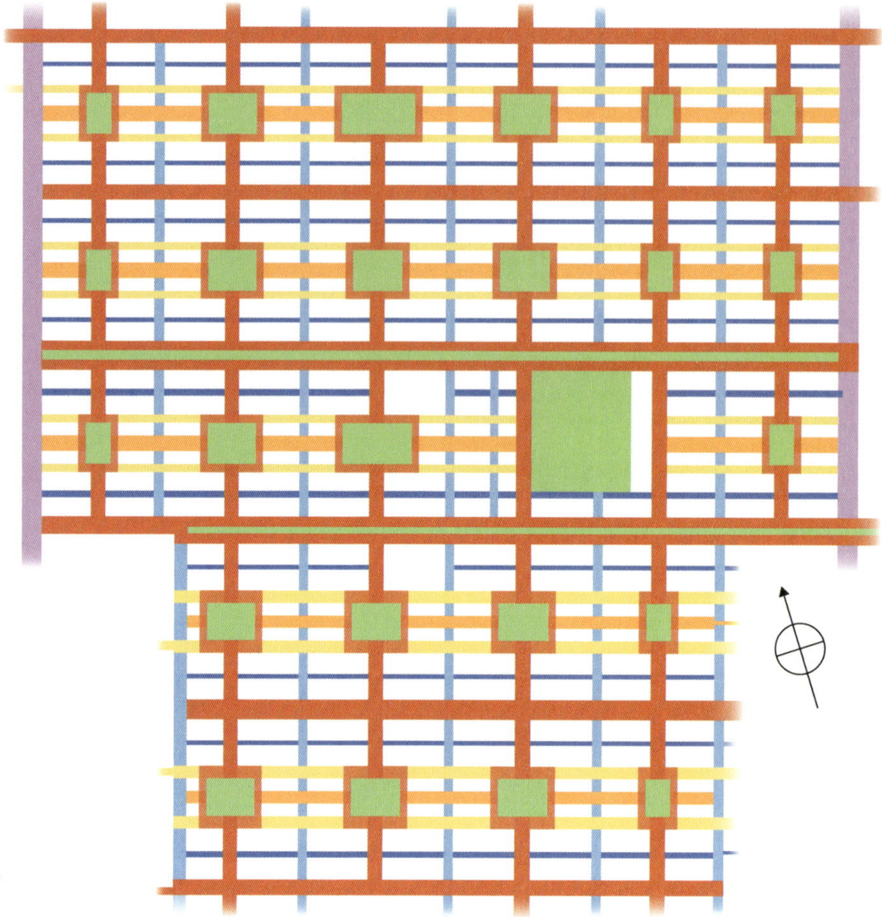

FIGURE 49. Tartan plan of Savannah. Diagram by Robin B. Williams.

block is 300 by 90 feet, some blocks are as small as 60 by 60 feet. By comparison, the blocks within the New York City Commissioners' Plan of 1811 range from 620 by 200 feet to 920 by 200 feet. If we interpret the streets and squares as representing the public realm and the building lots the private, then Savannah can be understood as having an extraordinarily generous amount of public space (almost 60 percent) with a high degree of "connectivity." Streets comprise about 45 percent of each ward; squares account for an additional 7 percent. If we also count the trust lots as public, only 40 percent of each ward would qualify as net developable acreage in today's terms.[1] Public space and connectivity are brought into high relief by Allan Jacobs's figure-ground maps depicting one square mile of a variety of cities at the same scale (figure 50). By representing building lots as solid figures and streets and squares as white ground, we can also compare the "textures" of

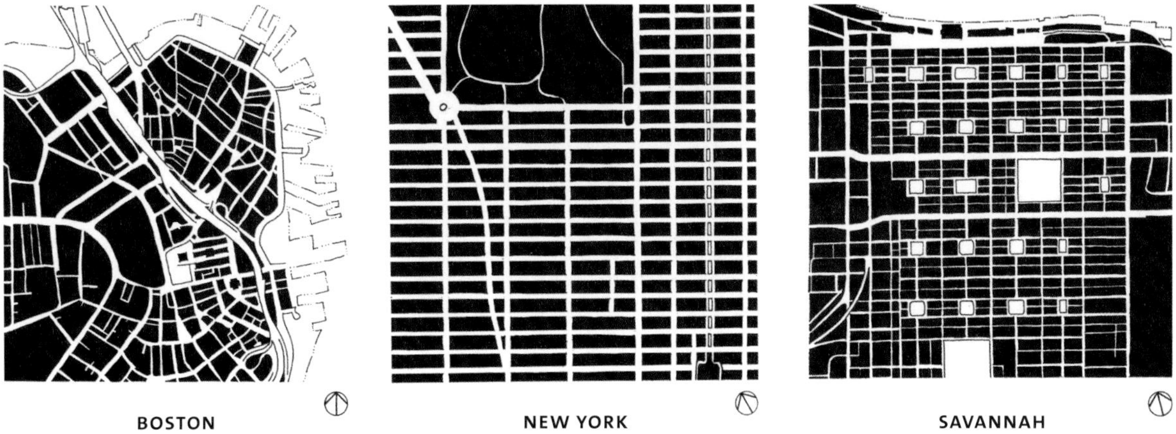

BOSTON (1980) · **NEW YORK** (Midtown Manhattan) · **SAVANNAH**

FIGURE 50. Comparative figure-ground city plans of Boston, New York, and Savannah showing one square mile of each. Adapted from Allan B. Jacobs, *Great Streets*, pp. 216, 232, 244. © 1993 Massachusetts Institute of Technology, by permission of the MIT Press.

various city plans. We quickly see in such a comparison that although Savannah's plan is, like many planned towns, orderly and predictable, it is also "fine-grained" and nuanced, like many "unplanned" preindustrial cities. The longer we peruse its urban fabric, the more we notice unpredictable interruptions or variations in its pattern.

The fine-grained patterns that form the Savannah Plan may be further understood by exploring the paradoxical patterns they produce. We notice, for example, that although the plan is dogmatically egalitarian, it allows for and even promotes significant hierarchies. Alluding perhaps to Plato's principle of geometric equality, the Salzburger minister Johann Martin Boltzius noted in 1734 that "all Houses and Gardens are laid out in a *Mathematical Equality*; which will make a fine shew, when they come to Perfection."[2] The Oglethorpe grid was implacably neutral: wards, trust lots, tythings, garden lots, and farm lots were laid out with a rigorous uniformity on a geography that seems to have been imagined as an abstract *tabula rasa*, and yet from this blind egalitarianism, hierarchies emerge. Certain wards, streets, squares, and lots have a status greater than others. These hierarchies are exploited and reinforced in the architecture that grows from the plan.

CHAPTER THREE

THE PARTS OF THE PLAN

The town is laid out for two hundred and forty freeholds; the quantity of lands necessary for that number is twenty-four square miles; every forty houses in town make a ward, to which four square miles in the country belong; each ward has a constable, and under him four tything men.
—FRANCIS MOORE, 1735

Just as the walls, the columns, etc., are the elements which compose buildings, so buildings are the elements which compose cities.
—JEAN-NICOLAS-LOUIS DURAND, 1802–1805

Wards

Many cities in the Anglo-American world employ the medieval term "ward" (literally, a "watch") to represent a neighborhood or district. The City of London was divided into twenty-four wards beginning in the eleventh century. In the Savannah Plan, the ward is a standardized neighborhood unit containing the formal, spatial, and political DNA of the city (figure 51). Formally, a ward is square in shape, symmetrically bisected in two directions by streets and divided into rectangular lots grouped on twelve blocks arranged around a central square. The crossing of major axes at a central square recalls a Roman castrum plan.[1] In this way, each Savannah ward is organized like an autonomous encampment, as opposed to the practice with other colonial towns, such as Philadelphia, that were formed as one large castrum. Like the plan as a whole, each ward involves a rhythmic pattern of repeated elements, both physical and abstract, public and private, active and passive, architectural and organic. The original six wards each comprised four tythings, with each tything containing ten house lots arranged in two rows of five, four trust lots for public buildings, a public square, six internal streets, and four bounding perimeter streets. Each ward offered a restricted mix of building types and uses.

Each of the original Savannah wards measures 675 feet on each side, forming an area of 10.5 acres. (If the wards are measured to the centerline of their outermost streets, the dimensions become 750 feet wide by 720 feet north to south—or about 12.5 acres.) Later wards vary in their dimensions, the largest growing to 765 feet north to south (or 840 feet to the street centerlines), with varied increases in street widths and tything block depths. The outer wards are compressed in their east–west dimension, the smallest being 555 feet wide.

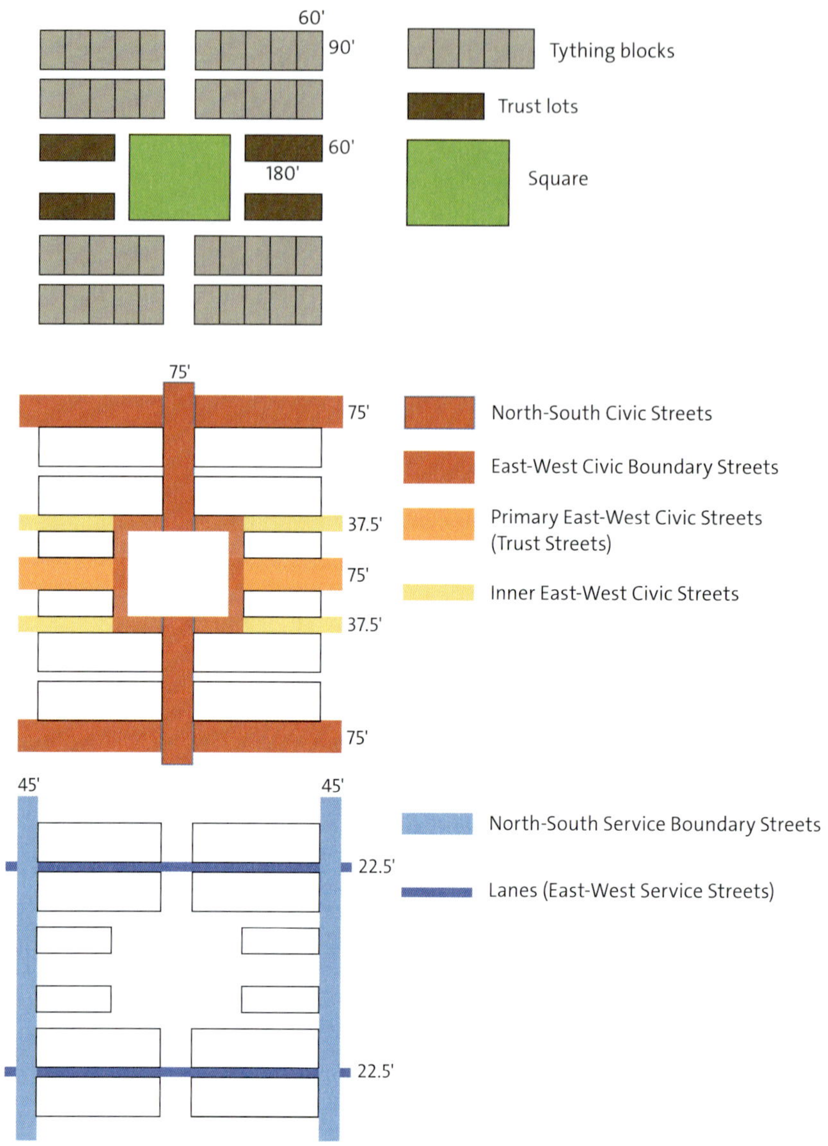

FIGURE 51. Components of a ward. Diagram by Robin B. Williams.

Politically, wards represent equal constituencies. They were conceived initially as military units; each ward had a captain or constable who would police and govern the affairs of his ward and muster its able-bodied male residents in the square when required. With the establishment of the city council in 1789, each ward had both a constable and an alderman to represent its residents on the council.[2] Savannah's wards are too small, however, to function as autonomous neighborhoods. Residents of each ward must rely on services offered in other wards to meet all urban needs.[3] Although the wards all have the same configuration and are roughly the same size, each one has a distinctive identity. The individualized character of each ward is the product of many things, including its location within the plan, its size, its landscape design, and the surrounding architecture. Some wards are centrally located; others are peripheral. Though nonhierarchical and noncentralized in its conception, the Savannah Plan contains several important hierarchical relationships. The wards bisected by the centralizing axis of Bull Street, for example, have the highest number of monumental buildings.

Important institutions and predominating uses further contribute to the individual character of each ward. Derby Ward (containing Johnson Square), with its several banks, is the city's financial district. In Decker Ward, Ellis Square operated as the city's principal market from at least 1757 until the destruction of the market building in 1954. Percival Ward, with its county and federal courthouses flanking Wright Square, has been a governmental center since the time of Oglethorpe. Some of the outer wards are more residential in character. The variety of uses characterizing the different wards has also given rise to significant differences in building heights, materials, architectural styles, and ornamentation.

The identity of each ward was assured by giving it a name (figure 52). The first four wards honored Trustees and philanthropists of the colony: Decker Ward was

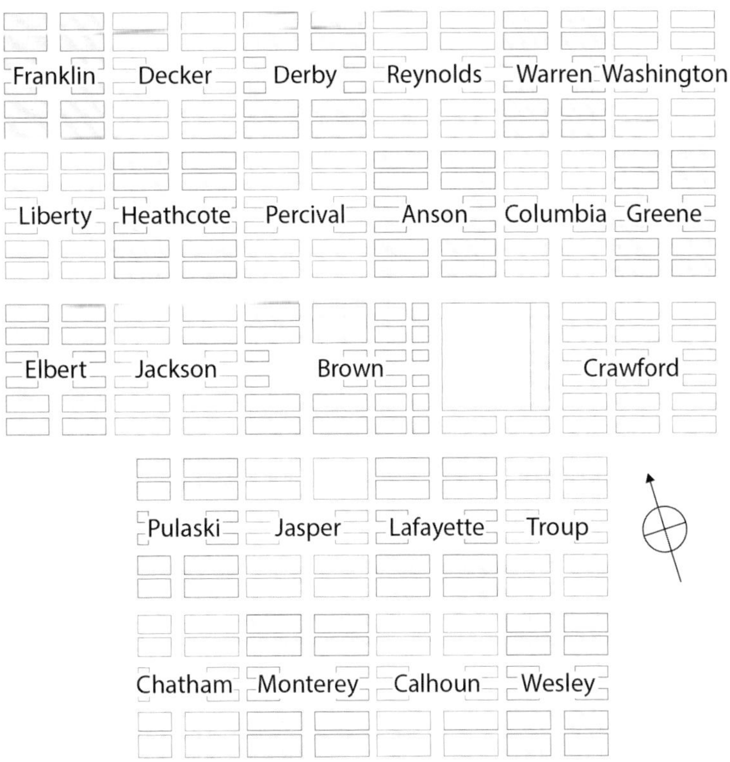

FIGURE 52. The twenty-four wards within the Savannah Plan. Diagram by Robin B. Williams.

named for Matthew Decker, first Baronet of Richmond Green in Surrey; Derby Ward honored James Stanley, tenth Earl of Derby; Percival Ward was named for John, Lord Viscount Perceval, first Earl of Egmont, who was the first president of the Trustees; and Heathcote Ward honored George Heathcote, an alderman in London and an active and influential Trustee.[4] Later wards commemorated national heroes or political leaders—Brown, Calhoun, Chatham, Crawford, Franklin, Greene, Jackson, Lafayette, Warren, and Washington; local heroes, governors, and political leaders—Anson, Elbert, Jasper, Pulaski, Reynolds, Troup, and Wesley; or, in the case of Monterey, a battle recently won (the battle took place in 1846; the ward was named in 1847). Two wards honored more generic patriotic identities—Columbia and Liberty. Representational identities were further entangled by naming squares, streets, and (in the first four wards) tythings after other illustrious figures or battles and then placing commemorative monuments to still other individuals or groups, transforming the tartan-like plan into an even more complicated civic memory map. For example, the Nathanael Greene Monument stands in Johnson Square in Derby Ward, which has tythings named Wilmington, Jekyll, Frederick, and Tyrconnel, while streets named Bull, Congress, St. Julian, and Bryan cross through the ward.

Each ward has what we might call its *genius loci*, or "spirit of the place." With the expansion of the plan to twenty-four wards, the relative size and location of the wards, the prevalence of certain institutions and uses, and the names of the wards confer a special identity on each ward and thus counterbalance potentially monotonous uniformity within the plan. Other factors that contribute to a ward's sense of place include landscape elements and the scale, size, style, materials, and purpose of surrounding buildings, as well as the historical time period of the ward's development. Who lived in each ward at any given time adds social, economic, and ethnic variables that are often explained by historical markers.

Squares

Many cities are renowned for their public parks, but no city has as many formal squares in such close proximity to each other as Savannah (figure 53). In the earliest maps of Savannah, no distinction exists between squares and streets; they appear as residual negative space between the building lots. The square in the colonial era was an implied, rectangular space bounded by the "inner" edges of the tything and trust lots, comprising approximately two acres of open space. The squares became enclosed entities within the circuit of sandy streets in 1810, when they were planted with trees and edged by a chain supported on short posts.[5] The Stouf map of 1818 depicts each square with a simple oval outline, while the McKinnon map of 1820 replicates the oval form, though it is now defined by a perimeter of trees (figures

FIGURE 53. (*Facing page*) Savannah's squares, showing eight different sizes. Diagram by Robin B. Williams.

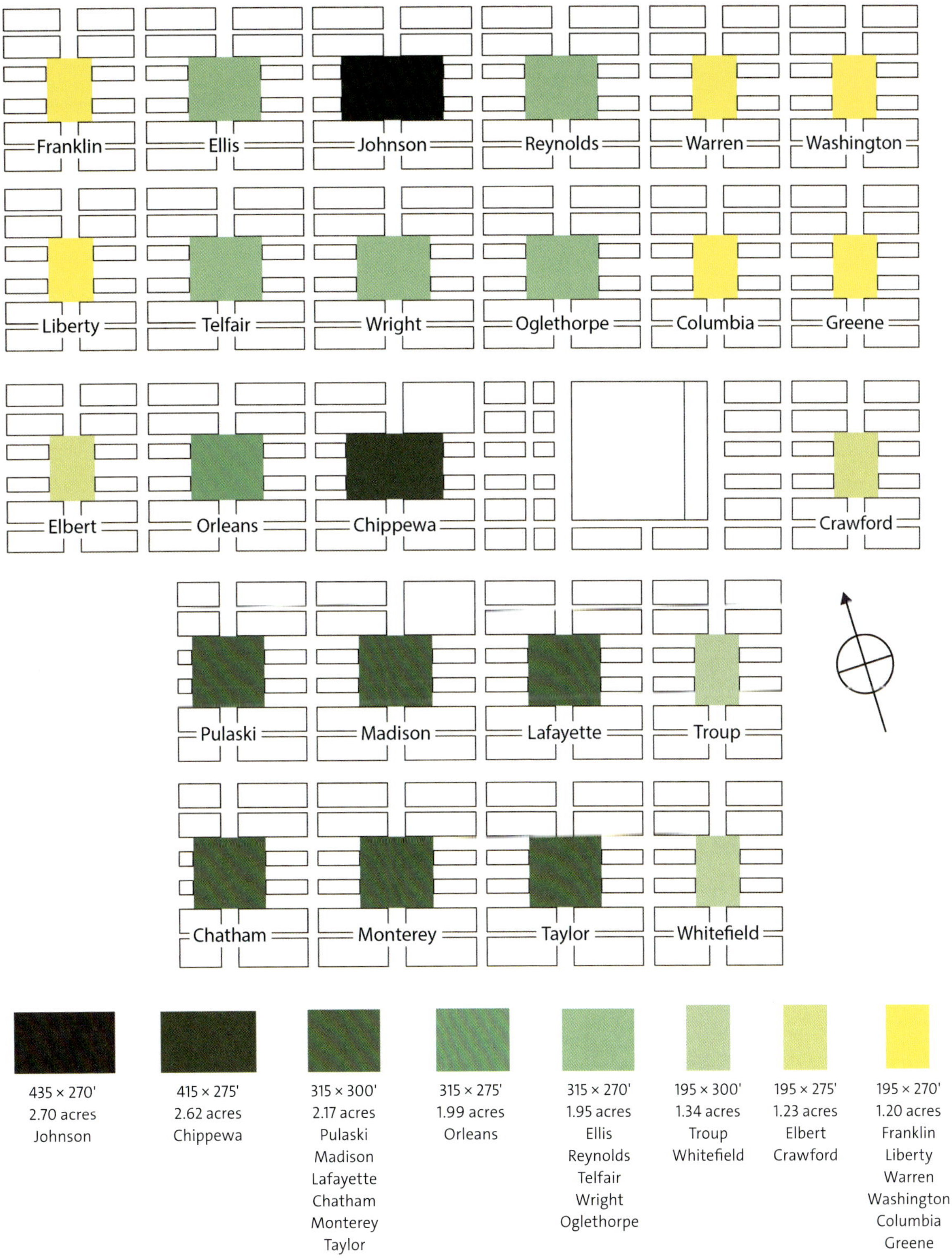
Franklin
Ellis
Johnson
Reynolds
Warren
Washington
Liberty
Telfair
Wright
Oglethorpe
Columbia
Greene
Elbert
Orleans
Chippewa
Crawford
Pulaski
Madison
Lafayette
Troup
Chatham
Monterey
Taylor
Whitefield
435 × 270'
2.70 acres
Johnson
415 × 275'
2.62 acres
Chippewa
315 × 300'
2.17 acres
Pulaski
Madison
Lafayette
Chatham
Monterey
Taylor
315 × 275'
1.99 acres
Orleans
315 × 270'
1.95 acres
Ellis
Reynolds
Telfair
Wright
Oglethorpe
195 × 300'
1.34 acres
Troup
Whitefield
195 × 275'
1.23 acres
Elbert
Crawford
195 × 270'
1.20 acres
Franklin
Liberty
Warren
Washington
Columbia
Greene

37 and 38). With the establishment of streets running around their perimeter and the planting of grass, trees, and shrubs inside, the squares became island parks averaging about one acre each. By the end of the nineteenth century the squares had evolved into their recognizable rectangular shape. Still, these islands retain a clear connection to the spatial envelope defined by the surrounding buildings that constitute the square as a whole.

Like the wards, Savannah's squares were named after prominent individuals and battles. The first to be named was Johnson Square, honoring South Carolina Governor Robert Johnson, who assisted Oglethorpe and the first settlers.[6] Each of the other five colonial squares was referred to by the same name as its ward until around 1762. Percival Square, or "the square in Percival Ward," came to be called Wright Square, after Georgia's third royal governor, James Wright, whose intermittent term was between 1760 and 1782.[7] The same 1762 document that first named Wright Square identified the square in Decker Ward as Ellis Square, after Wright's predecessor, Henry Ellis, whose term was from 1757 to 1760. Reynolds Square was named around this time as well—after the colony's first royal governor, John Reynolds (1754–57)—as were Oglethorpe and St. James Squares. Modern sources attribute the namesake of the latter to either St. James's Square or the nearby St. James's Park in London's West End. Three of the most prominent of the Georgia Trustees lived "within a stone's throw of St. James's Square."[8] Based on this reference, it seems reasonable to deduce that St. James Square and perhaps all of Savannah's squares were already thought of as landscaped parks, in the manner of London's St. James's Park, which was relandscaped by the innovative garden designer William Kent in 1733.[9] Savannah's St. James Square was renamed Telfair Square in 1883 to honor a venerable Savannah family. Only one other square has changed its name since then. Following acrimonious debates, the city council removed the name of Calhoun Square in 2022 and renamed it Susie King Taylor Square in 2023, in part to dissociate the neighborhood from the memory of slavery-supporting South Carolina Senator John C. Calhoun but also to honor Taylor, who was born into slavery near Savannah and served as a nurse in the Union army.

Savannah's squares derive from a long history of square building in the Western world, sharing qualities with various aspects of different sources but clearly not deriving from or corresponding to any single source or tradition. Geometrically conceived like Renaissance squares, neighborhood-focused like medieval squares, verdant and residential like London's squares, axial and monumentalized like Baroque squares, Savannah's squares are a unique amalgam of traditions and features. The inclusion of multiple squares in close proximity in Savannah may have been inspired by the multiplicity of squares that had emerged in London's West End through individual developments (figure 54). In contrast to most historic

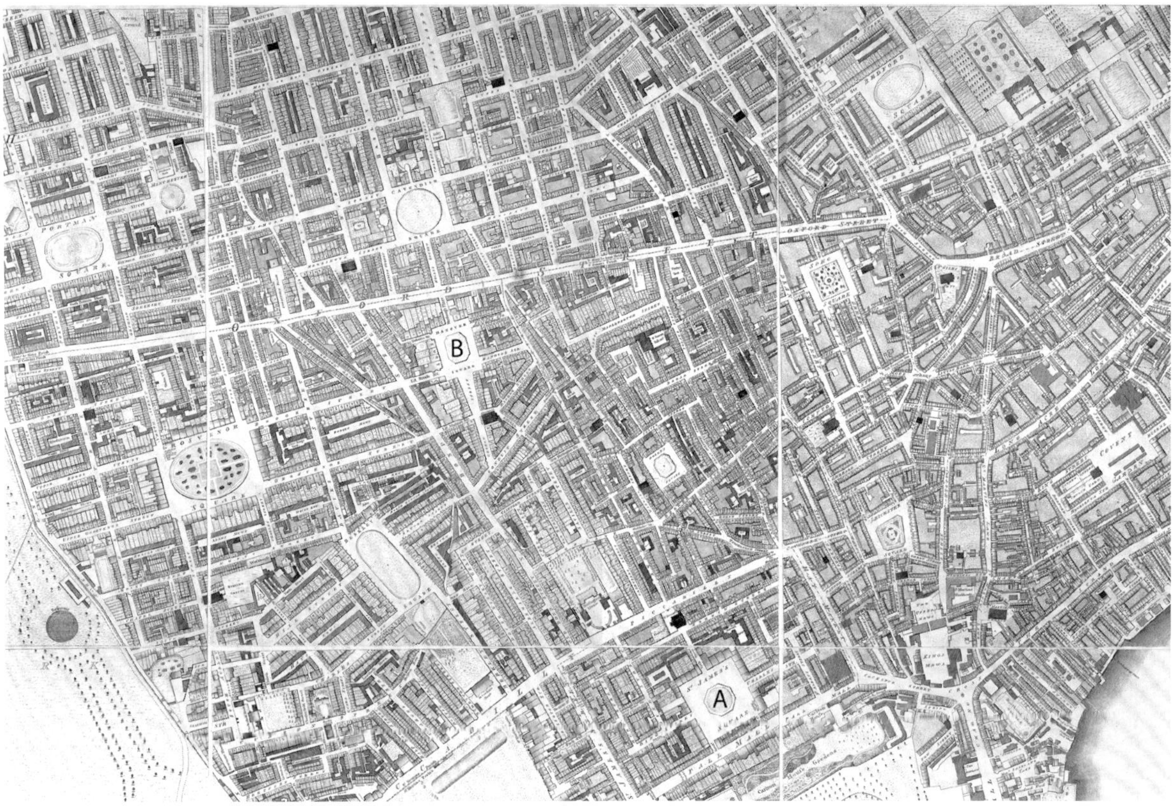

precedents, however, Savannah's squares are perceptually ambiguous, caught between figure and ground. Multiple openings, relatively wide streets, and proximity to nearby squares prevent them from being perceived as discrete urban rooms, as the squares of Rome, Paris, and London often are. Uniform, multistoried rowhouses were typical from the start in the development of London's squares. St. James's Square (labeled A on the Horwood map in figure 54), for example, is a decidedly contained space, with nearly 90 percent of its perimeter bounded by continuous facades (figure 55). Hanover Square (labeled B on the Horwood map) is closer to Savannah's squares in its size and permeability, with streets passing through its corners, but its continuous facades form an outdoor room that is more than 70 percent enclosed (figure 56). By contrast, only about 33 percent of Savannah's squares were bounded by building facades in the Trustee era, surrounded as they were by small wooden cottages. Even today, in a square such as Reynolds Square with fully built frontages, only about 62 percent of the perimeter is enclosed by building facades. Not only are Savannah's squares generally more porous

FIGURE 54. Map of London's West End showing the proximity of its residential squares. Detail from an engraved map by Richard Horwood, *Plan of the Cities of London and Westminster: The Borough of Southwark, and Parts Adjoining, Shewing Every House* (London, 1792–99), plates A2, A3, B2, B3, C2, C3. Carl H. Pforzheimer Collection of Shelley and His Circle, New York Public Library.

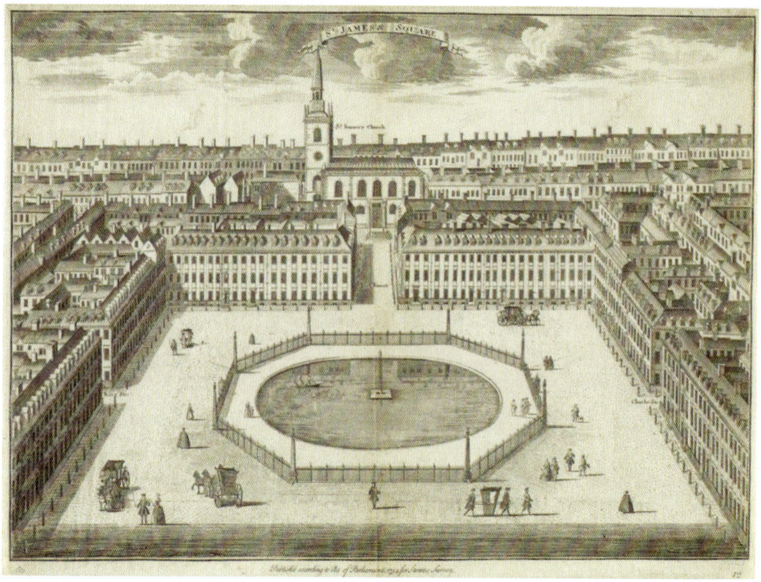

FIGURE 55. *Bird's-Eye View of St. James's Square*; engraved print by Sutton Nicholls, "published according to act of Parliament, 1754, for *Stowes Survey*." 13⅝" × 18½". Courtesy of the Lewis Walpole Library, Yale University.

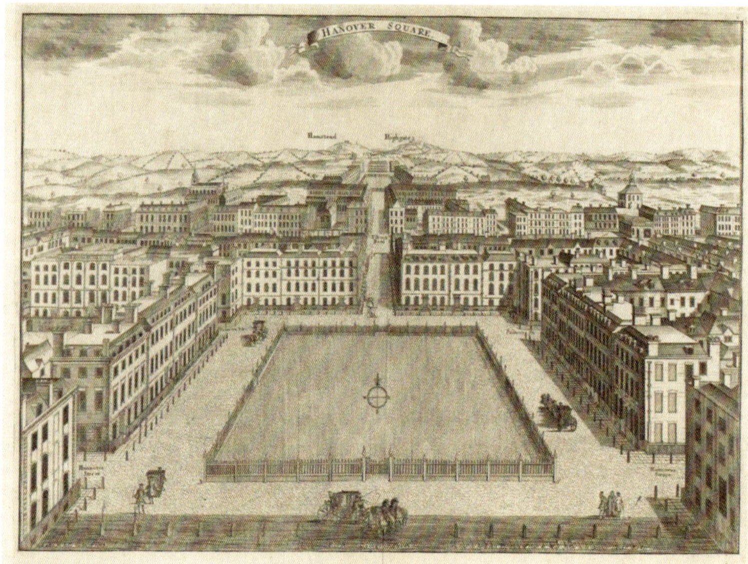

FIGURE 56. *View of Hanover Square*; etching and engraving drawn and printed by Sutton Nicholls for John Bowles, 1720–31. 13½" × 18⅛". Rijksmuseum, Amsterdam. Public domain via Wikimedia Commons.

than their European counterparts, but they are also closer and more strongly connected to each other.

The relative proximity of the squares ensures that the rhythmic quality of the plan is readily apprehended as one moves through the city. One is never more than two short blocks from a square. Savannah's squares were, from their beginning, unambiguously public (and remain so), unlike London's squares, many of which were fenced and locked to ensure their exclusive use by residents on the square—a custom followed in New York's Gramercy Park, which remains private and gated today.

From the city's founding, Savannah's squares have varied in size, shape, and character (figure 53). Of the six squares laid out by Oglethorpe, five conformed to a "standard" size of 315 feet wide (east–west) and 270 feet deep (north–south), measured from the edges of the facing lots. This is close to the average size of the squares in London's West End.[10] Despite the professed goal of ward equality, Oglethorpe made Johnson Square, at 435 feet in width, the most important square of the first row of wards, heralding a long tradition in Savannah of privileging the Bull Street axis within the town. Expansion of the Savannah Plan beginning in 1791 resulted in compressed wards to the east and west of the original town, with squares only 195 feet wide but maintaining the 270-foot north–south dimension. Southward expansions of the town included squares of all three widths (with Chippewa being slightly narrower than Johnson), but with their north–south dimensions increasing to 275 feet in the third row of wards and to 300 feet in the fourth and fifth rows as a result of increased east–west street widths. These modifications resulted in eight different square sizes across the eventual twenty-four squares. Within these open spaces, the actual size and shape of each square's perimeter after 1810 provides for even greater variety.

The shape of the square as a defined space bordered by perimeter streets changed over time (figure 57). Although the squares were given oval enclosures when first defined by 1820, they eventually became square in shape, as documented in the 1852 Vincent map. By the 1880s, as documented on Sanborn fire insurance maps, squares had acquired rounded corners.[11] The radii of their corners have varied at different times in history. For example, the 1884 Sanborn map depicts Wright Square with a circular enclosure; on the next Sanborn map published in 1888 (not shown in the diagram), it appears more square but has more generously rounded corners than any other square at the time. In the 1880s, the north–south dimension of Johnson Square was reduced by 35 feet to 235 feet in order to widen Bryan and Congress Streets that flank the square,[12] evidently to make room for the streetcar line that passed along the square's northern edge (visible in figure 136). The character of each square was further differentiated by its landscape and hardscape features, by the presence of monuments and fountains, and by the facades of the buildings surrounding it.

The intended purpose of the squares has been a matter of some debate. In *Some Account of the Design of the Trustees*, Oglethorpe states, "In the distribution of the Town the Streets should be spacious and laid out by Line and a large Square reserved for a Market place, and for exercising the Inhabitants."[13] Philip Georg Friedrich von Reck, in his diary of 1734, noted that "the Town is regularly laid

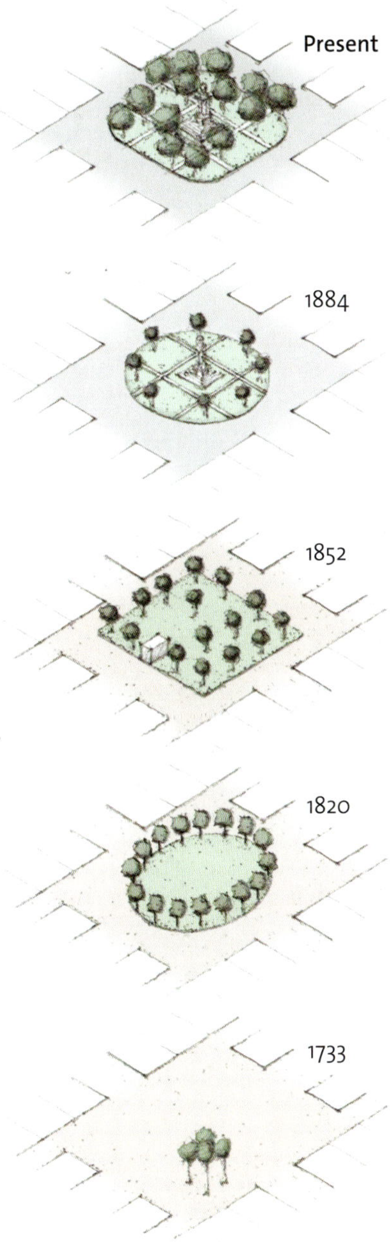

FIGURE 57. Wright Square in five stages of evolution. Drawing by Hamilton Brindley.

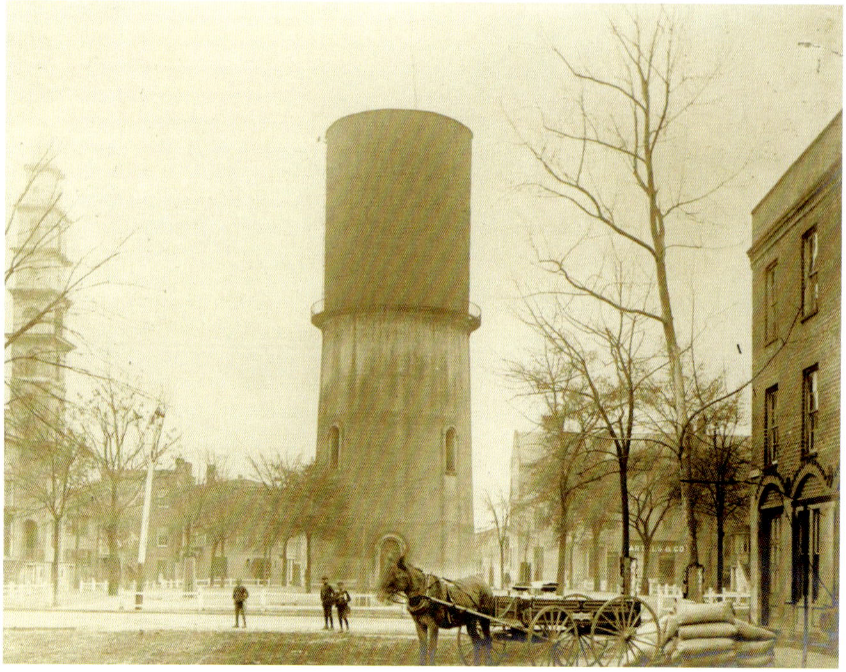

FIGURE 58. Photograph of Franklin Square looking north from Barnard Street, ca. 1890, showing the eighty-seven-foot-tall water reservoir erected in 1854 and demolished around 1900. Courtesy of the Georgia Historical Society, GHS 2126–PH-01–03 pg04, James S. Silva family papers.

out, divided into four Wards, in each of which is left a spacious Square, for holding Markets, and other public Uses."[14] Francis Moore's 1735 description of the Savannah Plan indicates another specific and practical purpose for the squares: "In case a War should happen, that the Villages without may have Places in the Town, to bring their Cattle and Families into for Refuge, and to that Purpose there is a Square left in every Ward; big enough for the Out-wards to encamp in."[15] The reserving of open space for markets and potential refugees suggests a rather utilitarian view of the squares, one that is confirmed by the subsequent placement of wells and cisterns in each square and of "engine houses" for firefighting equipment in seven of them by 1853.[16] A large water tower was built in Franklin Square in 1853 (figure 58), and a fixed market building occupied Ellis Square from at least 1757 until 1954 (figure 44), when it was replaced by a multilevel parking structure.

The belief that the squares were strictly utilitarian in conception led the Supreme Court of Georgia in 1871 to support a street railway company's bid, opposed by the city government at the time, to run streetcar tracks through Savannah's squares.[17] Streetcar tracks eventually bisected twelve of the twenty-four squares (those on Barnard, Abercorn, and Habersham Streets) and skirted three others (Franklin, Ellis, and Johnson Squares), setting an important precedent for the federal government's routing of U.S. 17 through three squares on Montgomery

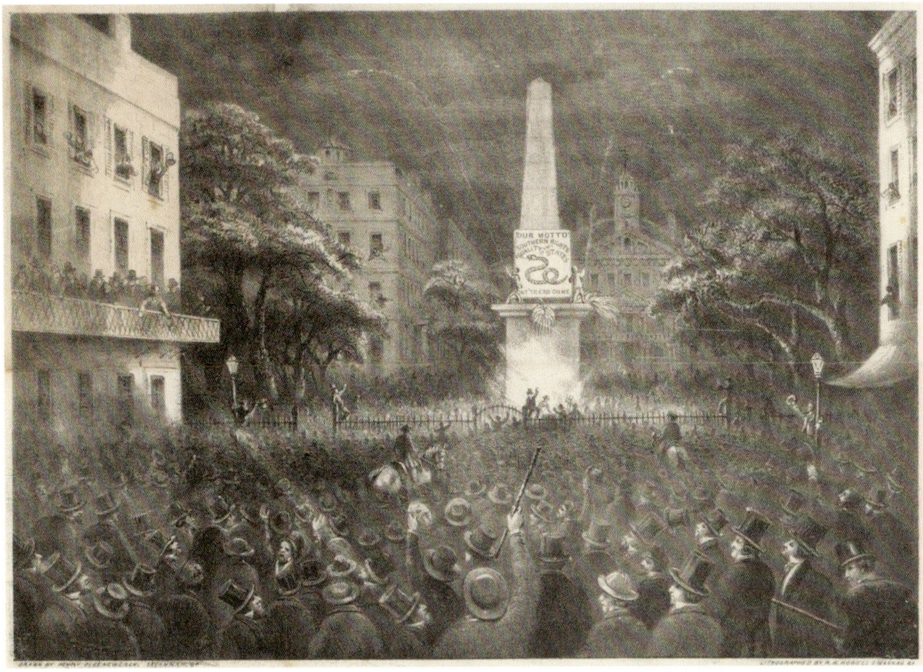

FIGURE 59. *The First Flag of Independence Raised in the South, by the Citizens of Savannah, Ga., November 8th, 1860.* Hand-colored lithograph by R. H. Howell, based on a sketch by Henry Cleenewerck, 13⅜" × 17". Library of Congress, Prints and Photographs Division.

Street in 1935, likewise opposed by the city and a majority of citizens (figure 42). These utilitarian uses do not exclude the possibility, however, that the squares also had an ornamental and civic role from the earliest years.

Of course, the squares were and remain places of public assembly. Oglethorpe's mention that the squares serve as places "for exercising the Inhabitants" suggests more a place of recreation than a merely utilitarian space. We are reminded, for example, of a newspaper account of July 7, 1733, describing an inaugural public ceremony in which "the people proceeded to the Square . . . [where] the Wards and Tythings were named," land grants were announced, and "all the people had a very plentiful Dinner."[18] Presumably the square referred to is Johnson Square, which was called "the Great Square" by John Wesley.[19] Shortly after establishing Savannah, Oglethorpe displayed civic awareness by installing a sundial in the center of Johnson Square and, in 1739, a burial monument in the center of Percival (now Wright) Square over the tomb of Tomochichi, the local Indian chief who was a key ally to the fledgling Georgia colony.[20] A temporary pavilion was erected in Johnson Square for a ball held on the occasion of President Monroe's visit in 1819.[21] An 1860 lithographic print entitled *The First Flag of Independence Raised in the South, by the Citizens of Savannah* depicts a clamorous nighttime rally in Johnson Square (figure 59). A photograph by Jerome Nelson Wilson portrays a public gathering in

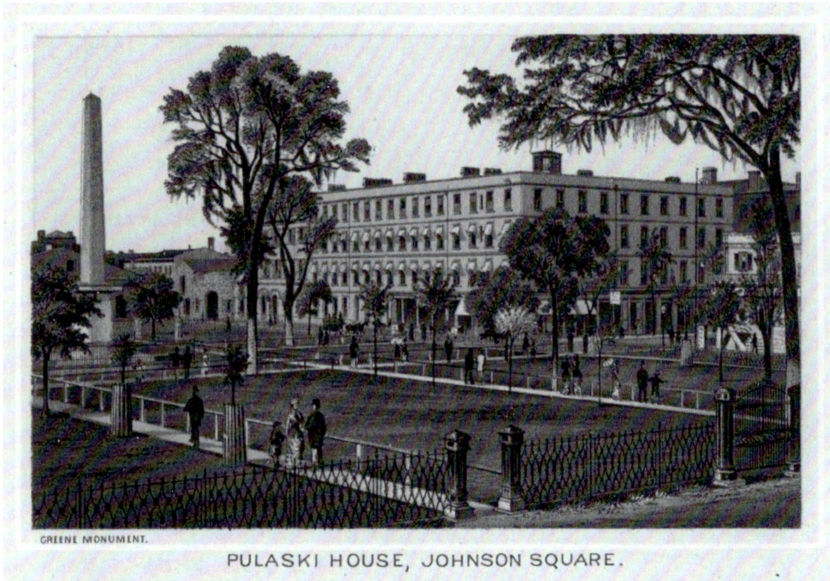

FIGURE 60. *Johnson Square Showing Enclosing Fence and People Promenading*, 1880; "photo-view" from a "Souvenir Album" by Louis Glaser entitled *Savannah* (New York, 1882). Jen Library Archives and Special Collections, Savannah College of Art and Design.

Wright Square on Election Day, November 3, 1868. Public auctions were held in Wright Square in front of the courthouse between 10 a.m. and 3 p.m. on the first Tuesday of each month for much of the nineteenth century.[22]

Both today and throughout much of the city's history, Savannah's squares have had the appearance and function of public parks. City council minutes mention trees in the squares as early as 1793.[23] Recreational and leisure uses of the squares are in evidence from the eighteenth century onward. William Stephens reported in his journal in 1741 that "it being Holiday Time, many of our Townsmen, Freeholders, Inmates and Servants, &c. were assembled in the principal Square, at Cricket, and divers other Athletick Sports."[24] Historic prints and photographs frequently depict citizens strolling or conversing quietly in the squares (figure 60). From the nineteenth century to the present, schoolchildren have used some of the squares as playgrounds. In more recent times, the squares have been used for a variety of public and semiprivate gatherings, such as weddings, luncheons, and receptions.

Tything Lots

Each ward comprises four *tythings*, an urban term peculiar to Oglethorpe's plan. A tything is a cluster of ten house lots that are grouped in two rows or blocks of five 60-by-90-foot lots (extended to 100 feet deep south of Liberty Street) separated by a lane running east–west (figure 51). Initially, the tythings functioned as subservient political associations within the ward system. A tything's residents were represented by a tythingman, who reported to the ward captain or constable. The concept of the tything is explained by Oglethorpe in *Some Account of the Design of the Trustees* as an ancient Saxon practice instituted by Alfred the Great, who had divided England into groups of hundreds subdivided into tythings of ten, each governed by a tythingman.[25] This, Oglethorpe explained, created an efficient form of policing for a "hardy race of Men in a woody and thinly peopled Country exposed to the frequent ravages of unexpected Enemys."[26] Oglethorpe's admiration for Alfred the Great is typical of the early eighteenth-century Whig Party's view of King Alfred as the founder of English constitutionalism and liberty.[27]

Tything lots represented the citizens of the city. They were uniform, repetitive, and dogmatically equal from the inception of the plan. The lots were first assigned by lottery, emphasizing the egalitarian ideals of the Trustees.[28] Of course, the restrictive policies supporting these ideals did not last beyond the Trustee era. Since that time, many tything lots have been subdivided and others combined, and many host a variety of building types. In wards laid out after 1815 (forming the fourth and fifth rows of wards), the depth of tything lots was increased to 100 feet, but the basic module and rhythm of the 60-foot frontage remained. A unique exception to this lot depth occurred in the southernmost row of tything lots in the fifth row of wards, those facing Gaston Street, which enjoy a generous depth of 120 feet, allowing houses on these lots to have front yards and forward-oriented staircases.

The building coverage and population density of the tythings have increased steadily since their inception. The first houses were built according to a standardized design with a footprint of twenty-four feet (width) by sixteen feet.[29] These timber and clapboard houses, represented at an exaggerated scale in the 1734 Gordon View (figure 9), apparently came to the front edge of the lots. The boundaries of each lot were further defined architecturally by a perimeter fence. Lot coverage and occupancy increased with the growth in the prosperity of the homeowners and with the advent of urban slavery.

Although zoned by Oglethorpe to be strictly residential in purpose, tything lots evolved to accommodate almost every kind of use. Skyscraper office buildings, retail stores, medium-rise apartment complexes, theatres, factories, hospitals, schools, and even government buildings and churches occupy tything lots. Such nonresidential buildings have adapted to the structure of the tything in various ways, often acknowledging the domestic paradigm and thus reflecting the legacy of the original tything DNA. For example, the Massie School, designed by John Norris on the southeast tything of Calhoun Ward in 1856, was expanded in 1872 and again in 1886 into three front-gabled house-like structures facing the square.

The orientation of buildings on tything lots also varies. In several cases, the north–south orientation of a tything is altered by structures that face east or west; this is especially true along Bull Street. On some tything lots at the end of a block, the principal building (typically a house) faces the east–west street, while the carriage house (sometimes incorporating a store) faces the north–south street instead of the lane, reflecting an even more nuanced variation.

The city's two largest churches, the Cathedral Basilica of St. John the Baptist and the Independent Presbyterian Church, occupy multiple tything lots and face the central north–south street of their respective wards, treating them in effect as supersized trust lots. Some tything lots have been combined across the lane, creating "superblocks." Chatham Academy on the northeast tything block of Brown Ward and the Oglethorpe Barracks (now occupied by the Desoto Hotel) on the northeast tything of Jasper Ward predated the platting of their wards. These tythings were never laid out with residential lots, and they never had lanes. A third example of a superblock is the southeast corner of Heathcote Ward, where the ten tything lots and lane laid out in 1733 were combined and completely covered by the Juliette Gordon Low Federal Building C in 1980–82.

Trust Lots

Each ward in the Savannah Plan has (or had) four trust lots to the east and west of the square; these oblong parcels of land were originally intended for public buildings approved by the Georgia Trustees (figure 51). Colonial-era records typically refer to these as "public lots" or "reserved lots," but by the mid-nineteenth century "trust lot" became the preferred designation, suggesting that the memory of the Trustee era—if not the egalitarian intentions of the Trustees—was worthy of commemoration.[30] Trust lots are among the most inventive and formative components of the Savannah Plan. By their position, orientation, and size, trust lots have a status greater than that of tything lots. They occupy places of prominence in each neighborhood, but none holds a fundamentally privileged position, with the original town of six wards containing twenty-four trust lots and the expanded town boasting ninety-eight. Like the plan as a whole, trust lots are dispersed and decentralized. They are limited in size and attenuated in their proportions, with a standard dimension of 60 feet wide by 180 feet deep, the equivalent of two tything lots back-to-back. Some trust lots are shorter in length due to their fronting larger squares, as in Derby and Brown Wards, where the trust lots run only 120 and 130 feet deep, respectively. Most extraordinary and illustrative of the plan's elasticity are the western trust lots in the two wards truncated on their west side by the irregular alignment of the Common's boundary (Pulaski and Chatham); they are 60 feet by 60 feet, surely among the smallest city blocks in the country.

Reserving building lots for unspecified public buildings is not unprecedented in the history of city planning. Designating lots fronting a city square as public is likewise a common strategy in the history of town planning, such as defined by the Laws of the Indies. An eighteenth-century map of nearby Beaufort, South Carolina, for example, shows a square flanked at its quadrants by lots labeled as "publick" (figure 19).[31] Distributing such lots equally throughout a city plan in accordance with the egalitarianism of its founders, however, seems to be unique to the Savannah Plan. Oglethorpe states in *Some Account of the Design of the Trustees* that on the "sides" of the square "may be the Church, Infirmary for the Sick, an House for new Comers, Town House and other publick Buildings."[32]

Rather than being granted by lottery, trust lots were assigned by the Trustees. The 1734 Gordon View shows four wards, with a total of sixteen trust lots (figure 9). By the end of that first full year of the colony's life, only the four trust lots of Derby Ward were in use. The southeast trust lot is shown empty but is labeled "The Lott for the Church." The southwest lot shows two simple structures, one of which is labeled "The House for Strangers," and the other, "The publick Oven." The northeast and northwest trust lots show buildings labeled "The publick Stores" and "The publick Mill," respectively. Although the engraving shows little detail, these were clearly the largest and most important buildings of their time. They represented the public institutions and practices most vital to the founding of the city. In 1740 William Stephens noted the existence of a courthouse, a jail, a stove-house or public oven, and a "large House for receiving the Indians."[33] All these structures occupied trust lots. A curious exception to this pattern, documented in the Gordon View, was "The Tabernacle & Court House" on the backside of a tything lot at Bay Lane and Bull Street. According to Francis Moore, the structure was "a hut thirty-six-foot-long and twelve-foot-wide, made of split boards, and erected on Mr. Oglethorpe's first arrival in the colony."[34] Oglethorpe's order in 1736 that it be replaced by a second tabernacle and courthouse in Percival (Wright) Square suggests that the first structure was likely to have been temporary.

When the Trustees relinquished control of the colony in 1752, several trust lots remained empty. In February 1755, Governor Reynolds and the colonial council, noting that "there were more Lots reserved for Publick uses in Savannah, than will probably ever be wanted for that Purpose, and there being several Persons in want of Lotts, who are willing to build thereon," made two important resolutions: first, "that the reserved Lotts in the Squares in Darby Ward, Reynold's Ward, and Deckers Ward [*sic*]"—that is, those trust lots closest to the waterfront—"be continued to be reserved for publick uses"; and second, "that such of the reserved Lots, as are not now built upon in Anson's Ward, Percival Ward and Heathcoate [*sic*] Ward, be divided into Lotts of 60 by 90 feet, and granted by the Board, to such Persons, as shall appear to them to be desirous to improve the same."[35] Over the succeeding months several petitioners were granted half of a trust lot. In April 1755, Governor Reynolds petitioned for and was granted a full trust lot for himself in Anson Ward.[36] New public institutions were also approved. The northwest trust lot of

Reynolds Ward was reserved for a "Publick School," while a group of "Dissenters from the Church of England" (who established the Independent Presbyterian Church) were granted the northeast trust lot of "Deckers" Ward.[37]

The council's "rezoning" decision heralded an important modification of Oglethorpe's town plan, with the vacant trust lots of the southern wards being reassigned and divided into residential lots. An exception was in Percival Ward (the central ward of the second row), where existing public lots were protected, as suggested by the council's response to a petition in November 1757 by Lewis Johnson, who requested permission to use a trust lot for private purposes. The council rejected his petition, because the "Court House that stands on the other Part of the Lot [requires] Additional Buildings."[38] Even so, Thomas Shruder's survey map shows that by 1770, fourteen (or 70 percent) of the twenty occupied trust lots were used for residential purposes.

Following the American Revolution, the city council of the newly formed municipal government clearly understood its responsibility to find public uses for public lots, though trust lots in the eastern and westernmost expansion wards seem to have been divided as private lots early on. In September 1790, the city council passed an act designating "a certain number of lots for the use of certain religious, literary, and benevolent institutions."[39] Most of these were trust lots. In 1791 the council ordered that a building be erected on "the Public lot in Wright Square, to secure the fire engine."[40] A succession of courthouses was built on the southeast trust lot of Percival Ward, beginning with a 1766 colonial courthouse that was damaged in the great fire of 1796; that building was replaced in 1832 by the first county courthouse, which was replaced in turn by a second county courthouse in 1889. Across the square, a federal courthouse and post office was erected on the southwest trust lot in 1894–99 and was expanded to encompass President Street and most of the northwest trust lot in 1935. The Planters Bank chose to locate in the renovated James Habersham Jr. residence (today the Pink House) on the northwest trust lot of Reynolds Ward in 1812, and in 1820 a branch of the Bank of the United States designed by English architect William Jay was built on the "back half" of the same lot, facing St. Julian Street (the central trust street).

Whether they are occupied by a church, a bank, a courthouse, or a private house, the size and configuration of trust lots within the town plan have directly conditioned the architecture of the buildings that inhabit the plan. Trust lot houses, for example, generally follow a different typological pattern from tything lot houses. Center hall plans with symmetrical facades, grand porticoes, and setbacks from the street line are more common on trust lot houses than they are on tything lot houses. Casual observation reveals that trust lot houses are among the most monumental and ornate houses in the city. Here we observe the Renaissance theory of magnificence in practice. When a private citizen built a house, its scale, use of materials, and ornamentation responded to the dignity of the place. Not surprisingly, many of these originally private dwellings have since been repurposed to serve as public or commercial institutions, as was the case with the James Habersham Jr. residence, conforming to the publicness of the trust lot dictated by the plan's urban genetic code (figure 72).

Streets

While orthogonal grid plans are common to many cities, especially in North America, Savannah possesses what is arguably the most intricate and tightly woven grid plan ever realized (figure 50). The interwoven hierarchy of its streets and the inward pull and outward thrust exerted by its squares and building lots combine to create its tartan-like appearance (figure 49). Each ward involves ten streets of six different types and four different sizes (figure 51). The post-Oglethorpe expansion of the plan introduced an additional nine street-width variations, bringing the total to thirteen and greatly enhancing the complexity of the urban tartan. To understand this complex weave, we must disentangle and isolate the differing threads.

CIVIC AND SERVICE STREETS

Two primary categories and six subcategories of streets can be identified. Civic streets constitute the first major category. These include the 75-foot-wide streets that bisect each ward along its central axes and their 37½-foot-wide counterparts, which define the inner boundaries of the tythings and flank the north and south edges of the squares. The boundary streets running east–west between wards are also civic (this category originally comprised only Broughton Street). Service streets constitute the second primary category. These include the 45-foot-wide streets that run north–south, bounding the east and west edges of the wards, as well as the 22½-foot-wide lanes that run east–west through the center of each tything block. The congruence of these dimensions attests to the careful intentionality of Oglethorpe's plan.[41]

NORTH–SOUTH CIVIC STREETS—KNOTTED STRANDS

The most distinctive individual components of Savannah's street grid are the primary civic streets running north–south and east–west and aligned with the center of the squares (figures 61 and 62). The intersection of streets in a grand public square is an ancient and symbolically rich motif in the history of urban form; examples can be found in Roman town planning, where the *cardo* and *decumanus* meet at a centrally located forum, or in Spanish colonial towns, where primary streets often cross at a central plaza mayor. Unlike in these examples, however, Savannah's primary civic streets cross through multiple squares in two directions.

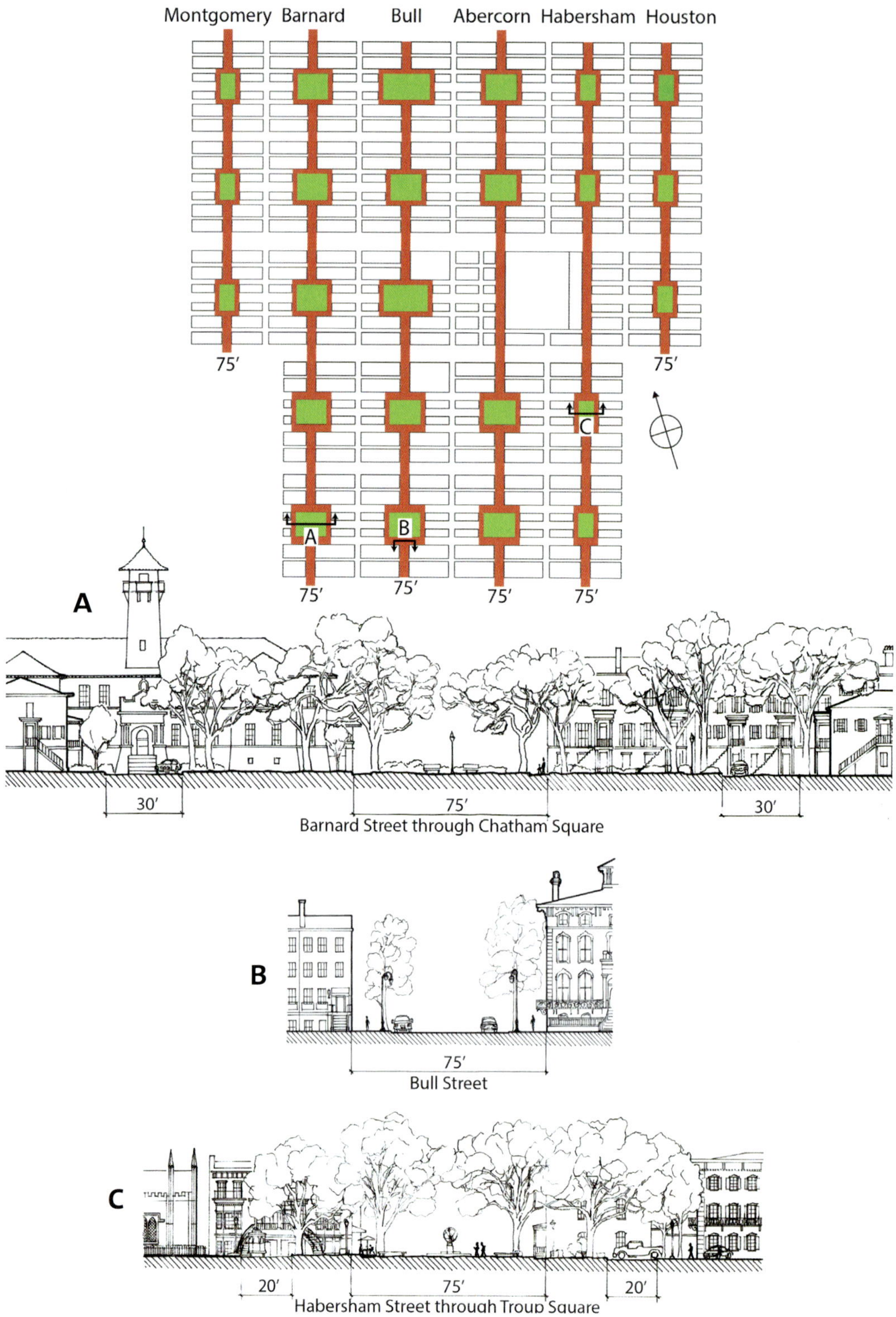

FIGURE 61. North–south civic streets. Diagram by Robin B. Williams and David Gobel.

Punctuated by these frequent interruptions, the streets are like knotted ropes or beaded chains.

Although north–south and east–west civic streets were created to be of equal status (they enjoy the same width and same axial centrality), it appears that from the time of Oglethorpe the streets running north–south enjoyed a higher level of priority. The six-ward town comprised three north–south central streets (Abercorn, Bull, and Barnard) but only two streets running east–west that intersected with the squares. Three more north–south streets (Houston, Habersham, and Montgomery) were added in 1791. The north–south civic streets stretch across a greater distance and a greater number of blocks and streets, conferring on them unmistakable priority over their east–west counterparts as well as a stronger sense of forward movement.

PRIMARY EAST–WEST CIVIC STREETS—TRUST STREETS

The central east–west axial trust streets bisecting the pairs of trust lots within each ward (St. Julian, President, McDonough, Macon, and Wayne Streets) are arguably the least necessary (figure 62). They were noticeably omitted in the later plans of Ebenezer and Augusta. Originally set at a generous 75-foot width to match the width of the north–south axial streets, they are the only streets that became narrower over time, being reduced to 60 feet within the fourth and fifth rows of wards. Part of their weakness stems from their short block lengths, as defined by the flanks of the trust lots, ranging from 180 feet to as little as 60 feet. In other words, the two-block run of such east–west streets between a pair of squares (defined by the front edge of the respective trust lots) ranges from 345 feet to 410 feet, depending on the size of the adjacent trust lots (compared to the distances between squares on the north–south civic streets, ranging from 480 to 565 feet). While trust streets do not make effective corridors for the movement of vehicles, which are forced to go around the square, they are highly effective for pedestrians, since their sidewalks align with the paths that cross the square.

More so than any other component of the plan, trust streets have experienced dramatic alterations. In 1916, the block of McDonough Street on the west side of Orleans Square was sacrificed to allow the Municipal Auditorium to straddle the pair of trust lots. This set a precedent for other public buildings and parking garages to follow, as well as for the closure of other central street blocks and their sale to adjacent churches—for example, in 1960 St. John's Episcopal Church acquired two blocks of West Macon Street, turning one block into a garden beside the church and absorbing the other into a parking lot. The conversion of two blocks of West St. Julian Street between Franklin and Ellis Squares into a pedestrian mall in 1985 exploited their shortcomings as streets for vehicular traffic. All these conversions reflect the elasticity of the Savannah Plan to adapt to changing social needs.

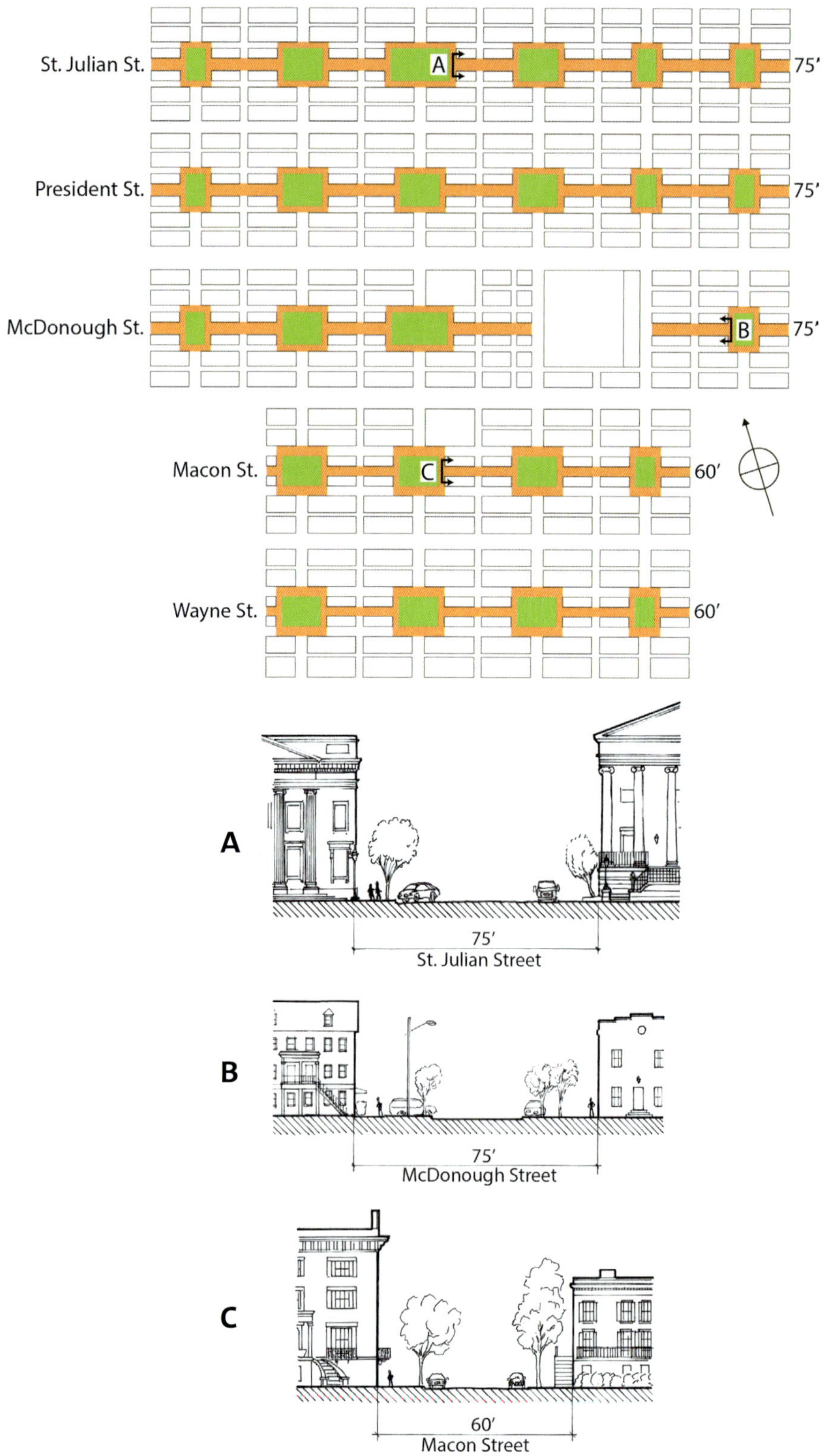

FIGURE 62. Primary east–west civic streets (trust streets). Diagram by Robin B. Williams and David Gobel.

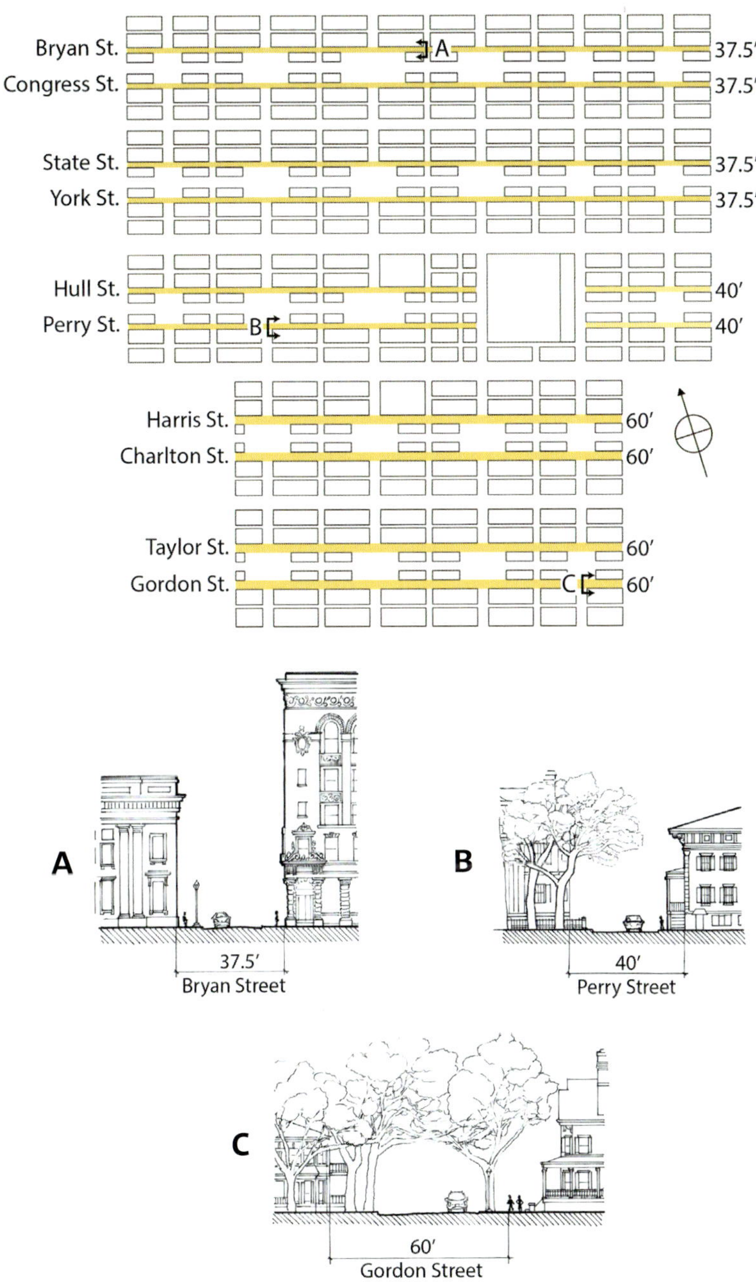

FIGURE 63. Inner east–west civic streets. Diagram by Robin B. Williams and David Gobel.

INNER EAST–WEST CIVIC STREETS—PAIRED LINEAR CORRIDORS

Paralleling the central trust streets, the east–west streets flanking the north and south edges of the squares—what we call inner civic streets—gradually grew in importance as the plan expanded (figure 63). Originally the inner civic streets were each 37½ feet wide. When viewed in pairs, their combined width of 75 feet equals that of the central civic trust street in each ward, as if the trust lots and the square were conceived as an extra wide median. As the Savannah Plan expanded southward, the inner civic streets grew to 40 feet wide in the third row of wards and to 60 feet wide in the fourth and fifth rows of wards. These streets possess the least clear sense of identity, however, bordering the outer flanks of trust lots and the square on one side of the street and the fronts of tything lots of differing status on the other.

EAST–WEST CIVIC BOUNDARY STREETS—CONNECTIVE LINEAR CORRIDORS

East–west boundary streets frame the north and south edges of the wards; four function as boundaries between wards—Broughton Street, Oglethorpe Avenue, Liberty Street, and Jones Street—and two serve as outer boundaries to the plan—Bay Street to the north and Gaston Street to the south. Although they are boundaries, these streets are also the city's longest continuous corridors, running across the entire plan. Each has a different width, character, and function (figure 64).

Broughton Street was the first and only east–west civic street defined in the colonial era. At 75 feet in width, it was the only continuous linear corridor with buildings on both sides, leading to its use as the main commercial street.[42] Remarkably, it has never lost that role. South Broad Street (now Oglethorpe Avenue) first functioned as an outer edge of the town facing the South Common, but when it was officially established in 1801 as a 140-foot-wide boulevard with a tree-lined pedestrian promenade running along its center, it began to function like a linear square, attracting prominent public and private buildings along its length (figure 7). Liberty Street, created in the 1830s at 130 feet wide, also boasts a tree-lined median, which briefly hosted a railway line.[43] Jones Street, laid out in the 1850s at a width of 95 feet, has extra wide sidewalks and tree lawns in place of a median.

As early maps of Savannah illustrate, the land along the outer edges of the plan was not originally defined by streets. Bay Street took shape incrementally as the City Exchange was built and an allée of trees was planted along its northern edge. It was first identified as "Bay Street" on the 1820 McKinnon map (figure 38). By the late nineteenth century, it had been established at sixty-five feet wide west of Barnard Street and eighty-two feet wide to the east with the construction of City Hall. Gaston Street, the southernmost boundary street, may have been planned at ninety-five feet (like Jones to its north), but its width was adjusted to seventy-five feet evidently in response to property owners requesting that twenty feet be added to the tything lots lining the north side of the street.[44] Its south side fronts the open green space of Forsyth Park on the blocks flanking Bull Street, further enhancing its feeling of spaciousness.

FIGURE 64. East–west civic boundary streets. Diagram by Robin B. Williams and David Gobel.

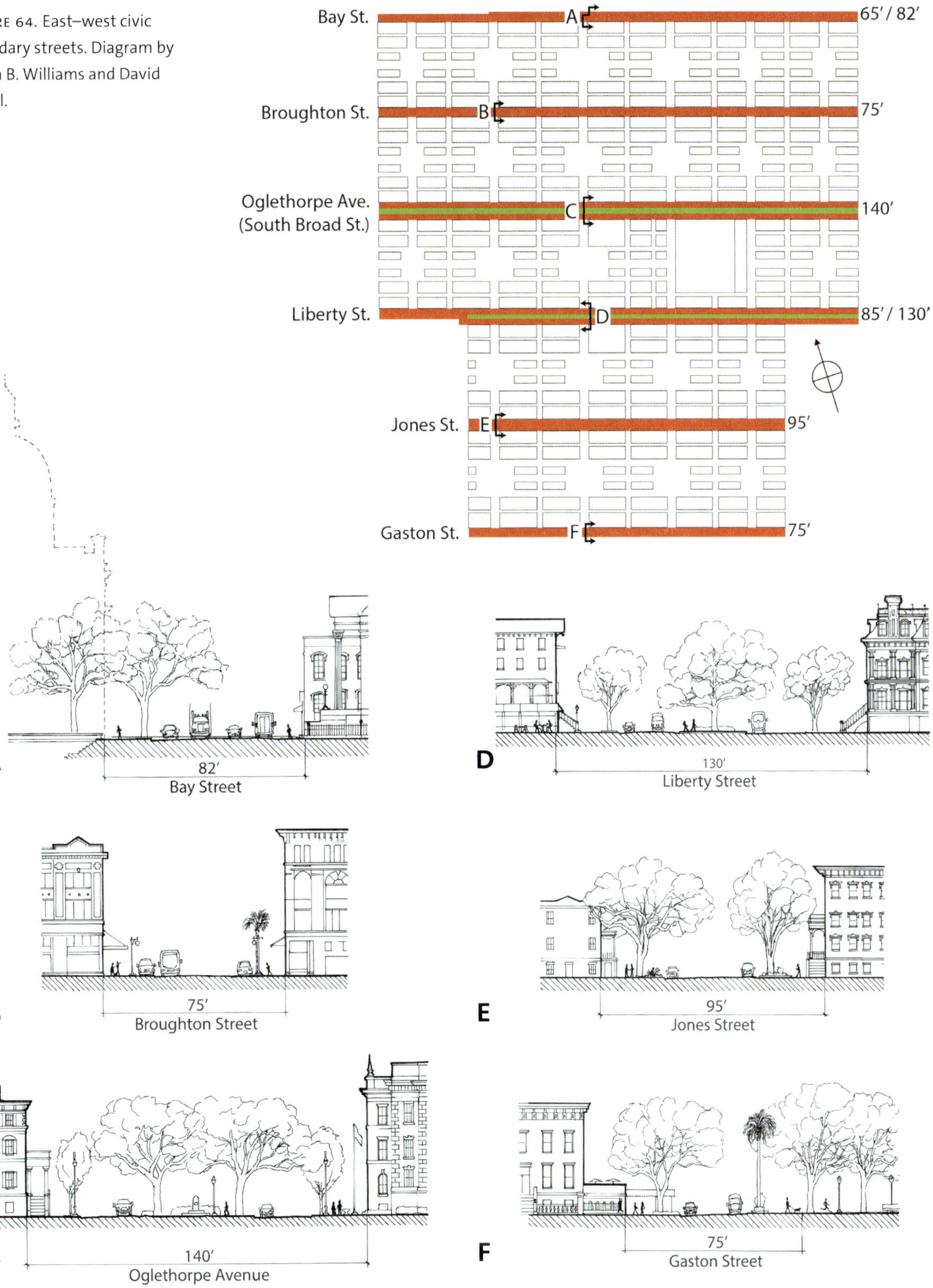

NORTH–SOUTH SERVICE BOUNDARY STREETS

The least celebrated component of Oglethorpe's plan of Savannah is the boundary streets (Jefferson, Whitaker, Drayton, Lincoln, and Price) defining the east and west edges of the wards and running north–south. These were first set at forty-five feet wide but were increased to a width of fifty feet in the ward expansion of 1791 (figure 65). As boundary streets, they form unbroken linear corridors that are intersected by a syncopated rhythm of alternating wide and narrow cross streets and have the rear halves of trust lots and end lots of the tything blocks that generally face away from such streets collectively.

OUTER BOUNDARY STREETS— EAST BROAD AND WEST BROAD STREETS

Unforeseen by Oglethorpe and unique among the streets constituting the Savannah Plan are East Broad and West Broad Streets, created at the outer edges of the Common in 1770. They exist in a kind of limbo between civic and utilitarian purposes. Their impressive one-hundred-foot width ensures a sense of civic grandeur, yet their location as north–south boundary streets makes them akin to streets like Whitaker and Drayton. The 1818 Stouf map of Savannah shows the two streets lined by trees (figure 37), yet they also became corridors for electricity wires (like the other service streets). Located at the edges of the Savannah Plan, they served marginalized populations of the city, becoming the focus of the African American community; West Broad Street (now Martin Luther King Jr. Boulevard) developed into a "Black Main Street," making it vulnerable to the wave of 1960s urban renewal highway projects that tore through historically Black areas in American cities. In Savannah the elevated Interstate 16 exit ramp cut across West Broad just outside the Savannah Plan area, interrupting the street's economic and social cohesion and paving the way for the even more destructive urban renewal projects of the Savannah Civic Center and the Chatham County Courthouse complex that effectively separate the street from the rest of downtown Savannah, sapping it of economic life (figure 46).

EAST–WEST SERVICE STREETS—LANES

Defined by Oglethorpe as 22½ feet in width, half the width of the original north–south boundary service streets, Savannah's lanes run east–west through each tything block, serving the back side of each house lot (figure 66). The lanes grew to 32½ feet wide in the third row of wards established in the early 1800s, rendering the lanes in this row almost as wide as the inner civic streets. But wider lanes proved unnecessary in the context of so many other civic streets, and in the subsequent fourth and fifth rows of wards, established in the 1830s and 1840s, respectively,

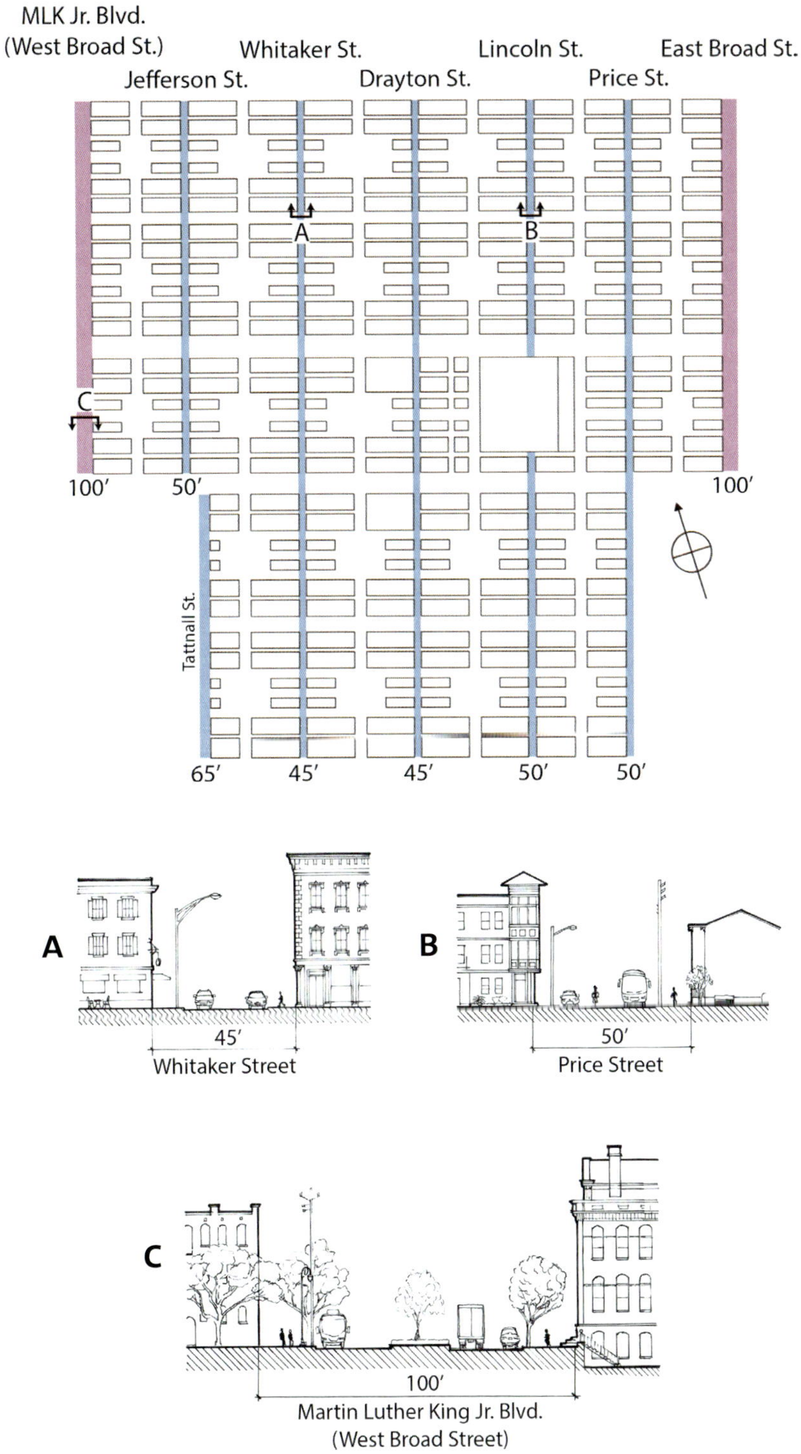

FIGURE 65. North–south service boundary streets and outer boundary streets. Diagram by Robin B. Williams and David Gobel.

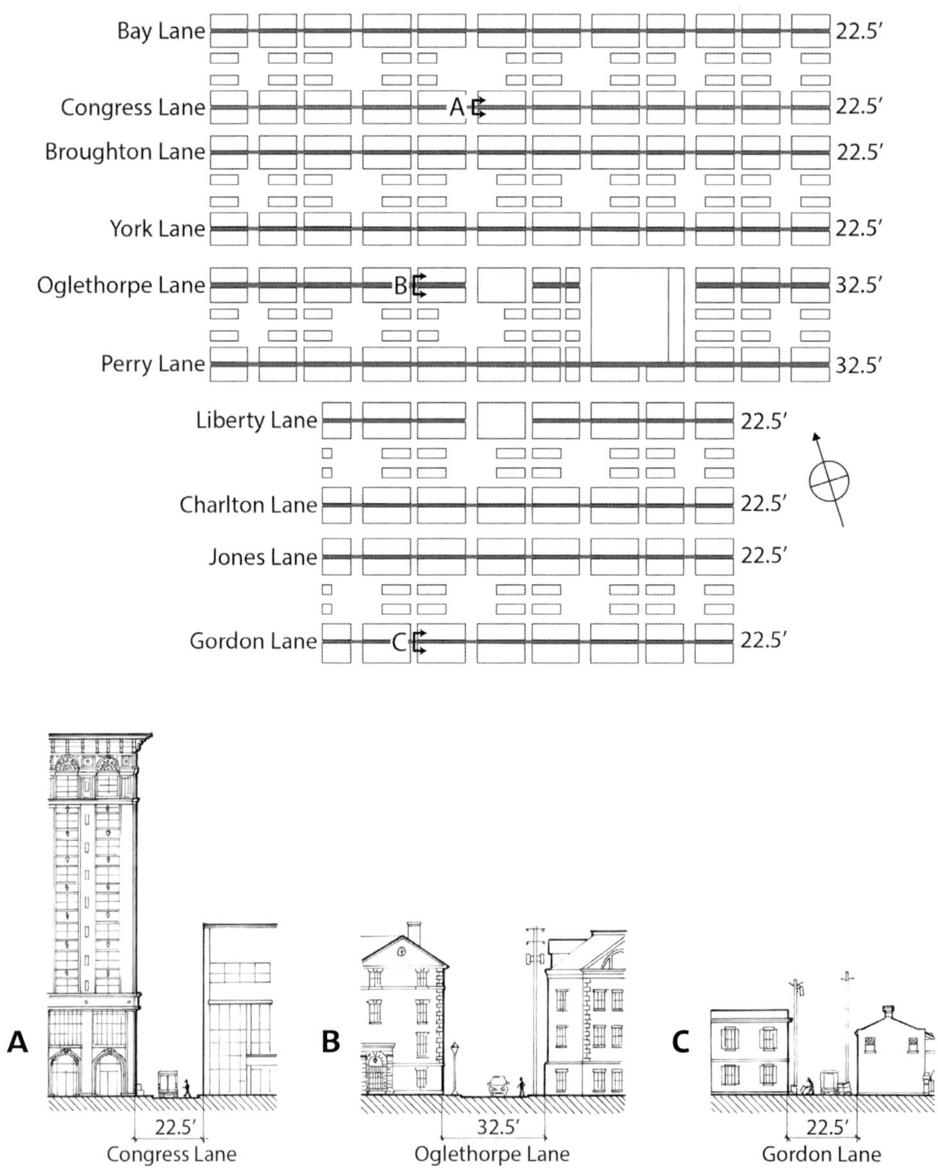

FIGURE 66. Lanes (east–west service streets). Diagram by Robin B. Williams and David Gobel.

the width of the lanes returned to 22½ feet, evidently to maximize their efficiency while consuming less land. As the most enduring elements of the Savannah Plan, lanes persisted as integral components of Savannah's urban planning until the mid-twentieth century, paralleling civic streets as far south as 66th Street, almost three miles south of downtown.

Savannah's lanes find their precedent in English mews, especially those in London. Unlike their British counterparts, however, which often form a dead end,

Savannah's lanes extend across the width of the plan, with only a few exceptions. Dexterous and adaptable throughout the history of the city, they have accommodated differing types of transportation technology, from horses and carriages to modern automobiles and delivery vehicles; differing social groups, from enslaved workers to students looking for affordable apartments; and an increasing selection of critical service infrastructure, beginning with sewers in the 1870s, then electricity wires in the 1880s, telephone wires in the 1900s, garbage collection in the 1920s, and recycling in the early 2000s. They function as the dropped ceilings of the Savannah Plan, neatly tucking the essential but messy services largely out of sight, and so allowing the civic streets to remain free of such urban detritus.

CHAPTER FOUR

HOW THE PLAN WORKS

Other plan factors of Savannah inherently possess double readings and interact with one another systematically in such ways as to resist any monolithic changes in use and meaning.
—STANFORD ANDERSON, 1993

Oglethorpe's plan for the city combines a variety of well-proportioned streets and spaces in an intelligent layout that shows how rich a grid can be: its regular rhythm of squares and streets of varying widths give a hierarchy, order, and majesty to the grid.
—VICTOR DOVER AND JOHN MASSENGALE, 2013

Potent as it is, the Savannah Plan is fundamentally an abstraction. Like all urban and architectural plans, it is merely a two-dimensional diagram representing geometric relationships, accompanied by a set of written and unwritten instructions for how to use the diagram. Understood in this way, it is a noteworthy contribution to the history of city planning. So alluring is the diagram of a Savannah ward that the city adopted stylized versions of it as the City of Savannah's official logo (figure 67). But the spatial-temporal reality of the Savannah Plan is composed not by lines on paper but by the buildings, monuments, trees, and pavement surfaces. Diagrammatic analysis of the city's urban plan can reveal much about the paradoxical patterns inherent in its composition, but Savannah can be fully understood experientially only by walking (or driving) its streets and squares. In this chapter we investigate the plan from both perspectives: as an abstract ideal but also as it is experienced on the ground.

Modular-Centric Grid Versus Orthogonal-Linear Plan

The Savannah Plan presents urban researchers with a parade of paradoxes. Its design is simple yet complex, rigid yet flexible, egalitarian yet hierarchical, noncentralized yet multicentered. Anderson suggests that the plan possesses inherent "double readings," endowing Savannah with innate ambiguity that he considers one of its greatest virtues—and that we see as yet another manifestation of Savannah's elastic urbanism, its ability to adapt while retaining its essential integrity. Among the double readings is his observation that the plan functions as two

FIGURE 67. City of Savannah logos from 2006 (at top) and 2020 showing a simplified ward diagram. Courtesy of the City of Savannah.

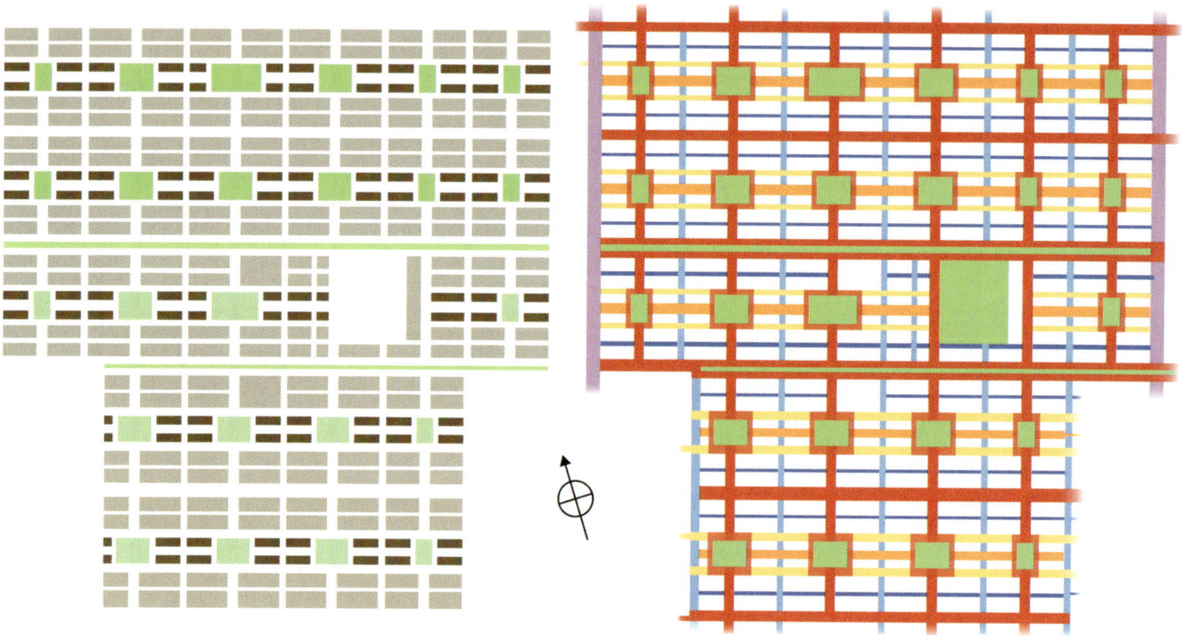

FIGURE 68. The Savannah Plan as a linear orthogonal grid (at left) and as a modular grid. Diagram by Robin B. Williams.

simultaneous systems of organization—the centric quality of the ward he calls "isomorphism" and "the alternative linear, street-oriented reading of the plan."[1] This centric yet linear dualism lies at the heart of the many paradoxes (or double readings) inherent in the Savannah Plan (figure 68).

Sibyl Moholy-Nagy, in her sweeping analysis of the history of urban form, identifies a similar distinction between the "modular grid plan" and the "orthogonal-linear plan."[2] The modular grid, she maintains, belongs to the largely preindustrial category that includes "geomorphic" and "concentric" town plans. It is tied to authoritative regimes and often has cosmological significance. The orthogonal-linear plan, she contends, was conceived in Assyrio-Hellenistic antiquity of the fifth through second centuries BC and developed in medieval market towns during the tenth through fourteenth centuries, ultimately becoming the dominant paradigm for the modern city. Anticipating Anderson's analysis, Moholy-Nagy notes that Savannah is a synthesis of the modular and orthogonal-linear paradigms.[3]

The implicitly hierarchical nature of a centric plan, as embodied by the Renaissance city of Palmanova (figure 4) or by Ebenezer Howard's Garden City diagram, is effectively contradicted through replication in a multicentered plan. Meanwhile, the grid of perpendicular streets in Savannah that connects the wards involves an intricate interweaving of streets coded with different functions (either civic or utilitarian), with each street implemented in both full- and half-size versions and with subsequent width variations introduced as more wards were added. The result is an array of overlapping planes and lines forming a tartan-like pattern more complex, nuanced, and elastic than most other grid plans in history.

A Modular and Multicentric Grid

Irony, ambiguity, and serendipity can be found in the multicentric nature of Savannah's modular grid. Each modular unit (the ward) is centralizing within itself, but because the wards are of relatively equal size and none occupies a privileged or central place within the ensemble, the grid as a whole lacks a discernible center and offers no obvious axial alignments to highlight positions of authority or power. Nevertheless, a strong central axis punctuated with monuments and lined with authoritative institutions developed along Bull Street. Linked by the strong axial vistas to the squares of their bisecting streets, Savannah's wards are simultaneously inward and outward in their centric organization (figure 69). This ambiguous relationship is strengthened by the arrangement of the residential tything lots, half of which face inward toward the square, while the other half face outward toward adjacent wards and bordering through streets. Many of the trust lots are similarly Janus-like in their orientation. Each of these qualities deserves further elaboration.

AXIAL PLANNING

Like an ancient Roman castrum, each ward is bisected by central axes running east–west and north–south that cross at the middle of the ward. The seventy-five-foot width of these streets reinforces their importance. Although these streets do not traverse the space of the square, their hypothetical intersection came to be marked, in several squares, by a monument, fountain, or gazebo. From within each square, a person can look outward along these broad axial streets to see another square a short distance away. Within the original six-ward town plan, each of the four outer wards allowed one to look out in two directions to adjacent squares, while the two central wards provided axial views to three other squares. This practical advantage for the central wards guided a privileging of the Bull Street north–south axis within Oglethorpe's purportedly egalitarian town plan following his addition in 1734–35 of two wards to the east of the original four laid out in 1733.

The town founder immediately recognized the potential of the Bull Street axis, erecting a sundial in the center of Johnson Square and a funerary monument to Tomochichi in Percival (now Wright) Square (figure 29). From these squares, Bull Street runs southward through the center of three additional squares and continues through Forsyth Park before becoming a central spine for the nineteenth-century expansion of the city, reinforcing its status as what the Romans would have called a *cardo maximus*. The Latin word *cardo* literally means "hinge," an apt metaphor for Bull Street. Clear evidence of Oglethorpe's conferral of this status can be seen on maps showing that the forty-five-degree hypotenuses of the original garden lots are symmetrically reflective on opposing sides of Bull Street (figure 35). The City of Savannah reinforced the street's centrality by making Bull Street the centerline of a new address system in November 1896, dividing the city into eastern and western halves.[4] By 1910, every square along Bull Street had a commemorative monument in its center, and many of the city's most prestigious public buildings and grandest churches defined its edges. The Bull Street axis functions today as it has historically, as Savannah's processional or ceremonial pathway, its *via triumphalis*.

Reinforcing the primacy of the Bull Street axis are terminating structures placed outside the plan in what seems to be a contradiction of the plan's original intent. The centrifugal effect of broad axial streets extending out from each square within Oglethorpe's six-ward town obviated the erection of any centrally placed buildings, such as are found in numerous European and American cities with squares. Savannah's central axes lead only to more squares. However, a public market structure, initially called the Vendue House but renamed the Exchange by 1757, was erected just outside the town's northern boundary atop the bluff overlooking the river and aligned with Bull Street (figure 29). With its construction, Savannah acquired a singular urban focal point that reinforced Bull Street's centralized authority. Endowed with such power, this site later accommodated the City Exchange (constructed in 1799–1802), which was replaced by the current City Hall in 1904–6 as an assertion of growing municipal self-confidence (figures 104 and 105).

CENTRIPETAL AND CENTRIFUGAL EFFECTS

Each ward exerts both an inward pull toward its center and a simultaneous outward thrust connecting it to the network of wards and streets beyond its borders, an effect we have attempted to diagram in figure 69. The centrally located public squares play the leading role in this effect, drawing people and buildings toward them like equally placed magnets across the plan. Buildings near to a central square are drawn to face it with suitable architectural adornment; those farther away are less obligated to face the center or to present high levels of embellishment or refinement. Those on the periphery, however, shift their allegiance away from the center, orienting themselves outward, facing adjacent wards and streets. These centripetal and centrifugal forces introduce architectural, social, and economic hierarchies throughout the Savannah Plan. The result is a dynamic richness in the city's urban and architectural landscape that is far from the egalitarian uniformity envisioned by the founding Trustees but which is admired by many today.

The inward orientation of the tything and trust lots around each square is clear. The status of lots along the periphery of a ward, especially those abutting the north–south service streets, is ambiguous, prompting one to wonder how much of each ward effectively relates to or "belongs" to the square. Buildings occupying entire trust lots emphatically address the square they face by their adornment,

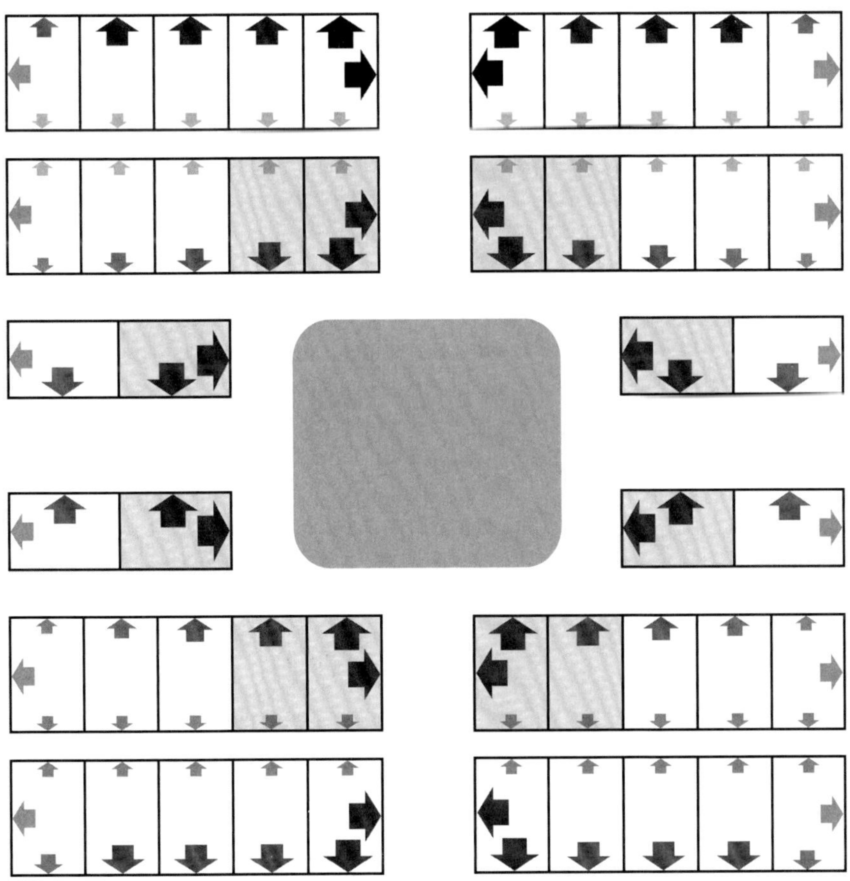

FIGURE 69. Savannah ward diagram showing the general inward and outward orientation of building lots. The lots clearly "belonging" to the square are shaded gray. Within a typical ward, the orientation of each lot to civic and utilitarian streets and lanes is indicated with arrows. The size and opacity of the arrows represent the relative strength of that orientation. Diagram by Robin B. Williams.

composition, and scale. Adding nuance to this orientation, however, is the pull of the east–west civic street that separates the pairs of trust lots in each ward. Several trust lot buildings have primary or secondary entrances facing these trust streets. Trust lots that are divided into two or more building lots are less emphatic in their orientation. Some have multiple rowhouses facing either north or south. Trust lots that have been divided into "front" and "back" portions often have service or retail buildings on the rear portion that face outward toward the service street that borders the ward.

With the tything blocks, the situation is even more fractured. Only half of each tything faces "inward" toward the middle of the ward, while the other half faces away from the center. The outward-facing tything lots perceptually belong less to their ward than to the east–west boundary street they share with buildings of the adjacent ward across the street.[5] The periphery of each ward, moreover, contains as many building lots that face outward as those that face inward. This high level of ward permeability provides strong "connectivity" with neighboring wards.

Each tything lot, moreover, differs from its neighbors by its relative position on the block. The inner lots closest to the central north–south street and with a direct view of the square enjoy a better urban situation than the lots at the other end of the tything block that are nearest to the outer edge of the ward and face the side of the trust lot. In several wards, the tything lots abutting the central north–south street function as pseudo trust lots occupied by freestanding buildings that rival the scale of adjacent trust lot buildings. Such lots enjoy an ambiguous status, belonging to the linear corridor spanning the ward and connecting to adjacent wards while also reinforcing the centripetal modular focus on the center of the ward. Lacking direct contact with the square, the more peripheral of the inward-facing tything lots possess not only lesser status but also an ambiguous state of allegiance. The outermost lots of the tything block exist in a kind of urban limbo, neither truly a part of the square nor tied strongly to the north–south service street that they abut. The centric attraction of each of its multiple squares transforms the Savannah Plan into a kind of urban cocktail party in which groups of people gather around small tables for conversation. As at any such party, some of the guests turn away from their own tables to make conversation with neighboring groups, while still others float in between conversations, their attention divided.

The centripetal pull of the square within a ward is reinforced by the circuit of streets that bound the square, effectively forming a traffic roundabout. This effect became stronger in the early twentieth century when the city began to require automobile traffic to move around the squares in a counterclockwise direction (figure 70).[6] Their effectiveness as traffic circles became stronger still in the 1950s when the corners of each square were cut back with a larger radius to permit more efficient traffic movement around them.

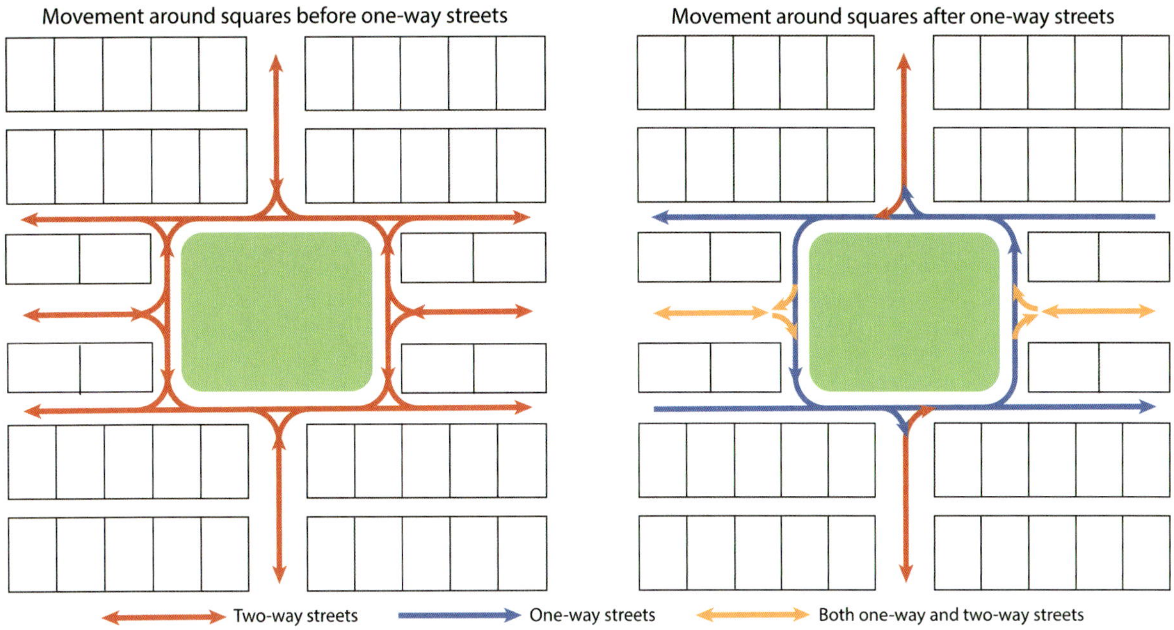

FIGURE 70. Automobile traffic patterns around a typical Savannah square before and after the implementation of one-way streets. Diagram by Robin B. Williams.

MULTICENTERED PLANNING

Despite the allure of its axial alignments and the effective inward focus of each square, Oglethorpe's plan of Savannah was conceptually and emphatically noncentralized, or perhaps multicentered. The replication of centralized squares with no ward occupying a truly central location makes the Savannah Plan striking in the history of city planning. Having the axes focus on an open green space and not a building at the center of each ward, while also multiplying their number, distinguishes Savannah from other concentric modular plans. No doubt this arrangement appealed to the Trustees as an expression of egalitarian society, where each resident had access to the commonly held public space of a square within each ward. The presence of multiple trust lots similarly downplays the hierarchical significance of any public institution.

The multicentered nature of the Savannah Plan became more pronounced as the town expanded from six wards to twenty-four. The allocation of trust lots within each ward established the principle of distributed power as part of the plan's DNA, which would remain a defining practice even as land use restrictions loosened over time. In contrast to the clustering of multiple churches on the central green in New Haven, for example, at least thirty churches and synagogues in Savannah (though not all coexistent) ended up spread across eighteen of the twenty-four wards, with no more than three houses of worship in any single ward (figure 71). At least seventy-six five-bay, center hall mansion houses have stood

FIGURE 71. Distribution of houses of worship. Diagram by Robin B. Williams.

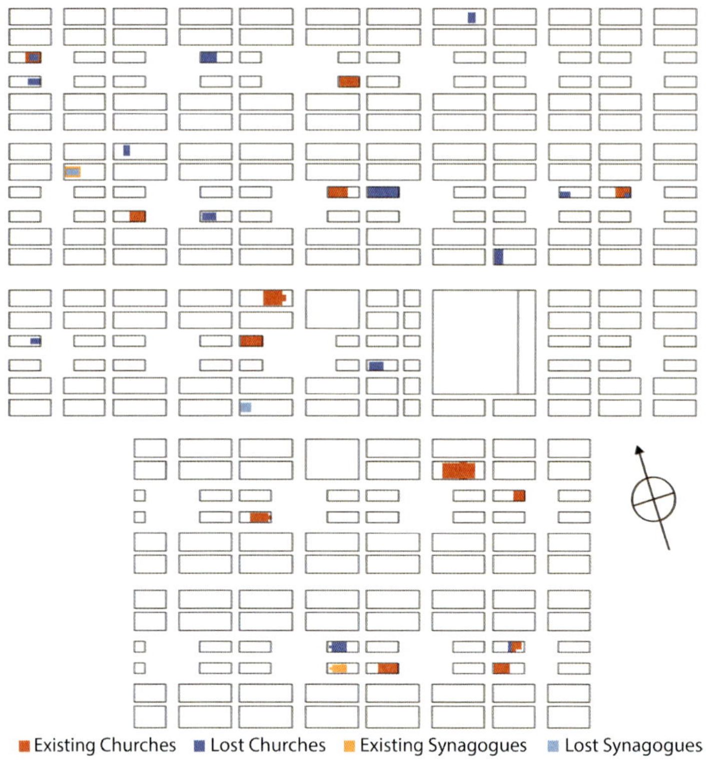

FIGURE 72. Distribution of five-bay, center hall mansion houses. Diagram by Robin B. Williams.

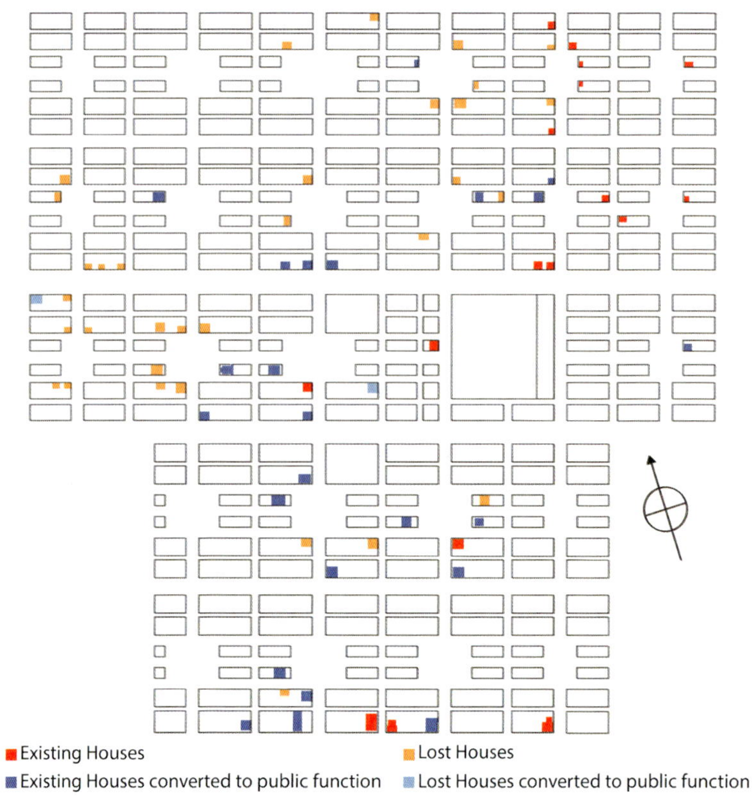

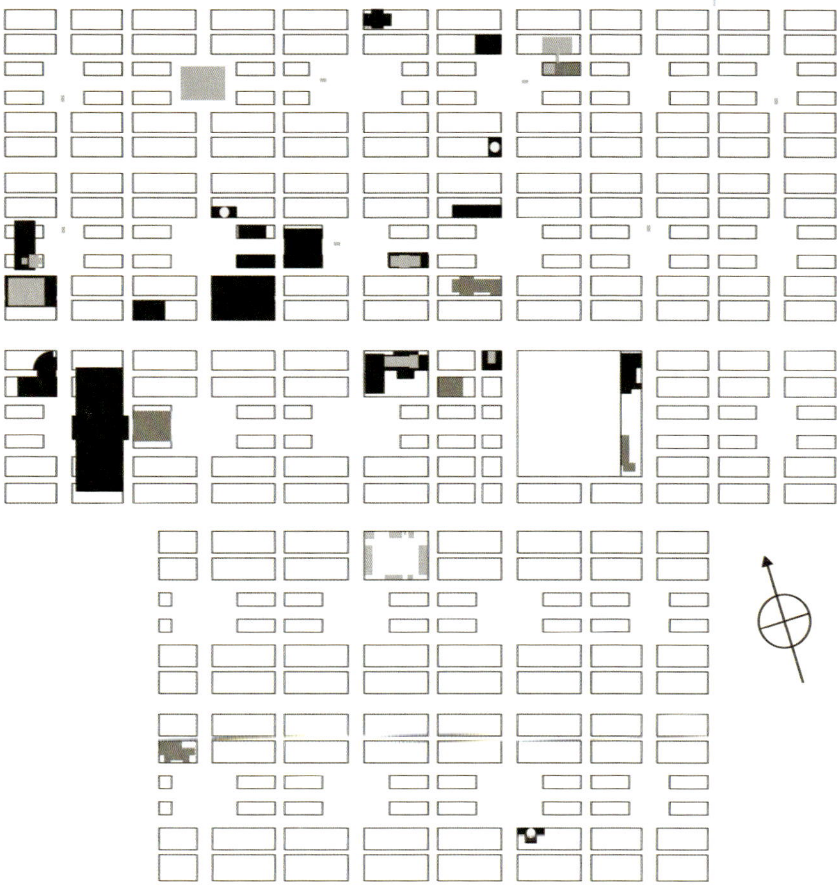

FIGURE 73. Distribution of civic buildings erected (or used) by local, state, or federal government. Diagram by Robin B. Williams.

in twenty wards within the plan area, mostly clustered around squares or fronting the major east–west boundary streets between the wards (figure 72). Of those houses, roughly a third were converted to publicly accessible functions (offices, inns, restaurants, museums) across fourteen of those wards. Civic buildings have been erected (or used) by local, state, or federal government entities in fourteen of the wards, concentrated mainly north of Liberty Street (figure 73).

A Linear and Porous Grid

The Savannah Plan is not just a network of multicentric wards; it is simultaneously a linear grid of streets. Savannah's complex street grid binds together its multicentered modular plan but also gives it a porous quality, allowing for the free flow

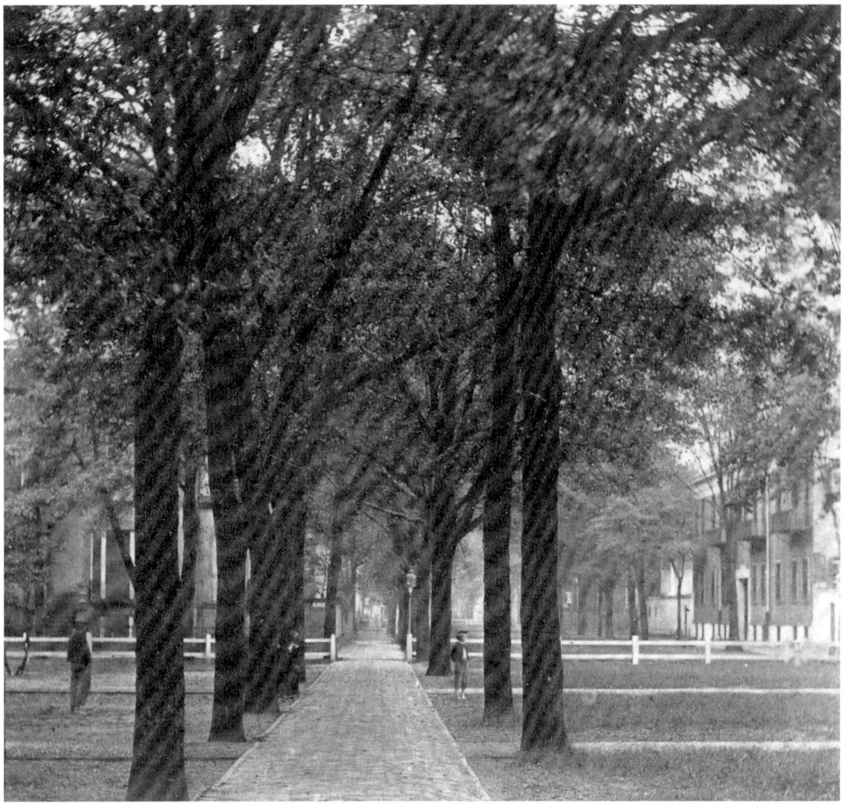

FIGURE 74. View northward through Madison Square to Bull Street showing the alignment of the path through the square with the street sidewalks. Photo by Jerome Nelson Wilson, ca. 1870. Savannah Stereoview Collection, MS 018, Jen Library Archives and Special Collections, Savannah College of Art and Design.

of people and vehicular traffic. Each street type functions differently, and yet their functions also overlap.

North–south civic streets tie the wards and squares together. Their axial alignment and breadth play a formative role in establishing the city's multicentric plan. This quality is strengthened when they intersect with a square, around which they must circumnavigate. At this point, however, the north–south civic streets overlap the narrower east–west inner civic streets. To facilitate the safe and efficient flow of automobile traffic, the city designated these inner civic streets as one-way streets in the 1920s. The southern inner civic streets of each ward were designated to flow from west to east, while their northern counterparts flow in the opposite direction. This results in a counterclockwise traffic flow around each square. Pedestrians, meanwhile, are encouraged to walk on sidewalks that pass in straight lines through the square (figure 74).

East–west streets are more numerous than north–south streets, and in general they are less affected by the multicentric pull of the Savannah Plan, contributing greatly to the porosity of its linear grid. Unlike the north–south streets, Savannah's east–west streets and lanes experienced numerous adjustments to their widths with the town's expansion southward, as municipal engineers refined the roles and usability of such corridors (figures 51, 63, 64, and 66). The prominence and coherence of these east–west corridors increase as one moves from the center of the ward due to the lessening impact of the square, establishing yet another unintended hierarchy within the plan.

The inner civic streets have an ambiguous status. They provide frontage for the tything lots that face inward, and yet despite their relatively narrow width, they have proved efficient for crosstown movement, with each pair flanking a square becoming one-way streets oriented in opposite directions. In the expansions of the plan, they were widened to forty feet in the third row of wards and to sixty feet in the fourth and fifth rows of wards.

Farthest from the center of each ward, the broad east–west boundary streets framing the north and south edges of the wards are the most strongly defined linear corridors within the Savannah Plan. These uninterrupted civic streets have equal tything lots fronting them on both sides, but each street has a different character and function.

For the east–west boundary streets and lanes, the presence of relatively equally sized buildings on both sides reinforced their effect as linear corridors more than as parts of the wards. The dissolution of the legibility of the ward structure is most apparent on Broughton Street, which more than any other street in the plan reads as an elongated outdoor room (figure 75). Anyone taking a stroll or shopping on Broughton Street would be unaware that each block is defined by buildings from two different wards, and that after every second block one encounters another set of wards. Across its full length from East Broad Street to West Broad Street (now Martin Luther King Jr. Boulevard), Broughton comprises parts of twelve wards—a fact invisible to drivers and pedestrians alike.

The porosity of the Savannah Plan derives ultimately from the quantity of its streets and their generous width. Wide streets were certainly seen as desirable by other colonial town planners. Puritan New Haven, for example, was noteworthy for the 66-foot-wide (four rods) streets defining its nine-square plan, but Savannah's five 75-foot-wide civic streets were even more prodigious. Other planned colonial towns had one or two broad streets. Philadelphia's Broad and High Streets were each 100 feet wide, as was Williamsburg's Duke of Gloucester Street, and the two intersecting streets in the 1672 "Grand Model Plan" for Charleston were each 66 feet wide. These streets acted as primary routes through their respective cities, often leading to important nodes. Colonial Savannah's five civic streets, by contrast, formed a multidirectional network of broad streets punctuated by multiple squares.

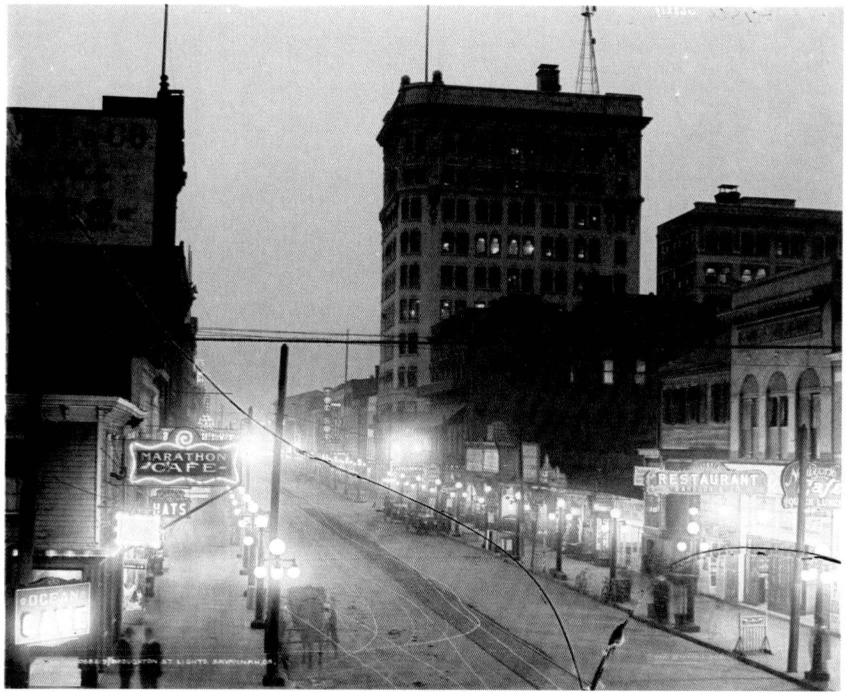

FIGURE 75. Broughton Street with streetlights at night, ca. 1900–1910. Photographic print from 8" × 10" glass negative, Detroit Publishing Company. Library of Congress, Prints and Photographs Division.

Oglethorpe's motives for endowing Savannah with so many wide streets are unknown. Fire protection may have been a concern. The City of London legislated a hierarchy of relatively wide streets for this purpose following the Great Fire of 1666.[7] Oglethorpe may also have had the hot climate in mind, with wide streets allowing for the planting of trees to provide shade; the circa 1740 map of Savannah appears to include trees lining all the civic streets and squares (figure 5). Accommodating vehicular traffic could hardly have been a concern in 1733, but the quantity and width of Savannah's streets has helped the city accommodate automobiles, trucks, and buses more easily than many other historic urban environments for both circulation and on-street parking.

The sheer quantity of Savannah's streets endows the city with a very fine-grained urbanism. As Allan Jacobs has noted, Savannah has a greater concentration of street intersections and blocks than any other American city.[8] Each Savannah ward comprises a total of twenty-six intersections: eight T-shaped intersections around the square and eighteen regular cross intersections around the perimeter of the ward. The greatest distance between two streets in the Savannah Plan is 300 feet, considerably shorter than the 675-foot block lengths in Penn and Holme's

Philadelphia plan or the 850-foot intervals of New Haven's nine-square plan. Pedestrians and motorists need not travel far in the Savannah Plan before encountering an alternate route.

Public and Private Space in Dynamic Balance

In most cities, public space within an urban environment mainly takes the form of streets and sidewalks and a rare public square, while privately owned land for building lots, parking lots, and so on constitutes a large majority of the land area. In Savannah, the relationship between public and private is markedly different, not only in terms of the high percentage of land devoted to public space but also in terms of the complexity of that relationship. Related to the inward-outward polarity of the Savannah Plan is a deft balance of public and private space. At nearly 50 percent of the land, Savannah's public space represents an extraordinarily generous endowment that few communities enjoy. But designating something as "public" versus "private" is not so simple. The squares, of course, belong to the city as a whole; they are "public" squares and may be occupied and enjoyed by individuals and groups who do not live in the neighborhood. Yet the squares can also be understood as semiprivate, "belonging" to their wards, as reflected in the ongoing tradition of residents of some wards, such as Pulaski, Warren, and Washington, gathering at 5:00 p.m. on a given evening for cocktails and conversation. Even though all of Savannah's squares are open to the public, modern-day ward captains in the form of nosy neighbors are ever vigilant for leash-law violators and reckless skateboarders, acting as "eyes on the street" to police their squares. Architectural features on houses—balconies, porches, and monumental staircases—facilitate this dialogue between private space and the public realm.

A paradoxical result of the high percentage of public space is an overall low building density at the scale of a ward. Yet the small block sizes motivated relatively dense construction within each block, as seen by the prevalence of rowhouses. The result is an eminently walkable built environment that evokes a sense of enclosure or openness depending on where one is within a ward.

Savannah's sidewalks illustrate the complex nature of the public-private relationship within the public realm. While sidewalks in many cities have shared public-private status as walkways accessible to the public, responsibility for their maintenance, such as the obligation to keep them clear of snow (in Northern cities), can sometimes fall on the adjacent property owners. In Savannah, that sense of the sidewalk as shared space is more complex and nuanced. As in other cities, residents historically paid all or part of the cost of pavement, reflected in the material change from house to house, as seen along Bay Street in 1837 in Cerveau's

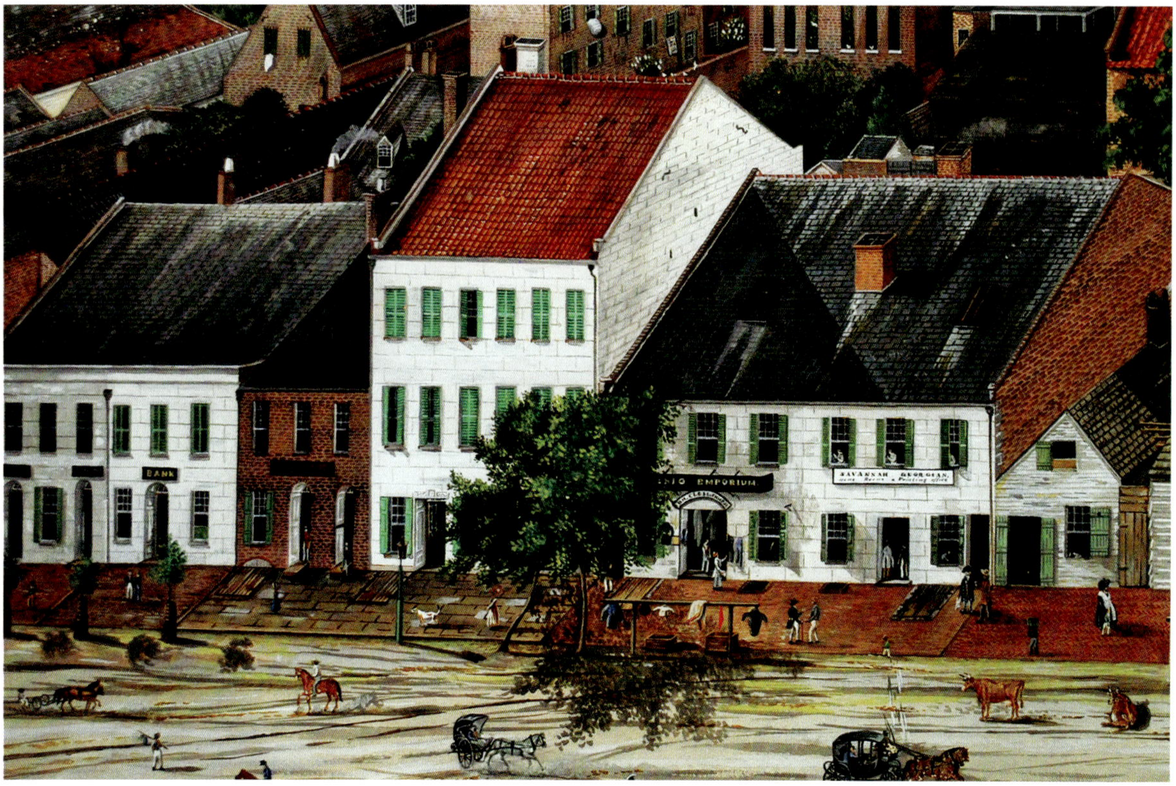

FIGURE 76. Detail of Cerveau, *Panorama of Savannah*, showing sidewalks on Bay Street. Courtesy of the Georgia Historical Society.

Panorama of Savannah, for example (figure 76).[9] Beginning in the eighteenth century, Savannah also permitted residents to erect the projecting private staircase and stoop of an elevated house on the public sidewalk by means of an encroachment agreement. The narrow strip of grass or garden between the sidewalk and street—the "tree lawn"—that developed with the introduction of street pavement in the later 1800s is fully within the public realm, but the adjacent property owner is responsible for maintaining it. Yet when one resident on East Broad Street attempted in 2013 to fence in her tree lawn as a private garden, public complaints led to the creation of a municipal tree lawn ordinance that prohibited such explicitly private use.[10]

The high degree of publicness within the Savannah Plan extends to areas that in most cities would be among the most private. By bisecting the tything blocks, the city's lanes provide both public access and visibility to the interiors of residential blocks (figure 77). Such openness also makes the rear end of private lots more accessible, allowing direct access to the lane. On a majority of tything lots, accessory

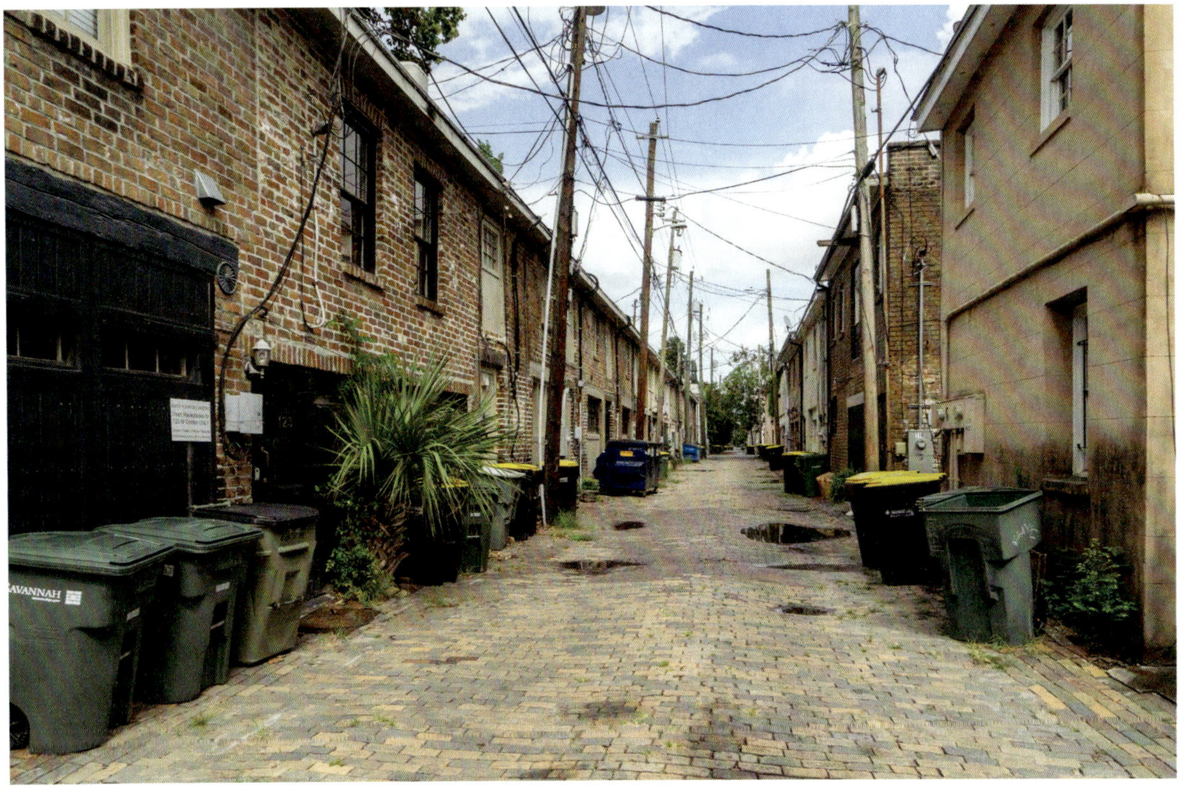

buildings in the form of carriage houses, cottages, or garages face the lane. While a carriage house gives access to both the lane and the rear yard, cottages generally front only the lane and could exist independently of the larger building oriented to the front of the lot.

FIGURE 77. Gordon Lane. Photo by Robin B. Williams, 2023.

In antebellum Savannah, this accessibility afforded enslaved African Americans, who typically lived on the lanes in carriage houses or lane houses, some freedom of movement, because the lanes connect with the north–south utilitarian streets to form their own network within the city's urban tartan (figure 51). By comparison, in nearby Charleston the large urban blocks generally lacked lanes, and access to the rear of a property came via a private driveway entered from the front of the property. In the case of a Charleston single house, this forced all movement to or from the property through the gate adjoining the front of the house, which for the enslaved population meant entering or exiting under the watchful gaze of anyone on the house's side porches. Today, Savannah's lanes allow maintenance crews, garbage and recycling collectors, and delivery trucks to provide services without needing to enter private yards or cluttering the civic frontage. Savannah's lanes accommodate the messy necessities of urban life yet stand in plain view (at least for those who care to look) where they intersect with the main civic streets.

An Experiential Plan

The Savannah Plan is a diagram of geometric relationships representing social and architectural ideals, but the diagram is not the reality of Savannah. On the ground, a pedestrian experiences the plan by walking along a public sidewalk that skirts past private stairways protruding from the ground floor of rowhouses that form the forty-foot-tall wall of a tything block, or along the brick pathways that cross a square and continue along a sidewalk interrupted by streets of varied sizes toward the next square. In both cases, trees shade the pedestrian's journey. Utilitarian corridors, by contrast, offer little or no such shade. The variety of experiences within this repetitive plan is extraordinary. Perceptive people on foot will likely notice the recurring patterns of the plan while also noting the varied responses of architects, builders, and patrons in addressing these patterns. We note also that the plan has largely remained intact over nearly three centuries, even as social, political, and architectural habits and practices have changed. The variety and vitality of our experiences are the unpredictable effects of the modular, centric, and linear patterns embedded in the Savannah Plan.

Drivers and passengers in vehicles experience a different set of choices as they move through the plan. The hierarchy of streets and their avoidance or contact with squares guide the path chosen. While pedestrians on a central civic street can continue on a straight path across a square, vehicles must skirt the square, forcing them to slow down. Even with the corners of the squares being cut back with a broader radius in the 1960s, vehicular movement around the squares remains slow enough to negate the need for traffic lights or even stop signs. Motorists wishing to move more quickly through the town learn to use the service corridors running between the wards, which were changed into one-way arterial streets at the same time. Bicycle paths are now being inserted along some of these linear corridors. The Savannah Plan continues to adapt to changing modes of movement, offering a growing number of ways to experience the city.

SECTION TWO CONCLUSION

A GRID LIKE NO OTHER

Oglethorpe's distinctive town plan is proof that grids can be much more than dull blueprints of land division. And it held its own for more than a hundred years. . . . Among the densely gridded towns of America, the city stood out as a picture of gracious urbanity, and does still.
—SPIRO KOSTOF, 1987

Of all the colonial plans, this was not only the most sophisticated, but also the most long-lived.
—WITOLD RYBCZYNSKI, 2010

Like a family recipe that relies on conventional ingredients, the Savannah Plan uses elements common to most cities—straight streets, squares, and rectangular blocks—yet they come together in a way unlike any other place. The plan belongs to a tradition of gridded city planning that extends back over 2,500 years, a tradition that shaped the majority of North America's cities. Even in its modest six-ward form laid out between 1733 and 1735, however, Savannah possessed qualities that set it apart from other gridded cities.

Among the ways it differed from other planned cities was the scale of its components. As political administrative units, its wards were individually too small to serve as autonomous neighborhoods that could support all the needs of their residents. As a result, the Savannah Plan necessitated an interdependence across multiple wards. Savannah's block sizes likewise are smaller than those in most cities. This was a result of the greater-than-normal allocation of land to public streets, which cover more than half the land area. Indeed, Oglethorpe employed a multiplicity of 75-foot-wide civic streets at a time when most streets were half that width. The expansion of the plan between 1791 and 1851 only accentuated its fine-grained scale, with individual blocks as small as 60 by 60 feet, and consolidated blocks as large as 222½ by 300 feet, which is still not a large city block compared to many other cities. The ward expansions saw the introduction of even wider streets, particularly South Broad (Oglethorpe Avenue) and Liberty.

Many commentators and travelers have noted, with varying degrees of admiration or disdain, how American cities are predominantly laid out according to a grid plan. Some, such as Dell Upton, have attempted to explain this predilection as a sign of an American spatial imagination, suggesting that the grid embodies a republican and mercantilist understanding of the world, informed by an Enlightenment desire for systematic order.[1] Orthogonal grids dominate the layout of American cities built throughout the nineteenth century. The renowned Commissioners' Plan for New York City is held up by John Reps as "the apotheosis of the gridiron," with its twelve avenues crossed by 155 streets yielding 2,028 uniform blocks, as Dutch architect Rem Koolhaas wryly noted.[2] In an attempt to vindicate and celebrate the achievement of surveyor John Randel Jr. and the New York commissioners on the bicentennial of their plan, the Museum of the City of New York hosted an impressive exhibition of maps and surveying equipment in 2011. The exhibition was confidently entitled *The Greatest Grid*.[3] We respectfully wish to contest this superlative title, claiming not that the Savannah Plan can compete with the immensity of Manhattan's gridded island but that the subtleties of its interwoven tartan of streets, blocks, and squares exceed those of any other American grid plan.

The Savannah Plan also informed a complexity of spatial arrangements and experiences that has few counterparts in other cities. Combining centripetal and centrifugal forces of the modular concentric grid tradition with linear paths of a conventional orthogonal grid, the plan further complicates matters by replicating the central focal point many times over to create a multicentric yet uncentered result.

The plan's unusually small-scale blocks, generous public space, elasticity, and spatial complexities inform the city's architectural developments. While climate, external building traditions, and technology all had a hand in shaping the architecture of Savannah's downtown area, it is our assertion that the plan also played a significant role, and this helps account for the city's harmonious and cohesive built environment, an example we believe to be highly unusual and potentially informative of how an urban plan can be an active design agent.

SECTION THREE

A SYMPHONY WITHOUT A SOLOIST

THE ARCHITECTURE OF THE SAVANNAH PLAN

The sheer number of distinguished buildings is astonishing for a city of Savannah's size.
—JOHN BERENDT, 1997

Architecture, as the music of the plastic arts, has, just as music, a rhythmic, harmonic, and melodic element.
—FRIEDRICH VON SCHELLING, 1809

For those seeking spectacular displays of architecture, Savannah is likely to disappoint. No truly exceptional masterpiece can be found. None of its buildings is a virtuoso performance of architectural design. Stylistically, Savannah's architecture is largely conventional, exemplifying trends and motifs made popular elsewhere. What is exceptional, however, are the abundant quantity and consistent quality of its historic buildings. With well over one thousand "contributing" historic buildings, the city's historic urban core was designated by the National Park Service as a National Historic Landmark District in 1966, and it is still counted as one of the nation's largest. But it is not merely the quantity or even the quality of its "historic" buildings that demands our attention here; it is how those buildings function together as a complete architectural fabric—or, to use a musical analogy, a symphonic performance, with no dominant soloists in the form of internationally recognizable iconic buildings. Our analysis would remain incomplete, however, if we failed to consider the profuse landscape elements that line the streets and fill the squares. The city's trees regularly receive more notice than do its buildings. The musical mode of Savannah's architectural composition is decidedly pastoral.

The Savannah Plan is the musical score orchestrating the performance of this architectural symphony. Its buildings and landscape elements, understood in this way, are the instruments, and their architects and builders are the musicians. In musical performance, the interpretation of a historic composition depends on the skill and temperament of the performers and the preferences and predilections of their time period. So it is with Savannah's architecture. The plan remains essentially fixed, but its architectural interpretation evolves. To understand and appreciate the complete symphony requires familiarity not only with the score but also with the modes and methods of its performance. Here, it must be remembered that architects, like musicians, are trained to practice within a tradition. The builders and designers of Savannah's architecture have worked for almost three centuries within the typological, material, and ornamental traditions of their predecessors. However, our analogy fails to account for the vital difference between the temporal art of music and the spatial art of architecture. Savannah's architectural symphony is cumulative and ongoing. Its buildings are not one-time performances. The stylistic preferences of many designers over many years collaborate to form a synthetic yet evolving whole. For those interested in how buildings can be designed in consort with one another under the orchestration of a strong and compelling plan, the study of Savannah delivers rich rewards.

Designing with Constraints

Preeminently, the plan acts as a constraint. Its fine-grained pattern of small lots and small blocks, for example, prevents the introduction of the kind of big-box architecture that prevails in many other American cities today, including in suburban Savannah. Its numerous streets and squares provide extensive street frontage for its building lots, conferring Savannah's architecture with a greater public presence than is found in most of today's urbanism. The rhythmic, hierarchical orientation and sequencing of these building lots choreographs Savannah's architecture, silently coaxing buildings to "face" toward or "turn away" from certain streets and squares. Hierarchies and adjacencies in the plan shape and determine the location, alignment, and level of ornamentation of buildings throughout the city.

Like all cities, Savannah contains a predictable assortment of building types, including houses, churches, and civic and commercial structures, among others. How they were designed and are dispersed is the result of a dialogue between the plan, which establishes the ground rules, and each architect, who brings shared notions of typology and stylistic trends. With its simple distinction between trust and tything lots, the Savannah Plan was initially "zoned" for two basic building types: public and private. As the city grew, this tacit zoning code became jumbled: private houses were built on public trust lots and public buildings were built on private tything lots. Today, nearly half of the trust lots are occupied by private residences, while more than half of the tything lots are occupied by nonresidential uses. Commerce was given no explicit place in the original plan, but retail, commercial, and entertainment-oriented buildings have found their places, scattered throughout the plan. Despite this typological reshuffling, however, the insistent and peculiar discipline of the plan exerts its will on the design of the city's buildings today as it has done since the eighteenth century.

The Architectural "Rules" of Tything Lots and Trust Lots

Tything lots constitute the essence of Savannah's private realm. Intended as the residential domain of original freeholders, the 60-by-90-foot rectangular area (5,400 square feet) of tything lots (expanded to 60 by 100 feet south of Liberty Street) continues to the present day to afford modest but ample room for residential architecture in a wide variety of configurations, even as more than half of the plan's tything lots are now occupied by commercial, institutional, and even industrial buildings. Many tything lot buildings have served multiple uses during their lifespan. A majority of Savannah's tything lots have been modified in their dimensions. Many have been subdivided into smaller lots, typically 30 or 20 feet wide (producing lots of 2,700 and 1,800 square feet, respectively, the latter among the smallest urban lots in American cities).[1] Others have merged to form larger lots, usually as multiples of the 60-foot lots. Within the modular structure of each ward, half of the lots in each tything "face" inward toward the square; the other half face outward toward an east–west street that connects them with an adjacent ward (figure 69). Because they are grouped in rows, tything lots lack the autonomy of a trust lot, and because of the latent hierarchies of the plan, their place in the block matters in the way that the plan shapes the architecture that occupies them. Amid this variety, certain building types and architectural features develop on tything lots that make them distinctive products of the Savannah Plan. Continuity and adaptability, characteristics of the plan in general, are also hallmarks of its tything lot buildings.

Trust lots are inherently public parcels, initially held in trust for civic uses by the Georgia Trustees during the early years of the colony. Their designation is made manifest not only by their name but also by their design as autonomous blocks fronting the public realm on all four sides—an altogether rare level of autonomy from neighboring buildings. Trust lot buildings normally face the public realm on the short side nearest the square. Like tything lots, their "back" sides are typically occupied by service entrances, carriage houses, or private gardens. The "inner" side of a trust lot—the one facing the wide central trust street—is typically treated as a more public facade than the "outer" side, which faced a much narrower street in the original wards. The primacy of the inner face of trust lots was recognized by the mapmaker of the eighteenth-century Moravian plan (figure 5), who showed rows of trees wrapping around the front and inner sides of each trust lot. These inner sides would accommodate secondary entrances, and in a few cases a building would face the trust street rather than the square.

The standard trust lot dimensions of 60 by 180 feet impose what is an undeniably challenging design constraint. A buildable floor area of 10,800 square feet is more than adequate for anyone constructing a private house and for many commercial and public enterprises, but the 3:1 oblong proportion introduces both limitations and opportunities. So prescriptive are the location, orientation, and size of the trust lots that they have generated distinctively Savannahian versions of the building types that occupy them, most notably the frequent combination of a house of worship coupled to a rear education building.

Apart from a few exceptional cases, trust lot facades that stretch across the full sixty-foot frontage are composed of five symmetrical bays with a centered primary entrance. While the central hall plan is dominant for trust lot buildings, public or private, some buildings place a tower or other projecting architectural feature to emphasize the leading inside corner, reflecting the "pull" toward the center of the square. More peculiarly, trust lot houses and churches are often elevated on a partial or fully raised basement, while commercial and governmental buildings are built closer to grade level.

Most of Savannah's trust lots have been subdivided into multiple properties and thus cannot be analyzed as unified design compositions. The "front" buildings of subdivided trust lots generally follow the patterns we have described, but the buildings behind them do not. In many cases, the back half of a trust lot has been divided into rowhouses running perpendicular to the long axis of the trust lot. In such cases, the "pull" of the central trust street is countered by the impulse to orient the row toward the rowhouses across from the "outer" edge of the trust lot. In later wards where the central trust street is equal in width to that of the inner civic streets flanking the trust lots, no such clear hierarchy exists, resulting in a few wards in which the trust street becomes a kind of lane, servicing back doors and automobile parking (figure 95).

Trust lot buildings jockey politely for attention within the rhythmic beat of the Savannah Plan. Tything lot buildings establish its ongoing melody line. Together they form a structured urban arrangement that has fostered inventive architectural responses comparable to musical variations on a theme. The architectural music of the Savannah Plan, however, is produced by individual buildings playing within the traditions and rules of their building type in a structured landscape setting. It is to these that we turn next.

CHAPTER FIVE

HOUSES

If (as the philosophers maintain) the city is like some large house, and the house is in turn like some small city, cannot the various parts of the house . . . be considered miniature buildings?

—LEON BATTISTA ALBERTI, 1452

Savannah is a town made of houses. That might sound banal, but in most great cities it's the public buildings which impress. Savannah's houses are architecture on a human scale, an idealised version of the 18th-century Age of Reason. Or perhaps the opposite of that—the ideal rendered real. Either way, it's hard not to gaze at the shuttered windows and say to yourself: "Yes, this is how people are supposed to live."

—ANTHONY McGOWAN, 2010

The private house is the fundamental building type of Savannah. Coming in a variety of forms and costumes that have evolved over time, Savannah's domestic architecture is nevertheless unified in its basic forms, a unity attributable largely to the power of the Savannah Plan. No building type is more profoundly influenced by the plan. None reflects the complex urban and architectural dialogue that takes place between public space and private property more clearly. Today Savannah's houses occupy both tything and trust lots, and as in most cities, they appear in a variety of configurations—from detached single-family homes to rowhouses and multifamily blocks. Yet the residential architecture of Savannah—especially its elevated rowhouses, single houses, and trust lot mansion houses—is sufficiently distinctive that it deserves recognition as a local form, analogous to the Charleston single house, the New York brownstone, and the New Orleans shotgun.

Savannah's houses come in four main types: the cottage, the rowhouse, the single house, and the mansion house. The origins of each lie outside Savannah, as they found their initial expressions as an echo of conventional patterns from other cities. All but the single house type saw their earliest manifestations built at grade, but by the 1790s rowhouses and mansion houses began to be elevated, with an aboveground or raised basement and a prominent exterior staircase; by the mid-nineteenth century even cottages were following this pattern. The Savannah Plan is the principal driver of these architectural developments, as house carpenters, builders, and, later, architects responded to its constraints. Beyond typology, a Savannahian language of design is clearly discernible in the massing, scale, materials, design composition, and ornamental details of Savannah's houses, a language that is continually evolving as it is shaped by local construction and design practices and, of course, by the city's distinctive plan. The result is a variety of expressions of each of these four residential types. As Savannah grew in the nineteenth and twentieth centuries, its houses became larger, more complex, and more densely fitted into the Savannah Plan, though their relative uniformity and local character remain to the present day.

The Savannah Cottage

The humblest of Savannah's four housing types, the Savannah cottage was also the first to emerge and, ironically, the least shaped by the plan. Although more vulnerable to demolition than other housing types, it never disappeared as a viable housing option for residents with modest means. In fact, the cottage type may be as relevant as ever in light of recent interest in the tiny house phenomenon and the increasing need for affordable housing options. Typical of Savannah's architectural traditions in general, cottages nimbly adapted to changing needs and urban situations (figure 78). The first houses in Savannah were small and uniform in design. The 1734 Gordon View depicts eighty-seven identical cottages, all of them freestanding side-gabled houses, and all centered on the front edge of their respective tything lots like the houses on a Monopoly gameboard (figures 9 and 78A). Thomas Causton, in a 1733 letter, describes them as being "of one floor, only a cock-loft over it sufficient to hold two beds, the lower part will make one large room and two smaller ones. . . . [The houses] are all of timber and very few have glass windows or brick chimneys."[1] Francis Moore recorded in 1735 that the houses are "a Frame of sawed Timber, 24 by 16 foot, floored with rough Deals, the Sides with feather-edged Boards unplained [*sic*] and the Roof shingled."[2] In form, they were similar to the small wood-frame cottages in other English colonies, such as those preserved at Colonial Williamsburg. Among Savannah's oldest surviving examples of the basic cottage form is a pair of houses on East York Street near Greene Square—the Susannah R. Clarke House (1801–8), and its smaller neighbor to the east, the Edward White House (1812) (figure 79). Both are loosely symmetrical one-story wood-frame vernacular cottages with moderately steep side-gabled roofs, each with a single small dormer.

The earliest extant house in Savannah—the Christian Camphor House (122 East Oglethorpe Avenue), dating to the 1760s—began as a one-story cottage (figure 78B). Only a few feet wider than the first houses, its frame and clapboard construction and its two-rooms-plus-loft configuration show continuity into the era

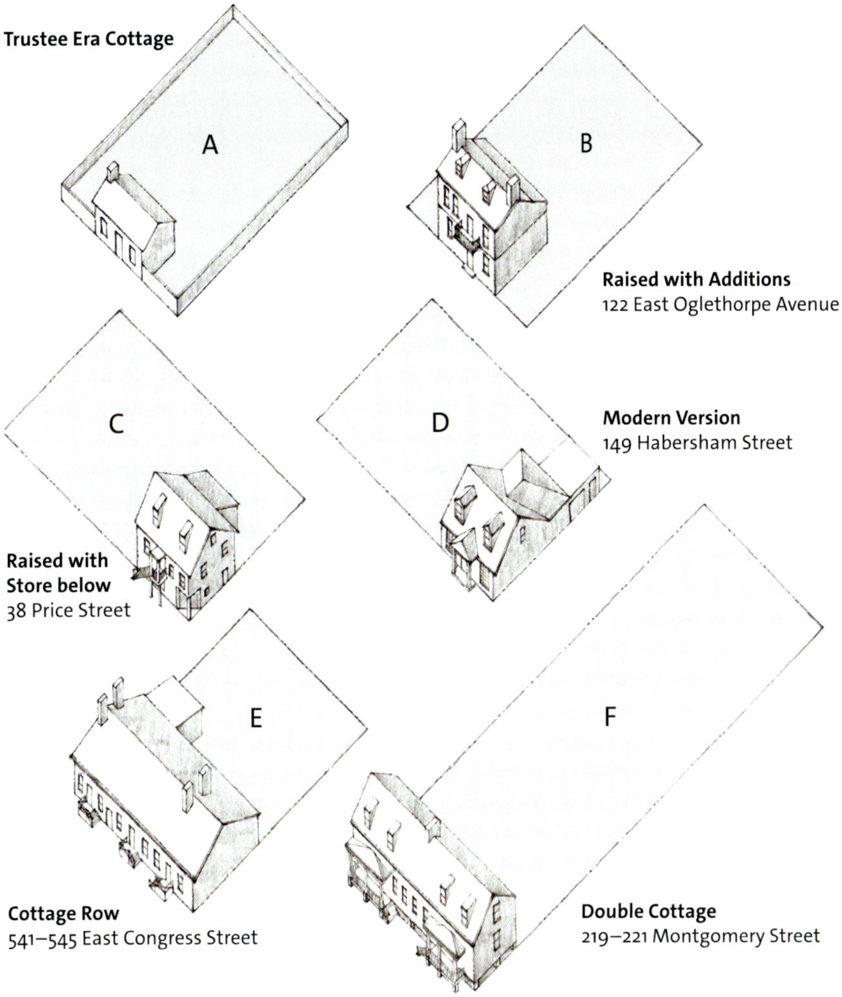

FIGURE 78. Six variants of the Savannah cottage. Each gray rectangle indicates the cottage's position on a tything or trust lot. Drawing by Hamilton Brindley.

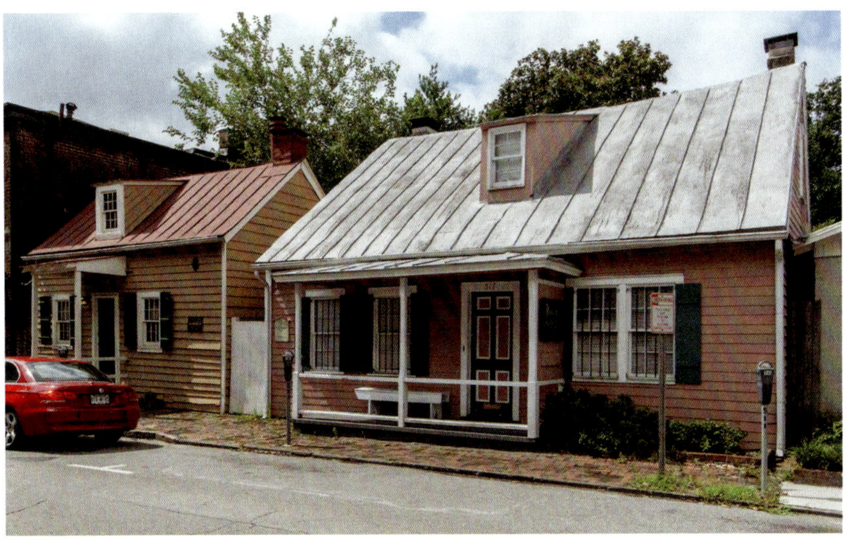

FIGURE 79. (*left to right*) The Edward White House (1812) and the Susannah R. Clarke House (1801–8), at 519 and 517 East York Street, respectively. Photo by Robin B. Williams, 2014.

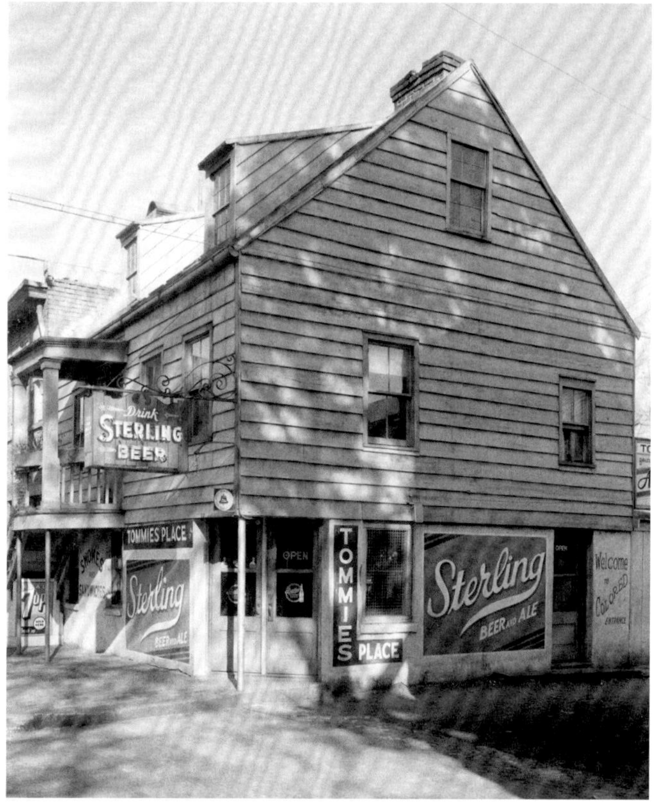

FIGURE 80. An 1841 Savannah cottage is perched above a corner sandwich shop at 38 Price Street in this 1939 photograph by Frances Benjamin Johnston for the Carnegie Survey of the Architecture of the South. Note the "Colored" entrance at the rear. Library of Congress, Prints and Photographs Division.

of Crown rule. The Camphor House originally sat at grade but was raised one full story above a brick ground floor in 1871. It was also expanded on the backside by continuing the roof gable in a saltbox configuration, a pattern found on several other early Savannah houses.[3] Other raised wooden cottages with aboveground brick basements adopted the exterior staircase to an elevated entrance introduced with rowhouses and mansion houses, reflecting the plan's influence and an evident desire to convey a sense of higher status.[4] A striking variant at 38 Price Street involved an 1841 cottage perched atop a stucco-covered sandwich shop with a chamfered corner entrance, as documented in a 1939 photograph (figures 78C and 80). The house stands today, though the shop and signage are gone.[5]

Savannah's cottages, like the larger rowhouses that would follow, were frequently erected in pairs as double cottages with symmetrical mirrored entrances that were either centered for each house or offset in the manner of a side hall plan. The Timothy Bonticou Double House (ca. 1815; moved 1971) at 418–420 East State Street follows the former arrangement of a centrally located door for each house. A larger and more grandly situated double cottage, predating 1888, once occupied the northwest trust lot facing Elbert Square (figure 78F).[6] The structure's wood-frame, side-gabled form was typical of Savannah cottages, while its set of three front windows per house followed the pattern of larger cottages, such as the Camphor House. Perhaps because of its prominent site, this pair of cottages had wider-than-normal stoops spanning both a window and the door. Other variations or longer rows of wooden Savannah cottages may have existed but have disappeared due to their modest stature. Unusual for its brick construction, a row of three conjoined cottages (evenly dividing the sixty-foot lot) survives at 541–545 East Congress Street; each cottage follows the pattern of two windows divided by a central door that is fronted by a low stoop accessed by steps rising parallel to the facade (figure 78E).

One-story and one-and-a-half-story cottages were numerous throughout the late nineteenth century, mostly lining the lanes as documented by Sanborn fire insurance maps. Different from carriage houses, which functioned as garages with habitable space above and logically connected to the service function of the lanes, cottages oriented to lanes provided lower-income residents with an independent housing option. The 1884 Sanborn map of Savannah, which surveyed only the northern half of the downtown area, labeled lower-income houses as "shanties" and distinguished those occupied by African Americans as "Negro shanties" or "Negro tenements" (figure 81). Of the fourteen wards surveyed in the 1884

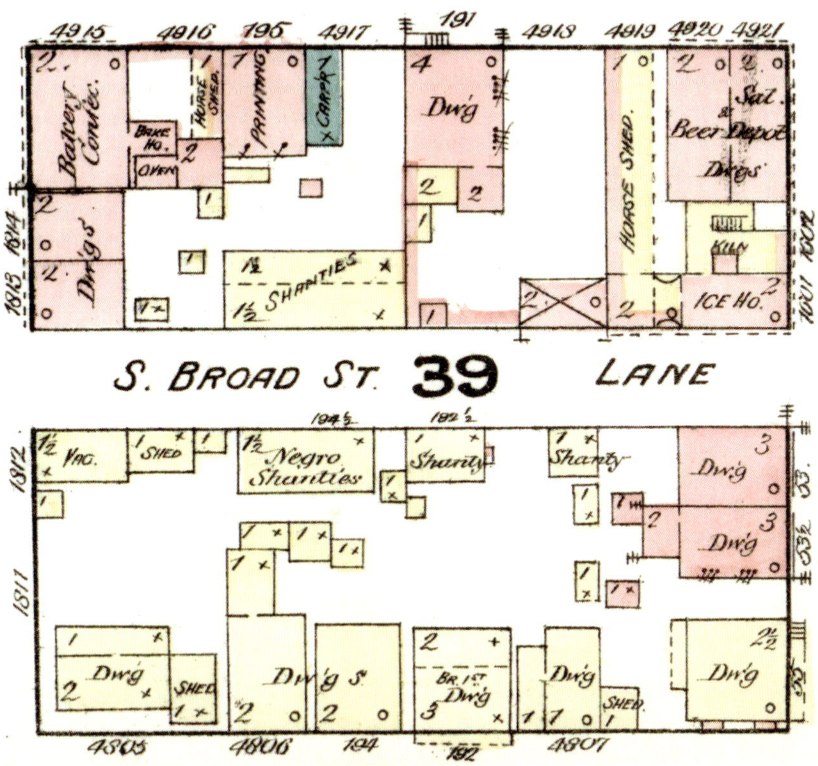

FIGURE 81. Detail of plate 12 of *Sanborn Fire Insurance Map from Savannah, Chatham County, Georgia* showing "Negro shanties." Sanborn Map Company, March 1884. Library of Congress, Geography and Map Division.

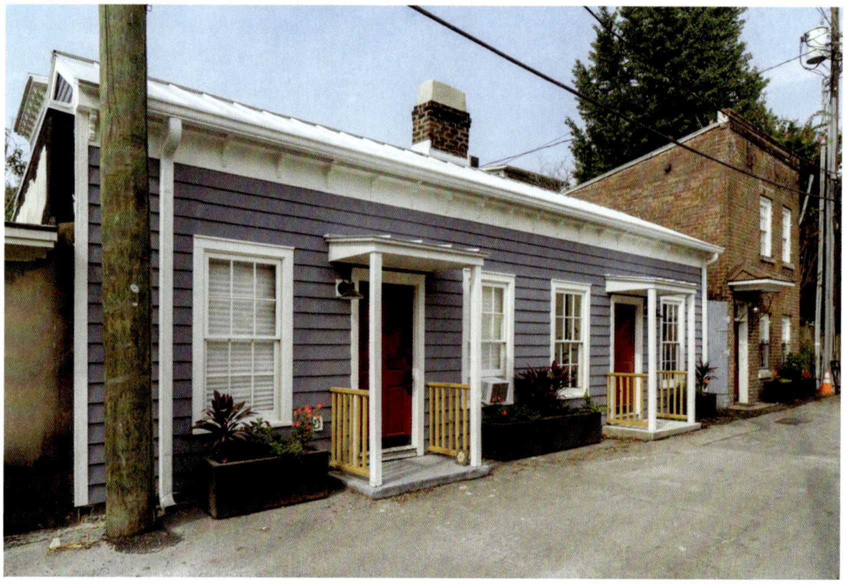

FIGURE 82. Savannah double cottage at 317A and 317B East York Lane. Photo by Robin B. Williams, 2023.

Sanborn map (ten completely and four partially), eleven included such shanties as one-story wood-frame cottages. This illustrates how lower-income housing was not restricted to one area but existed throughout the Savannah Plan. A higher concentration of shanties, however, can be found in the expansion wards on the plan's periphery, a further reflection of the plan's overall hierarchy.

At least one pair of lane houses labeled "shanties" on the 1884 Sanborn map still stands—the double cottage at 317A and 317B East York Lane (figure 82), which is among the rare surviving cottage types within the plan. Despite their modest size and location, the paired cottages display formal symmetry, with a central door flanked by a pair of windows (just like the cottages erected under Oglethorpe) and a bracketed cornice. Such architectural characteristics distinguish them from purely utilitarian buildings (let alone crudely built shacks such as the label "shanty" implies). Yet these cottages, along with the neighboring two-story brick house at 315 East York Lane (whose brickwork shows no sign of a large opening, indicating it never served as a carriage house), have entrances barely inches above grade, reinforcing the lower status of lane housing.

Beginning as the city's essential house form, the Savannah cottage is a persistent reminder of Savannah's modest and egalitarian origins. Variations of the Savannah cottage continued to be built into the mid-twentieth century (figure 78D). Their adaptive embrace of the trend toward elevated and double house forms and rows of identical residential units with covered entry stairs projecting into the public sidewalk show them to be a small but key component in the city's essential kit of residential types.

The Savannah Rowhouse

The most prevalent architectural form within the downtown area is the Savannah rowhouse, a noteworthy product of the city's growing prosperity after 1800 and a variant of a building type that proliferated in growing American cities to the north, such as Boston, Providence, Philadelphia, New York, and Baltimore in the early Federal period.[7] As in these other cities, Savannah's rowhouses come in a variety of expressions. We shall consider three basic variants: the detached rowhouse; the double house (the smallest row); and the row of three or more (figure 83). What unifies these variants is their simple boxy shape, narrow footprint, and side hall entrance. A majority are distinguished further by an elevated entrance accessed by a prominent exterior stair rising parallel to the facade (as opposed to the perpendicular stairs common in New York and elsewhere).

With the rowhouse becoming the city's most identifiable housing form, we encounter another paradox in the Savannah Plan. The conceptualization of Savannah's public squares undoubtedly owed some debt to the residential squares of London, and yet, as noted earlier, the founding Georgia Trustees favored low-density, individualized dwellings and prohibited speculative real estate investment altogether. Under Crown rule, however, speculative residential real estate development appears to have grown, though mostly in the peripheral "suburbs" of the Trustees' Garden and Yamacraw zones to the east and west of the Savannah Plan. When the town began to develop new Oglethorpe-style wards in the Common

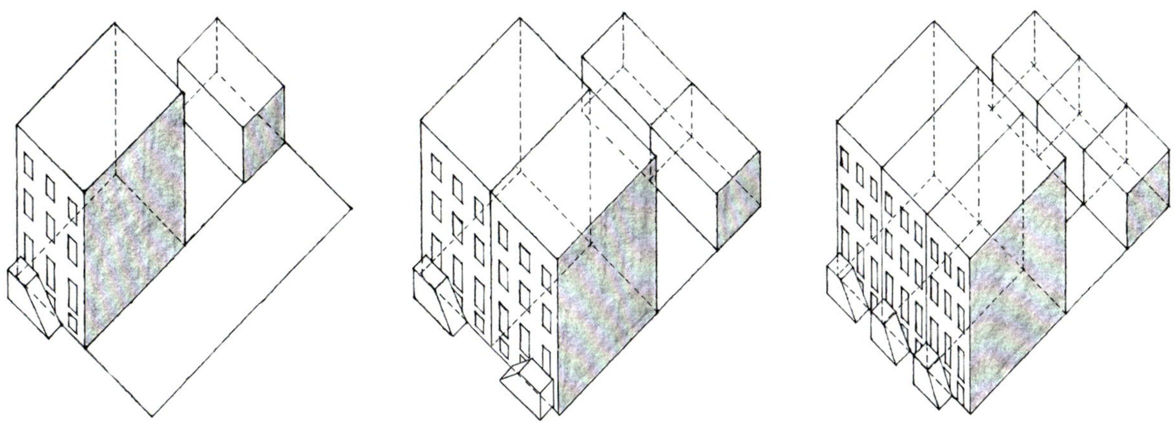

FIGURE 83. Three variants of the elevated Savannah rowhouse on a sixty-by-ninety-foot tything lot. Drawing by Hamilton Brindley.

during the 1790s, it did so for the explicit purpose of raising capital to cover municipal expenses.[8] To facilitate this, the city offered properties on a quit-rent system, which allowed purchasers to pay in annual installments, much like mortgage payments. Investors could buy on credit and then sell their property "with improvements." Dividing tything lots into two or three properties by building uniform rows of attached units was an attractive strategy for real estate developers seeking to maximize the return on investment. Urban walls of contiguous houses were certainly not part of the original vision for Savannah, but they became one of its defining architectural features. Savannah's rowhouses are like Savannah's urban plan: They are inherently uniform, and yet subtle hierarchies, telling details, and lyrical elements emerge in their architectural design.

Savannah's rowhouses are tall and narrow boxes, typically three or four stories or thirty-five to forty-five feet in height and either twenty or thirty feet wide, that are situated along the front edge of their lot. Most rowhouse facades are divided into three equal bays (as they are in most other cities whose rowhouses derive from Georgian English models), though variants of two or four bays do occur, with tall sash windows evenly spaced both vertically and horizontally, creating a solid-to-void ratio from 80:20 to 65:35. Most Savannah rowhouses have a low sloping side-gabled roof hidden by parapets, enhancing their boxlike purity of form. While rowhouses are most often paired double houses or rows of three or more units, detached versions can also be found. These were usually built in close proximity to and in alignment with their multiunit counterparts and can be read as part of them, though some freestanding rowhouses were built with elaborate side porches facing private gardens (what we call single houses). Most of Savannah's rowhouses are constructed of load-bearing brick walls, sometimes stuccoed and scored to imitate ashlar masonry, though clapboard-covered wood-frame construction occurs as well. An open work yard between the main house and its carriage house was used by servants to perform household chores.

National trends in the adoption of popular styles of architecture are plainly evident in Savannah's rowhouses, as one sees numerous examples ranging across the nineteenth century—from Federal style to Greek Revival, Italianate to Queen Anne—resulting in some variation in facade treatments, but the Savannah rowhouse is made distinctive by its elevated entry. Savannah's earliest rowhouses are nearly identical to their Federal-style counterparts in Northern cities. The four-bay, three-story detached rowhouse at 123 West Oglethorpe Avenue, built circa 1820, is of this kind, with its red brick and simple round-arched entrance one step above grade (the second entrance was adapted from a window) (figure 84).[9] Other Savannah rowhouses of the same era, however, chose a different approach, elevating the entry level a full story above grade. The detached Federal-style wood-frame house built around 1809 by Frederick Ball, another New Jersey builder, on

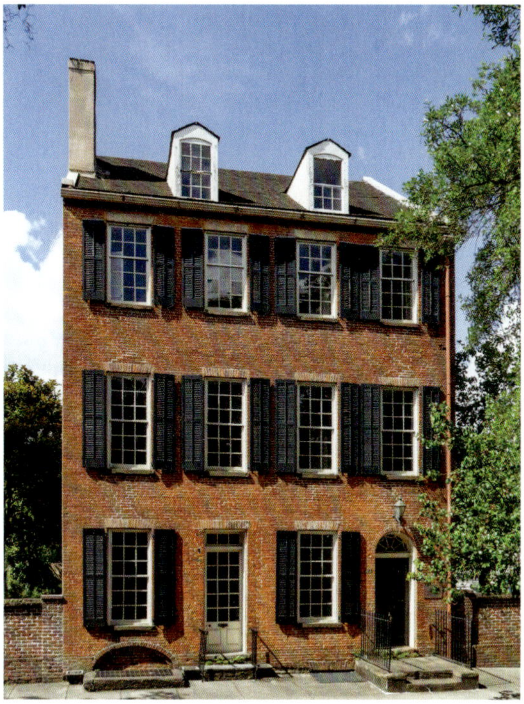

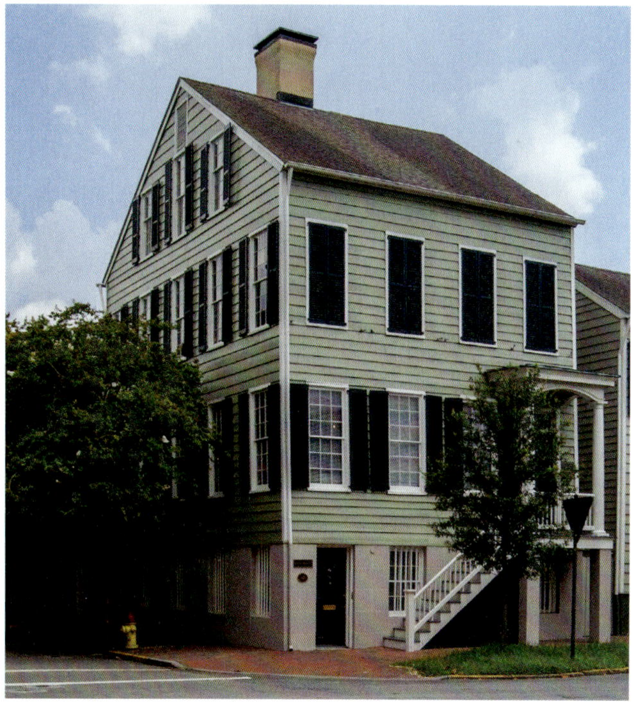

Columbia Square (136 Habersham Street) exemplifies this trend, which became one of the city's defining characteristics (figure 85).

Approximately 70 percent of downtown Savannah's roughly six hundred rowhouses are elevated one full story above the street and accessed by a stair rising parallel to the facade. Examples of rowhouses with partially raised "English" basements are prevalent in London, New York, Philadelphia, and Baltimore, where the stairs rise and descend perpendicular to the sidewalk, but full-story, aboveground basements are less common. Built in 1882, the two rows forming Sylvan Terrace in the Washington Heights section of New York are the closest analogues to Savannah's pervasive form, but similar examples are rare in American cities. So what accounts for the predilection of Savannah builders for the elevated form with a partially or fully raised basement and a prominent projecting exterior stair rising parallel to the facade?

It's tempting to point to the use of elevated ground floors accessed by prominent stairs that had become a hallmark of elite residential architecture in South Carolina as a model for urban homebuilders in Savannah. This Lowcountry tradition could be attributed to the land being near sea level and prone to flooding, but this is clearly not the case in Savannah's historic center, which stands on high ground

FIGURE 84. (*Left*) Samuel J. Brown House, 123 West Oglethorpe Avenue (moved from its original location across the street), 1821. Photo by Robin B. Williams, 2024.

FIGURE 85. (*Right*) Frederick Ball House, 136 Habersham Street, 1809. Photo by Jeffrey Klee, 2006. Courtesy of Jeffrey Klee.

at least forty feet above the river. It's also tempting to assume that being elevated helped houses take advantage of cooling breezes, which certainly influenced the development of Charleston's single houses. But Savannah, being considerably farther from the coast and more densely treed, does not benefit from ocean breezes to the same degree. Rising above dirt streets is also an unlikely reason, as all cities had such streets.

Rather, a combination of the orchestrating role of the plan and a reflection of economic status gave rise to Savannah's elevated house configuration. With the typical tything lot measuring only ninety feet deep, elevating the house provided room in the raised basement for utilitarian activities such as cooking, washing, and storage, which in the antebellum era were normally carried out by enslaved staff. Elevating this level also provided direct access to the service space from the front street—a practical advantage since both the main house and the carriage house at the rear typically filled the width of the lot, limiting ready access to the service area in between.

Being elevated also served as a status symbol. A majority of Savannah's elevated rowhouses are in the city's most fashionable wards closest to Bull Street and descend in number and height as one moves away from Bull Street. Our survey of extant downtown elevated houses revealed that more than three-quarters stand within the wealthier central six blocks flanking Bull Street, while less than a fourth of them stand in the outermost six blocks.[10] Anyone who climbs the stairs of a Savannah rowhouse immediately understands their exalted and privileged status as they are rewarded with commanding views of the public realm.

EXCURSUS: STAIRCASE DESIGN IN THE PUBLIC REALM

Parallel stairs are not unique to Savannah; nonetheless, their prevalence and variety are striking. Indeed, no other city can claim the feature as so defining a characteristic. Just as the relative shallowness of residential tything lots within the Savannah Plan led to houses meeting the zero lot line and to the establishment of a raised basement and elevated principal story (called the first floor in Savannah), the correspondingly wide public streets permitted generous sidewalks and private encroachments thereon.

From an early date, the distance a house could encroach into the public realm was calibrated to the width of the street. In March 1819, the city passed an ordinance to "fix the number of feet, which persons may occupy in the streets, squares, and Lanes, of the City for Steps, Porticos, and Railings, or Enclosures."[11] The ordinance superseded earlier legislation dating back to the first planning regulations of 1760. While authorizing the right to build in the public right-of-way, it nonetheless established restrictions on encroachments based on the street hierarchy within the Savannah Plan. The ordinance stipulated the maximum permissible distance one could extend beyond the lot line based on the width of the street.

Street Width	Encroachment Allowance	Street Names (ca. 1819)
37½'	4½'	Bryan, Congress, State, York, Hull, Perry
45' & 50'	5'	Drayton, Whitaker, Price, Jefferson, Lincoln
75' & 85'	6'	St. Julian, Broughton, President, McDonough, Bull, Abercorn, Habersham, Barnard, Montgomery, Houston
100'	6'	East Broad, West Broad (MLK)
140'	10'	South Broad (Oglethorpe)
Trust Lot Fronts	10'	

For example, the parallel stairs on the John Ash Houses, which face a 37½-foot residential street, protrude about 4 feet, while the frontal stairs of the contemporaneous John Hunter Houses on the 140-foot-wide Oglethorpe Avenue extend nearly 10 feet from the lot line. The ordinance explains how these examples were permitted and suggests, as building ordinances inevitably do, that the design of stairs was a matter of some debate in Savannah during the building boom of the early years of the republic (ca. 1790–1819). As full-story, above-grade basements became increasingly popular, staircases paralleling the front facade to fit within these constraints became predominant even on houses on trust lots and boulevards.

The arrangement of the distinct exterior staircases followed three patterns within rows: (1) stairs all ascending in the same direction; (2) staircases ascending in opposite directions and forming a symmetrical V; and (3) staircases ascending toward each other and forming a symmetrical A. Variations on these patterns are randomly scattered throughout the plan. In many double houses, the "A" pattern involves a shared raised stoop with a staircase ascending from either side, giving the impression that the paired houses are a single larger house.

Despite this relatively limited range of patterns, the shape of the staircase, the choice of materials, the treatment of the area under the stairs, the presence or absence of an architectural covering over the stoop, and the style employed have offered architects, builders, and homeowners a tremendous variety of possibilities for how a staircase can appear (figure 86). Most staircases rise parallel to the facade of the house in a straight line, but many staircases incorporate a curve, either throughout the rise or just near the bottom. Much less common is a dogleg form, where the lower part of the staircase rises perpendicular to the facade to a landing and then turns ninety degrees so that the upper part of the staircase rises parallel to the facade. Counterbalancing the relative uniformity and simplicity of the rowhouses themselves, their staircases offer moments of whimsy, employing a variety

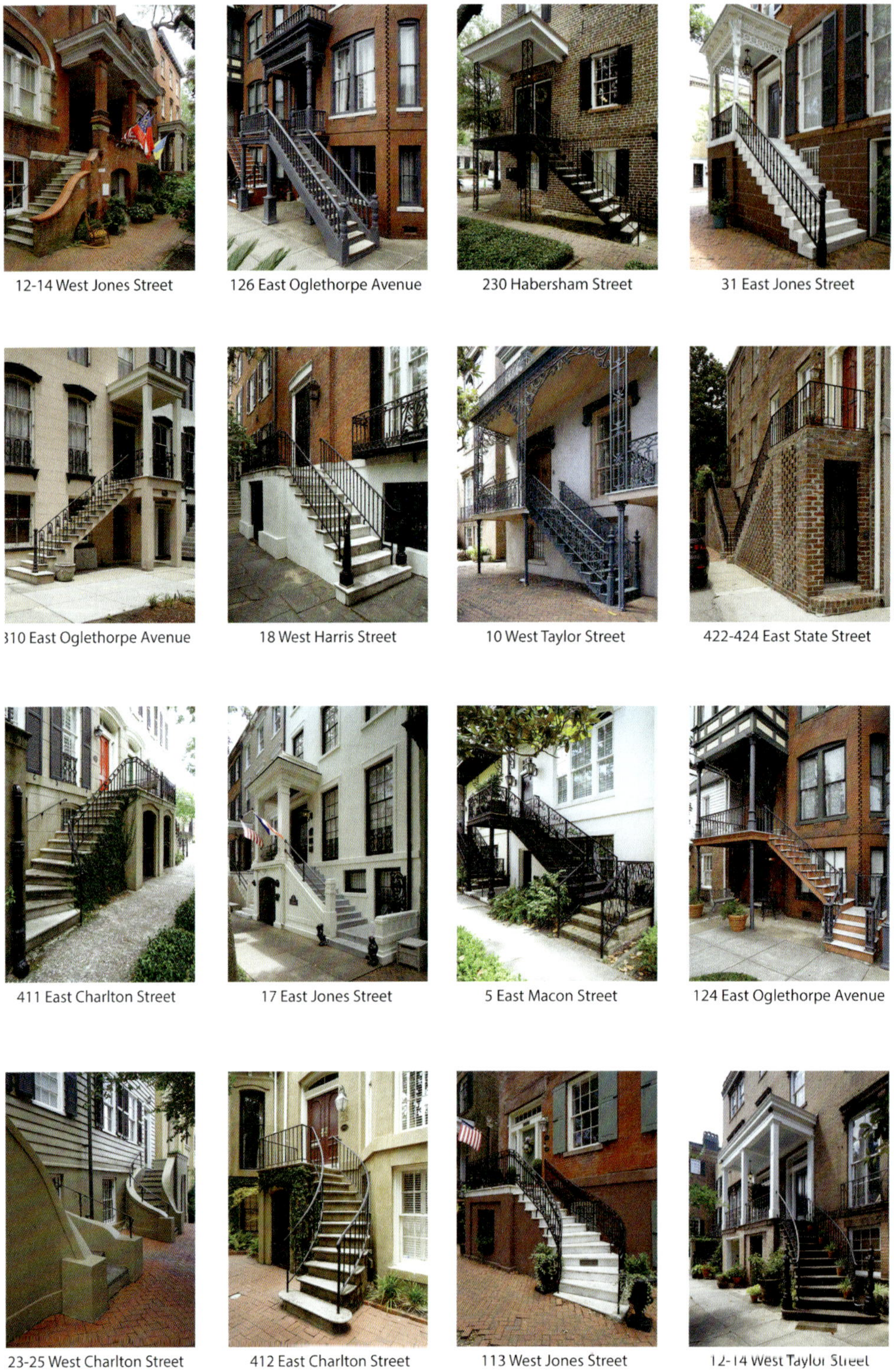

FIGURE 86. Elevated rowhouse stairs, showing parallel, dogleg, and curving variants. Photos by Robin B. Williams, 2024.

of materials, including stone, brick, concrete, stucco, wood, or metal (or combinations thereof), and are handled with varying degrees of solidity or openness. Many elevated staircases are completely open below both the stairs and the stoop, while others, mostly of brick, are enclosed. Some have a door below, while others do not. Similarly, it is just as common for a stoop to be an uncovered top landing as it is to be covered. Stylistic variety further enhances the seeming free-for-all that emerges among the hundreds of elevated staircases. The passage of time and the changing preferences or budgets of building owners have meant that staircases undergo modifications or replacement, giving an otherwise uniform row a touch of random playfulness. Here is the result of Savannah's elastic urbanism—a surprising variety of architectural refinement within a relatively limited framework.

THE DOUBLE HOUSE

Many of Savannah's early rowhouses were double houses, a subtype involving two side-by-side units symmetrically composed and attached by a party wall in a manner not commonly seen in other American cities. The form was evidently a response to the standard sixty-foot width of a single tything lot, which was generally too wide for an economical use of land. We see speculative property development with the first expansion of 1791, but its initial heyday was in the years immediately following the War of 1812, especially with the development of Jackson and Brown Wards and South Broad Street (Oglethorpe Avenue). This was a period of economic prosperity and of architectural sophistication brought not only by the arrival of talented architects such as William Jay from Bath, England, but also by increasing numbers of master builders who functioned as their own real estate developers, such as Isaiah Davenport from Rhode Island. We presume that the earliest double houses, as with other rowhouses, stood close to grade, though few survive. One example stands at 117–119 Houston Street (1810) above a short brick crawl space. Perhaps because of the self-contained quality of their symmetrical composition, double houses took on a greater variety of forms and styles than any other house type in Savannah.

Another early example of an elevated double house was built in 1817 by master builder John H. Ash on the middle lot of the northeast tything of Jackson Ward, at 114–116 West Hull Street (figure 87). Each house is approximately twenty-seven feet wide, allowing for a small setback on the east side of the lot. The Ash Houses were originally thirty-eight feet deep, but both have been extended in the rear. The primary two floors are arranged in a double-pile (two rooms deep), side hall plan. They sit high on a slightly sunken basement. Each unit is accessed via an exterior stair, which encroaches into the sidewalk and runs parallel to the facade before reaching a stoop. The two stairs converge at the center (the "A" configuration), giving access to the side-by-side doorways, each topped by a rounded arch transom. An attic floor is

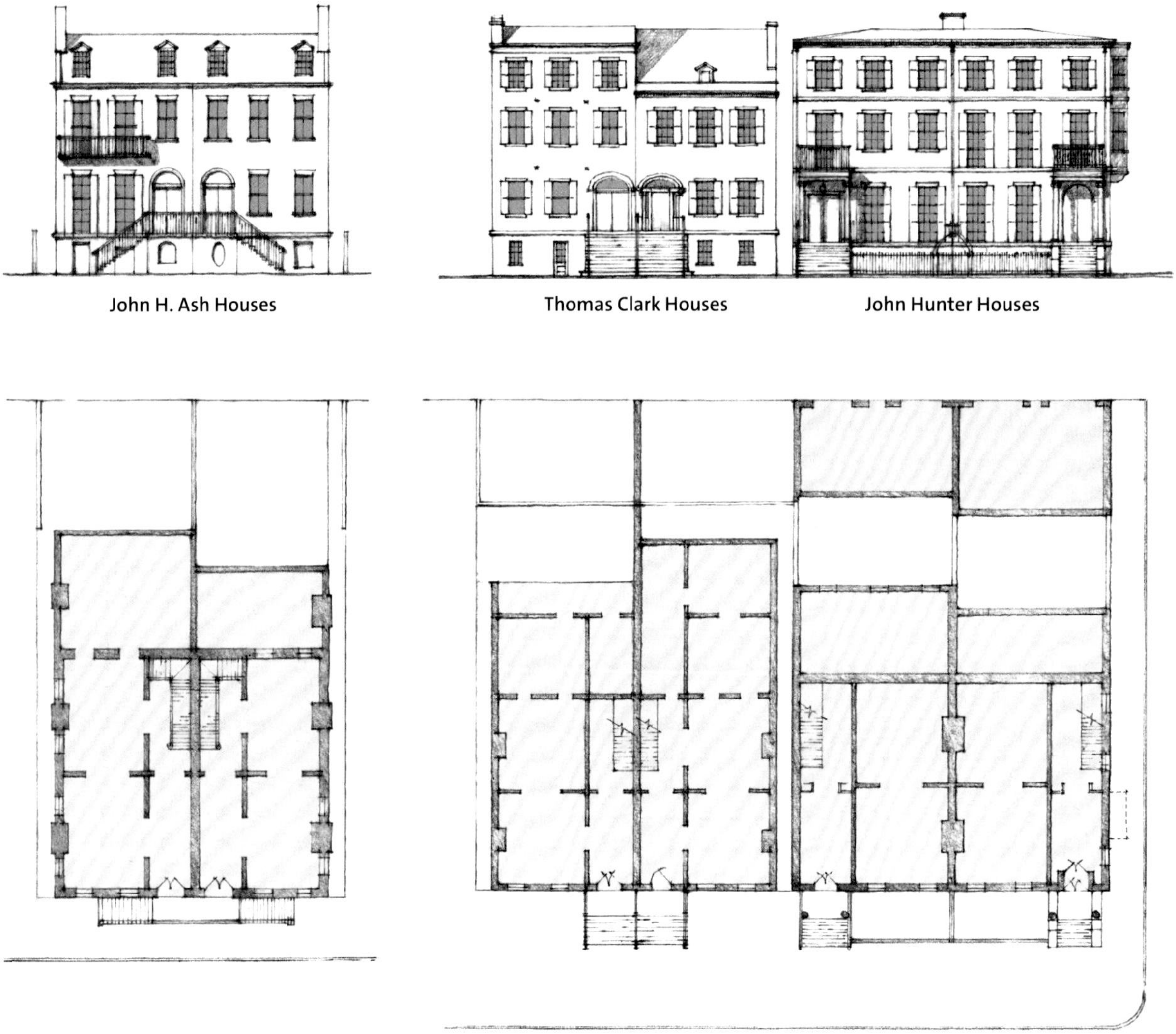

FIGURE 87. Early nineteenth-century Savannah double houses. The John H. Ash Houses (1817) stand at 114–116 West Hull Street, and the Thomas Clark Houses (1820–22) and John Hunter Houses (1821–22) sit side by side at 101–109 East Oglethorpe Avenue. Drawing by Hamilton Brindley.

lit by pairs of dormer windows on both slopes of the side-gabled roof. The end walls extend above the edges of the roof, forming parapets that incorporate a chimney at the side of each house. The 1852 Vincent map (figure 40) shows a carriage house stretching the full sixty feet across the back of the shared tything lot, with a yard in the remaining space between the main houses and the carriage house.

Larger and more sophisticated double houses appeared by the 1820s, such as the pair erected in 1821–22 at 101–105 East Oglethorpe Avenue, at the corner of Drayton Street, by John Hunter, a Savannah merchant who lived in the western half until his death in 1825. In this pair, the side halls are at the extremities, and the parlors share a party wall and a chimney. The front doors are protected by marble

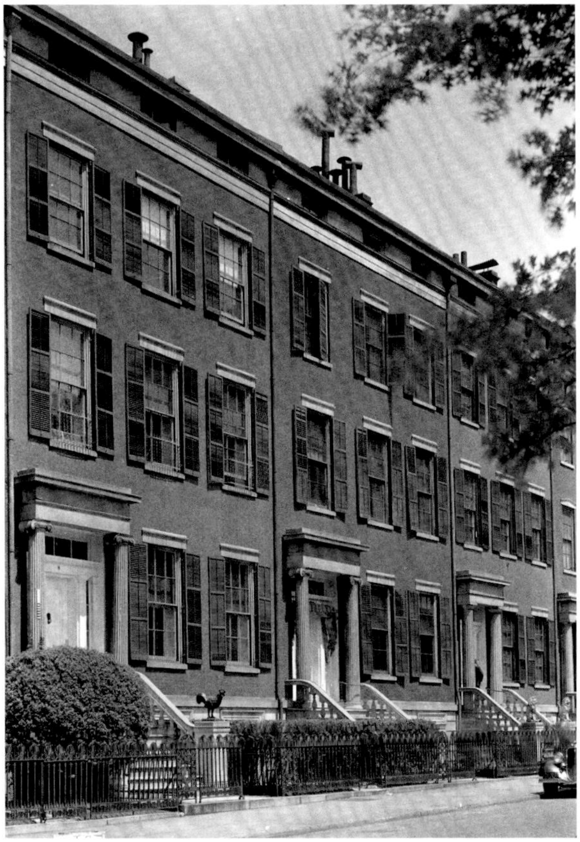

FIGURE 88. 7 & 8 Washington Square, part of "The Row," New York, 1832–33. Photo by E. P. MacFarland, 1934. Historic American Building Survey, Library of Congress, Prints and Photographs Division

porticoes supported by Ionic columns, with a balustraded balcony above. The porches are raised about four feet on a partial basement, and each porch is accessed by a perpendicular marble stair. Between the two stairs is a sunken light well that is protected by an ornamental iron fence. This arrangement is reminiscent of London terrace houses that became popular in New York, such as "The Row" at 1–13 Washington Square North (1832–33) (figure 88), which closely resembles the earlier pair in Savannah. The Thomas Clark double house at 107–109 East Oglethorpe Avenue was built next door to the Hunter Houses just as the latter were being completed in 1822. This pair sits on a higher basement that rises about six feet and is accessed by a wide frontal staircase; the houses lack covered porches and are inverted in plan, with front doors and side halls abutting at the center.

Double houses inspired more stylistic experimentation than other Savannah house types. Adopting the bracketed cornices and cast-iron ornamentation of the fashionable Italianate style, many of Savannah's grandest double houses erected in the 1850s occupied the blocks on either side of Bull Street. The Charles Rogers

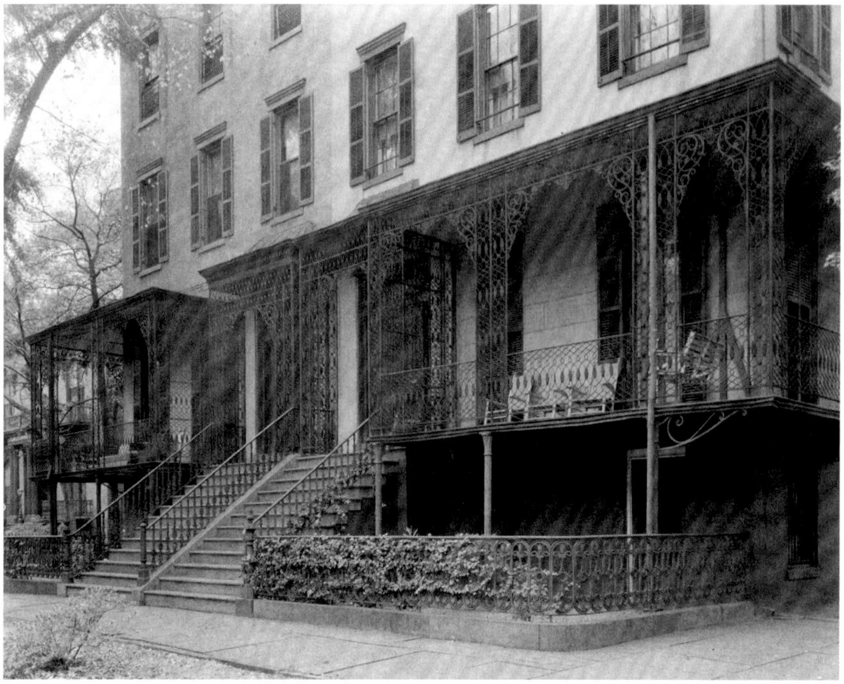

FIGURE 89. Charles Rogers Houses, 423–425 Bull Street, designed by John S. Norris, 1858. Photo by Frances Benjamin Johnston, 1939 or 1944. Carnegie Survey of the Architecture of the South, Library of Congress, Prints and Photographs Division.

Houses at 423 and 425 Bull Street (1858), on the northwest trust lot fronting Monterey Square, are the most impressive examples (figure 89). Designed by New York architect John Norris, these conjoined houses bear a striking resemblance to 3 and 4 Gramercy Park West in New York City, an 1840s double house attributed to Alexander Jackson Davis that was likely familiar to Norris. In both cases, wide joined sandstone staircases lead to a high stoop framed by lacy ironwork over a full-story basement. The Rogers Houses take advantage of their trust lot location by stepping back from the lot line, allowing for enclosed gardens across the front. As in other parts of the country, increasing ornament and stylistic experimentation became popular after the Civil War. Designed by architect Alfred Eichberg, the double house at 12–14 West Jones Street (1891), just west of Bull Street, displays a fascinating Queen Anne style variation on the traditional boxy double-house composition. The paired staircases follow the "A" format and meet in the middle, but the railings employ the curving shapes of Baroque architecture, and together they read as a Dutch gable typical of the Queen Anne style. Above, the paired side halls are crowned by a tower that rises above the main body of the houses. Even more exuberant are the Daniel J. Purse and Daniel Thomas Houses, a double house at 12–14 East Taylor Street erected in 1869 but boldly remodeled in 1897 to reflect contemporary interest in Paris-inspired Beaux-Arts classicism (figure 90).

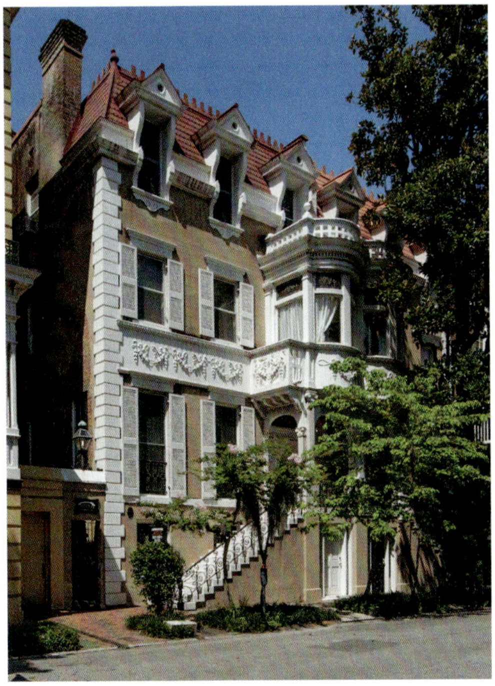

FIGURE 90. Daniel J. Purse and Daniel Thomas Houses, 12–14 East Taylor Street, 1869; remodeled 1897. Photo by Robin B. Williams, 2014.

The double house experienced considerable popularity in the late nineteenth century and continued architectural experimentation beyond the Savannah Plan area, particularly in the Victorian District flanking Forsyth Park.

ROWS (OF THREE OR MORE)

Rows of houses attached side by side proliferated in all wards of the Savannah Plan throughout the nineteenth century. Like their double house cousins, rows of three to fifteen units vary in size and style; they are located on both tything and trust lots, and most of them are elevated one full story above the street. Classic expressions of the Savannah elevated rowhouse are represented by two examples from the 1850s. The first is the Marshall Row, an austere block of four southward-facing dwelling units—actually, two pairs of double houses—occupying two lots in the southeast tything of Anson Ward at 230–244 East Oglethorpe Avenue (figure 91). The row was built in 1855–56 by Mary Marshall, a prosperous entrepreneur and real estate developer. Each unit is thirty feet wide and forty feet deep, three bays across, and four stories high, including a full-height raised basement. Each had a brick carriage house running across the back of the lot, though none survive. The four houses are grouped in reflecting pairs, with the side hall pushed to the outer edge of each pair, creating a rhythmic effect emphasized by the substantial

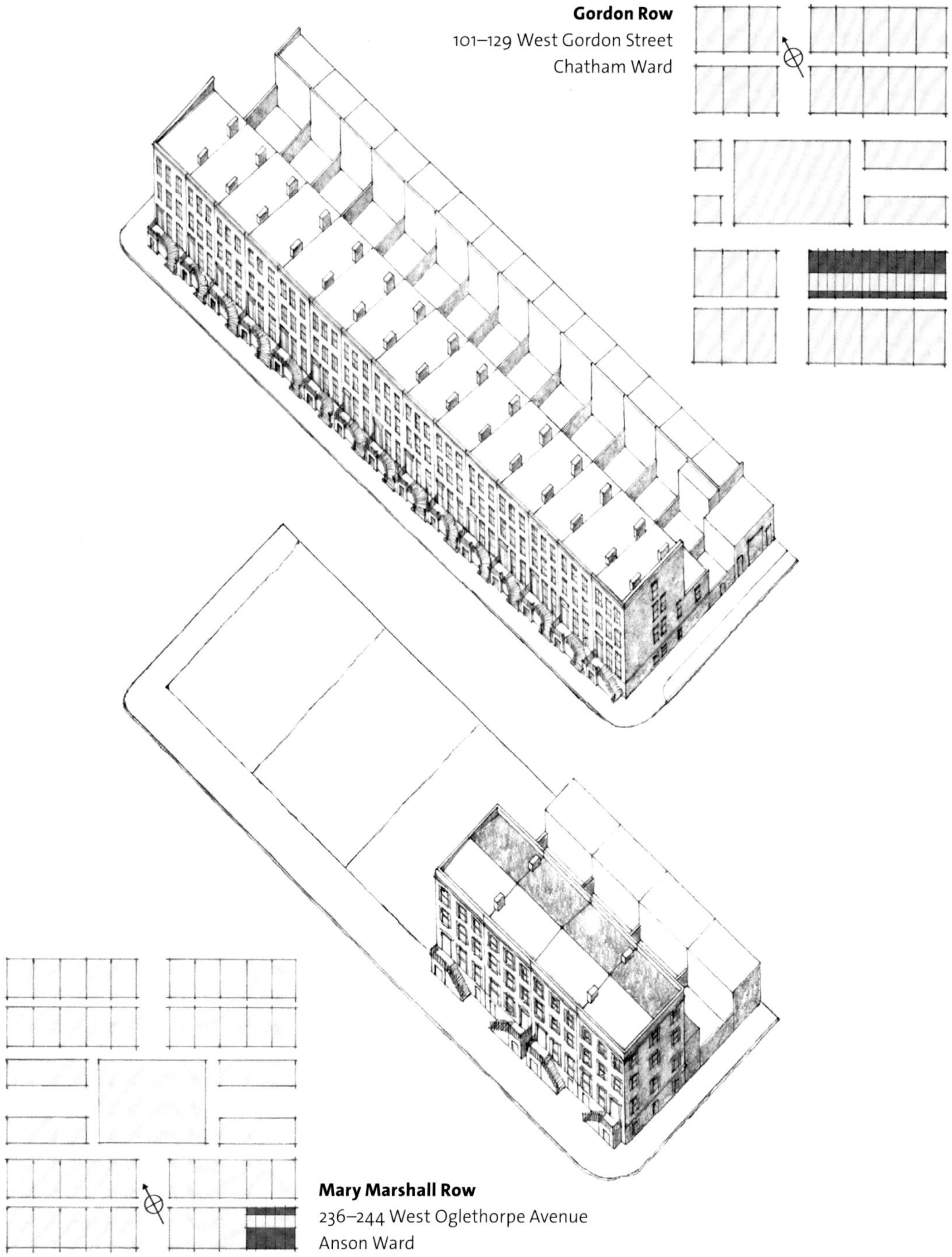

FIGURE 91. Gordon Row, 101–129 West Gordon Street, 1853–54, and the Marshall Row at 230–244 East Oglethorpe Avenue, designed by Charles Cluskey for Mary Marshall, 1855–56. Drawing by Hamilton Brindley.

projecting parallel stairs with their marble risers and treads and simple iron railing on a brick base. The low-pitched side-gabled roof is masked by a parapet, completing the visual transformation of four houses into a unified monolithic structure.

Even more powerful in its prismatic purity is Gordon Row, an unbroken chain of fifteen houses covering all five lots of the inner half of the southeast tything of Chatham Ward at 101–129 West Gordon Street (figure 91). Built in two phases between 1853 and 1854, Gordon Row epitomizes the Savannah elevated rowhouse form in many ways. Each unit is simple, uniform, and compact; a vertical emphasis—at twenty feet in width, these houses are one-third narrower than the units of the Marshall Row—is countered by the horizontality of the block as whole. Each house is raised a full story, with grade-level access to the raised basement under the stoop and a parallel stair that curves as it meets the sidewalk (except for the last house alongside Barnard Street, which has a straight staircase). The stoops are uncovered, enhancing the clarity of the block as a whole. Remarkably intact, the two-story carriage houses likewise form a continuous row on the lane.

The staircases on the Marshall Row and Gordon Row illustrate yet another example of subtle, rhythmic variety granted to Savannah's architectural symphony by the design decisions of practical yet imaginative builders working within the constraints established by the urban plan. In Gordon Row, all the staircases face the same direction. Each is asymmetrically placed on the left edge of the unit, corresponding to its side hall entrance. The lower six treads of each staircase curve to avoid crowding into the lower porch of its neighbor and project just beyond the basement wall, emphasizing a cascading effect. The benefit of this small detail is threefold: It creates a smoother, more gracious ascent for the visitor, it opens much-needed wall space for a basement window near the base of the stair, and it adds visual delight by introducing a curvilinear counterbalance to the otherwise relentless repetition of rectilinear elements. The shorter Marshall Row comprises two patterns, having the staircases descend toward one another in a "V" configuration, with the middle two staircases standing back-to-back in an "A" configuration—though in this case with separate staircases.

Whether a single, a double, or a row of three or more, the location of houses on a tything block has an impact on their relative prominence and apparent value. The inner southwest tything block of Jasper Ward dramatically illustrates the progressive diminishment of land value and prominence as one moves away from Bull Street (figure 92). On the lot closest to Bull Street, directly facing Madison Square, stood a freestanding mansion house, taking full advantage of what we call "pseudo trust lots." This house was replaced by the imposing 110-foot-tall Scottish Rite Temple that now stands at 341 Bull Street, an exuberant and polychromatic Beaux-Arts classical Masonic lodge designed by Savannah architect Hyman Witcover and constructed in 1912–23. Rowhouses fill the middle three lots of the five-lot block and

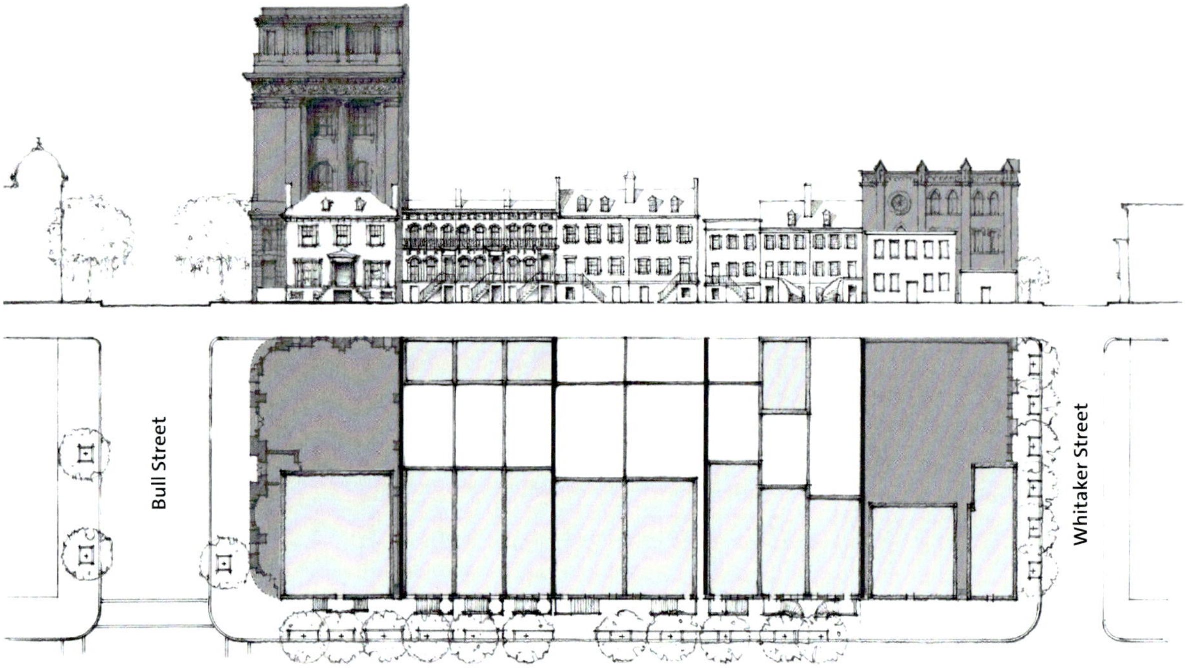

FIGURE 92. Facades along the southwest tything block of Jasper Ward, showing the descending hierarchy of scale and ornament from the inner to outer lots. The innermost mansion house was replaced in 1912 by the 110-foot-tall Scottish Rite Masonic Temple, shown in gray. On the opposite (west) end of the block, Cranmer Hall (also in gray) replaced the two previous buildings on the fifth tything lot in 1953. Drawing by Hamilton Brindley.

illustrate a progressive reduction in height and architectural elaboration as their distance from Bull Street increases. Closest to the Scottish Rite building, the set of three 20-foot-wide Italianate houses on the second lot west of Bull Street have the tallest cornice and showcase a more elaborate surface embellishment of iron balconies and sculptural cornice than is displayed on the slightly shorter pair of sober, 30-foot-wide Federal-style brick townhouses on the third lot over from Bull Street. The fourth lot west of Bull Street accommodates three modest 20-foot-wide townhouses that continue the downward stepping of cornice and sill lines and the trend of increasing simplicity. The fifth lot terminated the row by hosting a simple two-story unraised house and a one-story store until 1953, when the historical pattern was broken by the current three-story building (dramatically renovated into its Gothic Revival form in 2005) erected by St. John's Church as part of its campus.

ROWHOUSES ON TRUST LOTS

Not surprisingly, rowhouses on tything blocks generally face the front edge of their lot, but a few rows are built on trust lots, allowing for a variety of orientations. In contrast to a public building situated on a trust lot, which naturally fronts the square, rowhouses typically follow their tything lot brethren by facing an east–west inner civic street—that is, one of the streets along the flanks of the trust lot. While tything lots have an obvious front and back, there is less clarity with a trust lot when it is not occupied by a public building. Cassel Row, comprising eight attached three-story houses, occupied the northeast trust lot in Reynolds Ward (across the square from the Pink House) and logically faced the wider central civic street, St. Julian. The 1888 Sanborn map showed each house with a small outbuilding, likely a privy, which disappeared by 1898, presumably with the arrival of plumbing. The 1916 Sanborn map included staircases, set in pairs in the "A" formation, for all the houses in the row, except for the westernmost house closest to the square, where the elevated entrance was on the side fronting the square.[12]

South of Liberty Street, where the three interior east–west streets are uniformly 60 feet wide (as opposed to the original 37½, 75, and 37½ pattern, which privileged the central trust street), the lack of clear hierarchy resulted in sets of elevated rowhouses with varied orientations (figure 93). In Jasper Ward, the rows of houses

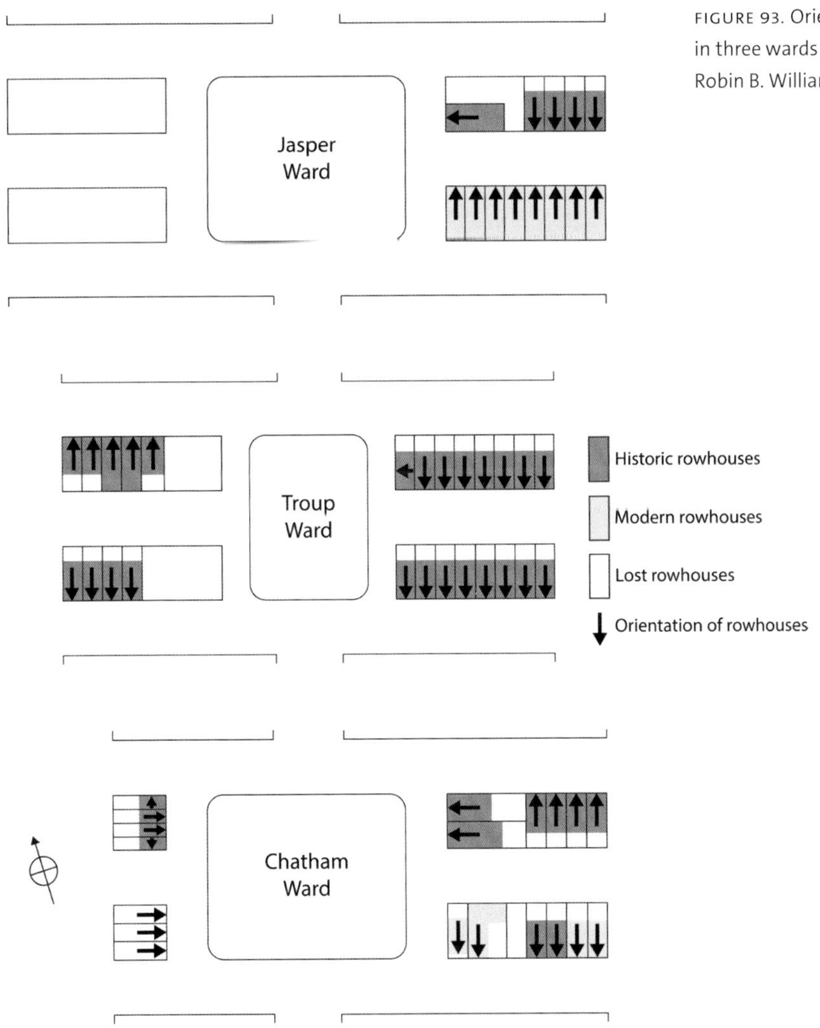

FIGURE 93. Orientation of rowhouses on trust lots in three wards south of Liberty Street. Diagram by Robin B. Williams.

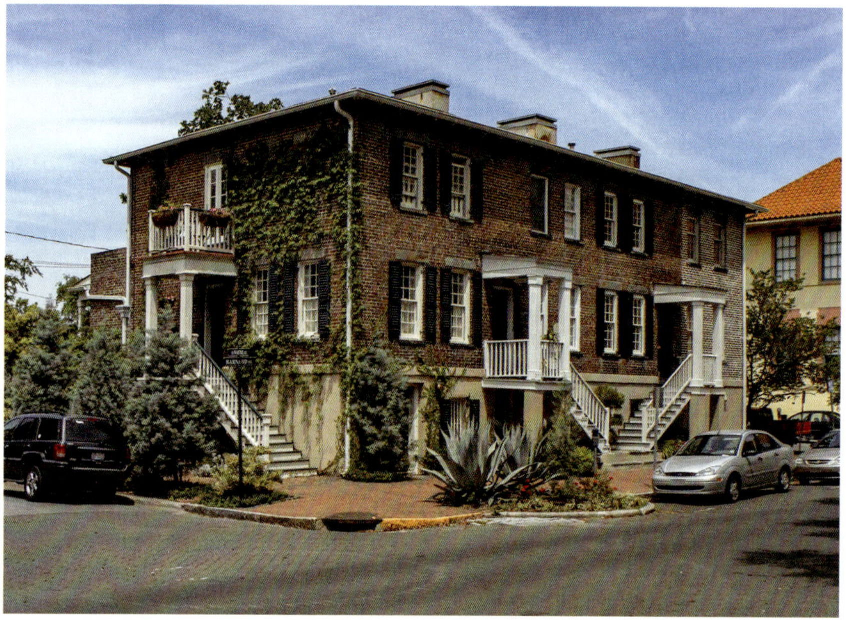

FIGURE 94. William Kine Houses, 419–425 Barnard Street, 1854, view looking northwest. The four small rowhouses in this unique cluster on an abbreviated trust lot face three different directions. Photo by Brian Jolley, Virtual Historic Savannah Project, 2004.

on the pair of eastern trust lots flanking Macon Street face inward toward one another. In Troup Ward, the rows on the western trust lots face away from each other, turning the central street effectively into a lane, while the rows on the eastern trust lots face southward, even though the middle street provides the parking area for both rows. An even looser arrangement appears on the eastern trust lots in Chatham Ward, where rowhouses face outward in three directions. The nimblest placement of rowhouses on a trust lot can be found across the square on the northwestern trust lot in Chatham Ward, where in 1854 William Kine built what appears to be a pair of conjoined and elevated five-bay, center hall houses (like the actual pair on the northwest trust lot in Washington Ward) but which in reality is a cluster of four 15-foot-wide elevated rowhouses (figure 94). While the inner pair of three-bay rowhouses have elevated entrances facing the square, the outer two-bay houses are accessed on the north and south flanks (not visible from the front), taking full advantage of the 60-foot width and island quality of the trust lot and further illustrating the flexibility possible within the Savannah Plan.

The essential form of the elevated Savannah rowhouse developed in the antebellum era and continued in popularity, with adaptation, throughout the later nineteenth century. The late twentieth century saw a resurgence of interest in the rowhouse, which continues to the present. Since relatively few unbuilt lots remain within the boundaries of the Savannah Plan, most of the city's newest rowhouses have been built on the fringes of the plan, especially in Berrien Ward to the west

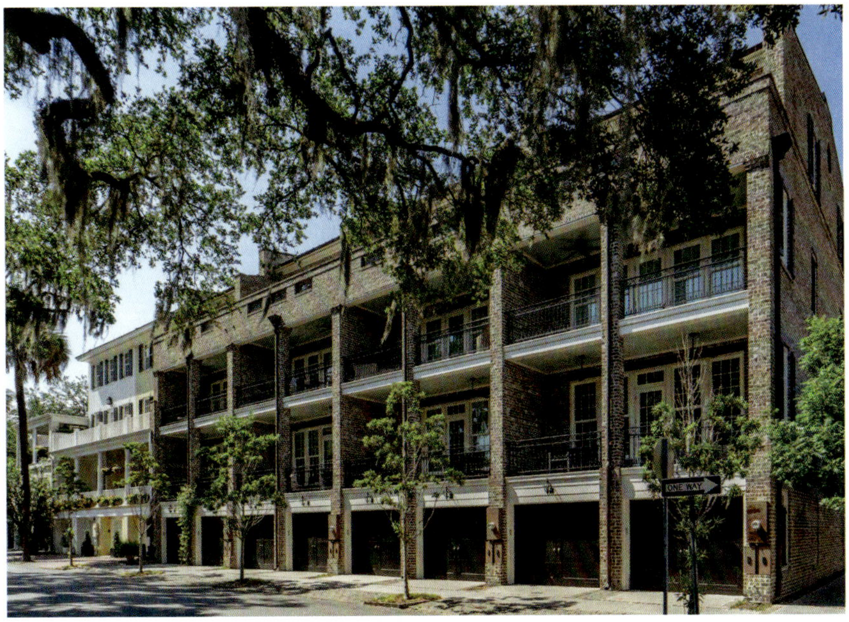

FIGURE 95. Madison Square townhouses, 9–15 East Macon Street, rear facades facing Charlton Street, designed by John Deering, Homeline Architecture, 2016. Photo by Robin B. Williams, 2024.

of Chatham Square and into the Victorian District to the south. As recently as 2019, however, a row of four houses was completed on the rear (eastern) half of the southeastern trust lot of Jasper Ward, complementing two pairs erected on the western half of the lot in the 1980s and early 2000s, respectively. Designed by Savannah architect John Deering, these "luxury townhomes" are adapted to twenty-first-century demands for convenience and comfort. They extend the full 60-foot depth of the lot and face the central trust street (Macon), incorporating a garage at the back (facing Charlton Street), rear porches on the second and third floors, and open terraces on the uppermost floor (figure 95). According to Deering, the design "respond[ed] to the Savannah plan and the building patterns that exist. We did borrow the galleries from John Norris."[13] As noted by the developer, they include amenities "to let residents age in place," such as elevators and walk-in showers.[14]

The Savannah Single House

Detached rowhouses, which appeared in Savannah in the early nineteenth century, are usually nested among their double and multiunit counterparts. Being freestanding, such houses take advantage of their unencumbered side elevations by having windows and porches on one side or the other. The Frederick Ball House (1809), for example, illustrates how a detached rowhouse exploited its location within the plan in the early nineteenth century (figure 85). It occupies the north end of a tything lot that technically fronts East York Street, yet the house (like its neighbors to the south on the same lot) fronts the central north–south street, Habersham, allowing it to capitalize on its corner location overlooking Columbia Square by having thirteen windows on its north facade. Its orientation reminds us that builders strayed early on from the pattern established by Oglethorpe that houses face east–west streets. By the middle decades of the nineteenth century, expanded detached rowhouses became an alluring alternative to center hall mansions as a means of expressing wealth with the addition of multilevel porches often overlooking a side garden. Based on their resemblance to their regional cousin, the Charleston single house, we shall refer to these as Savannah single houses.

The Charleston single house is an idiosyncratic residential building type, the origins and meaning of which have been debated by architectural historians.[15] Appearing first in the mid-eighteenth century, it is essentially a shallow (single-pile)

FIGURE 96. Charleston single house compared with a Savannah single house. Drawing by David Gobel.

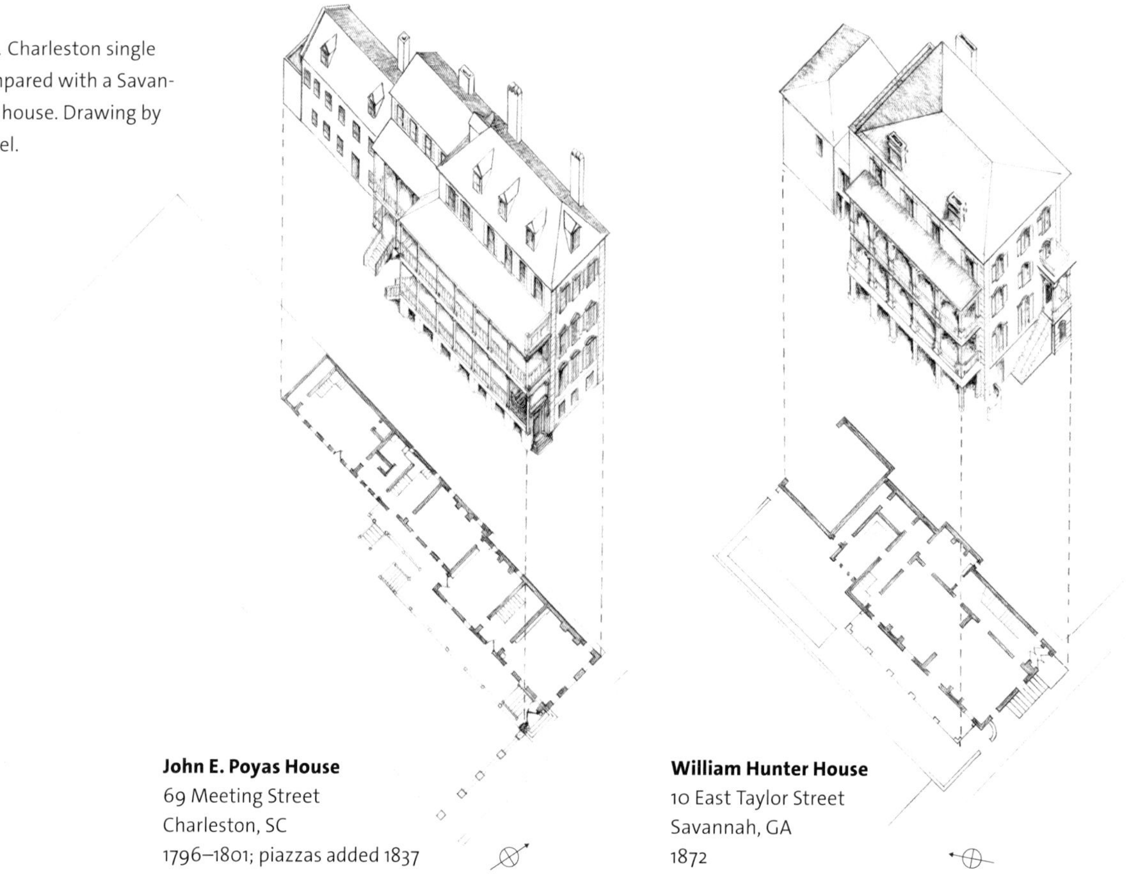

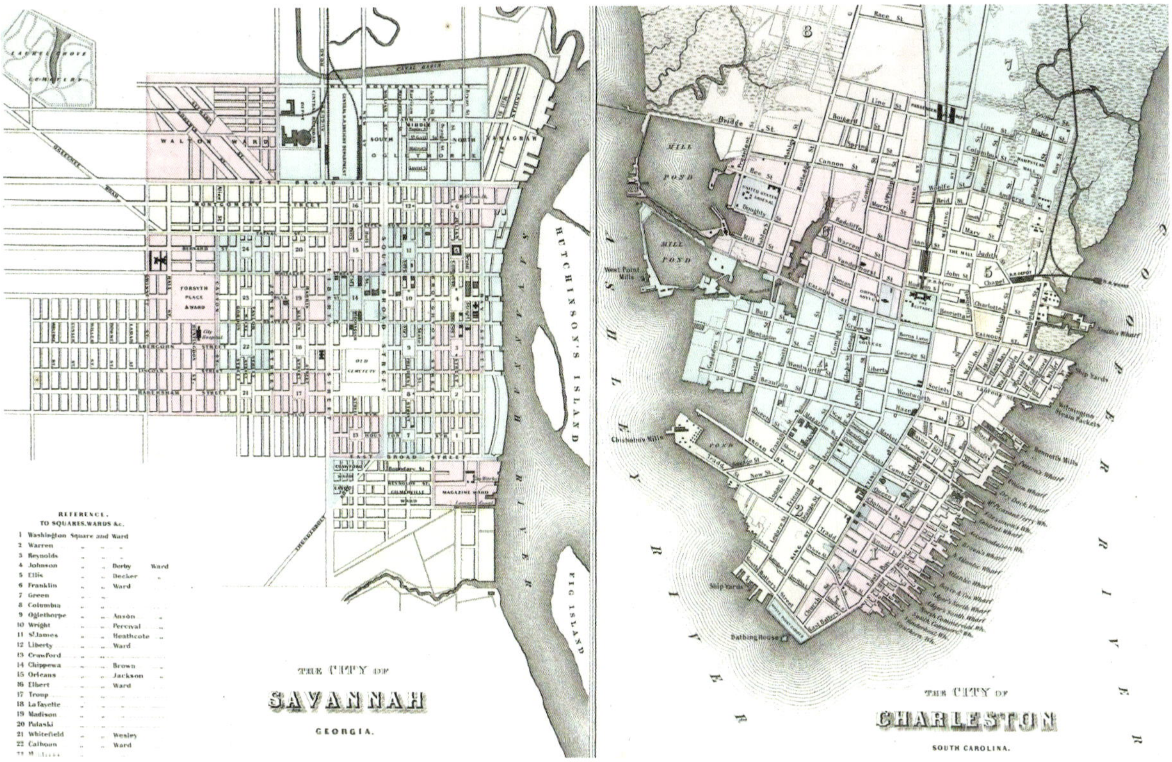

central-hall-plan house turned sideways on its building lot so that its narrow side faces the street (figure 96). The entire "front" of the house is typically shaded by a two-story covered porch (known as a "piazza" in Charleston) facing a walled side yard (usually to the south). Perhaps the most curious feature of the Charleston single house is the "false" main entrance door that typically faces the street, giving access not to the house itself but to its piazza.

The Savannah single house is less quirky. It is simply a freestanding side hall rowhouse with an elevated front entrance and embellished with a side porch extending from the parlor side of the house. In both cities, the single house form is a direct response to their respective urban plans—specifically large, deep blocks facing narrow streets with no rear lanes in Charleston versus the small, shallow blocks facing wide streets with rear lanes in Savannah (figure 97). That the mapmaker, New York–based George W. Colton, compared the two cities at the same scale on one plate speaks to the close geographic and cultural connections between these two cities, but it also visually underscores how radically different their urban layouts were.[16] In Charleston, where blocks could be almost as big as a whole

FIGURE 97. *The City of Savannah Georgia [compared with] The City of Charleston South Carolina.* From George W. Colton, *Colton's Atlas of the World, Illustrating Physical and Political Geography*, vol. 1 (New York, 1855). Wikimedia Commons.

Savannah ward, urban lots were typically narrow and deep and required a private driveway to access the rear portions of the property, where a separate kitchen and outbuildings stood. This necessitated houses to stand separate from their neighbors, while the block proportions encouraged the narrow end of each house to face the street. The house would typically occupy the northern half, leaving the south half to accommodate the driveway, a side yard, and the porches that framed the south elevation to provide shade and catch ocean breezes. Charleston's narrow streets surely played a role in the development of the false door entryways placed at grade and flush with the street facade. Savannah's shallow lots and wide streets with generous sidewalks gave rise to the protruding stairs and elevated doorways of the city's single houses, many of which face public squares. The side garden of the Charleston single house functions as a private substitute for that city's relative lack of public squares. Private side gardens viewed from multistory side porches in Savannah were an extravagance. Possibly the architects and owners of these houses were inspired by the Charleston single house, but whatever the source of their inspiration, Savannah's side porches and gardens became increasingly prevalent in luxurious single houses and mansions beginning in the mid-nineteenth century.

At least twenty-three examples of Savannah single houses with side porches still stand in the six central residential wards south of Liberty Street; historic Sanborn maps attest to the presence of many more in the past. More than half of the extant houses boast multistory porches in the manner of Charleston single houses, and another ten have a single-story side porch. The Hugh Moss Comer House (1880) on the inside lot adjacent to Bull Street at 2 East Taylor Street in the northeast tything of Monterey Ward exemplifies this type. Its elaborate double-height side porch looks onto its own garden as well as the garden of the William Hunter House at 10 East Taylor (1872), its mirror image on the adjoining lot (figure 96).

Compelling evidence of the direct correlation between townhouse architecture and the Savannah Plan can be found along the north side of Gaston Street, the southern boundary of the plan. The lots in the southern half of the tythings within the fifth row of wards were platted in 1850 with a depth of 120 feet, while the other lots within these wards retained the 100-foot depth south of Liberty Street. This added depth encouraged developers and homeowners along the north side of Gaston to push their houses back from the property line by roughly 20 feet, permitting front gardens and grand staircases descending perpendicularly from the facade. The effect is an expression of wealth and status uncommon for town lots and formerly only possible for trust lot mansions on their deeper lots. At least twelve Savannah single houses stood along the north side of Gaston Street by the end of the nineteenth century, almost all set well back from the street line to enjoy a double benefit of adjacent greenery.[17] Designed by John Norris in 1857, 20 West Gaston is representative in having its entry stair rise straight up perpendicular to the facade and in providing more privacy to the side porches on its east side. Next door, 24 West Gaston (1861) presents an inventive reinterpretation of the single house formula. Unlike most other houses on the street, it meets the lot line, where substantial gate piers frame a monumental entry walk that fills the side garden on the east side of the house, leading to the entrance at the end of the lower porch.

The Charleston single house type is rare in Savannah; only one example survives—the William Battersby House at 119 East Charlton Street (1852). Tellingly, its basement is only half raised, rejecting the local fashion of fully raised basements. Consistent with the house type, its side porch overlooks a side garden. A chic, contemporary interpretation of the Charleston (and not Savannah) single house designed by Daniel Snyder was built in 2007 at 320 East Jones Street (figure 98). Here, an unadorned, two-story box follows the massing of a single house—complete with a carriage house–like garage at the back—by having the main entrance at grade and leading to the outdoor porch on the west side of the house. The western facade, defined by monumental abstract piers, functions as an open frame of three bays, shading the actual western wall of the house, which is predominantly glass. This allows for a strong connection with the walled side garden that fills the entire depth of the western half of the tything lot.

FIGURE 98. Brower House, 320 East Jones Street, designed by Daniel E. Snyder, 2007. Photo by Robin B. Williams, 2024.

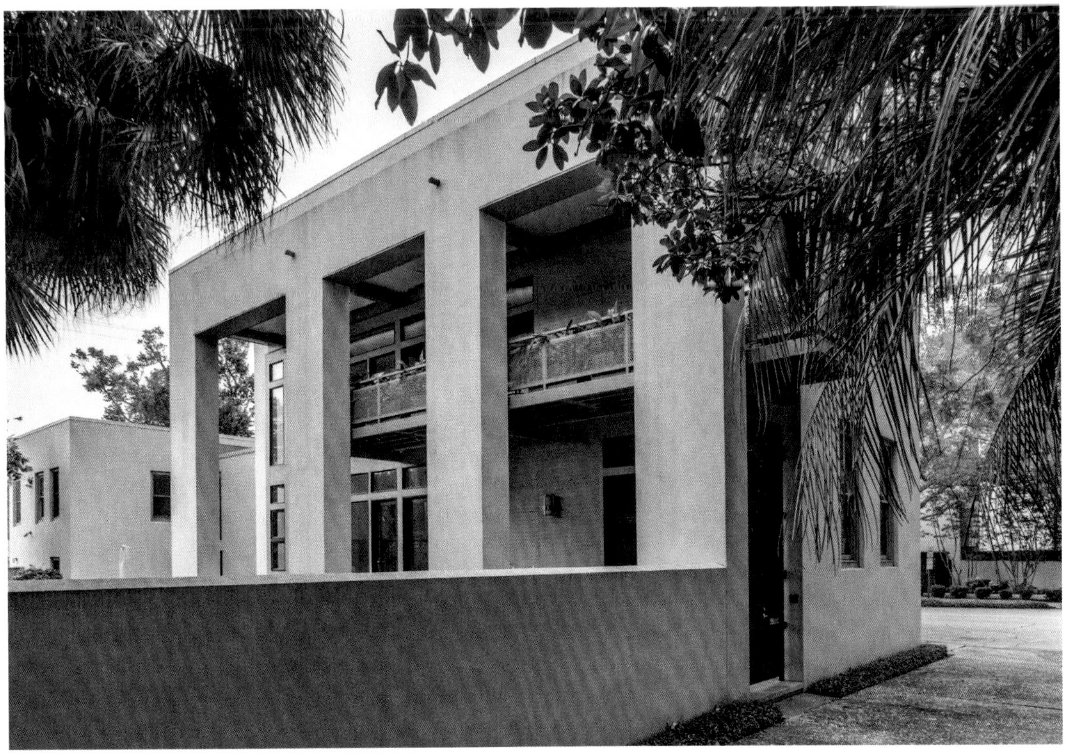

The Savannah Mansion House

As in other cities, the center hall house, expressed on the exterior with five bays, appeared in Savannah by the late eighteenth century. The symmetrical composition of these mansion houses was obviously suitable for trust lot sites, but many are found on tything lots, often located on the inner end of the tything block closest to the central north–south street and facing the square. Reflecting their expression as status symbols, most were built in the prestigious middle wards aligned with Barnard, Bull, and Abercorn Streets (figure 72). Some are rather modest in their materials and decoration; others are elaborate and ostentatious in their design. Like the Savannah rowhouse, many mansion houses have an elevated entrance accessed by a prominent exterior stair or pair of stairs. Many also have multilevel porches spanning their rear facade and facing a garden. A few follow the single house formula of having porches on one side facing a side garden, as exemplified by the Minis House at 204 East Jones Street. As with the elevated rowhouse, the golden age of the grand mansion house in Savannah came in the antebellum era.

TRUST LOT MANSIONS

Savannah's most architecturally renowned houses are built on trust lots, which were conceived and coded as public lots, yet they employ stylistic variants on the five-bay formula of private houses (figure 99). Not surprisingly, these trust lot mansions tend to have been designed in a more "public" manner, usually through the inclusion of a monumental portico. In fact, all but one of the twelve grandest mansion houses on trust lots are no longer private residences, having yielded to the public coding in such lots' DNA, and instead now serve as museums, inns, a restaurant, church offices, and a commercial office building. Such adaptability testifies to the high esteem with which these houses were and continue to be held by Savannahians. In fact, only one trust lot mansion appears to have been demolished in the city's history: the celebrated Archibald Bulloch House on the southwest trust lot on Orleans Square. Designed by William Jay in 1819, it was razed in 1916 to make room for the Municipal Auditorium, which in turn was demolished in 1971 to make room for the current Civic Center parking lot.

Trust lot mansions varied in how much of the trust lot site they utilized. The earliest trust lots used for residences were split into two sixty-by-ninety-foot properties. Dating perhaps to 1789, the James Habersham Jr. House (now the Pink House) facing Reynolds Square is among these; its fifty-foot-wide, five-bay Palladian-style facade hugs the inner corner of the property line of the northwest trust lot. When the building was converted into a bank in 1812, it was extended to the north, completing the lot's sixty-foot frontage. Its projecting Doric portico and window lintels were added at that time as well. Many other modifications have

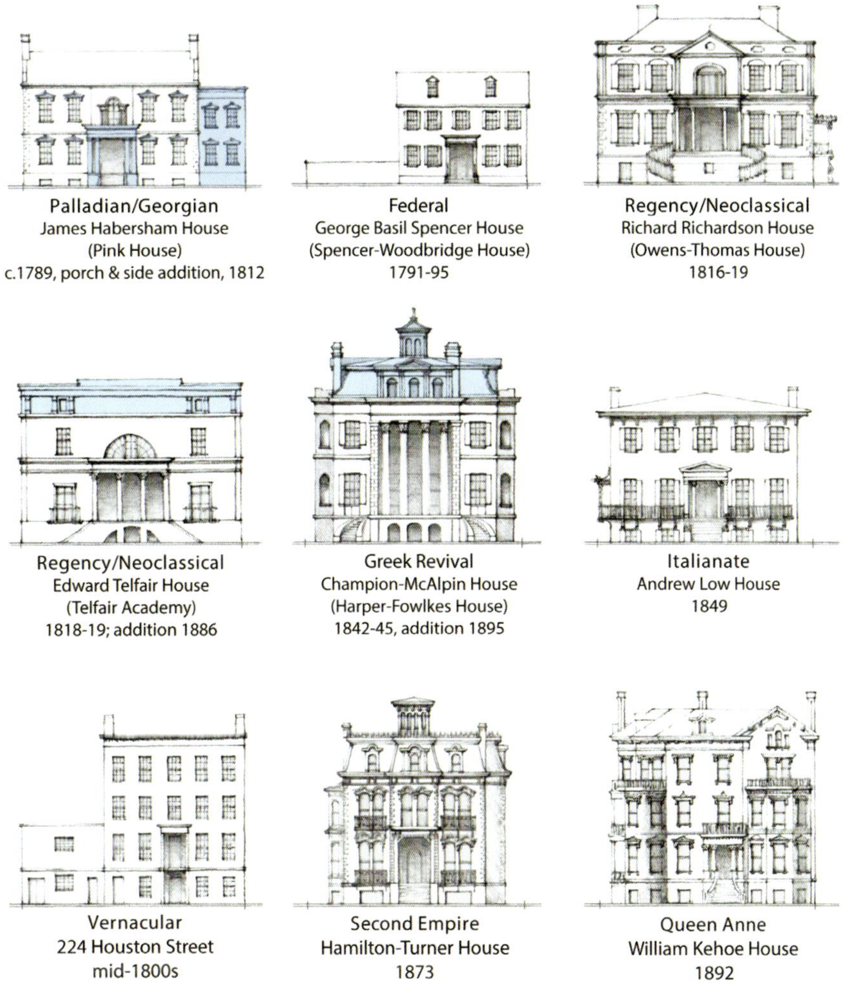

FIGURE 99. Trust lot mansion facades. Blue shading indicates additions to the original building. Drawing by Hamilton Brindley.

been made since then, including a major addition in 2007, when the remainder of the half trust lot was built out to expand its current use as a restaurant. The George Basil Spencer House, a five-bay, wood-frame structure built circa 1791–95, stands as a more modest example of this type. It sits on the inside corner of the northeast trust lot facing Warren Square, measuring approximately thirty-five feet wide by twenty feet deep in its original form, leaving a substantial side yard facing the square. Among the last trust lot mansions erected were two that occupied only the front half of a trust lot: the Hamilton-Turner House at 330 Abercorn Street (1873), designed by John D. Hall in a Second Empire style on the southeast trust lot facing Lafayette Square; and the Kehoe House at 123 Habersham Street (1892), designed by DeWitt Bruyn in a Queen Anne style.

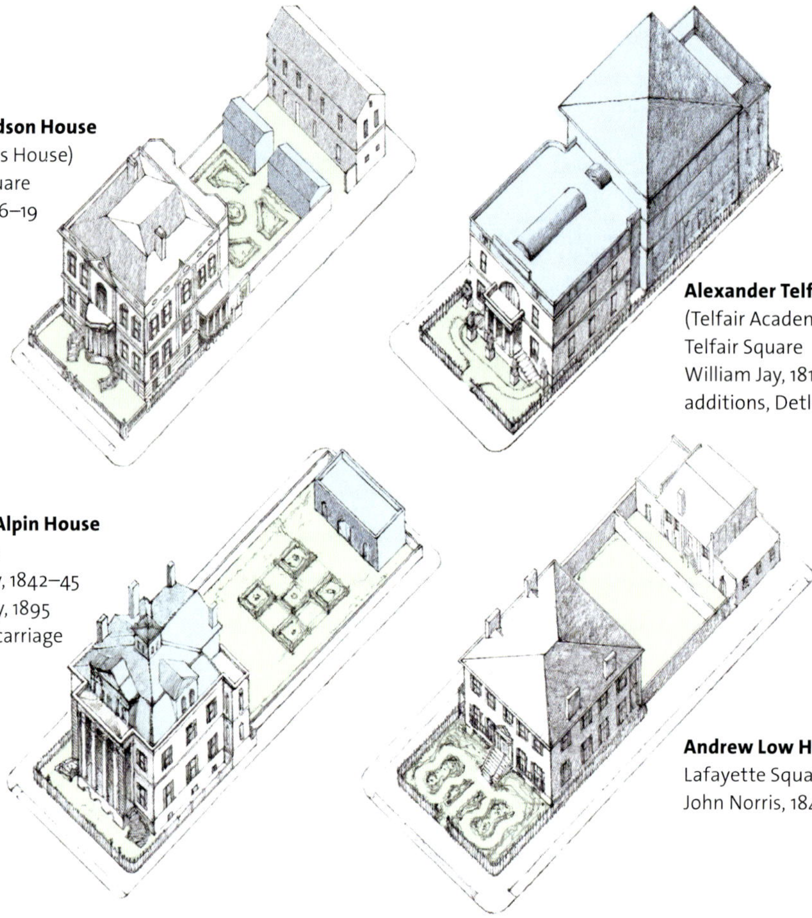

FIGURE 100. Trust lot mansions occupying full lots. Blue shading indicates additions to the original building. Drawing by Hamilton Brindley.

The Richard Richardson House (now known as the Owens-Thomas House) was designed in 1816 by William Jay and completed in 1819; it demonstrated the potential of a mansion house on a trust lot and set a standard of architectural achievement in Savannah. Effectively an urban villa, the house, together with its carriage house and yard, makes full use of the entire northeast trust lot facing Oglethorpe Square (figure 100). The primary facade, aligned with the site's central axis, sits approximately fifteen feet back from the front edge of the lot to create a small front garden, defined by a low wall with a Coade stone balustrade. The front door is framed by a projecting portico raised almost seven feet above grade and accessed by reflecting curving stairways. The mansion's sixty-foot-wide, five-bay facade announces the generous thirteen-foot-wide central hall with a dramatic staircase and flanked by entertaining rooms about twenty feet wide; the remaining seven feet of the house's span involved the formidably thick tabby concrete walls to support multiple cisterns that supplied its indoor plumbing. Acknowledging the hierarchical pull of the central trust street, the one-story cast-iron porch (an early use of that building material in the United States), linked to the master bedroom in the rear corner, extends into the adjacent sidewalk on President Street. Perhaps intended as a less formal side porch, its use as the platform from which the Marquis de Lafayette, staying in what was then a rooming house, purportedly delivered two public speeches in 1825 underscores the innate public nature of this house.

Behind the Owens-Thomas House is a garden that originally functioned as a work yard, accommodating a privy and storage building. The simple two-story, side-gabled rear outbuilding, laterally dividing the carriage house inside from the quarters for enslaved Africans, extends across the lot's back side, completing the trust lot. Unlike carriage houses on lanes, this carriage house faces the main house and is accessed via a gate facing the large central street. Most subsequent trust lot mansions followed the model of the Owens-Thomas House, some filling the full trust lot, including others designed by William Jay. This model centered the house on the lot, set back with a front garden and fence, and employed an impressive portico on the main facade facing the square. In the rear, outbuildings and work yards later may have become formal gardens (as happened at the Owens-Thomas House).

Two of Savannah's trust lot mansions deviate from this pattern. The Moses Eastman House, designed by Charles Cluskey in 1844–47 as a five-bay, central hall mansion, faces West McDonough Street, the central trust street. Like the Owens-Thomas House, this house has a raised projecting one-story portico (though Doric instead of Ionic) and flanking curved staircases (figure 101). However, acknowledging the public pull of Chippewa Square, Cluskey included a one-story semicircular Ionic porch centered on the east side of the house facing the square. This architectural gesture toward the public realm was grander both in scale and in architectural order than that of the house's entry porch, an effect that was made even more imposing by architect Henrik Wallin in 1911, when he rebuilt the side porch into its current form using double-height (colossal order) columns as part of a renovation that added a third story to the house.

The Gothic Revival Charles Green (Green-Meldrim) House, designed by John Norris in 1853, is perhaps the most unusual of Savannah's trust lot mansion houses (figure 102). It sits thirty-five feet back from the edge of Bull Street to accommodate a fenced formal garden. A shallow iron veranda wraps across both the eastern and southern facades, punctuated on center by the cast-iron entrance portico on the south side facing Macon Street, the central trust street. The service wing extending to the rear of the trust lot (to the west) is organized along the north side of the lot to frame a small garden on the southern "inner" half. This unusual

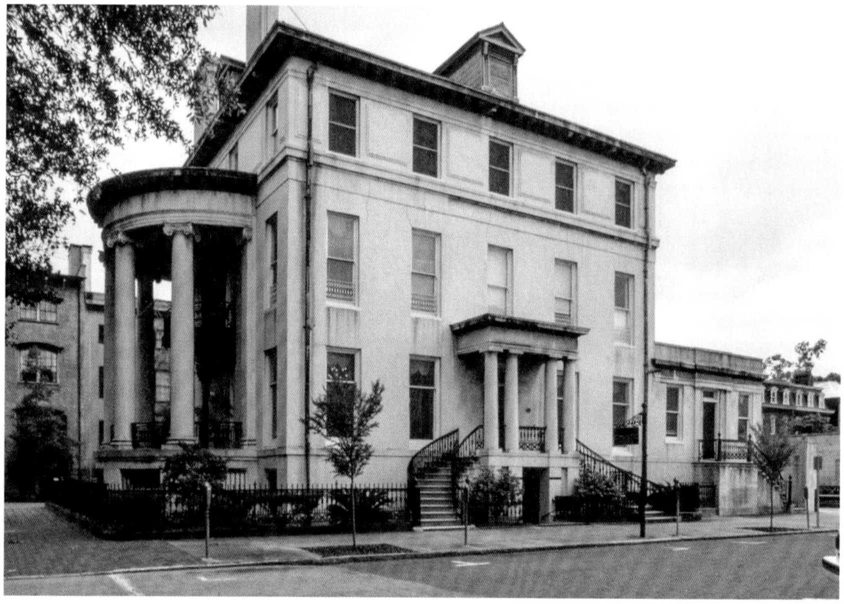

FIGURE 101. Moses Eastman House, 17 West McDonough Street, designed by Charles Cluskey in 1844–47; renovated and enlarged for Joseph Hull by Wallin & Young, 1911. The monumental Ionic porch replaced a smaller one in the 1911 renovation, and a third story was added. Photo by Robin B. Williams, Virtual Historic Savannah Project, 2001.

design inspired the vestry of St. John's Episcopal Church, which had purchased the house in 1943, to acquire the intervening section of Macon Street from the city in 1960 and create a formal garden, designed by local landscape architect Clermont Lee, thus enhancing the mansion's exotic urban villa character. Along the garden's western edge, a Gothic-style arcaded portico connects the church to the service entrance of the Green-Meldrim House.

Beginning with the James Habersham Jr. House, trust lot mansions one by one yielded, as it were, to the public-use "zoning" inherent in a trust lot site. In most cases, this did not alter the exterior appearance of the houses. The notable exception is the Telfair House at 121 Barnard Street upon its conversion in 1886 into the Telfair Academy of Arts and Sciences, the South's first art museum (figure 100). The Telfair Academy was founded by the bequest of Mary Telfair, heir to the estate of her father, the Revolutionary War hero and Georgia governor Edward Telfair. Mary stipulated that the Telfair mansion, designed by William Jay in 1818–19, be transformed into an academy of art and science upon her death. To accomplish this, the academy's first director, Carl Brandt, hired New York–based architect Detlef Lienau to modify the house and design a large addition. Opened to the public in 1886, Lienau's addition follows an "engine and caboose" pattern of growth, producing a tripartite sequence of linked structures, from the mansion to the skylit exhibition hall to an administrative section at the rear western end of

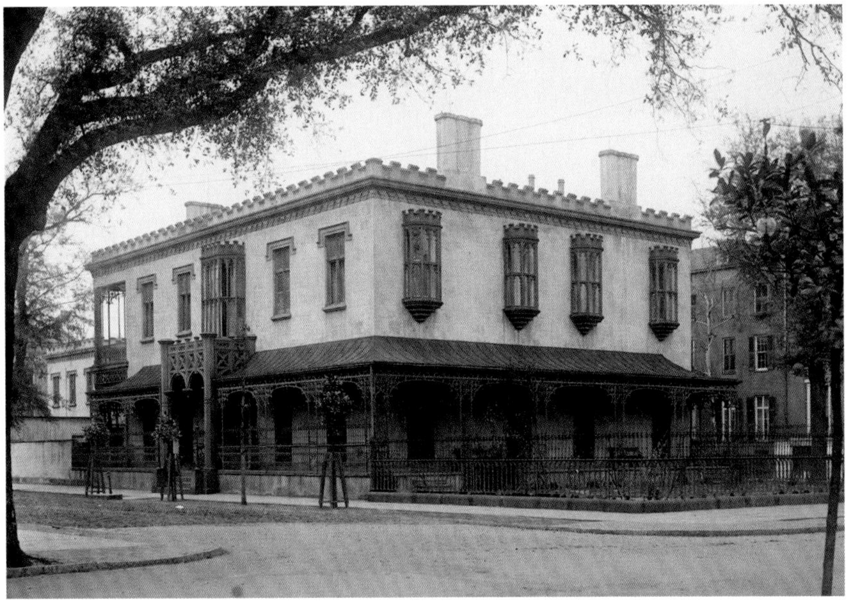

FIGURE 102. Charles Green (Green-Meldrim) House, 327 Bull Street, designed by John S. Norris, 1853. Photo ca. 1900, Detroit Publishing Company, Library of Congress, Prints and Photographs Division.

the trust lot. This final section gives the appearance of an austere rowhouse, with its bay windows and recessed entry portico accessed by a stair facing the central trust street.

TYTHING LOT MANSIONS

As the most public examples of residential architecture in Savannah, trust lot houses are eye-catching, but an equal number of mansions are located on tything lots. As a rule, end tything lots abutting central north–south streets were preferred for mansions, which could be sited fronting the square, rendering them pseudo trust lots (figure 61). A majority of tything lot mansions occupy a double lot, which allows space for a side garden (figure 103). Five of Savannah's grandest surviving tything lot mansions are sited on the innermost lot, directly facing a square. The Isaiah Davenport House at 324 East State Street (1821) on Columbia Square is the earliest example of this type. Both the Sorrel-Weed House at 6 West Harris Street (1840) on Madison Square, designed by Charles Cluskey, and the Abraham Minis House at 204 East Jones Street (ca. 1856), designed by Stephen Decatur Button, offer a variation and elaboration of this same basic building type, including having a side garden.

A dozen more freestanding mansion houses following the center hall, five-bay formula occupy the inner end of a tything block that faces outward from its ward,

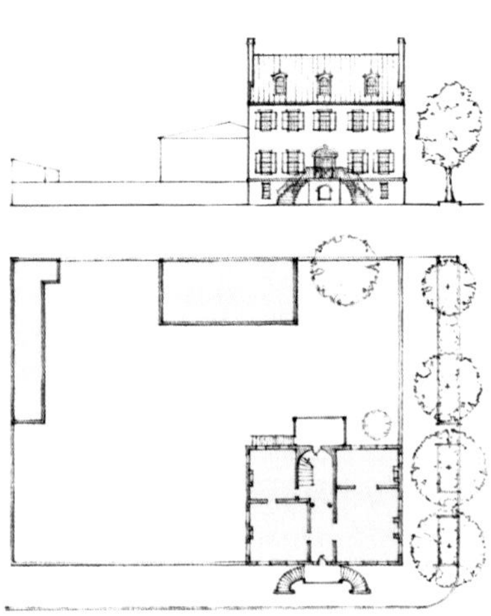

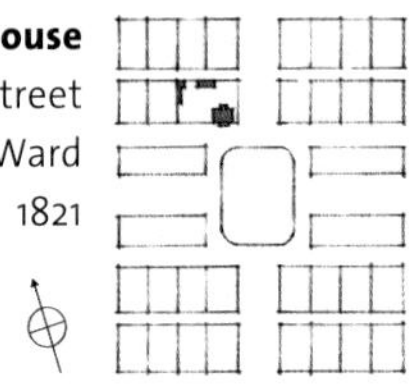

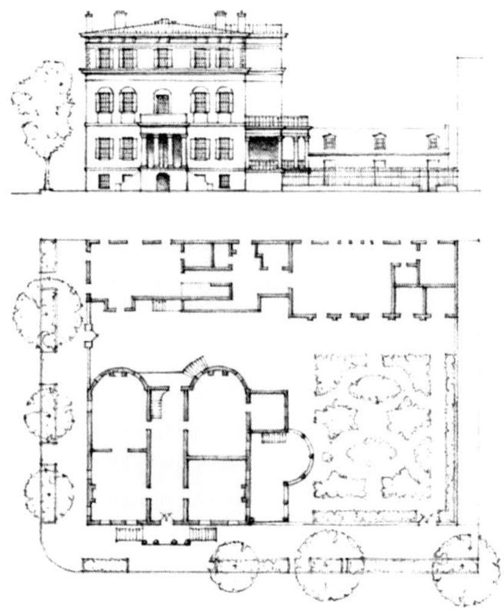

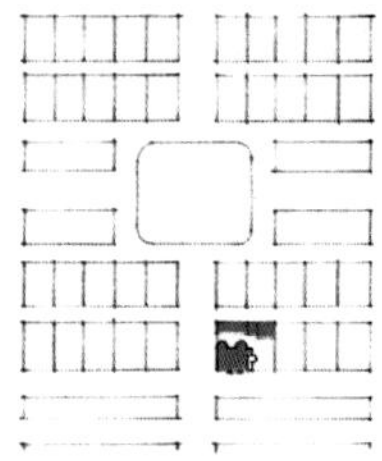

Isiah Davenport House
324 East State Street
NW Tything, Columbia Ward
1821

James Wayne Moore House
(Juliette Gordon Low Birthplace)
10 East Oglethorpe Avenue
SE Tything, Percival Ward
1820; third story and side porch additions 1886

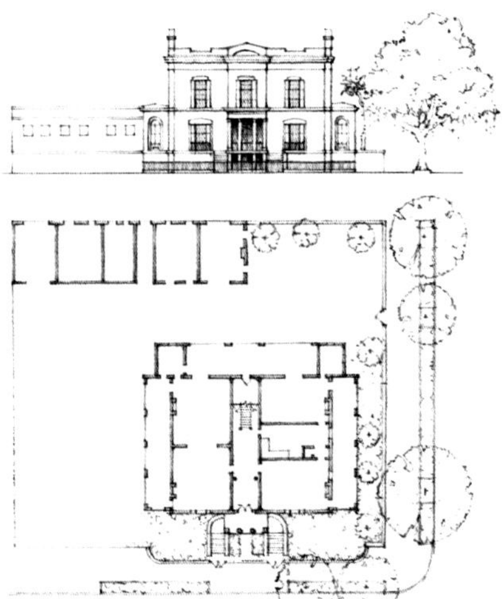

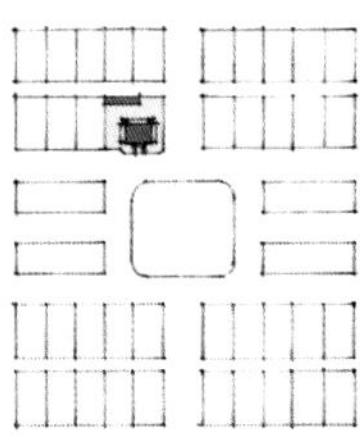

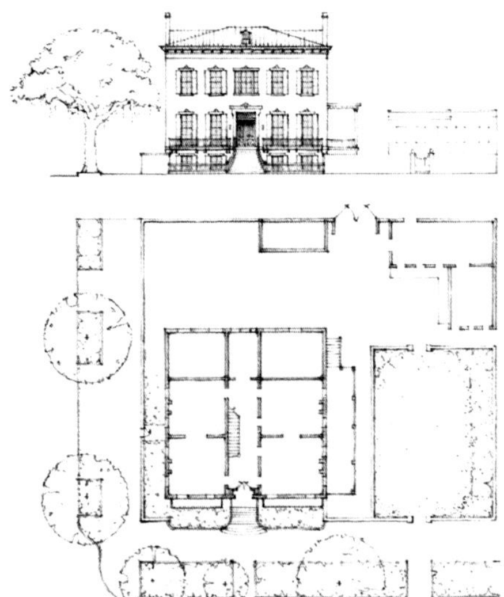

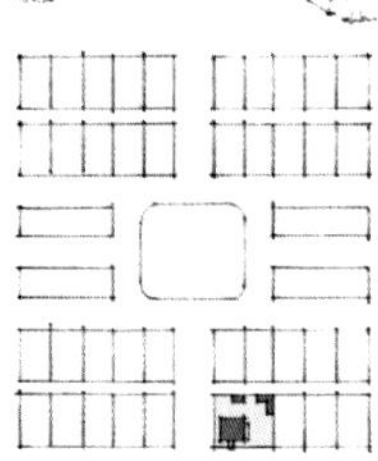

Francis Sorrel House
(Sorrel-Weed House)
6 West Harris Street
NW Tythig, Jasper Ward
1839–43

Abraham Minis House
204 East Jones Street
SE Tything, Lafayette Ward
1859–61

toward one of the grand east–west, tree-lined avenues—Oglethorpe Avenue, Liberty Street, Jones Street, and Gaston Street. Half of the houses have galleries on one side, similar to those on Savannah single houses. In nine of the twelve cases, the house abuts the central north–south street.

The James Moore Wayne House (now designated the Juliette Gordon Low Birthplace; 1820), abutting Bull Street on the north side of Oglethorpe Avenue (at 10 East Oglethorpe), further demonstrates the adaptability of Savannah's architecture to its plan (figure 103). The Wayne House originally resembled a trust lot mansion, with five bays, a center hall, and two stories over a raised basement. In 1886, the Gordon family commissioned New York architect Detlef Lienau to add a third story and a substantial porch on the east side to overlook the adjacent private garden. Tything lot mansions, like many of the city's single houses, often expand outward with side gardens or side porches, or both. Five other mansion houses have side porches facing Bull Street, addressing its importance as Savannah's primary processional route.[18]

SAVANNAH'S COTTAGES, rowhouses, single houses, and mansions embody the social and economic structure of the city in the antebellum era, including its widespread adoption of institutionalized slavery. Approximately three-quarters of the historic district's rowhouses were built before the Civil War. Their ground-floor workspaces, yards, and carriage houses were developed to facilitate the use of enslaved people that made possible the levels of comfort and luxury enjoyed by their enslavers. While cottages, intended to house low-wage workers, mostly disappeared from the immediate Savannah Plan area, numerous examples survive along the plan's margins, extending into suburban neighborhoods. And yet all four building types have persisted into the present era. Their compositional and decorative features were incorporated into late nineteenth-century rowhouses, single houses, and even worker housing projects, not to mention commercial and institutional buildings. Many trust lot houses now serve as public institutions, but antebellum rowhouses continue to function as private residences. Workspaces once designed to separate and hide enslaved laborers from the privileged families they worked for have been reconfigured to suit the needs of today's less formal, comfort-craving urban dwellers. Upstairs kitchens and breakfast rooms have been added; work yards have become intimate gardens and patios, and basements and carriage houses have been turned into rental properties.

FIGURE 103. (*Facing page*) Savannah mansion houses on "inner" tything lots facing a square or an east–west boundary street. Drawing by Hamilton Brindley.

Savannah's single, double, row, and mansion houses are variations of a unified Savannah house typology. They all share the same basic cubic geometries and common features—elevated entries with exterior stairs, tall ceiling heights, and, occasionally, side galleries and side gardens. In fact, several have mutated from one subtype to another, such as the Anderson House at 2 West Oglethorpe Avenue, which began as a side hall rowhouse and through a series of additions became a five-bay mansion house with side galleries. Like the city's urban plan, the Savannah house is standardized in its basic dimensions and regularized in its primary forms, making it expandable and adaptable to changing uses. The house is the primary building type of the city; its forms and patterns are routinely appropriated by the city's commercial and civic architecture. Together, Savannah's houses form the primary melody line of the city's architectural symphony.

CHAPTER SIX

CIVIC BUILDINGS

Wherever the temple is to be built, however, its principal facade should be towards the piazza or the noblest street.
—SEBASTIANO SERLIO, 1547

With her broad, well paved streets, intersecting at right angles, as originally planned by Oglethorpe; with her thousands of shade trees, many parks, squares and open places, constructed on a comprehensive scale, and in a beautifully artistic manner; with her churches, schools, libraries, art galleries, public buildings and monuments, Savannah is a delight to the eye and the admiration of visitors and residents alike.
—Savannah Chamber of Commerce, 1911

The prominence, abundance, and distribution of its "Publick lotts" are evidence of an innate civic spirit infused into the geometry of the Savannah Plan from its inception. For the Trustees and royal governors in Savannah's early days, and even for the elected city council following the American Revolution, the public realm included religious, charitable, medical, educational, and market usages. Governmental institutions themselves are surprisingly invisible in these early years. Lacking buildings of their own, legislative proceedings and court activities took place in buildings built for other purposes. Such a robust understanding of public life, though different from our own, was not unusual in the eighteenth or nineteenth centuries, but the city's urban plan ensured that the public realm was accommodated in ways that were both prominent and pervasive throughout the town (figures 71 and 73). The coding of a civic spirit into the plan has in turn energized and disciplined the design of Savannah's civic buildings, even for the few that have been built on sites beyond the public lots initially reserved for them. Like the city's residential architecture, Savannah's civic and religious buildings are typical of their type and time, but their placement, scale, and massing, and in some cases their design details, are unmistakably determined by the city plan.

Savannah's civic buildings are more varied and changeable in their architectural design than are its domestic buildings. The earliest descriptions of the town reveal an assortment of purpose-built and adaptively reused structures serving a blend of religious, civic, and governmental purposes. As in other colonial American towns, churches and synagogues played a vital role in Savannah's civic and social life; they are naturally among its most prominent and monumental structures. Savannah's nonreligious civic buildings began as nonspecialized structures, serving multiple and often incompatible purposes. For example, the Filature, a wooden structure built on the northeast trust lot of Reynolds Ward sometime before 1751 and then rebuilt in 1769, was intended for the processing of silk, but it also served as a courthouse, a council meeting hall, a theatre, and even a ballroom.[1] Prior to the early nineteenth century, judicial proceedings took place in a variety of locations, including the Filature, the City Exchange, a tavern, churches, and even private residences.[2] An assortment of other civic buildings appear in colonial records, but none survived the great fire of 1796. The nineteenth and early twentieth centuries saw grander scale and more specialized civic buildings, some located on trust lots but others finding tything lots more accommodating. The postwar era—the age of "urban renewal"—saw civic architecture abandon traditional "civic" modes of representation and scale, producing buildings that fragmented the civilizing geometry of the Savannah Plan.

City and county governments beginning in the nineteenth century oversaw the construction of courthouses, market structures, jails, fire stations, schools, and performing arts facilities. The federal government built a custom house, a combined courthouse and post office, a marine hospital, a military barracks, and, in the 1980s, a campus of generic federal buildings. Numerous private charitable institutions in the nineteenth century constructed orphanages, homes for the poor, hospitals, and schools. Fraternal orders, militia companies, social clubs, and academies erected meeting halls, lodges, libraries, armories, and museums, often sharing facilities.[3] Although Savannah's civic buildings have evolved in many ways, they have not failed to reveal the orchestrating influence of the Savannah Plan.

Government Buildings

CITY HALL

Savannah's most prominent civic building today is literally an outlier. Designed by Hyman Witcover and completed in 1906, the domed City Hall (the dome was gilded in 1987) stands as the terminal focal point of the Bull Street visual axis. The 160-foot-tall concrete, stone, and steel structure rises on the north side of Bay Street, straddling the 40-foot bluff that descends to the river, while its alignment with Bull Street links it with the orderly grid of squares and blocks of the city above the bluff that it faces. The present City Hall occupies the same location as two earlier civic structures. The first was the Vendue House, a wooden structure built during the era of the royal governors for the purpose of accommodating public auctions, including the selling of enslaved Africans. Its destruction in the great fire of 1796 led to the construction of the City Exchange, Savannah's first monumental civic building. The Exchange was a multipurpose building commissioned by the municipal government but funded by a combination of public funds and private investment (figure 104). Designed by a French-born builder named Adrian Boucher in 1799 and completed in 1802, it was a three-story brick-and-stone structure with a central clock tower and a tripartite, seven-bay facade calibrated to the width of Bull Street that was aggrandized in 1855 by a two-story portico and spired cupola. It was "the most notable building in the city," according to a newspaper account of 1879.[4] In 1903, against significant public opposition, the city council voted "to raze and replace the Exchange" with Witcover's City Hall building, stating that the "Exchange has served its time and must fall before this progressive century."[5] Reflecting the influence of the 1893 World's Columbian Exposition in Chicago, Witcover's fashionable Beaux-Arts classical design included crowning sculptural groups of four-horse chariots (*quadrigae*) that were not carried out (figure 105).

FIGURE 104. (*Left*) City Exchange, designed by Adrian Boucher, 1799–1802. Photo by Edward Wilson, 1904 (prior to demolition). Courtesy of the City of Savannah Municipal Archives.

FIGURE 105. (*Right*) Watercolor rendering of City Hall as proposed in 1903 by architect Hyman W. Witcover. Courtesy of the City of Savannah Municipal Archives, City of Savannah, Clerk of Council's Office, Savannah, Georgia.

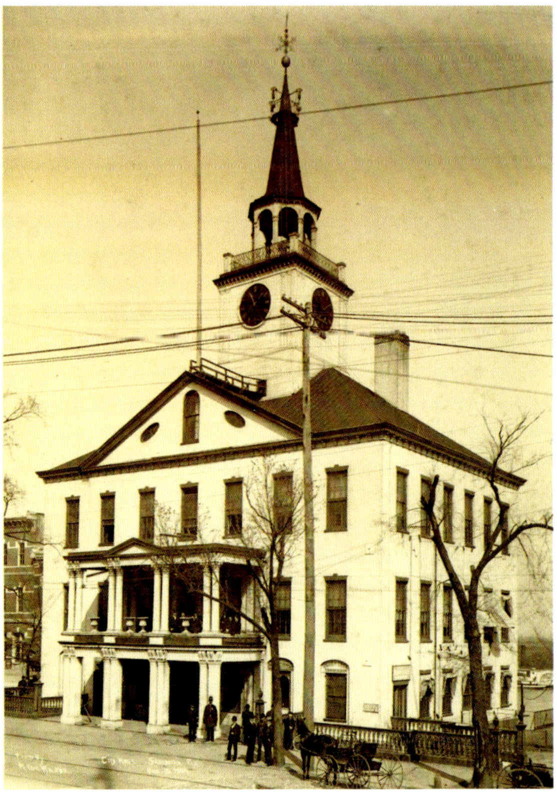

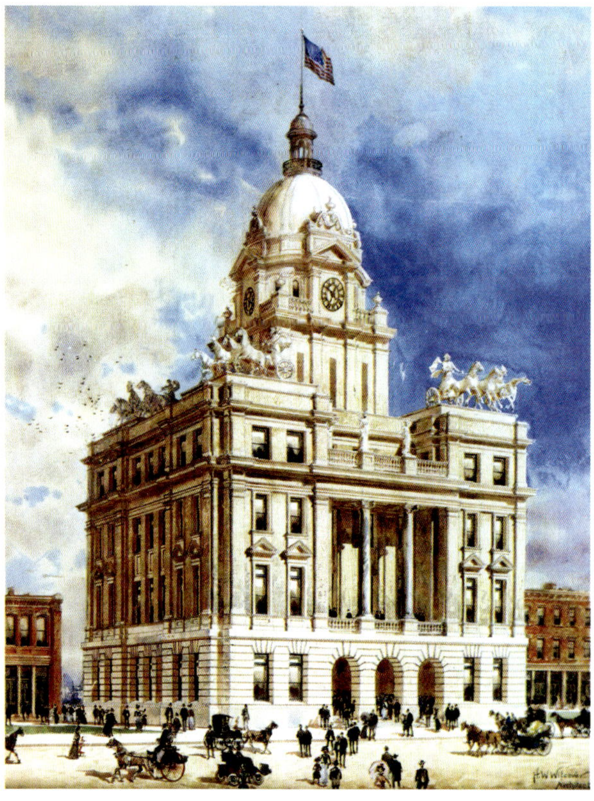

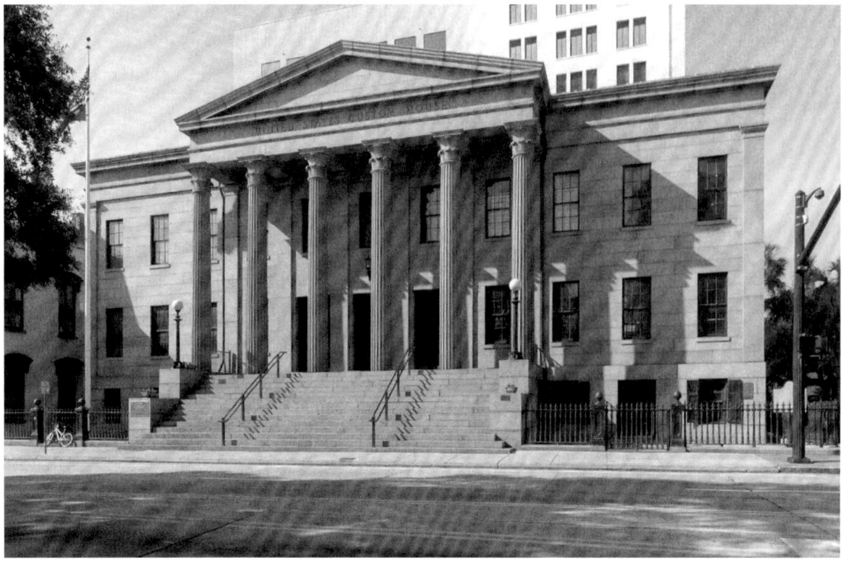

FIGURE 106. United States Custom House, 1–5 East Bay Street, designed by John Norris, 1848–52. Photo by Robin B. Williams, 2014.

THE UNITED STATES CUSTOM HOUSE

The monumental character and dramatic placement of City Hall established a vital connection to the Savannah Plan, even though the building stands *outside* the plan's boundaries. Obliquely across from City Hall is the similarly monumental U.S. Custom House, a building that sits *inside* the city plan but resolutely faces away from it, toward the Savannah River and the wharf lots and warehouses. The Custom House stretches across the two tything lots closest to Bull Street, fronting Bay Street in the northeast tything of Derby Ward. Its orientation to the port was clearly motivated by its function of collecting customs duties. The broad cruciform building, designed by New York architect John Norris in 1848 and completed in 1852, rises two stories above a tall at-grade basement and nearly fills the full width of the site with its eleven bays; at the rear it is set back by five feet from the lane (figure 106). In front, the stern gray granite pile boasts a monumental hexastyle portico of monolithic Tower-of-the-Winds order columns, accessed by a steep flight of steps that extends a few feet beyond the property line onto the public sidewalk. The encroaching staircase, in concert with the severe Greek Revival style and the imposing monumental portico, boldly asserts the federal government's presence at the head of Bull Street.

COURTHOUSES: STRUGGLING TO FIT IN

The Gordon View of 1734 shows that Savannah's first courthouse was a small multipurpose building occupying part of a tything lot now occupied by the U.S.

Custom House (figure 9).[6] Multiple locations and buildings have served as courthouses since then. In 1736, a wooden building serving as both a church and a courthouse was built on the southeastern trust lot facing what is now Wright Square.[7] This building was replaced in 1766 by a more substantial, single-purpose courthouse featuring a columnar portico on the same lot.[8] That building was heavily damaged, first during the Revolutionary War and again in the great fire of 1796, prompting plans to build a new courthouse as early as 1804. A variety of economic and political problems delayed the construction of a new Chatham County courthouse until 1832. Built on the same site as the previous courthouse and designed in a Greek Revival style by Providence architects Russell Warren, William Tallman, and James C. Bucklin, this structure filled most of the western two-thirds of the trust lot, with Doric porticos on all four facades. The two-story building stood a short pair of steps above grade, perhaps to facilitate easy accessibility. The rear third of the trust lot served as a walled yard (figure 107).

This building was replaced in 1889–90 by the current three-story courthouse designed by Boston architect William Gibbons Preston, a building that more than fills the trust lot, encroaching slightly into the public realm—by six feet, three inches on the west and by eight feet on the north.[9] Adopting a playful Romanesque style, the massing of the structure is broken into five sections of alternating heights. Asymmetry is introduced by adding a tower on the northwest corner, responding to the centripetal pull toward the center of the square, while the main entrance facing the square, framed by a generous Richardsonian round arch, acknowledges the lot's central axis. By the 1970s this courthouse proved to be inadequate for the needs of the growing county, leading commissioners to build the present courthouse, along with a new jail and parking garage, on a superblock assembled on the western half of Liberty Ward (figure 46). Displacing approximately twenty buildings and destroying the original street grid, this government complex stands out for its refusal to cooperate with the orchestrating geometry of the Savannah Plan.

Across from the county courthouse on Wright Square is a prodigious federal courthouse that originally served also as a post office and as offices for the U.S. Army Corps of Engineers and the U.S. Weather Bureau. The Tomochichi Federal Building and United States Courthouse, as it has been known since 2005, stands as yet another anomaly in the Savannah Plan. Designed by Jeremiah O'Rourke and William Aiken in an ornate Neo-Renaissance style, the building occupied the entire southwest trust lot when it was originally constructed in 1894–99, with its primary entrance in the center of the long facade fronting President Street, the central trust street (figure 108). Rising from the center of this original building is a 150-foot-tall marble tower. In 1930–32, the government almost tripled the size of the building so that it spanned the trust street and most of the adjacent trust lot (figure 109), perhaps using the Municipal Auditorium and its consolidation of trust

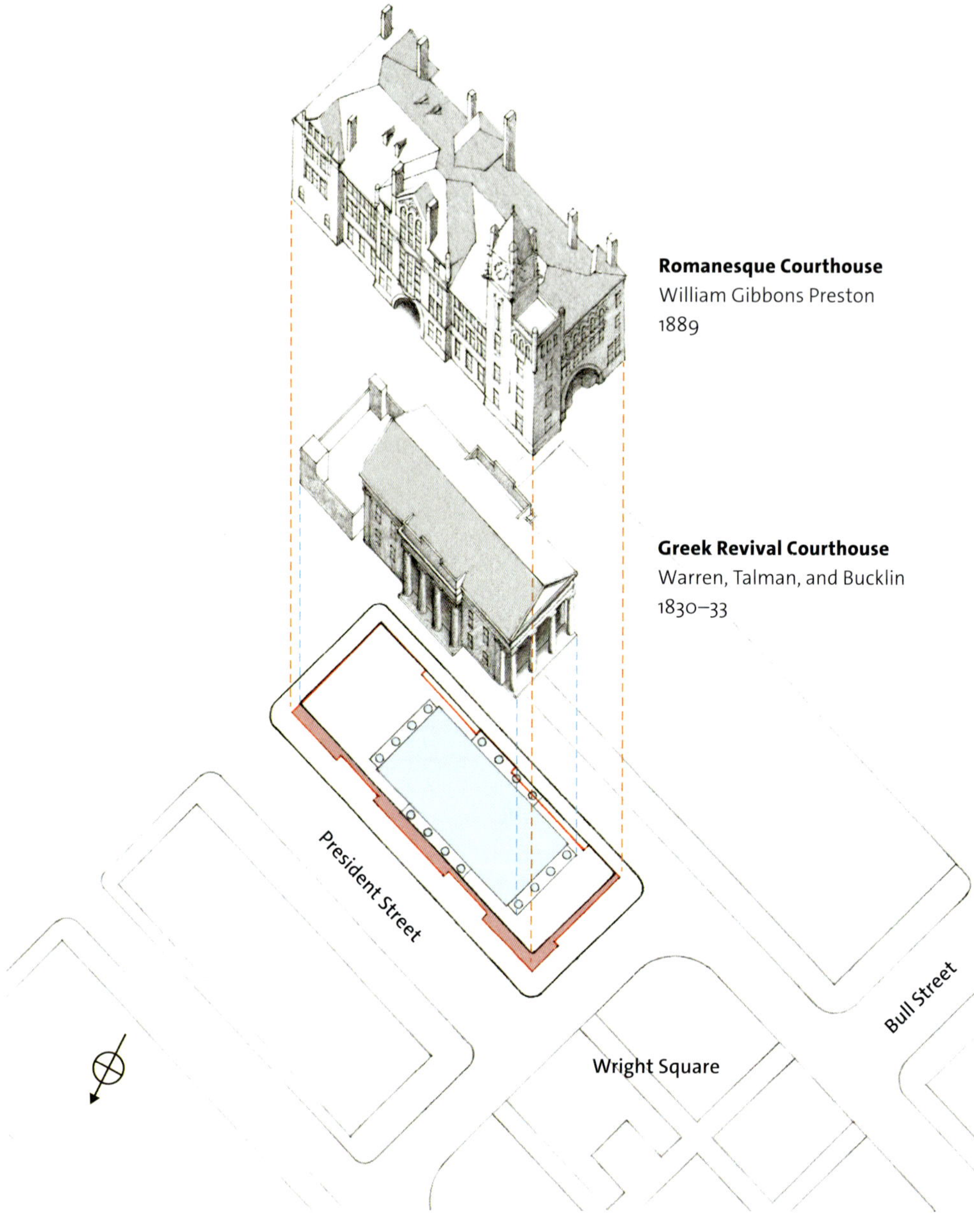

FIGURE 107. Two successive Chatham County courthouses on the southeast trust lot of Percival Ward facing Wright Square. The red area represents encroachments onto public sidewalks. Drawing by Hamilton Brindley.

lots overlooking Orleans Square in 1916 as a model. The expanded building faces Wright Square with rather understated arched entrances at either end. A loading dock for the post office delivery trucks shifted from the original rear facing York Street (where the opening was filled) to the new broadened rear facing Whitaker, a more appropriate utilitarian street for such a purpose. Using the same materials, architectural forms, and ornamental motifs, the expanded design so seamlessly continues the appearance of the original building that few observers can tell it

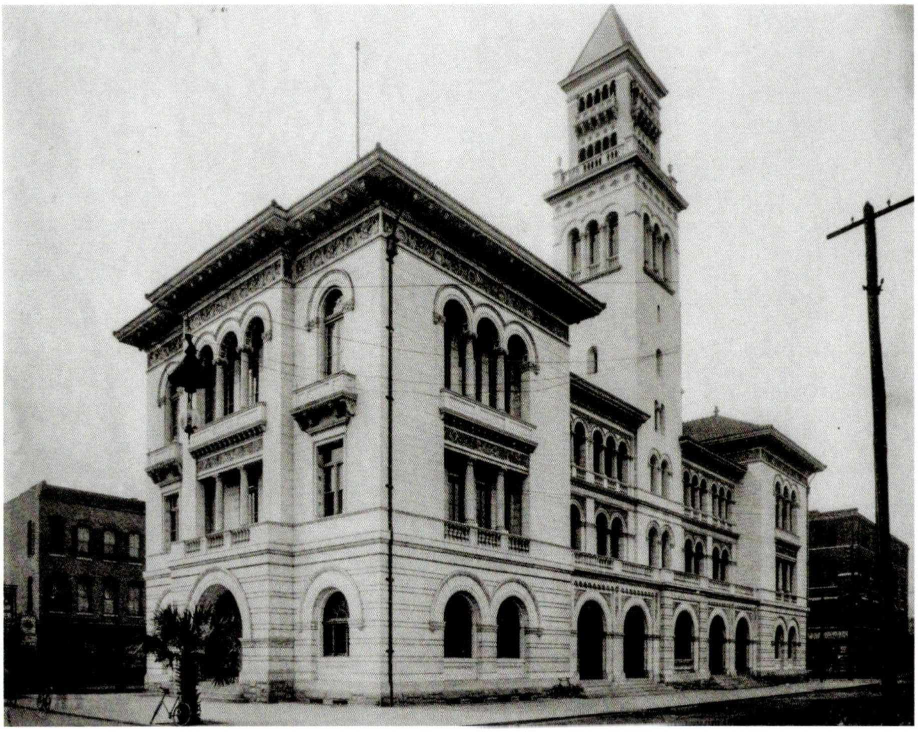

FIGURE 108. Federal building (U.S. courts, post office, Army Corps of Engineers, and Weather Bureau) on southwest trust lot of Percival Ward facing President Street, designed by Jeremiah O'Rourke and William Aiken, 1894–99. Photo from Charles Edgeworth Jones, *Art Work of Augusta and Savannah, Georgia* (Gravure Illustration, 1902).

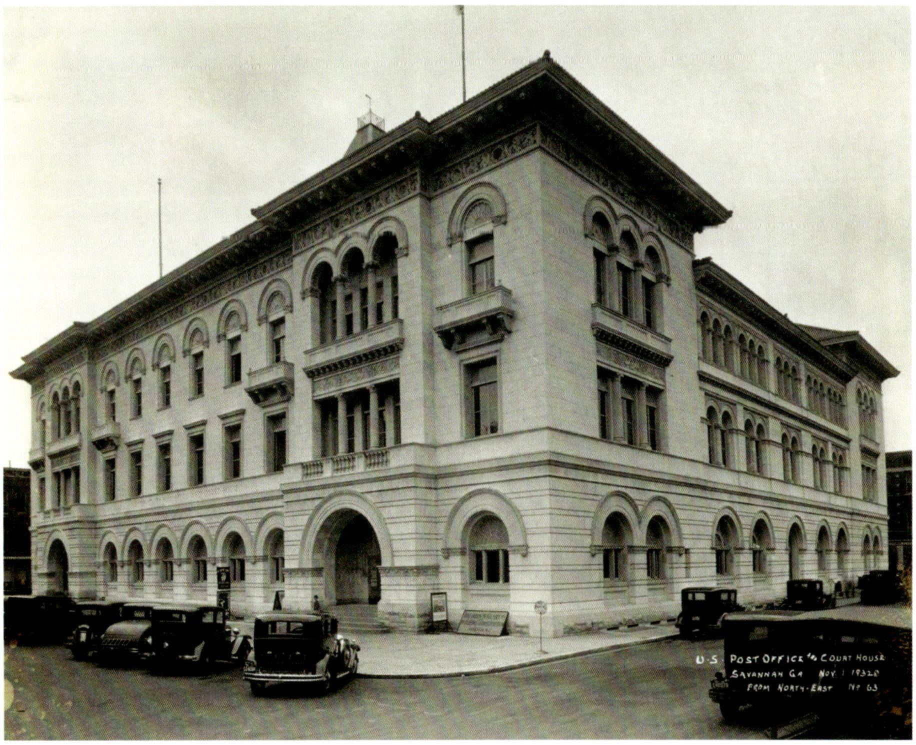

FIGURE 109. U.S. post office and courthouse after expansion under Supervising Architect of the Treasury Department James A. Wetmore, 1930–32. Renamed the Tomochichi Federal Building and United States Courthouse in 2005. National Archives, RG 121–BS, Box 19, Folder B. Wikimedia Commons.

was an addition. Its large scale, expensive materials, and refined ornamentation endow the building with an air of dignity, but lacking a central entrance in its main facade, it presents a visual puzzle for those viewing it from Wright Square. The 150-foot-tall former entrance tower remains, but its placement in the composition appears arbitrary. Rather than settle for a campus of multiple buildings, the federal government opted to create a building lot bigger than the Savannah Plan allowed. It is currently undergoing a major renovation in conjunction with the construction of yet another courthouse directly across Whitaker Street in the adjoining Heathcote Ward.

MULTISITE COMPLEXES: JULIETTE GORDON LOW FEDERAL BUILDINGS

The story of the Tomochichi Federal Building is tied to a neighboring federal building project. In the 1980s, needing space primarily for the district offices of the Army Corps of Engineers, the federal government built a campus of three buildings in Heathcote Ward, directly across Whitaker Street from the historic federal courthouse and post office (figure 110). The buildings, known today as the Juliette Gordon Low (JGL) Federal Buildings, were designed by the Atlanta firm of Stevens and Wilkinson in 1985. Clad with six-inch ceramic tiles, they became derisively known as the "bathroom tile buildings" by locals and were subjected to much criticism from the Historic Savannah Foundation and other concerned citizens for displacing historic buildings and for lacking architectural refinement.

Beyond aesthetics, the group of three buildings illustrates both the potential and the shortcomings of the plan's constraints. Building A (still standing) and Building B (replaced) occupied the pair of trust lots on the east side of Telfair Square and conformed to traditional trust lot buildings with their three-story rectangular massing that filled the front three-quarters of each lot and their orientation with monumental porticos facing the square. Their playful but glibly contrived porticos announced the nearly twin buildings to be postmodern descendants of the classical trust lot buildings on Johnson Square. Though it was closed to traffic, President Street between these trust lot buildings remained in use as a semiprivate parking lot. The main building (C) covers the entire southeast tything, obliterating its lane. Despite its normative three-story height and alignment with the property lines, a fenestration pattern meant to evoke Savannah rowhouses, and the use of traditional channeled masonry on the ground floor, Building C's otherwise unarticulated three-hundred-foot-long main facade with its flush-mounted windows presents a profound lack of sensitivity to the traditions of tything lot buildings. The recessed central entrance hides behind the open ground-floor piers, while the inside (northwest) corner ignores the presence of the

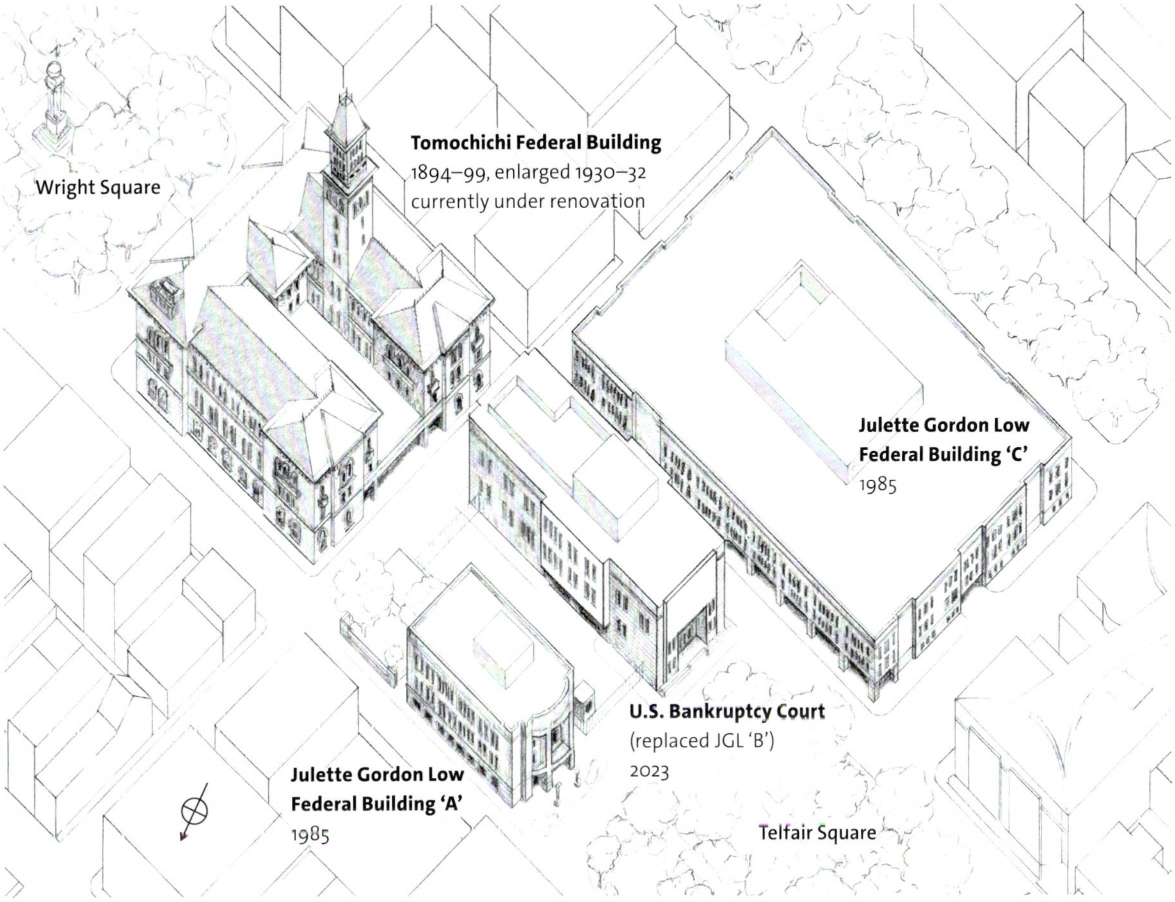

FIGURE 110. Federal buildings on Wright Square and Telfair Square. Drawing by David Gobel.

square. Along Barnard Street, a series of modestly recessed sections of that facade fails to reduce the building's unrelenting bulk.

The need to secure more space for court functions continued to guide the evolution of this federal building campus. In 1999, the post office vacated the Tomochichi Federal Building for more modest facilities, repurposing a nineteenth-century commercial building fronting Barnard Street in the tything immediately north of JGL Building A. In 2018, in an effort to provide yet more space to supplement the Tomochichi Federal Building, the General Services Administration (GSA) announced plans to raze the two JGL trust lot buildings for a single-building replacement that would also cover the block of President Street.[10] As noted in chapter 2, local opposition to the squat proportions and low height of the proposed new building and to its modernist abstraction of glass and metal, internal parking, and destruction of a further piece of the urban plan prompted the GSA to alter its plans. Instead, it replaced the southern trust lot building (JGL Building B) with a taller single building clad in marble and brick that presents a more formal face to the square. Most significant, the revised plan preserved President Street (albeit behind gates). At one point in the negotiations with the local committee, the GSA proposed using the north trust lot for a walled parking lot, but this too met with opposition. In the end, the GSA recognized the merit of preserving JGL Building A for the purposes of "swing space" during the renovation of the Tomochichi building.

The resulting campus of four buildings (five if the current post office is included) extended over two wards constitutes one of Savannah's most convoluted architectural ensembles. In its thirst to continually expand its facilities over the course of nearly a century as a laudable commitment to remain in downtown Savannah, the federal government made repeated attempts to fit its buildings within the constraints of the Savannah Plan, but it pushed beyond those limits by covering portions of both a lane and a street. By contrast, the 1977 Chatham County Courthouse complex failed to fit in, choosing rather to ignore and dismantle its portion of the Savannah Plan.

"Fitting in" has been a problem for government institutions in the Savannah Plan from the city's origins to the present day. The dispersed, nonhierarchical nature of the plan provides them with no obvious place of prominence. As experienced on the ground, governing institutions have no obvious priority over other public institutions—with the exception of City Hall. The small scale of the plan's building lots limits their expansion. In Savannah, governmental institutions are governed by the plan.

Churches and Synagogues

Religious institutions have played a defining role in the social life of Savannah and in its architectural landscape from the city's founding to the present day, a role more recognizable and defined than that of governmental institutions. The distribution of thirteen extant churches and two synagogues (though one is now the SCAD Student Center) among thirteen of the current twenty-four wards of the Savannah Plan illustrates this point; it also reflects the variety of Savannah's faith traditions and the distributive, noncentralized nature of the plan (figure 72). Seven of the sixteen documented lost churches and synagogues stood on an additional five wards, bringing that total to eighteen. Savannah's dispersed placement of religious buildings is emblematic of the Georgia Trustees' commitment to the "free exercise" of religion. Building on this legacy in the days of the early republic, the newly formed city government in the 1790s granted lots "for the use of certain religious, literary and benevolent institutions."[11]

The number of religious institutions and their locations have changed over the years, but a few observations can be made about their current distribution: All but two of the current houses of worship occupy trust lots. The locations of these religious bodies also reflect social, economic, and racial hierarchies discernible in the plan. Nearly half of the current houses of worship are located on the prestigious Bull Street axis. Among these are historically prominent Episcopal, Lutheran, Presbyterian, and Baptist churches and the synagogue of the third-oldest Jewish congregation in the country. The two Methodist churches and the Roman Catholic cathedral are located on Barnard and Abercorn Streets, the next most central streets. Further east on Habersham Street, Unitarian and Congregationalist meetinghouses are found. In the outermost wards are the city's two most historic African American Baptist churches, one to the west on Montgomery Street and the other to the east on Houston Street. A third African American Baptist church occupies the back half of a trust lot in Wesley Ward.

TRUST LOT CHURCHES AND SYNAGOGUE

Trust lots are naturally suited for religious buildings, a use explicitly intended by the Trustees. The architectural design of the eleven extant churches and one synagogue occupying trust lots is shaped by the history of the building type, by ecclesiastical doctrines and traditions, by stylistic trends, and, of course, by the constraints of the plan. In their most essential form, these houses of worship are the simplest building type in Savannah: an oblong box housing a large auditorium preceded by an entry hall or narthex. Despite the variety of creeds, they mostly follow a consistent design formula: They face the square with a monumental entrance facade that, unlike the city's private houses, prominently displays a front gabled roof; they are aligned on the lot's central axis; and most feature a symmetrically composed facade (figure 111). Steeples of varying heights and placement are a common architectural feature. Stylistically, Gothic Revival is most prevalent with five existing churches and one synagogue. Four churches were built in classical temple forms, of which three remain. The two African Baptist churches are relatively plain variations on classical forms. First African Baptist once had a much taller multistaged steeple rising to 125 feet (visible in figure 58), but it was destroyed by a hurricane in 1893. Second African Baptist Church is the most austere church building in the Savannah Plan. It maximizes its half-trust-lot site by rising abruptly from the sidewalk to a pair of doors just two steps up that lead to the sanctuary on the second floor.

The two oldest extant church buildings, Christ Church (Episcopal) on Johnson Square and First Baptist Church on Chippewa Square, were built on trust lots shorter than the normal 180-foot depth—120 feet deep for Christ Church and 130 feet deep for First Baptist—as those squares are larger than squares in

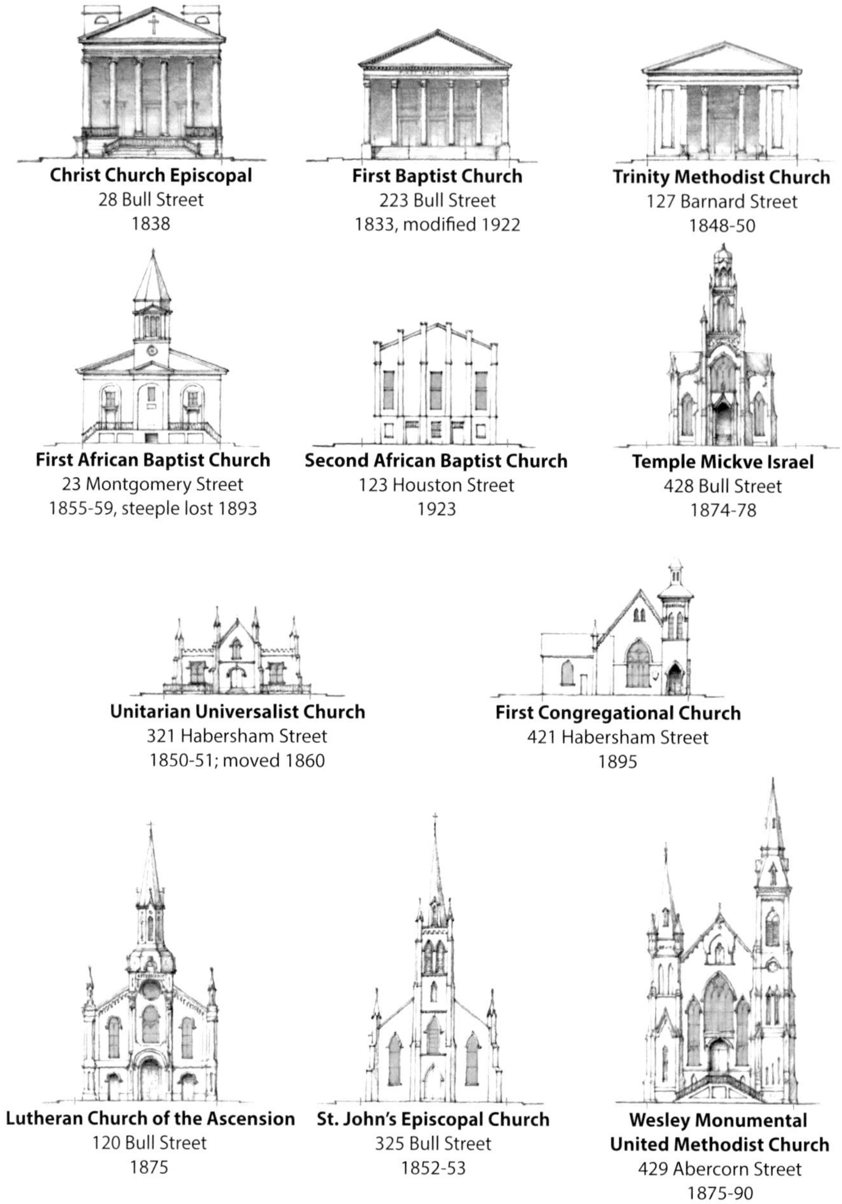

FIGURE 111. Comparative facades of houses of worship on trust lots. Drawing by Hamilton Brindley.

other wards. Both buildings occupy their entire lot. The churches and synagogue on standard trust lots range from about 65 feet to 110 feet in length; that is, each of those structures is less than two-thirds of its lot's length, with the exception of St. John's Episcopal, which is 145 feet long. Five of the churches and the synagogue have utilized the remaining property by building adjoining structures to accommodate activities supporting the ministry of the institution. In each case the

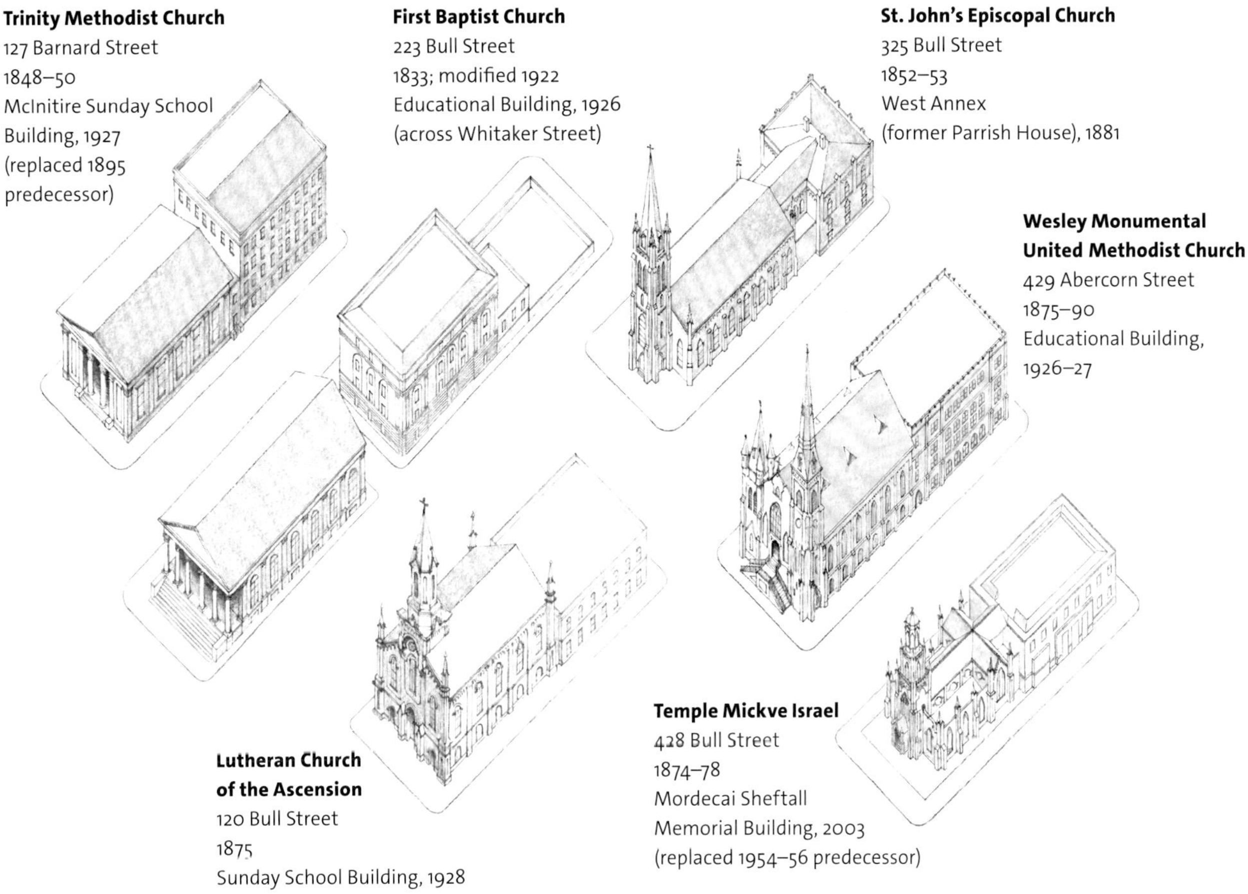

FIGURE 112. Churches and synagogue with ancillary buildings on trust lots. Drawing by Hamilton Brindley.

architectural style of the support building is harmonious with the primary building, yet deferential in its level of refinement and detail. The result is a distinctive Savannahian building composition, one that gives the appearance of a locomotive pulling a railroad car behind it (figure 112). So powerful is this pattern that First Baptist Church—which occupies the entirety of its abbreviated trust lot—erected an educational building behind its sanctuary building but across Whitaker Street, on the rear half of the northeast trust lot of neighboring Jackson Ward.

While the engine-and-caboose pattern is not unique to Savannah's houses of worship, it is a vivid example of how the Savannah Plan shapes, guides, and limits the growth of institutional building complexes. When a congregation needs to expand its facilities, it must work within the constraints of Savannah's small lot and block sizes. The plan prohibits buildings with large footprints and provides no single building site large enough to accommodate a campus of multiple structures. A church (like educational, governmental, and health-care institutions) is a clear example of an institution with such needs. Given the sixty-foot-width limitation of a trust lot and the avoidance of overly long proportions for the buildings themselves (all are well under a 2:1 ratio), the maximum seating capacity of a trust lot church is about four hundred to five hundred persons. This can be increased by adding an upper gallery, potentially allowing an additional two hundred congregants, but congregations with more than six hundred to seven hundred people are excluded altogether. A church reaching that size would be forced to move to a non–trust lot site (which happened with the two largest churches in the historic district), move to a location outside the plan altogether, or plant a new congregation within the plan (which occurred when St. John's Episcopal Church was founded by members of Christ Church).[12]

Another consequence of the small site imposed by the dimensions and orientation of trust lots is the pattern of elevating the sanctuary above grade (usually a full story) to allow space for offices, fellowship halls, and Sunday school rooms on the ground floor. Prominent external staircases at Christ Church, First African Baptist Church, and Wesley Monumental United Methodist Church broadcast this configuration. Evidently to save space and better fill the site, at least two churches—Second African Baptist and the Lutheran Church of the Ascension—have incorporated the stairs to the second-story sanctuary into the interior.

MULTISITE RELIGIOUS INSTITUTIONS WITHIN THE SAVANNAH PLAN

Adding a caboose-like building behind the main auditorium is not the only method used by trust lot church designers to increase support space for the church's ministry. Most Savannah churches own other buildings on nearby lots to support additional space requirements. Some of these are adaptively reused structures, but many were purpose-built, most often in a sympathetic but deferential architectural style. In this way, churches can create a campus of buildings, but one that is interrupted by and yet knitted into the city plan. An example of this can be seen at St. John's Episcopal Church, which added a parish house onto the back side of its trust lot in 1881 and then converted it into offices, a chapel, and an extension of the chancel in the 1950s (figure 113). In 1943 the church acquired the Green-Meldrim House on the neighboring trust lot to the north for use as a parish house and converted the former servant quarters into a rectory. In 1953 the church built an educational building on the full tything lot at 27 West Charlton Street, across from the parish house at the west end of the block. Originally designed in a modern International Style with a stylized Gothic entrance, this building was remodeled in a more traditional Gothic style in 2005 to unify it with the other buildings of the institution. The intervening section of Macon Street between the church and the Green-Meldrim House was purchased from the city in 1960 and transformed into a garden. At the same time, St. John's also acquired half of the

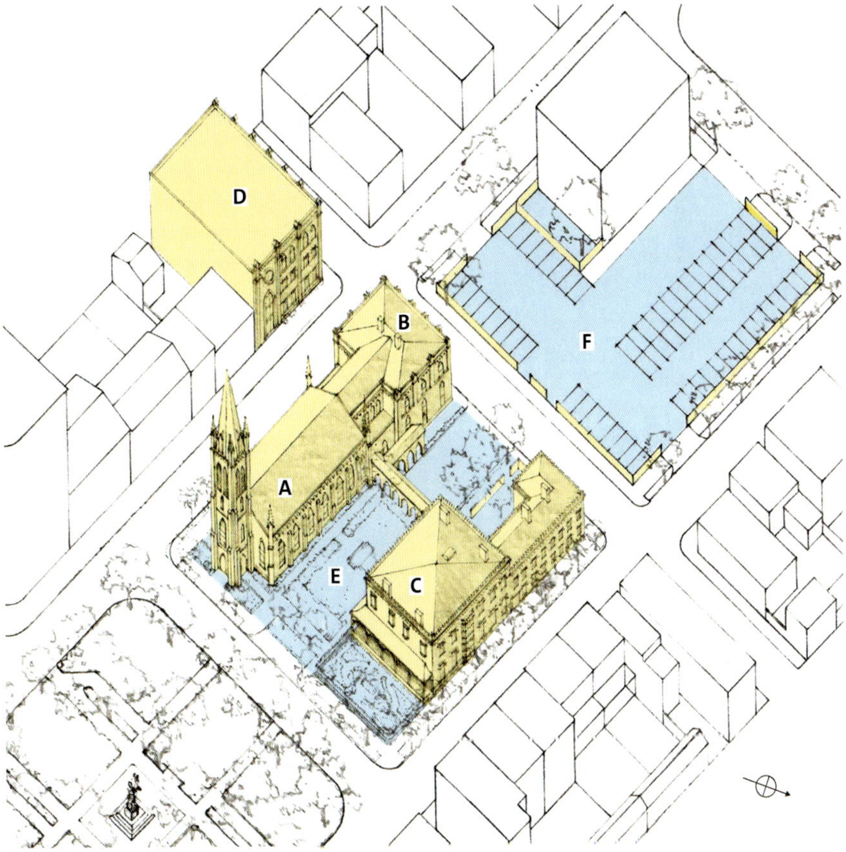

FIGURE 113. St. John's Episcopal Church and its campus of buildings. Drawing by Hamilton Brindley. (A) St. John's Episcopal Church, Calvin Otis, 1853; chancel added 1914. (B) Original parish house (west annex), 1881. (C) Green-Meldrim House (current parish house), John S. Norris, 1853, acquired 1943. (D) Cranmer Hall, 1953; enlarged and remodeled by Greenline Architects, 2005. (E) Garden (formerly Macon Street), Clermont Lee, 1961. (F) Parking lot, ca. 1960.

southeast and the entire northeast trust lots of Pulaski Ward and the section of Macon Street in between, demolishing several buildings to create a surface parking lot for staff and parishioners. Made of salvaged historic Savannah Grey bricks (possibly from buildings on the site), the low wall enclosing the parking lot serves as a meager attempt to contextualize its large expanse of asphalt that will soon be the largest surface lot within the plan once the Civic Center lot is redeveloped in the coming years.

TOO BIG FOR A TRUST LOT: CHURCHES ON GROUPED TYTHING LOTS

Two of Savannah's most prominent downtown churches were too large to fit on trust lots, so their leaders chose to build on multiple tything lots instead. Although they deviated from the expected norms dictated by the Savannah Plan, their architects adapted the trust lot formulas to a larger scale. The results in both cases are inventive responses to the plan's constraints, providing models for how large and growing institutions can flourish within the plan.

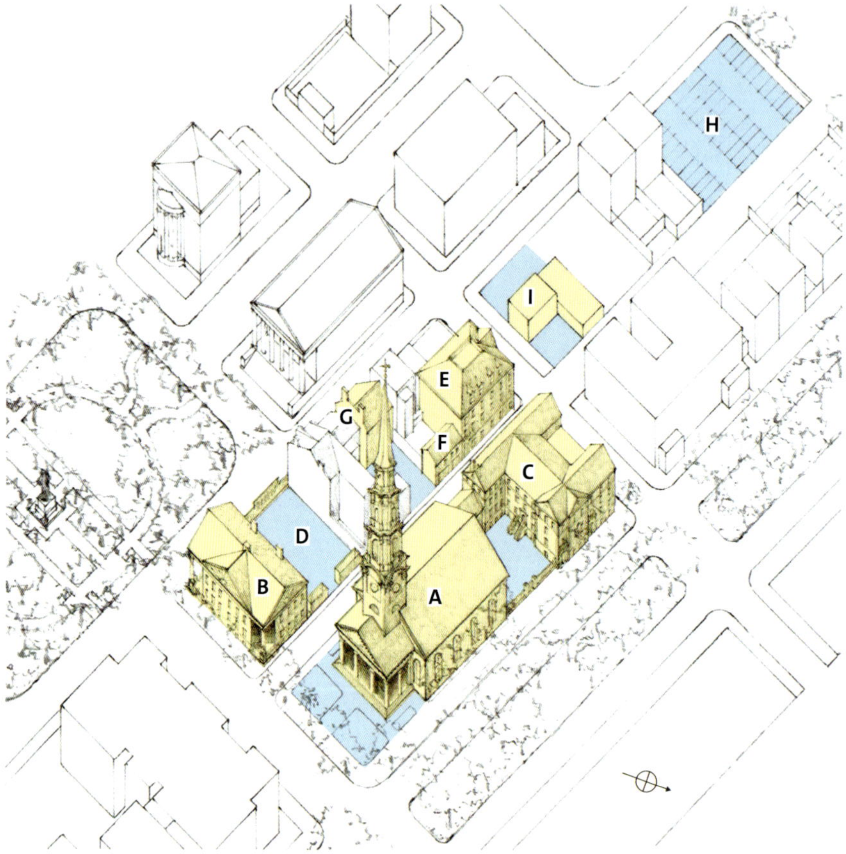

FIGURE 114. The Independent Presbyterian Church and its campus of buildings. Drawing by Hamilton Brindley. (A) Independent Presbyterian Church, John Holden Green, 1819; rebuilt by William Gibbons Preston after fire, 1891. (B) Administration building, Charles Henry, 1894. (C) Axson Memorial Building, Cram and Ferguson, 1928. (D) Parking lot, ca. 1971. (E) Whitaker Street building, Hansen Architects, 2010. (F) Intern residence (former carriage house built by John Scudder, ca. 1858), acquired 2017. (G) Adapted rowhouse (18 Hull Street), ca. 1869, acquired 2023. (H) Existing parking lot, acquired 2023. (I) Adapted gas station (ca. 1910) and parking lot, acquired 2024.

The Independent Presbyterian Church

The Independent Presbyterian Church provides an instructive case study of a public institution that grew beyond the limits of a trust lot (figure 114). In 1756 King George II granted "Lot K" in Decker Ward (the northeast trust lot, facing what is now Ellis Square) to a group of "Dissenters from the Church of England and Professors of the Doctrines of the Church of Scotland," upon which they built a brick meetinghouse that would serve them until its destruction in 1796.[13] They then built a new church on the southeast trust lot of Heathcote Ward (facing what is now Telfair Square), which survived until its destruction in 1804. No images remain of the latter building.[14] Despite hardships, the congregation was growing, and so in 1815 it purchased five contiguous lots of the northwest tything block of the newly platted Brown Ward flanking South Broad Street and commissioned John Holden Greene to design a new church similar to the architect's own First Congregational Church in Providence, Rhode Island, then under construction.

Completed in 1819, the granite structure was a premier example of the Wren-Gibbs-inspired Protestant church type so popular in early nineteenth-century America, and it became the most monumental church building in Savannah at the time. Greene's church burned in 1889 and in 1891 was replaced by the present building, designed by William Gibbons Preston as a replica of its predecessor but built with more fireproof materials. The footprint of the Independent Presbyterian Church is 80 feet wide and 135 feet deep (too wide for a trust lot). With a large upper gallery, the main auditorium was said at the time of its completion to accommodate twelve hundred persons. Its monumental Doric entrance portico faces Bull Street but sits about 45 feet back from the sidewalk, fronted by a lawn in the manner of a trust lot building facing a square.

The Independent Presbyterian Church and its front green occupy the three eastern tything lots on the block. The westernmost lot was used for the church's manse, an Italianate house designed by John Norris (1855–58) with a garden separating it from the church. In 1833 the church purchased the tything lot closest to Bull Street, across Oglethorpe Lane from the church green and facing Chippewa Square to the south. Here, a Greek Revival Sunday school building was erected, only to be replaced by a larger Victorian-style building in 1885. Just four years later, in 1889, this building was destroyed in the same fire that destroyed the church. It was replaced in 1894 by the current structure, designed by Charles Henry in a classical mode that borrows motifs directly from the church but in a simplified manner (figure 115). The building is understated but astute in its deferential acknowledgement of the monumental church to its north and public square to its south, linking them visually by the interlocking views afforded through its chamfered corner entrance porches, each supported by a single monumental Doric column.

In 1928 the church razed its venerable manse—to the protest of many—and replaced it with a Sunday school building designed by renowned Boston architect Ralph Adams Cram. The four-story Axson Memorial Building harmonizes with the classical language of the church and turns the five tything lots into a unified architectural composition that includes a formal garden and follows the engine-and-caboose configuration. Still growing, the Independent Presbyterian Church acquired the westernmost tything lot across Oglethorpe Lane from the Axson building in 2006 to build yet another Sunday school building.

This last project inspired the leadership of the church to repave the one-block length of Oglethorpe Lane in brick and granite and relandscape its borders to turn it into a pedestrian-friendly space for church members crossing from one building to another. This enhancement of the lane takes advantage of two unusual urban features: The lanes in the third row of wards, including this one, are 32½ feet wide, 10 feet wider than a typical lane within the plan, making them more like civic

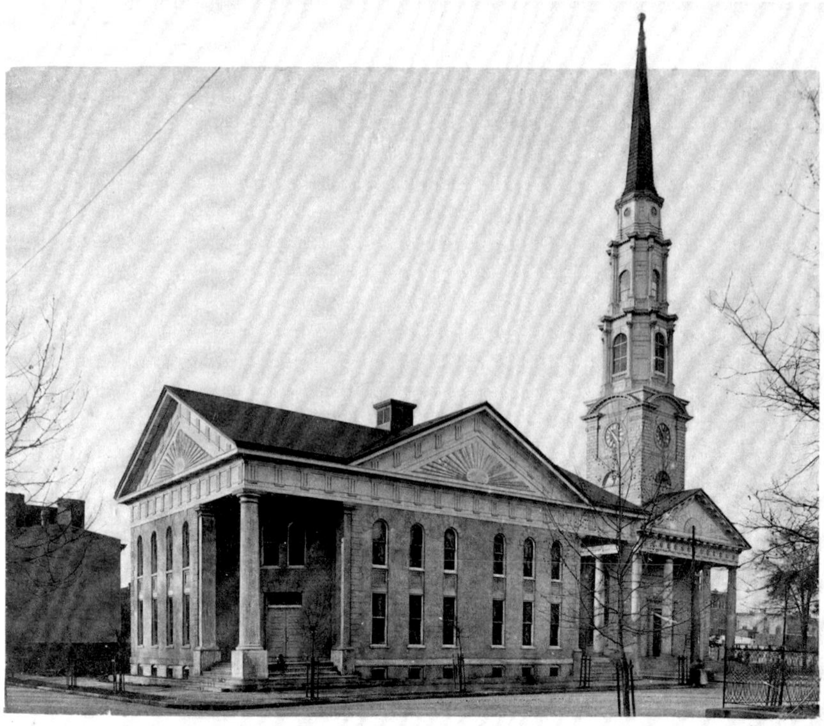

FIGURE 115. View of the Independent Presbyterian Church through a corner porch of its administration building. Photo from *Souvenir of Savannah: Photo-Gravures* (Brooklyn, 1898). Anonymous private collection.

streets in size; additionally, this one section of lane aligns with the board of education building across Bull Street to the east, whose monumental tetrastyle portico closes the vista down the lane. In 2017 the church acquired an antebellum carriage house facing Oglethorpe Lane, employing it as a residence for a church intern, and in 2023 it purchased an adjacent rowhouse at 18 Hull Street that also opens onto Oglethorpe Lane, further activating it as shared public space. Around this same time, to accommodate the parking needs of its growing congregation, the church acquired two nearby tything lots in Jackson Ward, one that was already serving as a parking lot and another housing a small, vacant building that was originally built in the early twentieth century as a gas station.

The Cathedral Basilica of St. John the Baptist

Having been excluded from the English colony of Georgia by the Georgia Trustees, Roman Catholics first arrived in Savannah in the late eighteenth century, after the American Revolution. On May 30, 1799, the city granted the front half of the northwest trust lot of Liberty Ward at the western edge of the plan to a Catholic congregation, which completed a building there in 1801.[15] By 1837 the church had moved, constructing a Greek Revival building in the Brown Ward

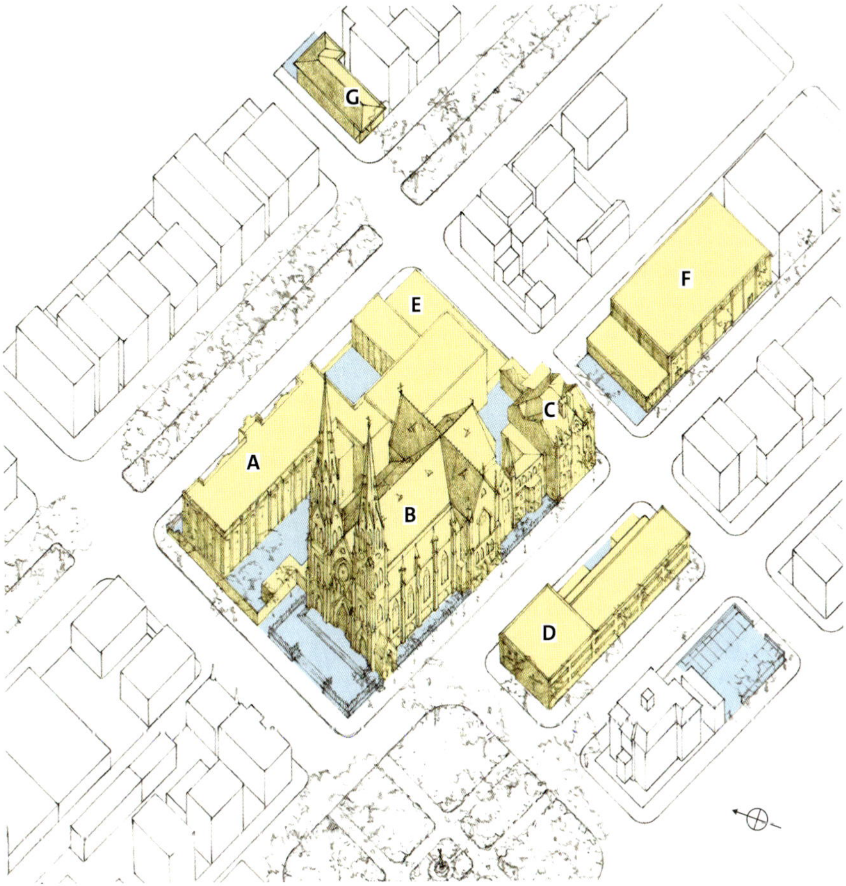

FIGURE 116. The Cathedral Basilica of St. John the Baptist and its campus of buildings. Drawing by Hamilton Brindley. (A) Convent and Academy of St. Vincent de Paul, Charles Cluskey, 1845; 1869. (B) Cathedral of St. John the Baptist, E. Francis Baldwin, 1872–76, spires 1896; interior rebuilt 1900–1914. (C) Bishop's residence (rectory), E. Francis Baldwin, 1872. (D) Cathedral Parochial School, Benjamin P. Ritzert, 1954. (E) St. Vincent's Academy (SVA), Thomas, Driscoll, and Hutton, 1955; 1960. (F) Sister Jude Walsh Hall (SVA), Benjamin P. Ritzert, 1968. (G) Peg F. Dressel Library (SVA), reused office building, 1955 (acquired 1989).

extension facing Drayton Street; it used that building until 1876, when it moved to its current site.[16] The cathedral occupies nearly four of the five lots in the northeast tything of Lafayette Ward, property conferred to the bishop by the Sisters of Our Lady of Mercy, whose convent was built on the northern half of the same tything in 1845. The cathedral was designed by Baltimore architect E. Francis Baldwin as a French Gothic–style cruciform basilica; it is two hundred feet long with a one-hundred-foot-wide transept, the largest ecclesiastical building in the historic district, able to accommodate more than a thousand worshipers (figure 116). Soon after its completion, the lane separating it from the convent was acquired by the church, thus converting the two tything blocks into a unified tything superblock.

The cathedral's imposing twin-towered facade faces west toward Abercorn Street, asserting its presence on Lafayette Square by sitting on an open forecourt (or parvis) extending forty feet from the sidewalk. Attached to the apse is a Gothic-style rectory built in 1888, once again in the engine-and-caboose configuration.

In 1954 the diocese erected a parochial school building that covers the entire northeast trust lot due south of the cathedral. Designed by Benjamin Ritzert in a tropical modernist idiom, this school building supplemented contemporaneous educational structures (St. Vincent's Academy) attached to the east end of the convent and a 1968 gymnasium across Lincoln Street on the tything lot behind the rectory. Together with an adaptively reused one-story former store across Liberty Street (now the St. Vincent's library) and a chancery building at 225 Abercorn (not shown in figure 116), the buildings of the Sisters of Our Lady of Mercy Convent, the academy, and the cathedral form a campus of related Catholic structures.

Educational Institutions

Education was a significant concern of the Georgia Trustees, who sent several schoolmasters to the colony. In 1755 the minister of Christ Church, Bartholomew Zouberbuhler, requested that the governor allocate a trust lot for a public school, noting that "he had understood, that one of the Publick Lotts in Savannah was always intended for a Publick School."[17] Although the governor's council responded by designating Lot R in Reynolds Ward for such a school, there is no evidence that a school was ever built there.

PRIMARY AND SECONDARY SCHOOLS

The first purpose-built school building in the Savannah Plan was the Chatham Academy, erected in 1813. Chartered by the Georgia Assembly in 1788, the Chatham Academy was granted a parcel of land in 1810 that was identified in the ordinance as tything lots but which was then part of the south Common (figure 36).[18] The Chatham Academy building stretched across the center three lots of the future northeast tything, with its four-story, five-part facade facing South Broad Street. Set back from the streets by a grassy border, this educational complex solved the problem of limited lot size by seizing a full tything superblock before the rest of Brown Ward was platted in 1815. This structure was replaced by the current two attached buildings, both designed in a Beaux-Arts classical style by Henry Urban, with the elementary school facing South Broad in 1901 and the high school facing Bull Street in 1906. The Chatham County school board converted these buildings into administrative offices in the 1970s, as school populations were moving to the suburbs.

Two other purpose-built elementary school buildings can be found in the downtown area of the plan today, though both have been repurposed for different educational uses. The older of the two is the Massie Common School, which consists of three structures connected by covered walkways and stretching across the two innermost lots in the southeast tything of Calhoun Ward facing the square at 207 East Gordon Street. The buildings were clearly designed for phased growth

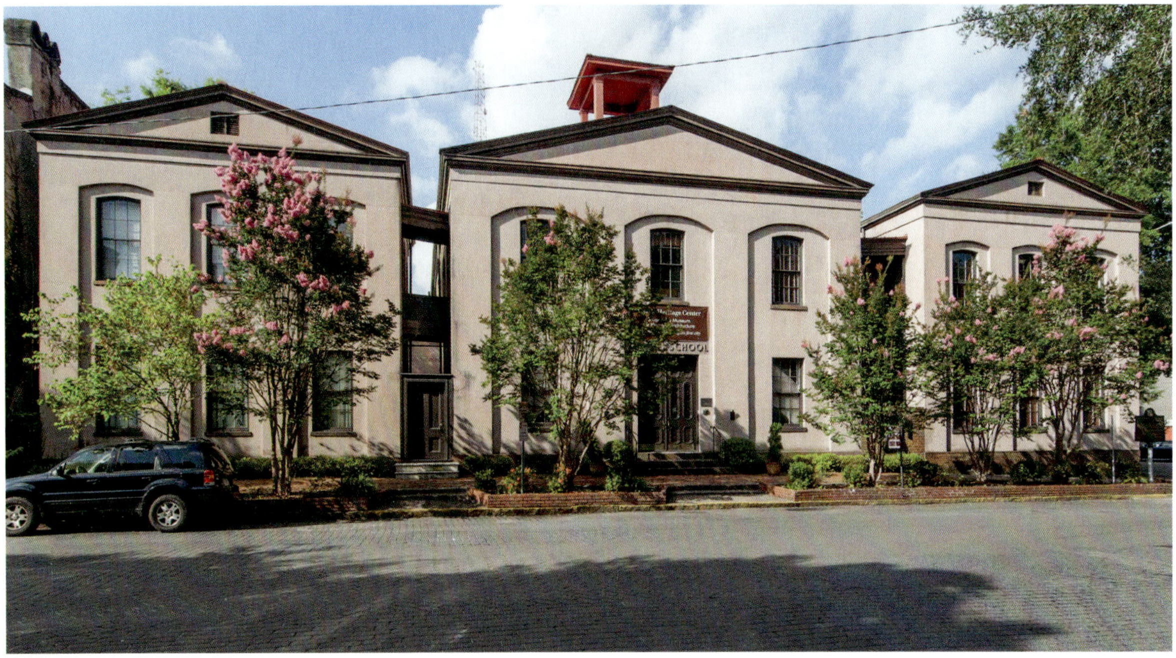

FIGURE 117. Massie Common School (now the Massie Heritage Center), 201–213 East Gordon Street, center structure designed by John S. Norris, 1856; flanking pavilions added 1872 and 1886. Photo by Robin B. Williams, 2014.

by the school's original architect, John Norris, whose center building of 1856 is the largest of the three; the western wing was added in 1872 based on plans by John B. Hogg, and the eastern wing was built in 1886 (figure 117). The three austere façades are nearly identical, presenting themselves with the dignity of a public trust lot building but evoking the domestic scale and repetitive patterns of tything lot houses. Since 1975, the Massie School has functioned as a historic school museum and study center for the public school system focusing on the city's architectural and cultural history.

The Barnard Street School, built in 1906 at 212 West Taylor Street on the northwest tything of Chatham Ward, takes full advantage of an irregularity in the Savannah Plan along its western edge (figure 118). Chatham Ward, like Pulaski Ward to its north, is asymmetrically truncated due to the boundary of the city Common aligning not with Jefferson Street (the western edge of the wards to the north of Chatham and Pulaski Wards) but with Tattnall Street, 120 feet to the east. As a result, the tythings in the western halves of these two wards comprise only three lots. Architect Gottfrid L. Norrman exploited this anomaly by aligning the center of the school—marked by a tall, tapering bell tower above the entrance—with the centerline of Barnard Street as it wraps around the west side of Chatham Square. This axial closing of the northward vista could have been readily appreciated at the time when traffic flowed in both directions around the square.

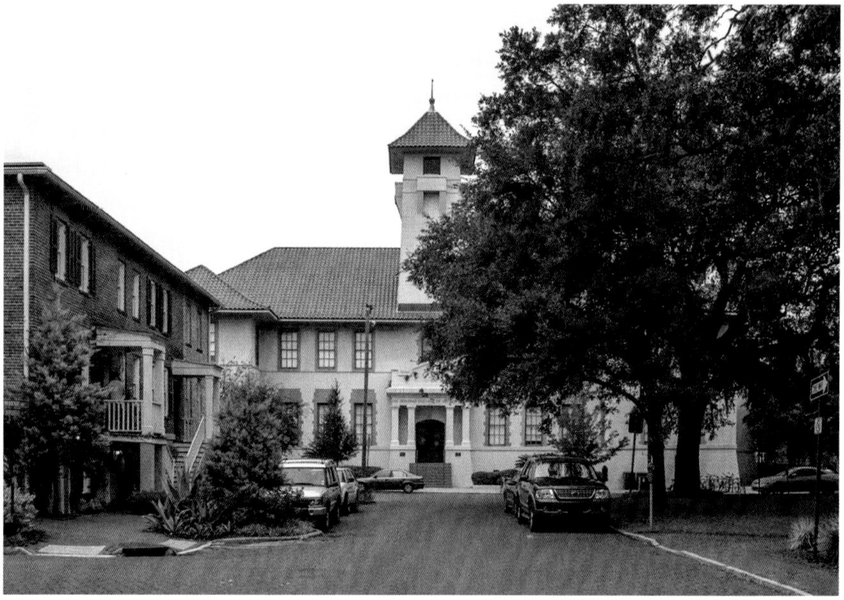

FIGURE 118. Barnard Street School (now Pepe Hall, SCAD), 212 West Taylor Street, designed by Gottfrid L. Norrman, 1906. Photo by Robin B. Williams, 2007.

MULTISITE COLLEGE CAMPUSES

Multibuilding campuses became the defining characteristic of two academic institutions established in Savannah: Armstrong Junior College (now part of Georgia Southern University) and the Savannah College of Art and Design (SCAD). At the bidding of Savannah's mayor, the widow and daughter of shipping tycoon George Ferguson Armstrong deeded the house and property at 447 Bull Street to the city in 1935 to be used as the flagship building for the newly established Armstrong Junior College. That same year the neighboring townhouse, the Italianate Brantley House at 20 West Gaston Street, designed by John Norris in 1857, was donated to the college, and a three-story auditorium building (later named Herschel V. Jenkins Hall), designed by Henrik Wallin to harmonize with the scale and massing of the Armstrong mansion, was constructed on the former rear garden, forming a campus of three buildings (figure 119).[19] A science building was constructed on the northeast trust lot on Monterey Square in 1941, replacing the First Presbyterian Church, which had burned down, sometime after which the church's congregation relocated to Washington Avenue in one of the city's early twentieth-century suburbs.[20]

As the college grew, other properties were acquired in close proximity. The sumptuous Noble Hardee House (1869), across Gordon Lane from the Armstrong House, was acquired in 1945.[21] In addition, the college library was moved to the Georgia Historical Society in Hodgson Hall in the next block facing Whitaker Street.

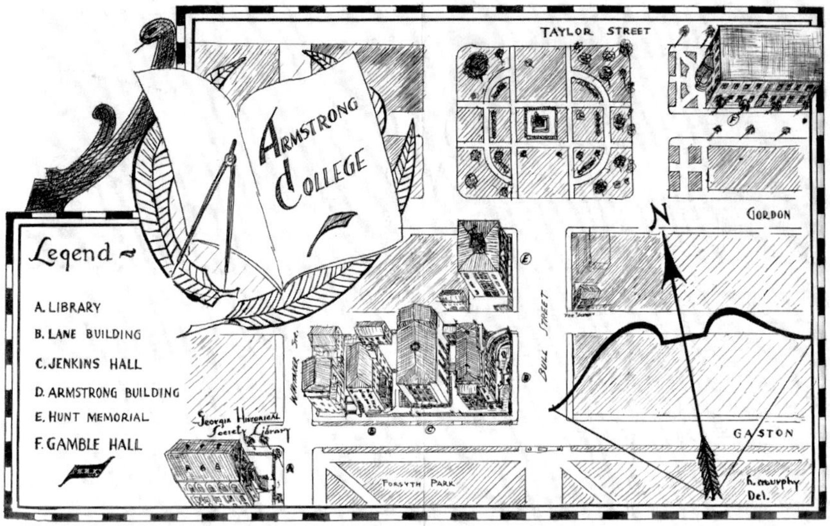

FIGURE 119. Armstrong College campus map, 1949. "Armstrong State College, 1 of 2," vertical file, Kaye Kole Genealogy and Local History Room, Live Oak Public Library, Savannah.

In 1961–62, the college's regents planned to expand the campus to the west and south in an ambitious scheme that would have replaced twenty-five blocks spanning most of Chatham Ward (including Chatham Square) and the area between Howard and Jefferson, Jones and Gwinnett with a modernist campus of asymmetrically arranged buildings and pedestrian walkways (figures 120 and 121), similar to the Illinois Institute of Technology in Chicago, which was designed by architect Ludwig Mies van der Rohe and completed in 1958.

In response to this sizable threat to numerous historic buildings, as well as to part of the city's plan, philanthropist Mills B. Lane Jr. donated 250 acres of land ten miles to the south to create the school's present campus. Having undergone two major renovations, the Armstrong mansion has recently been returned to a private residence, and its garden has been reconstructed and embellished. For thirty-two years Armstrong Junior College was able to function and grow without the benefit of a conventional college campus by adaptively reusing existing buildings within the constraints of the Savannah Plan. Ultimately, however, the school's administration determined this model to be unsustainable for the long-range growth of the school.

Less than twelve years after Armstrong College left Savannah's historic district for the suburbs, the Savannah College of Art and Design employed that same model to create a distributed urban campus in the heart of the historic district. Founded by an energetic young couple from Atlanta with one building in 1978, SCAD has grown from its first group of 71 students to over 17,000 students in Savannah served by more than seventy repurposed historic buildings that are scattered across

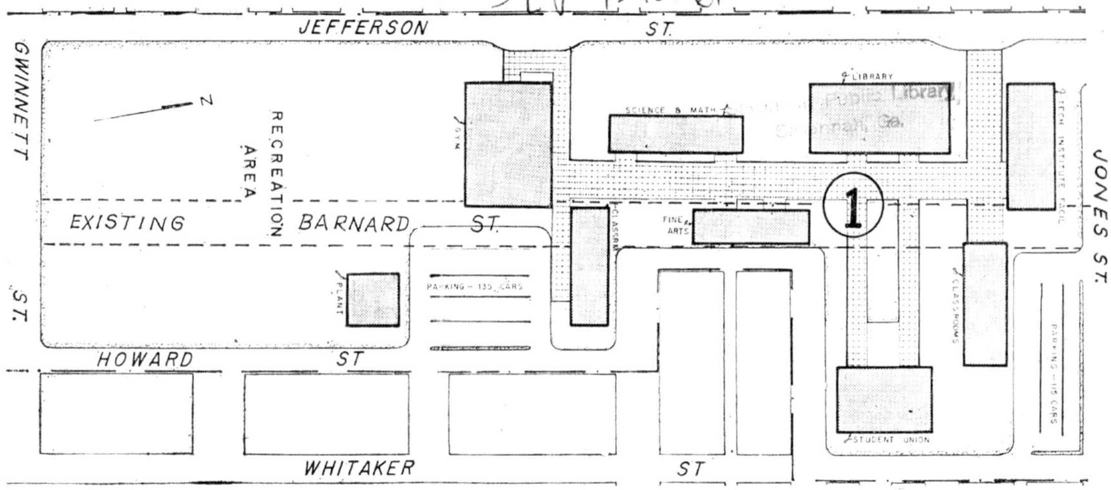
16—Savannah Evening Press, Tuesday, Sept. 12, 1961

ARMSTRONG COLLEGE CAMPUS EXTENSION PLAN TO BE DISCUSSED AT REGENTS' MEETING TODAY IN ATLANTA

Drawing Shows Area Under Consideration. Numeral "1" Is Present Chatham Square Area

FIGURE 120. (*Above*) Proposed Armstrong campus expansion in Chatham Ward and blocks south, newspaper clipping, *Savannah Evening Press*, September 12, 1961. "Armstrong State College, 2 of 2," vertical file, Kaye Kole Genealogy and Local History Room, Live Oak Public Library, Savannah.

FIGURE 121. (*Right*) Proposed Armstrong campus showing its size and relationship to the existing city plan. Diagram by Robin B. Williams.

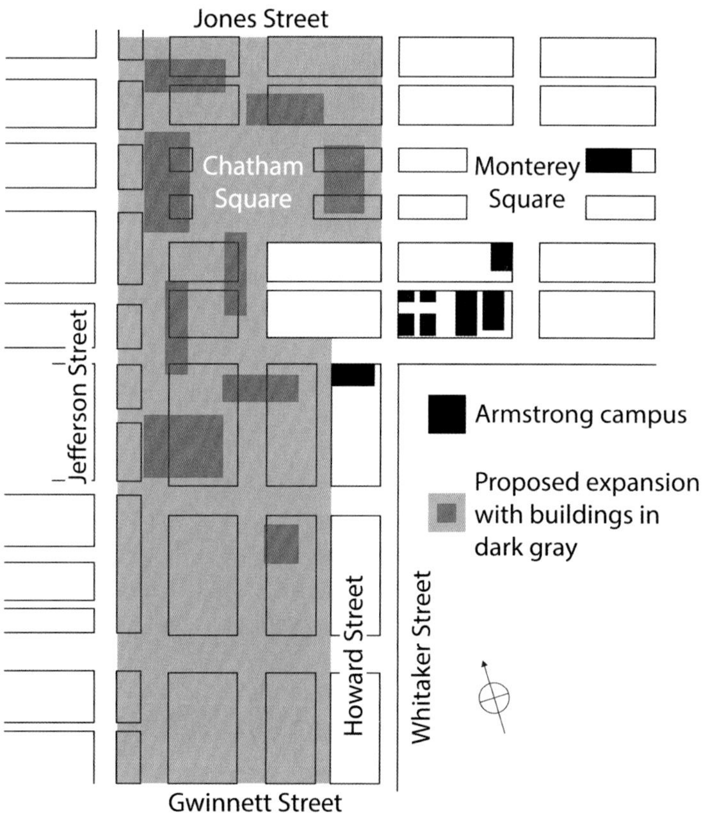

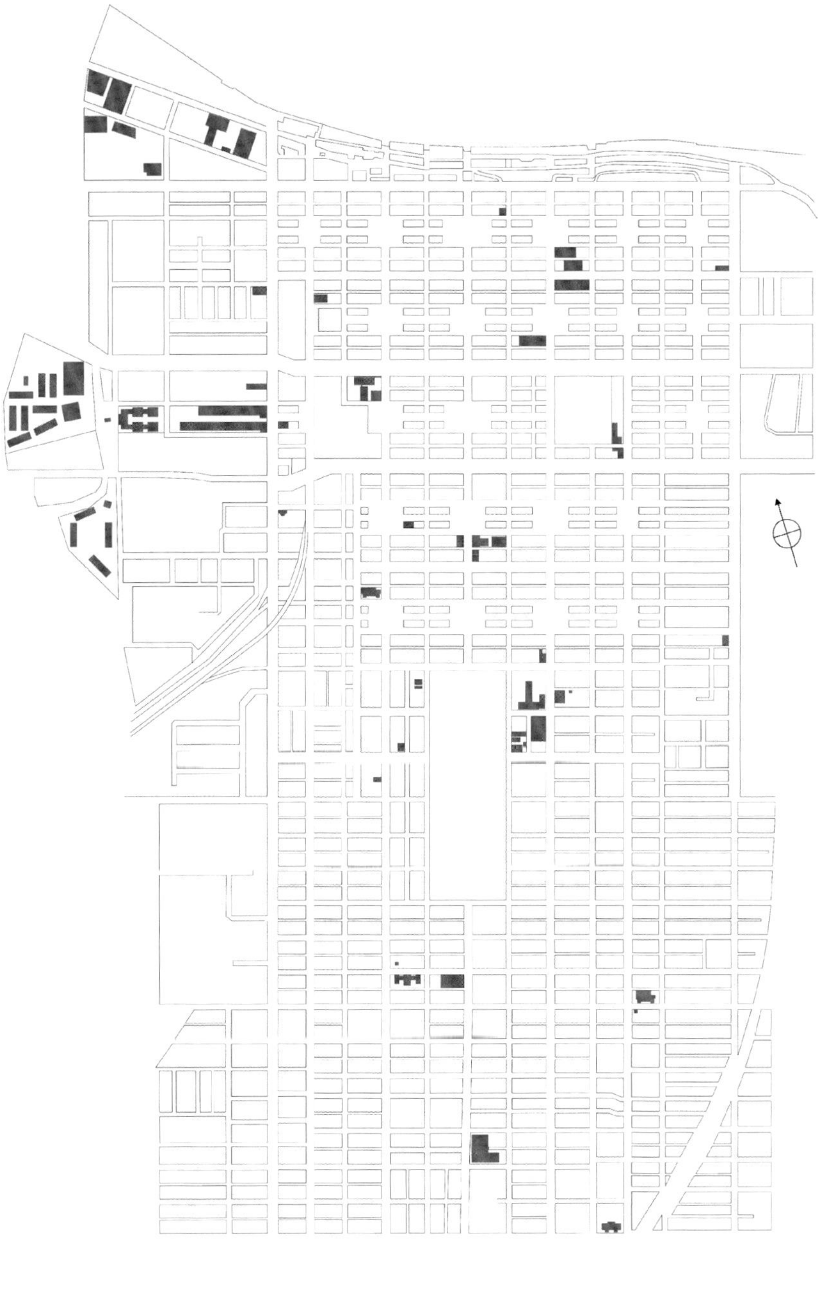

FIGURE 122. Savannah College of Art and Design campus as far south as 37th Street. Additional buildings along Victory Drive and Montgomery Street are not shown. Diagram by Robin B. Williams.

the city but concentrated within the walkable historic core, to which the college has more recently added several purpose-built residence halls. Twenty SCAD buildings are situated within the strict limits of the twenty-four-ward Savannah Plan, with several others along its edges (figure 122). The distributive nature of the Savannah Plan has surely inspired and facilitated SCAD's innovative model of growth for a world-class arts university, transforming the plan itself into a college campus.

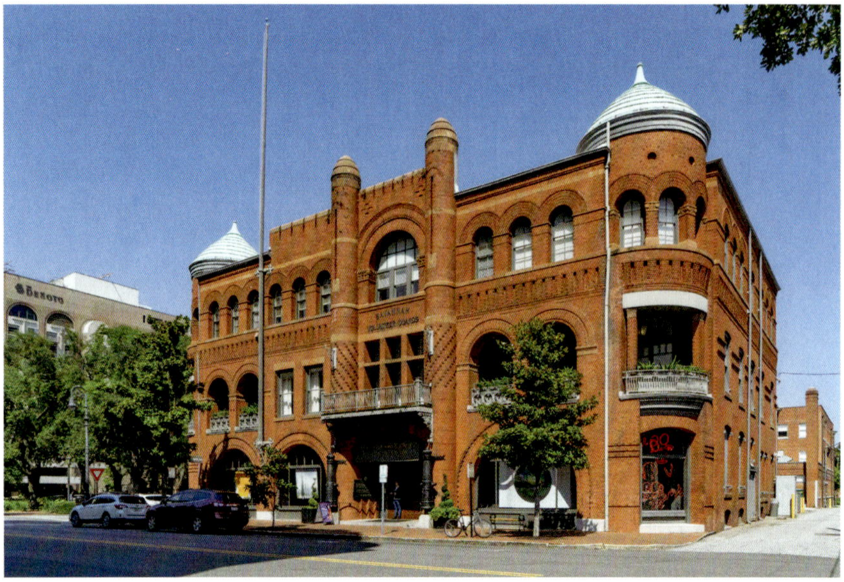

FIGURE 123. Savannah Volunteer Guards Armory (now Poetter Hall, SCAD), 342 Bull Street, designed by William Gibbons Preston, 1892–93. Photo by Robin B. Williams, 2024.

A key to SCAD's success has been not only the quantity and quality of Savannah's architecture but also its adaptability over time. In some cases, the appropriate reuse of one building type for another has been obvious and nearly seamless in its conversion. For example, public school buildings have been used for college classrooms, hotels have become dormitories, a movie theatre has become an auditorium, and an office high-rise has become administrative offices. Other examples have required more imaginative adaptation. The first building restored and adapted by SCAD was the Savannah Volunteer Guards Armory, designed by William Gibbons Preston in 1892–93 (figure 123). Known today as Poetter Hall, it initially served all of the college's functions, housing its classrooms, offices, and library; now it hosts a store selling artwork by students and faculty, a reception hall, and SCADstory, an immersive telling of the college's history. Other adaptive reuses by SCAD include a synagogue transformed into a student center, a department store turned into a library, a hospital converted into admissions facilities and classrooms, a bank repurposed as an art gallery, and numerous historic houses used for a variety of purposes, including offices, classrooms, and guesthouses.

The pattern of development set by Armstrong College and SCAD is now being repeated by Ralston College, which opened in 2022 and offers an innovative program in graduate education rooted in the classical liberal arts. Ralston currently owns or leases three historically significant buildings in the historic district. The school's website states that Savannah

> serves as a symbol for what Ralston College aims to provide: the welcoming warmth of fellowship, free thought and speech, and an intermingling of beauty and history and life. . . . Savannah is a revivifying place for the weary truth-seeker in us all.[22]

There can be little doubt that the urban and architectural virtues of the Savannah Plan have played a major role in shaping the vision and implementation of these three institutions for higher learning.

Cultural Institutions: Theatres and Museums

THEATRES

In the colonial era and the days of the early republic, social assemblies and theatrical performances were held in multipurpose buildings such as the Filature and the Exchange. In the nineteenth century, the city's churches were often used for civic and cultural gatherings. Privately funded, purpose-built theatres were erected in Savannah as early as the 1790s. One of the first such buildings, on Franklin Square, was converted into a council house and courthouse after the catastrophic fires of 1796. Its successor was built on a trust lot in Wright Square.

In 1818, the Savannah Theatre, a grand playhouse designed by William Jay, was completed on the northeast trust lot in the newly platted Brown Ward, facing Chippewa Square, where it stands today, having been rebuilt twice.[23] Jay's theatre had rather plain exterior walls, dressed only on the west facade fronting the square, where a one-story canopy sheltered the sidewalk. In its current configuration, the building covers more than the entirety of its 130-foot-deep trust lot, extending 10 feet into the public realm on its western front (the area occupied by the canopy on earlier iterations of the theatre).

The Savannah Theatre was dramatically remodeled in 1906 following a fire and then almost completely rebuilt in 1948 following another fire, leading to the building's current Art Moderne style, completed in 1950 (figure 124). Local architects Helfrich and Grantham displayed awareness of traditional trust lot hierarchies when they placed their architectural emphasis on the west and south facades, the two most visible from Chippewa Square. These facades receive grand yet abstract expression, with a vertical panel of rusticated ashlar masonry on the west facade and a projecting covered staircase rising diagonally in the middle of the south facade, which together frame the eye-catching marquee projecting from the southwest corner. As if tracing a centripetal line of force leading to the center of the square, the marquee projects from the theatre at a forty-five-degree angle, evoking through its angled massing and mast-like neon blade sign the prow of a ship sailing to the square, an allusion reinforced by the wave patterns in the terrazzo pavement.

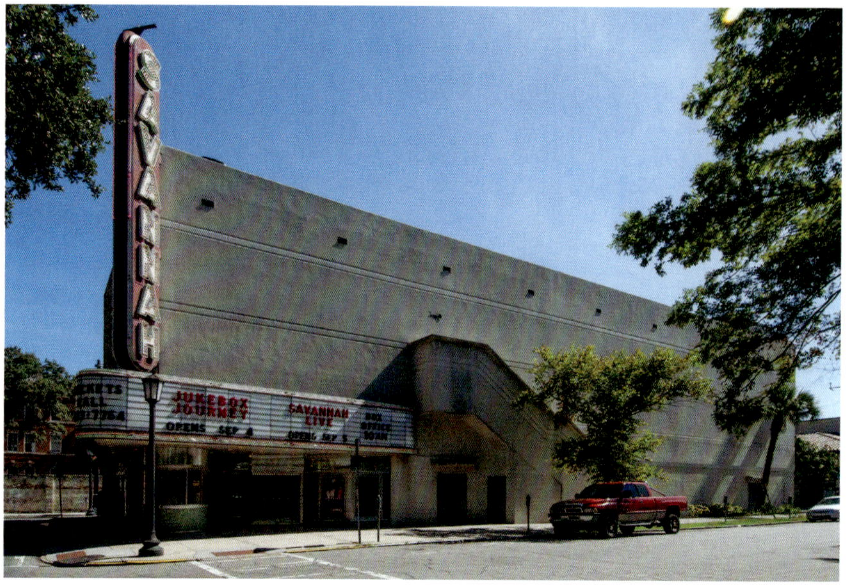

FIGURE 124. Savannah Theatre, 222 Bull Street, originally designed by William Jay; remodeled 1906 and rebuilt 1948–50 by Helfrich and Grantham. Photo by Robin B. Williams, 2014.

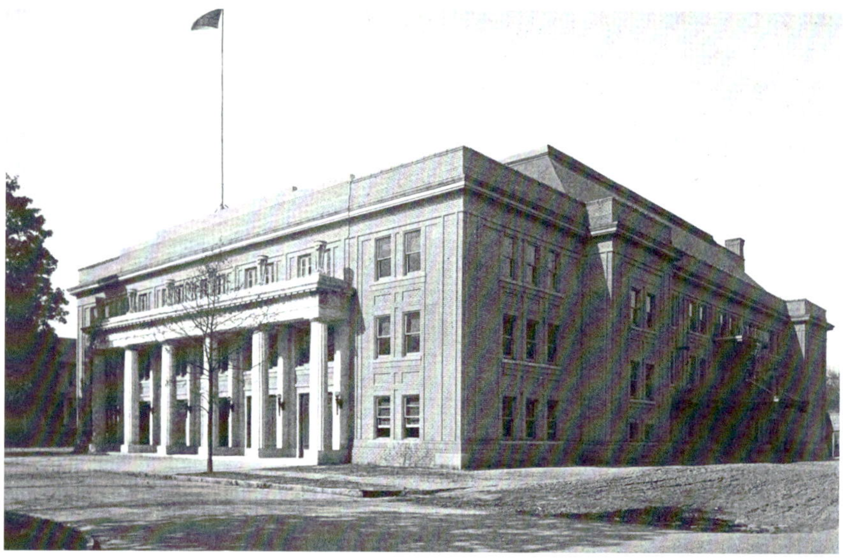

FIGURE 125. Municipal Auditorium, straddling the two western trust lots facing Orleans Square, designed by Wallin & Young, 1911–17, demolished ca. 1968. Photo from *American Architect* 116, no. 2271 (July 2, 1919), plate 7. Public domain, Google digitized.

The north side facing narrow Hull Street and the rear facade on Drayton Street are blank walls, articulated only by thin incised horizontal lines. Cramped as it is for space, the 525-seat Savannah Theatre continues to be a popular venue for theatrical performances and social events. Its success has been helped by its location and orientation on a public trust lot, facing a public square.

The small size of trust lots constrained their use for buildings meant to serve larger audiences, as we have seen with the two largest churches within the plan.

The city's development of the Municipal Auditorium, essentially a large theatre, in 1916 offered a creative solution to this problem by combining two trust lots and the trust street in between into a single larger building site (figure 125). Centered on the east–west axis of McDonough Street, the Municipal Auditorium covered only the inner halves of the two trust lots, allowing each of the flanking inner civic streets (Hull and Perry) to be widened to seventy-five feet to allow ample room for the movement of people and vehicles near the building. Designed by Henrik Wallin, the auditorium faced the square with a monumental hexastyle Doric portico that mitigated the large scale of the otherwise simple brick construction. At 135 feet wide, it enjoyed a more capacious site than any other public gathering space within the plan, churches included, and was able to accommodate between 1,735 to 2,149 people.[24] Perforated by windows on three sides and a large skylight in the ceiling, the auditorium differed from conventional theatres that avoided natural light inside.

Despite the apparent logic of erecting an auditorium on a trust lot, no subsequent theatres in Savannah have done the same. It appears that later theatre builders recognized that, as a building type, it is a poor fit on a trust lot with its four public facades. A theatre, after all, is about its interior, with the point of entry being the only part of the exterior needing to attract public attention. Later Savannah theatres migrated north to Broughton Street, where the more densely packed commercial surroundings provided an appropriate setting for theatergoers.

Beginning in the 1890s with the construction of the midblock Tivoli Hall, a music hall and beer garden, the area around the intersection of Broughton and Abercorn Streets became Savannah's theatre district (figure 126). By the mid-twentieth century, a succession of nine theatres had been erected on the four tything blocks clustered around this intersection, the southern tythings of Reynolds Ward and the northern tythings of Anson Ward, with as many as six theatres coexisting. But all but one had their entrances on Broughton, the most clearly defined linear corridor in downtown Savannah (figure 127).

The theatres employed dexterous ways to fit into the regular rectangular armature of tything blocks. Three of the earliest theatres—the Bijou, the Odeon, and the Polly—replaced livery stables, as documented on the 1898 Sanborn map. Most extraordinary of these was the Bijou, which presented a midblock marquee and entrance on the north side of Broughton, from which a narrow (twenty-foot-wide) passageway traversed the depth of the tything lot northward and bridged the lane to reach the theatre auditorium, which was oriented on an east–west axis to better fit the lots. Hidden from view from Broughton Street, the auditorium occupied the middle two-fifths of the northern half of the tything block—that is, the section with less urban presence than the lots at either end. This nimble solution was repeated in 1945 with the Avon Theatre on a tything lot across Broughton Street,

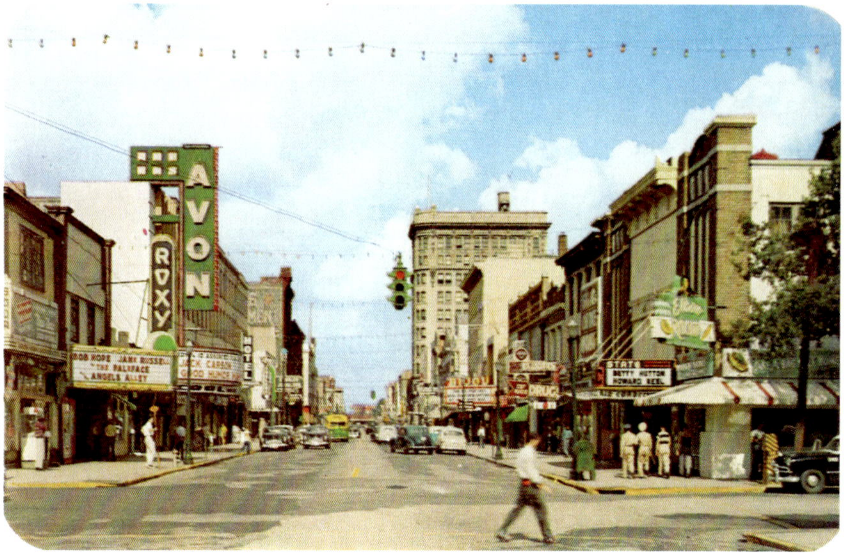

FIGURE 126. View of Broughton Street from Abercorn, looking west, with four theatre marquees, from a postcard ca. 1950. Courtesy of the City of Savannah Municipal Archives, item 656a_1121–070_Palumbo collection.

where a slightly wider marquee and passageway bridged Broughton Lane to the large midblock auditorium, which, like the Bijou, was oriented on an east–west axis to provide greater depth of seating.[25] While the auditorium of the Avon Theatre south of the lane was demolished sometime after the theatre's closing in 1970 to make room for the current parking garage and planning commission offices erected in 1983, the passageway served until recently as a diminutive theatre, but it has since been converted into a sports bar. The grandiose marquee survives as the sole record of the site's theatrical history.

A variation on the passageway-auditorium formula, though constrained within the depth of a half tything block, was used by two theatres. The Arcadia, erected before 1916 and occupying one and a half lots at the east end of the block just east of the Avon, oriented its auditorium on an east–west axis also, while a narrow lobby gave access to the center of its north side. Shops fronting Broughton flanked the theatre entrance and filled the areas north of the auditorium. The Weis Theatre (now SCAD's Trustees Theatre) employed a variation with the marquee and foyer leading northward to the rear of the auditorium, which extended eastward across the two tythings (also on an east–west axis to maximize auditorium depth) north of a one-story row of shops and greenroom spaces fronting Broughton Street.

Unique among this group is the Lucas Theatre, which fronts Abercorn Street and occupies the western three-fifths of its tything block in Reynolds Ward, closer to the square (figure 128). Its facade spans the full ninety-foot width of the block and presents a generously broad marquee. As a result, it has enjoyed a greater urban presence than any of the other theatres, a benefit exploited by Arthur Lucas, who

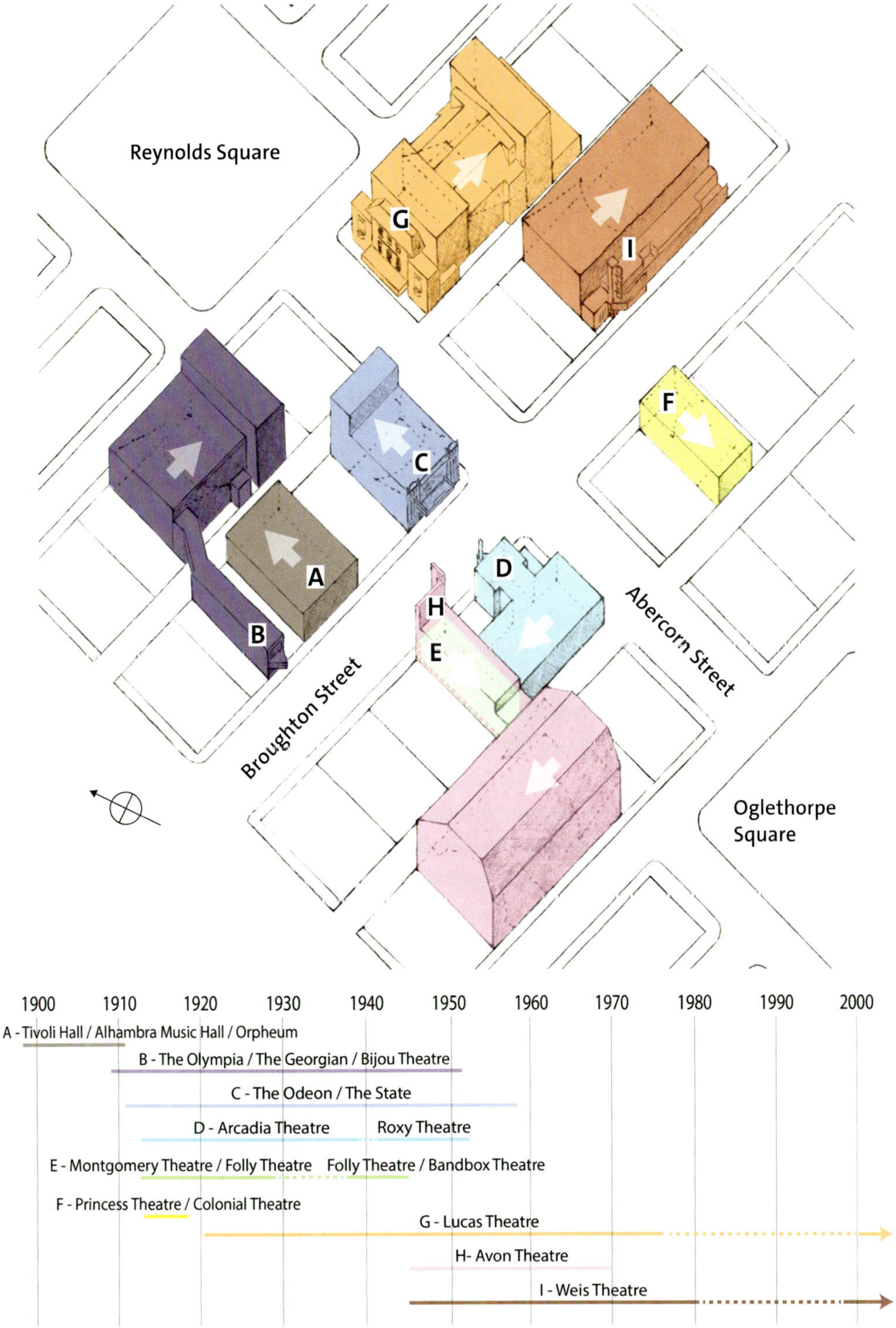

FIGURE 127. Theatres clustered around East Broughton Street and Abercorn Street showing their varied configurations and internal orientation relative to the Savannah Plan. Drawing by Hamilton Brindley, diagram by Robin B. Williams.

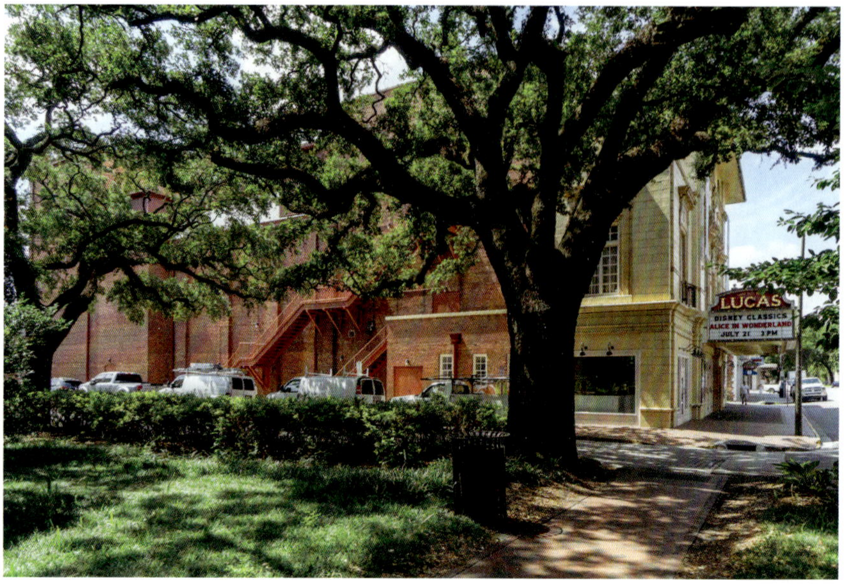

FIGURE 128. Lucas Theatre, 32 Abercorn Street, designed by Claude K. Howell, 1921, view looking southeast from Reynolds Square. Photo by Robin B. Williams, 2024.

built the theatre in 1921 with an ornate Spanish Baroque exterior. Like most of the other theatres, its auditorium is oriented on an east–west axis to take best advantage of the plan, but without the circuitous path the others required. Instead, visitors are greeted by a spacious double-height foyer and a broader interior than that of the neighboring Trustees Theatre. The potential negative effect of a starkly utilitarian windowless facade and metal fire escapes facing Reynolds Square was deftly diminished by an architectural sleight of hand: The main facade and a short stretch of the north facade at the corner are so eye-catching, with their yellow glazed terra-cotta surfaces and exuberant Baroque ornament, that one hardly notices the plain dark brick walls beyond. By day, the overhanging live oak branches from Reynolds Square provide further camouflage. At night, the contrasting treatments of the facades are even more successful, as the side elevation disappears into the darkness while the large marquee blazes brightly.

TELFAIR MUSEUMS AND THE JEPSON CENTER FOR THE ARTS

The museum as an institution exploded in popularity during the nineteenth century and has become a defining civic presence in the early twenty-first century. Savannah has several museums and no shortage of art galleries; not surprisingly, nearly all of them are set within existing historic structures. The Telfair Academy of Arts and Sciences, the oldest public art museum in the South, however, is a hybrid. It opened in 1886 with the completion of a rear addition and numerous other

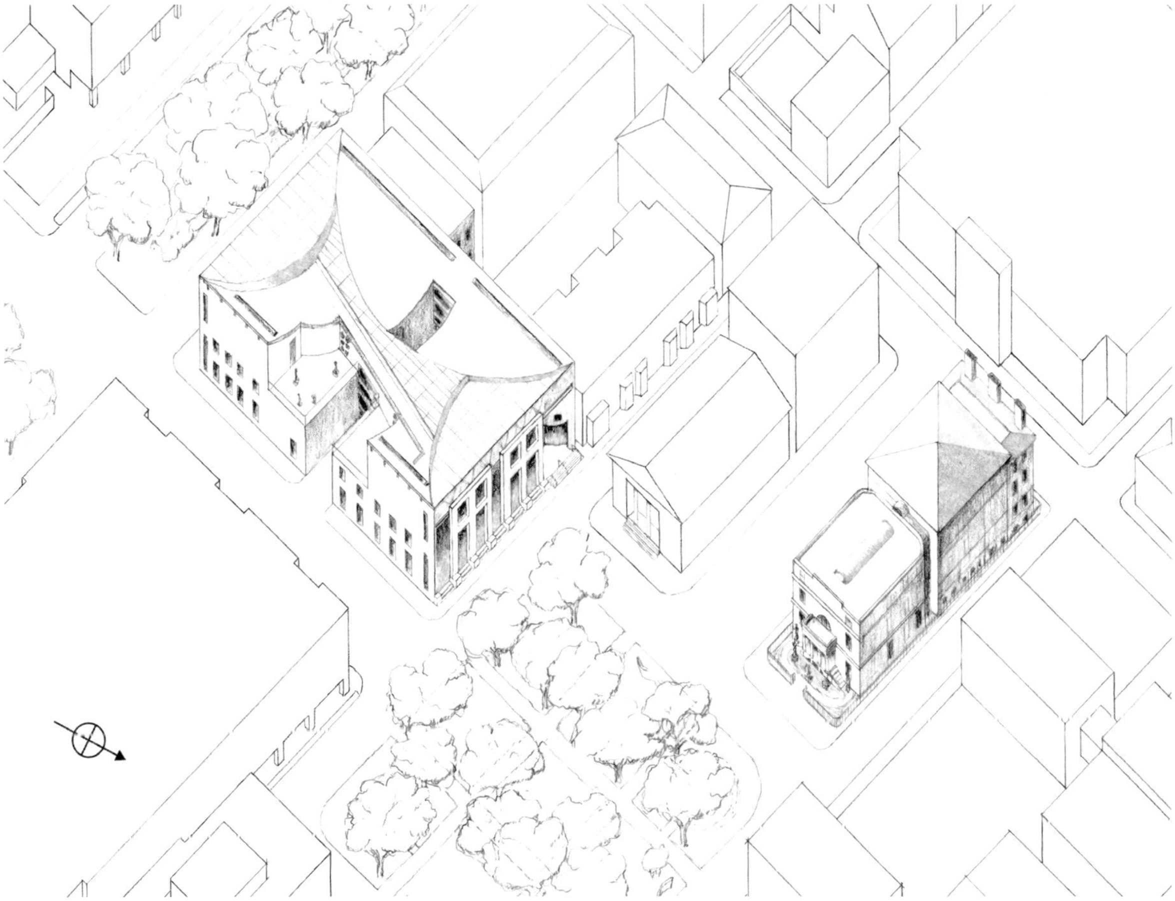

modifications to the Alexander Telfair mansion designed by Detlef Lienau with Augustus Schwab, becoming Savannah's first purpose-built museum.

In 2006 the Telfair Academy built a satellite museum nearby, on the eastern end of the southwest tything of Heathcote Ward, also facing Telfair Square. Designed by internationally acclaimed Israeli-Canadian-American architect Moshe Safdie, the Jepson Center and Telfair Children's Art Museum is daring for its pristine abstraction and boldly curving surfaces, offering an intriguing departure from the compositional and representational traditions that shape much of Savannah's architecture (figure 129). It is also novel in how it adapts to the rules of the Savannah Plan. The Historic District Board of Review rejected an earlier design for a single-volume box that would have covered two back-to-back pairs of tything lots and the service lane between them. Safdie's inventive response to the review

FIGURE 129. The Jepson Center and Telfair Children's Art Museum (at left), 207 East York Street, designed by Moshe Safdie (2006), and the Telfair Academy of Arts and Sciences, designed by William Jay (1819), with additions by Detlef Lienau with Augustus Schwab (1886); both face Telfair Square. Drawing by David Gobel.

board's demands was to split the building into two parts and connect them with two bridges that span the lane. This enabled him to design a spectacular stairway that ascends across the bridge to the primary galleries, traversing a distance greater than otherwise allowable within a single tything lot. Visitors thus experience the two buildings as one. The building responds to the Savannah Plan by presenting its principal front to Telfair Square with a monumental "portico" of joined concrete piers. Surprisingly, the entrance is located at the west end of the facade, aligning it with the sidewalk leading to the Telfair Museum. This alignment ignores the traditional centripetal emphasis on the innermost corner of the tything and leaves the building with a relatively blank facade fronting Barnard Street, the central civic street.

LIKE ITS PLAN, the civic architecture of Savannah has evolved and adapted over nearly three centuries to accommodate the changing demands and priorities of the city's civic institutions. Its governmental institutions have had difficulty finding a place in the plan as their spatial requirements have continued to grow. Its religious institutions have been its most stable and monumental, their multisite campuses granting them an ability to grow within the constraints of the plan. Indeed, multisite campuses and the adaptive reuse of existing buildings have proved to be powerful tools for civic institutions of many kinds. Multisite strategies of growth have kept vital institutions of all kinds from abandoning the city's historic core in favor of commuter-based suburban sites. Adaptive reuse has ensured that Savannah's historic district is not a museum-like collection of historic specimens but a living city in which changing institutions, social practices, and technologies are part of ongoing architectural and urbanistic traditions. Through many changes over many years, Savannah's rigorous yet flexible urban plan has judiciously guided its civic architecture.

CHAPTER SEVEN

COMMERCE AND TOURISM, INDUSTRY AND TRANSPORTATION

Although the centre of an extensive commercial business, and having a lively appearance, yet, from the fact that its streets are not paved, but sandy, it is as noiseless as a country village. Its public buildings are tasteful, and about its private residences, which are generally approached, even in winter, through beds of flowers, there is an air of home-like comfort which is quite refreshing; and its hotels are well kept, and not inelegant in their accommodations.
—CHARLES LANMAN, 1856

Savannah is pre-eminently a city where trade, commerce, manufactures, are charmingly intermingled with the highest culture, with unusual devotion to the beautiful, with deep appreciation of art, where the aesthetic side of life is cultivated while business opportunities are being seized and trade expanded in all directions.
—MAYOR HERMAN MYERS, 1904

Commercial Architecture

Apart from markets being held in the squares, commerce was given no assigned place in the original Savannah Plan.[1] The agrarian-minded Trustees were deeply suspicious of commerce and trade. The plan thus privileges private and public institutions, obliging the unrelenting forces of commercial development to adapt and defer. Commercial establishments are therefore dispersed throughout the plan. They change often both in location and in their architectural forms and finishes. They often occupy buildings built for other purposes, and when new commercial construction occurs, it borrows from the formal typology and the ornamental features of residential and institutional architecture. Still, patterns of commercial development do occur. In Johnson Square, Savannah has its financial center; on Broughton Street it has a retail corridor; and Bay Street traditionally housed port-related businesses. No matter where they are found, however, Savannah's commercial buildings are disciplined by the insistent, fine-grained, human-scaled nature of the city plan.

MARKETS AND SHOPS

The only commercial activity explicitly given a place in the Savannah Plan by the Trustees was public markets, which, of course, were originally intended to be established in the squares. The de Brahm map of 1757 shows a "Beef Market" in a square building in the middle of Ellis Square (figure 29). In 1759 the royal council ordered that a market house "sixty feet square" be built on the site of Tomochichi's tomb in the middle of Wright Square, either around or displacing Savannah's first commemorative monument.[2] In 1763 the public market was moved back to Ellis Square, where it would remain in a succession of buildings until the last was demolished in 1954. In its final form, designed by Muller and Schwaab and erected 1870–72, the brick and heavy timber structure occupied most of the square, which had been slightly reduced from its original dimensions to permit wider streets and more room for vehicles and vendors around its exterior (figure 44). Large gabled pavilions with projecting eaves framed large arches aligned with the bisecting streets of the ward that led to the cross-axial interior passageways. Carriages and later trucks could enter the cavernous hall. In effect, it was covered urban space.

The public market in Ellis Square acted as a catalyst for private retail development in the blocks surrounding the square, which gradually displaced institutions and residences. After their building was destroyed in the 1796 fire, the trustees of the Independent Presbyterian Church, for example, moved the church from its trust lot on Ellis Square to a trust lot on the adjacent Telfair Square to the south. They then built a speculative commercial block on the former church site to fund construction of the new church.[3] In 1802 a second public market was built in Warren Square, and yet another was built in 1820 on the median of South Broad Street, which for a period of less than three years was called Market Street.[4]

Most private retailing, however, occurred on private tything lots, predominantly on outward-facing lots. In a 1981 study, Anderson noted a fundamental pattern of commercial development within the urban plan that began in the early years of the Trustees.[5] Commercial and trading establishments clustered first along Bay Street, facing the port, and secondarily along Broughton Street. The former constellation of businesses was oriented outward, whereas the latter catered more to the needs of the inhabitants. This pattern largely remains into the present. By the early nineteenth century, houses, shops, and taverns lined the south side of Bay Street, forming a nearly continuous facade wall facing the river, as seen in Cerveau's 1837 *Panorama of Savannah* (figure 1). Many of these commercial buildings borrow their rectangular massing from the rowhouse typology, though none sports a raised entry, since retailing occurs on the street level. They are also deeper, offering greater lot coverage than is found in domestic architecture. We see this pattern clearly represented in Vincent's figure-ground map of 1852 (figure 40). The city's northernmost tythings are almost completely built up. Lots surrounding Ellis and Johnson Squares are similarly dense in their building footprints compared to the more residential wards.

Continuous facades and dense building footprints emerge similarly along the west end of Broughton Street, a corridor that began to develop commercially in the eighteenth century. By the later nineteenth century, Broughton Street had become one of Savannah's most architecturally dynamic zones, a commercial corridor lined with retail stores, restaurants, coffee shops, and theatres—buildings that were and still are constantly changing in ownership, use, and architectural design.[6] By the first decade of the twentieth century, multiglobed streetlamps contributed to the visual unity of Broughton Street, transforming it into an illuminated promenade at night, an electrified counterpoint to the older tree-lined allées on Bay and Liberty Streets and Oglethorpe Avenue (figure 75). Trees would not be planted on Broughton Street until the 1970s.

The earliest of Broughton Street's retail businesses began in houses transformed for commercial use. Purpose-built, speculative commercial buildings appear as early as the 1840s, but the formal characteristics of the tything lot rowhouse are invoked, revealing once again the power of the urban plan, in consort with a shared culture of building, to orchestrate Savannah's architectural fabric. Domestic scale and architectural traditions began to disappear, however, with the rise of mass merchandising.

As family businesses were transformed into regional and even national corporations, and as consumer demand grew for ever-greater quantities of goods, Broughton Street became a regional shopping area in the late nineteenth century. National retailers such as F. W. Woolworth (1912), S. H. Kress (1913), McCrory's (1925), Sears and Roebuck (1929), J. C. Penney (1939), and Lerner Shops (1947) came to Broughton Street, initially occupying existing buildings but later building new (or radically renovated) structures following their corporate models, though fitted to the scale of Savannah's tything blocks. During the 1970s, however, Broughton Street was supplanted as a retail destination by the rise of automobile-oriented shopping centers and big-box retailers in the suburbs.

One local retailer, Levy's, having outgrown three earlier buildings, constructed a three-story, 53,000 square foot department store in 1924–25 on the corner of Broughton and Abercorn (occupying the western two tything lots). In 1947 Levy's was bought out by the pioneering department store ownership group Allied Stores, which in 1953–54 combined the existing building with new reinforced concrete construction on the three lots to the east to create a modern, air-conditioned, and largely windowless store occupying a complete five-lot half tything (figure 130).[7] Designed by local architects Levy and Kiley (who in 1954 designed a new, equally modernist Woolworth's store across the street), Levy's became the largest retail emporium in the city and remains one of the few buildings within the Savannah Plan where the scale of the tything block can be read as a single, simple volume. After closing in 1987, the building was acquired by SCAD in 1996 and, after extensive renovations, reopened in 1999 as the college's main library.

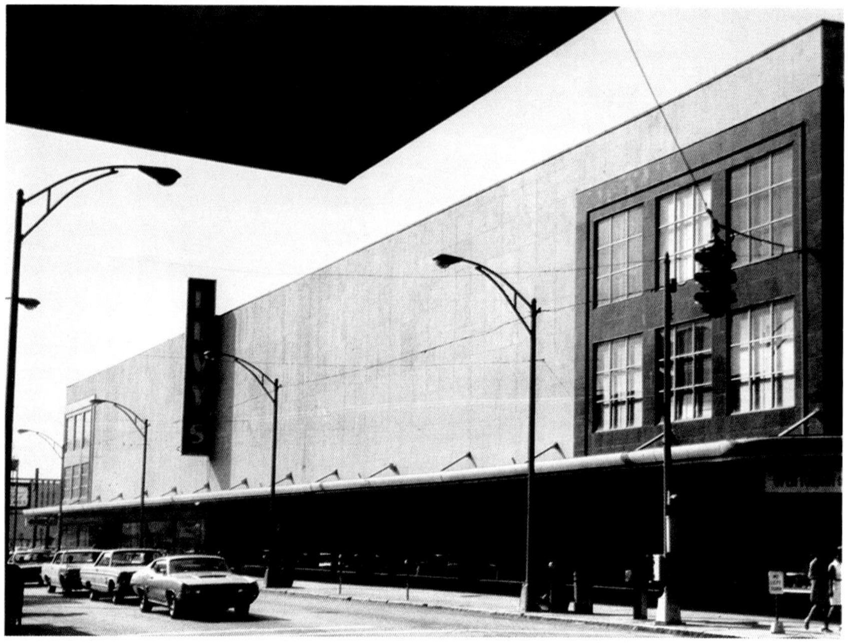

FIGURE 130. Levy's department store (now Jen Library, SCAD), 201–229 East Broughton Street, designed by Levy and Kiley, 1953–54. Undated photo, Metropolitan Planning Commission, Savannah.

BANKS AND OFFICE BUILDINGS

Savannah's banks stand out among the city's commercial architecture. Eschewing the expedient and ephemeral qualities of the marketplace, the city's earliest banks presented themselves with an air of grandeur and durability. Trust lots, of course, ensured urban prominence, and their use for publicly accessible functions responded to the public nature of such sites as defined by the colonial trustees. A pair of trust lots located back-to-back and fronting Reynolds and Johnson Squares welcomed two of the city's earliest banks. (The first bank in Georgia, a branch of the first Bank of the United States, was established in Savannah in 1802, but its location is unknown.)[8] The Planters Bank of Savannah received its charter in 1810 and two years later converted the James Habersham Jr. House (now the Pink House) for its use, adding a wing to the north end for additional space (figure 99). To give the house a more public face, the bank also added the single-story Doric portico and ornate window lintels. The Bank of the State of Georgia, which was created as part of the chartering of the Planters Bank and the Bank of Augusta, erected its own branch in Savannah in 1819 on the trust lot to the west fronting Johnson Square. The cubic two-story red brick building, designed by Isaac H. Robins, a builder from Maine, resembled a mansion more than a civic building, with marble quoining and five ample fanlight windows on its facade, and a one-story

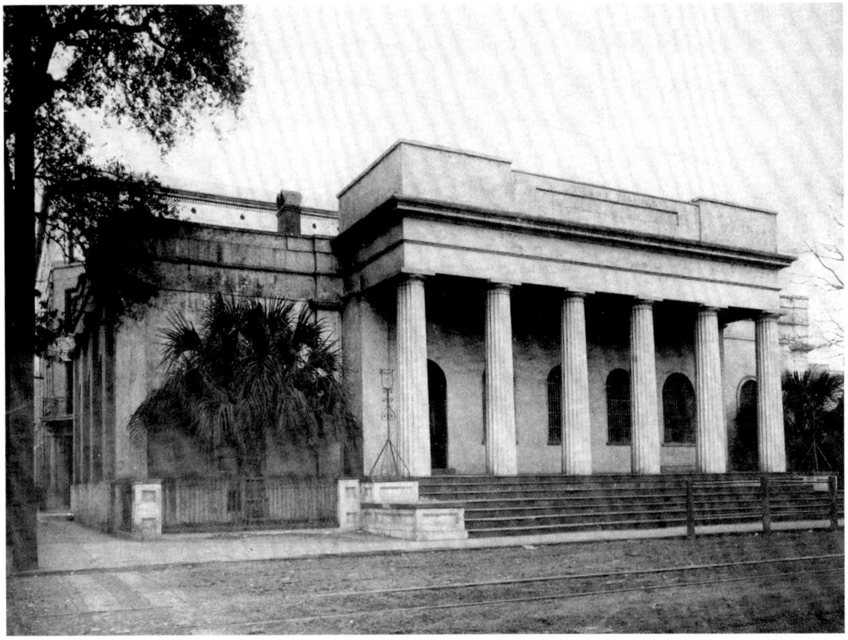

FIGURE 131. Bank of the United States, facing St. Julian Street, designed by William Jay, 1821; demolished ca. 1925. Photo from Charles H. Olmstead, *Art Work of Savannah* (Chicago, 1893). Anonymous private collection.

portico similar to that on the Planters Bank (partially visible in the left middle ground in Cerveau's *Panorama of Savannah*—see figure 1).

The first bank building to fully harness the language of civic architecture was William Jay's Bank of the United States (1821), located on the rear half of the trust lot fronted by the Planters Bank but oriented to the south to face St. Julian Street, the wide central east–west trust street that bisects the ward (figure 131). An early Greek Revival building in America, its Doric portico anchored the lot line, while a broad staircase spilled generously onto the public sidewalk. A second portico of equal width, but recessed into the north facade, addressed the narrower Bryan Street to the rear. The bank's orientation to the central trust street, as opposed to fronting a square, may have been selected to allow the building to have a more imposing and broader facade in the tradition of classical public buildings. Like Jay's other Savannah buildings, it would establish a new standard of design for civic architecture in the city.

A century later, the Citizens and Southern National Bank replaced the more residential character of its predecessor, the former Bank of Georgia building, on the northeast trust lot on Johnson Square with a more expressively civic presence. Designed by the New York firm of Mowbray and Uffinger in 1908, the marble-clad building (now a Bank of America) employed the Beaux-Arts classical style

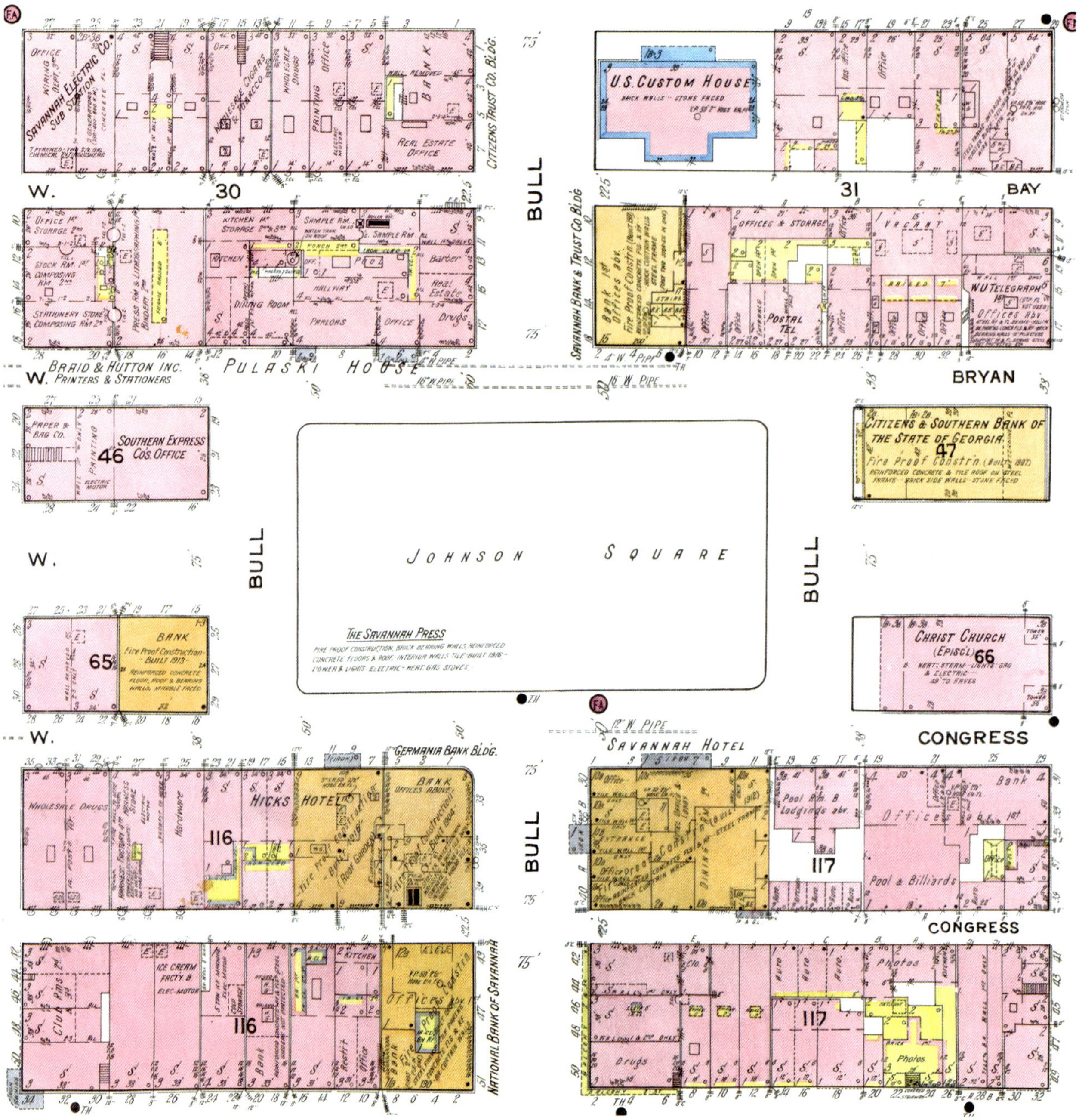

FIGURE 132. Detail from *Sanborn Fire Insurance Map from Savannah, Chatham County, Georgia* showing early skyscrapers made of fireproof construction (orange color) clustered around Johnson Square in Derby Ward. Sanborn Map Company, 1916, vol. 1, sheets 4, 5, 14, and 15. Digital Library of Georgia.

to embrace the civic spirit of the trust lot and directly enter into an architectural dialogue with the neighboring Christ Church; both present an Ionic temple front facing Johnson Square, and both occupy their full trust lot.

SKYSCRAPERS AND THE ECONOMIC HIERARCHIES OF THE PLAN

The earliest of Savannah's steel-frame high-rises, the six-story former Citizens Bank of Savannah, designed by Gottfrid L. Norrman in 1895, occupies a corner site at Bryan and Drayton Streets overlooking the earlier shorter banks to its immediate south flanking Drayton. The center of gravity for the city's business sector, however, would soon shift to Johnson Square with a clustering of early skyscrapers (buildings of ten stories or more with a steel frame and an elevator and made of fireproof construction) housing financial institutions and hotels (figure 132). One wonders what James Oglethorpe would have thought if he knew that the tything lot at 2 East Bryan Street behind where he once lived would one day be occupied by a fifteen-story, steel-framed skyscraper. At 200 feet tall (later raised to 225 feet by a small rooftop addition), it remains the tallest building in the city (figure 133). Designed by Mowbray and Uffinger in 1911, the Savannah Bank and

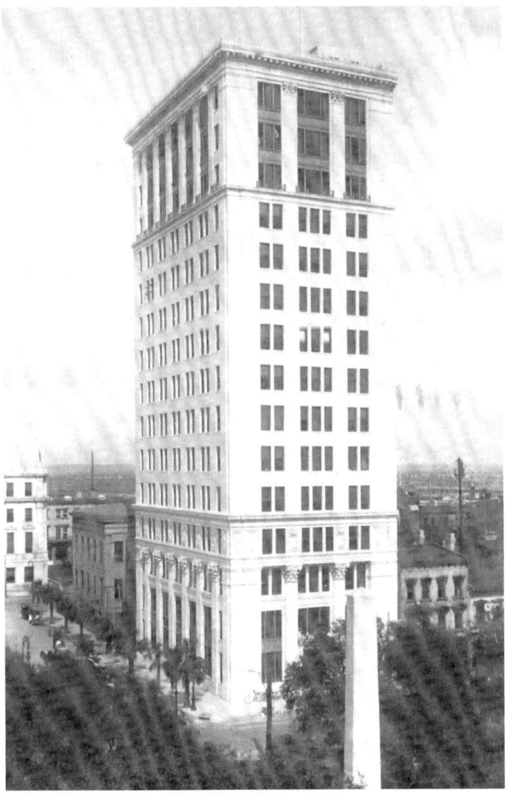

FIGURE 133. Savannah Bank and Trust Company, 2 East Bryan Street on Johnson Square, designed by Hyman Witcover, 1911. Early twentieth-century photo by George Raymond Foltz. Courtesy of the City of Savannah Municipal Archives, 1121–057 0253 V. & J. Duncan Postcard Collection

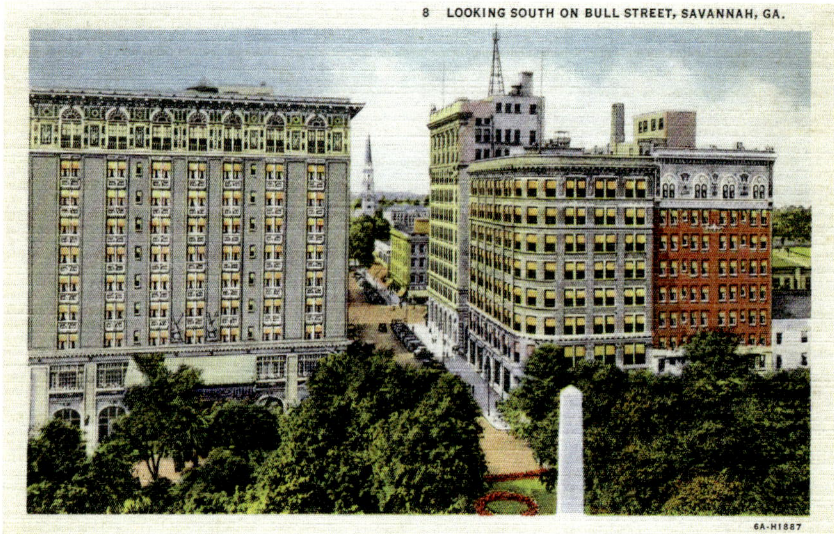

FIGURE 134. Johnson Square ca. 1940, historic postcard showing four of Savannah's early skyscrapers, view looking south. Robin B. Williams personal collection.

Trust Company building filled its 60-by-90-foot tything lot and tested the limits of the Savannah Plan to accommodate large commercial architecture. Like many other early twentieth-century skyscrapers in American cities, it is currently being converted into a luxury hotel.

Directly across Johnson Square from the Savannah Bank building is a ten-story high-rise, the Hotel Savannah, designed by Atlanta architect William Lee Stoddart and built in 1912. Three more early skyscrapers, two bank buildings and another hotel—including the first two skyscrapers on Bull Street, erected in 1904 and 1906—once occupied the inner lots of the southwest tything of Derby Ward (figure 134), but they regrettably were razed in 1975. The early twentieth-century skyscrapers around Johnson Square represent an exuberant era in the city's architectural history. Little about their design is specific to Savannah's architectural traditions, though by their scale and massing, they seem to fit comfortably on their 60-by-90-foot tything lots and, by their location, reinforce the effect of Johnson Square as a large urban room. Their gravitation to the innermost tything lots flanking Bull Street reinforced the hierarchical nature of tything blocks. Although such buildings rise considerably taller than their older neighbors, the experience of the differences in scale within Johnson Square is softened by the dense live oak tree canopy (figure 146).

Following World War II, bank architecture embraced the abstract minimalism of the International Style and its use of concrete and glass, which also symbolized the industry's greater transparency. The First Federal Savings and Loan building,

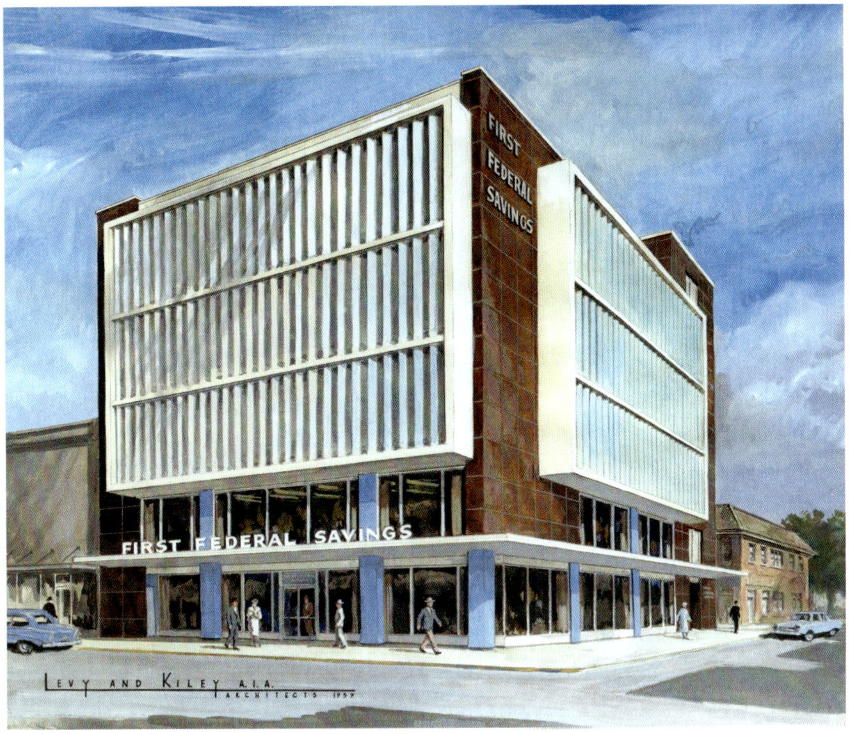

FIGURE 135. First Federal Savings and Loan Association, 132 East Broughton Street, designed by Levy and Kiley, 1959–61. Mixed media presentation rendering by Levy and Kiley. Anonymous collection, Savannah.

filling its tything lot on the northwest corner of Abercorn and Broughton (replacing the Odeon Theatre), captures the dynamism of the postwar years with its original operable louvers, regrettably removed by the 1990s (figure 135). Designed by Levy and Kiley in 1959, the bank catered to customers of more modest means who might shop at Woolworth's across the street. Located on the retail corridor of Broughton Street among theatres and department stores and away from the majority of banks around Johnson Square, the bank sensitively exploited its position on the inside end tything lot by a central north–south civic street (Abercorn), presenting its cantilevered canopy and reinforced concrete frameworks to both streets.

Like the former Savannah Bank and Trust and the Hotel Savannah (which served as a bank and office building in subsequent decades), the First Federal Savings and Loan Building has been transformed into a hotel. Reflecting a national trend, Savannah's growing demand for hotel rooms is being met felicitously by a waning demand for banking and office space. Savannah's architecture appears to be particularly adaptable to the inherently changeable nature of commerce.

HOTELS

Hotels have played a vital role in Savannah since the early nineteenth century. Early hotels in Savannah borrowed from the architectural forms of residential architecture. And in keeping with the intended land use patterns defined by Oglethorpe and the trustees, those early hotels, like almost all the hotels built since then, were erected on tything blocks, whose pattern of 60-foot-wide lots exerted a strong influence on the buildings' shape, size, and gradual expansion. That the earliest hotels clustered near Johnson Square suggests that business travelers constituted much of their clientele.

Opened in 1837, the Pulaski House is representative in being located on multiple tything lots. Originally occupying the two lots closest to Bull Street facing Johnson Square, the hotel expanded to a third lot in the 1880s, illustrating the rapid growth of this building type (figure 136). Its four-story, stucco-covered block adopted the formal patterns of the Savannah rowhouse, though it has ground-floor access from the sidewalk. It was demolished in 1956. The Marshall House Hotel at 123 East Broughton Street, opened in 1851, is similar in its residential pedigree (figure 137). Originally occupying two central tything lots in its block, it too has the massing and fenestration of four rowhouses (expanding in 1880 to add a fifth). A row of large windows framed by granite piers runs across the ground floor,

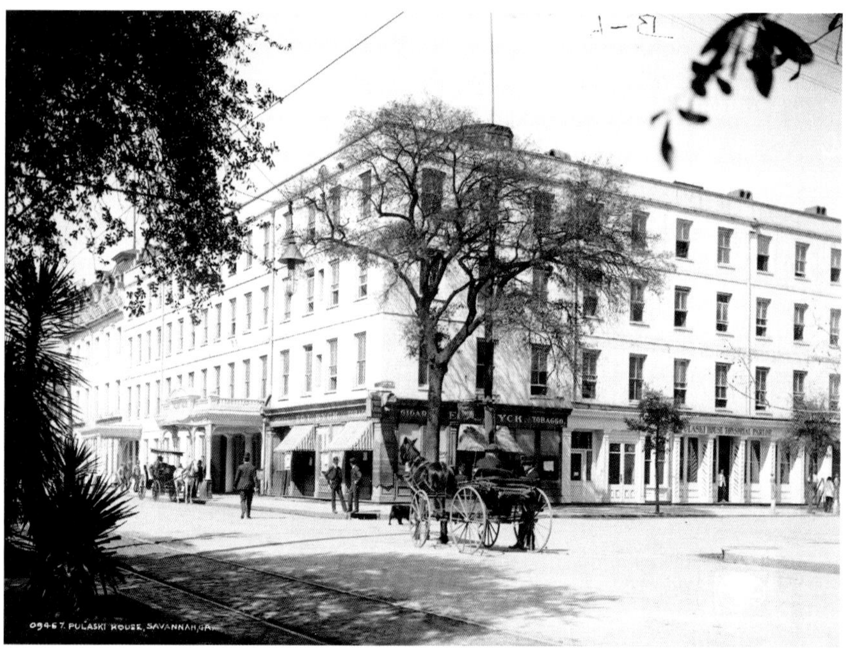

FIGURE 136. Pulaski House Hotel, northwest tything, Derby Ward, 1837 and later additions. Photo from the southeast, Detroit Publishing Company, 1906. Library of Congress.

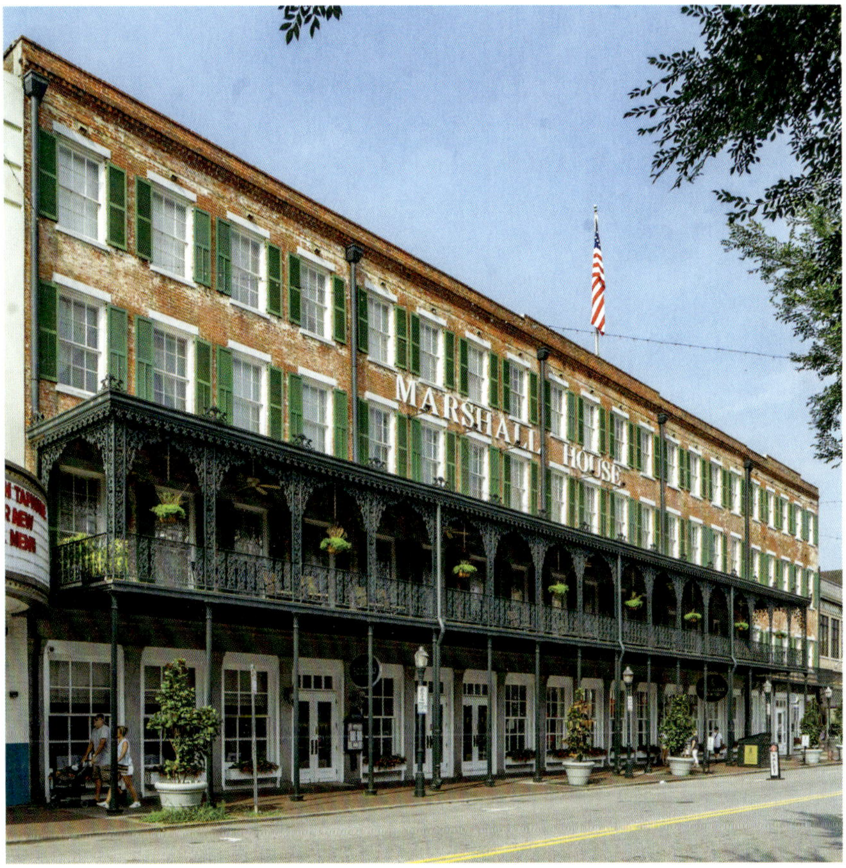

FIGURE 137. Marshall House, 123 East Broughton Street, 1850, ironwork added 1857, recreated 1998–99. Photo by Robin B. Williams, 2023.

clearly communicating the building's commercial function and visually opening the hotel to passersby. Added in 1857, its striking and effusively ornamented two-story cast-iron veranda is more evocative of New Orleans than Savannah. Perhaps it was added to communicate a "Southern" identity for visitors.[9] Its location on Broughton Street in what was then a residential section of Savannah suggests that Marshall House catered to a different clientele from those who patronized the hotels on Johnson Square.

Savannah's most successful hotel is an anomaly. The Desoto Hotel, like its predecessor the Hotel Desoto, occupies a complete tything block in Jasper Ward, the equivalent of ten house lots and a lane (figure 138). This was possible because the property was never subdivided: It was a large, unified parcel carved out of the Common for the Oglethorpe Barracks in 1834. The first version of the Hotel Desoto opened in 1890 and reflected the growing scale of architecture at the end of the nineteenth century. Designed by Boston architect William Gibbons Preston,

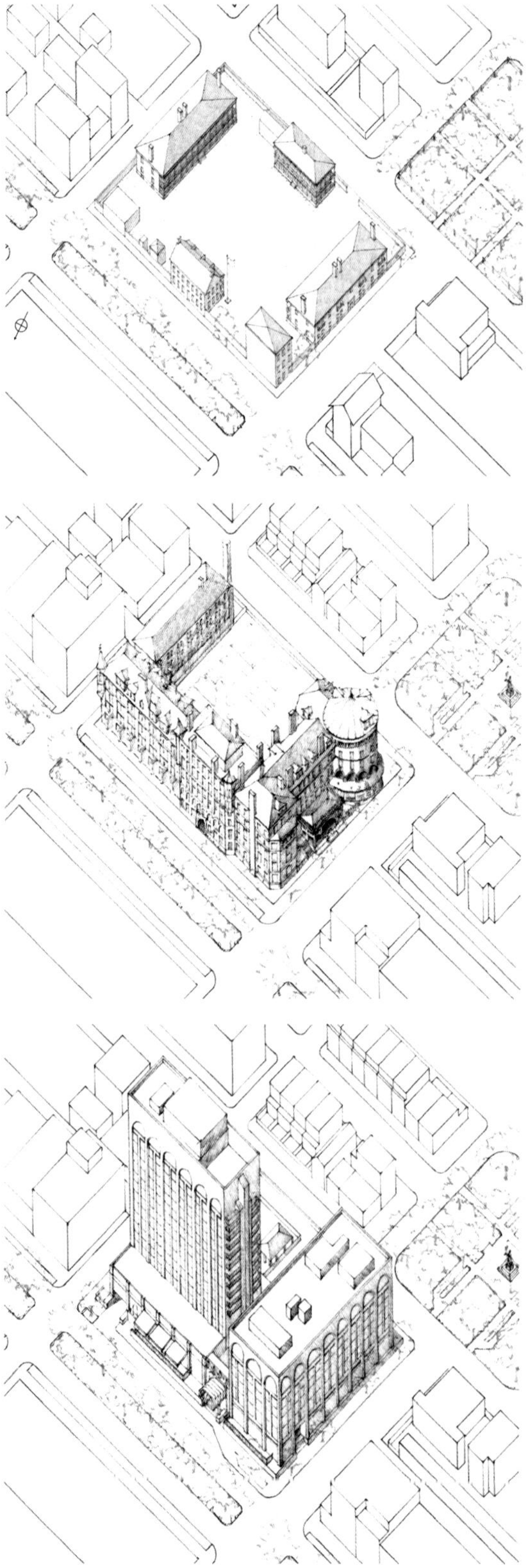

Oglethorpe Barracks, U.S. Army
Established 1833, Decommissioned 1888

Hotel Desoto
Designed by William Gibbons Preston,
Opened 1890, demolished 1966

Desoto Hotel and offices
Designed by Richard Aeck 1968

FIGURE 138. Evolution of the northeast tything of Jasper Ward. Drawing by Hamilton Brindley.

it was by far the largest structure erected within the Savannah Plan to date. Preston exploited the picturesque nature of the Richardsonian Romanesque style by breaking up the massing of the building to reduce its apparent size with a series of pavilions and a stepped roofline. The C-shaped building presented its largest mass along its north side fronting Liberty Street, where it rose to seven stories (seventy-four feet). The principal front faced Bull Street, rising to sixty-four feet; here, a curved pavilion turned the corner to provide views of Madison Square, politely recognizing the centripetal pull toward the center of the ward. At the east end of the site, the service wing appropriately fronted the adjacent utilitarian street, Drayton. With its ballrooms, restaurant, swimming pool, and miniature golf course, the hotel was an entertainment center for the city. By the 1960s, however, it was deemed unfit for continued use. It was replaced in 1968 by a larger mixed-use concrete and brick structure designed by Atlanta architect Richard Aeck, who combined a sixteen-story hotel block fronting Liberty Street and a seven-story bank and office building modestly addressing Bull Street. Typical of new construction in downtown Savannah during the 1960s, the buildings largely turn their backs on adjacent Madison Square. Only a low-ceilinged circulation space between the two buildings, passing north–south through the block and expressed with canopied entries on both Liberty and Harris Streets, provides a connection.

While the waterfront area has been the focus of the hospitality industry since the 1980s, with hotels fitted neatly on nine of the twelve tything blocks fronting Bay Street and with more hotels nearby, just outside the plan, other hotels have sought a more central location, despite the challenge of finding a sufficiently large site. Among Savannah's more recently built hotels, the Perry Lane Hotel has adopted the multisite campus approach as a solution, constructing two buildings on either side of Perry Street in the short extension blocks of Brown Ward. Taking a cue from the recent renovation of Ellis Square, the buildings, and Perry Street between them, sit atop an underground parking garage that spans the whole site.[10] To gain more square footage, the north building exploited a long-standing practice in Savannah of encroaching on the public realm (with the city's permission), extending a few feet southward into East Perry Street and about fifteen feet northward into McDonough Street (taking advantage of McDonough's generous seventy-five-foot width as a central trust street). The hotel building boom continues today, but the Savannah Plan itself continues to temper hotels' designs, though it has recently needed the help of an activist citizenry to pressure enforcement by city agencies. Developers and designers must innovate to fit the demands of the modern hospitality industry on Savannah's tything lots or else locate outside of the plan.

With the explosive growth of tourism in the late twentieth century up to the present, hotel construction has expanded at such a pace in downtown Savannah that many citizens have become alarmed. In response, the city created a "Savannah

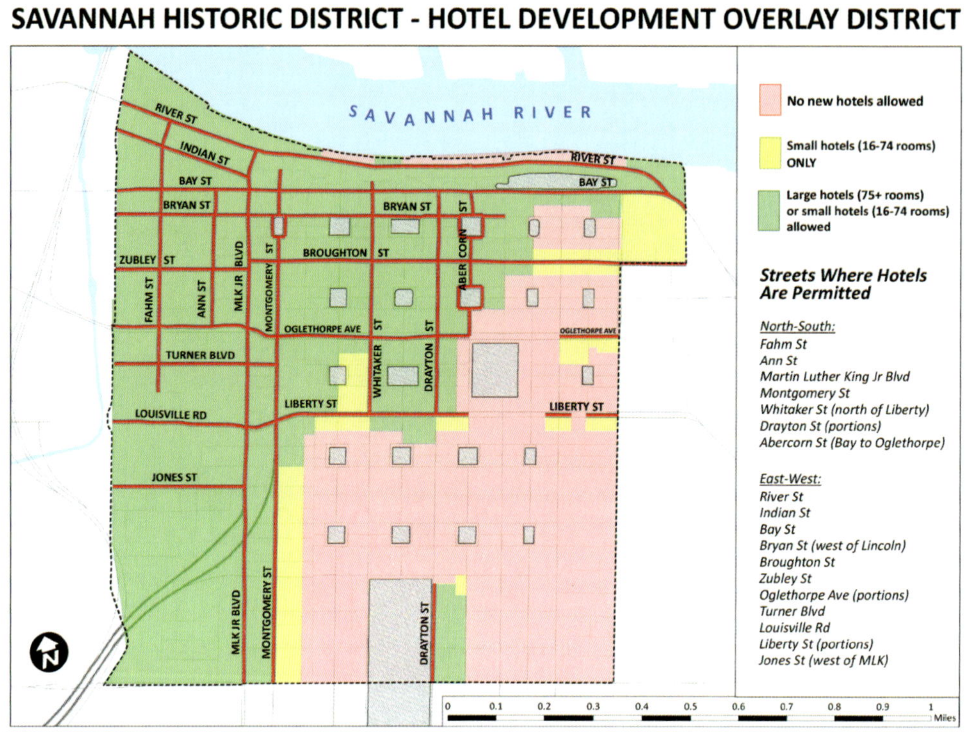

FIGURE 139. Savannah Historic District, Hotel Development Overlay District map, 2019. Courtesy of the City of Savannah.

Downtown Historic Overlay District" in 2019 to regulate future hotels and ensure they work within the historic development patterns and architectural scale of the Savannah Plan (figure 139).[11] The district divides downtown roughly into two halves, bisecting it diagonally from the northeast to the southwest, and allows both small and large hotels (sixteen to seventy-five rooms and over seventy-five rooms, respectively) in the northwest half, while generally prohibiting any hotels in the southeast triangle, other than a few areas in which only small hotels are allowed.

Industrial Buildings: Factories and Warehouses

Within the wide range of building functions accommodated within the Savannah Plan historically, factories and warehouses, more than any other functions, have largely disappeared from Savannah's urban center. This trend is typical of most cities, as production and transportation changes, in tandem with stricter zoning requirements and concerns over pollution, drove industry away from city centers. It's easy today to overlook the remarkably close proximity that factories, workshops, and warehouses had to other building types within the traditional urban landscape. Yet in Savannah, the urban plan exerted an influence on their location, their orientation, and even their architectural expression.

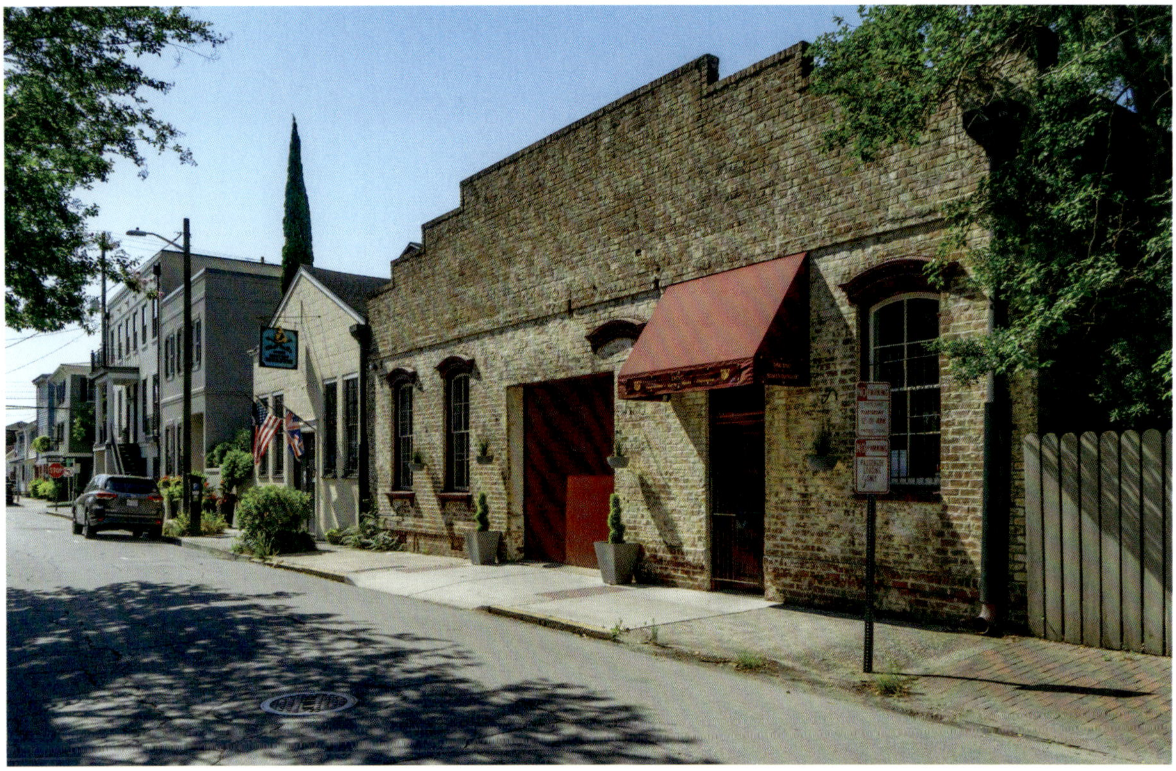

FIGURE 140. Early twentieth-century industrial buildings in Columbia Ward on East York Street. Photo by Robin B. Williams, 2024.

Traditional small-scale industrial buildings appeared in many parts of the Savannah Plan but were concentrated in the more peripheral wards, where they supported nearby larger-scale industrial complexes just outside the plan. Examples of small industrial buildings survive around Franklin Square, on East Bay Street, and on East York Street (figure 140). Typical of many such buildings historically in Savannah's downtown area, they fill the middle lots of tything blocks, leaving the end lots for more public or residential purposes. These low (usually one-story) utilitarian structures covered the entire depth of their lot, allowing for an entrance on both the front and the back. A similar pattern, but on a trust lot, survives on West St. Julian Street (now part of the City Market pedestrian mall area—see figure 48). When a warehouse occupied the end lot of a tything block, as was the case with the two-story warehouse at Bay and Lincoln Streets (now part of a Staybridge Suites hotel), it could have entrances on three sides, as the segmental arches reveal. By the late nineteenth century, warehouses serving the port filled the tything blocks along the south side of Bay Street. Yet such warehouses stood only a few feet from notable financial institutions and prominent residences facing the squares two blocks away.

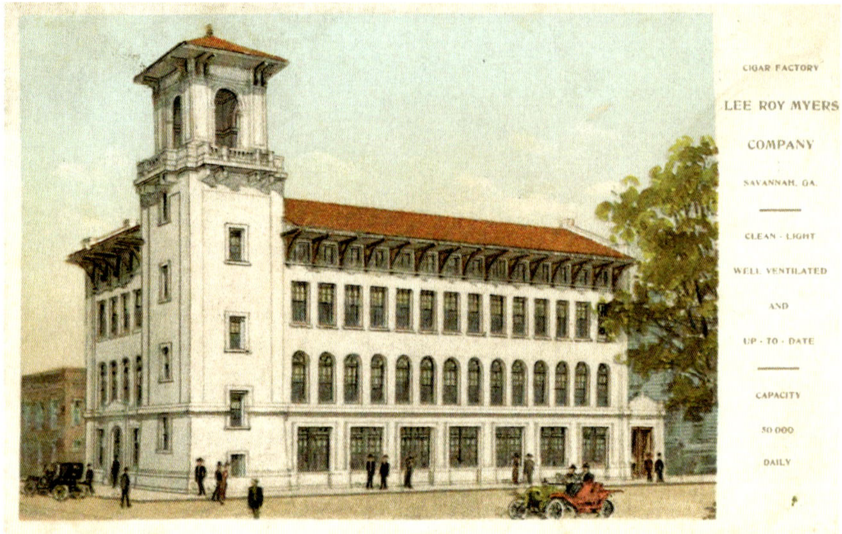

FIGURE 141. Lee Roy Myers Company cigar factory (now Christ Church Parish House), 18 Abercorn Street, designed by Wallin and Young, 1911. Rendering by Wallin and Young, from a postcard dated March 12, 1912, Detroit Publishing Company. Courtesy of the Georgia Historical Society, postcards collection, GHS 1361–PC-06–0437.

Notable among Savannah's early twentieth-century industrial buildings is the Lee Roy Myers Company cigar factory, designed by Henrik Wallin in 1911 in a lyrical Mediterranean style (figure 141). Commanding a prominent location on the two innermost northeast tything lots overlooking Reynolds Square, the factory featured a corner tower that was originally crowned by a belvedere rising sixty-five feet above the street. As a testament to the its handsome and respectful design, the building was acquired by Christ Church in 1940 and renovated soon after for its Sunday school and offices.

Transportation-Related Buildings

Changing modes of transportation have had a substantial impact on Savannah's architecture, as they have in all cities. We see this in the numerous carriage houses, service stations, and parking garages that remain scattered throughout the city. Savannah's extensive street grid, especially its network of north–south service streets and east–west lanes bisecting the tything blocks, has accommodated these continually evolving technologies with alacrity, from the outset of the colony to the present day.

CARRIAGE HOUSES

Located at the rear of all residential tything lots, most lanes have carriage houses on both sides. These intimate corridors provide the strongest expressions of the linear connectivity from ward to ward across the breadth of the plan, especially when the street walls of carriage house fronts are intact and form continuous walls, such as in Gordon Lane (figure 77). On its opposite side, each carriage house faces its main house across a small work yard. Here we are reminded of the profound impact the Savannah Plan had on the architectural development of residential properties: a principal house at the front of the property, usually taking up half the lot; a carriage house typically occupying the rear quarter of the lot and fronting the rear lane; and an open space in between on the remaining quarter of the lot (figure 83). This pattern established the formula—still in effect as part of Savannah's planning code for downtown—that residential lots have a 75-percent lot coverage maximum. An exception to this pattern, however, often occurs on the end tything lots, especially along the central north–south civic street, where the building at the rear (often serving a commercial purpose) fronts that civic street instead of the lane, reflecting the innate flexibility inherent in the Savannah Plan and the magnetic draw to the wider civic streets.

Though no longer housing horses or wagons, carriage houses remain an essential component of Savannah's architectural landscape. Typically two stories tall, utilitarian in form, and fronting the rear lane, they are a pervasive building form in downtown Savannah. Yet, like the lanes themselves, they are mostly hidden from view. Given their architectural simplicity, they have proven remarkably adaptable to changing technological and social needs. Most of the extant carriage houses within the Savannah Plan area predate the Civil War, with the oldest being the one designed by William Jay to accompany the Richard Richardson (Owens-Thomas) House in 1816–19. Like other carriage houses, this carriage house opened into a work yard, but different from carriage houses on lanes, it had windows but no door facing the rear, where it backed onto the fifty-foot-wide service corridor of Lincoln Street. Carriage houses typically had at least one large ground-floor opening facing the lane, with wooden doors for horses and a carriage. Above was a hayloft or storage area accessed through a large second-floor loading door with a bracket and pulley above (some of which survive) and living quarters for enslaved workers or other servants. By the early twentieth century, horses and carriages had been replaced by automobiles, and the living quarters above became less useful. But the revitalization of downtown Savannah in the late twentieth century spurred a boom of carriage house apartments.

GAS STATIONS

As automobiles began to supplant horses and animal-powered vehicles at the turn of the century, Savannah's carriage houses and livery stables began to be transformed into parking garages, auto sales showrooms, and service stations. The earliest service or filling stations were often combined with facilities for the sale and storage of automobiles. By the late 1910s and early 1920s, purpose-built gas stations began to appear, not surprisingly, along Savannah's service streets. Of the twenty-two stations known to have stood within the Savannah Plan area between the 1910s and the early 1970s, fifteen were located on the two most central of the north–south service streets, Whitaker and Drayton (figure 142); one was on Price Street; and five others were located along the outer edges of the plan on East Broad and West Broad Streets.[12] The lone exception was a gas station on Montgomery Street, which by the time the station was built had become part of U.S. 17. Of those twenty-two structures, seven survive, but only one continues to function as a gas station, the others having been converted to other commercial functions. Fifteen of the twenty-two were located at the outer end of a tything block.

The oldest extant gas station in Savannah is a simple two-story brick and stucco structure at 222 Drayton Street sporting a Mediterranean-style canopy with a

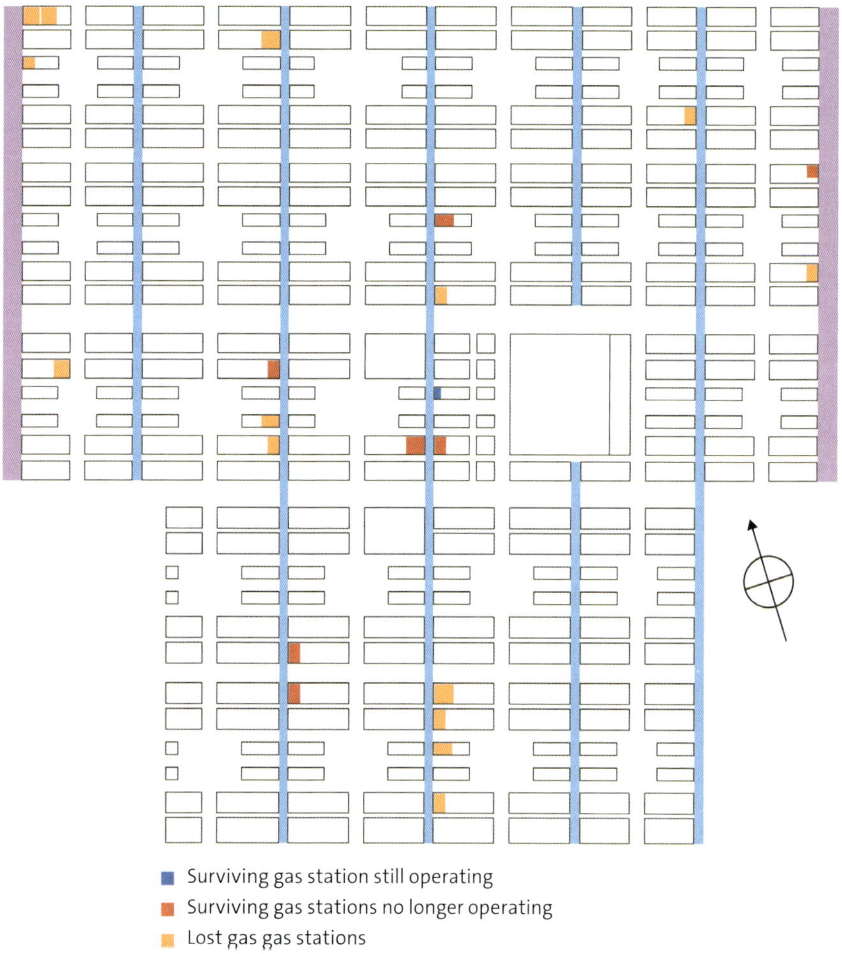

FIGURE 142. Distribution of gas stations in the 1950s–1970s as documented on 1955–73 Sanborn maps. Diagram by Robin B. Williams.

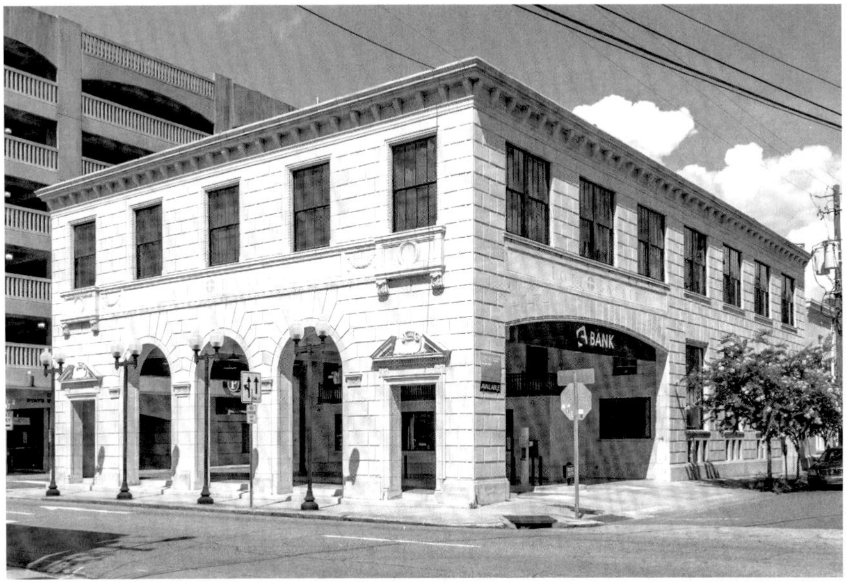

FIGURE 143. Standard Oil station, 110 East President Street, northwest trust lot in Anson Ward, fronting Drayton Street, 1924. Photo by Robin B. Williams, 2014.

gasoline pump under each of its three arches. Still selling gas today, but with a gourmet convenience store in the primary structure, it appears to have been given its present configuration by local architect Arthur F. Comer around 1920, when it served as a Peerless auto sales and service shop for the Georgia Auto and Supply Company. Other early gas stations followed a similar pattern, with a canopy extending toward a service street: a pair of modest early commercial vernacular stations on Whitaker flanking Jones Street, and a 1936 Art Deco former Texaco station at 236 Drayton Street. These three buildings have served a wide variety of functions following their roles as gas stations.

The most nuanced insertion of a gas station into the Savannah Plan is a 1924 Standard Oil station with offices above as a two-story Renaissance palazzo block filling the rear half of the northwest trust lot in Anson Ward fronting Drayton Street (figure 143). A driveway carved out of the first floor allowed cars access to pumps that filled the arches at the edge of the sidewalk. Since ceasing operation as a gas station, the building has served as a bank and as the offices of an architecture firm.

PARKING GARAGES AND PARKING LOTS

The introduction of automobiles brought the need to store them somewhere. Many of Savannah's carriage houses were converted to garages for this purpose. Another option was to store one's vehicle at a dealership. The Bryson Automobile Garage, built in 1904 (and still standing) at 5 East Perry Street on a single tything

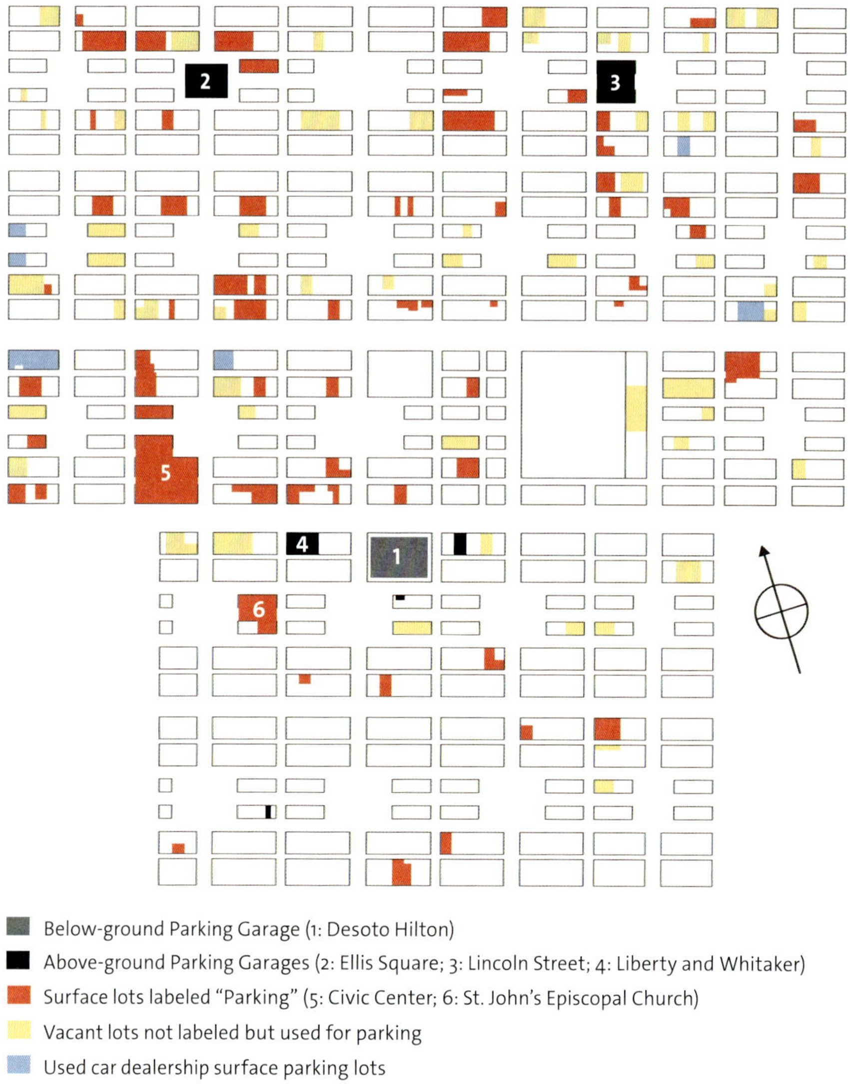

FIGURE 144. Surface parking lots, parking garages, and used car dealership parking lots documented in Sanborn maps, 1955–73. Diagram by Robin B. Williams.

lot just one lot in from Bull Street, is a striking early example of the latter. Its three-story concrete frame is adorned with an elegant arcuated facade of brick and stone facing Chippewa Square. Later parking garages have been less architecturally grand while still fitting within the confines of the Savannah Plan, such as a cluster of three modest garages in the northeast tything of Reynolds Ward, documented in the 1916 Sanborn map. Other garages have had destructive effects on the plan.

As in every North American city, the zeal to accommodate automobile parking—particularly during the postwar years, as more people commuted into downtown from the suburbs—led to the demolition of scores of historic buildings to create surface parking lots. Sanborn maps document that by the early 1970s, every ward within the Savannah Plan had at least one surface parking lot, and some wards had several, especially among the wards north of Liberty Street (figure 144).[13] With the exception of the Civic Center parking lot in Jackson Ward ("5" in figure 144) and the St. John's Episcopal Church parking lot in Pulaski Ward ("6"), all the lots fit within the confines of the Savannah Plan, with many unobtrusively tucked midblock on a full or partial tything lot. Structured parking garages, however, proved even more destructive to the integrity of the plan. In 1955 a garage replaced the historic City Market on Ellis Square ("2"), and in the same year the Lincoln Street Garage ("3") covered the two western trust lots and the central trust street (St. Julian) in Warren Ward. The Lincoln Street Garage set a precedent for sacrificing a street segment to assemble a larger parking area. The Chatham County Courthouse garage (1978) covers most of the northwest tything, including the lane, in Liberty Ward (figure 46); also catering to that courthouse is the Robinson Garage, erected by the city in 1985, which covers the eastern pair of trust lots and the central trust street (President).

Some parking garages, however, successfully integrate into the spatial confines of the Savannah Plan, occupying all or a large portion of a five-lot half tything, while nimbly adjusting the location of their entrances and exits depending on which tything they stand on and the direction of surrounding one-way streets. The oldest of these, erected in 1969 and filling the western half of the northwest tything block in Jasper Ward fronting Liberty and Whitaker ("4" in figure 144), is also the most architecturally self-confident. A pair of large brick arched openings demarcate the entrance from Liberty Street and the exit to Whitaker Street, while the elongated vertical openings, rounded at both top and bottom, reveal the concrete parking decks beyond the brick facades.

Two parking garages erected in the 1980s, both postmodernist in style, fill a whole ninety-by-three-hundred-foot block and in fact stand on the same southern half of the northwest tything in their respective wards (figure 145). Despite their equal bulk and similar style, the Bryan Street Garage in Reynolds Ward and the State Street Garage in Anson Ward employ dramatically different configurations, illustrating the flexibility possible within a seemingly limited setting. The Bryan Street Garage has an entrance and exit at each end, fronting Whitaker and Abercorn Streets, and a third exit on its south facade aligned with Abercorn as it runs along the western side of Reynolds Square. To the east of that exit, a small portion of the first floor in the corner of the building closest to the square serves as the offices for the city's parking services, reflecting the growing desire to activate street-level uses in such large structures. The State Street Garage was even more ambitious, allocating most of its first floor to the offices and hearing room of the Chatham County–Savannah Metropolitan Planning Commission. As a result, a

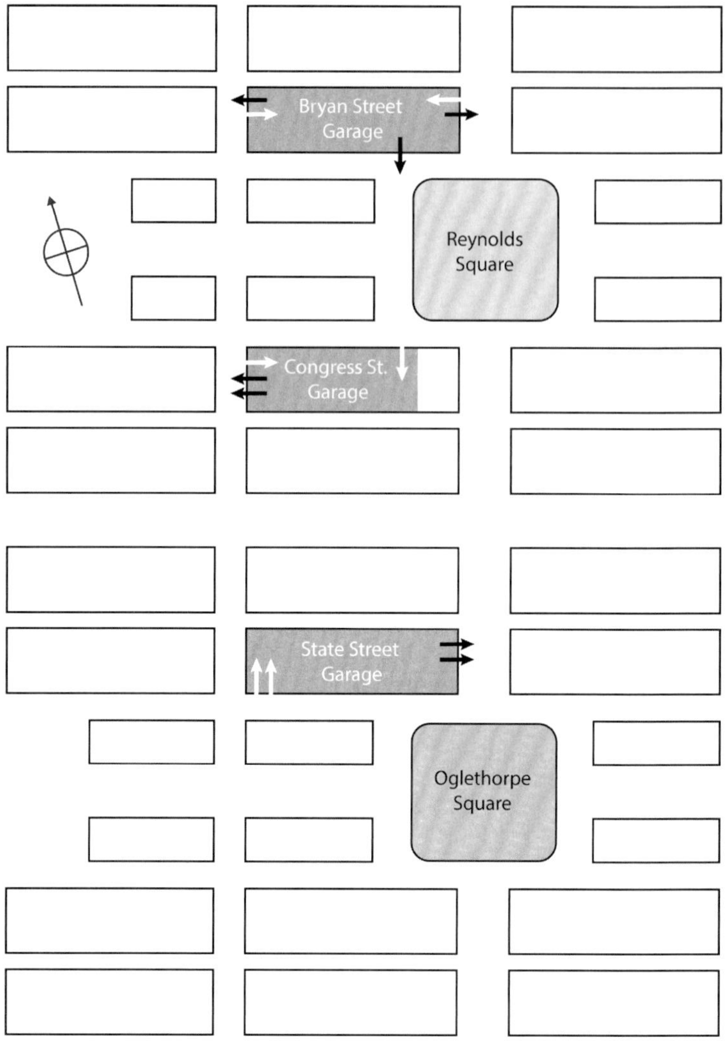

FIGURE 145. Structured parking garages with differing entrances and exits. Diagram by Robin B. Williams.

double car entry is accessed from State Street near the Drayton Street end of the building, complementing a double exit onto Abercorn at the building's east end. The slightly older Congress Street Garage, occupying four tything lots between the other two garages, illustrates yet another configuration of entries and exits.

As part of the recent move to restore the Savannah Plan, the City of Savannah in 2008 undertook the daring and expensive construction of a one-thousand-vehicle underground parking structure (figure 44). Arguably the city's greatest act of urban atonement, the project aimed to correct the destructive decision to tear down the historic City Market building on Ellis Square in 1954 and to grant a fifty-year lease for a two-story parking deck to cover the square from 1955 to

2005. This restoration project involved a public-private partnership consolidating the area underneath Ellis Square and the privately owned adjacent half tything block and northeast trust lot that had become surface parking lots. The project also included the area under the intervening streets. Demonstrating the lengths to which the city has gone to restore and preserve the integrity of the architectural fabric of the Savannah Plan, the Whitaker Street Parking Garage at Ellis Square has become a model for how to accommodate parking within other large-scale projects, such as the Perry Lane Hotel, where the underground garage is discreetly accessed from Perry Lane and exits onto utilitarian Floyd Street.

Commerce, industry, and transportation have been vital to Savannah's flourishing as a city from its beginning, dexterously finding their places within the plan. Retailing and hospitality businesses have sought to cluster or fit in by imitating domestic architectural forms or by inserting themselves into existing structures. Industrial structures have been located mostly at the margins or along utilitarian streets. Parking lots and gas stations have attempted to hide themselves by disguise or location. The inherent hierarchies within the Savannah Plan favor civic and residential uses, granting them urban prominence and pride of place while accommodating commerce, industry, and transportation in their supporting roles.

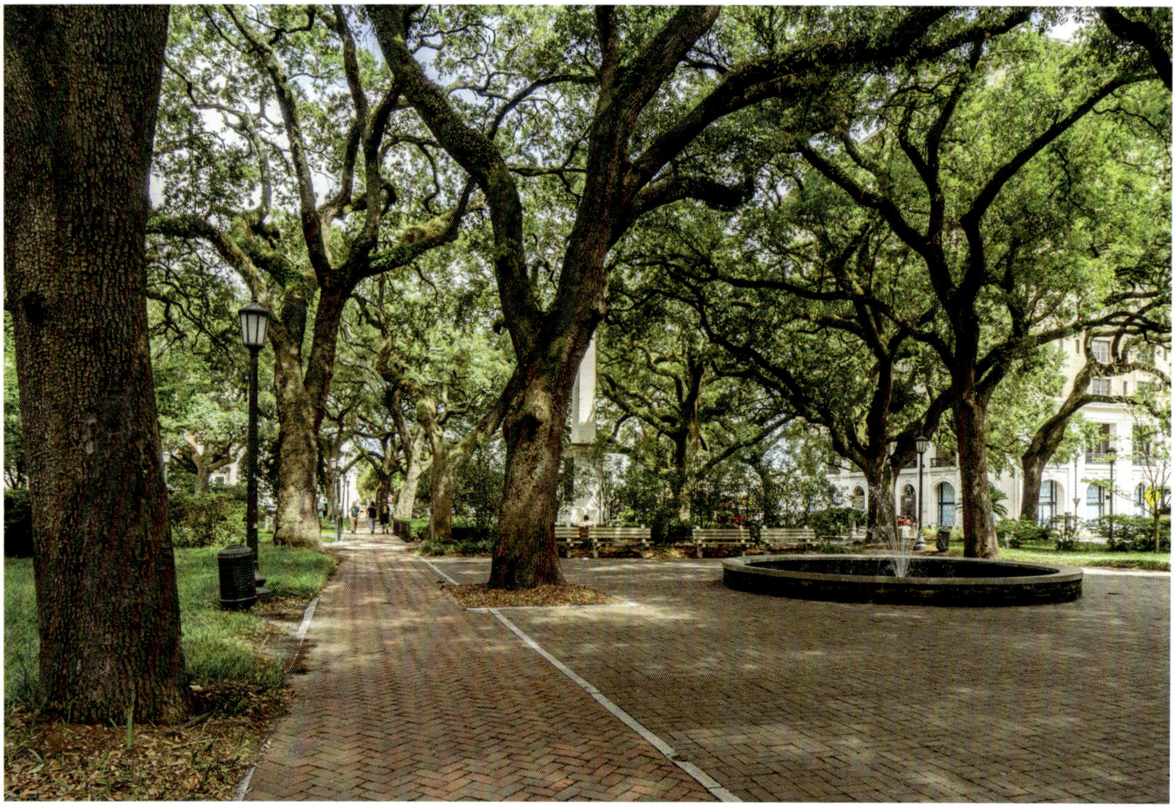

FIGURE 146. Live oaks in Johnson Square.
Photo by Robin B. Williams, 2024.

CHAPTER EIGHT

THE LANDSCAPE ARCHITECTURE OF THE PLAN

Savannah is called the Forest City, on account of every main avenue, being planted on each side with grand and stately trees, and having a public square, or ornament by a fountain or monument.
—*Savannah Morning News*, August 29, 1877

Savannah consists almost entirely of large squares, which are like as many paradises. They follow on, one after another, in a straight line, and you always pass from one to the next by means of a shady avenue. Trees, trees, you'll see them everywhere. They call Savannah a forest-town. And flowers. Roses and jasmine at every street corner. I should like to live here and never leave the place.
—JULIEN GREEN, 1916

Becoming a Forest City

Live oak trees draped with Spanish moss never fail to enchant visitors to Savannah. The massive evergreens (called "live" because they are never dormant or leafless) loom about fifty feet high and form a broad, diaphanous, leafy canopy with their sturdy arched branches spreading to about eighty feet in diameter, wide enough to visually obscure if not overwhelm the city's architecture. Planted at regular intervals in squares and along civic streets, they create an animated architecture of their own, a counterpoint melody to the city's buildings. Replacing the pride of India trees that had dominated the city's green spaces since the 1790s, the "majestic live oak" was identified together with "the grandiflora magnolia and the picturesque palmetto" as one of Savannah's official street trees in 1896 by the city's Park and Tree Commission, founded the previous year.[1] The live oaks and the commission that planted them are evidence of the vital role that landscape architecture has played in the making and nurturing of the Savannah Plan.

Savannah has been cultivated as a garden city since its founding in 1733, but the nature and purpose of its horticulture have changed radically. The Trustees' vision of industrious and productive citizen farmers living and working in an egalitarian, agrarian paradise was wildly unrealistic. The hot, humid climate and sandy soil of Savannah were not conducive to such an enterprise, and its urban-born colonists were hardly equipped or motivated to succeed as farmers. What is surprising then is how the misplaced dream of an agrarian utopia was transformed into the reality of a town praised by countless visitors for its luxuriant vegetation. Despite its initial missteps, Savannah came to epitomize what James Machor describes as the pastoral dream of American urbanism, a "blend of grid and garden, of civilization and nature in the Utopian city."[2] As one visitor wrote in 1852, "Here, more than in, perhaps, Any other city may be seen 'rus in urbe.'"[3]

The Trustees' agrarian vision appears at first to have lacked an aesthetic dimension. They issued no instructions about garden design in the Georgia colony, nor do they discuss landscape beauty in their pamphlets or correspondence. They were undoubtedly aware, however, of the writings of Joseph Addison, Alexander Pope, and others of their day extolling the virtues of landscape gardening.[4] Published in 1731, Pope's "Epistle to Richard Boyle, Earl of Burlington" became a manifesto, calling for an embrace of "Nature" as a guide for garden design.[5] Lord Burlington was at that time transforming his famous garden at Chiswick House under the direction of the painter-architect William Kent, regarded by many as one of the founders of the English landscape garden. In 1733, as Oglethorpe was laying out Savannah, Kent was reconfiguring the formal parterres of London's St. James's Park, very near the residences of at least three of the Georgia Trustees.[6]

Evidence of the Trustees' interest in garden design is manifested in a variety of ways. A rather fantastic view of the Georgia colony, drawn and engraved by artist John Pine and published by the Trustees in 1732, serves as an example (figure 147).

FIGURE 147. *A Prospective View of Savannah*, drawn and engraved by John Pine in 1732 and first published in the second edition of *Some Account of the Designs of the Trustees for Establishing the Colony of Georgia in America* (London, 1732), and then again in *Reasons for Establishing the Colony of Georgia* (London, 1733). Courtesy of the John Carter Brown Library at Brown University.

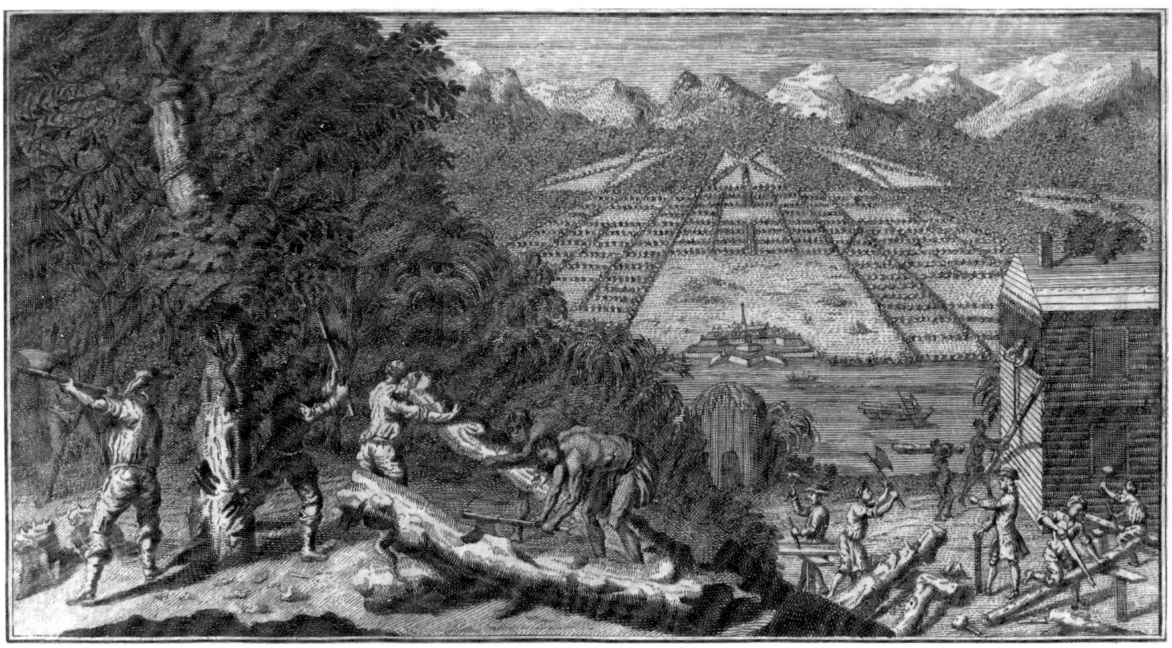

The print depicts robust colonists felling trees and constructing a log building in the foreground. Across a river, in the middle ground, a walled city appears to be a prevision of Savannah. The city is surrounded by an empty common and set within a vast grid of tree-lined fields in the background. Anderson argues that Pine's bird's-eye view adopts an artistic convention popular at the time for depicting gardens of great aristocratic estates.[7] This observation leads him to suggest numerous possible sources of influence on the development of the Savannah Plan from the world of gardening. The elevated one-point perspective became a canonic method for depicting Savannah, beginning with the Gordon View of 1734, the Cerveau watercolor *Panorama of Savannah* (1837), the 1855 lithographic print based on Charles Parsons's view from Monterey Square, and numerous photographs looking south from City Hall.

We should note that London engraver Paul Fourdrinier, who printed the Gordon View, produced illustrations for many architectural books, including Robert Castell's *Villas of the Ancients Illustrated* (1728), a key publication promoting landscape garden design that also played a pivotal role in the founding of the Georgia colony. Four future Georgia Trustees, including Oglethorpe, were subscribers to this landmark book, which was dedicated to Lord Burlington.[8] It was Oglethorpe's anger at Castell's senseless death in a debtors' prison that energized his work as a prison reformer in Parliament and led to his work in founding the Georgia Trustees.[9] William Harden even suggested that Castell's garden designs were an inspiration for Oglethorpe's design of Savannah, though this seems unlikely.[10] Further evidence of the Trustees' interest in garden design is found in the fact that the ill-fated Trustees' Garden was referred to in its day as a "Publick Garden" and was described by Francis Moore as being "laid out with Cross-walks planted with Orange-trees, . . . [and] in the Squares between the Walks, were vast Quantities of Mulberry-trees."[11] Although a specific theory of landscape design does not emerge from the writings of Oglethorpe or the Trustees, they were surely informed about the subject as they began to implement their plans for a city that would become famous for its interweaving of the urban and the rural.

Trees play a preeminent role in the landscape design of the Savannah Plan. They are an integral feature, carefully woven into the geometric fabric of the plan. We are therefore surprised to see in the Gordon View that Savannah began with the eradication of a dense pine barren; the land is shown as a bare, flat surface, bereft of foliage apart from two clusters of trees (figure 9).[12] However, in the Moravian plan, tentatively dated to 1740, we see rows of circles with hatch marks—evidently representing trees—lining all the principal seventy-foot-wide civic streets, as well as the fronts of the trusts lots to the east and west of every square and the first two lots of each tything block facing the square (figures 5 and 10). Trees also line both sides of Broughton Street, the one wide east–west street between the rows of wards. In short, trees define the *civic* realm, as distinct from the treeless utilitarian streets running north–south between wards and the lanes that bisect all the tything blocks. The 1740 plan indicates a precise tree planting scheme that is integral to the geometric structure of the Savannah Plan. Whether any of this was executed is unknown, but it is an early indication of what would happen as Savannah's streets and squares were planted with trees and populated with a variety of landscape elements over the next two centuries.

So successful were its tree planting efforts that by the middle of the nineteenth century Savannah had already begun to assume the moniker of "Forest City."[13] It was among the pioneering American cities to plant street trees in the eighteenth century, and it was one of the first to define planting pattern standards, to recognize their health benefits, and to advocate for tree protection. Yet Savannah's tree planting and landscaping efforts have not been uncontested endeavors. Concern about air quality and public health, the exclusion of people of color from some green spaces, the incursion of streetcars and automobiles into public squares, debates about passive and active uses for landscaped squares and promenades, and the erection of commemorative monuments have all had a bearing on the landscape architecture of the Savannah Plan.

Like the plan itself, Savannah's landscape architecture is the creation of many authors over a long period of time. It too is a work in progress. Since little is known about the actual landscape features executed under the Trustees or the royal governors, our account must begin in the 1790s with the early days of the city government. Various street, lane, and tree committees spearheaded the city's landscape plans, initiatives, and ordinances throughout the nineteenth century before the Park and Tree Commission was created in 1895. A succession of citizens and organized groups has played a vital role in landscaping the city as well. Private citizens planted many of Savannah's trees and shrubs. Savannah merchant John Hunter created a botanical garden in 1822, and William B. Hodgson established in 1846 what was later described as "a place for public and common resort for recreation and exercise," both within the Common.[14] Charitable groups such as the Daughters of the American Revolution, the Trustees' Garden Club, and the Historic Savannah Foundation have engaged in landscape beautification efforts. More recently, the Savannah Tree Foundation, established in 1982, has led the way in improving Savannah's urban forest. Public monuments were generally initiated and often paid for by private groups of citizens. Professionally trained landscape designers have played an increasingly important role ever since Bavarian gardener Wilhelm Christian Bischoff was hired to design Forsyth Place in 1851. The design and cultivation of Savannah's landscape architecture has always been collaborative.

Municipal ordinances have been the primary tool employed by the city to guide the design and implementation of landscape features in Savannah. Tree ordinances can be found in other American cities by the 1780s, but curiously, the earliest of these sought to limit (if not eliminate) trees along city streets. Political battles over street trees grew out of struggles over fire insurance and the belief that trees were a fire hazard.[15] A Pennsylvania law enacted in 1782, for example, required the removal of all trees along the streets of Philadelphia, but public protest forced the repeal of the law within two years. In May 1791, New York City attempted to ban street trees from everywhere in the city, but this effort too met stiff opposition and was repealed after only ten days. New York civic officials progressively warmed to trees and by 1806 were actively encouraging city residents to plant trees. Dating to 1793, Savannah's earliest tree ordinance differed from its Northern counterparts by advocating the planting of trees, regulating how they should be planted along the city's streets, and explicitly supporting "the inhabitants who choose to plant trees in the streets or squares."[16] The ordinance aimed to "contribute to the ornament of the city as well as its safety in case of fire by preventing the spreading of the same, that trees should be planted at regular distances and in a straight line on each side of the streets and in the squares." It is ironic that the Savannah City Council, in contrast to public officials in Northern cities, saw trees as a method of containing fires.

More significantly from an urban design perspective, the 1793 ordinance defined aesthetic guidelines for how trees should be planted—not just in straight lines, but with their distance from the property line calibrated to the width of the street. On 75-foot-wide streets, trees had to be planted 12 feet from the lot line, while on narrower streets, trees had to be 6 feet from the lot line.[17] The ordinance also regulated the planting of trees in squares, requiring that they be set 31½ feet in front of the building lot lines, since the current edges of the squares defined by curbs had not yet been established.

Savannah's city council passed progressively more ambitious tree-protection ordinances in 1796, 1803, and 1810, this last year being the same one in which New York City passed its first ordinance protecting trees.[18] By 1810, all of Savannah's trees were placed "under the special protection of council."[19] The protection of trees was tied to their impact on the health of the city. In 1807, a committee that was organized to address the health of Savannah advised the city council "that a square of trees planted around the wall of the city cemetery would have a very salutary influence by imbibing the impurities of the surrounding atmosphere."[20] The 1810 ordinance provides an explicit accounting of the real and perceived benefits of trees:

> Experience has fully proved that great advantages are derived to the Inhabitants of the City from trees being planted in the streets and squares, from the shade they afford, the heat of a very sultry climate is lessened, and by the power which they possess of absorbing the noxious vapour which arises

> from the marshes and other Low Grounds in its vicinity, the prolific source of Fevers so fatal in this climate, they afford a shield by disarming in a Great degree the said vapour of its noxious principles; thereby affording to the Inhabitants the means of comfort and security.[21]

Landscaping the Streets

The concept of a "forest city" is an American manifestation of the urban-rural synthesis advocated by American writers, artists, and political theorists from the nation's founding to the present—from William Penn's "greene Country Towne" to contemporary calls for "urban tree equity." Savannah is not the only American city famous for its trees. Portland, Maine, and Cleveland, Ohio, are also known as "Forest City"; Springfield, Massachusetts, is known as the "City of Trees"; and New Haven is known as "Elm City." The arboreal virtues of American cities were on the mind of an 1852 visitor to Savannah who extolled the city for its resemblance to "New Haven—indeed, whilst some of its streets very nearly equal the sylvan-arched thoroughfares of the City of Elms, the universal diffusion of trees and shrubbery through all the streets gives Savannah decidedly the advantage."[22]

Trees were largely absent from European cities until modern times. The earliest references to urban tree planting trace back to Italian court cities of the fifteenth century.[23] The mile-long Cours-la-Reine commissioned by Marie de' Medici in 1614, located just outside the walls of Paris along the River Seine, became an important model for later public, tree-lined, recreational promenades in other European cities.[24] Pall Mall in St. James's Park in Westminster, London, originated as a linear field for playing pall-mall (a precursor to croquet) in a royal pleasure park, but in the 1660s Charles II transformed it into a public promenade (figure 148). A Swiss visitor, writing at the time of the Georgia Trustees, described how "society comes to walk here on fine, warm days. . . . Some people come to see, some to be seen, and others to seek their fortunes."[25] Two of the original Trustees, John Perceval and John Laroche, lived in houses on Pall Mall. Also in London were the tree-lined public walks of Moorfields, just outside the Moor Gate, which were created in 1607 as "a pleasurable place of sweet ayres for Cittizens to walke in."[26] Elizabeth Milroy has shown how Moorfields became a model for William Penn in the layout of public squares in Philadelphia.[27]

The first formal planting of trees in American cities began in Boston in 1723 with a single row of English elms along Common (later Tremont) Street in the Boston Common. A fence was erected to protect the promenade in 1733, and a second row of trees was planted a year later to form an allée (figure 149).[28] It came to be called "the Mall," reflecting its European inspiration. Trees planted privately by the owners of adjacent houses appeared along some New York City streets by 1731

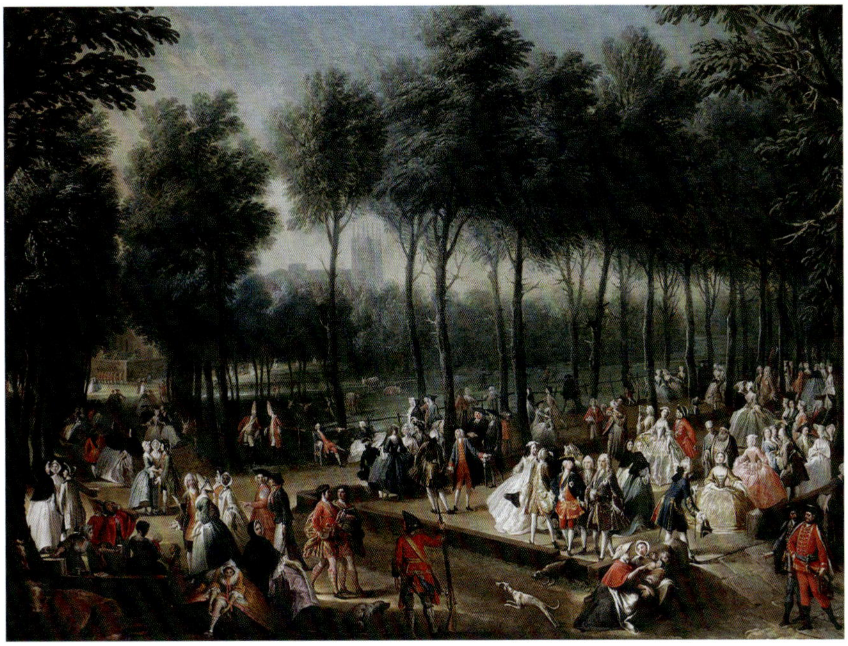

FIGURE 148. *St. James's Park and the Mall,* oil on canvas painting, attributed to Joseph Nickolls, ca. 1745, 40¾" × 54½". Royal Collection of the United Kingdom. Licensed under Wikimedia Commons.

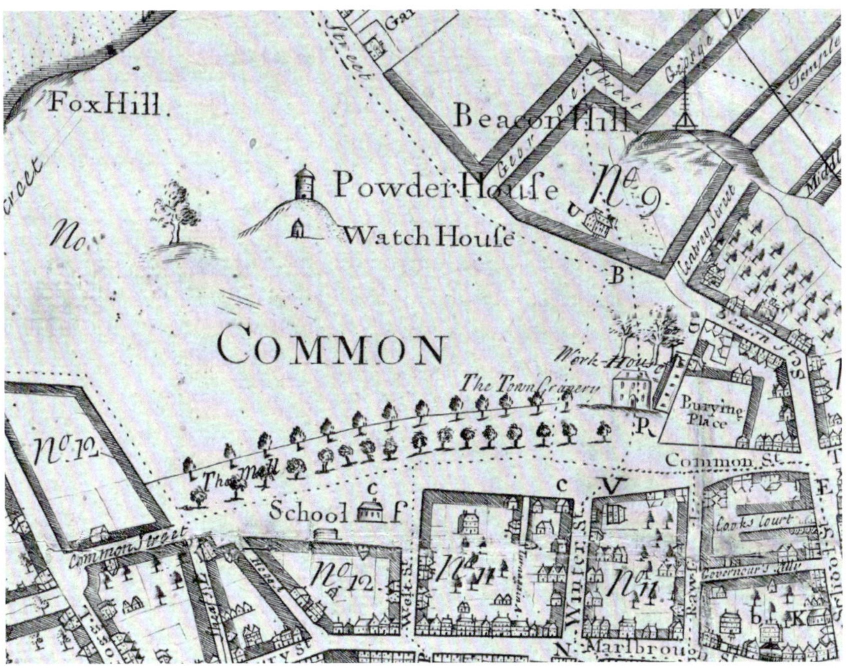

FIGURE 149. Detail from *A New Plan of Ye Great Town of Boston in New England in America, with the Many Additionall Buildings, & New Streets, to the Year, 1769,* engraved map by Thomas Johnston, published by William Price (Boston, 1769). Boston Public Library, Norman B. Leventhal Map and Education Center.

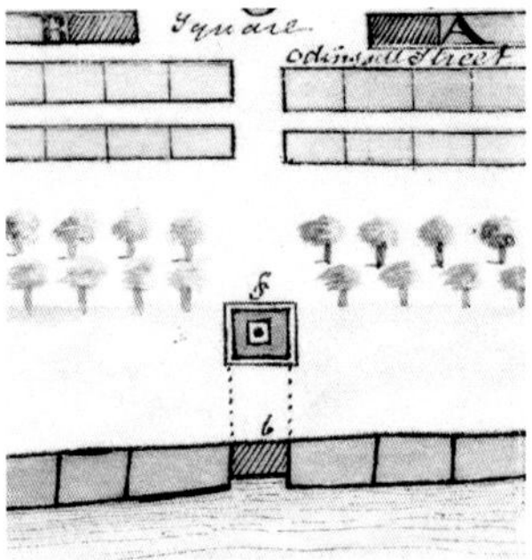

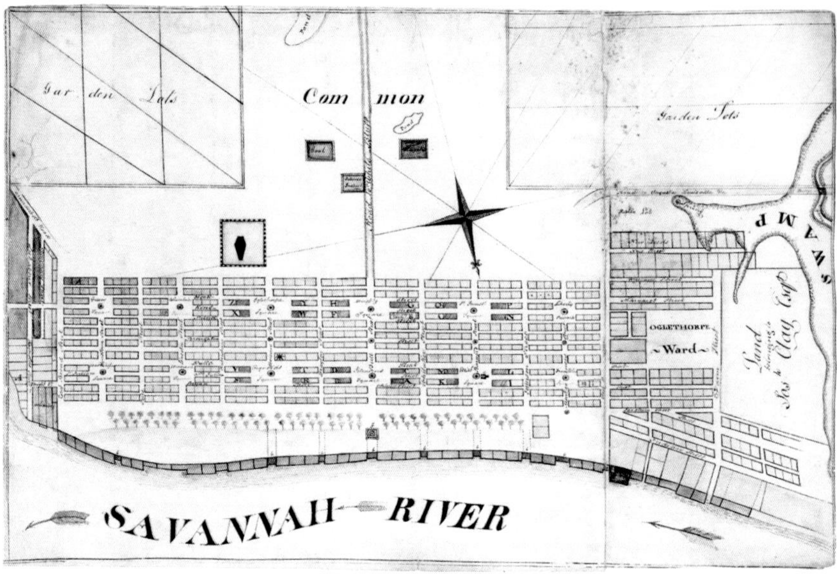

FIGURE 150. *Map of Savannah*, untitled, unsigned, dated 1802. *Above*: Detail of tree placement near river. Courtesy Beehive Foundation.

and in Philadelphia by the 1770s.[29] In Savannah, the 1793 tree ordinance guided the private planting of trees.

The first formally planted street trees in Savannah formed a public promenade, a double row of pride of India trees lining the north side of Bay Street atop the bluff above the Savannah River in the 1790s. The trees were planted, at least in part, by the harbor master, Captain George Throop, who was hired by the city in January 1799 "to complete the rows of trees on the Bay."[30] The allée was interrupted at the intersection with Bull Street to make way for the City Exchange, which was built the same year. A map of Savannah from 1802 documents these trees visually for the first time (figure 150). A local observer commented in 1806 that the rows formed "a pleasant walk in the summer months, adding to the beauty of that part of the city, and contributing to its healthiness in a considerable degree."[31] The double row of trees on "the Strand" created a clear northern edge for the city, separating it from the wharves below the bluff and providing a precedent for future tree-lined promenades within the town plan.

When the 1793 ordinance initiated the regular planting of street trees in the Savannah Plan, the streets were unpaved, so trees defined the edges of the streets, separating them from sidewalks, which likewise were unpaved ground between the street trees and the private building lots. As sidewalks were paved first, initially on an ad hoc basis with wood planks, flagstone, or brick, they were installed just inside the tree line. Cerveau's *Panorama of Savannah* of 1837 (figures 1 and 76) offers a detailed record of the city looking southward along the Bull Street

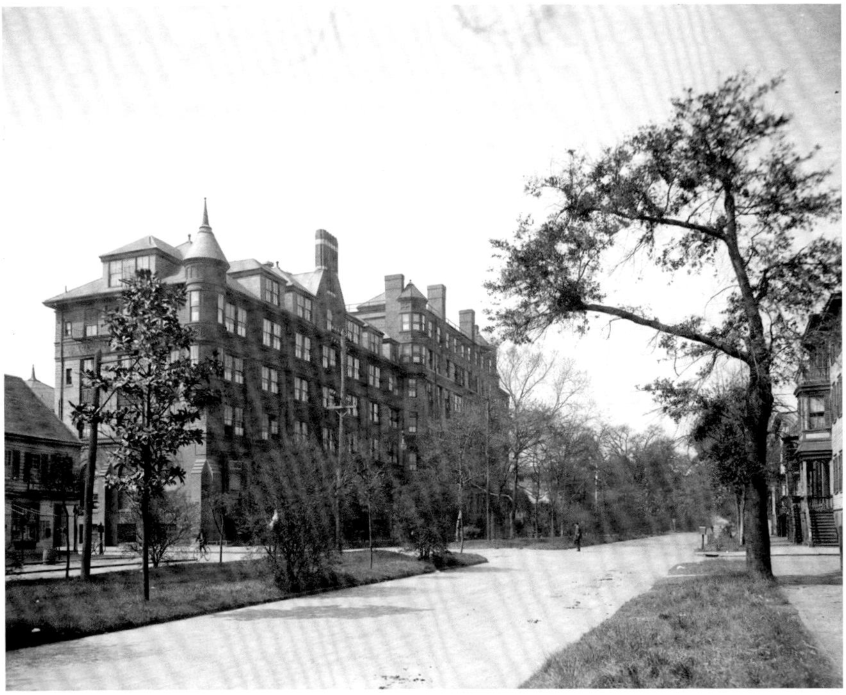

FIGURE 151. Liberty Street, looking west toward Drayton Street. The tree lawn appears prominently on the right, and the Desoto Hotel appears on the left. Detroit Publishing Company, ca. 1900–1915. 8" × 10" glass negative. Library of Congress, Prints and Photographs Division.

axis—nearly the same viewpoint as that represented in the Gordon View a century earlier. In this large watercolor painting, we see rutted streets, sidewalks, and curbs of various materials, reflecting property owner preference, and trees planted roughly as indicated in the ordinance.

Savannah's streets were paved incrementally beginning in the 1850s with a typical variety of surface materials—cobblestones, oyster shells, wood blocks, greywacke blocks, macadam, chert, pyrites, granite Belgian blocks, natural asphalt, vitrified brick, asphalt blocks, early concrete, and, finally, synthetic asphalt; six of these pavement types survive within the Savannah Plan area.[32] As the city faced the burden of paving such wide streets, the cost of pavement was reduced by extending sidewalks and curbs farther out into the roadway. Trees that had formerly lined the edges of dirt streets became part of the sidewalk, in a strip (locally called a "tree lawn") between the former outside edge of the sidewalk and the street, adding a new landscape feature to the plan (figure 151). So important are tree lawns to Savannah's urban identity today that they gained protection in a municipal ordinance passed in 2017. Responsibility for the maintenance of tree lawns, which are part of the public street corridor, rests with the adjacent property owners, who often turn them into diminutive gardens.

In a plan of Savannah published by Isidore Stouf in 1818, rows of trees are shown

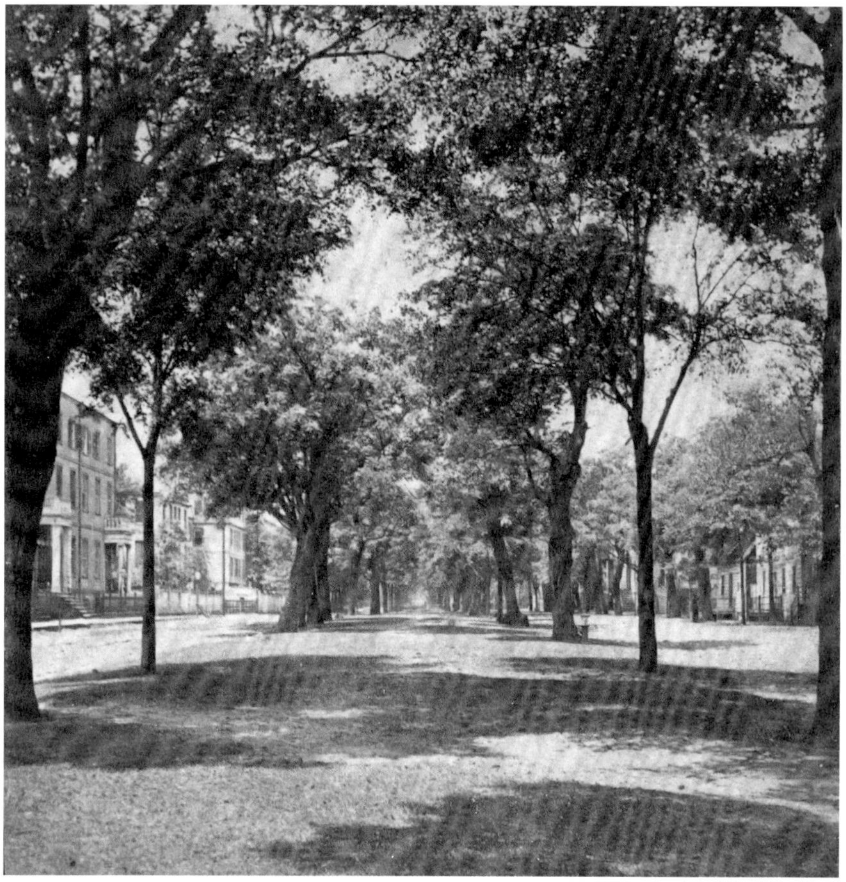

FIGURE 152. South Broad Street (Oglethorpe Avenue), looking west toward Drayton Street, albumen silver print on stereographic card by Jerome Nelson Wilson (active in Savannah ca. 1870–97). Library of Congress, Prints and Photographs Division.

along East Broad and West Broad Streets, creating strong edges to the city similar to that formed by the promenade on the Strand to the north (figure 37). The same map depicts the city's southern edge formed by the 140-foot-wide South Broad Street (now Oglethorpe Avenue), a magnificent tree-lined boulevard with a 45-foot-wide public pedestrian promenade running along its centerline (figures 7 and 152). Sadly, it was also a place of exclusion, as evidenced by an 1827 ordinance decreeing that "for the purpose of protecting the citizens while engaged in recreation upon the public walks from molestation or intrusion of improper persons from and after the passage of this Ordinance no negro, mulatto or other colored person shall be permitted to appear upon the public promenade in South Broad Street."[33] In the later twentieth century, just as legal racial segregation was coming to an end, everyone was effectively excluded from the public promenades of Oglethorpe Avenue and Liberty Street when masses of azaleas were planted, filling the space between the trees.[34]

The six principal east–west civic streets between the wards each acquired a distinct landscape cross section (figure 64). The north side of Bay Street is lined with trees, screening grassy parks, parking lots, and paved ramps to the riverfront, while its south side maintains a hard architectural edge that is free of trees. Broughton Street, as the main commercial corridor, has lacked trees for most of its history but acquired small ornamental trees in the 1970s. A recent renovation of its streetscape introduced a variety of hardscape features, more trees (including palmettos), and bioswale bump-outs planted with coastal grasses at each intersection. Unlike the grand boulevards of Oglethorpe and Liberty, Jones Street lacks a median; more than half (55 feet) of its 95-foot width was dedicated to the plan's widest combination of sidewalks and tree lawns, which amply accommodate the generous canopy of its flanking rows of live oak trees. Gaston Street, the 75-foot-wide southern boundary of the Savannah Plan, also has wide tree lawns, but its architectural edge lacks the visual clarity of many of Savannah's streets because the houses that front Gaston do so with less uniformity. Taking advantage of their extraordinary 120-foot tything lot depth, many of the houses on Gaston are set back from the street, but their setbacks and landscape features are inconsistent along the street's length. The south side of Gaston Street is variable as well; its central section, across from Monterey Ward, is defined by the vast garden spaces of Forsyth Park, which is tied to the central Bull Street axis by its capacious allées of live oaks.

Landscaping the Squares

Conceived by the Trustees as sites with both practical and recreational purposes, Savannah's squares functioned as miniature commons. Under Oglethorpe, they remained open fields for militia training and recreation and were largely devoid of vegetation. During the nineteenth century, their dual functions intensified, as utilitarian infrastructure features (water pumps, cisterns, and fire engine houses) were installed in the squares at the same time that their landscaping became more parklike.

The squares were set apart from the street grid when encircling fences were erected in 1810. That year Savannah merchant Robert Mackay wrote to his wife that "every square in town is now enclosed with light cedar posts painted white and a chain along their tops, trees planted within, and two paved footpaths across, the remainder of the ground they are spreading Bermuda grass over, and upon the whole the Town looks quite another thing and very enchanting."[35] City council minutes mention trees in the squares as early as 1793.[36] It appears, however, that prior to 1810 only Johnson Square enjoyed the presence of trees, since in that year the council decided that "all public squares shall as soon as council may deem it expedient be planted with Trees after the manner already adopted in Johnston [*sic*] Square."[37]

The squares have served a variety of uses. In general, active uses—public markets, political assemblies, auctions, playgrounds—have given way over the years to more passive uses—strolling, relaxing, reading, conversing—so that the squares have come to function primarily as landscaped parks for leisure and contemplation. Nineteenth-century travel writers lauded the squares primarily for their therapeutic and aesthetic benefits. Sara Hathaway, for example, described the squares in 1833 as "manifold grassy parks, or lungs of the city, [which] are very picturesque and inviting, and highly suggestive of health and comfort."[38] Charles Lanman in 1856 used a similar metaphor, referring to the squares as "ventilators."[39] The analogy of parks as lungs was regularly employed by nineteenth-century American reformers.[40] The health benefits of recreation and exercise, however, were considered of little importance by such reformers, who gave preference to the *vita contemplativa* over the *vita activa*. Gradually eliminating active uses has, more disturbingly, also had an exclusionary effect on some groups and individuals. In 1973, for example, Chatham Square was relandscaped at the prompting of the preservation-minded residents of the ward, who had argued that "the square should be renovated and returned to quiet park status."[41] In doing so, they banned the mostly African American children of the adjacent Barnard Street School, who had been using the square as a playground. Inclusive active uses have recently come back in favor in one square, as the restoration of Ellis Square in 2010 was designed to accommodate large-scale assemblies and a range of active uses (figure 44). The essential civic quality of Savannah's squares seems to demand increasingly accommodating designs.

Savannah's squares have undergone numerous reconfigurations over the years, but certain elements and compositional principles have persisted in their landscape design. Trees, planted according to the city's ordinances, have been found in all the squares since the early nineteenth century, though in the twentieth century a loosening of principles of symmetry and regularity has conferred on many of the squares a relatively informal quality. Pride of India trees were the most prevalent species in the nineteenth century, giving way to indigenous live oaks and magnolias in the 1890s, while a greater variety of species can be seen in recent times. Fences of various kinds surrounded the squares until the late nineteenth century, when street pavement and curbs provided them with a less restrictive boundary edge. Even so, shrubs or tall, ground-covering plants have been planted at the edges of some squares to form verdant boundary walls that create a sense of enclosure, making those squares feel like outdoor rooms. All the squares have specified entry points, which gives them a fundamental unity of composition.

Almost every square—Warren, Chippewa, Crawford, and Chatham being exceptions—follows a tic-tac-toe-like compositional structure formed by pathways aligned with the street grid, reinforced during the nineteenth century by rows of trees. Pedestrians can walk uninterrupted along the sidewalks of most any north–south or east–west civic street bisecting the wards from one square to the next across the entire Savannah Plan (figure 74). The pedestrian pathways are thus integral to the tartan plan. The resulting nine rectangular or square spaces are landscaped in a variety of ways in each of the squares; in some cases, they create rooms within rooms. In some squares, curved pathways are introduced within their nine-square structure.

The tic-tac-toe-like nine-cell structure reinforces the central focus of each square. In thirteen of the twenty-two extant squares, the center point is occupied by an architectural or sculptural object; two have a covered pavilion, three have a fountain, and eight have a monument. Since the time of Oglethorpe, Savannah has seen its public spaces aggrandized by public monuments, which have shaped the city's identity almost as much as the squares and trees have.

Until the early twentieth century, the city's monumental identity centered exclusively on the Bull Street corridor—from its head at Bay Street, where a prominent civic building has stood since the mid-eighteenth century, to Forsyth Park anchoring the Savannah Plan's south end. Oglethorpe reinforced Bull Street's primacy by setting the town clock, a sundial, at the center of Johnson Square, and in 1739, following the death of Tomochichi, he honored the Yamacraw chief's wishes to be buried in the town by placing his tomb in the center of Percival (now Wright) Square (figure 29). Taking the form of a pyramid of stone, the burial structure arguably constituted the first public monument in America, its formality reinforced by being located in the center of a square.[42] That monument disappeared most likely before the end of the eighteenth century and certainly by 1837, given its absence in Cerveau's highly detailed *Panorama of Savannah*. In 1899, Tomochichi was once again commemorated, this time with a large granite boulder located in the southeast corner of the square.

Savannah's current monumental identity began in 1825 when the Marquis de Lafayette laid the cornerstone for the Nathanael Greene Monument in Johnson Square. Designed by Philadelphia architect William Strickland and completed in 1830, the fifty-foot-tall obelisk was among the earliest large-scale monuments in the country.[43] A parade of monuments eventually emerged in the Bull Street squares: the even grander Casimir Pulaski Monument in Monterey Square (1855); the William Washington Gordon Monument in Wright Square (on the by-then-forgotten site of Tomochichi's tomb) in 1883; the Sergeant William Jasper Monument in Madison Square, completed in 1888 and inaugurated by President Grover Cleveland; and finally, and rather belatedly, the James Oglethorpe Monument (1910) in Chippewa Square by celebrated sculptor Daniel Chester French, working

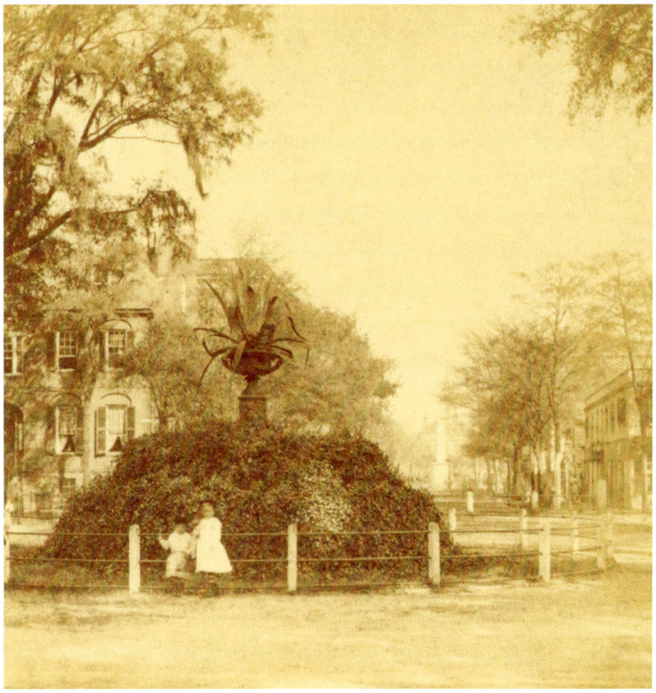

FIGURE 153. Mound in Wright Square, looking north along Bull Street. Albumen silver print on stereographic card by O. Pierre Havens, ca. 1875. New York Public Library, Miriam and Ira D. Wallach Division of Art, Prints and Photographs: Photography Collection.

with architect Henry Bacon, who also designed a new landscape plan to enhance the central statue.[44] It was not until the 1970s that other squares would begin to receive monuments or fountains.

The controversial introduction of streetcar lines through several squares beginning in 1871 challenged those who wished to enhance the aesthetic and therapeutic virtues of the squares. It also prevented the erection of centralizing monuments. Some activists rose to the occasion, however. A few weeks after the Georgia Supreme Court ruled against the city's attempt to block the streetcars in December 1871, Savannah alderman John Ferrill proposed erecting decorative mounds in some squares, including the two Bull Street squares lacking a monument or fountain at that time, Wright and Madison.[45] Essentially piles of rocks that could be erected quickly and therefore prevent the passage of tracks, these mounds were covered with vines, and each was crowned by a Warwick Vase, giving the mounds the imprimatur of decorative landscape features that captivated photographers at the time (figure 153). While the mounds successfully kept tracks off Bull Street, streetcars were running through nine of Savannah's twenty-four squares by 1877, and through twelve squares (while skirting three others) by the early twentieth century (figure 42).

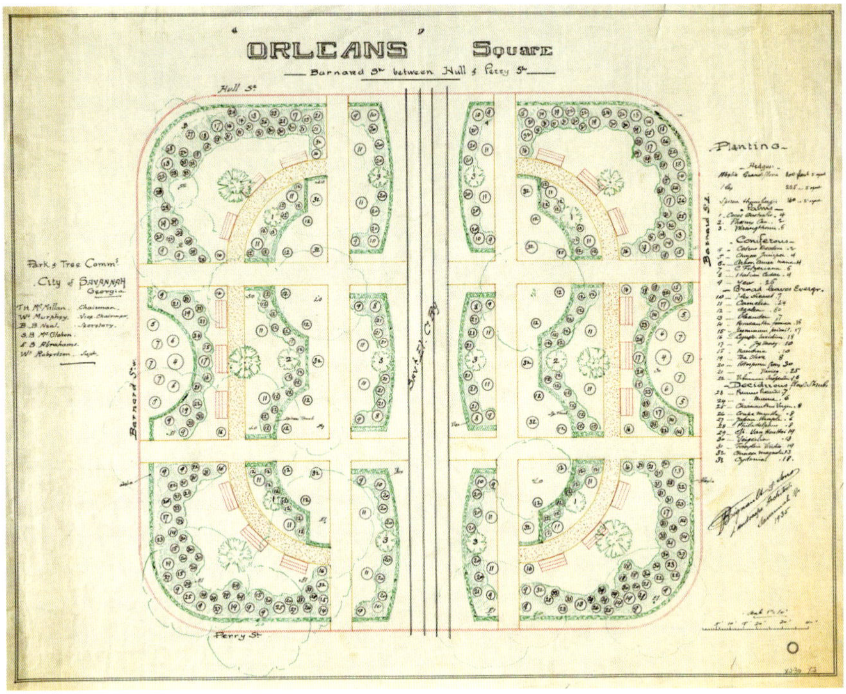

FIGURE 154. Design for Orleans Square, by Georges H. Bignault & Sons, 1935. Ink on paper. Courtesy of the City of Savannah Municipal Archives, item no. XJ-036.

The destruction of the city's three westernmost squares (Franklin, Liberty, and Elbert) in 1935 to accommodate the unimpeded traffic along U.S. 17 appears to have prompted the city's Paris-born landscape architect, Georges H. Bignault, to author plans for the beautification of at least ten squares between 1934 and 1938.[46] He proposed enlivening the outer parts of the squares with almost Baroque curving paths lined with benches and framed by elaborate plantings, most dramatically for the squares riven by streetcar tracks—Orleans, Pulaski, Lafayette, and Telfair (figure 154).[47] At least one of his designs, that for Telfair Square, was implemented in 1962 by the Garden Club of Savannah.[48]

Threats to the squares continued after World War II with proposals to run streets through the squares on Habersham and Barnard Streets, as well as through Oglethorpe and Whitefield Squares.[49] Even without formal streets, "fire lanes" (open grassy corridors) bisected several squares to allow emergency vehicles unimpeded paths through the squares. Lack of maintenance of the squares further contributed to their general decline in the mid-twentieth century. Efforts to run streets through the squares along Habersham were advanced by the Savannah Chamber of Commerce in 1945–46 and supported by the Merchants Council and the Savannah Real Estate Board but met stiff opposition from patriotic and preservation

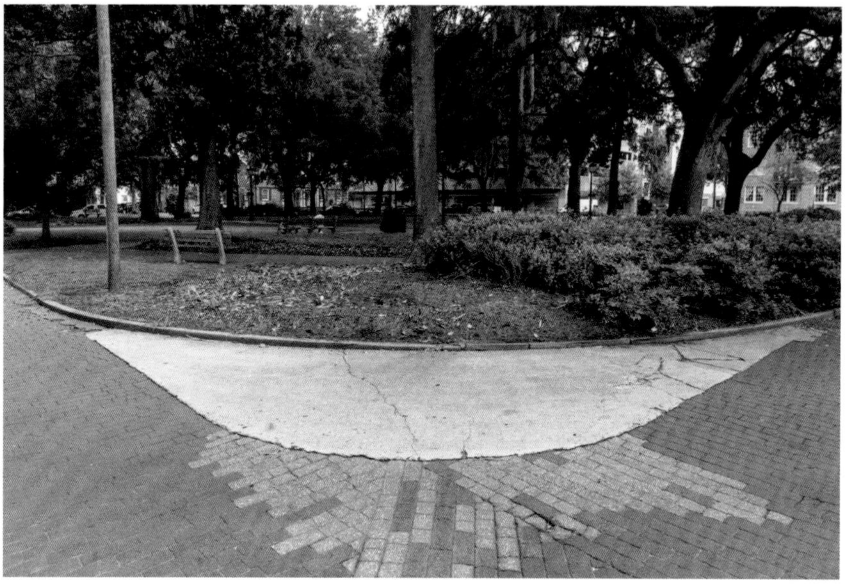

FIGURE 155. Southeast corner radius of Reynolds Square, altered in the 1960s with a concrete patch to allow easier traffic flow around the square. Photo by Robin B. Williams, 2023.

groups, as well as from local residents.[50] Despite the quelling of this initiative, the streets-through-squares idea returned in 1953 and in 1962, again focusing on the squares along Habersham and Barnard Streets, which had fire lanes crossing the squares even after the removal of the streetcar tracks; both efforts failed.[51]

The restoration of historic houses and their landscapes in the destitute northeast corner of downtown by local banker and preservationist Mills B. Lane Jr. beginning in the 1950s led to pioneering Savannah landscape architect Clermont Lee being commissioned in 1963 to relandscape Washington Square (Greene and Troup Squares would follow later in the decade, and Madison Square in the 1980s), perhaps inspired by the beautification of Telfair Square the previous year by the Garden Club of Savannah.[52] Pressured by the city and by private bus companies to keep the fire lanes open because modern emergency vehicles and buses were too big to navigate around the historic corners of the squares, Lee successfully argued (presumably as part of the 1962 debate over the squares) to close the fire lanes and instead round the corners of the squares, a solution still visible in multiple squares with concrete patches at their corners (figure 155).[53] This subtle adjustment, part of a long tradition of adjusting the shapes of the squares, further illustrates the principle of urban elasticity inherent in the Savannah Plan. It also definitively ended proposals to bisect the squares with streets. As seen in her design for Troup Square, Lee aimed to make the squares more usable by incorporating benches and retaining walls that reflect a modernist aesthetic, while reinforcing the historic pathways crossing the squares and the inclusion of a central monument (figure 156).

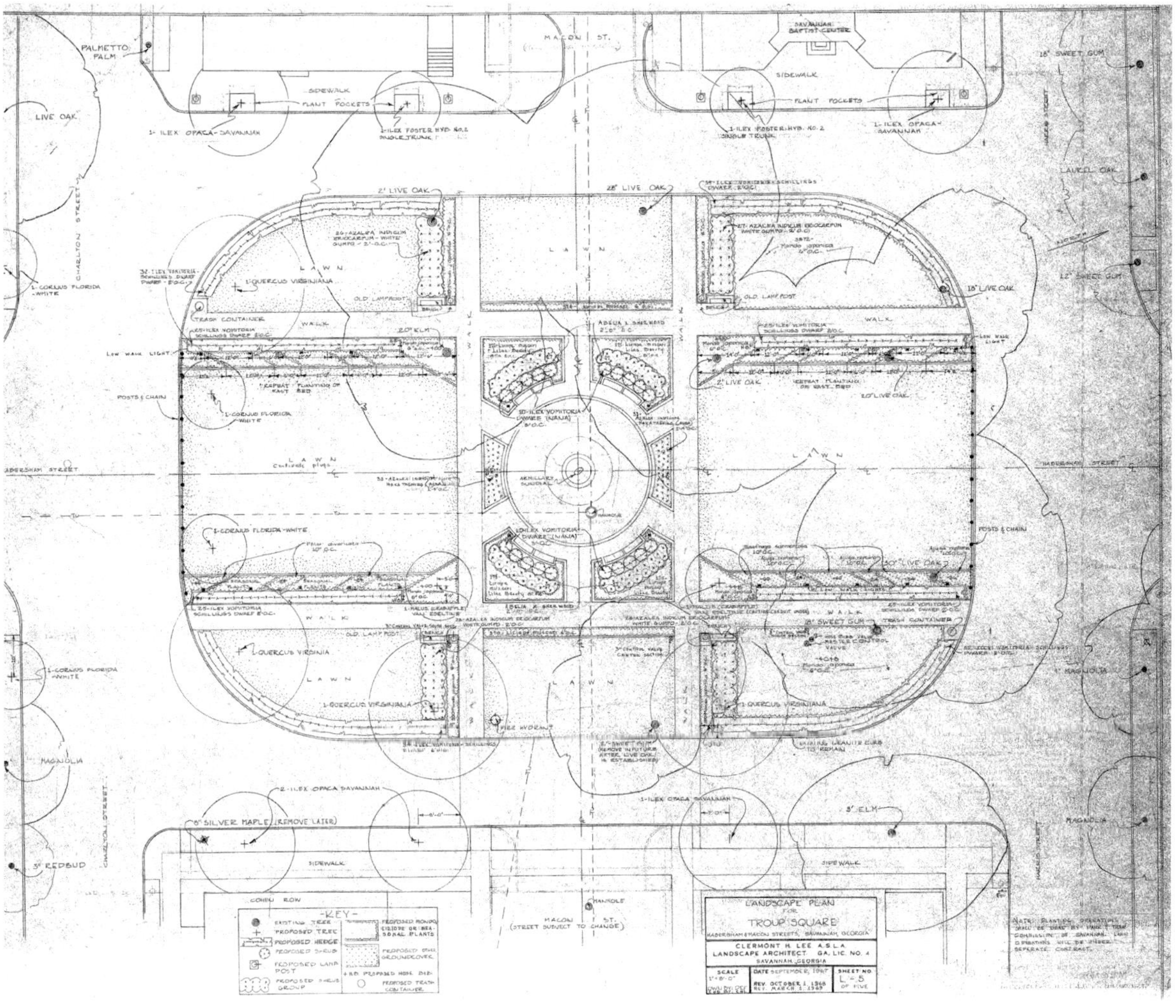

FIGURE 156. Troup Square landscape plan by Clermont Lee, 1969. Courtesy of the Georgia Historical Society, GHS 1480–217–001.

Other squares soon enjoyed a similar renewal of their landscape plans. Johnson Square, the city's most prominent square, was updated in 1967 with a design by Massachusetts-based Sasaki, Dawson, DeMay Associates that included a pair of circular modernist brick fountains (figure 146). Later square renovations emphasized usability, representing a return to the more active functions of squares in the nineteenth century: In 1973, Maryland-based designer Cy Paumier relandscaped Whitefield Square, setting the stage for the addition in 1975 of a central octagonal gazebo commissioned by Mills B. Lane Jr. and designed by local architect John LeBey; and in the south half of Crawford Square in 1981, Edward Pinckney/Associates from nearby Bluffton, South Carolina, installed a similar central gazebo and a playground set within a sunken area that revealed the top of the 1850 brick cistern. The demolition of the Ellis Square parking deck in 2005 allowed the city to restore yet another lost square. Completed in 2010 through a collaboration of EDAW/AECOM with local firm Lominack Kolman Smith Architects, the restored Ellis Square is an active-use public space, with interactive fountains, open spaces, a large chessboard, and restrooms, all set on top of a massive underground parking garage (figure 44).

Other Public Green Spaces Bordering the Plan

THE STRAND

One of the most unexpected green spaces in Savannah, and a by-product of the geometrical precision of the plan, is the irregular vestigial area between Bay Street (the plan's northern boundary) and the top of the bluff, historically called either the Strand or the Bay. Despite its adjacency to the historic port facilities of utilitarian warehouses and wharves along the river below, the dramatic change of grade caused by the forty-foot-high bluff assured the Strand a closer relationship with the formalized landscape of the plan, with which it shared the same elevation (figures 41 and 157). While the Common south of the city offered large open fields accommodating practical and utilitarian uses, the Strand lacked such practical usefulness, offering instead a long uninterrupted swath of green space, upon which the city introduced the first promenade in the 1790s. Its formality imbued the Strand with a square-like quality, but in elongated proportions. When a navigation range

FIGURE 157. The Strand, now called Salzburger Park and Emmet Park, view looking east. Photo by Robin B. Williams, 2024.

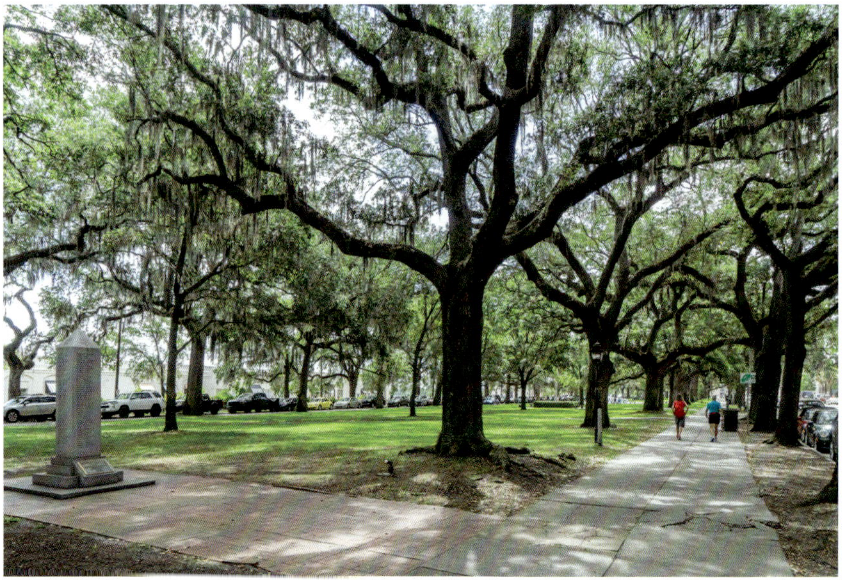

light—now called the Old Harbor Light—was installed in 1858 at the eastern end of the Strand, it was dressed up with elaborate cast-iron ornament in the manner of contemporaneous monuments. The survival of the Strand as green space in the context of the city's industrialization is admirable, as many other cities sacrificed their waterfronts to industry and trade. Beginning in 1905, the Strand has welcomed at least nine monuments (more than have been erected in any other green space in Savannah outside of cemeteries), with most installed since the 1950s.

COLONIAL PARK CEMETERY

From the time of its closure for burials in 1853 to its reinvention as a public park in 1895, the anomalous five-hundred-by-five-hundred-foot cemetery that had interrupted the southward expansion of the Savannah Plan had lain in a state of neglect. Mayor Thomas Gamble called it a weed-infested eyesore.[54] Following decades of debate concerning its future use, including lawsuits appealed to the Georgia Supreme Court, the old burial ground was turned over to the city in 1895 to be preserved as a historic cemetery but also as a public park.[55] The newly formed Park and Tree Commission hired Prosper J. Berckmans of Augusta, Georgia, to design and carry out the work, which included the introduction of picturesque, winding paved sidewalks and the removal of the cemetery's north, west, and south brick enclosure walls, transforming the cemetery from a place separated from the town to a spatial extension of the planned city (figure 158). The perimeter iron fences present today were installed in 1915 when the Daughters of the American Revolution built the monumental corner gate facing the intersection of Abercorn Street and Oglethorpe Avenue.

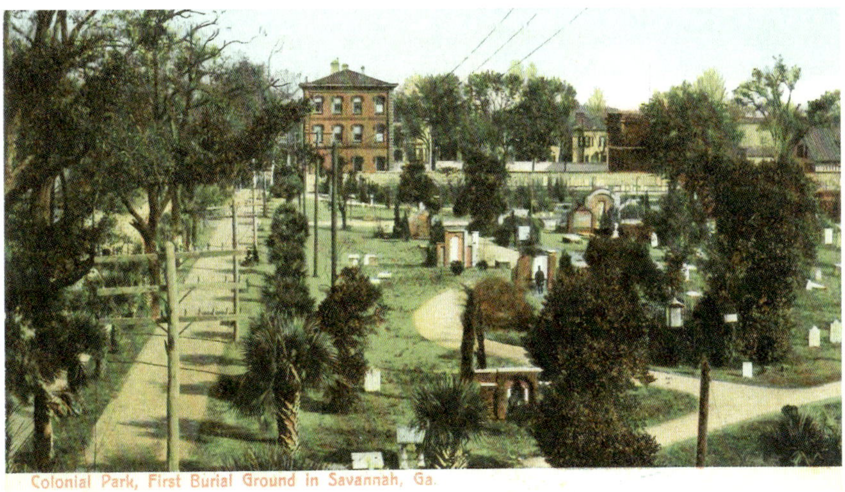

FIGURE 158. Colonial Park Cemetery, historic postcard. Courtesy of the City of Savannah Municipal Archives, V. & J. Duncan Postcard Collection.

FORSYTH PARK

The flexibility with which the Common accommodated expansions of the plan was further illustrated by the creation of Forsyth Park. On April 10, 1851, the city council approved a plan to "lay off" the remainder of the Common, which retained many of its old-growth pine trees, for a supersized square featuring a ten-acre park—the size of one of the original wards—at its center and aligning with the wards centered on Bull Street (figure 40). The site had already been partially developed as a park open to the public by William B. Hodgson, a prominent citizen who had been granted use of the land in 1846.[56] By 1851, the city took control of the land, formalizing it as a public park named Forsyth Place, and commissioned visiting Bavarian gardener Wilhelm Christian Bischoff to design a landscape plan, which was implemented (with modifications) by city engineer and architect John B. Hogg.[57]

The design followed the picturesque characteristics that emerged in eighteenth-century English country estate gardens, comprising "serpentine walks and grass-plots, interspersed with clumps of flowers, fanciful mounds and structures of ivy and other luxuriant runners and climbers" (figure 159).[58] Forsyth Place was an early American response to the emerging park movement that motivated its most important champion, landscape designer and horticulturalist Andrew Jackson Downing, to advocate for the need for a large municipal park in New York City, rather than small squares. Bigger than a traditional urban square, Savannah's Forsyth Place foreshadowed Frederick Law Olmsted and Calvert Vaux's vastly larger

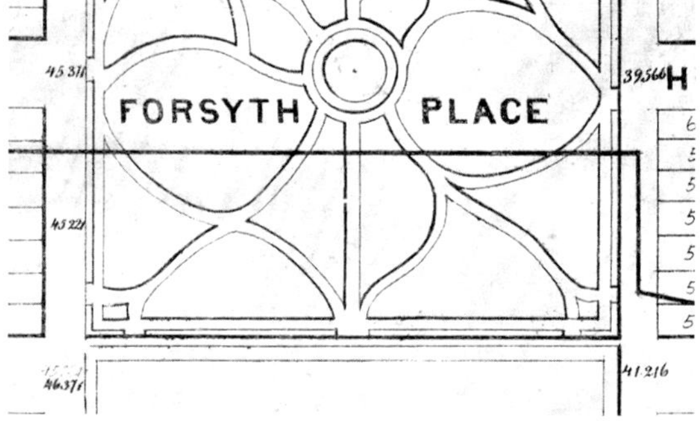

FIGURE 159. Forsyth Place as designed by Wilhelm Christian Bischoff, 1851. Detail of *Map of the City of Savannah & Vicinity, Showing Hydrographic Elevation & Lines of Drainage* by John B. Hogg (New York, 1868). Courtesy of Hargrett Rare Book and Manuscript Library, University of Georgia Libraries, Rare Map Collection.

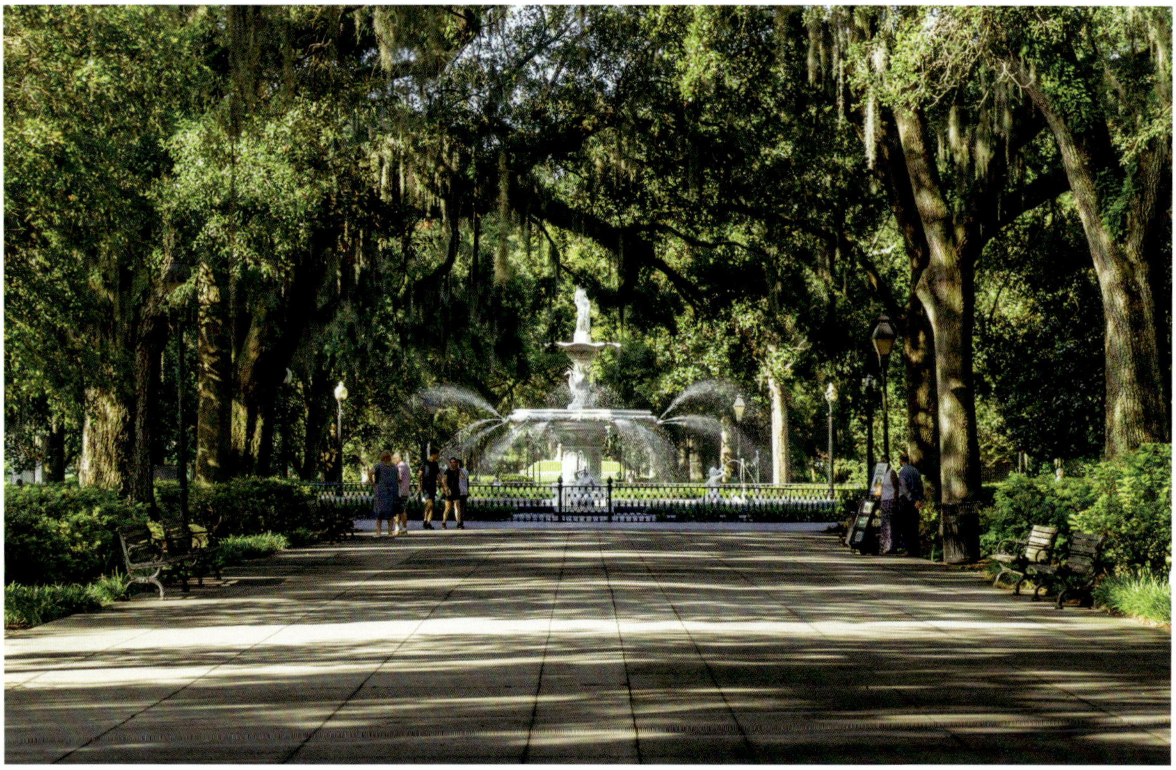

FIGURE 160. Forsyth Park, showing cast-iron fountain installed 1858. View looking south from Gaston Street. Photo by Robin B. Williams, 2024.

Central Park, begun in 1858. In 1853, Forsyth Place, renamed Forsyth Park, was expanded southward through the addition of a militia parade ground that tripled the park's size.

Forsyth Park extended the Bull Street axis southward and in 1858 followed the rhythmic spacing of monuments with the installation of the grandiose Forsyth Fountain at its center, a location equivalent to the center of a sixth row of wards and aligned with Huntingdon Street. Cast by Janes, Beebe and Company of New York, the fountain infused the urban formality of the Savannah Plan into the park space, definitively ending its role as a nature preserve (figures 8 and 160). The park extension offered the opportunity for a seventh monument along the Bull Street axis. The tall Confederate Monument, erected in 1874 and modified to its present design in 1879, aligns with Gwinnett Street, the original southern limit of the Common and roughly equivalent to the center of a seventh square—an appropriate place to culminate the monumental parade. The two Confederate busts displaced from Chippewa Square in 1910 were situated to the north and south of the monument (recently renamed the Civil War Memorial), further reinforcing the Bull Street axis.

From a small grid of open squares and town lots bounded by an extensive grid of gardens and farms, to a compact Forest City interlaced with leafy streets and luxuriant squares, the Savannah Plan has proved its ability to weave together *rus* and *urbs* into a hybrid fabric. As impressive as Savannah's architecture may be, travel writers, view makers, and photographers of the past two centuries have been captivated far more by the city's lush vegetation. The systematic planting of live oaks, magnolias, and palmettos along Savannah's numerous civic streets (and lately even along parts of its utilitarian north–south streets) and within its squares enlivens the city's architecture, simultaneously framing and obscuring it within a verdant trelliswork.

SECTION THREE CONCLUSION

AN UNFINISHED SYMPHONY

The noise produced at county fairs by many orchestras simultaneously playing different tunes is a true symbol for the architectural appearance of the typical modern city street.

—WERNER HEGEMANN AND ELBERT PEETS, 1922

One might imagine that buildings are normally "finished" simply because they are sufficiently desired, planned, and funded, and inversely that they remain incomplete when these necessities diminish or disappear.

—MARVIN TRACHTENBERG, 2010

The buildings and landscape components of the Savannah Plan constitute an architectural symphony remarkable for its harmony and rhythm. Its harmony is ensured by the commitment of its builders, architects, and designers to a shared language of form, texture, ornamental detail, and typology. Its rhythm is orchestrated by the city's urban plan. Although some buildings stand out, all have a part to play, and none are allowed to dominate. One building type, the Savannah rowhouse, like the stringed instruments of an orchestra, establishes the leitmotif for the city's architecture. An assortment of materials—brick, stucco, ironwork, with occasional wood and stone—are employed according to shared principles of design that we might describe as an everyday classicism. Stylistic fashions, technological inventions, and ever-changing building code requirements contribute to the making of Savannah's architecture, but these are tempered by tacit assumptions and long-standing practices.

Savannah's architectural symphony, unlike the symphonies of Mozart or Brahms, is constantly growing and changing. Old buildings are replaced with new ones; some buildings grow by rear additions, some by adding a new story on top; some are raised, with a new story inserted beneath; and some are adaptively reused and appropriately modified. Some institutions have grown within the plan by occupying multiple sites, acquiring or constructing additional buildings on nearby properties, but their expansion has been guided and constrained by the urban plan. Others have grown by literally pushing boundaries (encroachments into the public realm), by rising to greater heights, or by breaking the rules (the score). It seems significant that Savannah's civic buildings are almost all rule-breakers; the city's houses, however, generally play within the rules. Today, the "Design Manual for the Savannah Historic District," overseen by the Historic District Board of Review, guides rather than prescribes the form and character of modifications and new construction. The key concept is compatibility, in which the aim is to achieve harmony with the existing conditions while allowing variety and flexibility.

A chorus of designers, builders, council members, and critics over a period of almost three centuries has contributed to the symphonic unity of Savannah's architecture, but it is ultimately the Savannah Plan that is the conductor. Small block sizes, extensive street frontages, and the proximity of public squares or major civic avenues demand public visibility for some buildings more than others, but almost none escape the public realm. We have noted how the plan has precipitated creative strategies for some institutions with growing space requirements. Those unwilling or unable to work within the Savannah Plan—hospitals, correctional facilities, light industry, sports facilities, and some religious and educational institutions, for example—have left.

The Savannah Plan cannot accommodate all institutions or industries. This has been true even in earlier periods of the city's history. Shipping, railroads, and most industries have been located on the periphery. It is these marginal elements outside of the plan, and the influence of the plan beyond the Savannah Plan area, to which we turn in section 4.

SECTION FOUR

BEYOND THE SAVANNAH PLAN

ITS LEGACY AND LESSONS

A city, like a living thing, is a united and continuous whole. It does not cease to be itself as it changes in growing older, nor does it become one thing after another with the lapse of time, but is always at one with its former self in feeling and identity.
—PLUTARCH, first century AD

Many beautiful homes have been erected in these new subdivisions, and more are in course of erection and in contemplation. The rapidity with which the new section has grown is proof of Savannah's progress and an indication of the confidence which the public has in her future.
—Savannah Chamber of Commerce, 1911

Savannah is admirable because its urban plan has played a vital role in shaping its built environment and its landscape, but how has the plan shaped Savannah as it grew beyond the plan? How has the Savannah Plan shaped the building of cities beyond Savannah? What influence will it have on the future of cities elsewhere? These concluding chapters explore these questions as we investigate areas beyond the plan both geographically and chronologically.

The Georgia Trustees understood from the start that Savannah's town lots were merely part of an organized masterplan of common land, gardens, farms, villages, and forests—an urban and rural landscape that extended far beyond the town's original six wards and squares. The end of the Trustees' utopian experiment in the 1750s signaled the possibility of an alternative path for the city. While the plan expanded in a measured manner between the 1790s and the 1850s, unplanned growth took place along the periphery of the plan, as new residential districts, large-scale industry, and transportation networks developed. The continued expansion of the Port of Savannah and other industries along the Savannah River to the northwest was complemented by the development of shopping malls, big-box retail establishments, health-care complexes, and educational campuses along arterial traffic corridors mainly to the south that navigate through vast residential developments far from the walkable grid of squares in the city's celebrated downtown historic district. Chapter 9 explores how the city's suburban expansion connects with and was influenced by the Savannah Plan.

The influence of the Savannah Plan also extends far beyond Chatham County, Georgia. Enthusiasts of urban life throughout the country and around the world have long recommended Savannah as a model for other cities to follow. Remarkably, however, none has copied it outright—no city anywhere has been laid out with a plan quite like Savannah's. Our final chapter thus explores the widespread influence of the Savannah Plan on the one hand while attempting to account for its lack of imitators on the other. Chief among recent promoters of the plan as a model for future development elsewhere are followers of the New Urbanism, but even modernists from the 1960s to the present have advocated for its lessons.

CHAPTER NINE

THE PLAN AND THE CITY

Beyond the city limits, to the south, suburban settlements are fast growing up; and, at the present ratio of expansion, the city proper will soon comprise double its present area, the adjacent grounds being both eligible and available to an unlimited extent.

—W. V. THOMPSON, 1871

The Savannah region is at a pivotal point where our growth is outpacing our competitor regions, yet we still see even more opportunity in our future.

—BERT BRANTLEY, president and chief executive officer of the Savannah Area Chamber of Commerce, 2024

The City of Savannah is much more than its celebrated planned downtown area. In terms of pure geographic size, the Savannah Plan is modest—the roughly 1-square-mile area laid out according to the Savannah Plan represents less than 1 percent of the 108.7 square miles that make up today's Savannah—and in terms of people, the plan accommodates roughly 6 percent of the city's total resident population.[1] And yet the social, economic, political, and aesthetic impact of the plan on the rest of Savannah is disproportionately great. The relationship between the historic core defined by the Savannah Plan and its surroundings has changed dramatically over the years, especially as the city has grown, but it has always been a vital and codependent one. Central cities, of course, are never autonomous; they are always mutually reliant on their surrounding hinterlands. Savannah is no different. An analysis of this interdependent relationship will strengthen an understanding of the Savannah Plan.

A basic principle quickly becomes clear as we examine the codependence of the plan and its periphery: The compositional formality and clarity of the Savannah Plan depends on the informality and relative messiness of its surroundings. Put another way, the Savannah Plan is incapable of accommodating all the activities and structures required for its own prosperity. The fine-grained structure of the plan makes it less capable than other cities to serve the needs of shipping, industry, and recreation. In more recent times, the entertainment, hospitality, education, retail, and health-care industries have become more demanding in their spatial requirements than the plan is capable of accommodating. These constantly changing industries have grown up in locations surrounding the Savannah Plan to the north, south, east, and west.

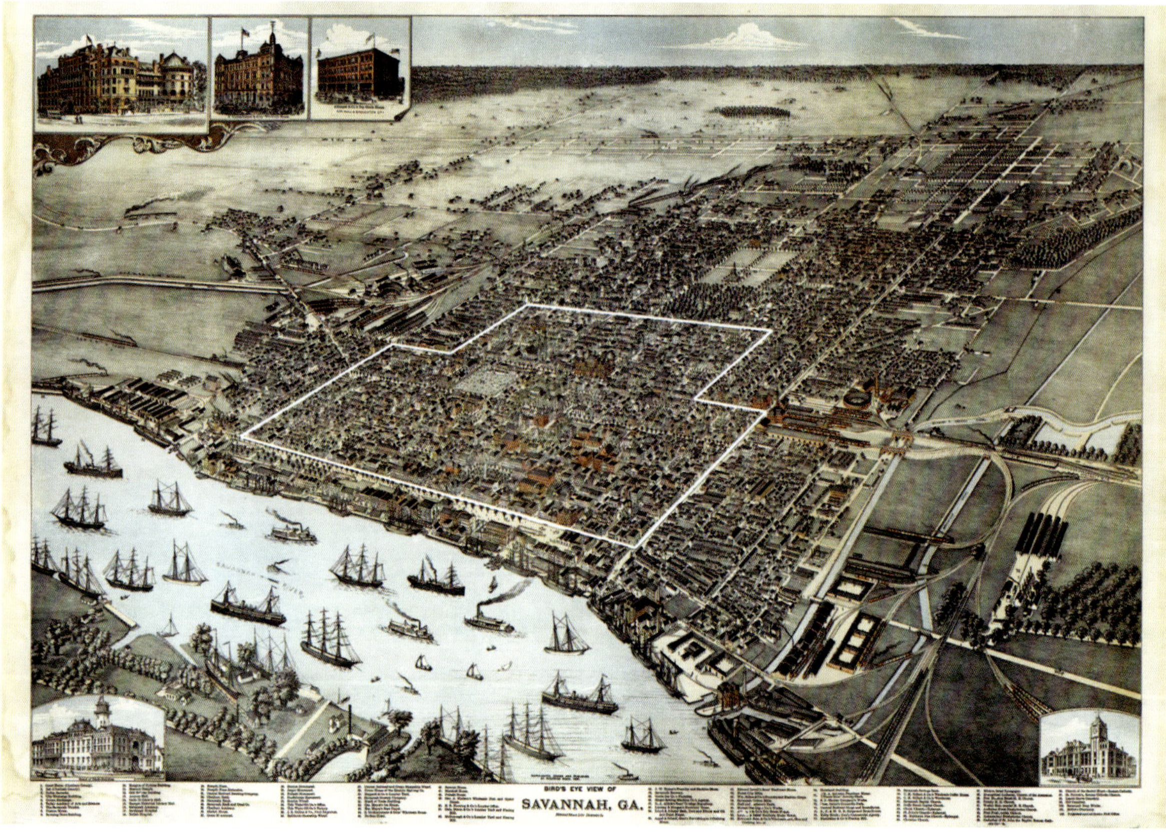

FIGURE 161. *Bird's Eye View of Savannah, Ga.*, multistone lithograph with added hand coloring, 29⅜" × 43⅞", copyrighted, drawn, and published by Augustus Koch, 1891. The white outline shows the boundaries of the Savannah Plan. Image from the Barry Lawrence Ruderman Map Collection, courtesy Stanford University Libraries. Diagram by Robin B. Williams

In their agrarian plan, Oglethorpe and the Trustees provided no clear place for industry or commerce, but they astutely recognized that town planning must be coordinated with regional planning. Like the town plan, the other colonial components have changed over time. The colonial features beyond the Common have been transformed into suburban neighborhoods, port facilities, a military airfield, commercial shopping centers, school and university campuses, recreational areas, and industrial complexes. The parts of Savannah that are beyond the Savannah Plan are in many ways quite ordinary, resembling similar features found in metropolitan areas nationwide, but the imprint and influence of the plan can be detected even in these outside zones, where urban and architectural features or patterns of downtown found expanded life. The ten-mile-wide grid established by the colonial plan, for example, extended some seven miles southward from the river and is remarkably close to the present size of the city. A map of Chatham County from 1875 vividly reveals how the city was even then growing according to the orthogonal land division laid out in the first years of the colony when compared to the 1735 county plan (figures 162 and 163). In fact, many later streets and roads fall on or near colonial alignments. Montgomery Cross Road, for example, parallels Bay

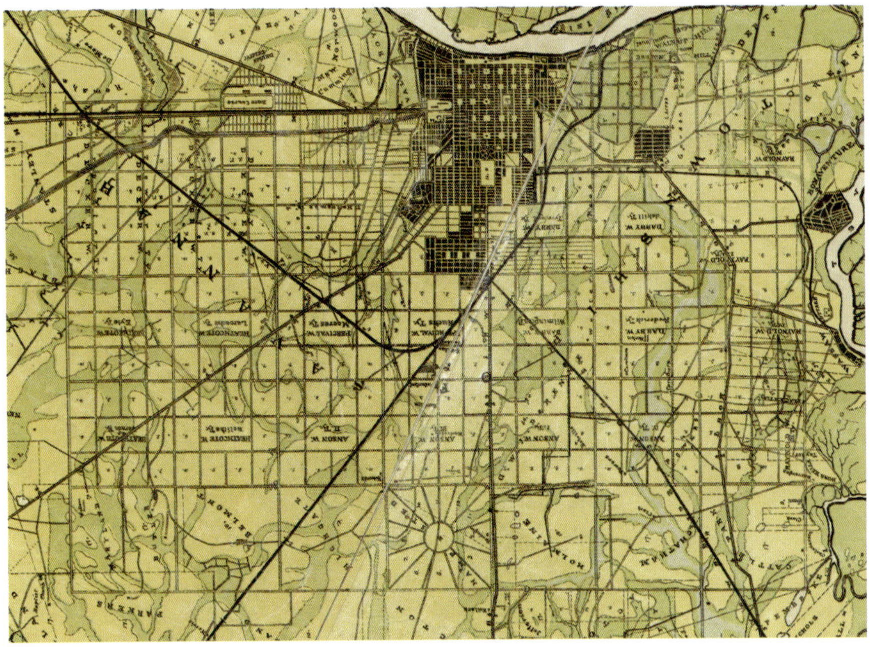

FIGURE 162. Detail of *Map of Chatham County, State of Georgia*, Charles G. Platen, 1875. Library of Congress, Geography and Map Division.

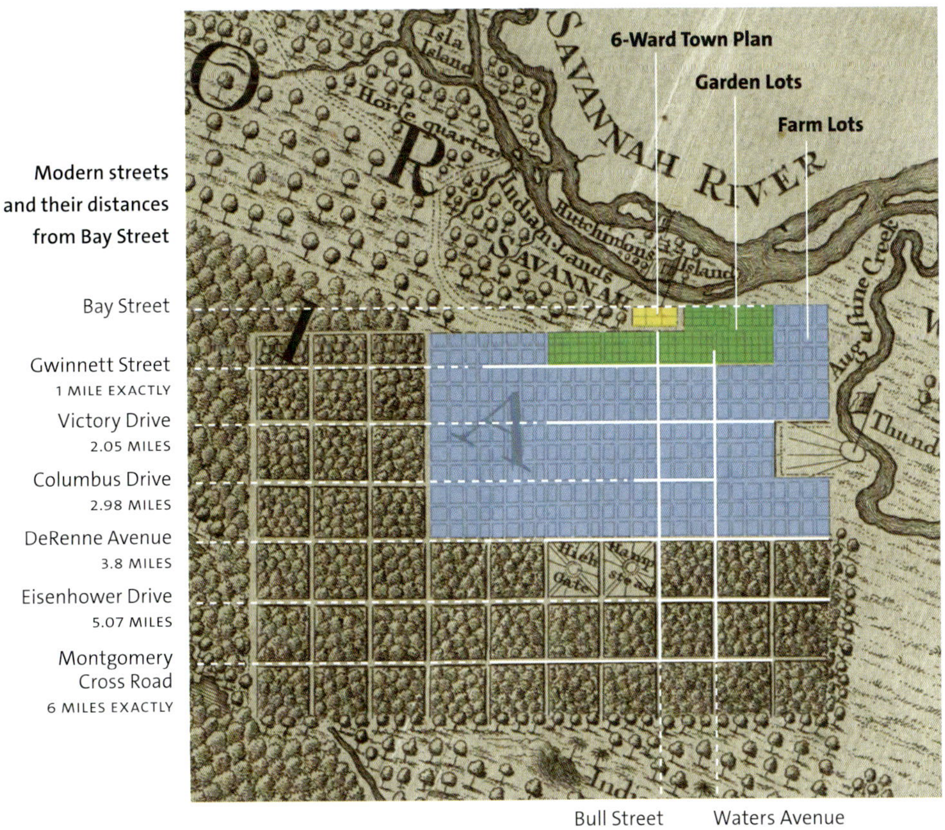

FIGURE 163. Savannah's existing streets aligned with those of the Georgia Trustees' original plan for Savannah and vicinity. Diagram by Robin B. Williams, overlaid on a detail from *A Map of the County of Savannah*, dated 1735, from Samuel Urlsperger, *Der Ausführliche Nachrichten von den Salsburgischen Emigranten* (Halle, 1747).

Street (the northern edge of the original town plan) exactly six miles to the south, just one mile shy of the seven-mile grid shown on the colonial map. Gwinnett Street, Victory Drive, Columbus Drive, DeRenne Avenue, and Eisenhower Drive are very close to being one, two, three, four, and five miles, respectively, from Bay Street. We shall return to these outer zones of the city, but first we consider the immediate edges of the twenty-four-ward plan.

The Four Edges of the Savannah Plan

Like the ideal city plans of the Renaissance, the Savannah Plan was conceived as a simple, geometric figure with clear boundaries. As the plan grew into the Common on three sides, it became more complicated, but its boundaries remained legible. Bay Street has never lost its function as a northern boundary, running parallel with the riverfront. Since their creation around 1770, the paired Broad streets, each one hundred feet wide and running perpendicular to the river, have provided the plan's east and west boundaries. South Broad Street (Oglethorpe Avenue), however, failed to hold a southern edge as the city expanded southward. Once the final wards were laid out in 1851, a new edge was established at Gaston Street. Though no longer a simple rectangle, the Savannah Plan retains clearly discernible edges. Unlike the impenetrable walls of a Renaissance city, however, those edges have always been permeable. Connective strands of the plan's tartan fabric extend across its edges, weaving it together with the surrounding city (figure 51). Each of the four sides connects in a different manner, partly due to the differing topographical conditions on each side, from steeply sloping ground to low-lying marshes. We get a vivid representation of the Savannah Plan connecting to its expanding, industrialized edges in Augustus Koch's *Bird's Eye View of Savannah, Ga.* from 1891 (figure 161).

THE RIVERFRONT

Until the early twentieth century, Savannah's riverfront served unambiguously as the city's front door, a threshold connecting the town to the world beyond. Its dramatic topography, wharf lots, warehouses, stone ramps, and retaining walls at first glance contrast dramatically with the polite and orderly architectural fabric of the town plan, even as the warehouse block lengths were defined by it. And yet the formal character of the Strand, the verdant buffer between the waterfront and the planned city, influenced the design of the warehouses. The embellished upper levels of the south-facing facades of the factors' warehouses, punctuated by the monumental City Hall (and the old Exchange that preceded it) and the Cotton Exchange that close northward vistas on Bull and Drayton Streets, acknowledge and engage the architecture of the Savannah Plan while standing apart from it (figure 164).

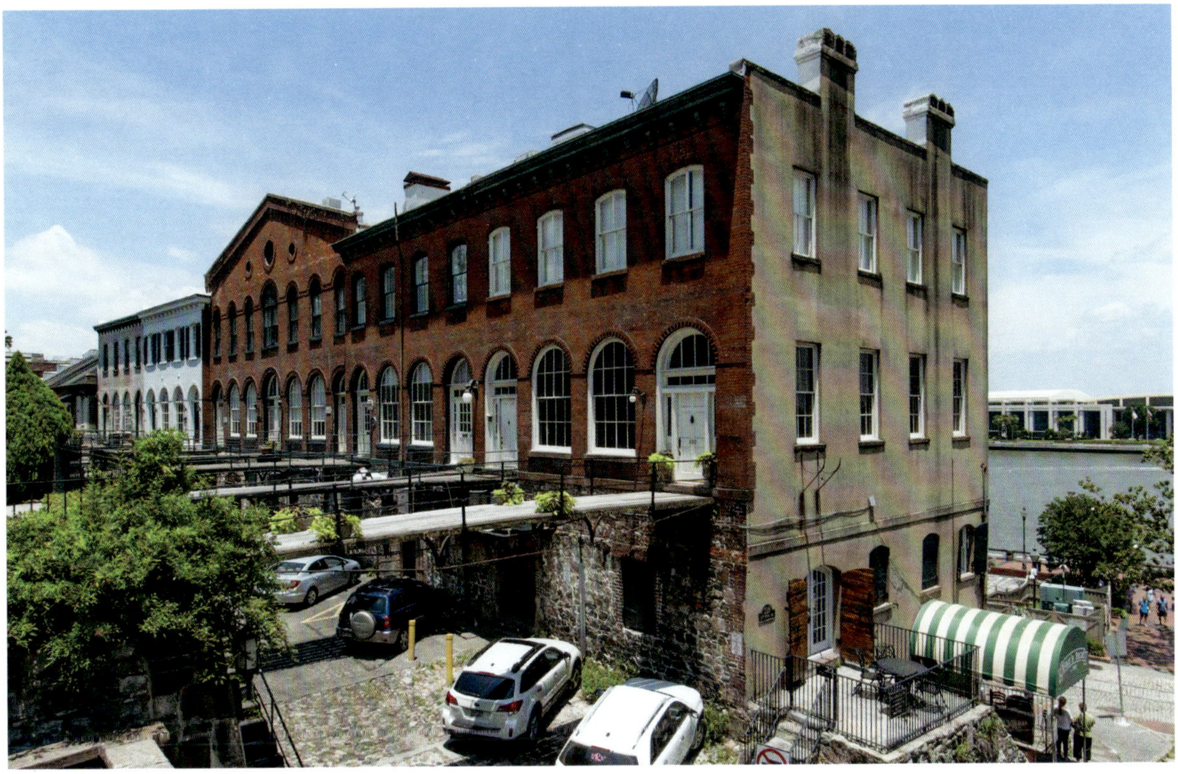

FIGURE 164. Stoddard's Lower Range Warehouses, just west of the Lincoln Street Ramp; built by John Stoddard, 1858–59. Photo by Robin B. Williams, 2014.

In 1975–77, the riverfront and its warehouses were transformed from a gritty industrial zone into a tourist-friendly retail and entertainment district, connecting them spatially and socially to the planned city atop the bluff as they had not been before. The area had become largely derelict as Savannah's port facilities moved upriver between the 1930s and 1950s. Under the leadership of Mayor John P. Rousakis (after whom the project would be named), local architects Robert Gunn and Eric Meyerhoff designed and supervised the construction of a thirty-acre waterfront plaza spanning about a half mile across the front of town, replacing the former private wharves north of River Street with landscaped terraces and discreet parking lots. They also restored the historic cobblestone ramps and Belgian block pavement on River Street. Private entrepreneurs repurposed many of the factors' warehouses as restaurants, shops, and small hotels, while retaining the buildings' gritty industrial patina. Inspired by a national trend to adaptively reuse industrial waterfronts that began in the early 1970s in places like San Francisco, Boston, and New York, Savannah's waterfront was transformed from a place of industry into a tourist destination. To tie the waterfront plaza to the planned city above, Gunn and Meyerhoff inserted a notable design feature at the base of each ramp aligned with the north–south street right-of-way—a trio of magnolia trees aligning with Lincoln Street; an anchor fountain with Abercorn; a diminutive tugboat in a sandbox with Drayton; and a ship fountain with Barnard.[2] The two missing alignments, with Bull Street and Whitaker Street, were completed later with the installation of the African American Monument in 2002 and the World War II Memorial in 2010, the latter designed by Meyerhoff.

A pair of prominent, privately developed hotel projects further integrated the waterfront into the planned downtown. Even before the waterfront renewal project was begun, developer Merritt Dixon III had purchased a large warehouse complex to the west of City Hall with plans to demolish it and replace it with a fifteen-story waterfront hotel. Faced with protracted opposition from the growing preservation community, Dixon reached a compromise with the Historic Savannah Foundation that the Hyatt Regency Hotel would rise no higher than the top floor of City Hall below the dome.[3] While the full impact of its enormous mass is partially hidden on Bay Street due to the bluff, the scale of the hotel nonetheless overwhelms the waterfront. Because it replaced the only block of warehouses that spanned River Street, the hotel was allowed to do the same. Despite its insensitive scale and massing, the hotel successfully spans the bluff, with entrances fronting both Bay Street and River Street four stories below. At the west end of the waterfront, the recently opened Plant Riverside, a 4.5-acre mixed-use hotel and entertainment complex, adaptively repurposed an early twentieth-century power plant. Northern extensions of Martin Luther King Jr. Boulevard (formerly West Broad Street) and Montgomery Street—the former as a quasi-public plaza and the latter as a monumental staircase leading down to River Street—effectively tie the popular destination to the planned city above.

WESTERN EDGE: YAMACRAW LANDS AND OGLETHORPE WARD

Industrial zones and marginalized residential neighborhoods developed beyond the western boundary of the plan by the end of the eighteenth century. Although not laid out in accordance with the planning paradigm of the Savannah Plan, this flanking area has long played an integral role in accommodating functions too big to fit within the small block sizes of the plan as well as low-income residents too numerous to be accommodated along its lanes. By 1787, lands west of the Common that were originally reserved for the Yamacraw Indian tribe were reorganized as Oglethorpe Ward, which was annexed by the city in 1838 and divided into three sections (North, Middle, and South) in 1856. The city's economy became increasingly dependent on industry and trade in the nineteenth century, but their needs could not be fully served by the urban and architectural forms of the Savannah Plan. The Central of Georgia Railway (established in 1833) was no exception, building an innovative multipurpose complex between 1851 and 1855

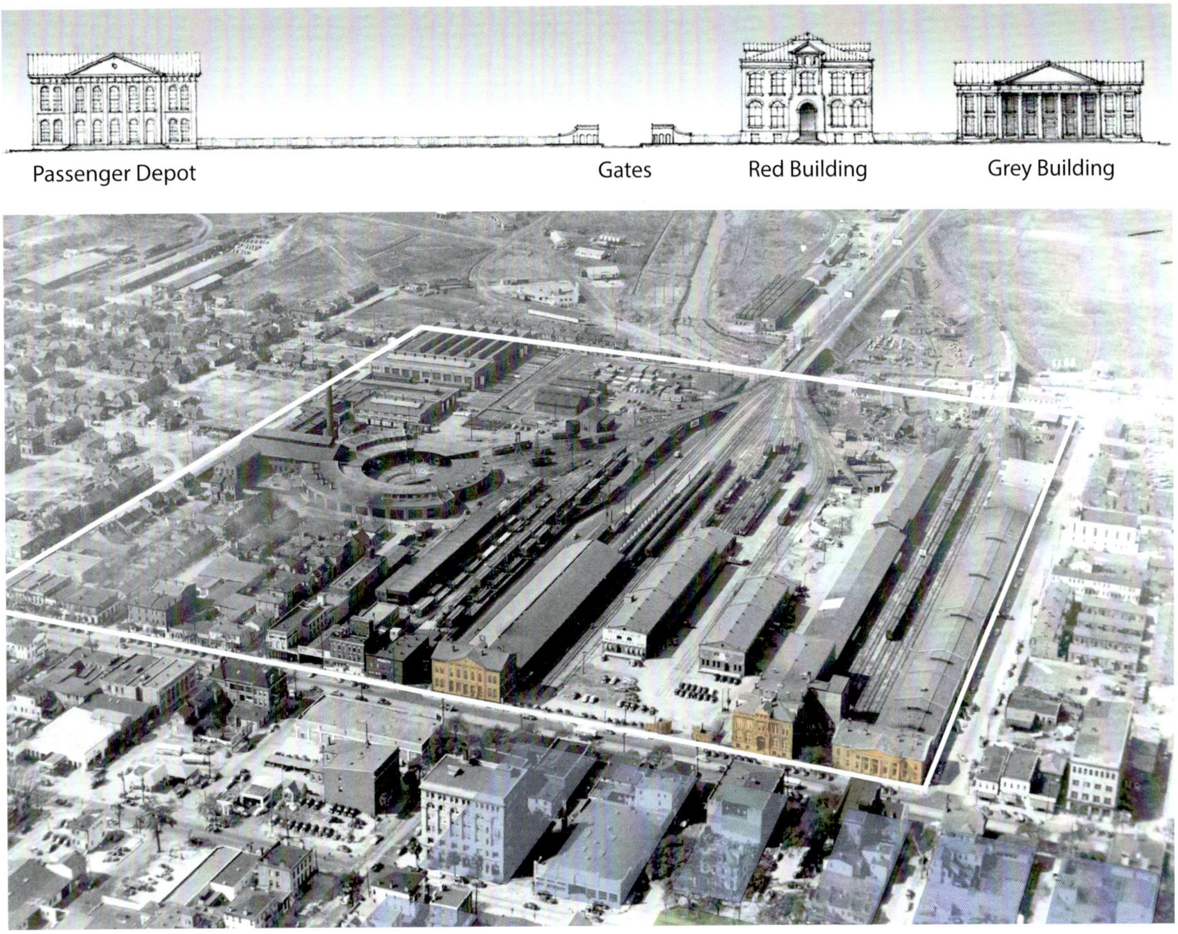

that integrated passenger, freight, and repair services with design and corporate offices (figure 165). At thirty-three acres, more than three times the size of a typical Savannah Plan ward, the complex dominated the land south of Oglethorpe Ward, its footprint representing a scale and design significantly distinct from the orderly tartan of streets and squares in the adjacent Savannah Plan. To tie the complex to the adjacent planned downtown, the Central of Georgia located its most public buildings—the passenger depot (designed by Augustus Schwaab, 1860–76), the Red Building (business and engineering, designed by Fay and Eichberg, 1887), and the Gray Building (company headquarters, 1851–56)—in the northern half of the complex along the section of West Broad Street that faced Elbert Ward, the southernmost part of the plan along its west side. Accordingly, this stretch of the railroad complex was dressed up in a variety of high styles, including castellated gates leading to a freight yard.

FIGURE 165. Central of Georgia Railway complex. Blue shading indicates tything and trust lot blocks of the Savannah Plan. Photo courtesy of the Central of Georgia Railway Historical Society; drawing by Hamilton Brindley; diagram by Robin B. Williams.

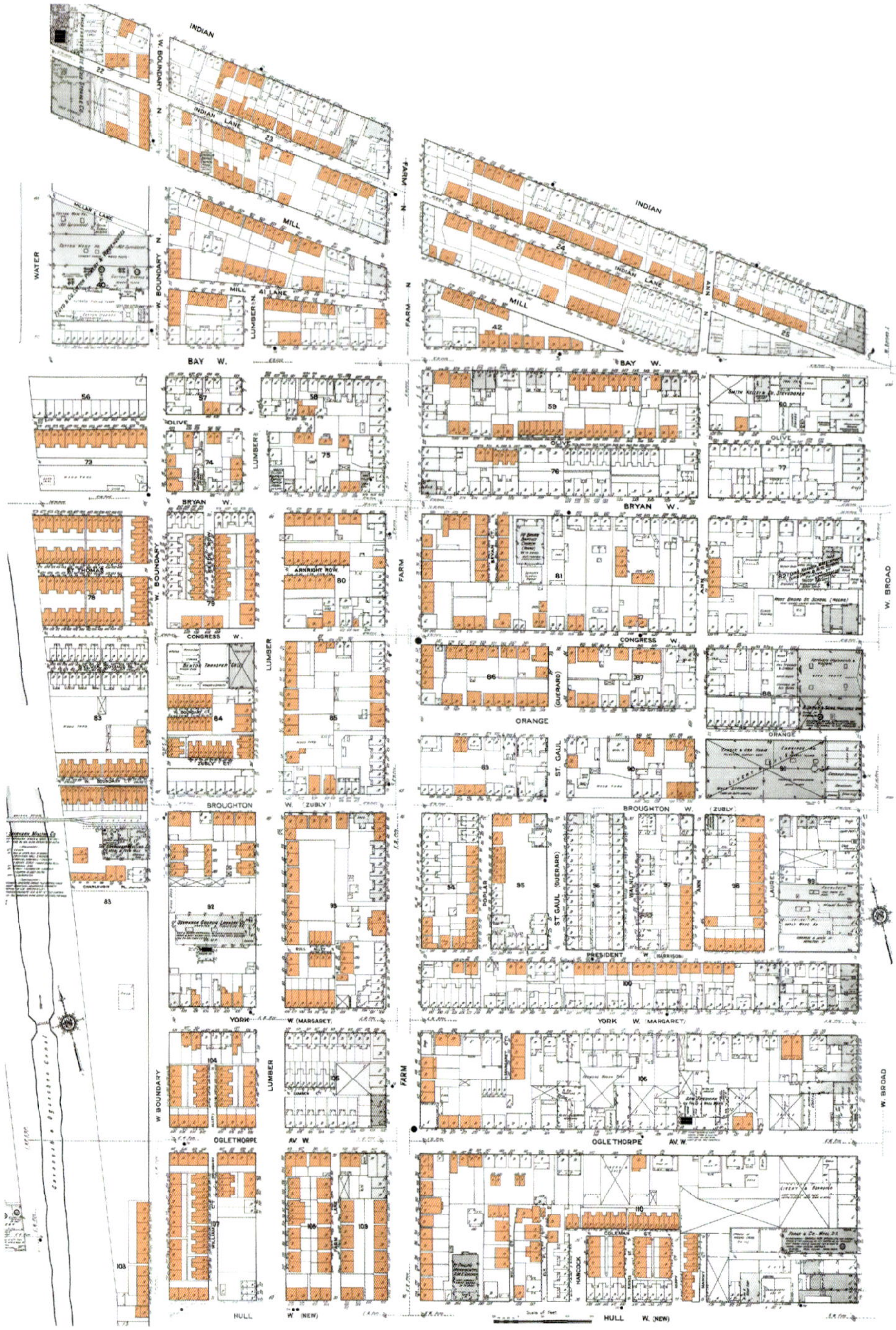

FIGURE 166. Savannah cottages (now lost) in the Yamacraw district bounded by Indian Street, West Broad Street (MLK Jr. Boulevard), Hull Street (Turner Boulevard), and the Springfield Canal, as documented on the *Sanborn Fire Insurance Map from Savannah, Chatham County, Georgia*. Sanborn Map Company, 1916, vol. 1, sheets 1, 2, 9, 10, 11, and 12. Diagram by Robin B. Williams.

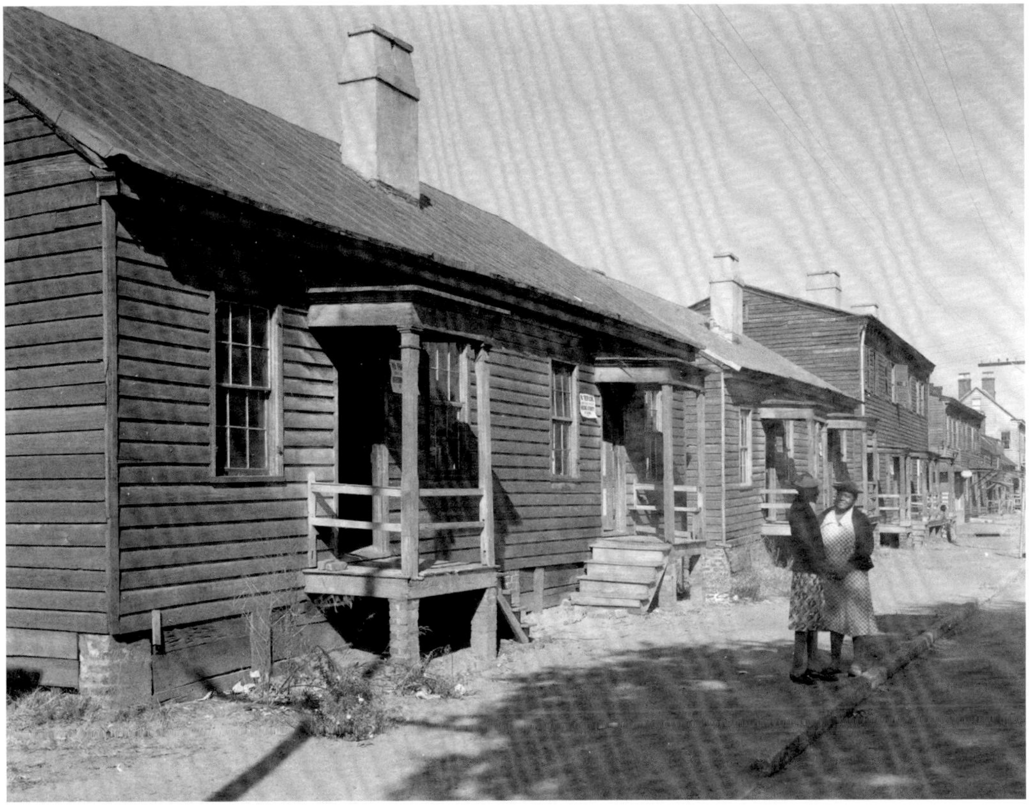

FIGURE 167. Savannah cottage double houses on Fahm Street shortly before their demolition, ca. 1935. Photo by Frances Benjamin Johnston, Carnegie Survey of the Architecture of the South, Library of Congress, Prints and Photographs Division.

Beginning in the late eighteenth century, the ad hoc development of the former Yamacraw lands absorbed waves of Russian, Norwegian, German, and Irish immigrants as well as free African Americans. Over the course of the nineteenth century, the Oglethorpe Ward area gained a reputation for squalor as the railway complex to the south and port facilities to the north grew around it. Although few of the ward's streets aligned with those of the plan, the area saw a proliferation of housing forms from within the plan. By 1916, more than 1,750 small, predominantly single-story freestanding and attached wooden houses and stores filled the informal urban grid of this area, along with several industrial and commercial buildings fronting West Broad. Most of these were one-story Savannah cottages, side-gabled, with a projecting covered entry stoop with stairs descending parallel to the facade, and organized in reflecting doubles or row configurations—all typical Savannah traits (figures 166 and 167). Occupied predominantly by African Americans, these houses were demolished in the mid-1930s in the name of slum clearance and replaced by a twenty-five-acre, segregated government housing project called Yamacraw Village, which is currently slated for demolition.

Two major east–west streets from the Savannah Plan were extended west of West Broad Street to form important transportation gateways to Savannah for automobiles—first Bay Street and then Oglethorpe Avenue. Extended by 1901, when it appears on a map of Chatham County, Bay Street carried both U.S. 17 and U.S. 80 into downtown Savannah beginning in the 1920s. With the construction of the first Talmadge Bridge over the Savannah River in 1953, U.S. 17 was rerouted along a widened and extended Oglethorpe Avenue. The construction in 1965 of a Greyhound bus station on Oglethorpe, one block west of West Broad, and its expansion in 2013 as the Joe Murray Rivers Jr. Intermodal Transit Center to accommodate multiple city bus transit and Greyhound Bus routes have enhanced this area's gateway status. To ease traffic flow between the misaligned sections of Oglethorpe as it crossed West Broad Street, a curving realignment was introduced west of Montgomery Street in 1983 (along with a similar realignment of Liberty Street), distorting the orthogonal fabric of the Savannah Plan at this point of entry (figure 46).

EASTERN EDGE: THE TRUSTEES' GARDEN AND THE BEACH INSTITUTE

A similar combination of industrial zones and marginalized residential neighborhoods developed along the eastern border of the Savannah Plan, including the former Trustees' Garden. Here a similar pattern and density of worker cottages developed to house the growing number of people working in nearby industrial buildings, including a gas works complex on the former Garden and, south of Liberty Street, a railroad complex developed by the Savannah, Florida and Western Railway.[4]

In an area just outside the plan known as the Beach Institute (bounded by Price, Liberty, East Broad, and Gaston), almost all east–west streets from the Savannah Plan south of Liberty were extended with their same widths to terminate at East Broad. This "extension" of the plan underscored the diminished status of central trust streets in the fourth and fifth rows of wards: Macon Street was reduced from a width of sixty feet to just twenty feet, and Wayne Street was eliminated altogether. At the south end of the Beach Institute area, Gordon Lane was reduced to eighteen feet wide, and Gaston Street was shifted northward and reduced to forty feet wide. Throughout this area, fronting both streets and lanes, pairs and rows of Savannah cottages, at least eighty-seven of which survive, further testify to the prevalence of this house form beyond its models within the plan (figure 168). The two rows on Macon Street all have their staircases descending in the same direction, creating a compact "sawtooth" effect emulating Savannah elevated rowhouses, while the three rows on Charlton Street comprise joined pairs of double cottages, resulting in a syncopated rhythm, just like that of their larger rowhouse counterparts. A row of seven houses of varying widths at 524–536 East

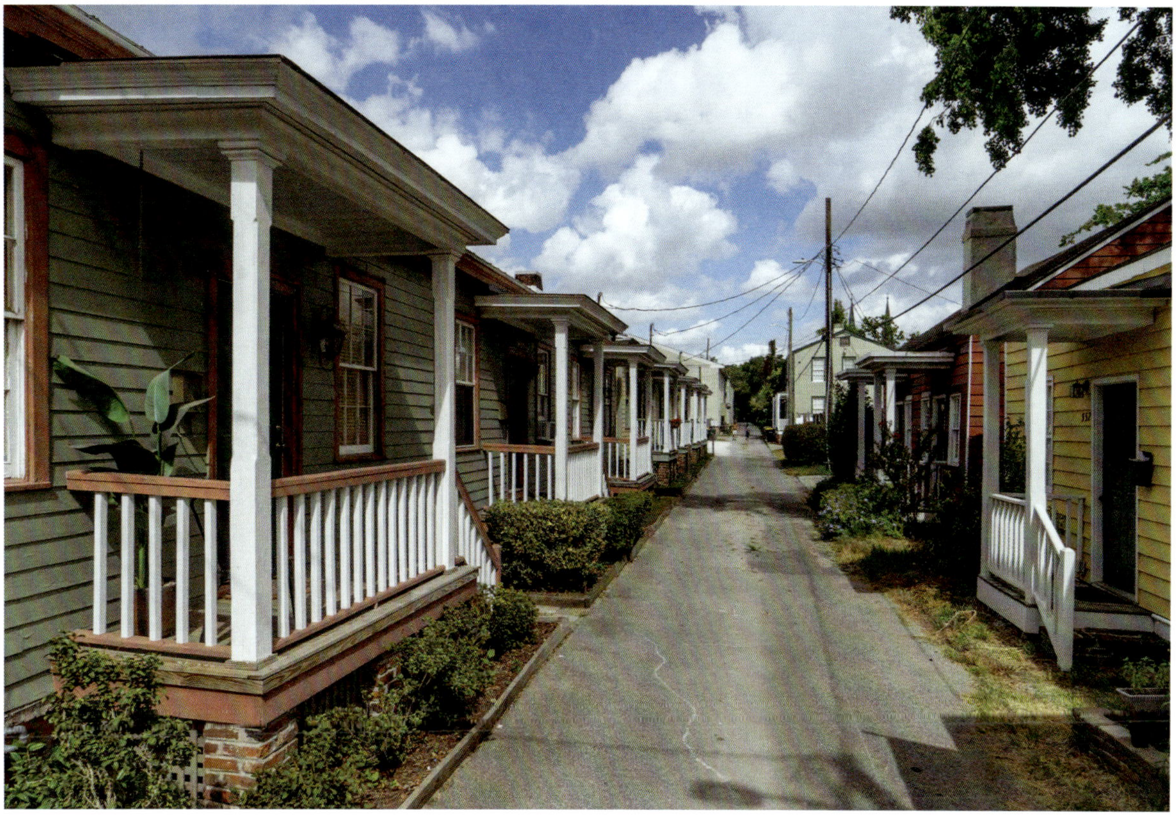

Gordon Lane includes a house (530) no wider than ten feet. The rehabilitation of the compact Beach Institute, with its largely intact urban fabric of scores of Savannah cottages and numerous two-story rowhouses, all of wood construction, illustrates how similar buildings in the Yamacraw district might have been rehabilitated had different social values and more vision existed in the 1930s.

FIGURE 168. Rows of Savannah cottages in the Beach Institute district on East Macon Street near East Broad, just south of Liberty Street. At twenty feet wide, East Macon is among the narrowest streets in Savannah. Photo by Robin B. Williams, 2024.

THE SOUTHERN EDGE

For the first century of Savannah's existence, the city's southern edge was determined by the South Common, a contingent space that accommodated activities and structures that were, for various reasons, deemed incompatible with daily life in the town. These included burial grounds, fortifications, large public gatherings and events, and public and private structures such as a city jail and workhouse, a hospital and poorhouse, a tobacco inspection station, a tree nursery, a female orphan asylum, a ropewalk, and a cotton packing facility.[5] Forsyth Park stands to this day as a remnant of the Common, tying the town plan to the suburban neighborhoods that developed in the second half of the nineteenth century. The park extends the monumental Bull Street axis beyond the Savannah Plan with its broad tree-lined promenade, punctuated by its spectacular fountain. This is the most dramatic visual connection between the Savannah Plan and the city that grew southward from its edge.

The Plan's Hinterland in the Suburbs

When the Savannah Plan reached its completion in the early 1850s, Savannah's southern city limit stood at Anderson Lane, immediately south of Anderson Street, the third civic street south of Forsyth Park (after Duffy and Henry). The ensuing suburban expansion of the city during the second half of the nineteenth century strengthened the connection of the suburbs to the Savannah Plan both symbolically and aesthetically. As suburban developments spread not just southward but increasingly to the southeast of East Broad Street, the city's address system required reform, since East Broad had served as "point zero," from which address numbers grew only westward. To allow for efficient address numbering into the future, in 1896 Bull Street became the new zero line from which addresses would be numbered east or west—yet another affirmation of Bull Street's primacy among north–south streets. The surveying of developments south of Anderson Lane just beyond the city limit included east–west streets initially named First Street, Second Street, and so on, up to Twelfth Street. In 1901, evidently occurring when the city limit was extended to Estill Avenue (now Victory Drive), these streets were renamed 31st, 32nd, and so on, subtly calibrating them to Bay Street—that is, 31st Street is the thirty-first street south of the river, with Bay Street (the plan's baseline) being the first street.

With the city's southward expansion, the housing forms that emerged within the Savannah Plan area found architectural reverberations beyond the plan into the early twentieth century. Savannah cottages, for example, continued to be a popular housing form for accommodating the city's poor. Following the Civil War, local judge and philanthropist Peter Meldrim erected eight long rows of Savannah cottages fronting two blocks of 33rd and 34th Streets from Montgomery Street to Burroughs Street, a block west of West Broad Street, to house newly emancipated African Americans (figure 169). Known as "Meldrim Row cottages," their twenty-four-foot width and central door flanked by windows can be traced back to the scale and form of cottages erected under Oglethorpe. Despite being in serviceable condition, the four rows east of West Broad Street (Martin Luther King Jr. Boulevard) were demolished by the city in 2015 for the construction of a new police station.

Numerous pairs and rows of Savannah cottages continued to be erected beyond Estill Avenue (Victory Drive), over a mile and a half south of Gaston Street.

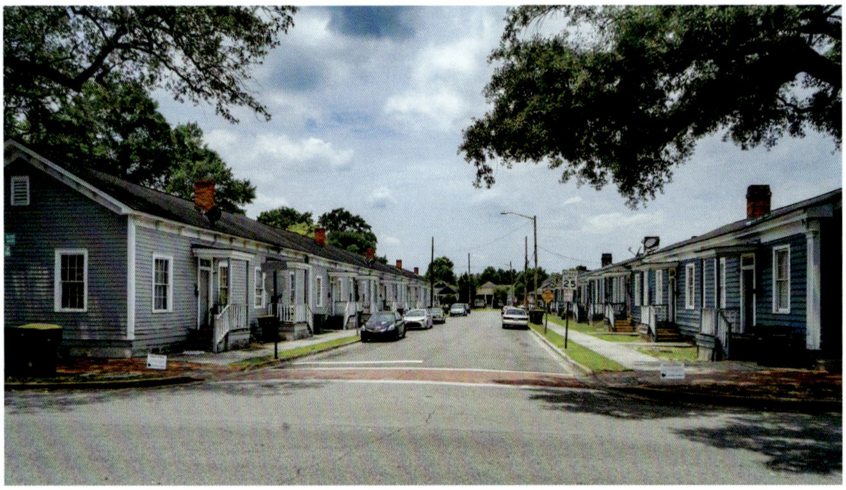

FIGURE 169. "Meldrim Row cottages": rows of Savannah cottages on West 33rd Street between Martin Luther King Jr. Boulevard and Burroughs Street, erected ca. 1865. Photo by Robin B. Williams, 2024.

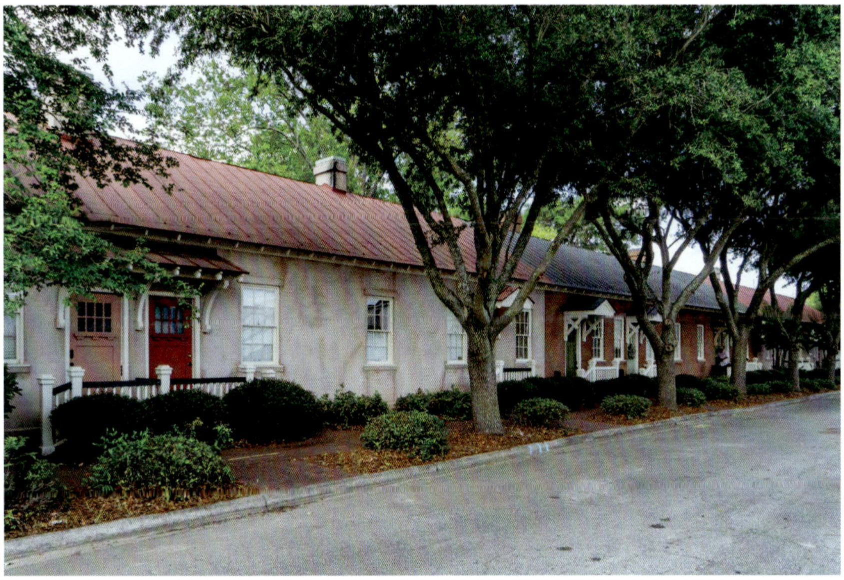

FIGURE 170. "Pearl Row": 101–121 Pearl Street, erected 1892. Row of eleven Savannah cottages arranged in both single and paired configurations. Photo by Robin B. Williams, 2024.

Surviving rows on Pearl Street (also now identified as West 46th Street), including "Pearl Row," a handsomely rehabilitated row of eleven houses erected in 1892, attest to the durability and flexibility of this housing type (figure 170).[6]

Although less prevalent, examples of Savannah elevated double houses and rowhouses from the later nineteenth century survive in the affluent Victorian suburb west of Forsyth Park. A row of six Italianate townhouses at 210–220 West Bolton Street is fully elevated in the manner of those erected within the Savannah Plan, with their parallel staircases encroaching on the public sidewalk. Two blocks

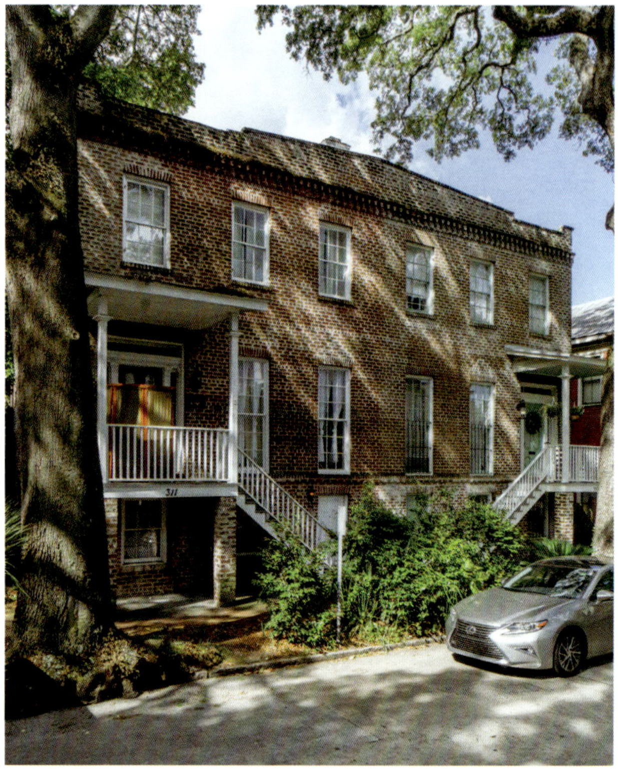

FIGURE 171. Elevated Savannah double house, 311–317 West Park Avenue, ca. 1870. Photo by Robin B. Williams, 2024.

farther south, at 311–317 West Park Avenue, stands a Greek Revival elevated Savannah double house—an outlier in terms of both its location and its late expression of that style (figure 171). Both sets of buildings predate 1888, when they appear on the earliest Sanborn map documenting this area. More innovative Victorian variations on double houses, such as the two pairs at 209–211 and 217–219 West Waldburg Street, involved full-width two-story porches across their facades. Several substantial and more stylistically expressive Second Empire, Queen Anne, and Italianate double houses populate the historically more affluent Victorian suburb east of Forsyth Park.

More enduring were the urban components and scale of the Savannah Plan, which exerted a continued influence on suburban developments beyond its boundaries until the mid-twentieth century. Its orthogonal grid continued to structure neighborhood street plans as the city grew southward and southeastward. The template of paired blocks measuring roughly one hundred by three hundred feet and divided by a lane was used in almost every neighborhood development until about 1900; thereafter the typical block doubled in length but retained the lane and similar lot depths until the Second World War. In fact, lanes proved to be the most persistent component of the Savannah Plan, being utilized at a recognizable scale and purpose throughout much of Savannah until the 1940s as far south as 66th Street, though they were left unpaved south of downtown and were mostly reduced to a width of sixteen feet.

Suburban developments included attempts at making squares, suggesting that private developers and city planners continued to be inspired by the Savannah Plan. As early as 1868, for example, a local banker, David R. Dillon, aimed to develop a one-hundred-acre tract in the farm lots west of White Bluff Road (Bull Street) between Anderson Street and what is now 42nd Street, naming it Dillontown and proposing three residential squares, which, like those downtown, were centered on the major north–south streets (figure 172).[7] Dillon's proposal included

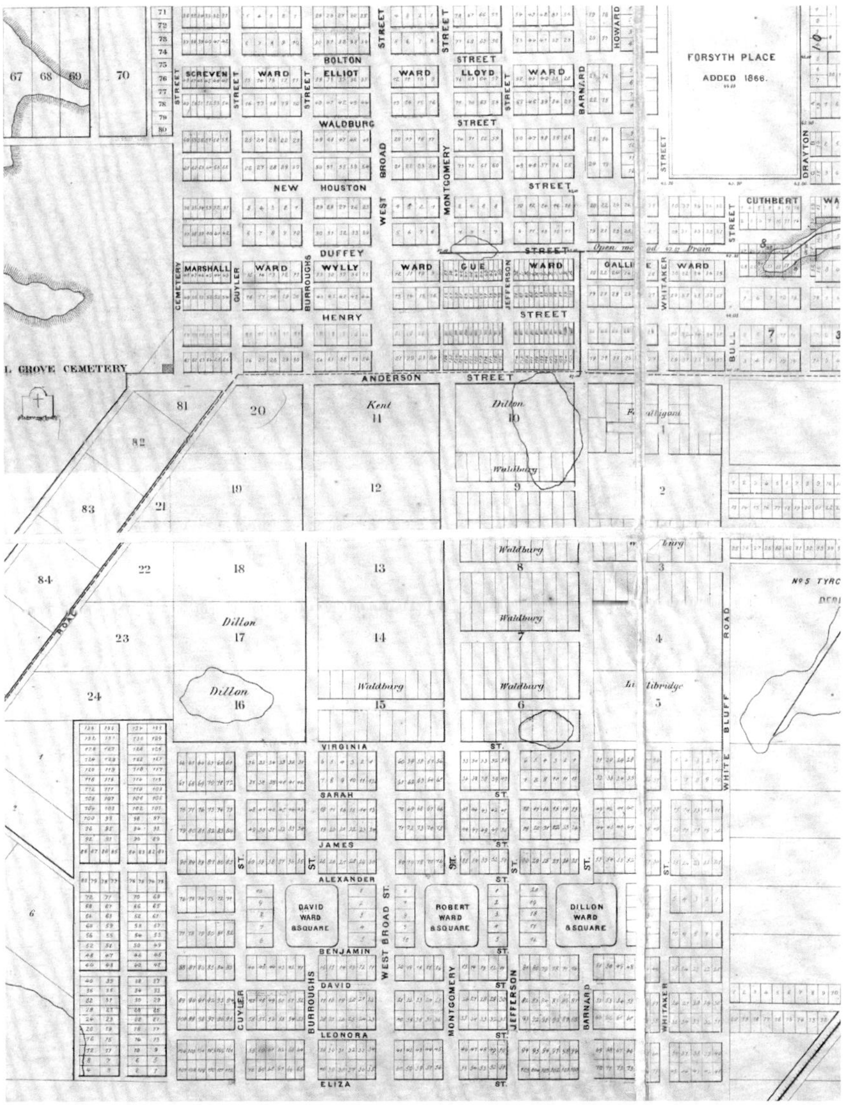

FIGURE 172. Unrealized plan for Dillontown, from a detail of *Map of the City of Savannah & Vicinity, Showing Hydrographic Elevation & Lines of Drainage* by John B. Hogg (New York, 1868). Courtesy of Hargrett Rare Book and Manuscript Library, University of Georgia Libraries, Rare Map Collection.

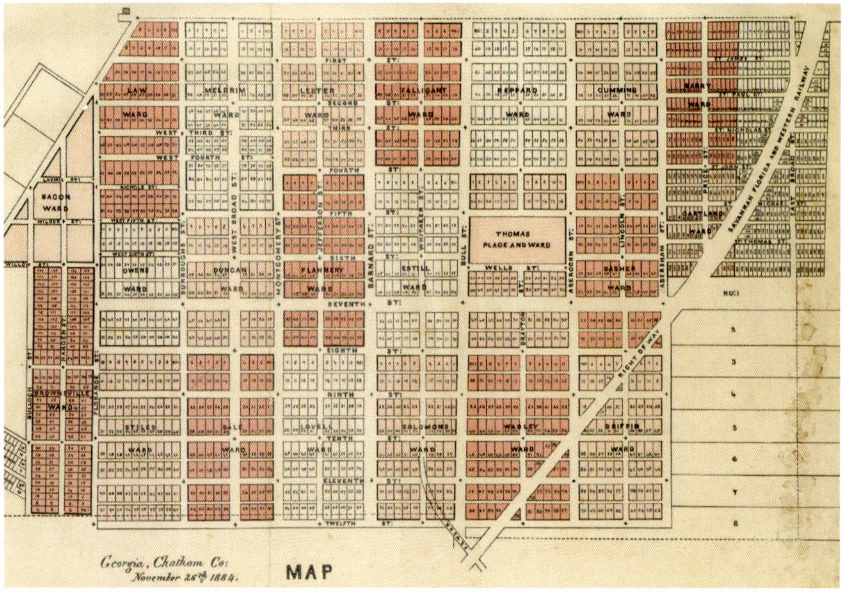

FIGURE 173. Detail of *Map of the Southern Extension of the City of Savannah* by John B. Howard, 1884, showing the original plan for "Thomas Place." The square was cut to half this size in 1886. Courtesy of Hargrett Rare Book and Manuscript Library, University of Georgia Libraries, Rare Map Collection.

orienting the lots to the east and west of the squares. Nothing appears to have come of the proposal, however. As streetcar lines enabled suburban development as far south as Estill Avenue (Victory Drive), a separate "Southern Extension" of the city for that area but extending farther east, authored by municipal engineer John B. Howard in 1884, eliminated the three squares proposed by Dillon.[8] Howard's survey plan instead included "Thomas Place," a square extending from Bull Street to Abercorn Street at 35th Street (figure 173). Initially proposed to span two city blocks and interrupt Drayton Street, Thomas Square was reduced by half to extend from Bull to Drayton. By 1898, "Wells Square," located slightly west of where the middle of the three squares proposed by Dillon would have been situated, appears on the 1898 Sanborn map, set between Montgomery, West Broad, Ninth (39th), and Tenth (40th) Streets, with picturesque curving paths radiating from a central circle to the outer corners. As with Thomas Square, this adjustment signaled the manner in which future squares, all to be called "parks," would most often be incorporated into the city grid—abutting rather than interrupting principal streets (figure 174).

The shift in nomenclature to "parks" reflects the perception of these spaces not as urban squares but as pockets of green space. At the prodding of the Park and Tree Commission, the city established similar parks in newly developing neighborhoods in the first decade of the twentieth century, including Myers Park (1901), Cann Park (1901), Dasher Park (1905, since replaced by the Thomas F. Williams

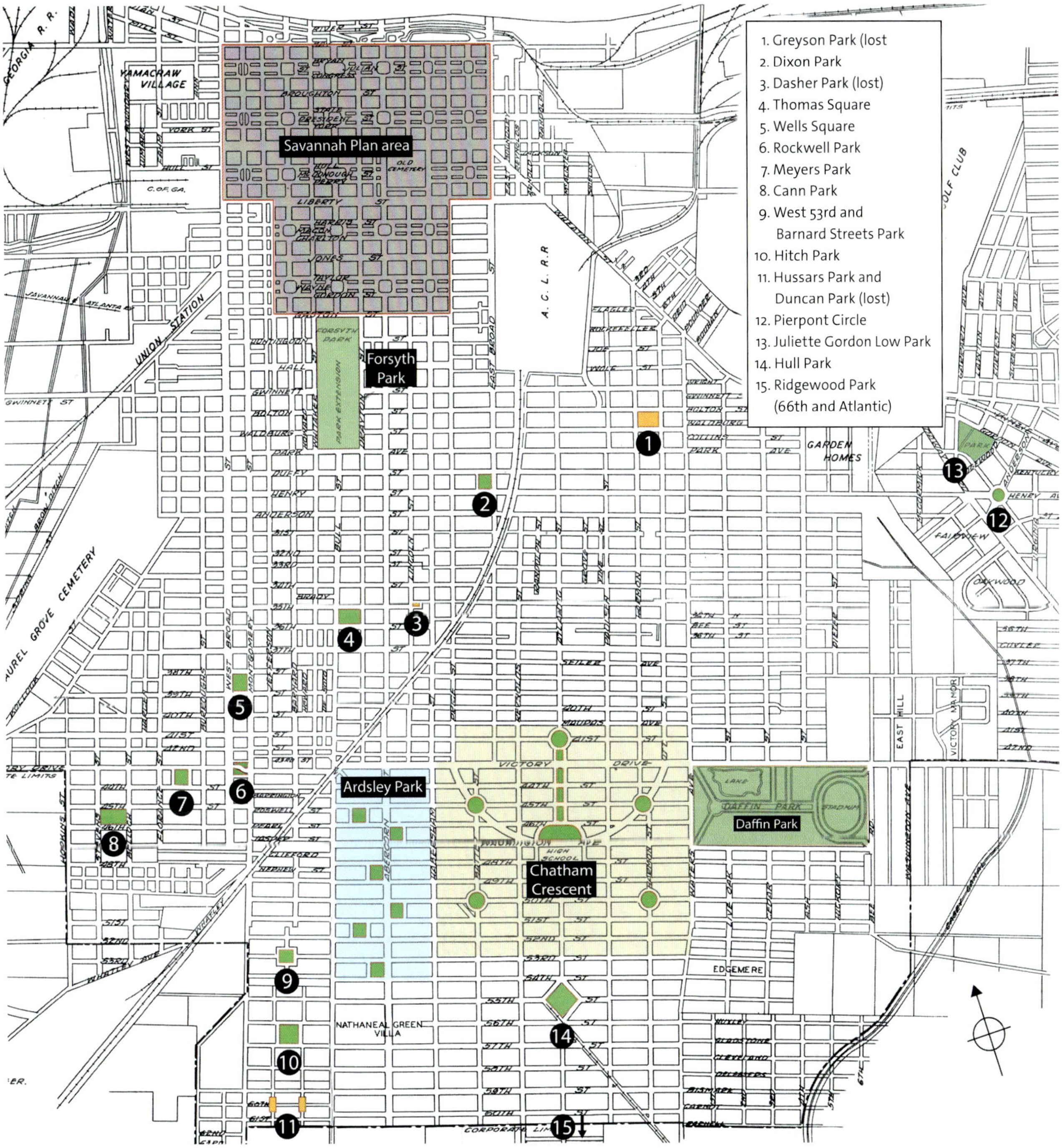

FIGURE 174. Map showing location of suburban square-like parks. Diagram by Robin B. Williams, overlaid on a detail from *Map of Savannah*, 1945. Courtesy of the City of Savannah Municipal Archives, Engineering Department, General Maps, Record Series 3121-007, Item #XA-036.

Court Apartments), Dixon Park (1906), and Grayson Park (1906, now the W. W. Law Community Center).[9] Nearly three miles south of the river, axially aligned along Barnard Street, four more parks appear on two city maps of 1910. In a neighborhood whimsically called "Bingville" is a square with the prosaic name of West 53rd and Barnard Streets Park. Further south and likewise bisected by Barnard Street, in the equally playfully named "Dithersville" neighborhood, is Hitch Park. Yet further south at 59th Street is the Hussars Tract, which was platted with twin oblong squares: Hussars Park, aligned with Barnard Street, and Duncan Park, aligned with Jefferson Street (figure 175). The latter two parks and the surrounding street patterns appear to be highly compressed versions of Oglethorpe-style wards. Although these squares were evidently carried out as planned, West 60th, Barnard, and Jefferson Streets would eventually bisect them, shifting diminutive patches of green to the corners as their only legacy. The farthest south and presumably the last neighborhood park following the scale of downtown squares is Ridgewood Park at 66th Street and Atlantic Avenue (figure 176).[10] Ironically, this park,

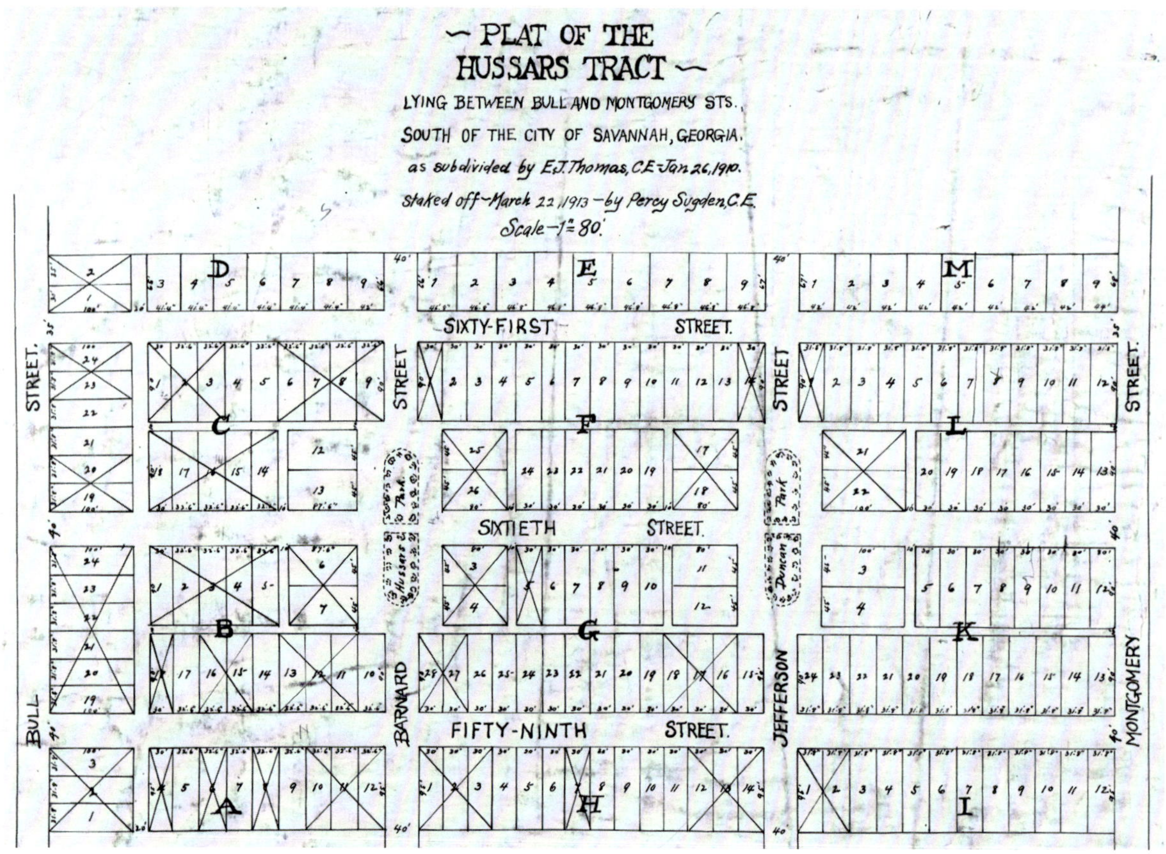

FIGURE 175. *Plat of the Hussars Tract, Lying Between Bull and Montgomery Streets, South of the City of Savannah, Georgia, as Subdivided by E. J. Thomas, C.E.—Jan. 26, 1910. Staked Off—March 22, 1913 by Sugden, Percy C.E.* Courtesy of the City of Savannah Municipal Archives.

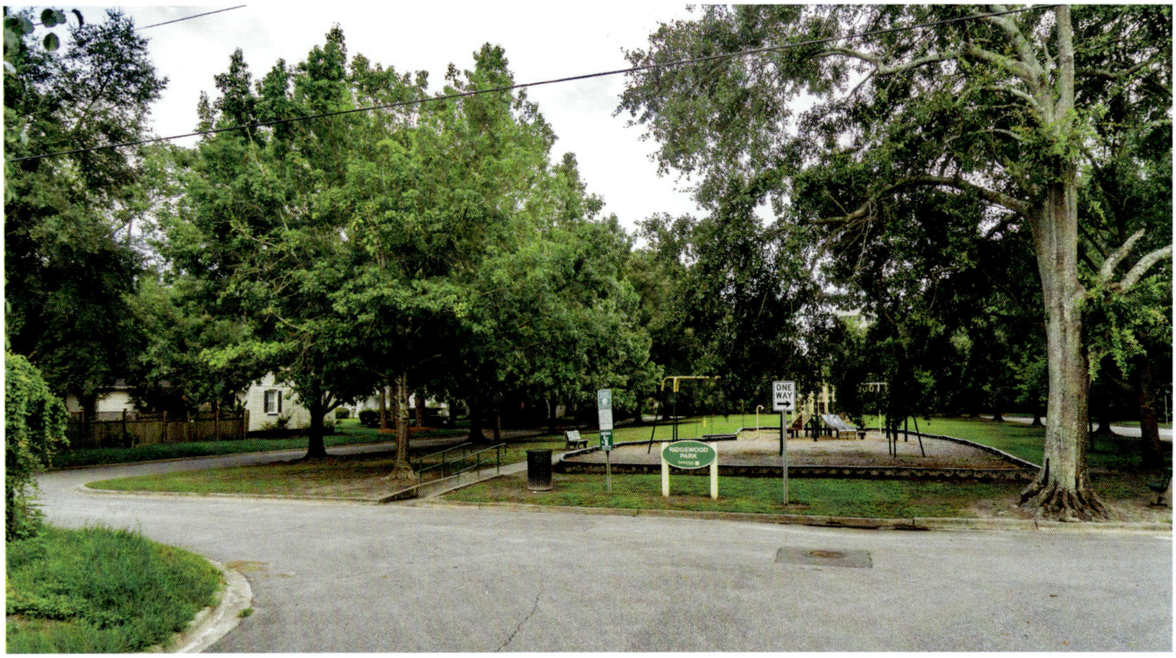

FIGURE 176. Ridgewood Park at 66th Street and Atlantic Avenue. Photo by Robin B. Williams, 2024.

more than any of the preceding suburban parks, most closely follows the Savannah Plan, with 66th and Atlantic both aligning on axis with the park, while 65th Street Lane and 66th Street Lane skirt its north and south sides in the manner of inner civic east–west streets.

The most ambitious expansion of green space by the city's Park and Tree Commission was the 1907 creation of Daffin Park just outside the city limit on the south side of Dale Avenue, the extension of Estill Avenue east of Waters Avenue. The year before, George Baldwin, a member of the commission and a progressive reformer, had invited landscape architect John Nolen, newly graduated from Harvard, to visit Savannah to consult about parks. Daffin Park was among the first major works in Nolen's illustrious career (figure 177).[11] Nolen's first visit to Savannah left a strong impression on him; he wrote to Baldwin of "the peculiar wealth of your city in centrally situated small parks and open spaces, in broad and interesting streets and in happily located public or semi-public buildings. In these matters Savannah—considering its population—stands unquestionably at the head of American cities." But Nolen also pointed out that the city had "certain limitations" and that public squares were "being omitted in newer areas."[12] Reflecting the Progressive Era's love of recreation, Daffin Athletic Park (as it was first called) would be "a general playground for the people of Savannah." Almost triple the size of Forsyth Park (eighty versus thirty acres), Daffin Park showcased

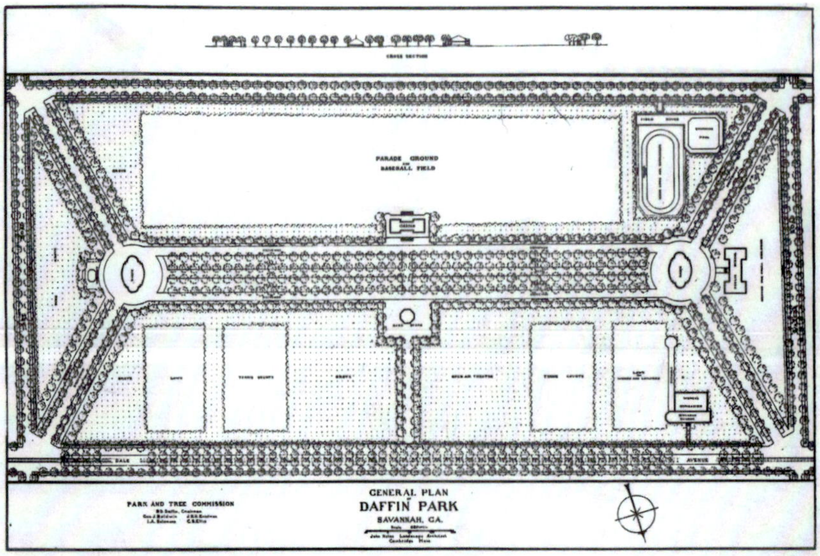

FIGURE 177. *General Plan of Daffin Park, Savannah, Ga.* by John Nolen, 1907. Courtesy of the City of Savannah Municipal Archives.

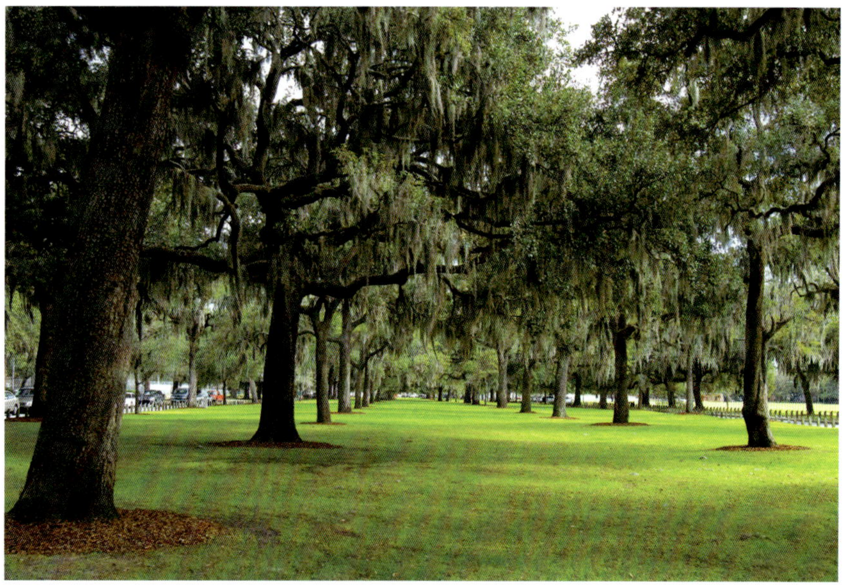

FIGURE 178. The Mall, central triple allée of live oaks at Daffin Park. Photo by Robin B. Williams, 2007.

the design principles of the City Beautiful movement with its central axial triple allée of live oak trees, called the Mall (figure 178)—an exaggerated version of the central median introduced a century earlier on South Broad Street (Oglethorpe Avenue)—and its radiating corner access roads, also flanked by rows of live oaks. Yet, in contrast to the increasingly passive use of the downtown squares, Daffin Park was designed to host active, athletic uses on broad open fields flanking the

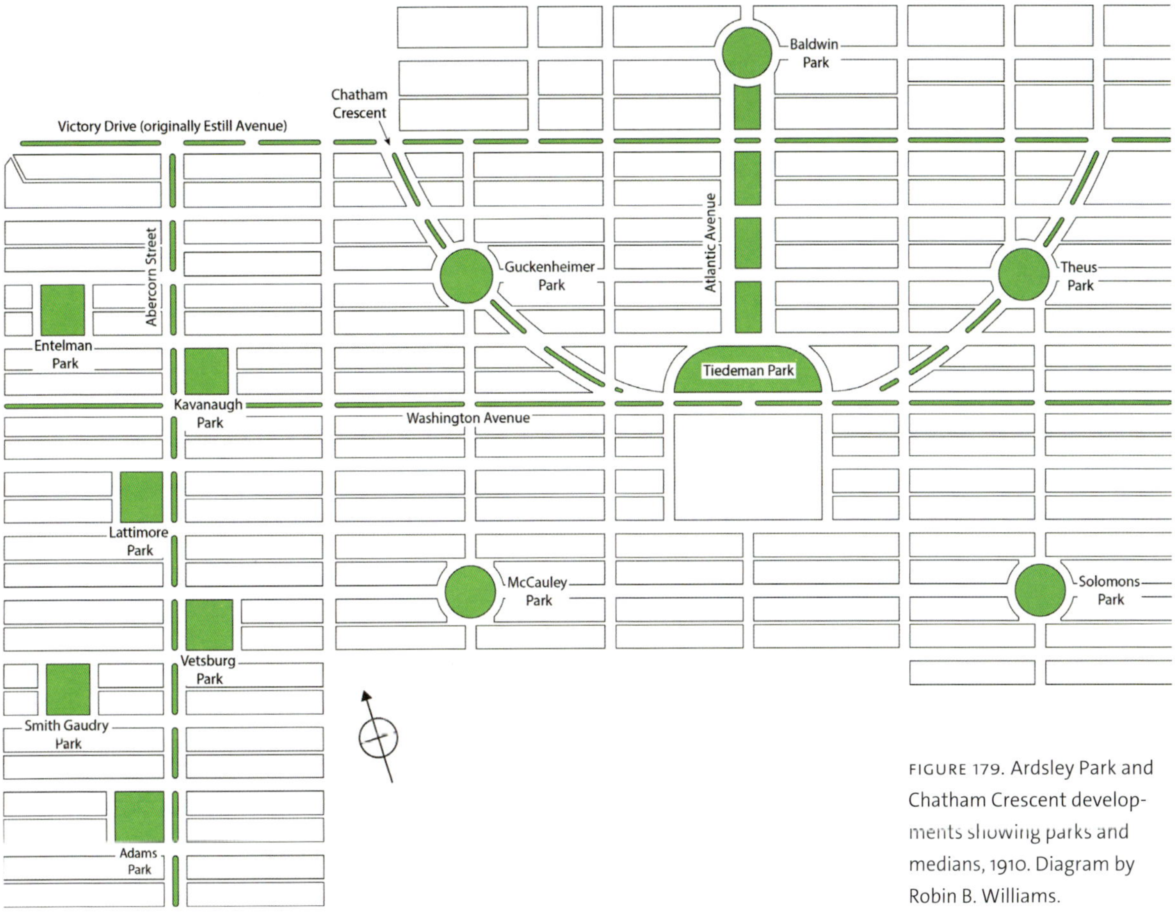

FIGURE 179. Ardsley Park and Chatham Crescent developments showing parks and medians, 1910. Diagram by Robin B. Williams.

Mall, purposes it continues to have, though the specific activities differ somewhat from those anticipated by Nolen, such as the introduction of a swimming pool in the form of an artificial lake by the 1920s.

In 1909, as the automobile age was taking hold, two private developments south of Victory Drive incorporated public squares, though now called parks, as they sought to cast a vision for modern suburban living. Developed by brothers William and Henry Hays Lattimore, Ardsley Park, south of Victory Drive between Bull and Habersham Streets, included six residential squares on alternating sides of Abercorn Street, with two of the four squares to the west set midblock and surrounded by houses (figure 179). Significantly, the squares were subordinated to the movement of automobiles, being pushed off axis to allow uninterrupted traffic flow along Abercorn Street, whose median echoed those downtown. Also begun in 1909 and adjacent to Ardsley Park is the larger Chatham Crescent, a

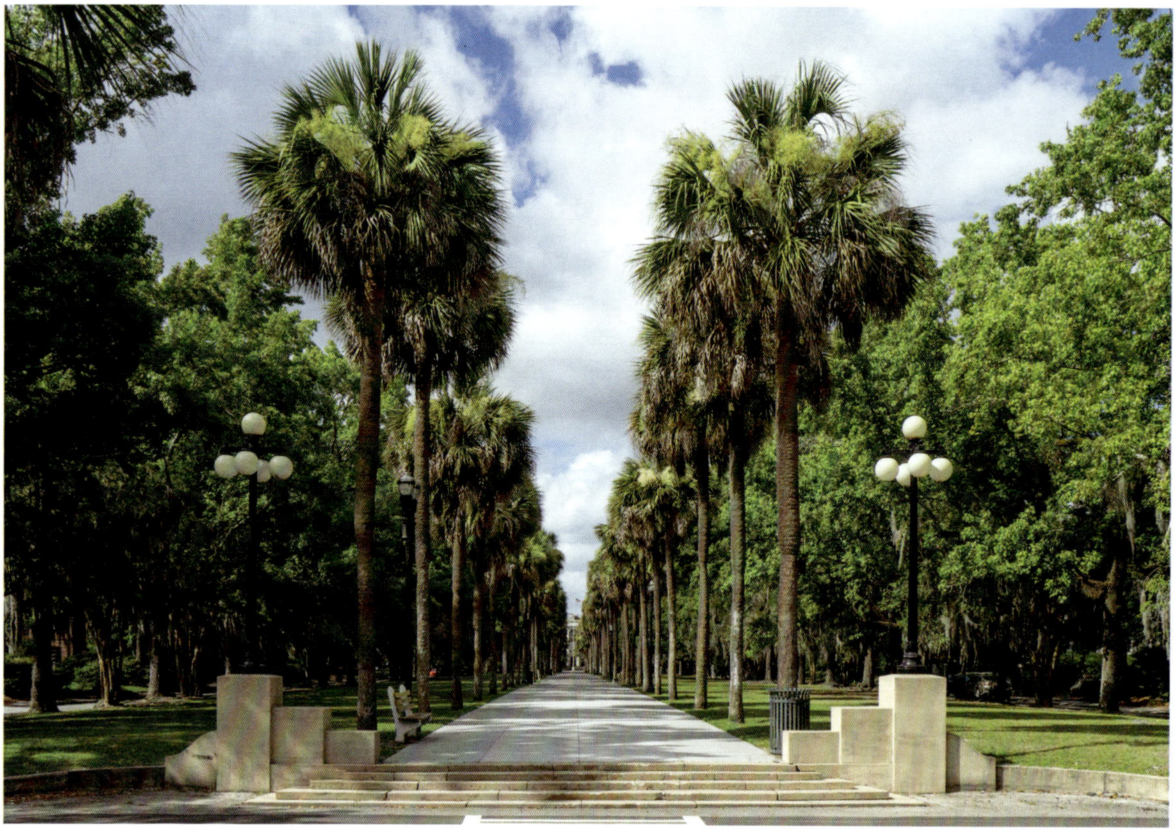

FIGURE 180. Atlantic Avenue Mall with palmetto trees laid out by Georges H. Bignault, Chatham Crescent development, 1910. Photo by Robin B. Williams, 2024.

Beaux-Arts-style development typical of the City Beautiful movement. The vision of automobile enthusiast Harvey Granger, this development incorporated five parks in the form of circles to facilitate the movement of cars.[13] Reflecting the influence of the automobile, both the Ardsley Park and the Chatham Crescent developments made use of longer blocks, eliminating Drayton, Lincoln, Price, and East Broad Streets south of Estill Avenue. Both developments also incorporated the prominent use of tree-lined medians in the tradition of Oglethorpe Avenue and Liberty Street within the plan, but with palmetto trees (one of the three tree species celebrated by the Park and Tree Commission) planted in the middle of Estill Avenue and the Atlantic Avenue Mall, a design feature introduced by the Paris-born and -trained landscape architect Georges Bignault (figure 180). The exclusive residential nature of these leafy neighborhoods, with their increased dependence on the automobile—with some houses sporting front-facing driveways and garages, even though both developments continued the local traditions of lanes and carriage houses—reflected a trend toward a more privatized kind of urbanism.[14]

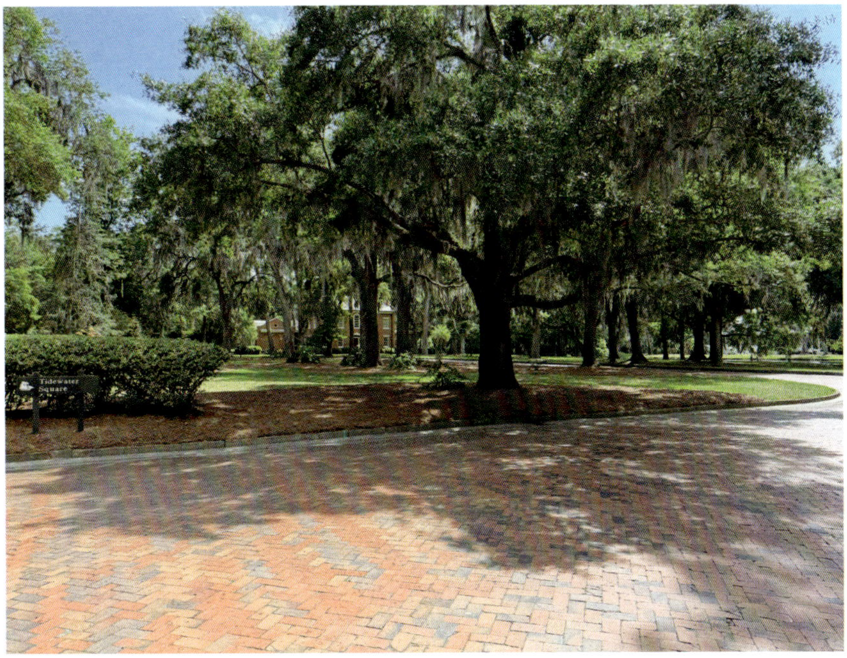

FIGURE 181. Tidewater Square, The Landings, 1984. Photo by Robin B. Williams, 2024.

Exclusively detached houses are modestly set back from the street, framed by private landscaping on all sides. The small parks and tree-lined mall of these neighborhoods serve the recreation needs of children, dog walkers, and picnickers.

Subsequent development found little use for the kind of urbanism in the Savannah Plan. In the postwar era, the city's suburbs instead adopted curvilinear street patterns; sprawling one-story "ranch style" house plans on ever-larger residential lots that focused outdoor life on the backyard; air-conditioning; and, most significantly, a comprehensive land use zoning code in 1960 that prevented any discernible influence of the Savannah Plan on the architecture or urban planning of mid-twentieth-century Savannah. In fact, the zoning code specifically disallowed many of the features and principles found in the architecture and urban design of the Savannah Plan, such as lanes, carriage houses, or other forms of housing, including accessory dwelling units and multifamily duplexes or quadplexes.

By the 1980s, however, a general rediscovery of the value of historic architecture and urbanism became noticeable in the downtown area and even in the outlying neighborhoods of greater Savannah. This can be seen in a rather token way in 1984 when Tidewater Square was made the center of the newly created neighborhood of Midpoint within the 4,500-acre gated community called The Landings on Skidaway Island, thirteen miles from the city's historic center (figure 181). An even more superficial but symbolically potent nod to Savannah's historic architecture

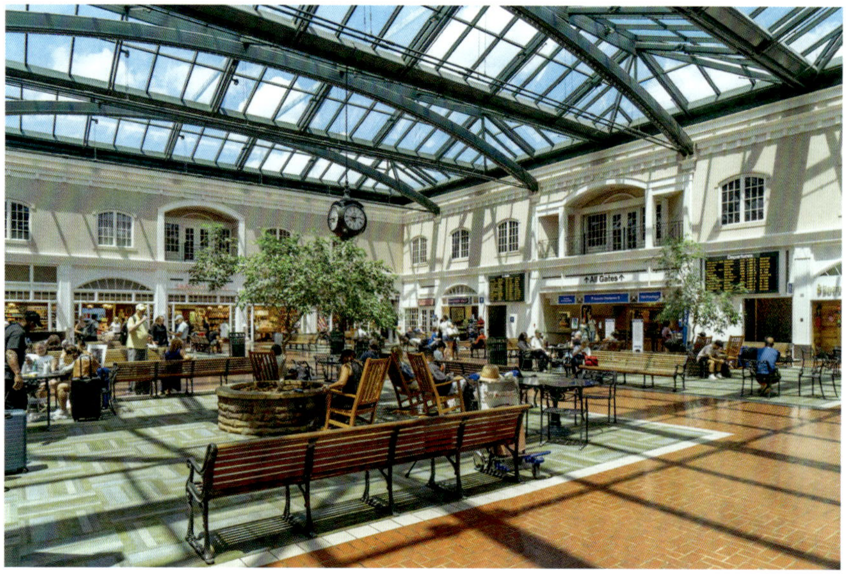

FIGURE 182. Savannah/Hilton Head International Airport terminal waiting area, designed by KBJ Architects, 1994. Photo by Robin B. Williams, 2024.

and urbanism can be seen in the 1994 Savannah/Hilton Head International Airport terminal, whose skylit waiting room was designed to evoke a Savannah square, complete with green-carpeted "lawns," park benches, potted trees, and brick pathways (figure 182).

A more serious attempt to replicate elements of the Savannah Plan occurred in 2006 when city officials collaborated with a consortium of private developers to extend the historic city street grid to the east of downtown in a project dubbed the Savannah River Landing (figure 183). Situated on a low-lying fifty-seven-acre site along the Savannah River, below the bluff where the original Trustees' Garden was located, the development, designed by Savannah architects Sottile and Sottile and inspired by the Savannah Plan, included five new squares connected by a grid of variable street types and blocks of building lots (though the blocks were larger than their historic precedents). Street curbs and sewers were already in place when a national economic downturn in 2008 bankrupted some of the investors, leaving this project a wasteland until recently; new developers have rebranded the project as "Eastern Wharf" and have begun to build according to a much-revised plan, which now features only two public squares.

Since the early 2000s, developers have returned to Savannah's historic housing typologies—elevated rows and double houses especially—both within the plan and beyond. Blocks of elevated rowhouses have been particularly popular, with Taylor Row, built in 2004 at 301–319 West Taylor Street between Jefferson and Montgomery (just outside the plan), being most impressive as a set of ten houses

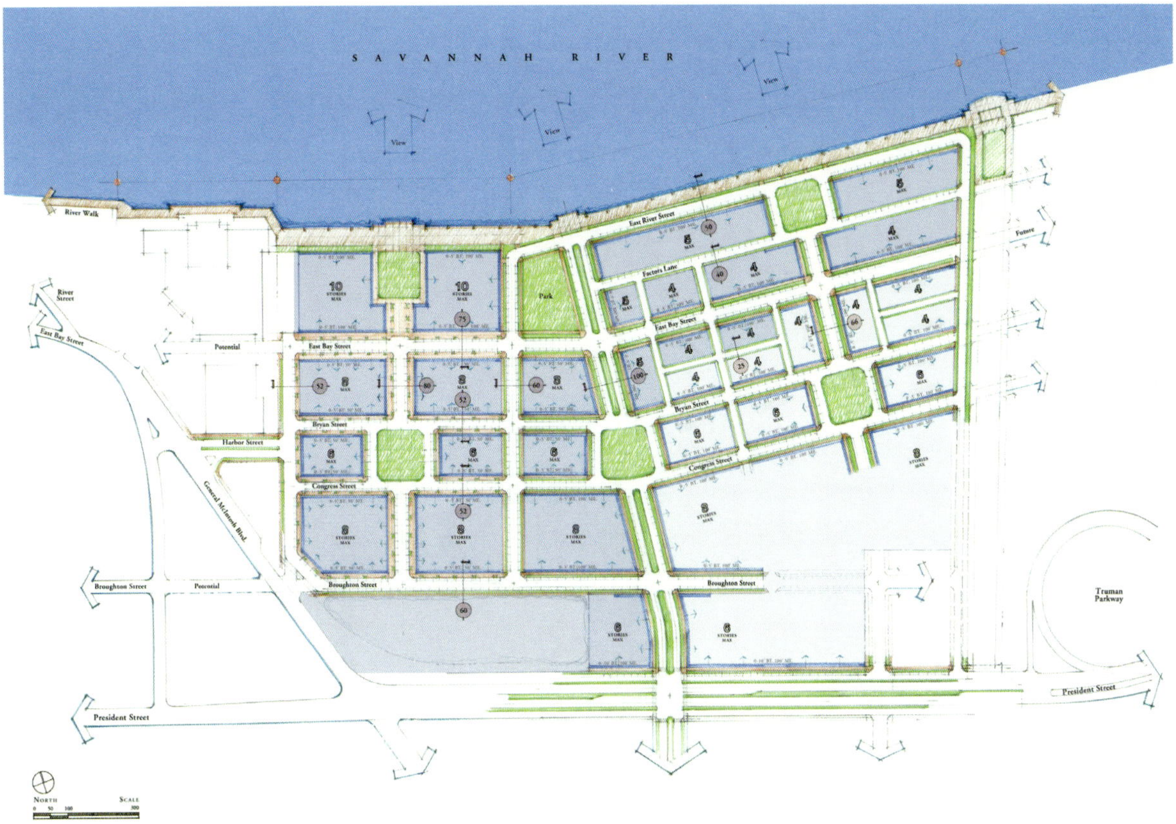

in which historic Italianate detailing is accurately employed for the five houses to the east and Federal style is employed for the western five. Both design styles were obviously borrowed from models within the plan (figure 184).[15] In keeping with the development patterns generated by the plan, these three-story rowhouses have two-story carriage houses (garage below, apartment above) across the rear, fronting West Wayne Street. The nearby Frogtown Lofts development just west of Martin Luther King Jr. Boulevard on Berrien Street, designed by Lominack Kolman Smith Architects, includes two adjacent rows that represent a thoughtful modern reinterpretation of the traditional Savannah elevated rowhouse form in exposed concrete and stained wood, with steel porches and staircases (figure 185). A recent pair of neotraditional reinterpretations of elevated Savannah double houses at 304–306 West Taylor Street and 303–305 Berrien Street, designed by Sottile and Sottile and completed in 2021, stand back-to-back, with a shared, private gated "lane" between them. The houses follow the symmetrical organization and raised main floor accessed by staircases in the "A" configuration, but they take creative

FIGURE 183. Civic masterplan for Savannah River Landing, Sottile and Sottile Architects, 2006. Courtesy of Sottile and Sottile.

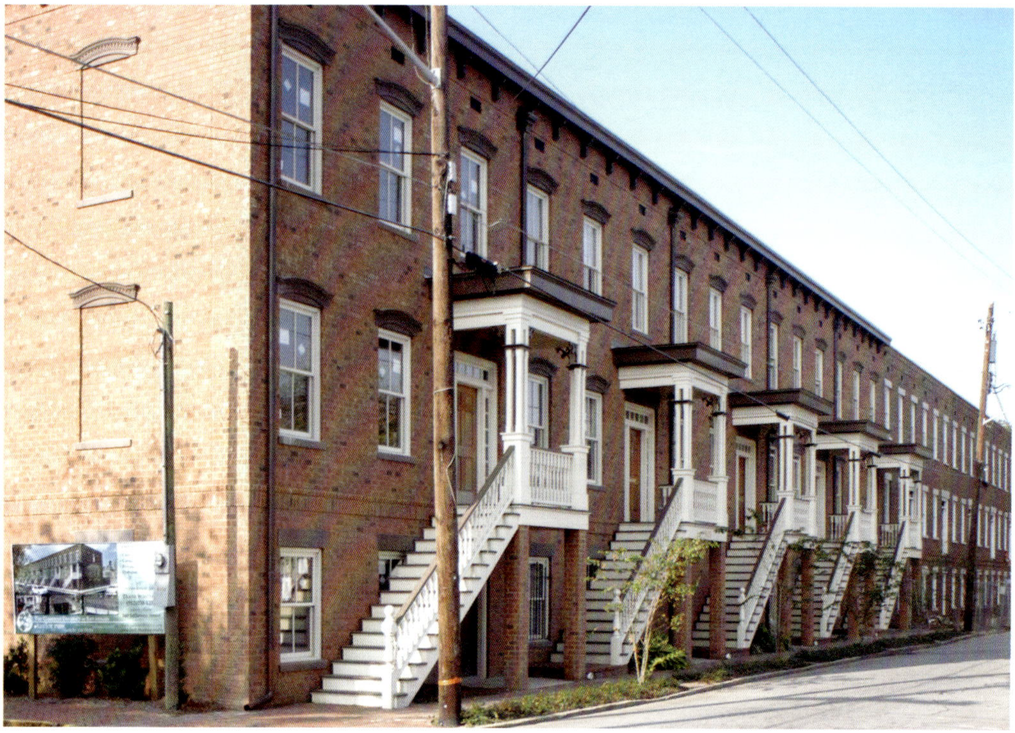

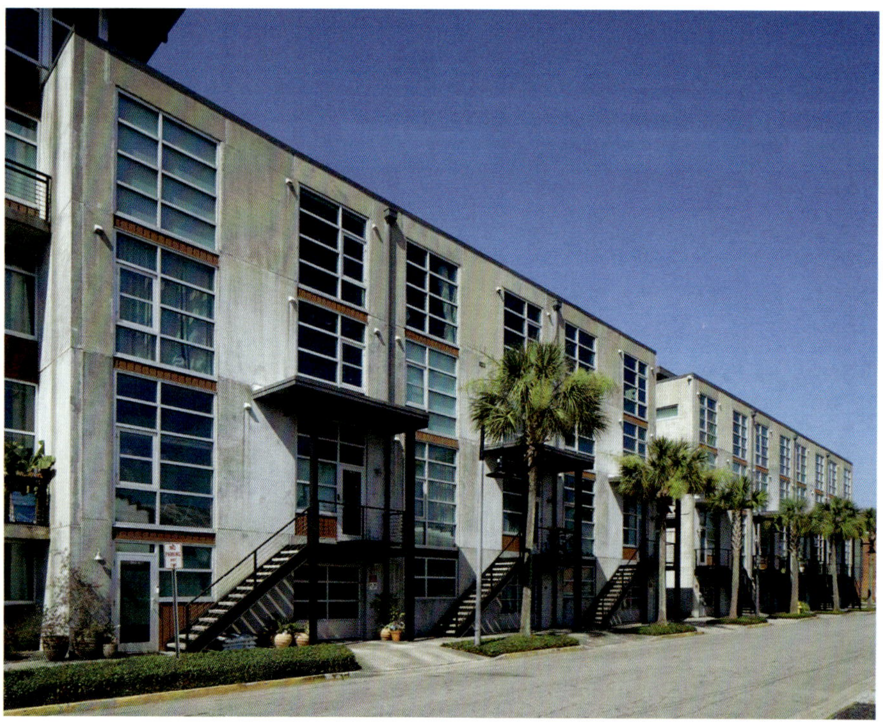

FIGURE 184. (*Above*) Taylor Row, 301–319 West Taylor Street, 2004. Photo by Robin B. Williams, 2004.

FIGURE 185. (*Right*) Frogtown Lofts rowhouses, 545–555 Berien Street, designed by Lominack Kolman Smith Architects, 2008. Photo by Robin B. Williams, 2024.

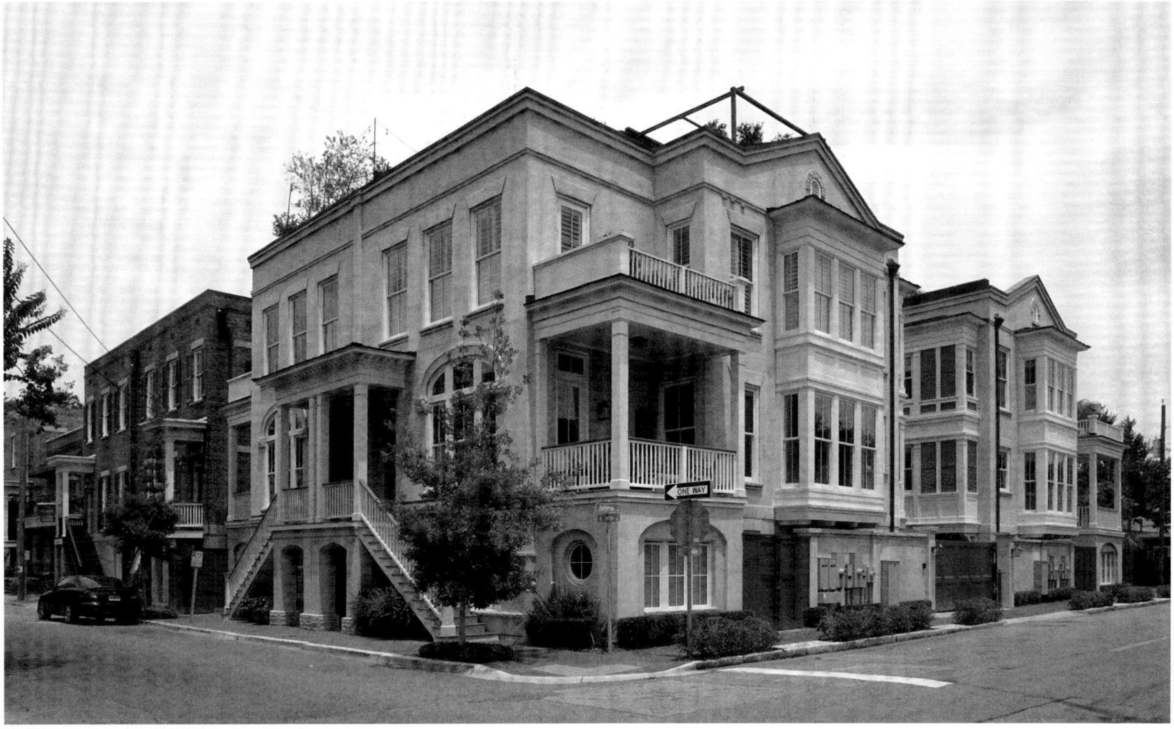

liberties with the fenestration and in the inclusion of side porches on the outer edges that extend halfway back, where they meet a T-shaped extension on the rear of each pair (figure 186).

FIGURE 186. Double house, 304–306 West Taylor Street, Sottile and Sottile, 2021. Photo by Robin B. Williams, 2024.

Although the Savannah Plan plays a very large role in shaping the identity of Savannah, it is inadequate to serve all the needs of the modern city. Hence, certain activities and building types must occur outside the harmonious, orderly, and fine-grained urbanism of the plan. Large-scale agriculture, industry, and transportation buildings have always been accommodated outside the plan. The growing demands of the entertainment and hospitality industries, sporting events, big-box retailing, health care, and education have made it increasingly difficult to accommodate such activities even with modification of the plan.

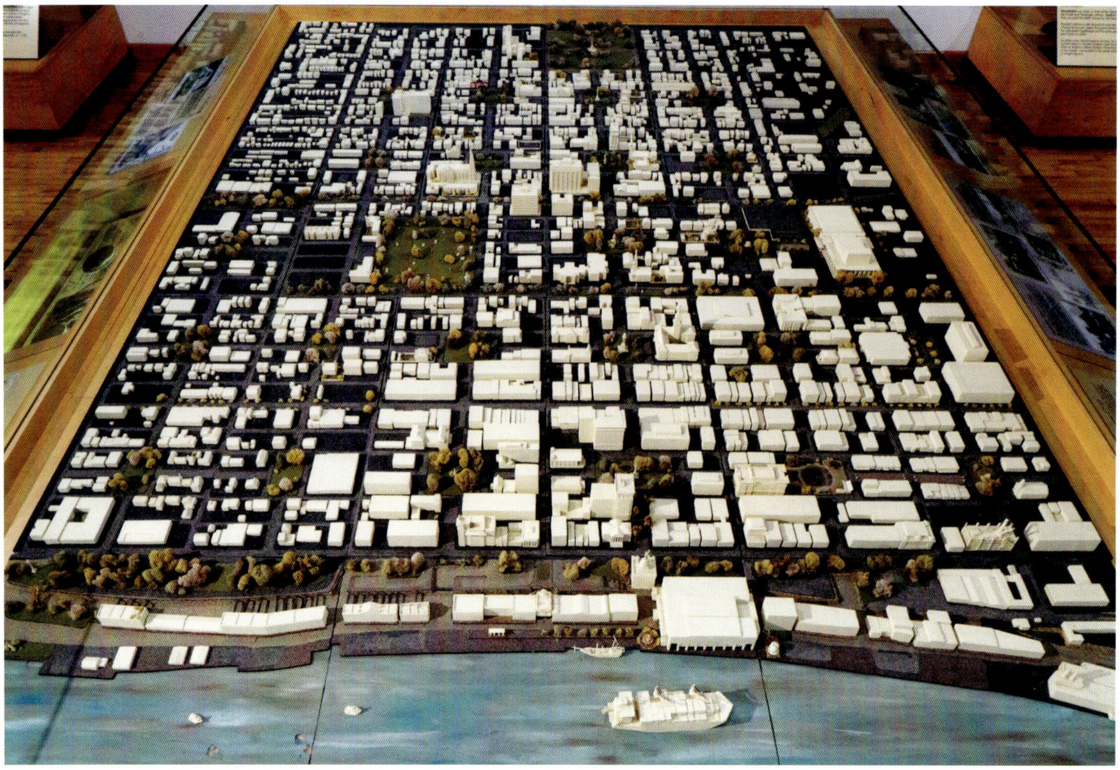

FIGURE 187. *Savannah Model*, on exhibit at the Massie Heritage Center; built to 1/50th scale by James W. Morton, 1982–85; updated in 2004 by Christian Sottile; refurbished by James Morton in 2011. Photo by Robin B. Williams, 2024.

CHAPTER TEN

THE SAVANNAH PLAN AS A MODEL

The plan of Savannah, with its patterned diversity, embodies principles of planning from which we still have much to learn.
—STANFORD ANDERSON, 1993

Savannah, Georgia, is a city on the architects' and planners' North American Grand Tour. The city's unique plan and eclectic architecture provide a PhD education on urban design. There is no limit to the lessons this city can teach, and I learn something new every time I have the opportunity to explore it.
—EDWARD ERFURT, 2024

One of the greatest conundrums presented by the Savannah Plan is its irreproducibility. Praised and admired though it has been, it has never been duplicated. No other city in the world follows the pattern of blocks, streets, and squares found in the Savannah Plan. John Reps calls this failure of influence "one of the great misfortunes of American town planning," speculating that "had Savannah been located, as were Philadelphia and New York, on the main routes leading to the interior, at least some of our midwestern cities might have achieved part of the charm and urbanity still retained in Oglethorpe's Savannah."[1]

The Savannah Plan's resistance to replication, however, seems to be built into its design. Small lot and block sizes, a surplus of streets, and an abundance of public squares can hardly be seen by today's developers and planners as features conducive to economically viable urban development. To be appreciated, the plan must be understood not merely as a diagram or planning formula but as a set of ideas and practices implemented over time by the construction of buildings and landscape features in a particular place. Like a non-fungible token, the Savannah Plan is impossible to counterfeit.

Our intention, therefore, is not to promote the Savannah Plan as a pattern to be copied elsewhere but to identify the lessons it has to offer for those who study, practice, or simply admire architecture and urban design. The Savannah Plan has captured the imaginations of urban and architectural theorists, designers, and builders for many years. In this final chapter we explore how the plan, though it has not been replicated, has been interpreted and implemented as a model.

Early Attempts to Imitate Savannah

The Trustee towns of Darien and New Ebenezer, both laid out in 1736, provide evidence that Oglethorpe himself believed that the Savannah Plan was a model worth repeating. Neither these nor any other Trustee-era towns, however, followed the model fully, and only Darien even remotely retains its original plan today. The port city of Brunswick, laid out under Crown rule in 1771 just eighteen miles south of Darien, also followed the pattern of the Savannah Plan, but at a larger scale. Its six wards and squares are nearly twice the size of those in Savannah (figure 188). As with Darien, however, elements of Brunswick's plan were modified significantly in the nineteenth and twentieth centuries, and what remains bears only a faint resemblance to the streets and squares of the Savannah Plan, with Hanover Square alone surviving intact.

One of the most mysterious Savannah-like town plans from the colonial era is found in the Moravian Archives in Bethlehem, Pennsylvania (not to be confused with the ca. 1740 plan of Savannah that is also in the Moravian Archives). Attributed

FIGURE 188. *City of Brunswick, State of Georgia: Showing the Recent Addition as Located in 1837*, plan by G. R. Baldwin, in *Report on the Brunswick Canal and Rail Road, Glynn County, Georgia* (Boston, 1837).

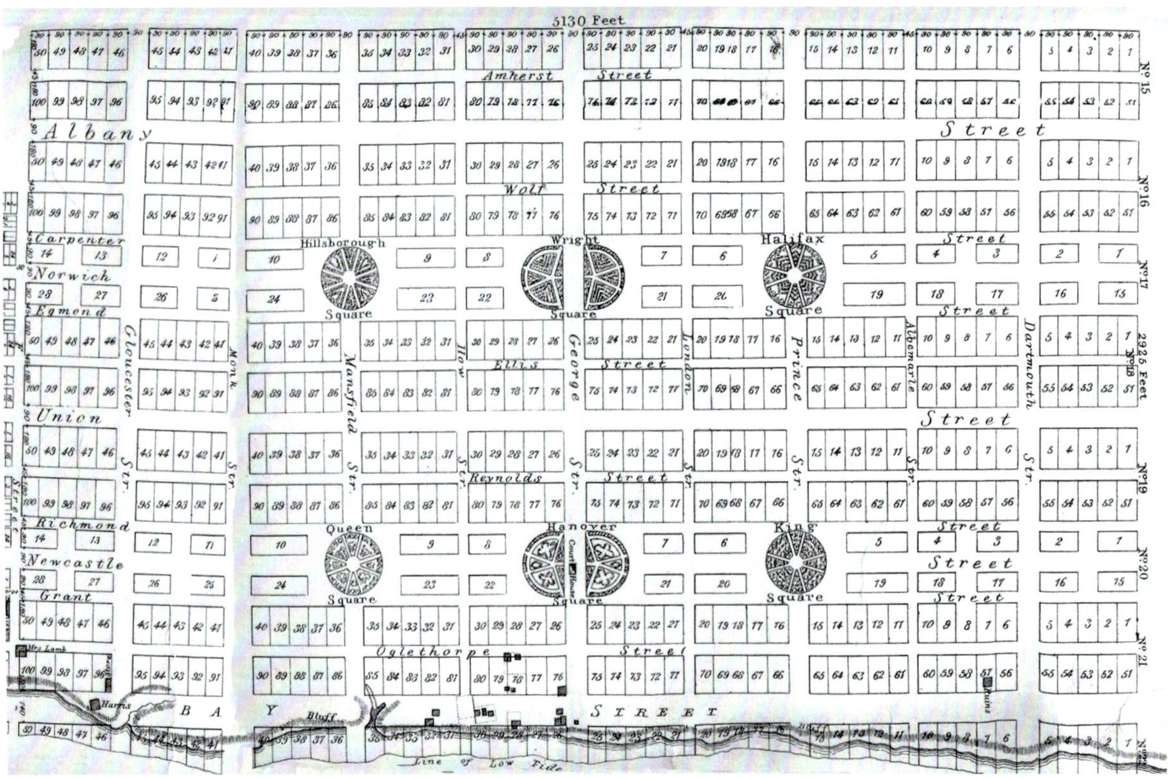

to Moravian surveyor and architect Christian Gottlieb Reuter and "copied" in 1765, it is labeled *Savanna Town in Georgien* (figure 189).[2] The drawing includes features such as the Savannah River, "Trustees Garden," and "Silk-House" that clearly identify the settlement as Savannah, but the plan itself, although similar in many details, differs significantly from that of Savannah by showing four "wards," no bisecting north–south streets, and no trust lots. At the invitation of the Trustees, the first group of Moravians arrived in Georgia in 1735 and were granted two tything lots, with associated garden and farm lots, and another five-hundred-acre site beyond the plan. It is believed that they intended to establish a town of their own, as their fellow German-speaking Protestants the Salzburgers would do at Ebenezer. But in 1740 the Moravians abruptly abandoned the Georgia colony, moving northward to colonies more accepting of their pacificism. Michael Lewis speculates that the *Savanna Town* plan was made by someone in the Moravian community wishing to remember and record the Savannah Plan twenty-five years after leaving Georgia.[3] Whatever the case, this puzzling drawing is clear evidence of the Moravian interest in city planning in general and in the Savannah Plan in particular. Together with Ebenezer, Darien, and Brunswick, it exemplifies how the Savannah Plan was admired and imitated in the colonial era, even if no attempt to replicate it was successful.

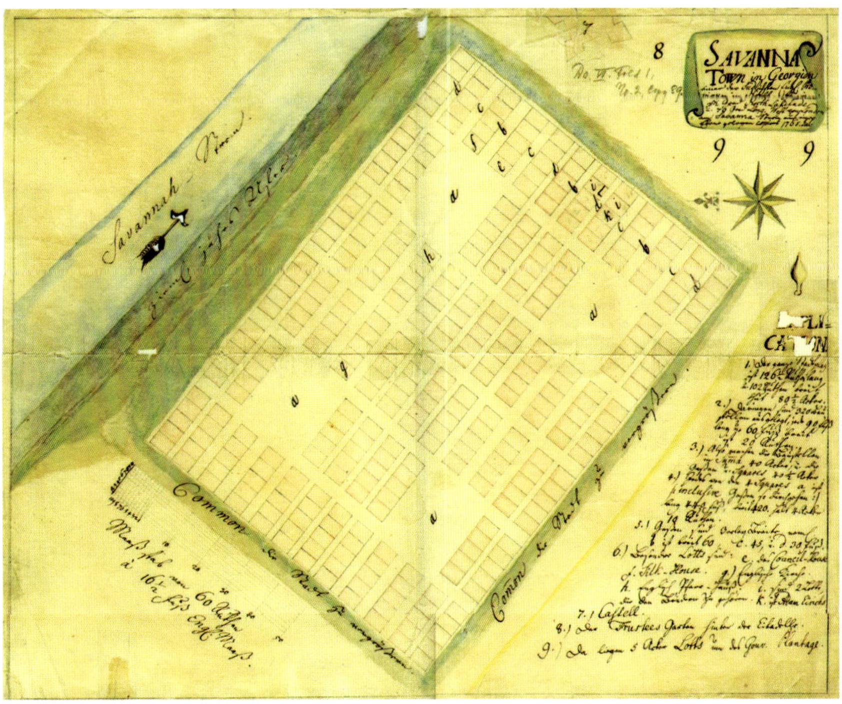

FIGURE 189. *Savanna Town in Georgien*, hand-drawn copy of a plan attributed to Christian Gottlieb Reuter, dated July 1765, ink and watercolor on paper, 14¼" × 16¼". By permission of the Archives of the Moravian Church, Bethlehem, Penn.

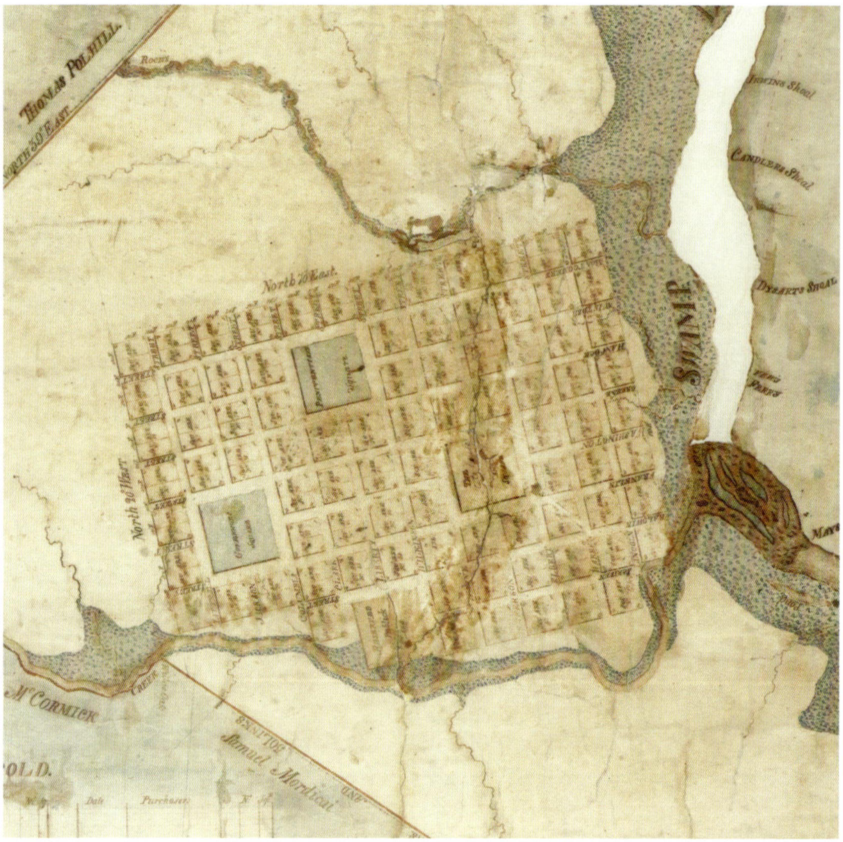

FIGURE 190. Detail of *A Plan of Milledgeville: The Capital and Permanent Seat of the Government of the State of Georgia.* "Copied from the original plan on the 2nd day of September 1808, by Daniel Sturges, sur. Genl"; ink and watercolor on paper. Courtesy of Hargrett Rare Book and Manuscript Library, University of Georgia Libraries.

Although no American town has replicated the model of the Savannah Plan, Joan Niles Sears, in her survey of the first century of town planning in Georgia, identifies four types of town plans, one of which is the "Savannah type plan."[4] Most of these, like most of Georgia's planned towns, were conceived as county seats, with only one square occupied by a courthouse, hardly employing the fine-grained, polycentric spirit of the Savannah Plan. Milledgeville, founded on the Oconee River in 1808 as Georgia's first planned state capital, was laid out with four public squares, each designated for a particular state building (figure 190). Sears suggests that "the planners may have hoped to produce a town similar in appearance to Savannah," but they failed because of the hilly topography.[5]

At least one realized town plan appears to reflect the influence of Savannah—Charlottetown, the capital of the province of Prince Edward Island in Canada. British surveyor Charles Morris laid out the original town in 1768, following a pattern he had used for other colonial settlements, with a single square centrally located within a regular grid of streets. In 1771, however, surveyor Thomas Wright

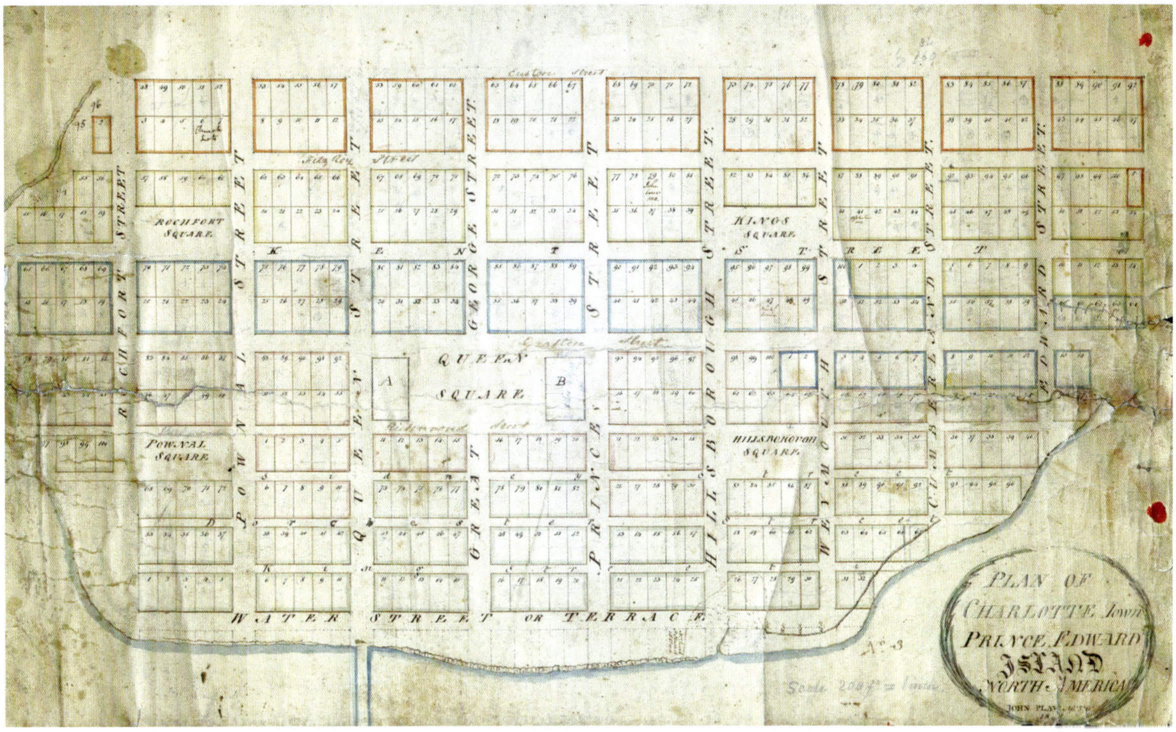

FIGURE 191. *Plan of Charlotte Town, Prince Edward Island, North America* by Thomas Wright, 1771; drawn 1810 by John Plaw; ink and watercolor on paper. Public Archives and Records Office, Charlottetown, PEI.

devised a new town plan that incorporated four additional squares (each slightly smaller than Johnson Square), evenly distributed within each of the town's four quadrants and following the oblong block proportions established by Morris (figure 191).[6] Upon arriving in North America from England in 1758, Wright "furthered his education with practical work under the surveyor general of Georgia," which could have been Henry Yonge or William de Brahm, since the two men shared that title at the time.[7] Wright's connection to Georgia (and surely to Savannah) makes the revised layout of Charlottetown with its multiple squares (which remain intact) compelling evidence of a direct influence.

If we consider the Savannah Plan less as a template and more as a set of principles and design strategies, we can see how it has had a decided effect on the theory and practice of American urbanism for nearly three centuries. Rational, regularized orthogonal grid plans punctuated by public spaces and permeated by trees and garden elements are not uncommon in American town planning history. Elements and concepts vital to the Savannah Plan, for example, can be found in Thomas Jefferson's influential vision of an egalitarian, agrarian, and anti-urban republic. The Land Ordinances of 1784, 1785, and 1787 followed Jefferson's scheme to impose a mile-square grid of land parcels in the Northwest Territory and, ultimately, across the nation. Jefferson's plan is reminiscent of the Georgia Trustees' employment of a mile-square grid to govern the settlement of towns, villages, and farmland. Reps suggests that Jefferson may have been inspired by the Savannah Plan in his advocacy for "checkerboard" town plans in which every other square would be reserved for public space.[8] Polycentric gridiron plans with multiple public squares appear regularly in American town plans from the Ohio territories to Sacramento, California, in the first half of the nineteenth century, but few were implemented. In Aiken, South Carolina, established in 1834, its grid of 150-foot-wide streets, with each boasting a broad central median to accommodate trees, bears a striking resemblance, writ large, to Savannah's earlier South Broad Street.[9] Echoes of the Savannah Plan reverberate throughout the history of American town planning, but nowhere else does the plan fully materialize.

In fact, the Savannah Plan's model for American urban planning became increasingly unfashionable in the century that followed its completion in 1851, as the English landscape garden supplanted the gridiron as a template for town planning. Transportation concerns and land use zoning practices gave rise to new modes of urbanism. Progressive-minded civic leaders sought to modernize Savannah itself by sending trolley lines and automobiles through its old-fashioned, disruptive squares.[10] Suburbanized, auto-centric architectural design prevailed in the age of urban renewal. The loss of historic buildings, streets, and squares that came with these modernizing trends, however, catalyzed a renewed appreciation for the architecture and urbanism of the Savannah Plan as early as the 1920s. Interest in preserving not just buildings but the urban plan has been growing ever since. Also growing has been an interest in the Savannah Plan as a model for urban designers of the present age.

Savannah as New Urbanism

Among the Savannah Plan's greatest admirers in recent times have been advocates for the New Urbanism. The Charter of the New Urbanism, signed in 1996 in Charleston, South Carolina, at the third meeting of the Congress for the New Urbanism (CNU), outlines principles of urban design that are intended to reverse the environmentally destructive and socially demoralizing effects of suburban sprawl and auto-centric urbanism and to restore urban design practices to a more connected, community-based, and human-centric approach. The charter emphasizes the continuity and connectedness of urban design from the scale of the building, block, street, corridor, neighborhood, city, and region.[11] Among the qualities espoused by the charter are walkability, connectivity, the importance of public space, the integration of diverse uses, a distinction between civic and private architecture, and the primacy of human-scaled design. Railing against the mono-zoned, automobile-oriented, nontypological principles of twentieth-century urbanism and architecture, New Urbanists have called for a return to the civic-minded principles of urban design that were developed over hundreds of years of planning history.

Despite its name, the New Urbanism is consciously rooted in historical practices, finding its paradigms in historic cities and neighborhoods that have received widespread acclaim for their livability, human scale, and beauty. Among its primary inventions is the traditional neighborhood development (TND), a reimagined and reconfigured version of the planned urban development (PUD) model that played a leading role in the configuration of the mono-zoned, auto-centric landscape of American suburban sprawl over the past century. Routinely acclaimed by New Urbanists as models for the TND are historic American cities such as Charleston, South Carolina; Alexandria, Virginia; Portland, Oregon; Santa Barbara, California; and of course Savannah, Georgia. New Urbanists have consistently praised Savannah's urban plan and its architecture and have looked to it for inspiration.

Seaside, a resort town on the Florida Panhandle, is recognized by many as the prototype of New Urbanist town planning (figure 192). Planned in 1981 by Andrés Duany and Elizabeth Plater-Zyberk, working closely with developer Robert

FIGURE 192. *Plan of Seaside, Florida, as Built in 2010.* Drawn by Eusebio Azcue for DPZ. Image courtesy © DPZ CoDesign.

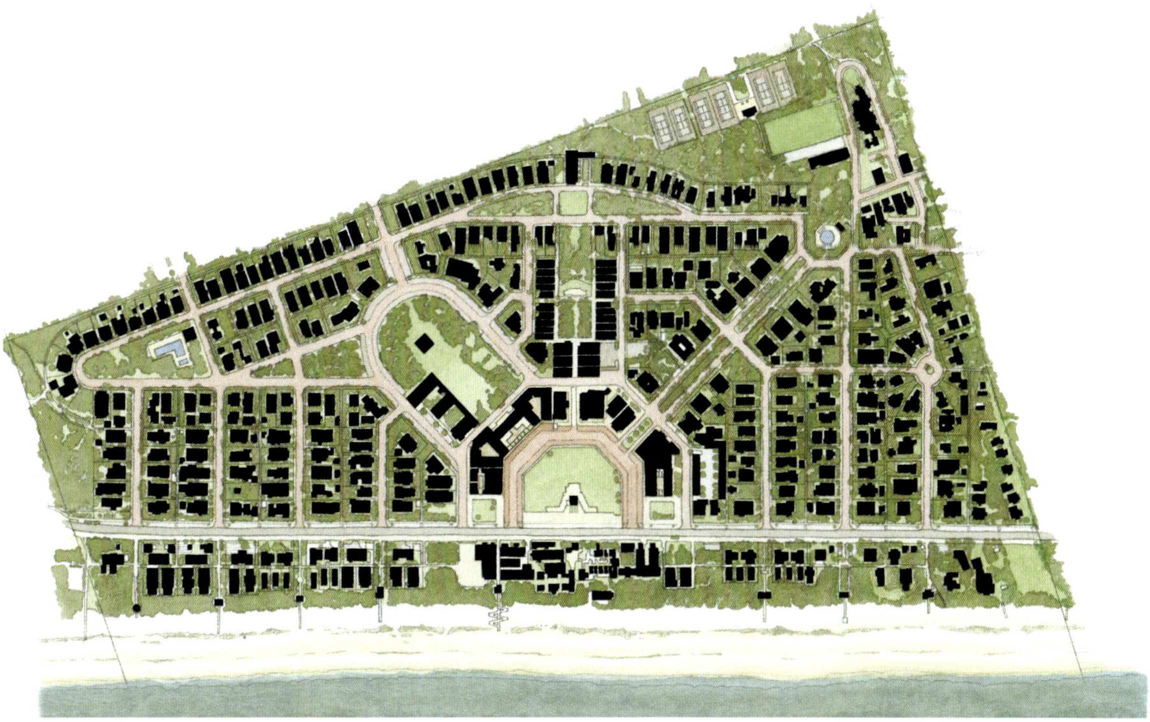

Davis, Seaside was conceived by studying traditional towns in the South and their architecture and distilling the most admirable urban and architectural features into the celebrated Urban Code, an innovation based on building typology that marks the beginning of what is now called form-based design coding.[12] The code was conceived as a means of achieving the "coherence, cohesion, and strong sense of place" that could be found in much-admired American towns such as "Cape May, Charleston, Key West, Nantucket, and Savannah," according to architect Dhiru Thadani, who has been documenting Seaside from its earliest days.[13] Our exploration of the architecture of the Savannah Plan has been, in effect, a study of Savannah's tacit "urban code." Savannah must also be considered a source of inspiration for Seaside's public spaces connected by radial streets to a central square.[14]

A more intriguing and ultimately more significant connection between Seaside and Savannah has been suggested by architect and theorist Philip Bess in his 1997 essay "Virtuous Reality: Aristotle, Critical Realism, and the Reconstruction of Architectural and Urban Theory."[15] Bess begins by agreeing with architect and CNU charter member Patrick Pinnell, who cheekily proposed that the chief planner of Seaside was the ancient Greek philosopher Aristotle. What Pinnell meant by this outlandish claim, Bess explains, is that the designers of Seaside "conceived both its formal and social order" in a way that was "essentially Aristotelian." Elaborating on this reading, Bess suggests that the "traditional architecture and urban design" principles employed at Seaside can be seen as "formal expressions" of an "understanding of human nature" that is rooted in Aristotle's moral and political philosophy. Invoking a venerable company of Aristotelian political philosophers, including Thomas Aquinas, Alexis de Tocqueville, and Alasdair MacIntyre, Bess argues for an approach to urban and architectural design that is informed by an understanding of the city as a principled community of citizens who seek a common good.

New Urbanism's emphasis on pedestrian-scaled, mixed-use developments is clearly aligned with such a communitarian approach. Seaside's "multicentered formalism," Bess suggests, offers a peculiarly potent means to achieving such an end by introducing the Tocquevillian ideal of subsidiarity. This principle maintains that the city that flourishes best is one that comprises a diverse array of institutions—that is, subsidiary communities that make up the totality of the city. It is at this point that Bess turns to Savannah, the ultimate model of a city that is a "community of communities," a principled, but multicentered and multifunctioning assembly of communal spaces. We would add that the incremental, multigenerational growth of the Savannah Plan adds a temporal dimension to Savannah as the ultimate example of an Aristotelian-Tocquevillian city.

Thomas Wilson, writing from a less philosophical but more skeptical perspective than Bess, discusses the New Urbanism and its relationship to Savannah at length, asserting that "the Oglethorpe Plan" is "admired but not well understood by New Urbanists."[16] He identifies and discusses New Urbanist principles that he believes are "directly comparable to the Oglethorpe Plan," including the importance of discernible neighborhood centers; a connected network of relatively narrow, tree-lined streets of varied types; the need for buildings to define the street edge; the prominent placement of civic buildings; self-governance of neighborhoods; and the use of automobile roundabouts. For each of these points of comparison, Wilson argues that the Oglethorpe Plan, while similar, differs in significant ways from the practices and principles of the New Urbanism. For example, Savannah's automobile roundabouts—that is, its squares—are habitable and walkable places and thus are preferable to the traffic circles typically created today, which are "devoid of pedestrian activity."[17] His conclusion appears to be that the Savannah Plan offers a set of principles superior to those of the New Urbanism.

Savannah as a Model for New Urbanism

The New Urbanism is a controversial movement that is part of a more widespread revival of traditional modes of architecture and urbanism. The Savannah Plan has played an important role as a model for neotraditional urban development, especially in the South Carolina and Georgia Lowcountry. A key example is Newpoint, a modest fifty-four-acre residential community founded by local developers Vince Graham and Robert Turner in 1991 on Lady's Island, across the river from Beaufort, South Carolina, and just an hour's drive from Savannah (figure 193). Graham and Turner sought to create a neighborhood inspired not only by the historic Old Point neighborhood in Beaufort but also by historic Savannah. The town plan, designed by Savannah architect Gerald Cowart, is comparable to the Savannah Plan in rudimentary ways, such as its use of an orthogonal street grid with a variety of street types, including service lanes, and its ample designation of parklike public spaces. The rapid success of Newpoint led Turner to develop a larger TND north of Beaufort called Habersham, while Graham went on to develop an ambitious neighborhood called I'On in Mount Pleasant, just across the Cooper River from Charleston, South Carolina.

Habersham was planned during a design charette directed by Duany Plater-Zyberk and Company (DPZ) in 1996. Its casual grid of streets, rear service lanes, and house lots rambles across 276 acres, punctuated by numerous parklike public spaces. Near its mixed-use town center are a couple of streets lined with townhouses designed by Eric Brown (figure 194), whose website explains that "we drew our inspiration from the classic row houses of Savannah. Design elements include high ceilings, large windows, raised foundations, and durable materials."[18] Based in Savannah, Brown Design Studio has also created a catalog of residential designs

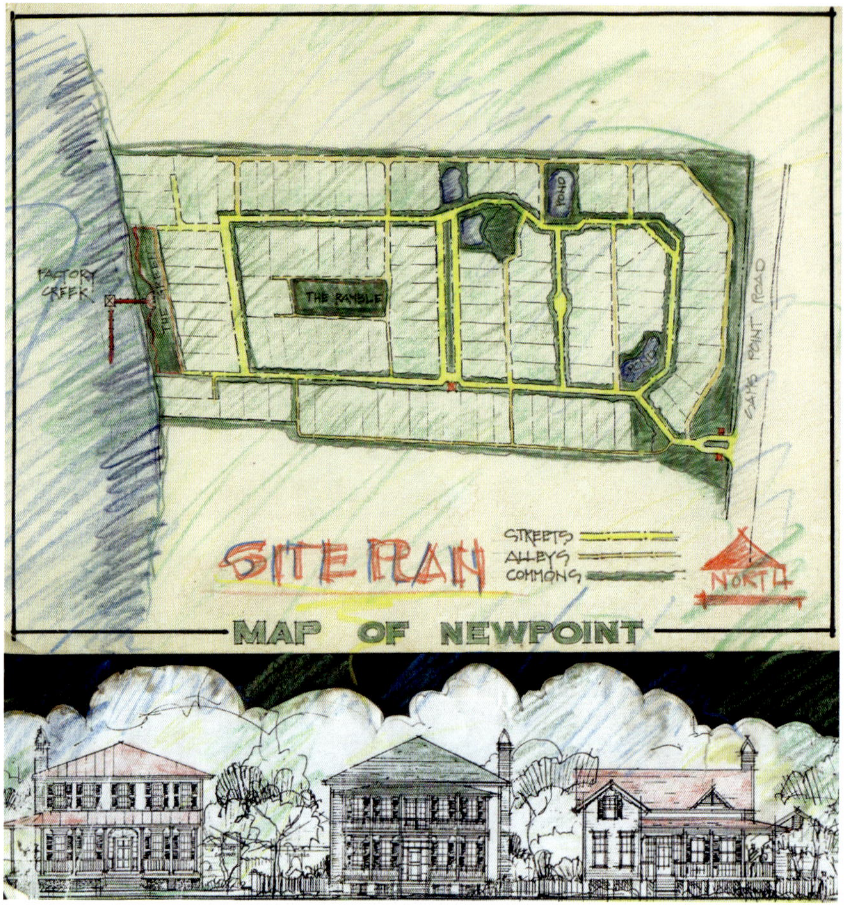

FIGURE 193. *Newpoint, Lady's Island, S.C., Conceptual Town Plan and Sample Elevations*, colored pencil sketch by Gerald Cowart, 1991. Courtesy Gerald Cowart, FAIA.

that borrow from Savannah's architectural lexicon, including single- and multi-family cottages and mansion houses (figure 195).

Vince Graham, his brother Geoff, and their father, Tom, invited DPZ and Dover, Kohl and Partners to collaborate on the original design of I'On in 1995 (figure 196). I'On comprises 244 acres and includes not only a variety of house types and grassy squares but also a significant number of commercial and institutional buildings, including a ten-room inn, two churches, and a school. Dover, Kohl and Partners' project profile for I'On explains that "the design team analyzed the building types and neighborhoods of Savannah, GA, Charleston, SC, and several other historic towns, then adapted their design conventions for the new neighborhood."[19] Admittedly, I'On draws more heavily from Charleston in its architectural and urban design than it does from Savannah, but Vince Graham's understanding of Savannah is deeper than one might expect of a typical real estate developer. In a 2001 CNU Council report, Graham expressed his admiration for

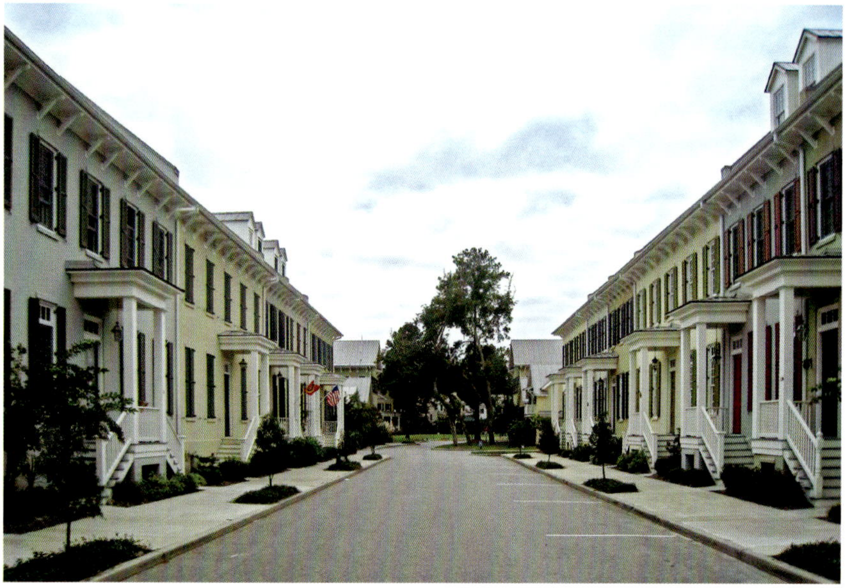

FIGURE 194. Assembly Row, Habersham, Beaufort, South Carolina, rowhouses designed by Brown Design Group, 2008. Photo courtesy Brown Design Group.

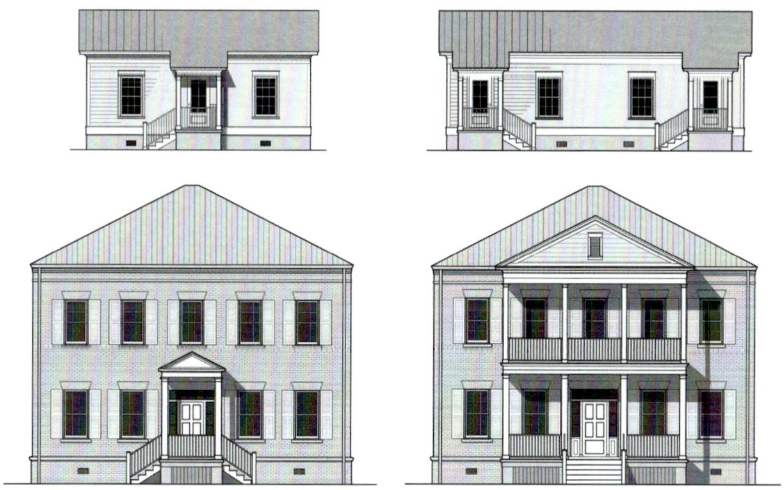

FIGURE 195. House types based on Savannah models. Courtesy Brown Design Group.

the Savannah Plan's ability to adapt and change over time: "We learn as we go, attempting to tinker our way to excellence. Savannah is a good example of this. Oglethorpe initially designed four wards on about 40 acres. Two more were added during his lifetime. Eighteen wards were added by later generations. The designers who built the later squares worked to adapt and improve Oglethorpe's original plan." Similarly, concerning the house types, he averred, "Again, thinking about Savannah, the first 100 houses were 16-foot by 24-foot log cabins on 60-foot by

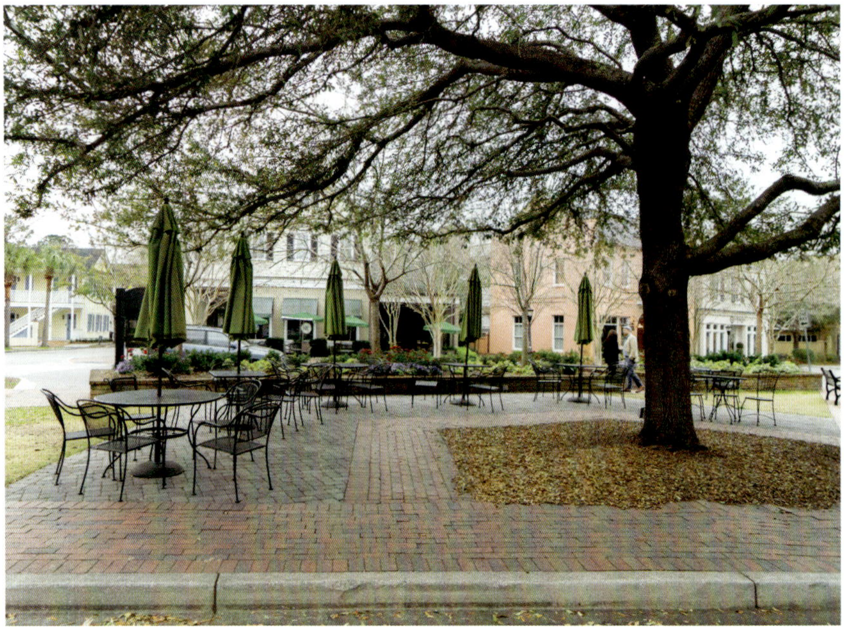

FIGURE 196. I'On, Mount Pleasant, South Carolina, photo by Robin B. Williams, 2017.

90-foot lots. Over time, these cabins were removed or torn down, and the lots subdivided to achieve the diversity you see today. In other words, be patient."[20]

Numerous examples of recent traditional urban design projects that owe a debt to the Savannah Plan can be found both in the Lowcountry and beyond. The acclaimed ten-thousand-acre town of Celebration, Florida, founded by the Disney Development Company, was planned by the prestigious New York firms of Cooper Robertson and Robert A. M. Stern Architects, together with the San Francisco–based landscape firm EDAW and Pittsburgh-based Urban Design Associates (UDA), in 1992. Several internationally recognized architects were asked to design public and commercial buildings. Brian Shea, who served as project manager for Cooper Robertson, explained that Celebration's town center, known as the Village, took "both town plan and architectural clues from a host of precedents found in Southeastern and Florida towns, including Charleston, Beaufort, Savannah, Madison, Coral Gables, Winter Park, St. Augustine, and New Orleans."[21] One of Celebration's public squares explicitly recalls Savannah. Surrounded by three-story rowhouses, Savannah Square is landscaped with azaleas, magnolia and live oak trees, park benches, a central fountain, and brick pathways laid in herringbone patterns, creating a stage-set version of Savannah (figure 197).

Specific references to Savannah can be found in many other New Urbanist TNDs, including Haile Village Center in Gainesville, Florida, founded and designed by Robert B. Kramer in 1992,[22] and Vermillion in Huntersville, North

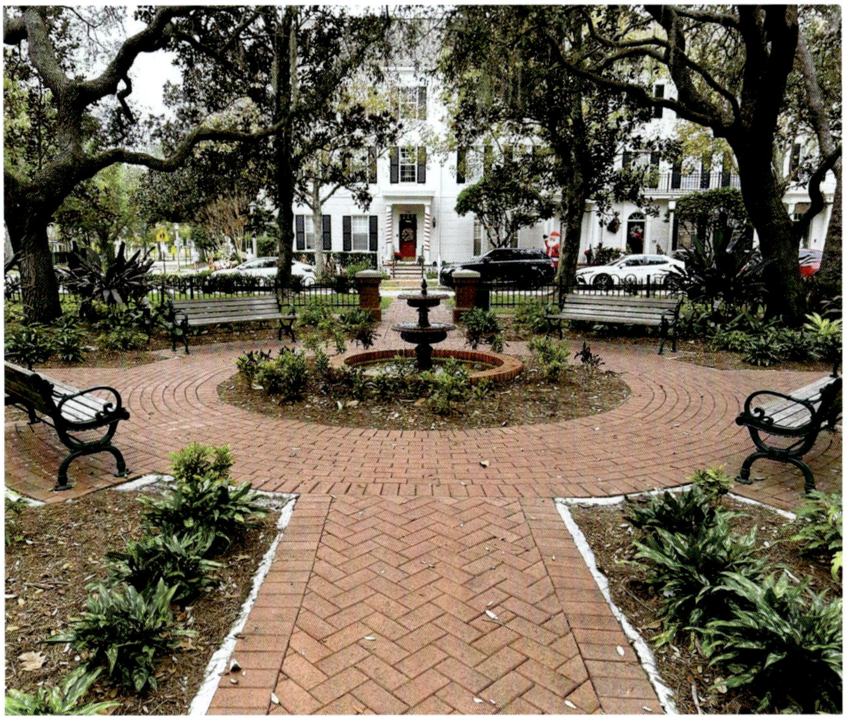

FIGURE 197. Savannah Square, Celebration, Florida, by Cooper Robertson and Robert A. M. Stern Architects, 1992. Photo by Will Hardy, 2023.

Carolina, planned by DPZ in 1996. The latter development has a "neighborhood square" boasting "Federal-style brick townhouses with tall, triple-hung second-story windows facing a green," which critic Catesby Leigh describes as being "inspired by James Oglethorpe's Savannah plan" (figure 198).[23]

One of the most direct imitations of the Savannah Plan can found in the borough of St. Laurent on the outskirts of Montreal, Canada. Bois-Franc is a 589-acre TND built on the site of a former airport owned by the manufacturing company Bombardier, which began developing the site in 1990 (figure 199). Working with Daniel Arbour and Associates, planner Louis Sauer "used the Savannah Historic District's pattern as the model for Bois-Franc."[24] What he designed is a high-density residential and commercial neighborhood with an orthogonal grid or varied street types structured around a series of landscaped public squares called "urban blocks." The project ultimately incorporated seven squares into the development, with the squares varying in the degree to which they conformed to the proposed diagram. Nonetheless, some connections to Savannah are apparent—most vividly in the way sidewalks align with the pedestrian paths crossing a square (figure 200). No one looking at Bois-Franc's buildings, however, will be reminded of Savannah. The neighborhood's architecture is mostly neotraditional, with an

FIGURE 198. (*Right*) Bowman Square, Vermillion development, by Andrés Duany and Elizabeth Plater-Zyberk, 1996, Huntersville, North Carolina. Photo by Robin B. Williams, 2024.

FIGURE 199. (*Below*) Diagrams comparing Bois-Franc, Quebec, with Savannah, Georgia, by Louis Sauer, ca. 1994. Courtesy of Louis Sauer.

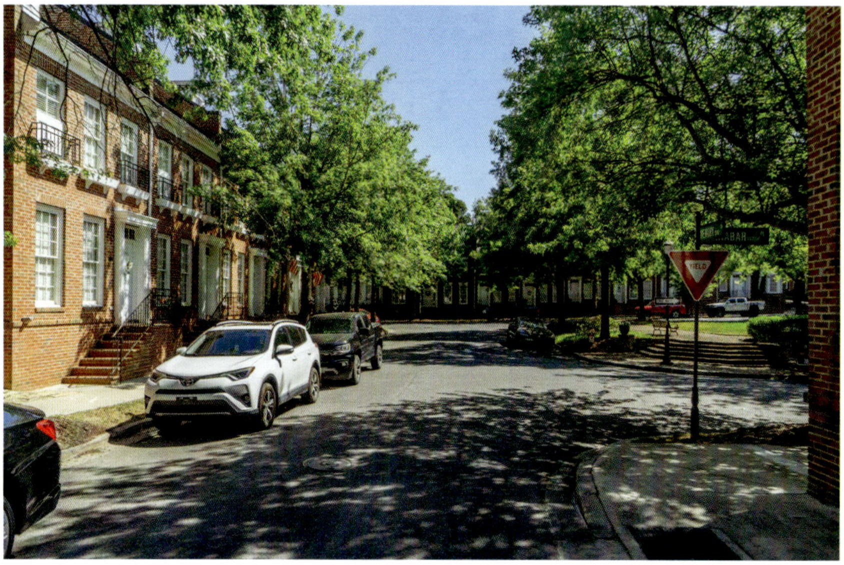

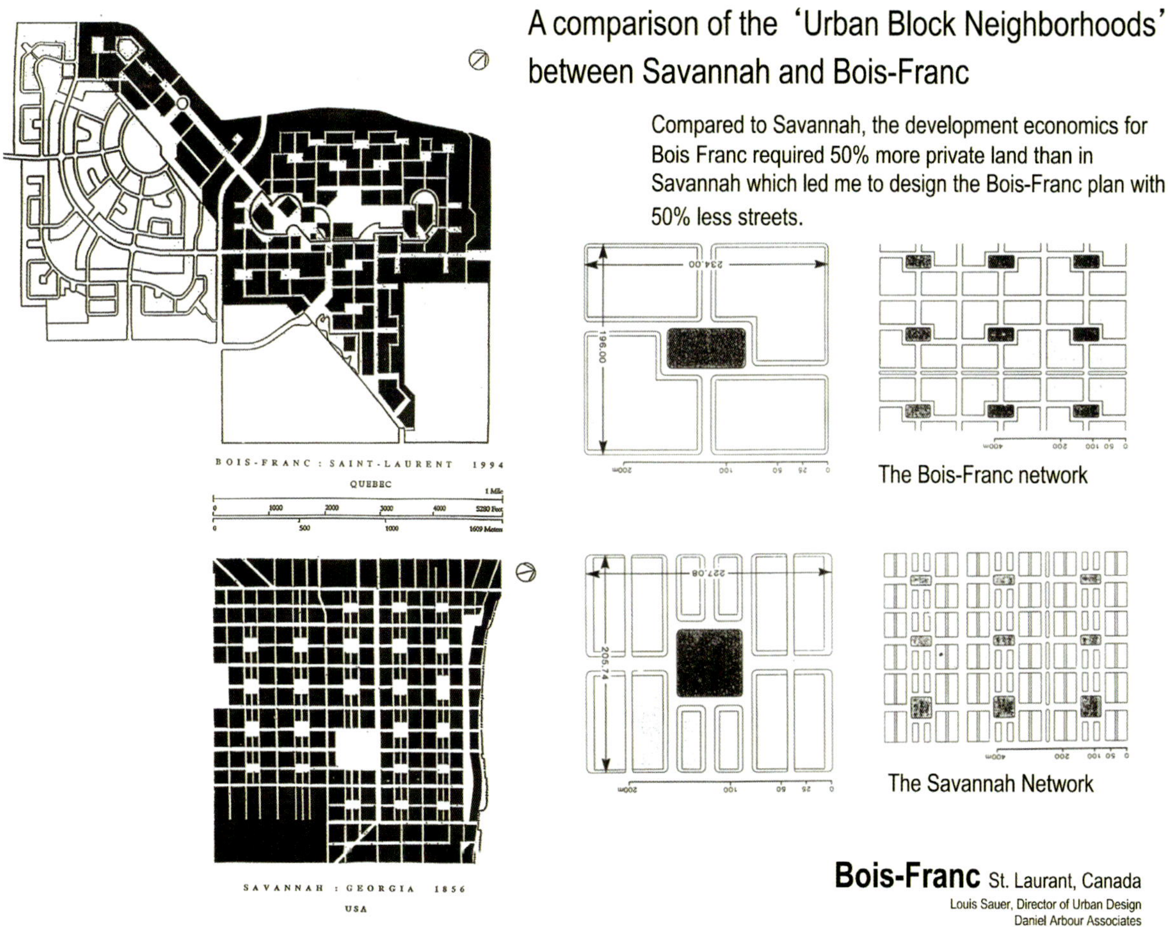

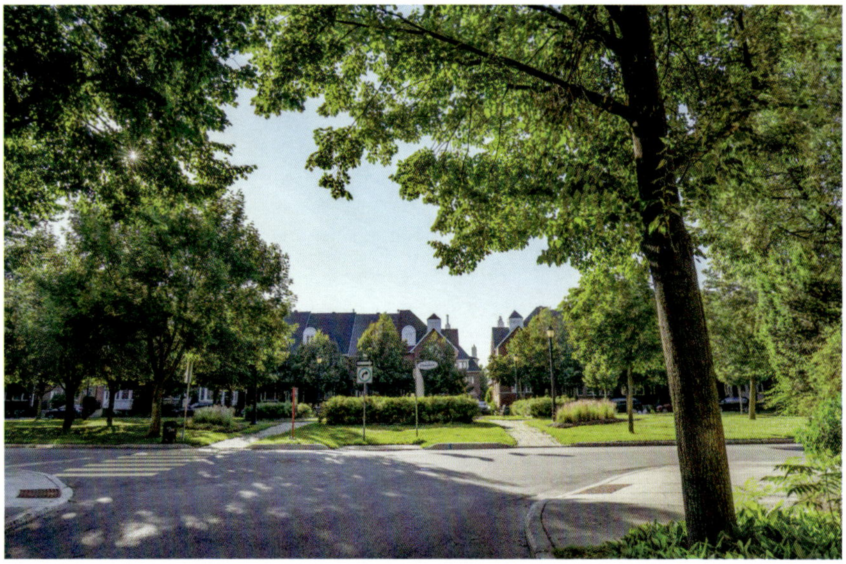

FIGURE 200. Square Jean-Rostand seen from the Rue de la Baltique, Bois-Franc, Quebec. Photo by Virginie Savage-Duguay, 2024.

abundance of red brick with white trim, dormer windows, and steeply pitched or mansard roofs that are decidedly French in inspiration. What we find in New Urbanist developments from Florida to Montreal are ad hoc references to the Savannah Plan—sometimes through direct citations of its architecture or landscape elements, sometimes by creating multiple neighborhood squares or a varied street grid—but no complete attempt to imitate its ward-based plan has yet been undertaken.

The Savannah Plan as a Model for Urbanism Today

Debates about the virtues of the New Urbanism abound, but admiration for the Savannah Plan as a model for urban design is nearly universal. Numerous planners, architects, and historians have recommended it as such, though the lessons they have extracted from it often differ. Stanford Anderson, who brought MIT students to study Savannah in the 1970s, sees the plan as exemplary of an approach to urban planning he calls "possibilism," an alternative to the deterministic or environmentalist models that he saw as prevalent in his day.[25] The possibilism of the Savannah Plan, as Anderson sees it, lies in its adaptability to use and circumstance and its inherent ambiguities or "double readings."[26] In the 1960s Philadelphia planner Edmund Bacon called the Savannah Plan "one of the finest diagrams for city organization and growth in existence."[27] Sibyl Moholy-Nagy touted it for its synthesis of modular and linear planning. Almost two generations later, in 2017, Harvard University architect and planning professor Joan Busquets brought a group of students from Harvard's Graduate School of Design to Savannah as part of a study of urban grids in more than one hundred cities around the world. Savannah, for Busquets, is noteworthy for its systematic "multi-scalar" adaptability.[28] More recently, a discursive book by Hong Kong architect and planner Peter Cookson Smith focuses on Savannah as the center of a conversation about the future of American urbanism.[29]

At this point, it seems fair to ask: If the Savannah Plan is so widely admired and recommended as a model for urban design, why has it not been copied? Three simple reasons for the reluctance to replicate the Savannah Plan can be offered. The first is economic. An obvious impediment for any real estate developer or municipality desirous of imitating the Savannah Plan is cost. The extensive amount of public space in the Savannah Plan—45 percent—is far beyond what most planners can afford to offer in a competitive real estate market. This appears to have been the case in Savannah itself, when the speculative Savannah River Landing project with five public squares succumbed to the economic downturn in 2008 and then was reborn in 2015 as Eastern Wharf, with only two squares. Compounding this expense is the cost of building and maintaining an excessive number of streets, which comprise the greatest percentage of Savannah's public realm. Small block and lot sizes are likewise unattractive to retailers, commercial developers, and hoteliers. The Savannah Plan makes little sense for developers or government officials seeking economic efficiency.

A second drawback is the scale of wards, a feature both admired by some and criticized by others. The Savannah Plan does not fit the model typically espoused by New Urbanists for a traditional neighborhood development. When compared to the paradigmatic TND, the walking radius from the center of each Savannah ward to its edge is too small. The street grid is overly generous in its connectivity. The public squares are too numerous. For many New Urbanists, these excesses are counterproductive to the design of livable neighborhoods.

A third reason is less tangible but more important. While the Savannah Plan might justly be admired as a fine "diagram," it is surely far more than that. The Savannah Plan is a dynamic set of ideas and practices that have been changed and refined over time by many constituencies as they have made it real. It is an ongoing project that cannot be deeply understood or appreciated through a cursory visit or a facile imitation. We believe that the plan has important lessons to teach all who design and build cities throughout the world, now and for ages to come. To merely copy the Savannah Plan is futile. To learn from it is imperative.

SECTION FOUR CONCLUSION

THE LESSONS OF SAVANNAH

Cities also believe they are the work of the mind or of chance, but neither the one nor the other suffices to hold up their walls. You take delight not in the city's seven or seventy wonders, but in the answer it gives to a question of yours.

Or the questions it asks of you, forcing you to answer, like Thebes through the mouth of the Sphinx.

—MARCO POLO, speaking to Kublai Kahn, in Italo Calvino's *Invisible Cities*, 1972

But Savannah is equally intriguing as a model of what urban life can be. Its green downtown squares cover the complete range of urban experience, from bustling commercial hubs to quiet residential oases, to battered victims of development and the automobile. The result is a bracing urban microcosm, surprising, diverse and supremely walkable, that still functions today as it did in Colonial times.

—PETER APPLEBOME, 1990

Savannah's urban plan poses an architectural and urbanistic riddle, one that has not ceased to entice architects and planners who seek to discover its secrets. What makes this brainteaser so enthralling is a belief that in its solution is found the key to a yet more vital endeavor: the quest to build the best city possible. Savannah has the appearance of an ideal city made real. Its urban plan is the key to this achievement.

In *Learning from Savannah*, we have identified principles that are at once specific to this place and universal to the project of building cities on this planet. We summarize our findings, therefore, by listing seven attributes of the Savannah Plan that we believe should be construed as principles worth pondering by all who study cities and buildings, as well as by those who are in the business of building cities. These attributes describe qualities that belong to the seemingly simple orthogonal grid of blocks, streets, and squares of the Savannah Plan. Like the physical features of the plan itself, the principles derived from it are interrelated and codependent. To understand these attributes is to learn the lessons of the Savannah Plan.

1. Elastic

Above all, the Savannah Plan is inherently elastic. Pulled by the opposing forces of the ideal and the real, it is lucid and insistent in its geometric regularity and uniformity even while being flexible and accommodating in its application. Although

Oglethorpe created the plan with the intention of guiding its development in a highly prescriptive manner, it soon evolved through a process of give-and-take, even while retaining its essential integrity for nearly three centuries. Its wards seem identical, but as their number grew from four to twenty-four, their dimensions were squeezed and stretched to fit the constraints imposed by existing conditions. The plan's streets, squares, and blocks have been manipulated and reconfigured, while retaining their essential form and function. The plan's elasticity extends even more profoundly to the arrangement of its building lots as they relate to the streets and squares. Responding to the geometry of the plan, buildings of different types, styles, and scales form a variety of spatial arrangements within a uniformly constituted whole. The dialogue between the architecture of Savannah's buildings and the architecture of its urban plan is likewise symbiotic, enabling the Savannah Plan to serve the needs and aspirations of its citizens while providing a model for other cities to emulate.

2. Collaborative

It seems most likely that the design of the Savannah ward in its original configuration is attributable to one man. James Edward Oglethorpe certainly deserves much of the credit and honor he has received as founder of the colony. He was likely thinking of his own achievement when he wrote in a promotional pamphlet that "the First Honours of the ancient World were paid to the Founders of Citys."[1] Nevertheless, we would like to gently remind Mr. Oglethorpe, and all those who attribute to him authorship of the Savannah Plan by continuing to call the final twenty-four-ward plan "the Oglethorpe Plan," that this is an inaccurate claim. Like all cities, Savannah was and remains a collaborative creation. Oglethorpe, we must remember, was one of seventy Trustees. Their collective plan for Georgia was, moreover, shaped by those who had inspired and enabled them to execute the plan. More important for the development of the Savannah Plan is that it is *not* the plan intended by the Trustees but rather a reimagined adaptation, expansion, and revision of it. City council members and surveyors of the postcolonial period deserve much of the credit for their commitment to continuity through adaptation. Even beyond these designers and decision makers, the actual plan and the architectural, infrastructural, and landscape features that make it a physical reality are the work of an unnumbered host of men and women of numerous professions and from many backgrounds: Native Americans, enslaved and free African Americans, landowners, religious dissenters, and immigrants. Savannah, though conceived by one man (or by a small group of men), is an ongoing, collaborative work. Finding a proper balance between authorship and collective action, between authority and freedom, is difficult. Savannah offers a model for how such a balance can be achieved.

3. Multicentric

For many planners and urban theorists, the multicentric nature of the Savannah Plan is its greatest virtue. Multiple neighborhood units that are relatively small, roughly equal in size and configuration, and equidistant from each other, but with each unit having its own identity and central focus, set Savannah apart from most other urban plans in the world. For nineteenth-century travel writers like Charles Mackay, Savannah appeared to be an assembly of "four-and-twenty villages" in the woods.[2] These "little republics" or "subsidiary communities" form a town plan evocative of the egalitarian principles of the colonial Trustees and yet even more congruent with the founding principles of the American republic. They also constitute a dynamic tension from one square to the next as the attention of the pedestrian is drawn alternately inward and outward, depending on their position in the plan. Social, religious, educational, and political institutions as well as commercial activities are thus dispersed throughout the plan, even as they are woven together into the total fabric of the plan. The multicentric organization of the Savannah Plan thus provides a potent template for all who seek a participatory, noncentralized form of polity.

4. Civic

The *res publica* is everywhere apparent in the Savannah Plan, ensured by the city's lavish allocation of public space. Its multiple public squares assert its civic spirit. Its numerous streets make it accessible to all from multiple directions. Generously wide sidewalks and tree lawns allow for the planting of trees and flowers and ably accommodate outdoor café tables. Private stairs stand self-assuredly in the public right-of-way. Pedestrian pathways tread uninterrupted throughout the plan. Private vehicles park on public streets. Schoolchildren play in public squares; nearby residents gather in those squares for five p.m. cocktails. Private houses adorn and face public garden parks.

The Savannah Plan stands as a rebuke to twentieth-century modernism's promotion of the "object building"—that is, the building that stands by itself, separated from the street grid, announcing its distinctive identity as the work of a creative genius. The restrictive scale of the plan's building lots together with its extensive street frontage oblige every building to make a prominent and appropriate appearance in the public realm. Savannah's architecture is encouraged by the plan to behave decorously, in a manner appropriate to the public realm. There's little room for architecture either to swagger or to hide from public perusal. This too is a lesson for cities striving to attain the common good.

5. Open/Porous

Lewis Mumford described the city in his magisterial book *The City in History* as "a container of containers."[3] This seems to be an apt metaphor for nearly all pre-industrial cities, which by necessity were walled enclaves, gated communities. They were containers that could be opened or closed. Savannah is not a container. Its plan is an unclosed, intertwined network or fabric. Its open weave acts more like a filter than a vessel. The tartan-like pattern of its varied streets creates an urban fabric that promotes free and open movement among people and vehicles. In this way, the Savannah Plan contrasts sharply with the "containment oriented" design of the gated residential communities and commercial pod developments that became characteristic of suburban sprawl. Each Savannah ward is open to the next one; none acts as an autonomous enclave; and none can be cut off from the whole. As Wilson observes, the "connectivity" of the Savannah Plan far exceeds even that promoted by the New Urbanists, both in terms of pathways for movement and in its "visual connectivity"—that is, in the views one gets from one square to the next.[4] The Savannah Plan is highly connected, not only within itself but beyond as well, as some of its streets extend into the suburban regions following paths established by the mile-square grid of the Trustee era, with the plan's block scale, coupling of civic and service streets, and landscape patterns persisting into the mid-twentieth century. These loose threads prevent Savannah from having a clear edge, as some urbanists might want, but they confer on Savannah an unbounded, uncontained, and unexclusive quality, which seems well suited to the openness and connectedness with which we must build cities in the twenty-first century and beyond.

6. Verdant

Conceived in the eighteenth century as an egalitarian, agrarian utopia, Savannah—despite the failure of this foundational dream—has been lauded for its luxuriant vegetation and leafy tree canopy ever since. Its renown is the achievement of numerous caretakers who for nearly three centuries have persistently cultivated Savannah as a garden city. Their achievement is made possible by the city's urban plan of generously wide streets, which functions as trelliswork, enabling *rus* and *urbs* to be woven together in an inimitable pattern. Its deliberate, orderly weave of garden elements into its streets, squares, and blocks differs from the nineteenth-century Romantic landscape garden approaches that placed architecture as an object in a garden that imitated nature in its curvilinear irregularity. The Savannah Plan stands equally in opposition to landscape design practices prevalent in the present day, in which we see the artificial importation of wild, "natural" elements into urban environments (such as recently occurred on Broughton Street). The Savannah Plan is not a city in a garden, nor is it an attempt to rewild the city to an imagined post-Anthropocene nature; it is, rather, an attempt to interweave the city and the garden into a synthetic and harmonious whole.

7. Humanistic

The Savannah Plan is fundamentally a humanistic endeavor. It is the product of a long-standing conversation about how we should live together in community. It is not an abstract diagram or a scientific solution to abstract economic, ecological, or social theories; it is, rather, a real place constructed by, lived in, and visited by real people, whose hopes, dreams, and fears are expressed in the dimensions, scale, materials, and ornamental details of its buildings. The origins of its design, regardless of possible sources identified by ongoing historical debates, are ultimately found in the tradition of the Renaissance humanists, who sought to know the place of human beings in the universe and among one another. The language of its architecture arises from this same tradition, a tradition that traces still further back to remote antiquity. In its squares we hear not only echoes of James Oglethorpe and Governor Wright but also Aristotle debating Plato, Vitruvius arguing with Andrew Jackson Downing, and Charles Mackay conversing with Alexis de Tocqueville, and we feel ourselves entering their conversations. When we walk through a public square along a brick-paved pathway that is shaded by massive live oak trees planted in uniform rows; when automobiles stop to let us pass; when we ascend the curved stairs leading to the Corinthian portico of a trust lot mansion house; or when we visit friends living in a converted carriage house, facing onto a lane lined with utility poles and dumpsters, we find ourselves palpably engaged in a tradition that is in pursuit of the best life possible.

NOTES

Introduction

Epigraphs are from Plato, *Republic*, 9.592a–b, trans. by Paul Shorey, Perseus Digital Library, http://data.perseus.org/citations/urn:cts:greekLit:tlg0059.tlg030.perseus-eng1:9.592a; and Johann Martin Boltzius's journal of 1734, published in part in *Our First Visit in America: Early Reports from the Colony of Georgia, 1732–1740*, introd. Trevor R. Reese (Beehive Press, 1974), 62.

1. This phrase appears in government documents, including a January 2014 Housing Authority of Savannah report, "East Savannah Gateway Transformation Plan," http://savannahpha.com/East%20Savannah%20Gateway%20Tranformation%20Plan%20-%20FINAL_052014update.pdf; in the Wikipedia entry "List of people from Savannah, Georgia" at https://en.wikipedia.org/wiki/List_of_people_from_Savannah,_Georgia; and on the websites of the local tour companies Old Town Trolley Tours (https://www.trolleytours.com/savannah/history) and Gray Line Savannah (https://savannahgrayline.us/savannah/).
2. Thomas D. Wilson, *The Oglethorpe Plan: Enlightenment Design in Savannah and Beyond* (University of Virginia Press, 2012). See also Wilson's more recent work *Charleston and Savannah: The Rise, Fall, and Reinvention of Two Rival Cities* (University of Georgia Press, 2023).
3. Wilson, *Oglethorpe Plan*, 99.
4. Charles Mackay, *Life and Liberty in America: or, Sketches of a Tour in the United States and Canada in 1857–8* (New York, 1859), 209–10.
5. William Caruthers, *The Kentuckian in New-York: or, The Adventures of Three Southerns*, vol. 1 (New York, 1834), 135–36.
6. Italo Calvino, *Hermit in Paris: Autobiographical Writings*, trans. Martin McLaughlin (Random House Digital, 2004), 117.
7. Roger K. Lewis, "Circulating Through the Restored, Palpable Joy of Historic Savannah," *Washington Post*, April 19, 1997, E3–E5.
8. Ed Rabey and Beverly Beyer, "Savannah's the City Sherman Thought Too Pretty to Burn," Travel, *Toronto Star*, February 22, 1986, Saturday First Edition, G22.
9. Edmund N. Bacon, *Design of Cities*, rev. ed. (Penguin Books, 1974), 219.
10. A. E. J. Morris, *History of Urban Form: Prehistory to the Renaissance* (George Godwin, 1972), 228.
11. See chapter 2, pp. 28–29.
12. Edward Erfurt, "Lessons on Development Patterns from America's Oldest Planned City," Strong Towns, March 8, 2024, https://www.strongtowns.org/journal/2024/3/8/lessons-on-development-patterns-from-americas-oldest-planned-city.
13. Bernard-Henri Lévy, "In the Footsteps of Tocqueville (Part IV): From the Storm Systems of Florida to Those of Washington, D.C.," trans. Charlotte Mandell, *Atlantic Monthly*, October 2005, 97.
14. See Nathaniel Robert Walker, "Savannah's Lost Squares: Progress Versus Beauty in the Depression-Era South," *Journal of the Society of Architectural Historians* 70, no. 4 (December 2011): 512–31.
15. Other streets with medians beyond the downtown historic district include 37th Street (in the Victorian District); Abercorn Street, Victory Drive, Washington Avenue, and Chatham Crescent (in Ardsley Park–Chatham Crescent); Columbus Drive (in Ardmore); Bull Street and Montgomery Street (in Sylvan Terrace); and White Bluff Road south of DeRenne Avenue.

Section 1. Being and Becoming Savannah

The first epigraph has numerous variations attributed in English criticism to writers such as W. H. Auden and E. M. Forster. Its origins are thought to derive from Leonardo da Vinci, but its modern formulation is generally credited to Paul Valéry, "Au sujet du Cimetière marin," *La Nouvelle Revue Française* (March 1933), 399. The second epigraph is quoted in George R. Collins, *Antonio Gaudí* (G. Braziller, 1960), 14.

Chapter 1. Conceiving and Implementing the Plan, 1732–1752

The first epigraph is from Benjamin Martyn, *Reasons for Establishing the Colony of Georgia* (London, 1733), 38–39. The second epigraph is from James Edward Oglethorpe, *Some Account of the Design of the Trustees for Establishing Colonys in America*, ed. Rodney M. Baine and Phinizy Spalding (University of Georgia Press, 1990), 36; this tract was published from a manuscript attributed to Oglethorpe and dated to 1731 or 1732 by Baine and Spalding.

1. A sweeping and dispassionate review of the scholarly literature on the Georgia colony appears in Julie Anne Sweet, "The Thirteenth Colony in Perspective: Historians' Views on Early Georgia," *Georgia Historical Quarterly* 85, no. 3 (2001): 435–60. Sweet has more recently published numerous articles on a variety of topics related to colonial Georgia, including a summary of the literature on Oglethorpe, "'These Difficulties . . . rather animate than daunt me': James Oglethorpe as a Leader," *Georgia Historical Quarterly* 99, no. 3 (2015): 131–55. Two more recent books of note are Noeleen McIlvenna, *The Short Life of Free Georgia: Class and Slavery in the Colonial South* (University of North Carolina Press, 2015); and Paul M. Pressly, *On the Rim of the Caribbean: Colonial Georgia and the British Atlantic World* (University of Georgia Press, 2013).
2. For a summary of primary sources, see Julie Anne Sweet, "'The natural Advantages of this happy Climate': An Analysis of Georgia's Promotional Literature," *Georgia Historical Quarterly* 98, no. 1/2 (2014): 1–25; and Harold E. Davis's bibliographic essay in *The Fledgling Province: Social and Cultural Life in Colonial Georgia, 1733–1776* (University of North Carolina Press, 1976), 259–76.
3. Albert Saye, ed., *Georgia's Charter of 1732* (University of Georgia Press, 1942).
4. Saye, *Georgia's Charter*, 10.
5. See Verner W. Crane, "Dr. Thomas Bray and the Charitable Colony Project, 1730," *William and Mary Quarterly* 19, no. 1 (January 1962): 49–63; and Albert B. Saye, "The Genesis of Georgia Reviewed," *Georgia Historical Quarterly* 50, no. 2 (1966): 153–61.
6. Martyn, *Reasons for Establishing*, 31.
7. See Julie Anne Sweet, "'The Excellency and Advantage of doing Good': Thoughts on the Anniversary Sermons Preached Before the Trustees of Georgia, 1731–1750," *Georgia Historical Quarterly* 90, no. 1 (2006): 1–34. On the promotion of international Protestantism, see Sugiko Nishikawa, "The SPCK in Defence of Protestant Minorities in Early Eighteenth-Century Europe," *Journal of Ecclesiastical History* 56, no. 4 (2005): 730–48; Katherine Carté Engel, "Connecting Protestants in Britain's Eighteenth-Century Atlantic Empire," *William and Mary Quarterly* 75, no. 1 (2018): 37–70; and Engel, "The SPCK and the American Revolution: The Limits of International Protestantism," *Church History* 81, no. 1 (2012): 77–103.
8. Martyn, *Reasons for Establishing*, 38.
9. Philip Bearcroft, *A Sermon Preached Before the Honorable Trustees for Establishing the Colony of Georgia in America, and the Associates of the Late Reverend Dr. Bray; at Their Anniversary Meeting March 16, 1737–8, in the Parish-Church of St. Bridget, Alias St. Bride, in Fleet-Street London* (London, 1738), quoted in Sylvia Doughty Fries, *The Urban Idea in Colonial America* (Temple University Press, 1977), 143.
10. On the Trustees' land policy, see Mart A. Stewart, *"What Nature Suffers to Groe": Life, Labor, and Landscape on the Georgia Coast, 1680–1920* (University of Georgia Press, 2002), 31–33.
11. Oglethorpe to the Trustees, November 2, 1739, in *The Colonial Records of the State of Georgia* (hereinafter cited as CRG), comp. and ed. Allen Daniel Candler et al. (Franklin Printing and Publishing, 1904–16), vol. 22, pt. 2:173.
12. On the political theory behind the Georgia colony, see Stewart, *"What Nature Suffers,"* 31–33; Fries, *Urban Idea*, 137–39; and Thomas D. Wilson, *The Oglethorpe Plan: Enlightenment Design in Savannah and Beyond* (University of Virginia Press, 2012), 20ff. On the neo-Harringtonians, see J. G. A. Pocock, "Machiavelli,

Harrington and English Political Ideologies in the Eighteenth Century," *William and Mary Quarterly* 22, no. 4 (October 1965): 569ff.

13. On rum restrictions, see Julie Anne Sweet, "'That Cursed Evil Rum': The Trustees' Prohibition Policy in Colonial Georgia," *Georgia Historical Quarterly* 94, no. 1 (2010): 1–29. On the institution of slavery in Trustee Georgia, see Betty Wood, *Slavery in Colonial Georgia, 1730–1775* (University of Georgia Press, 2007); Robert Scott Davis, "Wheels Within Wheels: Slavery and the Framework of the Social History of Eighteenth Century Georgia," *Journal of Backcountry Studies* 5, no. 1 (2010): 1–14, http://libjournal.uncg.edu/jbc/article/view/13/3; McIlvenna, *Short Life of Free Georgia*; and Andrew C. Lannen, "Liberty and Slavery in Colonial America: The Case of Georgia, 1732–1770," *Historian* 79, no. 1 (Spring 2017): 32–55.
14. *A New and Accurate Account of the Provinces of South-Carolina and Georgia* (London, 1732), 35ff.
15. See William L. Ramsey, *The Yamasee War: A Study of Culture, Economy, and Conflict in the Colonial South* (University of Nebraska Press, 2008), 219ff.
16. Cecil Headlam and Arthur Percival Newton, eds., *Calendar of State Papers, Colonial Series . . . Preserved in the Public Record Office*, vol. 37, *America and West Indies, 1730* (HMSO, 1937), 139ff (available online: http://www.archive.org/stream/calendarofstatep1730grea#page/139/mode/1up). On Johnson's township policy, see John W. Reps, "$C^2 + L^2 = S^2$? Another Look at the Origins of Savannah's Town Plan," in *Forty Years of Diversity: Essays on Colonial Georgia*, ed. Harvey H. Jackson and Phinizy Spalding (University of Georgia Press, 1984), 116. For a map and list of these towns, see http://www.carolana.com/SC/Royal_Colony/sc_royal_colony_townships_established.html (accessed July 1, 2011).
17. Arlin C. Migliazzo interprets this program as an attempt to "surround the plantation belt with an underdeveloped band of white settlements free of slavery. Intentionally small land grants in outlying (and less fertile) areas and officially sanctioned bounties on key commodities militated against the expansion of the plantation system and the institution of chattel slavery. Because poor Protestant immigrants would be freed from the religious persecution and economic privation of their European homelands, the provincial aristocracy reasoned that they would be compliant partners in this complex plan." See Migliazzo, *To Make This Land Our Own: Community, Identity, and Cultural Adaptation in Purrysburg Township, South Carolina, 1732–1865* (University of South Carolina Press, 2007), 43.
18. On the Trustees' Garden, see Julie Anne Sweet, "A Misguided Mistake: The Trustees' Public Garden in Savannah, Georgia," *Georgia Historical Quarterly* 93, no. 1 (2009): 1–29; and Zachary Dorner, "From Chelsea to Savannah: Medicines and Mercantilism in the Atlantic World," *Journal of British Studies* 58, no. 1 (2019): 28–57.
19. See Sweet, "Thirteenth Colony in Perspective," 436–37; and McIlvenna, *Short Life of Free Georgia*, 114–16.
20. "Tail male" meant that a freeholder could not sell his property, but upon his death it would be inherited by his eldest son. See Andrew C. Lannen, "Liberty and Authority in Colonial Georgia, 1717–1776" (PhD diss., Louisiana State University, 2002), 56. See also Phinizy Spalding, *Oglethorpe in America* (University of Chicago Press, 1977), 66. This was a feudal practice, but it was intended by the Trustees as a means of maintaining small, family-based landownership and preventing real estate speculation.
21. The text of Vitruvius quoted in Oglethorpe's pamphlet comes from Robert Castell's unpublished translation of Vitruvius's treatise. See Baine and Spalding's note in Oglethorpe, *Some Account*, 60n39.
22. Though most scholars have presumed Oglethorpe's authorship, Stanford Anderson argues that the plan must have been devised and likely drawn before Oglethorpe left England. As Anderson suggests, it seems improbable that no other Trustee contributed to the conceiving of its design. See his "Savannah and the Issue of Precedent: City Plan as Resource," in *Settlements in the Americas: Cross-Cultural Perspectives*, ed. Ralph Bennett (University of Delaware Press and Associated University Presses, 1993), 136–37.
23. "Journal of Peter Gordon," in *Our First Visit in America: Early Reports from the Colony of Georgia, 1732–1740*, introd. Trevor R. Reese (Beehive Press, 1974), 14.

24. Letter dated February 10, 1733, in CRG, 20:10. In his journal covering the early British settlement of the Georgia colony, Peter Gordon explained how Oglethorpe appointed four tythingmen "for the better regulation of our people" while on board the *Anne* and how those men continued to serve as armed guards in the months that followed; see E. Merton Coulter, ed., *The Journal of Peter Gordon, 1732–1735* (University of Georgia Press, 1963), 30–38.
25. See Thomas Gamble, "Col. William Bull—His Part in the Founding of Savannah," *Georgia Historical Quarterly* 17, no. 2 (1933): 111–26.
26. Henry Herbert (Savannah's first minister) in *The South-Carolina Gazette*, as quoted in Edward Chan Sieg, *The Squares: An Introduction to Savannah* (Donning, 1984), 27. According to Joan Niles Sears, "It seems likely that Col. William Bull, an experienced surveyor, chose the site of Savannah"; see Sears, *The First One Hundred Years of Town Planning in Georgia* (Cherokee, 1979), 35.
27. Oglethorpe to the Trustees, February 10, 1732–33, in CRG, 20:9–10. Quoted in Kenneth Coleman, "The Founding of Georgia," in Jackson and Spalding, *Forty Years of Diversity*, 13.
28. "Journal of Peter Gordon," in Reese, *Our First Visit*, 18.
29. Rodney M. Baine and Louis De Vorsey Jr. have shown that the engraving was based on a watercolor sketch by London artist George Jones from a since-lost plan; the sketch by Jones is now in the Hargrett Rare Book and Manuscript Library at the University of Georgia. See "The Provenance and Historical Accuracy of 'A View of Savannah as It Stood the 29th of March, 1734,'" *Georgia Historical Quarterly* 73, no. 4 (1989): 784–813.
30. Francis Moore, *A Voyage to Georgia: Begun in the Year 1735* (London, 1744), 29.
31. The original map has been lost, but numerous copies have been made, with three distinct variants of the map residing in several repositories. Based on the shape of the Common and garden lots and the accompanying list of names of lot holders, the version shown in figure 12 can be dated to ca. 1760–62. The actual document at the Hargrett Library at the University of Georgia (UGA Map 1777 S3 Neg 5187) is inexplicably dated 1777. It is signed by John McKinnon and dated 1798 as a true copy of an earlier plan by Thomas McCall. On the right, written with a typewriter, is a note that it is a tracing made in 1908. This is nearly identical to a map reproduced in facsimile for J. F. Minis, Esq., for private circulation at Stanford's Geographical Establishment, London, 1904 (UGA 1904 M2 Neg 205, McKinnon 1800 / Minis facsimile 1904).
32. The precise configuration of the garden lots as they were intended to be laid out is unclear from the available documents. Wilson assumes that each garden square is a furlong (660 feet, or 10 chains), which yields 5 acres exactly when bisected; see *Oglethorpe Plan*, 91ff. A seven-by-seven grid of such squares leaves a remainder of another 660 acres, which Wilson assumes was devoted to rights-of-way. In reality, the "5 acre" lots are not uniform. Dimensions written on the 1798 McKinnon manuscript plan (City of Savannah Municipal Archives, XA-37) yield dimensions of 693 feet, or 10.5 chains, for many but not all of the garden squares. A plat map prepared by John McKinnon in 1805 for the estate of Fair Lawn (Hargrett hmap1805m2), for example, shows several garden lots labeled with areas ranging between 5 and 6.5 acres.
33. See Farris W. Cadle, *Georgia Land Surveying History and Law* (University of Georgia Press, 1991), 12.
34. Oglethorpe settled twelve families, most of them French, in Highgate in the summer of 1733 and twelve German families in Hampstead. The subsequently founded village of Thunderbolt interrupts the grid, extending beyond it to the east with a radial fan plan. Joseph's Town, built by Lowland Scots to the northwest on the Savannah River, appears as a four-mile square, with a smaller, quadrated square. See Moore, *Voyage to Georgia*, 103. The village of Abercorn, further to the northwest, is about a mile square and has a radial fan plan. Of these villages, only Thunderbolt remains today.
35. Letter from Joseph Avery to the Trustees, in CRG, 23:411–12. See also Cadle, *Georgia Land Surveying*, 25.
36. This map is comparable to and may have the same source as a regional map engraved by Richard William Seale and published in Benjamin Martyn, *An Account*

Showing the Progress of the Colony of Georgia . . . from Its First Establishment (London, 1741).

37. See Cadle, *Georgia Land Surveying*, 13.
38. *South-Carolina Gazette*, n. 84, August 25, 1733, quoted in John W. Reps, *The Making of Urban America: A History of City Planning in the United States* (Princeton University Press, 1965), 186.
39. *Minutes of the Common Council*, Saturday, January 19, 1734. Each freeholder, lot, and deed is specified. See Charles Colcock Jones Jr., *The History of Georgia*, vol. 1, *Aboriginal and Colonial Epochs* (Boston, 1883), 155ff.
40. "Rules of the Year 1735," in *The General Account of All Monies and Effects Received and Expended by the Trustees for Establishing the Colony of Georgia in America*, in CRG, 3:409–10.
41. John Reps, for example, notes that "some of the Georgia Trustees were active participants in the development of these squares. Sir William Heathcote built what is now Chatham House in St. James's Square in 1734"; see *Making of Urban America*, 199. See also Reps's later discussion in "$C^2 + L^2 = S^2$?"
42. Turpin C. Bannister, "Oglethorpe's Sources for the Savannah Plan," *Journal of the Society of Architectural Historians* 20, no. 2 (May 1961): 55–56; and Anderson, "Savannah and the Issue," 127. On the 1666 rebuilding plans, see Lydia M. Soo, "A Baroque City? London After the Great Fire of 1666," in *Giambattista Nolli and Rome: Mapping the City Before and After the "Pianta Grande"*, ed. Ian Verstegen and Allan Ceen (Rome: Studium Urbis, 2013), 161ff, and Michael Cooper, *'A More Beautiful City': Robert Hooke and the Rebuilding of London After the Great Fire* (Sutton, 2003), 104. On the eighteenth-century reception of 1666 plans, see Nicholas Hudson, "Samuel Johnson, Urban Culture, and the Geography of Postfire London," *Studies in English Literature, 1500–1900*, 42, no. 3 (2002): 577–600; and Cynthia Wall, *The Literary and Cultural Spaces of Restoration London* (Cambridge University Press, 1998).
43. Two versions of this plan were published by different printers in Amsterdam in 1666. Lydia Soo has suggested that the plan has a Dutch origin, coming perhaps from the circle of Simon Stevin. See Soo's forthcoming book *Maps and Master Planning in Early Modern London: Recording and Re-envisioning the City Before and After the Great Fire.*
44. Anderson discusses Newcourt's plans in "Savannah and the Issue," 126–28. All three maps are in the London Municipal Archives. See Emily Mann, "In Defence of the City: The Gates of London and Temple Bar in the Seventeenth Century," *Architectural History* 49 (2006): 97n46.
45. The oblong rectangular parishes measured 575 feet by 855 feet, slightly larger in area than Savannah's wards.
46. Lydia Soo has kindly shared her research on Newcourt with the authors. See her forthcoming book, cited in note 43.
47. Reps, "$C^2 + L^2 = S^2$?," 111ff. His unpublished theory about Turin has been mentioned by several authors, including Wilson; see *Oglethorpe Plan*, 75.
48. Laura Palmer Bell, "A New Theory on the Plan of Savannah," *Georgia Historical Quarterly* 48, no. 2 (1964): 147–65.
49. Mark Reinberger, "Oglethorpe's Plan of Savannah: Urban Design, Speculative Freemasonry, and Enlightenment Charity," *Georgia Historical Quarterly* 81, no. 4 (1997): 839–62.
50. Anderson, "Savannah and the Issue," 134–37. See further discussion in chapter 8.
51. Bannister, "Oglethorpe's Sources," 60–61.
52. Nathaniel Robert Walker, "To Gather in War and Peace: The City Squares of Savannah, Georgia," in *Ordnance: War + Architecture & Space*, ed. Gary A. Boyd and Denis Linehan (Ashgate, 2013), 17–19.
53. Edmund N. Bacon, *Design of Cities*, rev. ed. (Penguin Books, 1974), 216–21. Though Bacon offers no evidence for Oglethorpe's use of this source, Malcolm Bell III made a compelling case for Oglethorpe's knowledge of and admiration for Cataneo's ideal plans in a public lecture entitled "European Sources of the Oglethorpe Plan" that he gave at the Savannah Symposium on the City Square on February 26, 1999.
54. A vast literature on both of these themes exists. On the American grid, see especially John R. Stilgoe, *Common Landscape of America, 1580–1845* (Yale University Press, 1982), 99–107. On the agrarian ideals, see James L. Machor, *Pastoral Cities: Urban Ideals*

and the Symbolic Landscape of America (University of Wisconsin Press, 1987).

55. Stilgoe, *Common Landscape*, 99–107.
56. See Morton and Lucia White's classic exposition of American anti-urbanism, *The Intellectual Versus the City* (Harvard University Press, 1962).
57. William Bradford, quoted in Fries, *Urban Idea*, 39.
58. "To James Madison from Thomas Jefferson, 20 December 1787" (letter), *Founders Online*, National Archives, https://founders.archives.gov/documents/Madison/01-10-02-0210. Original source: *The Papers of James Madison*, vol. 10, *27 May 1787–3 March 1788*, ed. Robert A. Rutland, Charles F. Hobson, William M. E. Rachal, and Frederika J. Teute (University of Chicago Press, 1977), 335–39.
59. On New Haven, see John Archer, "Puritan Town Planning in New Haven," *Journal of the Society of Architectural Historians* 34, no. 2 (May 1975): 140–49; John Warner Barber and Lemuel Swift Punderson, *History and Antiquities of New Haven, Conn., from Its Earliest Settlement to the Present Time* (New Haven, 1856), 65–88; and Elizabeth Mills Brown, *New Haven: A Guide to Architecture and Urban Design* (Yale University Press, 1976), 11–13.
60. See Archer, "Puritan Town Planning," 140–49; Anthony N. B. Garvan, *Architecture and Town Planning in Colonial Connecticut* (Yale University Press, 1951), 44–49; and Fries, *Urban Idea*, 65–67.
61. Fries, *Urban Idea*, 66–67.
62. On the subdivision of the nine-square plan, see Maureen E. Boyle, "The Failure of America's First City Plan: Why New Haven, the Colonies' First Planned City, Would Have Been Better Left Unplanned" (research thesis, Yale Law School, May 5, 2010), https://openyls.law.yale.edu/handle/20.500.13051/5574.
63. Martyn, *Reasons for Establishing*, 28.
64. These remarks come from a document entitled "Certaine Conditions or Concessions agreed upon by William Penn . . . & those who are the adventur[ers] and purchasers in the same Province," dated July 11, 1681, and also appear in "Instructions given by me William Penn Proprietor and Governor of Pennsylvania," September 30, 1681; both documents are found in *The Papers of William Penn*, ed. Richard S. Dunn and Mary Maples Dunn, vol. 2, *1680–1684* (University of Pennsylvania Press, 1982), 98–102, 118–21. Although they refer to a much more rural plan than is depicted in Holme's plan of 1683, they certainly suggest concerns that were important to Penn.
65. See Elizabeth Milroy, "'For the like Uses, as the Moore-fields': The Politics of Penn's Squares," *Pennsylvania Magazine of History and Biography* 130, no. 3 (July 2006): 257–82. On Holme's Philadelphia plan, see also Hannah Benner Roach, "The Planting of Philadelphia: A Seventeenth-Century Real Estate Development," pt. 1, *Pennsylvania Magazine of History and Biography* 92, no. 1 (1968): 3–47; Gary B. Nash, "City Planning and Political Tension in the Seventeenth Century: The Case of Philadelphia," *Proceedings of the American Philosophical Society* 112, no. 1 (1968): 61; Reps, *Making of Urban America*, 163; Perry L. Norton, "William Penn Plans His City," *Pennsylvania Heritage* 11, no. 2 (Spring 1985): 30; and Anthony N. B. Garvan, "Proprietary Philadelphia as Artifact," in *The Historian and the City*, ed. Oscar Handlin and John Burchard (MIT Press, 1963), 189–90.
66. Letter accompanying *A Portraiture of the City of Philadelphia in the Province of Pennsylvania in America* (map), in William Penn, *A Letter from William Penn Proprietary and Governour of Pennsylvania in America, to the Committee of the Free Society of Traders of That Province, Residing in London* (London, 1683).
67. This early introduction of landscape parks is discussed in Milroy, "'For the like Uses,'" 257–82.
68. Elizabeth Milroy, *The Grid and the River: Philadelphia's Green Places, 1682–1876* (Penn State University Press, 2016), 156–57.
69. See Frederic R. Stevenson, "Charleston and Savannah," *Journal of the Society of Architectural Historians* 10, no. 4 (December 1951): 3–9.
70. Thomas D. Wilson, *Charleston and Savannah: The Rise, Fall, and Reinvention of Two Rival Cities* (University of Georgia Press, 2023), 124.
71. Henry A. M. Smith, "Charleston: The Original Plan and the Earliest Settlers," *South Carolina Historical and Genealogical Magazine* 9, no. 1 (January 1908): 15.
72. See Smith, "Charleston: The Original Plan," 14–15.
73. See Henry A. M. Smith, "Beaufort: The Original Plan

and the Earliest Settlers," *South Carolina Historical and Genealogical Magazine* 9, no. 3 (July 1908): 150ff. The curious label "Castle" could be a reference to Beaufort Castle, the family home of Henry Somerset, Lord Beaufort, which is where the Lords Proprietors met in 1711 when they established the town of Beaufort.

74. On Purrysburg, see Migliazzo, *To Make This Land*; Lawrence Sanders Rowland, Alexander Moore, and George C. Rogers Jr., *The History of Beaufort County, South Carolina*, vol. 1, *1514–1861* (University of South Carolina Press, 1996), 118–27; Arlin C. Migliazzo, "A Tarnished Legacy Revisited: Jean Pierre Purry and the Settlement of the Southern Frontier, 1718–1736," *South Carolina Historical Magazine* 92, no. 4 (October 1991): 232–52; and Dan Elliott, "Huguenot Archaeology in South Carolina," *Mister Soapstone: Archaeology in the Post-Modern World* (blog), n.d., http://danelliott.wordpress.com/huguenot-archaeology-in-south-carolina/.
75. Jean Pierre Purry, *Memorial Presented to His Grace, My Lord the Duke of Newcastle . . . : Upon the Present Condition of Carolina, and the Means of Its Amelioration*, ed. Charles C. Jones (Augusta, Ga., 1880); reprinted in *The Most Delightful Country of the Universe: Promotional Literature of the Colony of Georgia, 1717–1734* (Beehive Press, 1972), 54–65.
76. In this he was preceded by Thomas Coram, a Georgia Trustee who had proposed the establishment of a colony called "Georgia" as early as 1717, although Coram's colony would have been in present-day Maine. See H. B. Fant, "Picturesque Thomas Coram, Projector of Two Georgias and Father of the London Foundling Hospital," *Georgia Historical Quarterly* 32, no. 2 (1948): 77–104.
77. Oglethorpe purchased three thousand of the twelve thousand acres of the venture for fifty pounds sterling; see Migliazzo, *To Make This Land*, 38.
78. Migliazzo, *To Make This Land*, 293.
79. See Migliazzo, *To Make This Land*, 61, and unnumbered illustration, "Plat Map of 'Purysburgh-Town' ca. 1765." Migliazzo notes than an earlier (though undated) map in the South Carolina Department of Archives and History is more "idealized."
80. On Montgomery, see Anthony W. Parker, *Scottish Highlanders in Colonial Georgia: The Recruitment, Emigration, and Settlement at Darien, 1735–1748* (University of Georgia Press, 2002), 16.
81. Sir Robert Montgomery, *A Discourse Concerning the Design'd Establishment of a New Colony to the South of Carolina, in the Most Delightful Country of the Universe* (London, 1717), 10, 11.
82. On the 1788 plan of Toronto, see J. David Wood, "Grand Designs on the Fringes of Empire: New Towns for British North America," *Canadian Geographer* 26, no. 3 (1982): 243–55.
83. John Perceval, *The Journal of the Earl of Egmont: Abstract of the Trustees Proceedings for Establishing the Colony of Georgia, 1732–1738*, ed. Robert G. McPherson (University of Georgia Press, 1962). According to Edward J. Cashin, "Jones did not complete his surveying of Augusta until July, 1737. At that time the ground was cleared for the fort and the town lots were laid off"; see Cashin, *The Story of Augusta* (Richmond County Board of Education, 1980), 10.
84. See Thomas Heard Robertson Jr., "The Colonial Plan of Augusta," *Georgia Historical Quarterly* 86, no. 4 (2002): 511–43.
85. The town was authorized on September 26, 1735, by order of the Common Council of the Trustees; see CRG, 1:231.
86. See Cadle, *Georgia Land Surveying*, 20.
87. See Reps, *Making of Urban America*, 192–95. The map is a manuscript resurvey signed by Joshua Miller and now in the Georgia Surveyor General Department, Georgia Division of Archives and History.
88. On Darien, see Bessie Lewis, *They Called Their Town Darien: Being a Short History of Darien and McIntosh County, Georgia* (Lower Altamaha Historical Society, 2002); Sears, *First One Hundred Years*, 41–43; and Parker, *Scottish Highlanders*.
89. See Sears, *First One Hundred Years*, 40, 189; Reps, *Making of Urban America*, 193; and Lewis, *They Called Their Town Darien*, 12.
90. "Rules of the Year 1735," in *General Account of All Monies*.
91. *Proceeding and Minutes of the Governor and Council*, June 2, 1767, in CRG, 10:215.

92. Buddy Sullivan, "Lachlan McIntosh," in *New Georgia Encyclopedia*, last modified February 21, 2018, https://www.georgiaencyclopedia.org/articles/history-archaeology/lachlan-mcintosh-1727-1806/.
93. On Ebenezer, see Philip A. Strobel, *The Salzburgers and Their Descendants: Being the History of a Colony of German (Lutheran) Protestants, Who Emigrated to Georgia in 1734, and Settled at Ebenezer, Twenty-Five Miles Above the City of Savannah* (Baltimore, 1855); and Charles Colcock Jones Jr., *The Dead Towns of Georgia* (Savannah, 1878), 11–44.
94. Strobel, *Salzburgers and Their Descendants*, 91–92.
95. John Wesley describes New Ebenezer in his journal: "The Huts, 60 in number, are neatly and regularly built; the little Piece of Ground allotted to each for a Garden, is everywhere put to the best Use, no spot being left unplanted. Nay, even one of the main Streets, being one more than was as yet wanted, bore them this year a crop of Indian Corn." Quoted in Jones, *Dead Towns of Georgia*, 22. The change in the layout of the farm lots is attributable to the work of surveyor Hugh Ross, who laid them out in a row of strips "measuring 6.60 by 75 chains." See Cadle, *Georgia Land Surveying*, 20–21.
96. See Daniel T. Elliott, *The Lost City Survey: Archaeological Reconnaissance of Nine Nineteenth Century Settlements in Chatham and Effingham Counties, Georgia* (LAMAR Institute, 1990), https://www.thelamarinstitute.org/images/PDFs/publication_19.pdf.

Chapter 2. Expanding and Adjusting the Plan, 1752–Present

The first epigraph is from *Minutes of Council*, City of Savannah Municipal Archives. The second epigraph is from *The Savannah Daily Republican*, February 10, 1851, p. 2.

1. Derby Ward was also the first to be settled; see Stanford Anderson, "The Plan of Savannah and Changes of Occupancy During Its Early Years: City Plan as Resource," *Harvard Architecture Review* 2 (Spring 1981): 64.
2. Francis Moore describes six wards in that year; see Moore, *A Voyage to Georgia: Begun in the Year 1735* (London, 1744), 29.
3. On Hardwick (Georgetown), see Charles Colcock Jones Jr., *The Dead Towns of Georgia* (Savannah, 1878), 224–32; and John W. Reps, *The Making of Urban America: A History of City Planning in the United States* (Princeton University Press, 1965), 195.
4. *Meeting of the President and Assistants in Council*, May 13, 1754, in CRG, 6:435–36.
5. *Proceedings and Minutes of the Governor and Council*, February 11, 1755, in CRG, 7:107–8.
6. *Proceedings and Minutes of the Governor and Council*, March 4, 1755, in CRG, 7:131–32.
7. *Journal of the Upper House of Assembly*, December 11, 1756, in CRG, 16:124.
8. See Farris W. Cadle, *Georgia Land Surveying History and Law* (University of Georgia Press, 1991), 40–41.
9. Charles Colcock Jones Jr., *History of Savannah, Ga.: From Its Settlement to the Close of the Eighteenthh Century* (Syracuse, N.Y., 1890), 171.
10. *Journal of the Commons House of Assembly*, November 11, 1760, in CRG, 13:443; *Report of the General Survey in the Southern Districts of North America*, now at Harvard University (MS Am 824. Houghton Library), dated "after 1771." The Georgia portion of this report was published as John William Gerard de Brahm and George Wymberley Jones De Renne, *History of the Province of Georgia: With Maps of Original Surveys* (Savannah, 1849); and more recently as *De Brahm's Report of the General Survey in the Southern District of North America*, ed. Louis De Vorsey Jr. (University of South Carolina Press, 1971).
11. *Statutes Enacted by the Royal Legislature of Georgia from Its First Session in 1754 to 1768*, in CRG, 18:455–60.
12. CRG, 13:563–64.
13. The garden lots were deeded to the city Common by Governor Wright in exchange for fifteen acres that were formerly part of the Trustees' Garden and had become part of the East Common but then became his property. See "An Act to Enable the Commissioners Appointed by the General Assembly of This Province, Entitled 'An Act for Regulating the Town of Savannah, and for Ascertaining the Common Thereunto Belonging' to Alien and Convey a Certain Portion of the Said Common in Exchange for Other

Land to the Said Common Adjoining,' March 4, 1762, *Statutes Enacted by the Royal Legislature of Georgia from Its First Session in 1754 to 1768*, in CRG, 18:526–28. On the evolution of the Common, see David W. Gobel, "Planned Obsolescence? The Role of the Town Common in the Making of Savannah's Urban Plan," *Journal of Planning History* 22, no. 2 (2022): 141–76, https://doi.org/10.1177/15385132211073471.

14. This plan corresponds to an act of the colonial council approved by Governor Wright on May 10, 1770, entitled "An Act for Further Amending an Act, Intitled 'An Act for the Better Regulating the Town of Savannah, and for Ascertaining the Common Thereunto Belonging,'" in CRG, vol. 19, pt. 1:202–4. Farris Cadle states that Shruder became surveyor in 1769; see *Georgia Land Surveying*, 51, citing *The Georgia Gazette* (Savannah), March 8, 1769, p. 2, col. 2.
15. This question is explored in greater detail in Gobel, "Planned Obsolescence?," 141–76.
16. James Edward Oglethorpe, *Some Account of the Design of the Trustees for Establishing Colonys in America*, ed. Rodney M. Baine and Phinizy Spalding (University of Georgia Press, 1990), 37.
17. Spanish colonial town planning is explicit about the intentional dual purpose of common lands. Law 129 of the Laws of the Indies states that "within the town, a commons shall be delimited, large enough that although the population may experience a rapid expansion, there will always be sufficient space where the people may go to for recreation and take their cattle to pasture without them making any damage." Translation from Dora P. Crouch, Daniel J. Garr, and Axel I. Mundigo, *Spanish City Planning in North America* (MIT Press, 1982), 16.
18. See Barratt Wilkins, "A View of Savannah on the Eve of the Revolution," *Georgia Historical Quarterly* 54, no. 4 (1970): 577–84.
19. Gobel, "Planned Obsolescence?," 163–64.
20. See Rita Folse Elliott and Daniel T. Elliott, "Savannah Under Fire, 1779: Expanding the Boundaries" (Coastal Heritage Society, April 2011).
21. "An Act for Better Regulating the Town of Savannah and the Hamlets Thereof," February 21, 1785, in CRG, vol. 19, pt. 2:419–33.
22. *Minutes of Council*, May 18, 1790, 26. City of Savannah Municipal Archives.
23. "An Act for the Better Regulating the Town of Savannah, and for Ascertaining the Common Thereunto Belonging," May 1, 1760, *Statutes Enacted by the Royal Legislature of Georgia from Its First Session in 1754 to 1768*, in CRG, 18:455–60.
24. *Minutes of Council, June 1791–December 1796*, 65. City of Savannah Municipal Archives.
25. On Houstoun, see Walter Charlton Hartridge, ed., *The Letters of Robert Mackay to His Wife: Written from Ports in America and England, 1795–1816* (University of Georgia Press, 2010), 295n161.
26. Canal Street in New Orleans dates to 1807 and at 171 feet would have been the widest street in the nation at the time.
27. On the original Jewish cemetery, see Marion Abrahams Levy, "Savannah's Old Jewish Burial Ground," *Georgia Historical Quarterly* 34, no. 4 (1950): 265–70; and B. H. Levy, "Savannah's Old Jewish Community Cemeteries," *Georgia Historical Quarterly* 66, no. 1 (1982): 1–20. M. A. Levy cites a petition to the Commons House in March 1770, which refers to the original grant made by Oglethorpe; cf. CRG, 15:145–46.
28. *Journal of the Upper House of Assembly*, April 7, 1770, in CRG, 17:573; quoted in B. H. Levy, "Savannah's Old Jewish Community Cemeteries," 4.
29. The Mordecai Sheftall Cemetery and the nearby Levi Sheftall Family Cemetery stand today near the intersection of Cohen and Coyle Streets.
30. Adelaide Wilson, *Historic and Picturesque Savannah* (Boston, 1889), 89.
31. *Minutes of the Common Council of the Trustees*, November 8, 1732, in CRG, 20:10.
32. Lots 2 and 3 of Holland Tything. A historical marker notes the spot today. On the origins of Colonial Park Cemetery, see Michael Trinkley and Debi Hacker, "Identification and Mapping of Historic Graves at Colonial Cemetery, Savannah, Georgia," Research Series 54 (Chicora Foundation, 1999), 13ff.
33. In 1762, in response to a report finding the cemetery with "little Vacancy left for future interments," the Georgia House of Commons resolved to extend the cemetery to Abercorn Street to the west and about

one hundred feet to the south, "bounding on the five Acre Lots in a Line with the Burial place for the parish of Christ Church for a Burial place for Negroes and other Slaves"; see *Journal of the Commons House Assembly*, November 9, 1762, in CRG, 13:720. An act was passed in April 1768 to enlarge it again; see CRG, vol. 19, pt. 1:75. On July 29, 1789, "An Ordinance for Enlarging the Cemetery or Public Burial Ground and for Laying Off 200 Feet of Land for a Negro Burying Ground" was passed; see *Ordinances, 1789–1842,* City of Savannah Municipal Archives.

34. This parcel was apparently used first as a "strangers burial ground"; see Trinkley and Hacker, *Identification and Mapping*, 17.
35. This parcel is labeled "City Pound" on several maps; see Trinkley and Hacker, *Identification and Mapping*, 19.
36. The width of Liberty Street is specified in city ordinance #1308 passed on March 28, 1837; see *The Code of the City of Savannah of 1907: Containing the Charter of City of Savannah with General State Laws Affecting Municipal Corporations, Also Ordinances Adopted by the Mayor and Aldermen of the City of Savannah, Now of Force, with an Appendix [. . .]* (Morning News Print, 1907), 317.
37. *Act of the General Assembly*, passed April 7, 1763, cited in Wilson, *Historic and Picturesque Savannah*, 89–90; *Ordinances, 1789–1842*, 7, Savannah Municipal Archives. See also "Act of Council, Repealing the 1789 Ordinance and Establishing a New and Larger Burial Ground on September 3, 1810," reported in *The Republican and Savannah Evening Ledger* (September 27, 1810), 4.
38. *Ordinances, 1789–1842*, 15, City of Savannah Municipal Archives; see also Thomas Gamble, *A History of the City Government of Savannah, Ga., from 1790 to 1901* (Savannah: s.n., 1901), 124, which cites the *Columbian Museum* of September 21, 1819, in which it was reported that "a plot of ground 455 feet in length and 240 feet in breadth, situated 565 yards south of the present burying ground, is set off for the interment of all strangers, or persons who have not relatives interred in the old cemetery."
39. *Proceedings of Council*, February 8, 1844, reported in *The Savannah Daily Republican*, February 12, 1844, 2.
40. Gamble, *History of the City Government*, 207.
41. City council minutes, April 25, 1851, published in *The Savannah Daily Republican*, April 12, 1851, 2.
42. See John Evelev, "Rus-Urban Imaginings: Literature of the American Park Movement and Representations of Social Space in the Mid-Nineteenth Century," *Early American Studies: An Interdisciplinary Journal* 12, no. 1 (Winter 2014): 174–201.
43. Andrew Jackson Downing, "The New-York Park," *Horticulturist* 6 (August 1851): 345.
44. See Dolores Boisfeuillet Floyd, *New Yamacraw and the Indian Mound Irene* (Savannah: Review Printing, 1936), 4–6.
45. CRG, 18:457.
46. On Musgrove's claim, see Andrew K. Frank, "Mary Musgrove," in *New Georgia Encyclopedia*, last modified October 6, 2019, https://www.georgiaencyclopedia.org/articles/history-archaeology/mary-musgrove-ca-1700-ca-1763/. See also William Stephens, *The Journal of William Stephens: 1741–1743* (University of Georgia Press, 1958), 47–48.
47. See Stephens, *Journal of William Stephens*, 47–48.
48. "An Act for Amending an Act Entitled 'An Act for the Better Regulating the Town of Savannah, and for Ascertaining the Common Thereunto Belonging,'" June 9, 1761, *Statutes Enacted by the Royal Legislature of Georgia from Its First Session in 1754 to 1768*, in CRG, 18:479.
49. February 10, 1787, in CRG, vol. 19, pt. 2:563–68.
50. Journal of Philip Georg Friedrich von Reck, published in *Tracts and Other Papers Relating Principally to the Origin, Settlement, and Progress of the Colonies in North America, from the Discovery of the Country to the Year 1776, ed. Peter Force, vol. 4* (Washington, D.C., 1846), 10. Reynolds's acquisition is recorded in the council minutes of February 4, 1755; see *Proceedings and Minutes of the Governor and Council*, in CRG, 7:101.
51. These lots were granted to Governor Wright in the act of March 4, 1762; see CRG, 18:526–28.
52. For example, in 1749, Francis Harris and James Habersham petitioned "to build a Wharf in the Front of this Town"; see CRG, 6:242.
53. A petition in February 1741, for example, recommends

fees for "all Live Stock that shall be Landed on the Wharf"; see *Proceedings of the President and Assistants from October 12, 1741, to October 30, 1754*, in CRG, 6:21. By 1743 the wharf was facing the "likelyhood of its falling to Decay"; see CRG, 6:67. A recommendation was made to the Common Council on March 25, 1748, to "enlarg[e] the Wharf at Savannah"; see CRG, 1:509.

54. Robin B. Williams, "'A Well-Paved City': Variety, Locality, and Modernity in Paving Savannah's Streets," *Arris: Journal of the Southeast Chapter of the Society of Architectural Historians* 24 (2013): 26–27.
55. Nathaniel Robert Walker, "Savannah's Lost Squares: Progress Versus Beauty in the Depression-Era South," *Journal of the Society of Architectural Historians* 70, no. 4 (December 2011): 517.
56. Walker, "Savannah's Lost Squares," 520–21.
57. Walker, "Savannah's Lost Squares," 525–26.
58. As a case in point, the block of Hull Street west of the Civic Center is labeled "Turner Blvd" on street signage, after the name of a separately developed street that runs westward from West Broad Street (Martin Luther King Jr. Boulevard) and with which it only partially aligns.
59. "Savannah Downtown Historic District Board of Review," Chatham County–Savannah Metropolitan Planning Commission, accessed January 29, 2024, https://www.thempc.org/Historic/Hdbr#gsc.tab=0.
60. "Design Manual for the Savannah Historic District," Chatham County–Savannah Metropolitan Planning Commission, updated August 2012, https://www.thempc.org/docs/lit/hist/designmanual.pdf.
61. Walker, "Savannah's Lost Squares," 528.
62. Kelly Gregg, "Conceptualizing the Pedestrian Mall in Post-War North America and Understanding Its Transatlantic Transfer Through the Work and Influence of Victor Gruen," *Planning Perspectives* 34, no. 4 (2018): 566. Gregg notes that the roots of pedestrian malls predate World War II (pp. 551–52).
63. According to Chris Morrill (then the assistant city manager) in a June 23, 2022, interview with Robin B. Williams, the traditional features, not included in the original design, were added in response to public feedback.
64. The local committee was formed at a meeting of the Historic District Board of Review and comprised Scott Barnard, architect; Daniel Carey of the Historic Savannah Foundation; Bill Durrence, District 2 alderman, City of Savannah; Ellen Harris, preservation officer, Chatham County–Savannah Metropolitan Planning Commission; Sonja Wallen of the Telfair Museum; and Robin B. Williams, architectural and urban historian.
65. An Urban Land Institute Technical Assistance Panel, convened on October 29–30, 2018, addressed the Savannah Civic Center Redevelopment, recommending in its final report that the whole of the Civic Center be demolished; see https://ulidigitalmarketing.blob.core.windows.net/ulidcnc/2019/06/FINAL-REPORT_Savanah-Civic-Ctr-TAP_v-4.1.19.pdf.
66. See the minutes of the council for June 27, 2024, https://agenda.savannahga.gov/publishing/june-27-2024-city-council-regular-meeting/minutes.html.

Section 1 Conclusion. Collaborative Elastic Urban Design

Epigraphs are from James Edward Oglethorpe, *Some Account of the Design of the Trustees for Establishing Colonys in America*, ed. Rodney M. Baine and Phinizy Spalding (University of Georgia Press, 1990), 3; and Aldo Rossi, *The Architecture of the City*, trans. Diane Ghirardo and Joan Ockman (MIT Press, 1982), 113.

Section 2. Paradoxical Patterns

The epigraph is from Charles Mackay, *Life and Liberty in America: or, Sketches of a Tour in the United States and Canada in 1857–8* (New York, 1859), 209–10.

1. A reference publication of the American Planning Association, by comparison, notes that "infrastructure may use 10 to 30 percent of a project's gross land area." See APA, *Planning and Urban Design Standards* (John Wiley & Sons, 2006), 186.
2. Johann Martin Boltzius and Philip Georg Friedrich von Reck, *An Extract of the Journals of Mr. Commissary Von Reck* (London, 1734), 41.

Chapter 3. The Parts of the Plan

The first epigraph is from Francis Moore, *A Voyage to Georgia: Begun in the Year 1735* (London, 1744), 29.

The second is from Jean-Nicolas-Louis Durand's *Précis of the Lectures on Architecture* (Paris, 1802–5), quoted in Aldo Rossi, *The Architecture of the City*, trans. Diane Ghirardo and Joan Ockman (MIT Press, 1982), 35.

1. A Roman castrum, or encampment plan, was defined by two main streets, the *cardo* and the *decumanus*, meeting at right angles at the center, which would typically be defined by an open square, or forum.
2. *Minutes of Council*, September 28, 1790, 49; April 29, 1794; and May 3, 1796, 144. City of Savannah Municipal Archives.
3. Stanford Anderson, "Savannah and the Issue of Precedent: City Plan as Resource," in *Settlements in the Americas: Cross-Cultural Perspectives*, ed. Ralph Bennett (University of Delaware Press and Associated University Presses, 1993), 128.
4. Charles Colcock Jones Jr., *The History of Georgia*, vol. 1, *Aboriginal and Colonial Epochs* (Boston, 1883), 149.
5. Robert Mackay to Eliza Anne Mackay, April 2, 1810, Georgia Historical Society, Coll. 1320; published in *The Letters of Robert Mackay to His Wife: Written from Ports in America and England, 1795–1816*, ed. Walter Charlton Hartridge (University of Georgia Press, 2010), 92.
6. See F. D. Lee and J. L. Agnew, *Historical Record of the City of Savannah* (Savannah, 1869), 8.
7. The first reference we can find to any of the current square names besides Johnson Square is from December 10, 1762, in *Journal of the Commons House of Assembly*, CRG, 13:755.
8. John Reps, "$C^2 + L^2 = S^2$? Another Look at the Origins of Savannah's Town Plan," in *Forty Years of Diversity: Essays on Colonial Georgia*, ed. Harvey H. Jackson and Phinizy Spalding (University of Georgia Press, 1984), 31.
9. See Laurence Pattacini, "André Mollet, Royal Gardener in St. James's Park, London," *Garden History* 26, no. 1 (Summer 1998): 14; and David Coombs, "The Garden at Carlton House of Frederick Prince of Wales and Augusta Princess Dowager of Wales: Bills in Their Household Accounts 1728 to 1772," *Garden History* 25, no. 2 (Winter 1997): 153–77.
10. Reps, "$C^2 + L^2 = S^2$?," 139.
11. The 1884, 1888, 1898, and 1916 Sanborn maps of Savannah are accessible through the Digital Library of Georgia at https://dlg.galileo.usg.edu/sanborn/CityCounty/Savannah.html?Welcome.
12. The 1884 Sanborn map, plate 4, shows Johnson Square with its original dimensions; the 1888 Sanborn map, plates 3 and 4, shows the altered dimensions and notes the width of Bryan and Congress Streets by the square as 55 feet, up from the original 37½ feet.
13. James Edward Oglethorpe, *Some Account of the Design of the Trustees for Establishing Colonys in America*, ed. Rodney M. Baine and Phinizy Spalding (University of Georgia Press, 1990), 36.
14. "An Extract of the Journals of Mr. Commissary Von Reck and of the Reverend Mr. Bolzius," published in part in *Our First Visit in America: Early Reports from the Colony of Georgia, 1732–1740*, introd. Trevor R. Reese (Beehive Press, 1974), 47.
15. Moore, *Voyage to Georgia*, 29.
16. Water pumps or wells are documented as early as the 1796 map. Cisterns appeared around 1830; see "Cisterns of Savannah," City of Savannah Municipal Archives, https://www.savannahga.gov/DocumentCenter/View/4534/City-Cisterns-1830-1848. Fire engine houses appear on the 1853 Vincent map of Savannah as small black rectangles, sometimes denoted by "EN," in Franklin, Johnson, Reynolds, Washington, Liberty, Wright, and Columbia Squares.
17. Nathaniel Robert Walker, "Savannah's Lost Squares: Progress Versus Beauty in the Depression-Era South," *Journal of the Society of Architectural Historians* 70, no. 4 (December 2011): 517.
18. *South-Carolina Gazette*, n. 84, August 25, 1733, quoted in John W. Reps, *The Making of Urban America: A History of City Planning in the United States* (Princeton University Press, 1965), 186.
19. "An Extract of the Rev. Mr. John Wesley's Journal," in *Our First Visit in America*, 231.
20. Both the sundial and Tomochichi's monument are documented in the 1757 de Brahm map of Savannah. On Tomochichi's tomb, see Robin B. Williams, "The Challenge of Preserving Public Memory: Commemorating Tomochichi in Savannah," *Preservation Education and Research* 5 (2012): 2.

21. *Savannah Daily Republican*, May 12, 1819, 2.

22. Mills Lane, *Savannah Revisited: A Pictorial History* (University of Georgia Press, 1969), 54, citing *Frank Leslie's Illustrated Newspaper*, March 23, 1867.

23. *Minutes of Council*, December 17, 1793. City of Savannah Municipal Archives.

24. William Stephens, *A Journal of the Proceedings in Georgia, Beginning October 5, 1740, by William Stephens, Esq.*, in CRG, vol. 4, Supp.: 117.

25. On tythingmen, see Larry E. Ivers, "Rangers, Scouts, and Tythingmen," in *Forty Years of Diversity: Essays on Colonial Georgia*, ed. Harvey H. Jackson and Phinizy Spalding (University of Georgia Press, 1984), 154–55. Edmund Spenser discusses lathes, tythings, and constables in relation to the laws of Alfred in *A View of the Present State of Ireland* (1596).

26. Oglethorpe, *Some Account*, 30.

27. See David Pratt, *The Political Thought of King Alfred the Great* (Cambridge University Press, 2007); and Paul Readman, "The Place of the Past in English Culture c. 1890–1914," *Past & Present* 186, no. 1 (February 2005): 147–99.

28. Oglethorpe, *Some Account*, 37. Oglethorpe wrote that colonists "should draw Lots for the lands."

29. See chapter 5 in this book and Mills Lane, *Architecture of the Old South: Georgia* (Beehive Press, 1986), 18, for a description of these early houses.

30. A city ordinance of March 4, 1847, for example, refers to "lots known in the plan of the city as trust lots"; see *The Code of the City of Savannah of 1907* (Morning News Print, 1907), 320. Confusingly, when the term "trust lot" appears in colonial documents, it generally refers to the Trustee-controlled ninety-acre farm lots in the center of each tything's block of farm lots. Surveyor William Gerard de Brahm, however, did use the term "trustee lot" to refer to the in-town lots that are now called trust lots; see John William Gerard de Brahm and George Wymberley Jones De Renne, *History of the Province of Georgia: With Maps of Original Surveys* (Savannah: 1849), 36.

31. See Henry A. M. Smith, "Beaufort: The Original Plan and the Earliest Settlers," *South Carolina Historical and Genealogical Magazine* 9, no. 3 (July 1908): 150ff.

32. Oglethorpe, *Some Account*, 36.

33. William Stephens, *A Journal of the Proceedings in Georgia, Beginning October 20, 1737, by William Stephens, Esq.: To Which Is Added, a State of That Province, as Attested upon Oath in the Court of Savannah, November 10, 1740*, in CRG, 4:664.

34. Moore, *Voyage to Georgia*, 25–26.

35. *Proceedings and Minutes of the Governor and Council*, February 11, 1755, in CRG, 7:108.

36. *Proceedings and Minutes of the Governor and Council*, April 9, 1755, in CRG, 7:168.

37. *Proceedings and Minutes of the Governor and Council*, June 3, 1755, in CRG, 7:183. Their grant was officially made by a royal charter signed on January 16, 1756, and received on May 17, 1756.

38. *Proceedings and Minutes of the Governor and Council*, November 1, 1757, in CRG, 7:650.

39. *Ordinances, 1789–1842*, 27–28. City of Savannah Municipal Archives.

40. *Minutes of Council, June 1791–December 1796*, 94. City of Savannah Municipal Archives.

41. Mark Reinberger offers an intriguing numerological explanation for the street widths in his article "Oglethorpe's Plan of Savannah: Urban Design, Speculative Freemasonry, and Enlightenment Charity," *Georgia Historical Quarterly* 81, no. 4 (1997): 839–62.

42. Stanford Anderson made this point in two insightful articles—see "Savannah and the Issue," 113, and "The Plan of Savannah and Changes of Occupancy During Its Early Years: City Plan as Resource," *Harvard Architecture Review* 2 (Spring 1981): 66–67.

43. A rail line was built in the center of Liberty Street to connect railroad stations on the east and west sides of Savannah during the Civil War. In a letter to the city council published in Savannah's *Daily News and Herald* on July 28, 1866, Colonel John Screven called for its removal. A streetcar line was opened on Liberty Street in 1881, as reported in the November 16, 1881, edition of the *Savannah Morning News*.

44. "An Ordinance in Addition to and Amendatory of an Ordinance Entitled an Ordinance to Lay Off Certain Portions of the South Common in Lots, and to Offer Them at Public Sale," July 31, 1851, in *A Digest of All the Ordinances of the City of Savannah Which Were*

of Force on the 1st July 1854, comp. and arr. Charles S. Henry (Savannah, 1854), 129–32.

Chapter 4. How the Plan Works

The first epigraph is from Stanford Anderson, "Savannah and the Issue of Precedent: City Plan as Resource," in *Settlements in the Americas: Cross-Cultural Perspectives*, ed. Ralph Bennett (University of Delaware Press and Associated University Presses, 1993), 118. The second is from Victor Dover and John Massengale, *Street Design: The Secret to Great Cities and Towns* (John Wiley & Sons, 2013), 173.

1. Stanford Anderson, "The Plan of Savannah and Changes of Occupancy During Its Early Years: City Plan as Resource," *Harvard Architecture Review* 2 (Spring 1981): 63–64.
2. Sibyl Moholy-Nagy, *Matrix of Man: An Illustrated History of Urban Environment* (Praeger, 1968); see especially pp. 198ff.
3. Moholy-Nagy, *Matrix of Man*, 190.
4. Prior to November 1896, addresses on east–west streets began at East Broad Street and counted upward in a westward direction.
5. Anderson, "Savannah and the Issue," 64.
6. The bidirectionality of the central east–west trust streets shown on the diagram is true of thirty-one of the surviving thirty-seven sections of trust streets. The remaining eleven sections have disappeared under buildings or are closed to vehicular traffic.
7. "Charles II, 1666: An Act for Rebuilding the Citty of London," in *The Statutes of the Realm*, vol. 5 [1625–80], ed. John Raithby (s.l., 1819), 603–12, http://www.british-history.ac.uk/statutes-realm/vol5/pp603-612.
8. Allan B. Jacobs, *Great Streets* (MIT Press, 1995), 262.
9. Robin B. Williams, "'A Well-Paved City': Variety, Locality, and Modernity in Paving Savannah's Streets," *Arris: Journal of the Southeast Chapter of the Society of Architectural Historians* 24 (2013): 24.
10. See the Petition of Parker Morgan for Hunter Maclean, 554 East Taylor Street, 13–000388–COA, Fence, in the minutes of the February 13, 2013, Savannah Historic District Board of Review regular meeting, https://www.thempc.org/eagenda/x/hrb/2013/FEBRUARY%2013,%202013%20HISTORIC%20DISTRICT%20BOARD%20OF%20REVIEW%20REGULAR%20MEETING%20on%20Wednesday,%20February%2013,%202013/59DBA3B2–4AAA-42C0–9EF2–4580EB08335AMinutes.pdf. The "City of Savannah Tree Lawn Compliance and Policy Guide" passed in 2017.

Section 2 Conclusion. A Grid like No Other

Epigraphs are from Spiro Kostof, *America by Design* (Oxford University Press, 1987), 151–54; and Witold Rybczynski, *Makeshift Metropolis: Ideas About Cities* (Scribner, 2010), 11.

1. Dell Upton, *Another City: Urban Life and Urban Spaces in the New American Republic* (Yale University Press, 2008), 113–44.
2. John W. Reps, *The Making of Urban America: A History of City Planning in the United States* (Princeton University Press, 1965), 297–98. Rem Koolhaas cites Reps at the beginning of his clever analysis of the Manhattan grid in *Delirious New York: A Retroactive Manifesto for Manhattan* (Monacelli Press, 1994), 18–19.
3. See Hilary Ballon, ed., *The Greatest Grid: The Master Plan of Manhattan, 1811–2011* (Columbia University Press, 2012).

Section 3. A Symphony Without a Soloist

Epigraphs are from John Berendt, foreword to *The National Trust Guide to Savannah,* by Roulhac Toledano (John Wiley & Sons, 1997), xvii; and F. W. J. von Schelling, *The Philosophy of Art*, ed. and trans. Douglas W. Stott (University of Minnesota Press, 1989), 174.

1. According to a study of real estate data, Philadelphia has the smallest lots at 1,089 square feet, Chicago was the next smallest at 1,699 square feet, and Washington, D.C., was third at 2,614 square feet; see Maria Gatea, "The American Backyard in the Last 100 Years: Lot Sizes in San Diego Get Bigger While Seattle Loses Yard Space," StorageCafe, July 29, 2021, https://www.storagecafe.com/blog/lot-size-home-size-in-top-20-biggest-us-cities/. The article is unclear about whether the figures represent average or smallest lot size.

Chapter 5. Houses

Epigraphs are from Leon Battista Alberti, *On the Art of Building in Ten Books*, rev. ed., trans. Joseph Rykwert, Neil Leach, and Robert Tavernor (MIT Press, 1991), 23; and Anthony McGowan, "Southern Belles," *Daily Mail* (U.K.), July 17, 2010.

1. Thomas Causton to his wife, March 12, 1733, quoted in Sarah B. Gober Temple and Kenneth Coleman, *Georgia Journeys: Being an Account of the Lives of Georgia's Original Settlers and Many Other Early Settlers* (University of Georgia Press, 2010), 8, 12–14.
2. Francis Moore, *A Voyage to Georgia: Begun in the Year 1735* (London, 1744), 23. See also John P. Corry, "The Houses of Colonial Georgia," *Georgia Historical Quarterly* 14, no. 3 (1930): 181–201; Harold E. Davis, *The Fledgling Province: Social and Cultural Life in Colonial Georgia, 1733–1776* (University of North Carolina Press, 1976), 33–35; and Temple and Coleman, *Georgia Journeys*, 12–14.
3. E. G. Daves Rossell and Marisa C. Gomez, eds., *Vernacular Architecture Forum 2007: Savannah and the Lowcountry; Field Guide for the 28th Annual Meeting; Savannah, Georgia, March 28–31, 2007* (Savannah College of Art and Design, 2007), 127–29.
4. Examples include 542 East State Street (built in 1818), 40 Price Street (1841), and 21 Houston Street (1852).
5. A similar cottage-on-corner-store once stood nearby at 34 Price Street.
6. The pair appears on the 1888 Sanborn map, plate 13.
7. Charles Duff argues that rowhouses are peculiar to cities on both sides of the North Atlantic, with the American half found mainly within fifty miles of the East Coast, and Savannah as a Southern outlier; see Duff, *The North Atlantic Cities* (Bluecoat Press, 2019), 10. On American rowhouses, see Mary Ellen Hayward and Charles Belfoure, *The Baltimore Rowhouse* (Princeton Architectural Press, 1999); Kenneth Ames, "Robert Mills and the Philadelphia Row House," *Journal of the Society of Architectural Historians* 27, no. 2 (1968): 140–46; and William John Murtagh, "The Philadelphia Row House," *Journal of the Society of Architectural Historians* 16, no. 4 (1957): 8–13.
8. *Minutes of Council, 1791–1804*, May 18, 1790, 26. City of Savannah Municipal Archives.
9. The buildings originally stood across the street at 122–124 West Oglethorpe Avenue; they were moved in order to preserve them before the federal government redeveloped that tything for the Juliette Gordon Low Federal Building C in 1985.
10. Our survey of 404 extant fully elevated rowhouses in the historic district identified 312 examples (77 percent) between Lincoln and Jefferson Streets versus 92 (23 percent) between Martin Luther King Jr. Boulevard and Jefferson Street to the west and Lincoln and East Broad Streets to the east.
11. *Ordinances, 1812–1839*, 40–41. City of Savannah Municipal Archives.
12. Cassel Row was demolished sometime before 1951, when a four-story building was erected on the whole trust lot for the U.S. Army Corps of Engineers, as documented in the Sanborn map of 1955.
13. John Deering, email message to authors, June 12, 2024.
14. "New Townhomes in the Heart of Downtown Savannah Offer Luxury, Convenience and Historic Charm," *Savannah CEO*, September 29, 2015, http://savannahceo.com/news/2015/09/new-townhomes-heart-downtown-savannah-offer-luxury-convenience-and-historic-charm/.
15. On the Charleston single house, see Gene Waddell, "The Charleston Single House: An Architectural Survey," *Preservation Progress* 22, no. 2 (March 1977): 4–8; and Bernard L. Herman, "The Embedded Landscapes of the Charleston Single House, 1780–1820," *Perspectives in Vernacular Architecture* 7 (1997): 41–57.
16. For an in-depth comparison of the two cities, see Thomas D. Wilson, *Charleston and Savannah: The Rise, Fall, and Reinvention of Two Rival Cities* (University of Georgia Press, 2023).
17. The 1898 Sanborn map shows two single houses in Chatham Ward, six in Monterey Ward, three in Calhoun Ward, and at least one in Wesley Ward.
18. Those other mansion houses are the Joseph Fay House (10 West Oglethorpe); the Sorrel-Weed House (6 West Harris); the Henry Brigham House (4 West Liberty); the Smets House (4 East Jones); and the Noble Hardee House (3 West Gordon).

Chapter 6. Civil Buildings

Epigraphs are from Sebastiano Serlio, *Sebastiano Serlio on Architecture*, trans. Vaughan Hart and Peter Hicks, vol. 1 (Yale University Press, 2005), 396; and Joseph F. Gray, comp. and ed., *Savannah: Founded 1733: Municipal, Financial, Commercial, Industrial, Agricultural, Residential & Historical* (Savannah Chamber of Commerce, 1911), 17.

1. See Hoke P. Kimball and Bruce Henson, *Governor's Houses and State Houses of British Colonial America, 1607–1783: An Historical, Architectural and Archaeological Survey* (McFarland, 2017), 377–76.
2. See Monica M. Gann, "Justice in Flux: The Evolving and Roving Early Court Houses of Savannah, Georgia, 1733–1888" (MFA thesis, Savannah College of Art and Design, 2020).
3. Kayla Hess, "Building Masculine Socialization: The Landscape of Men's-Only Organizations in Savannah, Georgia, 1840s–1930s" (BFA thesis, Savannah College of Art and Design, 2023).
4. "The City Exchange: A Brief History of the Landmark—Some Interesting Reminiscences," *Savannah Morning News*, March 14, 1879.
5. City council records, quoted in Luciana M. Spracher, "The Birth of City Hall, 1903–1906" (City of Savannah, Research Library and Municipal Archives, January 2006), 186.
6. Lot 1 in Jekyl Tything is labeled on this view as "The Tabernacle & Court House."
7. Gann, "Justice in Flux," 8–16.
8. A small image appears on *Plan of the City of Savannah* (ca. 1796) in the Marian S. Carson Collection, Library of Congress (figure 34). See Gann, "Justice in Flux," 16–25. The front elevation of this courthouse appears on the map.
9. 1890 city plat. E/W Maps 3121–008. City of Savannah Municipal Archives. See Gann, "Justice in Flux," fig. 21. The city council passed ordinances on October 3, 1888, and February 6, 1889, allowing these expansions; see Thomas Gamble, *A History of the City Government of Savannah, Ga., from 1790 to 1901* (Savannah: s.n., 1901), 487.
10. An earlier version of this project, designed by Robert A. M. Stern in 1998 and more closely mimicking the massing and style of the original courthouse, also would have displaced the one block of President Street, but it failed to secure government funding and was shelved.
11. *Ordinances, 1789–1842*, 27. City of Savannah Municipal Archives.
12. An example of a larger church located just outside of the plan was St. Patrick's Roman Catholic Church (erected before 1888; demolished before 1955) on the south side of Liberty Street, fronting West Broad Street on an irregular block lacking a lane.
13. *Proceedings and Minutes of the Governor and Council*, in CRG, 7:183. This church appears in the 1796 map of Savannah at the Library of Congress (Fig. 1.2.35).
14. Fragments that are most likely from this building were discovered during excavations for the Juliette Gordon Low Federal Building B in 1985 and were re-erected on a vacant tything lot owned by the Independent Presbyterian Church and facing Chippewa Square.
15. "An Ordinance for Laying Off into Lots Certain Parts of the Common Appurtenant to the City, and for Disposing of the Same," May 30, 1799, as published in the *Columbian Museum & Savannah Advertiser*, June 7, 1799. See also Andrew J. Remick, "Creating Sacred Space: The Nineteenth-Century Churches of Saint John the Baptist, Saint Patrick, and Saint Benedict the Moor of Savannah, Georgia" (master's thesis, Savannah College of Art and Design, 2011), 12.
16. The church used the lot facing Drayton for the Catholic Library Association, as well as the block to the east, which housed the parochial school until its replacement was erected adjacent to the cathedral. The eastern site now accommodates the diocese's chancery building, erected between 1955 and 1973.
17. *Proceedings and Minutes of the Governor and Council*, February 11, 1755, in CRG, 7:108.
18. It was one of three such academies in the state, along with Glynn County and Richmond County schools, established by an Act of the Georgia Assembly. The Chatham Academy leased this land jointly with Union Society. In 1816 the newly formed Sunday School Union, which is credited with establishing the first school system in Savannah, began to meet;

Savannah Republican, November 21, 1816. On the Chatham Academy, see Adelaide Wilson, *Historic and Picturesque Savannah* (Boston, 1889), 112–14.

19. The Brantley House was donated by Mills B. Lane, one of the college's primary benefactors, and was known as the Lane Building. Herschel V. Jenkins Hall was razed sometime between 1955 and 1973 (given its absence from the 1955 Sanborn map amended through 1973) so that the land could be used as a parking lot, most likely after Armstrong College had moved to the south side in 1966.
20. Originally known as Thomas Gamble Hall, the eastern half of the building, designed in a modernist yet compatible International Style, was added in 1958, according to the 1955 Sanborn map amended through 1973. It now serves as the office of United Way.
21. This building was known during the Armstrong years as the John W. Hunt Memorial Building.
22. "About," Ralston College, accessed August 2, 2024, https://www.ralston.ac/about.
23. A 1929 plaque commissioned by the Daughters of the American Revolution and affixed to the current building claims, "This theatre is the oldest in active use in the United States." That title more rightly belongs to the Walnut Street Theatre in Philadelphia, which opened in 1809 and is reputed to be the oldest theatre in continuous use in the English-speaking world.
24. Documents in the City of Savannah Municipal Archives quote different capacity numbers: 3121–010 Engineering Department Retrospective Plans and Designs Collection, Item Number 28.22a lists the auditorium's capacity at 2,149 (and as a convention hall at 2,914); 3121–010 Engineering Department Retrospective Plans and Designs Collection, Item Number 28.21 lists a capacity of 1,735 and up for the theatre and a capacity of 3,471 as a convention hall.
25. A similar solution was used by department stores fronting Broughton Street that bridged the lane to provide access to an annex on the adjacent tything block—Adler's in the northeast tything of Percival Ward, for example (documented on the 1916 Sanborn map), and Sears in the northwest tything of Heathcote Ward, where a simple wooden bridge (documented on the 1916 Sanborn map) was replaced by a surviving two-story space above the lane linking to a rear building.

Chapter 7. Commerce and Tourism, Industry and Transportation

Epigraphs are from Charles Lanman, *Adventures in the Wilds of the United States and British American Provinces* (Philadelphia, 1856), 2:99; and Herman Myers, *Savannah: A City of Opportunities* (Savannah Morning News, 1904), promotional brochure in SCAD Special Collections, https://scad.lunaimaging.com/luna/servlet/detail/SCAD~15~15~4~17655:Savannah,-A-City-of-Opportunities.

1. James Edward Oglethorpe, *Some Account of the Design of the Trustees for Establishing Colonys in America*, ed. Rodney M. Baine and Phinizy Spalding (University of Georgia Press, 1990), 36.
2. September 18, 1759, governor and council records, in CRG, 8:135–36. The council had ordered six weeks prior that a market house be built in Johnson Square, where markets had been held, but opposition to this location prompted it to be moved to Wright Square.
3. Joseph Frederick Waring, *Cerveau's Savannah* (Georgia Historical Society, 1973), 19.
4. See Thomas Gamble, *A History of the City Government of Savannah, Ga., from 1790 to 1901* (Savannah: s.n., 1901), 120–23. The market on South Broad also appears on the 1820 map of Savannah drawn by John McKinnon (figure 38).
5. Stanford Anderson, "The Plan of Savannah and Changes of Occupancy During Its Early Years: City Plan as Resource," *Harvard Architecture Review* 2 (Spring 1981): 65–67.
6. See Richard Longstreth, "The Continuous Transformation of Savannah's Broughton Street," in *Looking Beyond the Icons: Midcentury Architecture, Landscape, and Urbanism* (University of Virginia Press, 2015), 170–94.
7. See Longstreth, *Looking Beyond*, 177–79 and 184–86. Longstreth's figure 13.9 illustrates the earlier version of Levy's.
8. David Jack Cowen, *The Origins and Economic Impact of the First Bank of the United States, 1791–1797* (Garland, 2000), 204.

9. The veranda was removed in the 1950s and then re-created when the building was restored to a hotel in 1998–99.
10. This strategy for growth has already influenced another development on a full tything at 415 East Oglethorpe Avenue, between Habersham and Price Streets; the project was required to develop the site as two buildings in order to preserve the lane, with a large belowground parking garage underneath.
11. City of Savannah Code of Ordinances, division II, part 8, chapter 3, article 7.0, sec. 7.8; see http://online.encodeplus.com/regs/savannah-ga/doc-viewer.aspx#secid-5517. The district overlay map can be viewed at http://agenda.savannahga.gov/content/files/savannah-historic-district-hotel-development-overlay-district-map.pdf.
12. Statistics based on the 1955 Sanborn map and the 1955 map amended through 1973.
13. See the 1955 Sanborn Fire Insurance Map with "paste-in" updates through 1973, vol. 1, City of Savannah Municipal Archives.

Chapter 8. The Landscape Architecture of the Plan

The second epigraph is from Julien Green, *The Green Paradise: 1900–1916*, vol. 1 (Marion Boyars Publishers, 1993), quoted in David B. Calhoun, *The Splendor of Grace: The Independent Presbyterian Church of Savannah, Georgia, 1755–2005* (A Press Printing, 2005), 75.

1. "Report of Park and Tree Commissioners," Savannah, Ga., December 31, 1896, published in *Report of Mayor of the City of Savannah* (Savannah, 1896), 236. On the Park and Tree Commission, see Melanie Katia Jones, "The Urban Park Movement in the American South: Savannah, Atlanta, Nashville, 1850–1916" (PhD diss., University of Cambridge, 2014), 100. https://idiscover.lib.cam.ac.uk/permalink/f/t9gok8/44CAM_ALMA21433400480003606.
2. James L. Machor, *Pastoral Cities: Urban Ideals and the Symbolic Landscape of America* (University of Wisconsin Press, 1987), 28.
3. Extract from letter in *The Philadelphia Presbyterian*, June 9, 1852, as quoted in a manuscript by Walter Hartridge in the Georgia Historical Society, Hartridge Collection #1349, box 50, folder 749. *Rus in urbe* translates to "country in the city."
4. For a survey of this subject, see John Dixon Hunt, introduction to *The Genius of the Place: The English Landscape Garden 1620–1820*, ed. John Dixon Hunt and Peter Willis, 2nd ed. (MIT Press, 1988), 1–46.
5. Pope names Oglethorpe in his "Second Epistle of the Second Book of Horace," published in 1737. See Edward J. Cashin, "Glimpses of Oglethorpe in Boswell's Life of Johnson," *Georgia Historical Quarterly* 88, no. 3 (2004), 404.
6. Reps notes the proximity of the residences of the Earl of Egmont and John Laroche on Pall Mall and that of William Sloper on St. James's Place; see Reps, "$C^2 + L^2 = S^2$? Another Look at the Origins of Savannah's Town Plan," in *Forty Years of Diversity: Essays on Colonial Georgia*, ed. Harvey H. Jackson and Phinizy Spalding (University of Georgia Press, 1984), 131. On Kent's work at St. James's Park, see Laurence Pattacini, "André Mollet, Royal Gardener in St. James's Park, London," *Garden History* 26, no. 1 (Summer 1998): 14; and Jan Woudstra, "Landscape Gardening and the Metropolis: Reptonian Influences on John Nash's Transformation of St. James's Park, 1814–30," *Garden History* 47 (Spring 2019): 90–91.
7. Stanford Anderson, "Savannah and the Issue of Precedent: City Plan as Resource," in *Settlements in the Americas: Cross-Cultural Perspectives*, ed. Ralph Bennett (University of Delaware Press and Associated University Presses, 1993), 132–37.
8. The others were James, Earl of Derby; James, Lord Viscount Limerick; and Erasmus Phillips.
9. On Castell, see Yu Liu, "Castell's Pliny: Rewriting the Past for the Present," *Eighteenth-Century Studies* 43, no. 2 (Winter 2010): 243–57; and Pierre de la Ruffinière du Prey, *The Villas of Pliny from Antiquity to Posterity* (University of Chicago Press, 1994), 131–42. On Castell's incarceration and relation to Oglethorpe, see Rodney M. Baine, "The Prison Death of Robert Castell and Its Effect on the Founding of Georgia," *Georgia Historical Quarterly* 73, no. 1 (1989): 67–78; Alex Pitofsky, "The Warden's Court Martial: James Oglethorpe and the Politics of Eighteenth-Century Prison Reform," *Eighteenth-Century Life* 24, no. 1

(Winter 2000): 88–102; and Thomas D. Wilson, *The Oglethorpe Plan: Enlightenment Design in Savannah and Beyond* (University of Virginia Press, 2012), 30ff.

10. William Harden, *A History of Savannah and South Georgia* (Lewis, 1913), 6–8.
11. Francis Moore, *A Voyage to Georgia: Begun in the Year 1735* (London, 1744), 30.
12. Oglethorpe described "vast Woods of Pine-trees, many of which are an Hundred, and few under Seventy Feet high." Letter to the Trustees, February 10, 1733, in CRG, 20:9–10; quoted in Mart A. Stewart, *"What Nature Suffers to Groe": Life, Labor, and Landscape on the Georgia Coast, 1680–1920* (University of Georgia Press, 2002), 38.
13. *Savannah Daily Republican*, July 3, 1848, 2. The moniker was widely adopted by local businesses and organizations, including the Forest City Gun Club (established 1883). Savannah was also called "Forest City of the South," perhaps because Portland, Maine, had likewise become known as "Forest City" by the 1860s; see Thomas J. Campanella, *Republic of Shade: New England and the American Elm* (Yale University Press, 2003), 130. Another point of reference may have been Cleveland, Ohio, which had acquired the nickname "Forest City" by 1850; see Encyclopedia of Cleveland History, "Forest City," Case Western Reserve University, accessed July 4, 2022, https://case.edu/ech/articles/f/forest-city.
14. Hodgson's park was approved by the city council in April 1846, as reported in *The Savannah Daily Republican*, April 18, 1846, p. 2. The description of the park appeared in *The Savannah Republican*, June 24, 1850, p. 2.
15. Henry W. Lawrence, *City Trees: A Historical Geography from the Renaissance Through the Nineteenth Century* (University of Virginia Press, 2006), 161.
16. Ordinance of December 17, 1793, *City of Savannah Ordinances, 1787–1817*, 162–63.
17. Ibid.
18. "An Ordinance for the Protection of the Trees Planted and to Be Planted in This City by the Corporation," March 1, 1796, mentioned in *City of Savannah Ordinances, 1787–1817*, 194; ordinance of October 6, 1803, *City of Savannah Ordinances, 1787–1817*, 195.
19. "An Ordinance for the Protection of Trees in the City of Savannah," June 11, 1810, *City of Savannah Ordinances, 1787–1817*.
20. Thomas Gamble, *A History of the City Government of Savannah, Ga., from 1790 to 1901* (Savannah: s.n., 1901), 81, 144. Gamble notes (p. 205) that in 1846 more trees were planted around the burial ground to provide further protection from exposure to the feared miasmic vapors of the dead. We are indebted to Robin Miller, "Racism Does Not End at the Grave: A Case Study of Savannah's Laurel Grove Cemetery" (BFA thesis, Savannah College of Art and Design, 2022).
21. "Ordinance for the Protection of the Trees in the City of Savannah," June 11, 1810, *City of Savannah Ordinances, 1787–1817*, 225.
22. *Daily Morning News* (Savannah), June 9, 1852, 1.
23. Perhaps the earliest example is Via Santa Maria degli Angeli in Ferrara, which was paved and lined with poplar trees at the order of Borso d'Este between 1457 and 1461; see Charles M. Rosenberg, ed., *The Court Cities of Northern Italy: Milan, Parma, Piacenza, Mantua, Ferrara, Bologna, Urbino, Pesaro, and Rimini* (Cambridge University Press, 2010), 85. On this subject more generally, see Lawrence, *City Trees*.
24. See Sara Galletti, "Female Agency and Early Modern Urbanism: The Paris of Maria De' Medici," *Journal of the Society of Architectural Historians* 71, no. 2 (2012): 186–203.
25. César de Saussure, *Letters from London, 1725–1730*, quoted in Desmond Shawe-Taylor, *The Conversation Piece: Scenes of Fashionable Life* (Royal Collection Publications, 2009), 94.
26. Richard Johnson, *The Pleasant Walkes of Moore-fields: Being the Guift of Two Sisters, Now Beautified, to the Continuing Fame of This Worthy Citty* (London, 1607), quoted in Elizabeth Milroy, "'For the like Uses, as the Moore-fields': The Politics of Penn's Squares," *Pennsylvania Magazine of History and Biography* 130, no. 3 (July 2006): 266.
27. Elizabeth Milroy, "'For the like Uses, as the Moore-fields': The Politics of Penn's Squares," *Pennsylvania Magazine of History and Biography* 130, no. 3 (July 2006): 257–82.

28. Lawrence, *City Trees*, 115–16. Anne Beamish identifies 1725 as the date of the first row; see "A Garden in the Street: The Introduction of Street Trees in Boston and New York," *Studies in the History of Gardens & Designed Landscapes* 38, no. 1 (2018): 39.
29. Lawrence, *City Trees*, 118–19, 128.
30. George Throop, advertisement in *The Georgia Gazette*, January 17, 1799. He was still planting the double rows a year later when he advertised needing an additional 150 trees in the February 18, 1800, issue of the *Columbian Museum & Savannah Advertiser.*
31. J. E. White, "Topography of Savannah and Its Vicinity. A Report to the Georgia Medical Society, May 3, 1806," *Georgia Historical Quarterly* 1, no. 3 (1917): 237.
32. See Robin B. Williams, "'A Well-Paved City': Variety, Locality, and Modernity in Paving Savannah's Streets," *Arris: Journal of the Southeast Chapter of the Society of Architectural Historians* 24 (2013): 20–39.
33. "Ordinance Regarding Public Walks," 1827, *Ordinances, 1789–1842*, 183. City of Savannah Municipal Archives.
34. On these promenades, see also Victor Dover and John Massengale, *Street Design: The Secret to Great Cities and Towns* (John Wiley & Sons, 2013), 175–77.
35. Robert Mackay to Eliza Anne Mackay, April 2, 1810, Georgia Historical Society, Coll. 1320, published in *The Letters of Robert Mackay to His Wife: Written from Ports in America and England, 1795–1816*, ed. Walter Charlton Hartridge (University of Georgia Press, 2010), 92.
36. *Minutes of Council*, December 17, 1793. City of Savannah Municipal Archives.
37. "An Ordinance for the Protection of the Trees in the City of Savannah," June 11, 1810. City of Savannah Municipal Archives.
38. Sara Hathaway [Mrs. James Hine], "Georgia Reminiscences" (1833), published in *Old Homestead* 11 (1891), 395–96, and quoted in Mills Lane, *Architecture of the Old South: Georgia* (Beehive Press, 1986), 13.
39. Charles Lanman, *Adventures in the Wilds of the United States and British American Provinces* (Philadelphia, 1856), 2:116.
40. It is attributed first in 1808 to William Pitt, the first Earl of Chatham; see *The Parliamentary Debates from the Year 1803 to the Present Time*, vol. 9 (London, 1812), 1124. In America, Frederick Law Olmsted is often credited with this trope; see Geoffrey Blodgett, "Frederick Law Olmsted: Landscape Architecture as Conservative Reform," *Journal of American History* 62, no. 4 (March 1976): 878.
41. See Emily Polgardi, "'Keep off the grass': Beautification or Play in Savannah's Crawford and Chatham Squares, 1960–1980" (MA thesis, Savannah College of Art and Design, 2014), 18–24.
42. Robin B. Williams, "The Challenge of Preserving Public Memory: Commemorating Tomochichi in Savannah," *Preservation Education and Research* 5 (2012): 1–16.
43. A pair of monuments in Baltimore, the Battle Monument and the Washington Monument—both begun in 1815, and completed in 1822 and 1829, respectively—appear to be the earliest. The Bunker Hill Monument in Boston was begun in 1825 and completed in 1843. The residents of Boonsboro, Maryland, built a monument to George Washington on South Mountain in 1827.
44. This last monument displaced a fountain erected there in 1871, which was moved to Thomas Square in the suburbs; see *Mayor's Annual Report, 1910* (Savannah, 1910), 291. In addition, a pair of large busts of local Civil War heroes Major General Lafayette McLaws and Colonel Francis Bartow, installed in 1907, was moved to Forsyth Park.
45. "The Mound Builders," *Savannah Morning News*, January 17, 1872, p. 3, col. 1; cited in Williams, "Challenge of Preserving," 7.
46. Tourism may have been another reason for beautifying the squares; see "Landscapes of Clermont Lee, Savannah, Georgia," The Cultural Landscape Foundation, accessed June 12, 2022, https://www.tclf.org/sites/default/files/microsites/landslide2020/clermont-lee-landscapes.html.
47. XJ-40 etc. collection, City of Savannah Municipal Archives.
48. "Old Telfair Place Plans to Be Used by the Garden Club of Savannah," *Savannah Morning News*, September 30, 1962.
49. For Oglethorpe Square, see "Proposed Plan for Roadway Through Squares," *Savannah Morning News*; for Whitefield Square, see map document XJ-53,

December 19, 1946, Office of the City Engineer, City of Savannah Municipal Archives.

50. See listing of multiple newspaper reports from December 8, 1945, to December 28, 1946, in *Savannah Newspaper Index, 1945–46* (Works Progress Administration, n.d., ca. 1946), 219–20, copies at the Bull Street Public Library and the Georgia Historical Society.
51. Harry Murphy, "Savannah Squares Withstand Efforts to Open Them to Cars," *Savannah Morning News*, February 18, 1962, 1C and 3C.
52. Lane's beautification plan for Washington Square was announced at a city council meeting on November 20, 1963; see the council minutes for that date, p. 312. Lee's relandscaping design for Madison Square, commissioned in 1967, met with citizen opposition; see City of Savannah council minutes, November 21, 1967, 485. Lee completed the relandscaping of Madison Square two decades later, in 1988.
53. Ced Dolder, "Clermont Lee," in *New Georgia Encyclopedia*, last modified May 8, 2017, https://www.georgiaencyclopedia.org/articles/arts-culture/clermont-lee-1914-2006/.
54. Gamble, *History of the City Government*, 389–90.
55. Michael Trinkley and Debi Hacker, "Identification and Mapping of Historic Graves at Colonial Cemetery, Savannah, Georgia," Research Series 54 (Chicora Foundation, 1999), 13ff.
56. City council minutes, April 10, 1851, published in *The Savannah Daily Republican*, April 12, 1851, 2.
57. On Bischoff, see Charles A. Birnbaum et al., *Pioneers of American Landscape Design: An Annotated Bibliography, NPS Reading List* (Washington, D.C.: U.S. Department of the Interior, National Park Service, Cultural Resources, 1993).
58. Charles Colcock Jones Jr., O. F. Vedder, and Frank Weldon, *History of Savannah, Ga.: From Its Settlement to the Close of the Eighteenth Century* (Syracuse, N.Y., 1890), 533–34.

Section 3 Conclusion. An Unfinished Symphony

Epigraphs are from Werner Hegemann and Elbert Peets, *The American Vitruvius: An Architects' Handbook of Civic Art* (Architectural Book Publishing, 1922), 1; and Marvin Trachtenberg, *Building-in-Time: From Giotto to Alberti and Modern Oblivion* (Yale University Press, 2010), 401.

Section 4. Beyond the Savannah Plan

The first epigraph is from Plutarch's *Moralia*, quoted in Marvin Trachtenberg, *Building-in-Time: From Giotto to Alberti and Modern Oblivion* (Yale University Press, 2010), 67; the second is from Joseph F. Gray, comp. and ed., *Savannah: Founded 1733: Municipal, Financial, Commercial, Industrial, Agricultural, Residential & Historical* (Savannah Chamber of Commerce, 1911), 5, https://catalog.hathitrust.org/Record/100383706.

Chapter 9. The Plan and the City

The first epigraph is from W. V. Thompson, "Savannah," *Appletons' Journal: A Magazine of General Literature* 5, no. 106 (April 8, 1871): 407, 409; the second is quoted in Megan Houck, "Savannah Manages Explosive Growth," Federal Reserve Bank of Atlanta, July 10, 2024, https://www.atlantafed.org/economy-matters/regional-economics/2024/07/11/savannah-manages-explosive-growth.

1. As of the 2020 U.S. Census, Savannah's population was 147,780. The Savannah Plan area overlaps with three census tracts—117 (mainly downtown north of Liberty Street but extending west to West Boundary Street), 112 (between MLK Jr. Boulevard and Bull Street but extending south to Park Avenue), and 119 (between East Broad and Bull Streets but extending south to Park Avenue); see https://data.census.gov.
2. Eric Meyerhoff, interview by Robin B. Williams and students, Savannah, November 7, 2013 (recording to be donated to the City of Savannah Municipal Archives).
3. Edmund Bacon, the well-known urban planner from Philadelphia who admired Savannah, brokered the compromise.
4. As documented on Sanborn maps, this complex was owned by the Plant System of Railways by 1898 (plates 84 and 85) and by the Atlantic Coast Line Railroad by 1916 (plate 57).
5. David W. Gobel, "Planned Obsolescence? The Role of the Town Common in the Making of Savannah's Urban Plan," *Journal of Planning History* 22,

no. 2 (2022): 163–64, https://doi.org/10.1177/15385132211073471.

6. Such examples are documented in the 1916 Sanborn map but are absent from the 1898 map.
7. City of Savannah, "Cuyler-Brownsville Urban Redevelopment Plan" (Savannah, Georgia, December 18, 1997), 7.
8. John B. Howard is the former John B. Hogg, who changed his surname in 1879. See "Before Midnight, Bonaventure and the Bird Girl Exhibition Guide," Telfair Museums, accessed April 7, 2025, https://www.telfair.org/guides/before-midnight-bonaventure-and-the-bird-girl-exhibition-guide/.
9. On Savannah's parks, see Melanie Katia Jones, "The Urban Park Movement in the American South: Savannah, Atlanta, Nashville, 1850–1916" (PhD diss., University of Cambridge, 2014), https://idiscover.lib.cam.ac.uk/permalink/f/t9gok8/44CAM_ALMA21433400480003606.
10. Unnamed when it was platted, the park was officially named Ridgewood Park by a vote of the Savannah City Council in 2021; see Savannah City Council (preliminary) action meeting minutes, October 14, 2021, p. 11, https://www.savannahga.gov/DocumentCenter/View/22836/ActionMinutes_2021-10-14?bidId=.
11. See Thomas W. Hanchett, "John Nolen and the Planning of Savannah's Daffin Park, 1906–1909," *Georgia Historical Quarterly* 78, no. 4 (1994): 810–27.
12. Quoted in Hanchett, "John Nolen," 815.
13. Tanya A. Bailey notes that Granger was instrumental in securing Savannah as the site of international auto races, known locally as "The Great Savannah Races," in the years 1908 to 1911; see Tanya A. Bailey, *The First American Grand Prix: The Savannah Auto Races, 1908–1911* (McFarland, 2014), 44–45.
14. Their exclusivity was further enforced through racial covenants that prescribed White-only ownership of property in each development.
15. Other rows have been built at 511–525 East Liberty Street (within the plan), 518–526 West Gwinnett Street, 710–716 Barnard Street, 815–827 Howard Street, 302–310 Lorch Street, 314–318 West Taylor Street, and 301–305 and 309–313 East Huntingdon Street (adjacent separate developments).

Chapter 10. The Savannah Plan as a Model

Epigraphs are from Stanford Anderson, "Savannah and the Issue of Precedent: City Plan as Resource," in *Settlements in the Americas: Cross-Cultural Perspectives*, ed. Ralph Bennett (University of Delaware Press and Associated University Presses, 1993), 114; and Edward Erfurt, "Lessons on Development Patterns from America's Oldest Planned City," Strong Towns, March 8, 2024, https://www.strongtowns.org/journal/2024/3/8/lessons-on-development-patterns-from-americas-oldest-planned-city.

1. John W. Reps, *The Making of Urban America: A History of City Planning in the United States* (Princeton University Press, 1965), 202.
2. William J. Murtagh discusses this plan briefly and gives a translation of the text in *Moravian Architecture and Town Planning: Bethlehem, Pennsylvania, and Other Eighteenth-Century American Settlements* (University of North Carolina Press, 1967), 11–12.
3. Michael J. Lewis, *City of Refuge: Separatists and Utopian Town Planning* (Princeton University Press, 2016), 106–7. Lewis discusses Moravian missionary David Nitschmann, who spent time in Savannah with Oglethorpe and later drew his own ideal city plan, likely inspired by Savannah.
4. Joan Niles Sears, *The First One Hundred Years of Town Planning in Georgia* (Cherokee, 1979), 14.
5. Sears, *First One Hundred Years*, 170.
6. David M. Bulger, "Charlottetown: A Small, Quiet Seat of Government—No Boom, No Bust," in *Sites of Governance: Multilevel Governance and Policy Making in Canada's Big Cities*, ed. Martin Horak and Robert Young (McGill-Queen's University Press, 2012), 55.
7. H. T. Holman, "Wright, Thomas," in *Dictionary of Canadian Biography*, vol. 5, University of Toronto/Université Laval, 2003–, accessed July 6, 2023, http://www.biographi.ca/en/bio/wright_thomas_5E.html. J. David Wood also sees Charlottetown "as in the same tradition as Savannah"; see Wood, "Grand Designs on the Fringes of Empire: New Towns for British North America," *Canadian Geographer* 26, no. 3 (1982): 249.
8. John W. Reps, "Thomas Jefferson's Checkerboard

Towns," *Journal of the Society of Architectural Historians* 20, no. 3 (October 1961): 108.

9. Stanford Anderson, "Jefferson, Railroad Towns, and the Singular Plan of Aiken," *Places: Forum of Design for the Public Realm* 20, no. 3 (Fall 2008): 65–73.
10. See Nathaniel Robert Walker, "Savannah's Lost Squares: Progress Versus Beauty in the Depression-Era South," *Journal of the Society of Architectural Historians* 70, no. 4 (December 2011): 512–31.
11. The CNU charter can be found at https://www.cnu.org/who-we-are/charter-new-urbanism. A published version includes essays by the signers; see Congress for the New Urbanism, *Charter of the New Urbanism*, 2nd ed., ed. Emily Talen (McGraw-Hill Education, 2013). Victor Dover specifically mentions Savannah in his essay in the section "Block, Street, and Building," noting that its "530 intersections per square mile" exceed the density of street crossings in Rome (148).
12. See Emily Talen, "The Seaside Code," in *Visions of Seaside: Foundation/Evolution/Imagination; Built and Unbuilt Architecture*, by Dhiru A. Thadani (Rizzoli, 2013), 193–213.
13. Dhiru A. Thadani, *Reflections on Seaside: Muses/Ideas/Influences* (Rizzoli, 2021), 44.
14. Seaside's Central Square is more directly inspired by the Piazza del Campo in Siena, but Jay Walljasper, quoting Derrick W. Smith, former town architect at Seaside, mentions Savannah's squares as a source of inspiration in "How a Florida Beach Town Changed How We Live," *Public Square: A CNU Journal*, May 14, 2019, https://www.cnu.org/publicsquare/2019/05/14/how-florida-beach-town-changed-how-we-live.
15. Philip Bess, "Virtuous Reality: Aristotle, Critical Realism, and the Reconstruction of Architectural and Urban Theory," *Classicist* 3 (1996): 6–18. Bess cites Patrick Pinnell's essay "Organon" in Andrés Duany and Elizabeth Plater-Zyberk, *Towns and Town-Making Principles*, ed. Alex Krieger, with William Lennertz (Rizzoli, 1991), 105–8.
16. Thomas D. Wilson, *The Oglethorpe Plan: Enlightenment Design in Savannah and Beyond* (University of Virginia Press, 2012), 172.
17. Wilson, *Oglethorpe Plan*, 179.
18. "Habersham Townhouses," Brown Design Studio, accessed June 8, 2022, https://www.brownds.com/habersham-th.
19. I'On project profile, Dover, Kohl and Partners, accessed June 9, 2022, https://www.doverkohl.com/s/IOn_sm.pdf.
20. Vince Graham, "Vision Keeper," in *CNU Council Report*, ed. Diane Dorney (Congress for the New Urbanism, 2001), 40.
21. Brian Shea, "The Designer's Review of Celebration," in *CNU Council Report* (2001), 22.
22. Thomas J. Comitta, "A Model Village Center," in *CNU Council Report* (2001), 14.
23. Catesby Leigh, "It Takes a (Well-Planned) Village: In Praise of the New Urbanism," *National Review* 55, no. 13 (2003): 34–37.
24. Louis Sauer, "Creating a Signature Town: The Urban Design of Bois-Franc," *Plan Canada* 34, no. 5 (September 1994): 23.
25. Stanford Anderson, "The Plan of Savannah and Changes of Occupancy During Its Early Years: City Plan as Resource," *Harvard Architecture Review* 2 (Spring 1981): 60.
26. Stanford Anderson, "Savannah and the Issue," 121–22.
27. Edmund N. Bacon, *Design of Cities*, rev. ed. (Penguin Books, 1978), 219.
28. Joan Busquets and Dingliang Yang, *Savannah: Rethinking the Multi-Scalar Capacity of the City Project* (Harvard University Graduate School of Design, 2018); and Joan Busquets, Dingliang Yang, and Michael Keller, *Urban Grids: Handbook for Regular City Design* (ORO Editions, 2019).
29. Peter Cookson Smith, *Seeking Savannah* (ORO Editions, 2018).

Section 4 Conclusion. The Lessons of Savannah

Epigraphs are from Italo Calvino, *Invisible Cities*, trans. William Weaver (Harcourt Brace Jovanovich, 1974), 44; and Peter Applebome, "Savannah's Leafy Green Squares," *New York Times*, May 13, 1990, sec. 5.

1. James Edward Oglethorpe, *Some Account of the Design of the Trustees for Establishing Colonys in America*, ed.

Rodney M. Baine and Phinizy Spalding (University of Georgia Press, 1990), 3.

2. Charles Mackay, *Life and Liberty in America: or, Sketches of a Tour in the United States and Canada in 1857–8* (New York, 1859), 209.
3. Lewis Mumford, *The City in History: Its Origins, Its Transformations, and Its Prospects* (Harcourt, Brace & World, 1961), 16.
4. Thomas D. Wilson, *The Oglethorpe Plan: Enlightenment Design in Savannah and Beyond* (University of Virginia Press, 2012), 174–75.

BIBLIOGRAPHY

Savannah Plan

Anderson, Stanford. "Jefferson, Railroad Towns, and the Singular Plan of Aiken." *Places: Forum of Design for the Public Realm* 20, no. 3 (Fall 2008): 65–73.

Anderson, Stanford. "The Plan of Savannah and Changes of Occupancy During Its Early Years: City Plan as Resource." *Harvard Architecture Review* 2 (Spring 1981): 60–67.

Anderson, Stanford. "Savannah and the Issue of Precedent: City Plan as Resource." In *Settlements in the Americas: Cross-Cultural Perspectives*, edited by Ralph Bennett, 110–44. University of Delaware Press and Associated University Presses, 1993.

Anderson, Stanford. "Studies Toward an Ecological Model of the Urban Environment." In *On Streets*, edited by Stanford Anderson, 267–307. MIT Press, 1978.

Bannister, Turpin C. "Oglethorpe's Sources for the Savannah Plan." *Journal of the Society of Architectural Historians* 20, no. 2 (May 1961): 47–62.

Bell, Laura Palmer. "A New Theory on the Plan of Savannah." *Georgia Historical Quarterly* 48, no. 2 (June 1964): 147–65.

Berke, Arnold. "The Ideal City." *Preservation*, July/August 1998, 36–38, 110.

Bess, Philip. "Virtuous Reality: Aristotle, Critical Realism, and the Reconstruction of Architectural and Urban Theory." *Classicist* 3 (1996): 6–18.

Busquets, Joan, and Dingliang Yang. *Savannah: Rethinking the Multi-Scalar Capacity of the City Project*. Harvard University Graduate School of Design, 2018.

A City of Streets and Squares: Savannah Design Guidelines for the Historic District. Christopher Chadbourne and Associates with Clarion Associates, 1992.

De Vorsey, Louis. "The Origin and Appreciation of Savannah, Georgia's Historic City Squares." *Southeastern Geographer* 52, no. 1 (Spring 2012): 90–99.

Gobel, David. "Interweaving Country and City in the Urban Design of Savannah, Georgia." *Global Environment: A Journal of Transdisciplinary History* 9, no. 1 (Spring 2016): 108–48.

Gobel, David. "Planned Obsolescence? The Role of the Town Common in the Making of Savannah's Urban Plan." *Journal of Planning History* 22, no. 2 (2022): 141–76. https://doi.org/10.1177/15385132211073471.

Lee, Clermont H. "The Squares of Savannah." *Planning and Civic Comment* 17, no. 1 (1951): 24.

Reinberger, Mark. "Oglethorpe's Plan of Savannah: Urban Design, Speculative Freemasonry, and Enlightenment Charity." *Georgia Historical Quarterly* 81, no. 4 (Winter 1997): 839–62.

Reps, John W. "$C^2 + L^2 = S^2$? Another Look at the Origins of Savannah's Town Plan." In *Forty Years of Diversity: Essays on Colonial Georgia*, edited by Harvey H. Jackson and Phinizy Spalding, 101–51. University of Georgia Press, 1984.

Reps, John W. *The Making of Urban America: A History of City Planning in the United States*. Princeton University Press, 1965.

Reps, John W. "Thomas Jefferson's Checkerboard Towns." *Journal of the Society of Architectural Historians* 20, no. 3 (1961): 108–14.

Reps, John W. "Town Planning in Colonial Georgia." *Town Planning Review* 30, no. 4 (January 1960): 273–85.

Simo, Laura Beth. "Constructing Savannah's Cityscape, 1837–1854." Master's thesis, University of Delaware, 2008.

Smith, Peter Cookson. *Seeking Savannah*. ORO Editions, 2018.

Walker, Nathaniel Robert. "Savannah's Lost Squares: Progress Versus Beauty in the Depression-Era South." *Journal of the Society of Architectural Historians* 70, no. 4 (December 2011): 512–31.

Walker, Nathaniel Robert. "To Gather in War and Peace: The City Squares of Savannah, Georgia." In *Ordnance: War + Architecture & Space*, edited by Gary A. Boyd and Denis Linehan, 9–31. Ashgate, 2013.

Williams, Robin B. "Evolution and Adaptation: The Savannah Plan and Its Impact on Architectural

Development." In *Vernacular Architecture Forum 2007: Savannah and the Lowcountry; Field Guide for the 28th Annual Meeting; Savannah, Georgia, March 28–31, 2007*, edited by E. G. Daves Rossell and Marisa C. Gomez. Savannah College of Art and Design, 2007.

Wilson, Thomas D. *The Oglethorpe Plan: Enlightenment Design in Savannah and Beyond*. University of Virginia Press, 2012.

Savannah and Lowcountry Architecture and Urbanism

Adler, Lee, and Emma Adler. *Savannah Renaissance*. Wyrick, 2003.

Ayer, N. W. *A Description of Savannah and Its Surroundings, Including Chatham Crescent*. Chatham Land and Hotel, 1911.

Bell, Laura Palmer. "The Vanishing Gardens of Savannah." *Georgia Historical Quarterly* 28, no. 3 (September 1944): 196–208.

Corry, John P. "The Houses of Colonial Georgia." *Georgia Historical Quarterly* 14, no. 3 (September 1930): 181–201.

Cox, James A. D. *Savannah Tour of Homes and Gardens*. Christ Church and Historic Savannah Foundation, 1996.

Crane, Edward A., and E. E. Soderholtz. *Examples of Colonial Architecture in South Carolina and Georgia*. New York, 1895.

Duncan, John D., and Sandra L. Underwood. *"The Showy Town of Savannah": The Story of the Architect William Jay*. Mercer University Press, 2019.

Follett-Thompson, Jean Ames. *The Business of Architecture: William Gibbons Preston and Architectural Professionalism in Boston During the Second Half of the Nineteenth Century*. 2 vols. PhD diss., Boston University, 1986.

Hanchett, Thomas W. "John Nolen and the Planning of Savannah's Daffin Park, 1906–1909." *Georgia Historical Quarterly* 78, no. 4 (Winter 1994): 810–27.

Haughey, Patrick D. "The Historic Port of Savannah: A History from Slavery to Heritage Tourism." *PORTUS: The Online Magazine of RETE*, no. 38 (November 2019): 1–8. https://portusonline.org/the-historic-port-of-savannah-a-history-from-slavery-to-heritage-tourism/.

Jones, Carmie M., ed. *Historic Savannah: A Survey of Significant Buildings in the Historic Districts of Savannah, Georgia*. 3rd ed. Historic Savannah Foundation, 2005.

Lane, Mills. *Architecture of the Old South: Greek Revival and Romantic*. Beehive Foundation, 1996.

Lane, Mills. *Savannah Revisited: History and Architecture*. 4th ed. Beehive Press, 1994.

Levy, B. H. "Savannah's Bull Street: The Man Behind Its Name." *Georgia Historical Quarterly* 71, no. 2 (Summer 1987): 286–96.

Levy, B. H. "Savannah's Old Jewish Community Cemeteries." *Georgia Historical Quarterly* 66, no. 1 (Spring 1982): 1–20.

Linley, John. *The Georgia Catalog, Historic American Buildings Survey: A Guide to the Architecture of the State*. University of Georgia Press, 1982.

Longstreth, Richard W. "The Continuous Transformation of Savannah's Broughton Street." In *Looking Beyond the Icons: Midcentury Architecture, Landscape, and Urbanism*, 170–94. University of Virginia Press, 2015.

McDonald, Mark C., ed. *Architecture of the Last Colony: Georgia's Historic Places, 1733–2000*. Georgia Trust for Historic Preservation and University of Georgia Press, 2023.

Mitchell, William Robert, Jr. *Classic Savannah: History, Homes, and Gardens*. Golden Coast, 1991.

Morrison, Mary Lane. *John S. Norris, Architect in Savannah, 1846–1860*. Beehive Press, 1980.

Murtagh, William J. *Moravian Architecture and Town Planning: Bethlehem, Pennsylvania, and Other Eighteenth-Century American Settlements*. University of North Carolina Press, 1967.

Reiter, Beth Lattimore. *Victorian District Building Survey and Evaluation*. City of Savannah, 1980.

Rossell, E. G. Daves, and Marisa C. Gomez, eds. *Vernacular Architecture Forum 2007: Savannah and the Lowcountry; Field Guide for the 28th Annual Meeting; Savannah, Georgia, March 28–31, 2007*. Savannah College of Art and Design, 2007.

Sheehy, Barry, and Cindy Wallace. *Savannah, Immortal City*. With Vaughnette Goode-Walker. Emerald Book, 2011.

Souther, J. Mark. "'Green Spots in the Heart of Town': Planning and Contesting the Nation's Widest Streets in Georgia's Fall Line Cities." *Georgia Historical Quarterly* 104, no. 4 (Winter 2020): 286–322.

Souther, J. Mark. "Making 'The Garden City of the South': Beautification, Preservation, and Downtown Planning in Augusta, Georgia." *Journal of Planning History 20*, no. 2 (2019).

Toledano, Roulhac. *The National Trust Guide to Savannah*. John Wiley & Sons, 1997.

Waddell, Gene. *Charleston Architecture, 1670–1860*. Gibbs Smith, 2003.

White, J. E. "Topography of Savannah and Its Vicinity: A Report to the Georgia Medical Society, May 3, 1806." *Georgia Historical Quarterly* 1, no. 3 (September 1917): 236–42.

Williams, Robin B. "The Challenge of Preserving Public Memory: Commemorating Tomochichi in Savannah." *Preservation Education and Research* 5 (2012): 1–16.

Williams, Robin B. "Henry Ford, the Hermitage, and Slave-Made Savannah Grey Bricks in Twentieth-Century White Suburbia." In *Architectures of Slavery: Ruins & Reconstructions*, edited by Nathaniel Robert Walker and Rachel Ama Asaa Engmann, 284–308. University of Virginia Press, 2025.

Williams, Robin B. "Savannah, Georgia." In *Encyclopedia of Urban Studies*, edited by Ray Hutchison, 688–92. Sage, 2010.

Williams, Robin B. "'A Well-Paved City': Variety, Locality, and Modernity in Paving Savannah's Streets." *Arris: Journal of the Southeast Chapter of the Society of Architectural Historians* 24 (2013): 20–39.

Williams, Robin B., with David Gobel, Patrick Haughey, Daves Rossell, and Karl Schuler. *Buildings of Savannah*. University of Virginia Press, 2016.

Wilson, Thomas D. *The Ashley Cooper Plan: The Founding of Carolina and the Origins of Southern Political Culture*. University of North Carolina Press, 2016.

Wilson, Thomas D. *Charleston and Savannah: The Rise, Fall, and Reinvention of Two Rival Cities*. University of Georgia Press, 2023.

Savannah History

Abbot, William W. *The Royal Governors of Georgia, 1754–1775*. University of North Carolina Press, 1959.

Baine, Rodney M. "James Oglethorpe and the Early Promotional Literature of Georgia." *William and Mary Quarterly*, 3rd ser., vol. 45, no. 1 (1988): 100–106.

Baine, Rodney M. "The Prison Death of Robert Castell and Its Effect on the Founding of Georgia." *Georgia Historical Quarterly* 73, no. 1 (Spring 1989): 67–78.

Baine, Rodney M., and Louis De Vorsey Jr. "The Provenance and Historical Accuracy of 'A View of Savannah as It Stood the 29th of March, 1734.'" *Georgia Historical Quarterly* 73, no. 4 (Winter 1989): 784–813.

Bryant, William Cullen, ed. *Picturesque America; or, The Land We Live In*. Vol. 1. New York, 1872.

Buckingham, James Silk. *The Slave States of America*. London, 1842.

Cadle, Farris W. *Georgia Land Surveying History and Law*. University of Georgia Press, 1991.

Cashin, Edward J. *Governor Henry Ellis and the Transformation of British North America*. University of Georgia Press, 2007.

Crane, Verner W. "Dr. Thomas Bray and the Charitable Colony Project, 1730." *William and Mary Quarterly*, 3rd ser., vol. 19, no. 1 (January 1962): 49–63.

Davis, Harold E. *The Fledgling Province: Social and Cultural Life in Colonial Georgia, 1733–1776*. Published for the Institute of Early American History and Culture, Williamsburg, Va., by the University of North Carolina Press, 1976.

Davis, Robert Scott. "Wheels Within Wheels: Slavery and the Framework of the Social History of Eighteenth Century Georgia." *Journal of Backcountry Studies* 5, no. 1 (2010): 1–14. http://libjournal.uncg.edu/jbc/article/view/13/3.

DeBolt, Margaret Wayt. *Savannah: A Historical Portrait*. 3rd ed. Hallmark, 2001.

Denmark, Lisa L. "'At the Midnight Hour': Economic Dilemmas and Harsh Realities in Post-Civil War Savannah." *Georgia Historical Quarterly* 90, no. 3 (Fall 2006): 350–90.

De Vorsey, Louis. "The Origin and Appreciation of Savannah, Georgia's Historic City Squares." *Southeastern Geographer* 52, no. 1 (Spring 2012): 90–99.

De Vorsey, Louis, Jr. "Maps in Colonial Promotion: James Edward Oglethorpe's Use of Maps in 'Selling' the Georgia Scheme." *Imago Mundi: The Journal of the

International Society for the History of Cartography 38, no. 1 (1986): 35–45.
Dorner, Zachary. "From Chelsea to Savannah: Medicines and Mercantilism in the Atlantic World." *Journal of British Studies* 58, no. 1 (2019): 28–57.
Fancher, Betsy. *Savannah: A Renaissance of the Heart*. Doubleday, 1976.
Fraser, Walter J., Jr. *Savannah in the Old South*. University of Georgia Press, 2003.
Fries, Adelaide Lisetta. *The Moravians in Georgia, 1735–1740*. Edwards and Broughton, 1905. http://archive.org/details/moraviansingeorgoofrieiala.
Gamble, Thomas. *A History of the City Government of Savannah, Ga., from 1790 to 1901*. Savannah: s.n., 1901.
Gibson, Dot Rees. *Historic Savannah*. Dot Gibson Publications, 1976.
Gregory, G. A. *Savannah and Its Surroundings*. Savannah, 1890.
Harden, William. *A History of Savannah and South Georgia*. 2 vols. Lewis, 1913.
Harris, Leslie M., and Daina Ramey Berry, eds. *Slavery and Freedom in Savannah*. University of Georgia Press, 2014.
Hitch, Robert M. "Modern Savannah." *Georgia Historical Quarterly* 13, no. 3 (1929): 285–341.
Jackson, Harvey H., and Phinizy Spalding, eds. *Forty Years of Diversity: Essays on Colonial Georgia*. University of Georgia Press, 1984.
Johnson, Whittington B. *Black Savannah, 1788–1864*. University of Arkansas Press, 1999.
Jones, Charles Colcock, Jr. *The Dead Towns of Georgia*. Collections of the Georgia Historical Society, vol. 4. Savannah, 1878. Reprint, Oglethorpe Press, 1997.
Jones, Charles Colcock, Jr. *The History of Georgia*. 2 vols. Boston, 1883.
Jones, Charles Colcock, Jr., O. F. Vedder, and Frank Weldon. *History of Savannah, Ga.: From Its Settlement to the Close of the Eighteenth Century*. Syracuse, N.Y., 1890.
Jones, Melanie Katia. "The Urban Park Movement in the American South: Savannah, Atlanta, Nashville, 1850–1916." PhD diss., University of Cambridge, 2014. https://idiscover.lib.cam.ac.uk/permalink/f/t9gok8/44CAM_ALMA21433400480003606.
Lannen, Andrew C. "Liberty and Authority in Colonial Georgia, 1717–1776." PhD diss., Louisiana State University, 2002.
Lannen, Andrew C. "Liberty and Slavery in Colonial America: The Case of Georgia, 1732–1770." *Historian* 79, no. 1 (Spring 2017): 32–55.
Lee, F. D., and J. L. Agnew. *Historical Record of the City of Savannah*. Savannah, 1869.
Levy, Marion Abrahams. "Savannah's Old Jewish Burial Ground." *Georgia Historical Quarterly* 34, No. 4 (December 1950): 265–70.
Mackay, Charles. *Life and Liberty in America: or, Sketches of a Tour in the United States and Canada in 1857–8*. New York, 1859.
McCain, James Ross. *Georgia as a Proprietary Province: The Execution of a Trust*. Richard G. Badger; Copp Clark, 1917.
McDonogh, Gary Wray. *Black and Catholic in Savannah, Georgia*. University of Tennessee Press, 1993.
McIlvenna, Noeleen. *The Short Life of Free Georgia: Class and Slavery in the Colonial South*. University of North Carolina Press, 2015.
Migliazzo, Arlin C. *To Make This Land Our Own: Community, Identity, and Cultural Adaptation in Purrysburg Township, South Carolina, 1732–1865*. University of South Carolina Press, 2007.
The Most Delightful Country of the Universe: Promotional Literature of the Colony of Georgia, 1717–1734. Beehive Press, 1972.
Pressly, Paul M. *On the Rim of the Caribbean: Colonial Georgia and the British Atlantic World*. University of Georgia Press, 2013.
Ready, Milton. "The Georgia Concept: An Eighteenth Century Experiment in Colonization." *Georgia Historical Quarterly* 55, no. 2 (Summer 1971): 157–72.
Ready, Milton. "Land Tenure in Trusteeship Georgia." *Agricultural History* 48, no. 3 (July 1974): 353–68.
Rivers, Lou. *Remembering Crawford Square: Savannah, Ga*. AuthorHouse, 2005.
Robertson, Thomas Heard, Jr. "The Colonial Plan of Augusta." *Georgia Historical Quarterly* 86, no. 4 (Winter 2002): 511–43.
Rousey, Dennis C. "From Whence They Came to Savannah: The Origins of an Urban Population in the Old South." *Georgia Historical Quarterly* 79, no. 2 (Summer 1995): 305–36.

Russell, Preston, and Barbara Hines. *Savannah: A History of Her People Since 1733*. Frederic C. Beil, 1992.

Sears, Joan Niles. *The First One Hundred Years of Town Planning in Georgia*. Cherokee, 1979.

Sheehy, Barry, and Cindy Wallace. *Savannah, Immortal City*. With Vaughnette Goode-Walker. Emerald Book, 2011.

Sieg, Edward Chan. *Eden on the Marsh: An Illustrated History of Savannah*. Windsor, 1985.

Sieg, Edward Chan. *The Squares: An Introduction to Savannah*. Donning, 1996.

Smith, Henry A. M. "Beaufort: The Original Plan and the Earliest Settlers." *South Carolina Historical and Genealogical Magazine* 9, no. 3 (July 1908): 141–60.

Stevenson, Frederic R. "Charleston and Savannah." *Journal of the Society of Architectural Historians* 10, no. 4 (December 1951): 3–9.

Stewart, Mart A. *"What Nature Suffers to Groe": Life, Labor, and Landscape on the Georgia Coast, 1680–1920*. University of Georgia Press, 2002.

Stone, Janet D. *From the Mansion to the University: A History of Armstrong Atlantic State University, 1935–2010*. Armstrong Atlantic State University, 2010.

Sweet, Julie Anne. "'The Excellency and Advantage of doing Good': Thoughts on the Anniversary Sermons Preached Before the Trustees of Georgia, 1731–1750." *Georgia Historical Quarterly* 90, no. 1 (Spring 2006): 1–34.

Sweet, Julie Anne. "A Misguided Mistake: The Trustees' Public Garden in Savannah, Georgia." *Georgia Historical Quarterly* 93, no. 1 (Spring 2009): 1–29.

Sweet, Julie Anne. "'The natural Advantages of this happy Climate': An Analysis of Georgia's Promotional Literature." *Georgia Historical Quarterly* 98, no. 1/2 (Spring/Summer 2014): 1–25.

Sweet, Julie Anne. *Negotiating for Georgia: British-Creek Relations in the Trustee Era, 1733–1752*. University of Georgia Press, 2005.

Sweet, Julie Anne. "'That Cursed Evil Rum': The Trustees' Prohibition Policy in Colonial Georgia." *Georgia Historical Quarterly* 94, no. 1 (Spring 2010): 1–29.

Sweet, Julie Anne. "'These Difficulties . . . rather animate than daunt me': James Oglethorpe as a Leader." *Georgia Historical Quarterly* 99, no. 3 (Fall 2015): 131–55.

Sweet, Julie Anne. "The Thirteenth Colony in Perspective: Historians' Views on Early Georgia." *Georgia Historical Quarterly* 85, no. 3 (Fall 2001): 435–60.

Sweet, Julie Anne. "Thomas Causton: Cause or Casualty of Early Georgia's Troubles?" *Georgia Historical Quarterly* 97, no. 2 (Summer 2013): 139–75.

Sweet, Julie Anne. *William Stephens: Georgia's Forgotten Founder*. Louisiana State University Press, 2010.

Waring, Joseph Frederick. *Cerveau's Savannah*. Georgia Historical Society, 1973.

Weeks, Carl Solana. *Savannah in the Time of Peter Tondee: The Road to Revolution in Colonial Georgia*. Summerhouse, 1997.

Wilson, Adelaide. *Historic and Picturesque Savannah*. Boston, 1889.

American Urbanism

Attoe, Wayne, and Donn Logan. *American Urban Architecture: Catalysts in the Design of Cities*. University of California Press, 1989.

Bacon, Edmund N. *Design of Cities*. Rev. ed. Penguin Books, 1974.

Ballon, Hilary, ed. *The Greatest Grid: The Master Plan of Manhattan, 1811–2011*. Columbia University Press, 2012.

Bridenbaugh, Carl. *Cities in the Wilderness: The First Century of Urban Life in America, 1625–1742*. Ronald Press, 1938.

Bushman, Richard L. *The Refinement of America: Persons, Houses, Cities*. Alfred A. Knopf, 1992.

Busquets, Joan, Dingliang Yang, and Michael Keller. *Urban Grids: Handbook for Regular City Design*. ORO Editions, 2019.

Campanella, Thomas J. *Republic of Shade: New England and the American Elm*. Yale University Press, 2003.

Cardinal-Pett, Clare. *A History of Architecture and Urbanism in the Americas*. Routledge, 2016.

Carey, George Wescott, and Bruce Frohnen, eds. *Community and Tradition: Conservative Perspectives on the American Experience*. Rowman & Littlefield, 1998.

Clawson, Marion, and Peter Hall. *Planning and Urban Growth: An Anglo-American Comparison*. Johns Hopkins University Press, 1973.

Dover, Victor, and John Massengale. *Street Design: The Secret to Great Cities and Towns*. John Wiley & Sons, 2013.

Duany, Andres, Elizabeth Plater-Zyberk, and Jeff Speck. *Suburban Nation: The Rise of Sprawl and the Decline of the American Dream*. North Point, 2000.

El-Khoury, Rodolphe, and Edward Robbins. *Shaping the City: Studies in History, Theory and Urban Design*. 2nd ed. Routledge, 2013.

Fries, Sylvia Doughty. *The Urban Idea in Colonial America*. Temple University Press, 1977.

Gillette, Howard, Jr. *Civitas by Design: Building Better Communities, from the Garden City to the New Urbanism*. University of Pennsylvania Press, 2010.

Goodman, Phebe S. *The Garden Squares of Boston*. University Press of New England, 2003.

Hegemann, Werner, and Elbert Peets. *The American Vitruvius: An Architects' Handbook of Civic Art*. Architectural Book Publishing, 1922.

Hinshaw, Mark L. *True Urbanism: Living in and near the Center*. American Planning Association, 2007.

Jacobs, Allan B. *Great Streets*. MIT Press, 1995.

Kasson, John F. *Rudeness and Civility: Manners in Nineteenth-Century Urban America*. Hill and Wang, 1990.

Kornwolf, James D. *Architecture and Town Planning in Colonial North America*. With the assistance of Georgiana Wallis Kornwolf. Johns Hopkins University Press, 2002.

Kostof, Spiro. *America by Design*. Oxford University Press, 1987.

Krieger, Alex. *City on a Hill: Urban Idealism in America from the Puritans to the Present*. Belknap Press of Harvard University Press, 2019.

Lawrence, Henry W. *City Trees: A Historical Geography from the Renaissance Through the Nineteenth Century*. University of Virginia Press, 2006.

Lawrence, Henry W. "The Neoclassical Origins of Modern Urban Forests." *Forest & Conservation History* 37, no. 1 (January 1993): 26–36.

Lawrence, Henry W. "Origins of the Tree-Lined Boulevard." *Geographical Review* 78, no. 4 (October 1988): 355–74.

Leinberger, Christopher B. *The Option of Urbanism: Investing in a New American Dream*. Island Press, 2008.

Lewis, Michael J. *City of Refuge: Separatists and Utopian Town Planning*. Princeton University Press, 2016.

Lewis, Roger K. *Shaping the City*. AIA Press, 1987.

Longstreth, Richard W. *Looking Beyond the Icons: Midcentury Architecture, Landscape, and Urbanism*. University of Virginia Press, 2015.

Machor, James L. *Pastoral Cities: Urban Ideals and the Symbolic Landscape of America*. University of Wisconsin Press, 1987.

Milroy, Elizabeth. *The Grid and the River: Philadelphia's Green Places, 1682–1876*. Penn State University Press, 2016.

Moholy-Nagy, Sibyl. *Matrix of Man: An Illustrated History of Urban Environment*. Praeger, 1968.

Morris, A. E. J. *History of Urban Form: Before the Industrial Revolutions*. 3rd ed. Longman Scientific & Technical; John Wiley & Sons, 1994.

Mumford, Eric. *Designing the Modern City: Urbanism Since 1850*. Yale University Press, 2018.

Mumford, Lewis. *The City in History: Its Origins, Its Transformations, and Its Prospects*. Harcourt, Brace & World, 1961.

Mumford, Lewis. *The Story of Utopias*. Viking, 1962.

Muthesius, Stefan. *The English Terraced House*. Yale University Press, 1982.

Nobles, Gregory H. "Straight Lines and Stability: Mapping the Political Order of the Anglo-American Frontier." *Journal of American History* 80, no. 1 (June 1993): 9–35.

Passell, Aaron. *Building the New Urbanism: Places, Professions, and Profits in the American Metropolitan Landscape*. Routledge, 2013.

Ross, Benjamin. *Dead End: Suburban Sprawl and the Rebirth of American Urbanism*. Oxford University Press, 2014.

Rybczynski, Witold. *Makeshift Metropolis: Ideas About Cities*. Scribner, 2010.

Sauer, Louis. "Creating a 'Signature' Town: The Urban Design of Bois-Franc." *Plan Canada* 34, no. 5 (September 1994): 22–27.

Scully, Vincent. *American Architecture and Urbanism*. Praeger, 1969.

Stilgoe, John R. *Common Landscape of America, 1580 to 1845*. Yale University Press, 1982.

Stilgoe, John R. "The Puritan Townscape: Ideal and Reality." *Landscape* 20 (Spring 1976): 3–7.

Talen, Emily. *New Urbanism and American Planning: The Conflict of Cultures*. Routledge, 2005.

Thadani, Dhiru A. *Visions of Seaside: Foundation/Evolution/Imagination; Built and Unbuilt Architecture*. Rizzoli, 2013.

Upton, Dell. *Another City: Urban Life and Urban Spaces in the New American Republic*. Yale University Press, 2008.

Walker, Nathaniel Robert. *Victorian Visions of Suburban Utopia: Abandoning Babylon*. Oxford University Press, 2020.

Wilson, Thomas D. *Exceptional Places: A Comparative Field Guide to Iconic and Extraordinary Historic Districts*. Twyyst Books, 2025.

Winthrop, John. "A Modell of Christian Charity." In *An American Primer*, edited by Daniel J. Boorstin, 8–25. University of Chicago Press, 1966.

Zucker, Paul. *Town and Square: From the Agora to the Village Green*. Columbia University Press, 1959.

INDEX